RAND McNALLY

MW00445180

The C road atlas

TELL US
WHAT YOU THINK
comment card on last page

Contents

Cover photo: The Outer Banks of North Carolina. ©Panoramic Images/Getty Images.
Interior photos: page E, F, and G ©Rand McNally; page I Photo by Bill Russ, NC Division of Tourism Courtesy of Wilmingtop/Cape Fear Coast CVB; page J (tl) ©Bill Russ/Courtesy North Carolina Tourism, (bl) ©PhotoDisc, (tc) Courtesy North Carolina Tourism, (bc) Courtesy of the Chicamacomico Life-Saving Station Historic Site, (tr) ©DK. Khattiya/Alamy, (br) Crystal Cost Tourist Development Authority; page K (l) Carolyn Mason/Foundation for Shackleford Horses, Inc., (r) ©Ablestock/Hemera Technoligies/Alamy; page M, N and O courtesy of the Myrtle Beach Area Chamber of Commerce.

PageFinder™ Map   U.S. Patent No. 5,419,586
                     Canadian Patent No. 2,116,425
                     Patente Mexicana No. 188186

©2008 Rand McNally & Company. Portions ©2006 NAVTEQ. NAVTEQ ON BOARD is a trademark of NAVTEQ. All rights reserved. Rand McNally is a registered trademark of Rand McNally & Company. Published in U.S.A. Printed in China. All rights reserved.

RAND McNALLY

randmcnally.com

If you have questions, concerns, or even a compliment, contact us by visiting our website at go.randmcnally.com/contact

or write to:
Rand McNally Consumer Affairs
P.O. Box 7600
Chicago, Illinois 60680-9915

NAVTEQ
ON BOARD™

Mileage and Driving Times

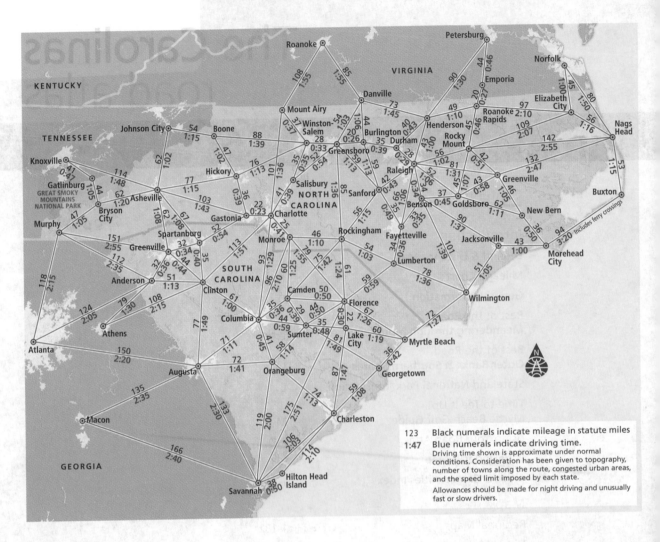

123	Black numerals indicate mileage in statute miles
1:47	Blue numerals indicate driving time.

Driving time shown is approximate under normal conditions. Consideration has been given to topography, number of towns along the route, congested urban areas, and the speed limit imposed by each state.

Allowances should be made for night driving and unusually fast or slow drivers.

Legend

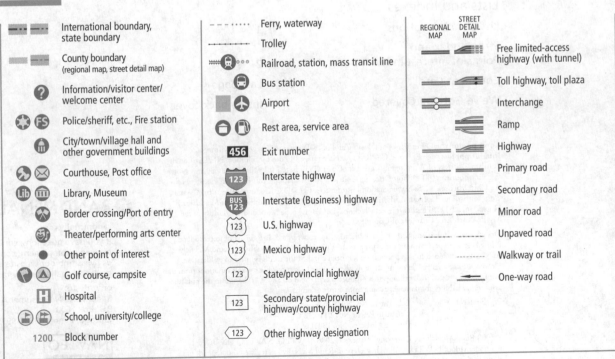

International boundary, state boundary	
County boundary (regional map, street detail map)	
Information/visitor center/ welcome center	
Police/sheriff, etc., Fire station	
City/town/village hall and other government buildings	
Courthouse, Post office	
Library, Museum	
Border crossing/Port of entry	
Theater/performing arts center	
Other point of interest	
Golf course, campsite	
Hospital	
School, university/college	
1200 Block number	

Ferry, waterway	
Trolley	
Railroad, station, mass transit line	
Bus station	
Airport	
Rest area, service area	
456 Exit number	
123 Interstate highway	
BUS 123 Interstate (Business) highway	
123 U.S. highway	
123 Mexico highway	
123 State/provincial highway	
123 Secondary state/provincial highway/county highway	
123 Other highway designation	

	REGIONAL MAP	STREET DETAIL MAP	
Free limited-access highway (with tunnel)			
Toll highway, toll plaza			
Interchange			
Ramp			
Highway			
Primary road			
Secondary road			
Minor road			
Unpaved road			
Walkway or trail			
One-way road			

Mileage Chart

	Anderson, SC	Asheboro, NC	Asheville, NC	Burlington, NC	Charleston, SC	Charlotte, NC	Clemson, SC	Durham, NC	Florence, SC	Georgetown, SC	Greenville, NC	Greenwood, SC	Hickory, NC	Hilton Head Island, SC	Jacksonville, NC	Kinston, NC	Mt Airy, NC	Myrtle Beach, SC	Roanoke Rapids, NC	Rocky Mount, NC	Sanford, NC	Spartanburg, SC	Statesville, NC	Wilmington, NC	Winston-Salem, NC	Zebulon, NC
ɔingdon, VA	194	196	101	195	365	193	188	226	296	366	329	216	99	417	369	328	103	364	312	305	229	167	154	380	145	270
bemarle, NC	171	38	162	83	220	44	172	115	93	163	189	179	91	273	195	168	101	153	196	165	67	112	57	173	64	130
nderson, SC	0	212	95	238	237	132	18	270	205	271	373	40	144	290	383	382	228	273	355	348	263	61	168	332	204	314
sheboro, NC	212	0	170	47	246	85	213	78	118	191	151	221	99	298	186	145	88	169	158	127	46	154	69	183	51	92
sheville, NC	95	170	0	192	265	129	88	224	233	299	326	116	77	318	366	325	162	301	309	302	226	67	102	330	147	267
thens, TN	201	342	174	364	430	289	184	396	398	464	499	281	250	447	539	497	289	466	481	474	398	232	274	490	319	439
ugusta, GA	102	244	184	270	174	160	111	302	148	208	338	60	209	151	325	325	260	215	359	327	270	119	200	274	236	302
arnwell, SC	135	241	215	267	110	156	154	298	125	143	317	93	205	107	304	304	256	176	338	306	249	150	196	253	232	281
eaufort, NC	427	218	398	210	262	317	428	176	225	202	86	373	328	406	47	74	293	167	178	128	176	386	298	95	256	141
enson, NC	319	85	280	92	245	199	320	58	118	169	77	266	210	298	90	64	175	149	98	66	38	268	180	101	138	41
ɔone, NC	188	135	87	133	299	101	189	165	209	279	268	196	47	352	308	267	89	276	250	243	167	130	73	319	88	209
amden, SC	159	132	188	203	145	92	160	222	50	111	240	106	141	198	228	227	192	118	261	230	127	123	132	176	168	204
harlotte, NC	132	85	124	111	207	0	133	143	104	174	245	140	58	259	285	244	100	172	228	221	135	73	40	197	77	186
hesapeake, VA	458	266	411	223	442	330	459	189	315	366	123	462	341	495	189	152	306	346	103	145	230	399	311	294	269	167
hester, SC	113	132	116	158	174	48	114	190	123	180	293	73	80	227	301	300	148	191	275	268	183	49	88	249	124	234
emson, SC	18	213	88	239	238	133	0	271	206	272	374	58	145	291	384	383	229	274	356	349	264	62	169	333	205	315
inton, SC	51	193	100	219	170	113	71	251	138	203	328	27	126	222	316	315	209	205	349	317	244	35	149	264	185	292
olumbia, SC	129	177	157	203	111	93	129	235	80	126	271	75	142	164	258	258	193	148	292	260	203	92	132	207	169	235
olumbus, NC	81	163	41	188	227	82	82	220	195	261	323	89	74	280	363	322	159	263	306	299	213	29	99	283	143	264
ommerce, GA	59	260	143	286	285	180	59	318	253	319	421	88	192	265	431	430	276	321	403	396	311	109	216	380	252	362
onway, SC	259	155	287	224	96	158	260	190	54	37	209	205	219	220	130	165	242	13	230	198	141	223	198	79	205	173
anville, VA	267	76	221	44	346	140	268	58	192	265	162	276	150	399	202	160	84	243	114	137	103	209	120	212	78	102
arlington, SC	201	108	230	153	137	95	202	179	9	80	197	147	156	190	185	184	195	77	218	187	101	165	135	134	157	161
urham, NC	270	79	224	35	303	143	271	0	176	227	99	279	153	356	145	103	118	207	87	74	56	212	123	155	81	40
izabeth City, NC	457	235	410	222	419	329	458	188	292	313	99	439	340	472	154	128	305	278	97	111	206	398	310	206	268	144
ijay, GA	140	319	151	341	366	261	124	373	334	400	475	177	226	367	512	474	311	402	458	451	375	190	251	461	296	416
nporia, VA	375	183	329	140	360	248	376	107	232	284	104	380	258	412	164	122	223	263	20	63	147	317	228	212	186	85
yetteville, NC	292	82	261	85	218	136	293	90	90	142	109	238	191	270	110	96	156	122	130	98	35	213	161	90	119	73
orence, SC	205	118	233	163	130	104	206	175	0	70	194	151	165	183	181	181	204	67	215	183	126	169	144	130	167	158
rest City, NC	101	145	62	171	248	64	102	203	172	281	305	109	62	300	345	304	147	240	288	281	195	34	86	265	131	246
astonia, NC	111	102	103	128	220	22	112	160	130	200	263	119	36	273	303	262	118	197	245	239	153	52	58	223	94	204
atlinburg, TN	174	256	89	278	345	203	131	310	313	378	413	196	164	397	453	412	231	380	396	389	313	146	189	404	233	354
oldsboro, NC	356	118	298	110	282	218	357	76	154	202	43	302	228	334	70	28	193	166	86	44	76	286	198	94	156	43
oose Creek, SC	224	232	252	303	19	193	225	289	91	62	308	165	242	120	220	295	293	98	329	297	240	187	233	169	269	272
reensboro, NC	221	29	171	20	300	93	222	52	146	219	155	229	100	352	195	154	65	197	138	131	59	162	70	206	28	96
reenville, NC	373	151	326	138	321	245	374	104	194	222	0	342	256	374	71	28	221	186	86	44	122	314	226	114	184	59
reenville, SC	32	183	62	208	212	102	29	240	180	245	343	54	115	264	357	342	198	247	326	319	233	32	138	306	174	284
reenwood, SC	40	221	116	246	179	140	58	278	151	212	342	0	153	231	329	329	236	219	362	331	271	63	176	278	212	306
ampton, SC	167	252	246	297	77	187	219	309	136	131	328	124	236	76	315	315	287	187	349	317	260	181	227	264	263	292
ckory, NC	145	99	77	121	256	58	145	153	165	236	256	153	0	308	296	255	92	233	238	231	155	86	31	258	76	197
gh Point, NC	208	23	160	36	287	81	209	68	140	212	171	217	90	340	211	170	55	190	153	146	67	150	60	222	18	112
ghlands, NC	63	233	71	255	284	167	45	287	252	317	389	104	140	336	429	388	225	319	372	365	289	108	165	378	210	330
llsville, VA	240	116	175	115	319	113	241	147	216	287	250	249	104	372	290	248	21	284	232	225	149	182	75	300	65	190
lton Head Island, SC	290	298	318	370	114	259	291	355	183	173	374	231	308	0	361	361	359	210	395	363	306	254	299	310	335	338
cksonville, NC	383	186	366	178	217	286	384	144	181	158	71	329	296	361	0	43	261	123	147	101	129	354	266	51	224	110
hnson City, TN	155	189	62	188	326	151	149	219	294	359	322	177	99	378	362	321	143	362	305	298	222	128	124	373	142	263
ke City, SC	208	141	236	186	87	127	209	198	22	52	217	155	188	174	177	204	227	60	238	206	149	171	167	126	190	181
ncaster, SC	143	125	157	151	175	41	144	183	73	150	234	103	90	228	249	221	141	141	268	224	124	79	81	197	117	187
urinburg, NC	228	79	221	104	188	93	229	110	61	120	152	193	154	241	154	139	165	98	173	141	55	170	133	103	128	118
mberton, NC	260	112	254	153	186	126	261	119	59	103	138	207	187	239	110	125	198	83	159	127	70	224	166	79	161	102
artinsville, VA	256	78	198	54	335	128	257	84	194	267	196	264	128	387	236	195	52	245	144	172	104	197	98	247	51	137
t Airy, NC	228	88	163	86	307	101	229	118	204	277	221	236	92	360	261	220	0	255	203	197	120	170	62	272	37	162
t Pleasant, SC	243	252	272	323	5	213	244	309	136	55	328	185	262	119	214	248	313	92	349	317	260	207	253	162	289	292
yrtle Beach, SC	273	169	301	240	96	172	274	207	67	36	186	219	233	210	123	158	255	0	246	214	157	237	211	72	218	189
gs Head, NC	489	268	443	254	452	362	490	221	324	338	132	472	372	504	179	160	338	303	172	144	239	431	343	231	301	177
w Bern, NC	416	179	359	171	255	278	417	137	215	196	46	363	289	395	37	35	254	160	131	88	137	347	259	88	217	102
wport, TN	153	236	68	258	324	183	147	290	292	358	393	175	144	377	433	392	202	360	375	368	292	126	168	384	213	334
angeburg, SC	167	221	196	247	74	137	168	263	90	108	281	109	186	127	269	268	237	141	302	271	214	131	177	218	213	245
ford, NC	298	106	251	63	328	171	299	30	200	252	101	306	181	380	169	110	146	231	60	69	85	240	151	180	109	42
nehurst, NC	222	48	214	94	220	93	223	84	92	151	151	223	144	272	156	130	135	129	158	126	29	164	114	136	98	91
leigh, NC	297	70	250	62	278	170	298	28	151	202	81	298	180	331	120	78	145	182	88	56	42	238	150	130	108	22
anoke Rapids, NC	355	158	309	120	342	228	356	87	215	266	86	362	238	395	147	105	204	246	0	45	130	297	208	195	166	67
ckingham, NC	207	57	199	102	189	71	208	111	61	134	175	188	132	241	177	162	143	112	185	154	56	148	111	126	106	119
cky Mount, NC	348	127	302	113	311	221	349	80	183	235	42	331	231	363	102	60	197	215	45	0	98	290	202	139	160	36
isbury, NC	168	44	133	69	247	41	169	101	132	202	204	177	62	300	244	203	72	182	187	180	94	110	29	255	35	145
nford, NC	263	46	226	50	254	135	264	56	126	178	123	271	155	306	129	103	120	157	130	98	0	204	125	140	83	63
vannah, GA	282	290	310	362	106	251	283	347	175	165	366	197	300	38	353	353	351	202	387	355	298	246	291	302	327	330
elby, NC	96	126	79	151	243	45	97	183	153	223	286	105	38	296	326	285	125	220	269	262	176	38	64	246	117	227
uth Hill, VA	340	148	293	105	351	212	341	72	224	275	112	348	223	404	193	141	188	255	55	71	117	281	193	203	151	73
uthport, NC	328	195	356	219	156	210	329	185	122	97	144	274	271	270	81	116	302	61	225	169	142	291	249	30	265	168
artanburg, SC	61	154	67	180	201	73	62	212	169	235	314	63	86	254	354	313	169	237	297	290	204	0	109	295	146	255
ring Lake, NC	301	73	252	76	227	123	302	71	100	151	118	248	181	280	119	105	147	131	139	108	26	194	152	100	110	71
tesville, NC	168	69	102	91	247	40	169	123	144	214	226	176	31	299	266	225	62	211	208	202	125	109	0	277	46	167
mter, SC	173	146	201	191	98	131	174	216	44	81	235	120	180	151	222	222	231	94	256	224	167	137	171	171	207	199
llace, NC	323	158	338	149	207	189	324	116	122	148	76	270	267	302	39	47	232	112	155	99	100	287	237	41	195	98
iteville, NC	285	137	279	190	140	151	286	156	84	80	136	231	212	264	99	110	223	60	196	164	107	249	191	47	186	139
liamston, NC	392	170	346	157	354	265	393	123	227	278	34	375	275	407	92	63	240	215	61	46	142	334	245	143	203	80
mington, NC	331	183	325	189	166	197	332	155	130	107	114	278	258	310	51	86	272	72	195	138	140	295	277	0	235	138
son, NC	339	117	292	104	290	211	340	70	163	214	33	310	222	343	84	42	187	194	62	18	88	280	192	121	150	25
nston-Salem, NC	204	51	147	49	283	77	205	81	167	240	184	212	76	335	224	183	37	218	166	160	83	146	46	235	0	125

ges in this chart are based upon the routes usually followed by motorists. Highway systems involved include interstate, U.S., and state highways.

General Information

HIGHWAY PATROL
In case of emergency, call 911

SPEED LIMIT ON RURAL INTERSTATE HIGHWAYS
North and South Carolina: 70 miles per hour

STATE MOTOR VEHICLE INFORMATION
North Carolina: (919) 861-3720; www.ncdot.org/dmv
South Carolina: (803) 896-3870; www.scdps.org

HOTLINES & WEBSITES
North Carolina Road Construction and Conditions
511; (877) 511-4662; www.ncdot.org/traffictravel/
South Carolina Road Construction and Conditions
www.dot.state.sc.us

CLEAR CHANNEL RADIO STATIONS
(AM band, 50,000 watts, Class A)
North Carolina: WPTF 680 Raleigh
South Carolina: WSB 750 Atlanta, GA

TOURISM INFORMATION

North Carolina Division of Tourism
(800) 847-4862
(919) 733-8372
www.visitnc.com

South Carolina Department of Parks, Recreation & Tourism
(888) 727-6453*
(803) 734-1700
www.discoversouthcarolina.com

*To request travel materials only
You can also get tourism information and road construction updates at randmcnally.com.

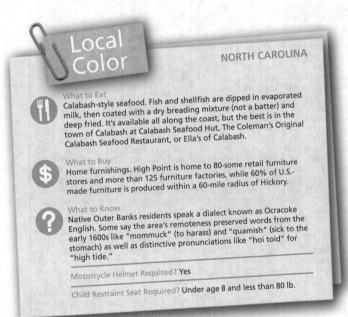

Local Color — NORTH CAROLINA

What to Eat
Calabash-style seafood. Fish and shellfish are dipped in evaporated milk, then coated with a dry breading mixture (not a batter) and deep fried. It's available all along the coast, but the best is in the town of Calabash at Calabash Seafood Hut, The Coleman's Original Calabash Seafood Restaurant, or Ella's of Calabash.

What to Buy
Home furnishings. High Point is home to 80-some retail furniture stores and more than 125 furniture factories, while 60% of U.S.-made furniture is produced within a 60-mile radius of Hickory.

What to Know
Native Outer Banks residents speak a dialect known as Ocracoke English. Some say the area's remoteness preserved words from the early 1600s like "mommuck" (to harass) and "quamish" (sick to the stomach) as well as distinctive pronunciations like "hoi toid" for "high tide."

Motorcycle Helmet Required? **Yes**

Child Restraint Seat Required? **Under age 8 and less than 80 lb.**

Local Color — SOUTH CAROLINA

What to Eat
Shrimp and grits. Combining a coastal specialty and a southern staple, this classic Charleston dish has become a South Carolina favorite. It's especially popular at restaurants in the Lowcountry.

What to Buy
Sweetgrass baskets. Gullah women weave sweetgrass into beautiful yet practical baskets, continuing a basket-making tradition begun in West Africa. Purchase baskets at stands along Hwy 17 North outside Mt. Pleasant, or in Charleston.

What to Know
On the barrier islands live the Gullah people, whose ancestors were transported to the Lowcountry as slaves. They speak a Creole dialect influenced by African languages and maintain distinct storytelling, cooking, and craft traditions.

Motorcycle Helmet Required? **Under age 21, all helmets must have reflectorization**

Child Restraint Seat Required? **Under age 6 and less than 80 lb.**

Meandering through
Mountains
A Best of the Road™ trip

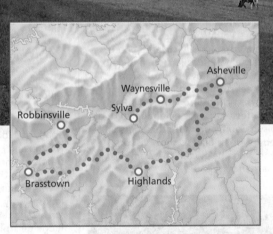

Cows graze in a pasture nestled among the foot-hills of the Great Smokies near Fontana Lake.

On a clear day, the entire area covered by this Best of the Road trip can be seen from atop Clingman's Dome, the 6,643-foot peak that sits on the Tennessee-North Carolina border. The route winds through a realm of ancient mountains mellowed by time, of deep hollows harboring isolated farms, of forests that stretch unbroken to the horizon, and of national treasures such as historic Asheville, the Blue Ridge Parkway, and Great Smoky Mountains National Park. Public markets, a subterranean lake, and fine dining are all here in the Editor's Picks, shown in bold, our way of sharing with you those special things we call "Best of the Road." ▸

Meandering through Mountains (cont.)

The trip begins just over the crest of the Smokies, at the Tennessee line. It descends on the North Carolina side, into the Cherokee Indian Reservation.

Asheville, a popular resort since the mid-1800s and site of the famous Biltmore Estate, is the first stop. Nestled in the Blue Ridge Mountains at an elevation of 2,200 feet, the city offers an unusual combination of Appalachian charm and cosmopolitan sophistication. Its devotion to the arts and culture earned it the nickname "Paris of the South."

Grove Arcade Public Market

Asheville's lively downtown streets brim with eclectic shops, top-notch restaurants, and elegant buildings that date back to the city's Gilded Age heyday. One such building, the Gothic Revival-style Grove Arcade, was recently renovated and reopened as the **Grove Arcade Public Market**. A pleasant anachronism in this age of chain stores and strip malls, the market consists of some 40 owner-operated businesses, many of which sell products and foods made or grown in western North Carolina. Food lovers flock to the area called The Stalls, where vendors offer organically grown fruits and vegetables, locally made cheeses, exotic spices and herbs, and gourmet pies. (The blueberry-peach pie is a favorite.)

The best-known spot for arts and crafts shopping in the area is the Southern Highland Craft Guild's Folk Art Center, located five miles east along the Blue Ridge Parkway. An excellent and less pricey alternative sits just off Pack Square in downtown

'Face jugs' from the Appalachian Craft Center

Asheville. **The Appalachian Craft Center** specializes in authentic mountain handicrafts, especially traditional pottery made by local artisans. A large part of the store's ample space is devoted to casserole dishes, plates, and pitchers, as well as the scary-looking "face jugs" once made by African-American slaves to ward off evil spirits. Among the other handicrafts on display are wooden bowls, "friendship" brooms, quilts, looper rugs, and rustic furniture. Many of the items come from the region's best-known artisan families, including the Coles, Owenses, and Teagues.

The Asheville area boasts several world-class gardens, most notably those at Biltmore and at the North Carolina Arboretum. It also has a number of "hidden" gardens—little-known places that are well worth a visit. One of these is **Jarvis Japanese Garden** near Mars Hill, which is located about 15 miles north of Asheville via I-26. Created by Jack Jarvis, a landscaper who became smitten with Japanese gardens after designing one for a client, the five-acre garden incorporates traditional Japanese elements of water, stones, and plants. Pathways wind around five koi-filled, lotus and lily-covered ponds, past a large bonsai collection, and among a riot of colorful flowers, shrubs, and exotic trees such as a Chinese pistachio and a dwarf cherry from Mt. Fuji. Jarvis, who confesses that his neighbors in rural Madison County don't quite understand his obsession, is glad to show visitors around when he's available. Admission to the garden is free.

Jarvis Japanese Garden

From Asheville, the route heads west on the Blue Ridge Parkway, then south on US 276 to the **Cradle of Forestry**. This 6,500-acre section of the Pisgah National Forest commemorates the beginnings of forest conservation in the United States. It lies some 20 miles from the Biltmore Mansion but, incredibly, it falls within the estate's original boundaries. At the **Forest Discovery Center,** visitors can examine forestry-related exhibits and watch an 18-minute film that tells how the once-deforested

1915 logging train at the Cradle of Forestry

landscape was nursed back to robust health by Gifford Pinchot and Dr. Carl A. Schenk around the turn of the 20th century. Two paved paths, each a mile long, meander through the surrounding woodlands, and guided tours introduce visitors to basic forestry concepts.

A few miles down the highway, a turn-off leads to perennially popular **Sliding Rock**. Here, the waters of the Davidson River shoot 60 feet down a slanting stretch of smooth granite and into a 6-foot-deep pool. On hot summer weekends, this natural waterslide often attracts crowds in the hundreds. Stepping into the frigid waters and scudding down the rock face takes some courage, and the word "foolhardy" might come to the mind of onlookers on the observation deck, but the experience is exhilarating.

South of Sliding Rock, the route joins NC 280 and heads south through Brevard before connecting with US 64, where it climbs to the "High Country" resort towns of Sapphire, Cashiers, and Highlands. Heavy local rainfall feeds rivers and streams that cascade down the steep Blue Ridge escarpment and give this area its other nickname, "Waterfall Country." One of the most notable cataracts is the curiously named **Dry Falls**, a 75-foot plunge along the Cullasaja River just west of Highlands. The falls are impressive enough when seen from the front, but a walkway allows visitors the bracing experience of walking behind the thundering curtain of water, where mist and air currents swirl against the black rock face.

Franklin, the next stop, has a rich gem-mining history that traces back to the 1870s. Today, numerous commercial mines offer amateur gem hunters the chance to find—and keep—rubies, sapphires, garnets, and amethyst.

The Franklin Gem and Mineral Museum, housed in an old brick jailhouse near the center of town, displays stones and minerals from North Carolina, the other 49 states, and around the world. One of

its highlights is the Fluorescent Room, where mineral specimens glow in a bright rainbow of colors under black lights.

Best L'il Corner Ice Cream Parlor

West of Franklin, US 64 enters sparsely populated Clay County and rolls through a wild, densely forested landscape where the pavement is often the only sign of human presence. Eventually, a Chamber of Commerce Visitor Center welcomes travelers to Hayesville, population 308, the county seat and largest town. Next door sits another welcoming place, the **Best L'il Corner Ice Cream Parlor.** Soda jerks at the old-fashioned soda fountain serve generously sized milkshakes, sodas, and sundaes. On Saturday nights, local musicians gather at 7 p.m. for a few hours of "country pickin'."

The **John C. Campbell Folk School** in nearby Brasstown ranks as Clay County's most famous attraction. People from all over the country come to the rustic campus to learn traditional Appalachian crafts such as quilting, wood carving, and pottery, as well as arts like watercolor painting and photography. Visitors are invited to shop in the excellent craft shop, observe classes in progress, wander the wooded pathways along Little Brasstown Creek, and have lunch or dinner in the sunny dining hall (reservations are required).

John C. Campbell Folk School

From Brasstown, the route zigzags northward, passing through Robbinsville and on to Yellow Branch, a bucolic valley that slopes down to Fontana Lake. This off-the-beaten-path spot is home to the Mountain Hollow B&B, a handsome

Victorian house situated on a grassy hillside. Just down the road lies **Yellow Branch Pottery and Cheese**. Husband and wife Bruce DeGroot and Karen Mickler use milk from their small herd of Jersey cows to make a delicious farmstead cheese and three variations: pepper, basil, and natural rind. Mickler's studio, where her hand-thrown stoneware is displayed and sold, also serves as cheese shop and tasting room.

Yellow Branch Pottery and Cheese

Just above the valley, a simple roadside stand called **Beckie's Country Corner** deserves a quick visit. Beckie Martell sells homemade jams, jellies, preserves, pickled foods, and condiments as well as a Southern specialty, boiled peanuts. The jewelry on display? Beckie makes that, too.

Beckie's Country Corner

Another great food stop lies a short drive west of Robbinsville. At **Stoney Hollow Farm**, the Boxberger family grows strawberries, raspberries, blackberries, blueberries, and grapes. Visitors can buy pre-picked fruit or grab a carton and pick their own while enjoying the views of Santeetlah Lake, the Great Smokies, and Nantahala National Forest.

Nestled within the national forest just west of the lake is a pocket of arboreal paradise called the **Joyce Kilmer Memorial Forest**. Through a combination of chance, falling lumber prices, and the foresight of the USDA Forest Service, this 3,800-acre tract of virgin hardwood forest escaped logging. It was dedicated in 1936 to the poet who penned the famous lines, "I think that I shall never see/A poem lovely as a tree." The two-mile-long Joyce Kilmer

National Recreation Trail shows off many of the most spectacular trees, including yellow poplars that measure more than 100 feet tall and 20 feet in circumference.

The road out of the forest leads to the **Cherohala Scenic Skyway**. Completed in 1996, this National Scenic Byway stretches some 36 miles between Robbinsville and the Tennessee town of Tellico Plains. True to its name, the skyway climbs more than 5,400 feet into the sky as it twists along high mountain crests. More than two dozen overlooks provide expansive views of the surrounding mountains and of forest blanketed valleys that seem untouched by civilization. Best of all, the Cherohala Skyway is practically undiscovered, and travelers can feel as if they have it entirely to themselves.

Instead of continuing into Tennessee, this route backtracks through Robbinsville and continues on to US 19/74. The destination is **Nantahala Outdoor Center (NOC)** deep in the Nantahala Gorge. One of the best-known names in outdoor adventures, NOC offers whitewater-rafting trips on the Nantahala and other rivers in the area. Even for people with no interest in rafting, NOC is fun to visit. For starters, there's always an interesting mix of river rafters, Appalachian Trail hikers, mountain bikers, locals, and tourists. The "campus" has an outfitter's store, a bike-rental shop, and a restaurant called River's End that overlooks the river. A low pedestrian bridge over the Nantahala provides an excellent vantage point for watching rafters.

Rafters at the Nantahala Outdoor Center

Some visitors and rafters arrive at NOC on an excursion train called the Great Smoky Mountains Railroad. Built in the late 1800s, the railroad runs 53 miles between the towns of Dillsboro and Andrews, passing through two tunnels and over 25 bridges along the way. It has appeared in numerous movies, including *The Fugitive*. Passengers take in the mountain scenery from reconditioned coaches, open-air cars, and dining cars pulled by either diesel-electric locomotives or a beautifully restored old Baldwin steam locomotive.

A short walk from the railroad station in Dillsboro is a small cluster of shops and galleries called **Riverwood Shops**. The upscale, tastefully decorated Oaks Gallery displays fine bowls, pottery, kitchenware, and jewelry.

A mile or so east of Dillsboro lies Sylva, the Jackson County seat. From atop a hill, the handsome, cream-colored county courthouse presides over Main Street and one of the region's best-known restaurants. **Lulu's Café** is a surprisingly sophisticated place to find in such a small town. Its eclectic menu draws from all around the culinary globe with offerings such as Indonesian chicken satay, tropical pork tenderloin, Szechwan salad, and that American staple, the hamburger. High ceilings, brightly painted walls, and comfortable booths create an inviting atmosphere in the spacious interior. Near the front of the restaurant, large glass doors open up for al fresco dining.

Mud Dabber's Pottery and Crafts, the next stop, sits unobtrusively along US 276 west of Waynesville. The first thing to greet visitors is a large sun mask affixed to the chimney, its purple tongue hanging out and its mouth frozen in a loopy grin. The mask is a fitting introduction to the work of potter Brad Dodson, whose parents started the business back in the

Mud Dabber's Pottery and Crafts

1970s. Dodson's other whimsical creations include face jugs, mountain gnomes, and impish creatures he calls "wood spirits." The shop also sells attractive tableware and kitchenware made by other members of the Dodson family.

The route continues on to Waynesville, one of the most appealing towns in western North Carolina. **Whitman's Bakery** is located among the galleries and boutiques on the town's handsome, brick-façaded Main Street. Dating back to 1945, Whitman's is an old-fashioned bakery where everything is made on the premises. Upon entering the store, customers are immediately tempted by a variety of pastries and baked goods arrayed in two glass display cases. There are Danishes, doughnuts, napoleons, apple turnovers, éclairs, and "fried pies"—a regional

specialty and perennial bestseller—which feature peach, chocolate, or coconut filling in a halfmoon-shaped pastry crust.

To find the **Grace Cathey Metal Art Gallery**, just head to Waynesville's Frog Level district and look for the "Phillips 66" sign. Cathey, an award-winning sculptor, displays her nature-themed art in the waiting room of her husband's service station. Frogs are a favorite theme, but she also sculpts other animals as well as leafy lamps, trellises, and benches. Along the edge of the parking lot, she has created a small sculpture garden with flowers, bushes, and a waterfall.

Grace Cathey Metal Art Gallery

From Waynesville, the route heads east toward Asheville. The drive takes only a half hour or so, but that's enough time to savor the highlights of this trip through a mountain wonderland.

Additional Information

Appalachian Craft Center
10 N. Spruce St.
Asheville, NC 28801
(828) 253-8499
www.appalachiancraftcenter.com

Best L'il Corner Ice Cream Parlor
4 Yellow Jacket Dr.
Hayesville, NC 28904
(828) 389-0164

Dry Falls
USDA Forest Service, Highlands Ranger Dist.
2010 Flat Mountain Rd.
Highlands, NC 28748
(828) 526-3765

Franklin Gem and Mineral Museum
25 Phillips St.
Franklin, NC 28734
(828) 369-7831
www.fgmm.org

Grace Cathey Metal Art Gallery and Sculpture Garden
136 Depot St. (in the Walker Service Station)
Waynesville, NC 28786
(828) 456-8843
www.gracecathey.com

The Grove Arcade Public Market
1 Page Ave., Ste. 225
Asheville, NC 28801
(828) 252-7799
www.grovearcade.com

John C. Campbell Folk School
1 Folk School Rd.
Brasstown, NC 28902
(800) 365-5724
www.folkschool.org

Lulu's Café
612 W. Main St.
Sylva, NC 28779
(828) 568-8989
www.lulusonmain.com

Mud Dabber's Pottery & Crafts
20767 Great Smoky Mountain Expwy.
Balsam, NC 28707
(828) 456-1916
www.muddabbers.com

Riverwood Shops at Craft Circle
c/o Oaks Gallery, 29 Craft Cir.
Dillsboro, NC 28725
(828) 586-6542

Stoney Hollow Farm
944 Ollies Creek Rd.
Robbinsville, NC 28771
(828) 479-9092
www.thestoneybrookcabin.com

Whitman's Bakery & Sandwich Shop
18 N. Main St.
Waynesville, NC 28786
(828) 456-8271

Yellow Branch Farm & Pottery
136 Yellow Branch Cir.
Robbinsville, NC 28771
(828) 479-6710
www.yellowbranch.com

Outer Banks &
Southern Shores

A Best of the Road™ trip

North Carolina

- Kitty Hawk
- Kill Devil Hills
- Manteo
- Cape Hatteras Nat'l Seashore
- Ocracoke
- Cape Lookout National Seashore
- Wilmington
- Carolina Beach

Wrightsville Beach dunes.

Mystery envelops so much of North Carolina's coastal history that it's hard to tell where fact ends and legend begins. But that's exactly what makes this trip magical. Who can resist the intrigue of pirates, a vanished colony, back-alley ghosts, and fly-gobbling plants? (And you thought this trip would be nothing but a good book and the almighty beach. Think again.) ▸

Outer Banks & Southern Shores (cont.)

What follows: unforgettable experiences on the Outer Banks and Southern Shores, beginning around Kitty Hawk and continuing south to the Cape Fear Coast around Wilmington. Some are new twists on old favorites, and some are memorable moments waiting to be had in nearly undiscovered places.

The Lost Colony Outdoor Drama

On Roanoke Island, the best way to escape summer crowds and still learn about the Lost Colony (Roanoke Island's most fascinating story) is by hiring a guide to lead a kayak eco-tour under the bow of the re-created 16th-century *Elizabeth II*. Locals have their own take on the popular story of the early explorers who mysteriously disappeared in Roanoke Sound. Along the way, great blue heron, nesting egrets, or backyard crabbing pots frequently come into view. Non-seafarers learn about the Lost Colony on board the (tethered) *Elizabeth II* or at the **Lost Colony Outdoor Drama at Waterside Theater**.

Wright Brothers National Memorial

Across Roanoke Sound lies a thin strip of land (and sand) reachable via US 64. Perched on a Kill Devil Hills hilltop, the **Wright Brothers National Memorial**, honoring Orville and Wilbur, marks the site of the world's first powered airplane flight in 1903. The visitor center includes a replica of the original "Wright Flyer."

Orville and Wilbur Wright telegraphed word of their first flight from a telegraph in Kitty Hawk. Once a lifesaving station

(with the town's only telegraph), the building now houses the **Black Pelican Oceanfront Café**. For travelers not into museums, this is the perfect stop. A copy of the telegraph and a few flight photos look down from the walls while visitors munch wood-fired gourmet pizza. The white seafood pizza, with shrimp, scallops, and a white sauce, is one of the most popular.

A couple of miles south, hang gliders swoop from the mountainous dunes of **Jockey's Ridge State Park**. Year-round gusty winds make this Nags Head park an ideal spot for kiteflying, too. Spectacular sunsets are visible from the Atlantic Coast's tallest sand dune.

Hang glider at Jockey's Ridge State Park

Sam & Omie's, also in Nags Head, serves a 7 a.m. breakfast favored by local fishermen and visitors, too. Locals say this quaint 70-year-old diner serves the best breakfast in the Outer Banks. Don't leave without trying the crabmeat Benedict—a weekend special.

A drive down NC 12 and through the Pea Island National Wildlife Refuge leads to the **Chicamacomico Life-Saving Station** in Rodanthe. Before the U.S. Coast Guard existed, life-saving station volunteers rescued crew members from ships sinking just off shore. Self-guided tours of the station, one of the Outer Banks originals, and its various buildings are offered April through November. June through September, visitors enjoy weekly programs such as rescue stories told during evening beach bonfires.

Chicamacomico Life-Saving Station

Cape Hatteras Lighthouse

More tourists flock to the 208-foot **Cape Hatteras Lighthouse** than to any other natural or historic attraction on the Cape Hatteras National Seashore, the country's first. In a monumental engineering effort, the lighthouse was moved 1,600 feet inland in retreat from the encroaching sea. Visitors can climb the black-and-white, spiral-striped lighthouse April through October.

NC 12 continues south via ferry from Pea Island to Ocracoke Island. According to locals, a government ordinance ensures that Howard Street, the island's oldest street and a modest dirt road, will never be paved. The best time for checking out the historic houses, old family cemeteries, moss-covered fences, and Village Craftsmen store is just after a rain, when the tree-canopied street drips a fresh, woodsy scent. **Teach's Hole**, Blackbeard's retail lair for kids, is packed with eye patches, pirate flags, and treasure chest booty of all kinds. Young mates actually enjoy learning history at the store's fun Edward Teach (a.k.a. Blackbeard) exhibit.

Maritime Museum

Back on the mainland and down US 70, Beaufort is home to the **North Carolina Maritime Museum**. Cannon balls and platters from Blackbeard's ship, *Queen Anne's Revenge*, are on display, along with other artifacts from the 18th-century vessel, discovered off the coast here in 1996. From atop this museum, visitors view the fishing village's historic homes with their rooftop widow's walks, balconies where wives of sailors and fishermen would wait

and watch for their husbands to return from sea.

The **Beaufort Grocery Company** decorates its walls with unusual art: whimsical fish and lobsters made from retired surfboards. By day this bistro in Beaufort's historic district serves homemade deli sandwiches. At night the restaurant turns slightly more upscale with excellent seafood burritos, crab cakes, and an extensive wine list.

Wild horses run free on **Shackleford Banks**, across the water from Beaufort. Ancestors of these Spanish horses survived

Shackleford Banks horses

Venus flytrap

16th-century shipwrecks by swimming to shore. There aren't any fences to separate you from the island's animals, whose coats shine red in the late afternoon light. (But remember, these are wild animals, not petting-zoo ponies.) Boats and private ferries run to Shackleford Banks from Harkers Island, Beaufort, or Morehead City. The horses can also be seen from Beaufort's waterfront.

A meander down the coast—you'll drive NC 24, NC 172, then US 17—brings Wilmington, famous for Hollywood studios and the Cotton Exchange. Perhaps less

well-known is the **Ghost Walk tour of Old Wilmington**. Guides recount shivering tales of murder and betrayal on this 1.5-hour tour of haunted back alleys, cemeteries, and historic landmarks. These same guides say people experience ghosts about 35 times each year on the walks. South of Wilmington, **Carolina Beach State Park** is home to fly-munching plants along the Venus Flytrap Trail. Within a 75-mile radius of Wilmington, the Venus flytrap is considered a native plant. If you're lucky, you'll hit lunchtime in the mostly-pine forest and see a fly gobbled by one of the carnivores.

At the tip of the Fort Fisher peninsula, the Cape Fear River's fresh water mixes with the salty ocean. Some say the wind whips 10 miles per hour faster there than at Wrightsville Beach (up near Wilmington), making it easier for kitesurfers to jump as high as 30 feet. Local sports outfitters help novices end their Outer Banks drive on an adventurous note.

Additional Information

Roanoke Island Festival Park
1 Festival Park
Manteo, NC 27954
(252) 475-1500
www.roanokeisland.com

Kitty Hawk Sports
US 158
Nags Head, NC 27959
(252) 441-6800
www.kittyhawksports.com

The Lost Colony Outdoor Drama
1409 National Park Dr.
Manteo, NC 27954
(252) 473-3414
www.thelostcolony.org

Wright Brothers National Memorial
800 Colington Rd.
Kill Devil Hills, NC 27948
(252) 441-7430
www.nps.gov/wrbr

Black Pelican Oceanfront Café
Milepost 4
Kitty Hawk, NC 27949
(252) 261-3171
www.blackpelican.com

Jockey's Ridge State Park
Nags Head, NC 27959
(252) 441-7132
www.jockeysridgestatepark.com

Sam and Omie's
7228 S. Virginia Dare Trail
Nags Head, NC 27959
(252) 441-7366
samandomies.net

Chicamacomico Life-Saving Station
23645 NC 12
Rodanthe, NC 27968
(252) 987-1552
www.chicamacomico.net

Cape Hatteras Lighthouse
Cape Hatteras Lighthouse Office
Manteo, NC 27954
(252) 473-2111
www.hatteras-nc.com/light

Frisco Native American Museum & Natural History Center
SC 12
Frisco, NC 27936
(252) 995-4440
nativeamericanmuseum.org

Village Craftsmen
170 Howard St.
Ocracoke Island, NC 27960
(252) 928-5541
www.villagecraftsmen.com

Teach's Hole
161 Back Rd.
Ocracoke Island, NC 27960
(252) 928-1718
www.teachshole.com

North Carolina Maritime Museum
315 Front St.
Beaufort, NC 28516
(252) 728-7317
www.ah.dcr.state.nc.us/sections/maritime

Shackleford Banks
131 Charles St.
Harkers Island, NC 28531
(252) 728-2250
www.shackleford horses.org

Beaufort Grocery Co.
115-117 Queen St.
Beaufort, NC 28516
(252) 728-3899
www.beaufortgrocery.com

The Cotton Exchange
321 N. Front St.
Wilmington, NC 28401
(910) 343-9896
www.shopcottonexchange.com

Screen Gems Studio
1223 N. 23rd St.
Wilmington, NC 28405
(910) 343-3500
www.screengemsstudios.com

Ghost Walk
Wilmington, NC
(910) 602-6055
www.hirchak.com/

Carolina Beach State Park
1010 State Park Rd.
Carolina Beach, NC 28428
(910) 458-8206
www.ils.unc.edu/parkproject/visit/cabe/do.html

State and National Park Information

Park	Page	Camping	Visitor Center	Lodging	Concessions	Trails	Fishing	Boating	Swimming	Boat Rental	Marina
NORTH CAROLINA											
State Parks											
Carolina Beach State Park	147	•	•		•		•	•			•
Cliffs of the Neuse State Park	83	•	•		•	•	•		•	•	
Crowders Mountain State Park	74	•			•	•	•		•		
Fort Macon State Park	113		•		•		•		•		
Goose Creek State Park	60	•	•		•	•	•	•	•		
Gorges State Park	95	•				•	•	•			
Hammocks Beach State Park	112	•			•	•	•	•	•		
Hanging Rock State Park	6	•	•	•	•	•	•	•	•	•	
Jockey's Ridge State Park	40		•			•			•		
Jones Lake State Park	107	•			•	•	•	•	•		
Kerr Lake State Recreation Area	11	•	•			•	•	•	•		•
Lake Norman State Park	49	•			•	•	•	•	•		•
Lake Waccamaw State Park	129	•	•			•	•	•			
Merchants Millpond State Park	16	•	•			•	•	•		•	
Morrow Mountain State Park	77	•	•	•	•	•	•	•		•	
Mount Mitchell State Park	45	•	•		•	•					
Pettigrew State Park	61	•				•	•	•	•		
Raven Rock State Park	81	•		•	•	•	•				
Stone Mountain State Park	3	•	•		•	•	•				
William B. Umstead State Park	55	•	•		•	•	•	•			
National Parks											
Cape Lookout National Seashore	114	•	•		•	•	•	•			•
Fort Raleigh National Historic Site	39		•			•					
Great Smoky Mountains National Park	42	•	•		•	•	•				
Moores Creek National Battlefield	130		•			•	•				
Wright Brothers National Memorial	40		•								
SOUTH CAROLINA											
State Parks											
Barnwell State Park	161	•	•		•	•	•			•	
Caesars Head State Park	96	•	•		•	•	•				
Cheraw State Recreation Area	125	•			•	•	•	•	•		
Devils Fork State Park	95	•		•	•	•	•	•	•		
Dreher Island State Recreation Area	137	•			•	•	•	•			
Edisto Beach State Park	178	•	•		•	•	•	•			
Givhans Ferry State Park	172	•			•	•	•				
Hickory Knob State Resort Park	148	•		•	•	•	•	•		•	
Hunting Island State Park	177	•	•		•	•	•	•	•		
Huntington Beach State Park	157	•	•		•	•	•	•			
Lake Greenwood State Recreation Area	135	•	•		•	•	•	•			
Lake Hartwell State Recreation Area	116	•			•	•	•	•			
Lake Warren State Park	169					•	•	•			
Lake Wateree State Recreation Area	122	•			•	•	•	•			
Little Pee Dee State Park	127	•			•	•	•			•	
Myrtle Beach State Park	158	•	•		•	•	•	•			
Oconee State Park	95	•	•		•	•	•	•	•	•	
Santee State Park	153	•	•	•	•	•	•	•			
Sesquicentennial State Park	138	•				•	•	•		•	
Table Rock State Park	96	•	•		•	•	•	•	•		
National Parks											
Charles Pinckney National Historic Site	173		•			•					
Congaree National Park	152	•	•			•	•	•			
Cowpens National Battlefield	72		•			•					
Kings Mountain National Military Park	74	•	•			•					
Ninety Six National Historic Site	135		•			•					

Many of the nearly 100 courses in the Myrtle Beach area have been designed by the best in the business: Pete and P.B. Dye, Robert Trent Jones, Greg Norman, and Jack Nicklaus, among others. It's ranked among the best places in the world to play, not just because of the sheer number of courses, but also for the access to tee times and local southern hospitality. Most of the courses are open to the public. The following golf courses are listed in alphabetical order by course name.

Aberdeen Country Club
701 Bucks Tr.
Longs, SC 29568
(843) 399-2660
Number of Holes/Courses: 27 holes make up three 18-hole courses

Arcadian Shores Golf Club
701 Hilton Rd.
Myrtle Beach, SC 29572
(843) 449-5217
Number of Holes/Courses: One18-hole course

Arrowhead Country Club
1201 Burcal Rd.
Myrtle Beach, SC 29579
(843) 236-3243
www.arrowheadcc.com
Number of Holes/Courses: 27 holes make up three 18-hole courses

Azalea Sands Golf Club
2100 US 17 S
North Myrtle Beach, SC 29582
(843) 272-6191
Number of Holes/Courses: One 18-hole course

Barefoot Resort & Golf
4980 46th Ave. S. Ext.
North Myrtle Beach, SC 29582
(843) 390-3200
barefootgolfresort.com
Number of Holes/Courses: Four 18-hole courses

Beachwood Golf Club
1520 US 17 S
North Myrtle Beach, SC 29582
(843) 272-6168
www.beachwoodgolf.com
Number of Holes/Courses: One 18-hole course

Black Bear Golf Club
2650 US 9 W Longs
North Myrtle Beach, SC 29568
(843) 756-0550
www.classicgolfgroup.com
Number of Holes/Courses: One 18-hole course

Blackmoor Golf Club
6100 Longwood Rd.
Murrells Inlet, SC 29576
(888) 650-5556
www.blackmoor.com
Number of Holes/Courses: One 18-hole course

Brick Landing Plantation Golf & Country Club
1882 Goose Creek Rd.
Ocean Isle Beach, NC 28469
(910) 754-4373
www.bricklanding.com/vacations.html
Number of Holes/Courses: One 18-hole course

Brunswick Plantation Golf Resort
US 17 N
Calabash, NC 28467
(910) 845-6928
www.brunswickplantation.com
Number of Holes/Courses: 27 holes make up three 18-hole courses

Burning Ridge Golf Club
US 501 W
Conway, SC 29577
(843) 347-0538
www.classicgolfgroup.com
Number of Holes/Courses: One 18-hole course

Time to Tee It Up! *(cont.)*

Caledonia Golf & Fish Club

Caledonia Golf & Fish Club
369 Caledonia Dr.
Pawleys Island, SC 29585
(843) 237-3675
www.fishclub.com
Number of Holes/Courses: One 18-hole course

Carolina National Golf Club
1643 Goley Hewett Rd., SE
Bolivia, NC 28422
(910) 755-5200
www.carolinanationalgolf.com
Number of Holes/Courses: 27 holes make up
three 18-hole courses

Crow Creek Golf Club
240 Hickman Rd., NW
Calabash, NC 28467
(910) 287-3081
www.crowcreek.com
Number of Holes/Courses: One 18-hole course
.

Diamond Back Golf Club
615 Log Cabin Rd.
Loris, SC 29569
(843) 756-3264
www.diamondback-golf.com
Number of Holes/Courses: One 18-hole course

The Dunes Golf & Beach Club
9000 N. Ocean Blvd.
Myrtle Beach, SC 29572
(843) 449-5236
www.dunesgolfandbeachclub.com
Number of Holes/Courses: One 18-hole course

Eagle Nest Golf Club
US 17 N
North Myrtle Beach, SC 29597
(843) 249-1449
www.eaglenestgolf.com
Number of Holes/Courses: One 18-hole course

Glen Dornoch Waterway Golf Links
4840 Glen Dornoch Way
Little River, SC 29566
(843) 249-2541
www.glendornoch.com
Number of Holes/Courses: One 18-hole course

Grande Dunes Golf Club
8700 Golf Village Ln.
Myrtle Beach, SC 29579
(888) 886-8877
www.grandedunes.com
Number of Holes/Courses: One 18-hole course
.

Heather Glen Golf Links
US 17 N
Little River, SC 29566
(866) 259-0558
www.heatherglen.com
Number of Holes/Courses: 27 holes make up
three 18-hole courses

Heritage Club
US 17 S
Pawleys Island, SC 29585
(800) 299-6187
www.legendsgolf.com
Number of Holes/Courses: One 18-hole course

Heron Point Golf Club
6980 Blue Heron Blvd.
Myrtle Beach, SC 29588
(800) 786-1671
www.heronpointgolfclub.com
Number of Holes/Courses: One 18-hole course

Indian Wells Golf Club
100 Woodlake Dr.
Garden City, SC 29576
(843) 651-1505
Number of Holes/Courses: One 18-hole course

The International Golf Club of Myrtle Beach
1560 Tournament Blvd.
Murrells Inlet, SC 29576
(843) 651-9995
Number of Holes/Courses: One 18-hole course

The Legends
US 501 W
Myrtle Beach, SC 29577
(800) 299-6187
www.legendsgolf.com
Number of Holes/Courses: Three 18-hole
courses

Litchfield Beach & Golf Resort
US 17 S
Pawleys Island, SC 29585
(843) 235-5505
www.litchfieldbeach.com
Number of Holes/Courses: One 18-hole course

Putting practice

Lockwood Folly Country Club
19 Clubhouse Dr., SW
Holden Beach, NC 28462
(877) 562-9663
www.lockwoodfolly.com
Number of Holes/Courses: One 18-hole course

The Long Bay Club
350 Foxtail Dr.
Longs, SC 29658
(843) 399-2222
Number of Holes/Courses: One 18-hole course

Man O' War Golf
5601 Leeshire Blvd.
Myrtle Beach, SC 29579
(843) 236-8000
www.manowargolfcourse.com
Number of Holes/Courses: One 18-hole course

The Wizard Golf Course and Man O' War Golf

Meadowlands Golf Club
1000 Meadowlands Trail
Calabash, NC 28467
(910) 287-7529
www.meadowlandsgolfclub.com
Number of Holes/Courses: One 18-hole course

Myrtle Beach National Golf Club
4900 National Dr.
Myrtle Beach, SC 29579
(843) 347-3333
www.mbn.com
Number of Holes/Courses: Three 18-hole
courses

Myrtlewood Golf Club
US 17 at 48th Ave.
North Myrtle Beach, SC 29577
(843) 913-4516
www.myrtlewoodgolf.com
Number of Holes/Courses: Two 18-hole
courses

Ocean Ridge Plantation
351 Ocean Ridge Pkwy., SW
Sunset Beach, NC 28469
(800) 233-1801
www.big-cats.com
Number of Holes/Courses: Three 18-hole
courses

Oyster Bay Golf Links
US 179
Sunset Beach, NC 28468
(910) 579-3528
www.legendsgolf.com
Number of Holes/Courses: One 18-hole course

Pawleys Plantation Golf & Country Club
US 17 S
Pawleys Island, SC 29585
(843) 237-6200
www.pawleysplantation.com
Number of Holes/Courses: One 18-hole course

Pearl Golf Links
1300 Pearl Blvd., SW
Sunset Beach, NC 28468
(888) 947-3275
www.thepearlgolf.com ·
Number of Holes/Courses: Two 18-hole courses

Pine Lakes International Country Club
5603 Woodside Ave.
Myrtle Beach, SC 29577
(843) 449-3321
www.pinelakes.com
Number of Holes/Courses: One 18-hole course

Possum Trot Golf Club
Possum Trot Rd.
North Myrtle Beach, SC 29582
(843) 272-5341
www.possumtrot.com
Number of Holes/Courses: One 18-hole course

Prestwick Country Club
1001 Links Rd.
Myrtle Beach, SC 29575
(843) 293-4100
www.prestwickcountryclub.com
Number of Holes/Courses: One 18-hole course

Sunshine on Myrtle Beach area greens

Quail Creek Golf Club
US 501 W
Myrtle Beach, SC 29578
(843) 347-0549
www.quailcreekgolfclub.com
Number of Holes/Courses: One 18-hole course

River Hills Golf & Country Club
3670 Cedar Creek Run
Little River, SC 29566
(800) 264-3810
www.riverhillsgolf.com ·
Number of Holes/Courses: One 18-hole course

River Oaks Golf Plantation
831 River Oaks Dr.
Myrtle Beach, SC 29577
(843) 236-2222
www.riveroaksgolfplantation.com
Number of Holes/Courses: 27 holes make up
three 18-hole courses

Rivers Edge Golf Club
2000 Arnold Palmer Dr.
Shallotte, NC 28470
(877) 748-3718
www.river18.com
Number of Holes/Courses: One 18-hole course

Sandpiper Bay Golf & Country Club
800 Sandpiper Bay Dr.
Sunset Beach, NC 28468
(800) 356-5827
www.sandpiperbaygolf.com
Number of Holes/Courses: 27 holes make up
three 18-hole courses

One of 100-plus Myrtle Beach area golf courses

Sea Trail
211 Clubhouse Rd.
Sunset Beach, NC 28468
(800) 546-5748
www.seatrail.com
Number of Holes/Courses: Three 18-hole
courses

Shaftesbury Glen Golf & Fish Club
681 Caines Landings Rd.
Conway, SC 29526
(866) 587-1457
www.shaftesburyglen.com
Number of Holes/Courses: One 18-hole course

Surf Golf & Beach Club
1701 Springland Ln.
North Myrtle Beach, SC 29597
(843) 249-1021
www.surfgolf.com
Number of Holes/Courses: One 18-hole course

Thistle Golf Club
8840 Old Georgetown Rd.
Sunset Beach, NC 28468
(800) 571-6710
www.thistlegolf.com
Number of Holes/Courses: 27 holes make up
three 18-hole courses

Tidewater Golf Club & Plantation
1400 Tidewater Dr.
North Myrtle Beach, SC 29582
(843) 249-3829
www.tide-water.com
Number of Holes/Courses: One 18-hole course

Tournament Player's Club of Myrtle Beach
1199 TPC Blvd.
Murrells Inlet, SC 29576
(843) 357-3399
www.tpc.com
Number of Holes/Courses: One 18-hole course

Tradition Golf Club
1027 Willbrook Blvd.
Pawleys Island, SC 29585
(877) 599-0888
www.traditiongolfclub.com
Number of Holes/Courses: One 18-hole course

True Blue Golf Club
900 Blue Stem Dr.
Pawleys Island, SC 29585
(843) 235-0900
www.fishclub.com/trueblue/
Number of Holes/Courses: One 18-hole course

Wachesaw Plantation East
911 Riverwood Dr.
Murrells Inlet, SC 29576
(843) 357-5252
www.wachesawplantationeast.com
Number of Holes/Courses: One 18-hole course

Waterway Hills Golf Club
9731 US 17 N, Restaurant Row
Myrtle Beach, SC 29578
(843) 449-6488
Number of Holes/Courses: 27 holes make up
three courses

Wedgefield Plantation Golf Club
US 701 N
Georgetown, SC 29440
(843) 448-2124
www.wedgefield.com
Number of Holes/Courses: One 18-hole course

Wicked Stick Golf Links
1051 Coventry Rd.
Myrtle Beach, SC 29575
(800) 797-8425
www.wickedstick.com
Number of Holes/Courses: One 18-hole course

Wild Wing Plantation
1000 Wild Wing Blvd.
Conway, SC 29526
(800) 736-9464
www.wildwing.com
Number of Holes/Courses: One 18-hole course

The Witch
1900 SC 544
Conway, SC 29526
(843) 347-2706; www.witchgolf.com
Number of Holes/Courses: One 18-hole course

The Wizard Golf Course
4601 Leeshore Blvd.
Myrtle Beach, SC 29579
(843) 236-9393
Number of Holes/Courses: One 18-hole course

World Tour Golf Links
2000 World Tour Blvd.
Myrtle Beach, SC 29579
(843) 236-2000
www.worldtourmb.com
Number of Holes/Courses: 27 holes make up
three 18-hole courses

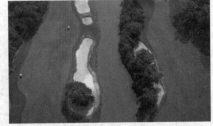

Golf from a bird's eye view

Using Your Road Atlas

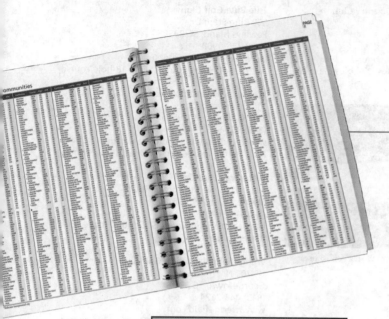

City Listings

- The Cities and Communities Index includes all communities large or small. County, page number, and grid location for each are listed.
- Find the community you're looking for in the list, then turn to the page number indicated.

STREET		
City	State	Map#-Grid
DAVENPORT CREEK RD		
SAN LUIS OBISPO CO CA		271-D6
DAVID AV		
MONTEREY CO CA		337-E4
PACIFIC GROVE CA		337-D5

FEATURE NAME		
City	State	Map#-Grid
1000 STEPS CO BCH		
PACIFIC COAST HWY, LAGUNA BEACH CA		365-G10
ALISO BEACH		
S COAST HWY, LAGUNA BEACH CA		365-F9
ANCHOR MARINA		
1970 TAYLOR RD, CONTRA COSTA CO CA		174-C2

Index

- Street listings are separate from points of interest.
- In the street listings, read across for city, state, page number, and grid reference.
- Points of interest include campgrounds, ski areas, and more.
- The grid reference, a letter-number combination such as D6, tells where on the map to find a listing.

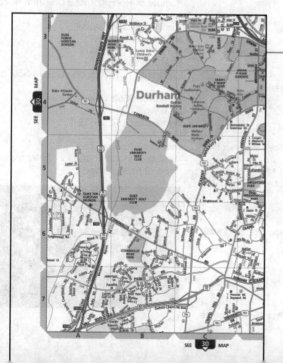

Working with the Maps

- The grid is created by combining letters running along the bottom of the map with numbers running along the side.
- To use a grid reference, follow the numbered row until it crosses the lettered column.
- To find an adjacent map, turn to the map number indicated on map edges.
- The Legend explains symbols and colors.

Using Three Types of Maps

PageFinder™ Map

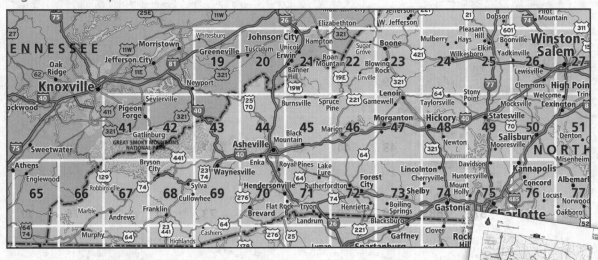

regional map

detail map

You will find numbered boxes on several different types of maps in this atlas. Each box indicates an area covered in greater detail on a subsequent page. If your area of interest falls within one of these boxes, turn to the indicated page to view in greater detail.

PageFinder™ Map

- The PageFinder™ map provides an overview of the entire area covered in this atlas.
- Use the PageFinder™ map to guide you to the page(s) showing your general area of interest.

Regional Maps

- Regional maps offer a general view of your area of interest.
- Use Regional maps for long distance planning and navigation.

Detail Maps

- Detail maps offer street detail as well as multiple points of interest.
- Use Detail maps for local planning and navigation and for locating many points of interest.

PageFinder™ Map

Use this map as a guide to the page(s) showing your general area of interest.
Use the chart to find regional and street detail maps of some of the cities featured in this book.

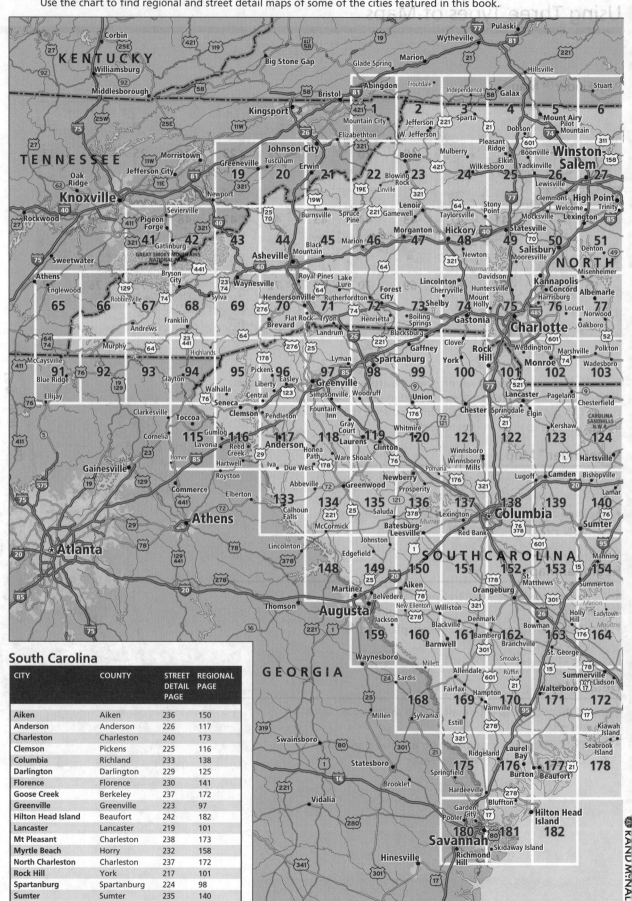

South Carolina

CITY	COUNTY	STREET DETAIL PAGE	REGIONAL PAGE
Aiken	Aiken	236	150
Anderson	Anderson	226	117
Charleston	Charleston	240	173
Clemson	Pickens	225	116
Columbia	Richland	233	138
Darlington	Darlington	229	125
Florence	Florence	230	141
Goose Creek	Berkeley	237	172
Greenville	Greenville	223	97
Hilton Head Island	Beaufort	242	182
Lancaster	Lancaster	219	101
Mt Pleasant	Charleston	238	173
Myrtle Beach	Horry	232	158
North Charleston	Charleston	237	172
Rock Hill	York	217	101
Spartanburg	Spartanburg	224	98
Sumter	Sumter	235	140

PageFinder™ Map
U.S. Patent No. 5,419,586
Canadian Patent No. 2,116,425
Patente Mexicana No. 188186

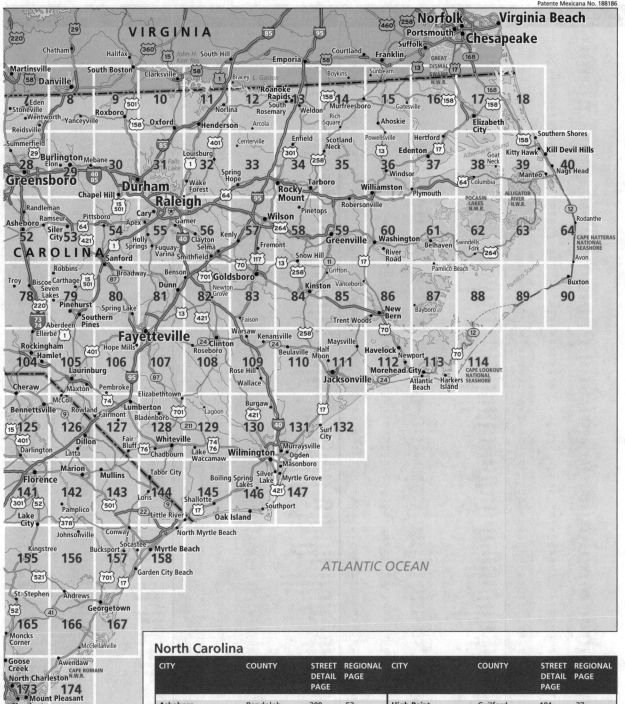

North Carolina

CITY	COUNTY	STREET DETAIL PAGE	REGIONAL PAGE	CITY	COUNTY	STREET DETAIL PAGE	REGIONAL PAGE
Asheboro	Randolph	209	52	High Point	Guilford	191	27
Asheville	Buncombe	206	44	Jacksonville	Onslow	227	111
Atlantic Beach	Carteret	228	113	Kinston	Lenoir	205	84
Boone	Watauga	185	23	Monroe	Union	218	102
Burlington	Alamance	192	29	Morehead City	Carteret	228	113
Chapel Hill	Orange	195	30	Mt Airy	Surry	183	5
Charlotte	Mecklenburg	216	75	Pinehurst	Moore	220	79
Concord	Cabarrus	210	76	Raleigh	Wake	199	55
Durham	Durham	194	31	Rocky Mount	Nash	201	34
Elizabeth City	Pasquotank	184	17	Salisbury	Rowan	208	50
Fayetteville	Cumberland	222	107	Southern Pines	Moore	220	79
Gastonia	Gaston	210	74	Spring Lake	Cumberland	221	80
Goldsboro	Wayne	204	83	Wilmington	New Hanover	231	146
Greensboro	Guilford	190	28	Wilson	Wilson	202	57
Greenville	Pitt	203	59	Winston-Salem	Forsyth	188	27
Harrisburg	Cabarrus	212	76				
Hickory	Catawba	207	48				

Cities and Communities

Community	County	Map#	Grid
A			
Aarons Corner	StkC	6	A4
*Abbeville	AbbC	134	B3
ABBEVILLE CO	AbbC	133	D3
Abbottsburg	BldC	128	D3
*Aberdeen	MreC	79	C7
Abingdon	CrkC	99	D3
Abingdon	CwlC	47	C1
*Abingdon	WasC	1	B1
Abner	MntC	52	B7
Abney Crossroads	KswC	123	C4
Abshers	WksC	3	D7
Acme	CbsC	130	A6
Acorn	MroC	66	A1
Acorn Hill	GatC	16	C3
Acre	BeaC	60	E4
Adako	CwlC	47	A1
Adams	WatC	23	A2
Adamsburg	UnnC	99	D6
Adams Mill	WsgC	20	D4
Adamsville Crossroads	MrlC	105	A7
Adcock Crossroads	VncC	11	C7
Addie	JakC	69	A2
Addington Mill	MacC	68	B7
Addison	McmC	65	A3
Addor	MreC	105	C1
Adger	FaiC	121	D5
Adrian	HryC	143	E6
Afton	WrnC	11	E6
Agnes	LncC	148	A3
Aho	WatC	23	B3
*Ahoskie	HtfC	15	B6
Al	PerC	9	D7
*Aiken	AknC	150	A6
AIKEN CO	AknC	150	A7
Aiken Summit	HenC	7	D2
Airlie	HlfC	12	D6
Airline	HarC	116	B6
*Alamance	AlmC	29	B5
ALAMANCE CO	AlmC	29	E4
Alarka	SwnC	68	A3
Albany	GreC	19	D2
*Albemarle	StnC	77	B3
Albemarle Beach	WshC	37	B6
Albrittons	LnrC	84	C5
Alcot	LeeC	140	C1
Alder Branch	CdnC	17	E6
Alert	FraC	32	D1
ALEXANDER CO	AlxC	24	D7
Alexander Crossroads	DlgC	141	B2
Alexander Mill	GreC	20	A4
*Alexander Mills	RthC	72	D4
Alfordsville	RobC	126	E1
Algary	GrwC	118	C6
ALLEGHANY CO	AlgC	3	C5
Allegheny	MdnC	20	C6
Allen	HryC	143	E6
Allen	MklC	76	B5
*Allendale	AlnC	169	B2
ALLENDALE CO	AlnC	161	B7
Allen Grove	CckC	42	E2
Allen Grove	HlfC	13	C7
Allens Crossroads	UnoC	102	E4
Allens Level	PerC	9	D7
Allenstand	MdnC	20	A7
Allensville	PerC	9	E6
Allensville	SvrC	42	A1
Allenton	RobC	128	A2
Allentown	GtnC	156	E5
All Healing Springs	AlxC	48	B1
*Alliance	PamC	86	E5
Alligator	TyrC	38	D5
Alligoods	BeaC	60	D5
Allison	CasC	8	B6
Allison Ferry	MklC	75	B3
Allreds	MntC	78	C1
Allsbrook	HryC	144	A5
Alma	RobC	105	E7
Almeda	HmpC	170	A5
Alston	FaiC	137	B1
Altamahaw	AlmC	29	B3
Altamont	AvyC	22	C6
Altapass	MhlC	46	B1
Altman	ScrC	168	B7
Alton	UnoC	102	C4
Alvarado	WasC	1	D2
Alvin	BrkC	165	D3
Amantha	WatC	22	E1
Amelia	AlgC	3	C4
Amherst	BkeC	47	C3
Amity Hill	IrdC	49	D4
Ammon	BldC	108	A5
Ammon Ford	BldC	107	E5
Amostown	StkC	6	D4
*Anderson	AndC	117	C4
Anderson	CasC	29	D1
ANDERSON CO	AndC	133	B1
Anderson Creek	HntC	81	A4
Andersons Crossroads	HlfC	13	B5
*Andrews	CheC	67	A6
*Andrews	GtnC	166	B1
*Andrews	WmbC	166	B1
Andy Cove	MdnC	44	B1
Angelus	ChfC	124	A2
*Angier	HntC	55	C7
Ankum	BrwC	12	D2
Anne	GtnC	157	B7
Annieville	GtnC	157	D7
Ansley Heights	WatC	23	A4
Ansley Mill	MdfC	148	A7
ANSON CO	AnsC	103	C3
*Ansonville	AnsC	77	D7
Antioch	BwkC	146	B4
Antioch	CbsC	144	D1
Antioch	HokC	106	B4
Antioch	KswC	139	D1
Antioch	LtrC	101	E7
Antioch	MdnC	43	E1
Antioch	RabC	94	D4
Antioch	WksC	25	A4
Antioch	WmbC	156	B7
Antlers	MkbC	11	C1
Antreville	AbbC	117	D7
Anvil Rock	LtrC	122	E3
Apalache	SptC	97	D3
Apalachia	PolC	65	D6
*Apex	WkeC	55	A3
Appleton	AlnC	169	A1
Aquadale	StnC	77	B5
Aquone	MacC	67	D6
Arabia	HokC	106	C3
*Arapahoe	PamC	86	E7
Arba	GrnC	84	B1
Arborville	AbbC	134	B1
Arcadia	DavC	27	A7
Arcadia	SptC	98	B3
Arcadia Heights	SptC	98	B3
*Arcadia Lakes	RldC	138	B5
Archdale	ClvC	73	E6
*Archdale	GlfC	28	A7
*Archdale	RndC	52	A1
Archer Lodge	JtnC	56	C4
Archville	PolC	65	A7
Arcola	WrnC	12	C7
Ard Crossroads	WmbC	156	D2
Arden	MroC	65	C2
Ardulusa	CumC	107	A2
Argura	JakC	69	B5
Argyle	MrlC	125	E4
Arial	PckC	96	C5
Ariel Cross Roads	MrnC	143	A4
*Arlington	YadC	25	C2
Armenia	CstC	100	B6
Armour	CbsC	129	E6
Arnold	DavC	51	A1
Arrwood Mill	CheC	66	E7
Arthurtown	RldC	138	A6
Asbury	ChaC	54	A5
Asbury	CrkC	99	B4
Asbury	MntC	52	C7
Asbury	StkC	5	E4
ASHE CO	AshC	24	A1
*Asheboro	RndC	52	B4
Ashebrook Park	GasC	74	C4
Ashepoo	ColC	171	C6
Ashepoo Crossing	ColC	171	B6
Ashepoo Siding	ColC	177	D1
*Asheville	BcbC	44	D6
Ashford	McdC	22	C7
Ash Hill	SryC	5	B6
Ashland	AshC	2	B6
Ashland	CasC	8	B7
Ashland	FrkC	115	C7
Ashland	LeeC	124	C7
Ashleigh	BrnC	161	B4
Ashley Heights	HokC	79	D7
Ashmont	HokC	105	D1
Ashton	ColC	170	B1
Ashton	PdrC	131	A4
Ashwood	LeeC	140	A4
Ashwood	PamC	87	B6
Aska	FnnC	91	E6
*Askewville	BrtC	36	C2
Askin	CvnC	86	B4
*Athens	McmC	65	A1
Atkins	LeeC	140	D5
*Atkinson	PdrC	130	B2
*Atlantic Beach	CarC	113	B6
*Atlantic Beach	HryC	158	D1
Auburn	DlgC	125	A6
Auburn	WkeC	55	E4
*Augusta	RmdC	149	A7
*Aulander	BrtC	35	E1
Aumans Crossroads	RndC	52	B7
Aurelian Springs	HlfC	12	E6
*Aurora	BeaC	87	A2
Austin	WksC	25	A1
Austin Mills	StnC	77	B2
Austral	PolC	65	A5
*Autryville	SamC	107	E2
*Avalon	SpnC	115	E4
Aventon	NshC	33	D2
Averett	MkbC	10	D2
Averill	AlnC	168	D1
AVERY CO	AvyC	22	C5
Avery Creek	BcbC	70	D1
Avon	DarC	64	D7
Avondale	RthC	72	E5
*Awendaw	ChsC	174	A2
Axtell	WmC	11	E5
*Ayden	PitC	59	A7
Ayersville	RocC	6	D5
Ayersville	SpnC	115	B3
*Aynor	HryC	143	B5
B			
Babbs Mill	GreC	20	A2
Bacchus	YanC	21	D7
Bachelor	CvnC	113	A2
Bachelors Hall	PtsC	8	A2
Bachman Chapel	NbrC	136	D1
Back Swamp	FloC	141	E1
Backwoods	CtrC	21	E3
*Badin	StnC	77	D2
Baggette Crossroads	ClnC	154	D5
Bagley	JtnC	57	A5
Bailey	MhlC	21	B5
*Bailey	NshC	57	B2
Bailey Camp	CwlC	23	B4
Baileys Landing	BftC	176	C6
*Baileyton	GreC	19	E1
Baker Crossroads	ClvC	73	D2
Baker Crossroads	HryC	143	E5
Baker Crossroads	WmbC	155	C2
Baker Hill	JprC	175	E6
Bakers	UnoC	102	B2
Bakers Crossing	ChtC	181	A5
Bakers Crossroads	RocC	7	C7
*Bakersville	MhlC	21	E6
Bald Creek	YanC	45	A1
*Bald Head Island	BwkC	146	E7
Bald Mountain	YanC	20	E7
Baldock	AlnC	168	E1
Baldwin	AshC	2	C7
Balfour	HdrC	70	E3
Ballard	MtnC	35	E6
Ballards Crossroads	PitC	58	E6
Ballentine	RldC	137	C3
Ballew Mill	FnnC	91	D5
Balltown	AknC	150	A6
Balltown	McmC	65	A4
Balm	AvyC	22	D3
Balsam	JakC	69	B2
Baltic	SamC	109	A1
Baltimore	BldC	129	C4
Baltimore	CckC	19	B6
*Bamberg	BamC	162	A4
BAMBERG CO	BamC	170	A1
Bamboo	WatC	23	B3
Bandana	MhlC	21	D7
Bandy	CwaC	48	E5
Banks	WkeC	55	C5
BANKS CO	BnkC	115	A6
*Banner Elk	AvyC	22	D3
Bannertown	FsyC	27	A2
Bannertown	SryC	5	B5
Bannock Burn	FloC	141	D3
Banoak	CwaC	47	E6
Baptist Hill	ChsC	172	B6
Barbecue	HntC	80	D3
Barber	RowC	50	A4
Barclaysville	HntC	81	D1
Barfield Mill	KswC	123	C4
Barham	WkeC	32	B6
Barium Springs	IrdC	49	B4
Barker Crossroads	BrwC	12	B1
Barkersville	HmpC	170	C7
Barker Ten Mile	RobC	106	E7
Barksdale	LarC	119	A3
Barley	GsvC	13	B2
Barnard	MdnC	44	A2
Barnes	AndC	133	B1
Barnes Station	AndC	133	B1
Barnesville	RobC	127	D5
Barnhill	GtnC	156	E3
*Barnwell	BrnC	161	A5
BARNWELL CO	BrnC	160	C5
Barr	LexC	137	B6
Barrelville	ChsC	172	A7
Barrett	AlgC	4	B4
Barretts Crossroads	HtfC	15	A3
Barriers Mill	CabC	76	D3
Barrineau Crossroads	ClnC	155	B1
Bartell Crossroads	WmbC	156	B3
Bartlett	CdnC	17	E6
Barton	AlnC	169	C3
Barton Crossroad	GsnC	3	A2
Bascom	ScrC	168	B5
Bascomville	CstC	122	B1
Bashan	JprC	176	B3
Bass Crossroads	DilC	126	D6
Bass Crossroads	NshC	33	A6
Batarora	BwkC	130	B7
Bat Cave	HdrC	71	C2
Batchelor Crossroads	NshC	33	C6
*Batesburg-Leesville	LexC	136	D7
*Batesburg-Leesville	SalC	136	C7
Bates Creek	CheC	66	C7
Batesville	GrvC	97	D5
Batesville	HabC	93	D7
Bath	AknC	149	D7
*Bath	BeaC	60	E6
Baton	CwlC	47	D2
Baton Rouge	CstC	100	B7
*Battleboro	EdgC	34	A4
*Battleboro	NshC	34	A4
Battlecreek	OcnC	94	D6
Battleground	AvyC	22	C2
Batts Crossroads	BeaC	60	A3
Baxter	HdrC	71	B4
Baxter	UniC	92	B7
Baxter Forks	HryC	143	E5
Bay	TyrC	38	A5
Bayboro	HryC	143	E5
*Bayboro	PamC	87	A5
Bay City	PamC	87	A4
Bayleaf	WkeC	31	D6
Baynes	CasC	29	E1
Baynham	AknC	149	E4
Bayshore	NhrC	131	B6
Bay Springs	ChfC	124	C2
Bayview	BeaC	60	E7
Baywood	GsnC	4	A3
Bazen Crossroads	FloC	142	B7
Beach Springs	PqmC	37	D1
Beaman Crossroads	SamC	82	C6
Beam Mill	ClvC	73	D3
Bear Creek	GhmC	67	C5
Bear Creek	OnsC	112	A7
Beard	CumC	81	B7
Beards Crossroads	ClnC	154	E1
*Bear Grass	MtnC	59	E2
Bear Paw	CheC	66	A7
Bearpond	VncC	32	B1
Bear Poplar	RowC	49	E5
Bears Bluff	ChsC	178	C1
Bearskin	SamC	108	C1
Bear Stand	CtrC	22	A2
Bearwallow	HdrC	71	B1
Beasley	WshC	37	C5
*Beaufort	BftC	177	A5
*Beaufort	CarC	113	C5
BEAUFORT CO	BeaC	59	E7
BEAUFORT CO	BftC	170	E7
Beaulieu	ChtC	180	E6
Beautancus	DupC	83	D5
Beaver Creek	AshC	2	D7
Beaverdam	BcbC	70	B1
Beaverdam	HlfC	13	B7
Beaverdam	HwdC	43	E7
Beckhamville	CstC	122	B2
Beckwith	BeaC	60	E5
Beech	BcbC	44	E4
Beech Bottom	AvyC	22	B5
Beech Cove Vista	TwnC	93	B3
Beech Creek	AvyC	22	C2
Beechertown	MacC	67	C5
Beech Glen	MdnC	44	E2
Beech Grove	HawC	19	C1
*Beech Mountain	AvyC	22	D3
*Beech Mountain	WatC	22	D3
Beechwood	MkbC	11	D1
Bee Log	YanC	21	A6
Belair Springs	PatC	5	C2
Belcher Crossroads	MccC	134	A5
Belcross	CdnC	17	C5
Belfast	WanC	83	D1
Belgrade	OnsC	111	E3
*Belhaven	BeaC	61	C5
Belin	GtnC	157	C6
Bell	ElbC	133	A6
Bellair	CvnC	86	A5
Bellamy	RobC	128	A2
Belle Mead	GrvC	97	A6
Bellemont	AlmC	29	C5
Belleview Estates	McmC	65	A4
Bells	ChaC	54	D3
Bells Crossroads	ColC	170	D2
Bells Crossroads	GrvC	97	D6
Bells Crossroads	IrdC	49	C5
Bells Crossroads	PdrC	130	E4
Bells Crossroads	PitC	59	A3
Bells Fork	PitC	59	B5
Bell Swamp	BwkC	146	C2
Belltown	GraC	31	D1
Bell Town	LtrC	122	C2
Belltown	MroC	65	E2
Belltown Hill	PolC	91	D2
Belltown Mill	MroC	65	E2
Bell View	CheC	92	C2
*Belmont	GasC	75	A5
Belmont	HlfC	13	B4
Belmont	RldC	138	A4
Belser Crossroads	ClnC	153	E5
*Belton	AndC	117	E4
Belva	MdnC	20	B7
Belvedere	AknC	149	C7
Belvedere Estates	BrkC	173	A3
*Belville	BwkC	130	D7
*Belwood	ClvC	73	D1
Benaja	RocC	28	D1
Ben Avon	SptC	98	D4
Benham	WksC	25	B1
Bennetts Point	ColC	177	E2
*Bennettsville	MrlC	125	E1
Bennington Mill	GsnC	3	C1
*Benson	JtnC	82	A2
Bent Creek	BcbC	70	C1
Bent Creek	YanC	21	B6
Bentonville	JtnC	82	D2
Berea	GraC	10	B7
Berea	GrvC	97	A5
BERKELEY CO	BrkC	173	C2
Berkeley Hills	BrkC	173	A3
Berlin	AknC	151	B4
*Bermuda Run	DveC	26	D6
Berry Hill	MklC	75	A6
Berry Hill	PtsC	7	E3
Berry Mill	MacC	68	D6
Berrys Crossroads	DilC	126	C7
Berryville	EffC	175	C5
Bertha	CurC	18	B5
BERTIE CO	BrtC	15	C7
*Bessemer City	GasC	74	B5
Bessie	JakC	68	E7
Best	WanC	84	A3
Beta	JakC	68	E3
Bethania	FsyC	26	E3
Bethany	GreC	20	B5
Bethany	RocC	28	B1
Bethany	YorC	74	B7
Bethany Crossroads	CumC	107	D1
Beth Eden	NbrC	120	B7
Bethel	CasC	8	B5
Bethel	CbsC	144	E3
Bethel	EffC	175	A5
Bethel	GtnC	166	C1
Bethel	HokC	106	A3
Bethel	HwdC	69	D1
Bethel	MdnC	44	E1
*Bethel	PitC	59	B1
Bethel	PqmC	37	D1
Bethel	WasC	1	D1
Bethel	WatC	22	D2
Bethel Hill	PerC	9	E4
Bethera	BrkC	165	D5
Bethesda	ChfC	124	D2
Bethesda	ChtC	180	E6
Bethesda	DavC	51	B1
Bethesda	DurC	31	A7
Bethlehem	AlxC	48	B2
Bethlehem	HtfC	15	C6
Bethlehem	MroC	65	D2
Bethlehem	UniC	92	C4

*Indicates incorporated city

Community	County	Map#	Grid
*Bethune	KswC	124	A5
Bettie	CarC	113	D4
Beufordtown	BrkC	165	E4
Beulah	GreC	19	A4
Beulah	HydC	61	E7
Beulah	LncC	133	C7
Beulah	PlkC	71	E4
Beulahtown	JtnC	57	A5
*Beulaville	DupC	110	B2
Beverly	ElbC	133	B4
Beverly	PckC	96	C6
Biddle	FaiC	122	C5
Big Cherokee	WsgC	20	E2
Big Creek	MroC	65	D2
Bigcreek	SalC	135	D5
Big Curve	CbsC	145	C1
Big East Fork	HwdC	69	E3
Big Fork	MkbC	11	E1
Big Hill	WasC	2	B2
Big Laurel	MdnC	20	B7
Big Laurel	SwnC	68	C4
Big Lick	StnC	76	E5
Big Pine	MdnC	44	A3
Big Ridge	JakC	69	B6
Big Sandy	WsgC	20	D1
Big Spring	CtrC	21	D1
Bilboa	DurC	31	A6
Bills Creek	RthC	71	E2
*Biltmore Forest	BcbC	44	D7
Bina	AshC	2	D5
Bingham	DilC	126	B5
Bird Cage	CbsC	128	B6
Bird Crossroad	SvrC	42	C1
Birds	EffC	175	C6
Birdstown Crossroads	DlgC	125	A4
Birdtown	LtrC	123	D2
Birdtown	SwnC	68	C1
*Biscoe	MntC	78	C3
Bishop	BwkC	146	C1
Bishops Cross	BeaC	61	B4
*Bishopville	LeeC	140	B2
Bitter End	CtrC	22	A3
Bixby	DveC	26	D7
Blackberry	HenC	6	D1
Blackberry Inn	BcbC	45	A4
Blackburn	CwaC	48	A6
*Black Creek	WlnC	57	D4
Black Jack	PitC	59	D6
Blackmans Mills	SamC	82	C4
Blackmon Crossroads	JtnC	82	B2
*Black Mountain	BcbC	45	B6
Blacknel	LeCo	54	C5
Blackridge	MkbC	12	B1
Blacks	SalC	136	B7
*Blacksburg	CrkC	73	D7
*Blackville	BrnC	161	B3
Black Water	SryC	5	A6
Blackwell	CasC	8	B5
Blackwood	OrgC	30	C6
BLADEN CO	BldC	107	D6
*Bladenboro	BldC	128	C3
Bladen Springs	BldC	129	B3
Blades	CvnC	113	A2
Blaine	MntC	77	D1
*Blairsville	UniC	92	D4
Blairville	YorC	100	A4
Blake	ColC	170	E7
Blakedale	GrwC	134	D2
Blakely	WmbC	155	D7
Blakley Crossroads	LtrC	122	C3
Blalock	RabC	94	A4
Blandford	EffC	175	C7
Blands	DurC	30	D7
Blands Crossroads	LnrC	84	C5
Blantyre	TrnC	70	C4
Bleases Crossroads	SalC	135	E5
*Blenheim	MrlC	125	E3
Blevins	CtrC	21	E2
Blevins Crossroads	AlgC	4	A4
Blevins Store	SryC	4	D5
Blizzards Crossroads	DupC	83	E6
*Bloomingdale	ChtC	180	B3
Bloomingdale	RobC	127	E4
Bloomington	StnC	77	A3
Bloomingvale	WmbC	156	A6
Bloomville	ClnC	154	D5
Blossom	FloC	142	B6
Blossomtown	MacC	68	B7
BLOUNT CO	BntC	41	B4
*Blowing Rock	CwlC	23	B4
*Blowing Rock	WatC	23	B4
Blue Brick	MrnC	142	C1
Bluefield	BldC	128	E3
Blue Heaven	AbbC	118	C6
Bluehouse Corners	ColC	171	A6
Blue Mill	CckC	43	C2
*Blue Ridge	FnnC	91	D5
Blue Ridge	GrvC	97	C2
Blue Ridge	HdrC	71	B3
Blue Ridge	TrnC	70	C7
Blue Ridge Forest	BcbC	45	B7
Blue Rock	YanC	45	D1
Bluff	MdnC	43	E2
Bluff Estates	RldC	138	B7
*Bluffton	BftC	181	D1
Bluffton	CckC	42	E3
*Blythewood	RldC	138	B2
*Boardman	CbsC	128	A4
*Bogue	CarC	112	C6
Bohaynee	TrnC	95	C1
*Boiling Spring Lakes	BwkC	146	C4
Boiling Springs	BrnC	160	E7
Boiling Springs	CheC	66	D6
*Boiling Springs	ClvC	73	B5
Bolen Town	OraC	162	A1
*Bolivia	BwkC	146	B3
Bolling	HlfC	13	B4
*Bolton	CbsC	129	C6
Bona Bella	ChtC	181	A5
Bonair	RmdC	149	A7
Bonaparte Landing	BwkC	145	B7
Bonds Crossroads	LarC	119	E5
Bones Ford	CumC	80	C7
Boney	RldC	138	B1
Bonham	UnnC	99	B6
Bonlee	ChaC	53	C5
*Bonneau	BrkC	165	B3
Bonneau Beach	BrkC	165	A3
Bonnerton	BeaC	86	D1
Bonnetsville	SamC	108	C2
Bonniview Estates	AknC	150	A7
Bonsal	WkeC	54	E4
Bookman	RldC	137	D3
Boomer	CckC	43	C2
*Boone	WatC	23	B3
Boone Fork	WatC	23	A4
Boones Creek	OcnC	95	D4
Boones Crossroads	NhnC	14	A6
Boones Hill	SryC	5	B5
Boone Trail	HntC	80	E2
Boonford	MhlC	21	E7
*Boonville	YadC	25	E2
Booth	HryC	143	D6
Bordeaux	MccC	134	A7
Borden	SmtC	139	D4
Bostian Heights	RowC	50	C7
*Bostic	RthC	72	D3
Bostick	FloC	142	C6
Boswellville	WlnC	57	D4
Bottom	SryC	4	D5
Bouknight	EgfC	149	D2
Bounty Land	OcnC	95	C7
Bowdens	DupC	83	B7
Bowditch	YanC	45	D1
Bowen Point	BwkC	145	D6
Bowers Corner	BrwC	12	C1
*Bowersville	HarC	116	B6
Bowlens Creek	YanC	45	C1
*Bowman	OraC	163	A3
Bowman Bluff	HdrC	70	D4
Bowmantown	WsgC	20	D1
Bowmore	HokC	105	E3
Bowyer	OraC	163	E3
Boxwood	HenC	7	D2
Boyd	NbrC	136	C2
Boyd Crossroads	PitC	59	E5
Boyds Fork	BeaC	60	E5
*Boydton	MkbC	11	B1
Boydville	SpnC	115	C3
Boykin	KswC	139	B3
Boykin	MrlC	105	A7
*Boykins	ShmC	14	D2
Boyles Chapel	StkC	5	E7
Boylston Creek	TrnC	70	C4
Bradburn Hill	GreC	20	A3
Bradford Crossroads	IrdC	49	A3
Bradleyville	AknC	149	C7
Braemar	CtrC	21	E1
Brake	EdgC	34	B6
*Branchville	OraC	162	D4
*Branchville	ShmC	14	C2
Brandon	AshC	2	D4
Brandon	GrvC	97	A5
Brannon	SptC	98	B1
Branon	YadC	25	E4
Brassfield	DurC	31	A7
Brasstown	OcnC	94	D7
Braswell	CbsC	128	B5
Braswells Crossroads	HlfC	35	B3
Breeden	MrlC	125	E1
Breezewood	GrwC	134	E4
Brendletown	MacC	68	C5
Brent	SmtC	139	E5
*Brevard	TrnC	70	B6
Brewers Crossroads	NhnC	13	C3
Brewerton	LarC	118	C5
Brewton	BftC	176	D1
*Briarcliffe Acres	HryC	158	D1
Briars	BftC	177	A2
Briar Thicket	CckC	19	A4
Brice	RthC	72	D6
Brices Creek	CvnC	86	A7
Brices Crossroads	DupC	109	B5
Brickhaven	ChaC	54	D6
Brickhouse Crossroads	NbrC	120	A5
Bricks	EdgC	34	B2
Brickton	HdrC	70	E2
Bridgeport	CckC	19	A7
Bridgersville	WlnC	58	B2
*Bridgeton	CvnC	86	B6
Bridgewater	BkeC	46	D4
Bridle Creek	GsnC	3	B2
Brief	UnoC	76	C6
Brier Creek Landing	ScrC	168	D6
Briertown	MacC	67	D5
Bright Hope	GreC	19	C5
Brighton	HmpC	175	C2
Brighton Beach	BftC	181	D1
Brightwater	HdrC	70	E4
Brindletown	BkeC	46	E6
Brink	GsvC	13	C1
Brinkleyville	HlfC	12	E7
Brisbon	BynC	180	C6
*Bristol	SulC	1	A3
Bristow	MrlC	126	A5
Britton	SmtC	154	B1
Brittons Neck	MrnC	142	E7
Brittontown	GreC	19	E2
Broad	WlkC	133	A7
Broad Creek	CarC	112	D5
Broadway	CbsC	128	B7
*Broadway	LeCo	80	D1
Brock	OcnC	116	B1
Brockington	WmbC	155	D3
Brocks	OnsC	110	E2
Brocks Mill	ChfC	104	A7
Brogden	JtnC	82	E1
Brogden	WanC	83	C3
Brogdon	SmtC	154	B2
Bronson Crossroads	DilC	126	E4
Brook Cove	StkC	27	B1
Brookdale	OraC	152	D7
*Brookford	CwaC	48	A4
Brookgreen Park	FloC	141	D1
Brooklyn	HalC	9	A1
Brooks Crossroads	YadC	25	D4
Brooksdale	PerC	9	D6
Brookside Mill	CckC	19	B6
Brookston	VncC	11	C6
Brooksville	HryC	144	E7
Brosville	PtsC	7	E2
Brown Bay	HryC	143	D7
Brownlee Crossroads	AbbC	133	D1
Brown Mill	FnnC	91	E3
Brown Mountain Beach	CwlC	47	A1
Browns	CckC	43	A3
Browns Crossroads	NbrC	120	D6
Browns Crossroads	RndC	53	A3
Browns Hill	AknC	159	D3
Brownsville	MrlC	126	A5
Brown Town	GasC	75	A5
Brown Town	PdrC	131	C5
Browntown Crossroads	GrnC	84	C2
Brownway	HryC	157	C2
Brownwood	AshC	23	C1
Broylesville	WsgC	20	D3
Bruce	PitC	58	E3
Bruner	RldC	138	D7
*Brunson	HmpC	169	D3
Brunson Crossroads	EgfC	149	A2
Brunson Crossroads	WmbC	156	C3
Brunsons Store	SmtC	154	B1
Brunswick	BrwC	12	D1
BRUNSWICK CO	BrwC	13	A1
BRUNSWICK CO	BwkC	130	C7
BRYAN CO	BynC	180	B6
Bryan Mill	FnnC	92	A4
Bryans Crossroads	WmbC	155	C5
Bryantown	NhnC	14	B7
*Bryson City	SwnC	68	B2
Buck	WksC	24	C4
Buckeye Ford	HdrC	71	A5
Buck Hall	ChsC	166	B7
Buckhead	CbsC	129	C5
Buckhead	ChtC	181	A6
Buckhorn	OrgC	30	A5
Buckhorn Crossroads	WlnC	57	B4
Buckingham Landing	BftC	181	E1
Buckland	GatC	15	E3
Bucklesberry	LnrC	84	B4
Bucklick	FaiC	122	C5
Buckner	MdnC	44	E2
Buck Shoals	YadC	25	C5
Bucksport	HryC	157	C3
Buck Stand	AbbC	134	B1
Bucksville	HryC	157	D3
Buena Vista	BrtC	36	B2
Buffalo	CheC	67	B6
Buffalo	IrdC	49	A4
Buffalo	MccC	134	B7
Buffalo City	DarC	39	B6
Buffalo Cove	CwlC	23	D6
Buffalo Springs	MkbC	10	C1
Buford	LtrC	102	B7
Bug Hill	CbsC	144	E3
Buie	RobC	106	B6
Buies Creek	HntC	81	E2
Buies Neck	RobC	107	A5
Buladean	MhlC	21	D4
Buladeen	CtrC	1	B5
Bullet Creek	MroC	65	C5
Bullock Creek	YorC	99	E5
Bullocksville	VncC	11	C4
*Bulls Gap	HawC	19	B2
Bullucks Crossroads	EdgC	34	B7
Bumpus Cove	UciC	20	E4
BUNCOMBE CO	BcbC	43	E5
Bunker Hill	DilC	126	D4
Bunker Hill	HryC	157	B4
Bunker Hill	UniC	92	C5
*Bunn	FraC	32	D6
Buntontown	JhnC	22	B1
Bunyan	BeaC	60	C5
Burbage Crossroads	BeaC	61	A7
Burbank	CtrC	22	A4
Burch	SryC	25	D1
Burden	BrtC	36	A1
Burgan	HryC	157	B1
*Burgaw	PdrC	130	E2
Burger	McmC	65	B2
Burger Town	CheC	91	D1
Burgess	HryC	157	D5
BURKE CO	BkeC	22	E7
BURKE CO	BurC	160	C7
Burke Chapel	BkeC	47	E4
Burkemont	BkeC	47	A5
*Burlington	AlmC	29	C5
Burnett	GilC	91	C5
Burnett Fields	MacC	67	E6
*Burnettown	AknC	149	D7
Burnett Siding	HwdC	69	D3
Burney	BldC	107	D6
Burningtown	MacC	68	A5
Burnside	ChtC	180	E6
Burns Mill	OcnC	95	B6
Burnsville	AnsC	77	B7
*Burnsville	YanC	45	C1
Burnt Chimney Corner	PlkC	71	D6
Burnt Chimneys	HenC	7	C1
Burnt Church Crossroads	ColC	171	D5
Burnt Mills	CdnC	17	B4
Burr Hill	ColC	171	D3
Burroughs	ChtC	180	C6
Burton	BftC	177	A4
Burton	DurC	31	A5
Burton Hills	GasC	74	D5
Burtons Ferry Landing	ScrC	168	D3
Busbee	BcbC	70	E1
Bush River	NbrC	119	E7
Bushy Fork	PerC	9	C7
Busick	YanC	45	D3
Butler Crossroads	CbsC	144	E3
Butler Crossroads	FloC	142	B6
Butlers	BrtC	36	B3
Butlers Crossroads	SamC	108	D2
Butters	BldC	128	B2
Butts	WasC	1	A1
Buxton	DarC	90	C2
Buzzards Crossroads	BrtC	36	C2
Bynum	ChaC	54	B3
Byrd	DorC	163	D6
Byrds Crossroads	FloC	141	C6
Byrdville	CbsC	129	E6
C			
Cabarrus	CabC	76	C5
CABARRUS CO	CabC	75	E4
Cabes Ford	OrgC	30	D4
Cabin	DupC	110	A2
Cades Cove	BntC	41	A6
Caesars Head	GrvC	96	C1
Cahaba	BrtC	35	D3
Caines	GtnC	167	B3
Cainhoy	BrkC	173	D3
Cairo	AnsC	104	A4
*Cajah's Mountain	CwlC	47	C2
*Calabash	BwkC	145	A7
Calahaln	DveC	26	A7
Caldwell	ColC	170	C1
Caldwell	MklC	75	C1
Caldwell	OrgC	30	D2
CALDWELL CO	CwlC	24	A7
Caldwell Crossroad	CstC	122	B3
CALHOUN CO	ClhC	152	C4
*Calhoun Falls	AbbC	133	C4
Calhoun Mill	MccC	133	E5
Calico	PitC	59	D7
Calico	SptC	98	E4
California	HtfC	15	B5
California	MdnC	44	E2
California	PitC	58	E4
Call	WksC	24	D4
Callahans Hills	PtsC	8	A2
Callison	GrwC	134	E5
Callisons	PamC	87	B6
Calvander	OrgC	30	B7
Calvert	SptC	98	B3
Calvert	TrnC	70	A7
*Calypso	DupC	83	B6
Cambria	McmC	65	A4
Cambridge	GrwC	135	C4
*Camden	KswC	123	B7
CAMDEN CO	CdnC	17	C4
Camelot	HdrC	70	D3
*Cameron	ClhC	153	A6
*Cameron	MreC	80	A3
Campbell	AndC	117	D4
Campbell	StkC	6	B4
Campbell Creek	BeaC	87	B2
Campbell Crossroads	ChfC	124	C1
Campbells Crossroad	HokC	80	A7
Camp Branch	FloC	141	C7
Camp Branch	HmpC	170	A5
Camp Bryan	CvnC	112	C3
Camp Cox	LtrC	101	C2
Camp Creek	BkeC	47	C6
Camp Creek	GreC	20	A4
Camp Creek	LtrC	102	A6
Camp Croft	SptC	98	D4
Camp Don-Lee	PamC	113	A1
Campfield	GtnC	157	B6
Camp Gravatt	AknC	150	C3
Camp Hardee	BeaC	60	C6
Camp Leach	BeaC	60	D7
Camp Long	AknC	150	B4
Camp Oak	OcnC	95	B5
*Campobello	SptC	71	E7
Camp Occoneechee	RthC	71	D2
Camp Rawl	AknC	150	E5
Camp Seagull	PamC	113	A1
Camp Springs	CasC	29	B1
Camp Tom Howard	SulC	1	B4
Campton	SptC	98	A2
Cana	DveC	26	B7
Canaan	DorC	172	B2
Canaan	OraC	162	B3
Canaan	SptC	98	C4
Canadys	ColC	171	B1
Canal Lake	UniC	92	D4
Candler Heights	BcbC	44	B7
*Candor	MntC	78	D4
Cane	YanC	45	B1
Cane Brake	TrnC	95	E1
Cane River	YanC	45	B1
Cane Savannah	SmtC	139	D7
Caney Branch	GreC	19	C5
Caney Creek	PolC	65	A7
*Canon	FrkC	116	A7
*Canon	HarC	116	A7
Canon Hill	HryC	157	B2
Cantey	KswC	123	A7
Canto	BcbC	44	A4
*Canton	HwdC	43	E7
*Cape Carteret	CarC	112	B6

*Indicates incorporated city

PAGE V

Cities and Communities

Community	County	Map#	Grid
Cape Fear	HntC	81	B1
Capella	StkC	6	A7
Capelsie	MntC	78	B4
Capels Mill	RchC	78	C6
Capernium	FsyC	26	D5
Capitol View	RldC	138	B6
Capwells Crossroads	ChsC	172	B6
Carbonton	ChaC	53	D7
Carem	UnnC	120	C1
Carlan	BnkC	115	B7
Carlisle	SptC	98	C1
*Carlisle	UnnC	120	E2
Carlock	McmC	65	A4
Carmen	MdnC	20	C6
Carmichael Crossroads	DilC	126	E5
Carnes Crossroad	BrkC	164	E7
*Carnesville	FrkC	115	D6
Caroleen	RthC	72	E5
Carolina	AlmC	29	C3
Carolina	DilC	126	C2
*Carolina Beach	NhrC	147	A4
*Carolina Shores	BwkC	145	A6
Caromi Village	BrkC	172	E2
Carpenter	WkeC	55	A2
Carpenter Bottom	AvyC	22	B5
Carr	OrgC	30	A2
*Carrboro	OrgC	30	C7
Carris	WmbC	155	C7
Carroll	DupC	109	B2
CARROLL CO	CrlC	5	B2
Carson Mill	SwnC	67	E2
Carsonville	GsnC	3	E1
Carter	CtrC	1	A6
Carter	GatC	16	A5
CARTER CO	CtrC	1	A6
CARTERET CO	CarC	114	B2
Carters Crossroads	DlgC	140	D3
Carters Crossroads	GtnC	157	A4
Carters Mill	PatC	5	C3
Cartersville	DupC	109	E5
Cartersville	FloC	140	E4
Cartertown	SvrC	42	A4
*Carthage	MreC	79	C4
Cartoogechaye	MacC	68	A7
Carvers	BldC	129	C4
Carvers Bay	GtnC	157	A4
*Cary	ChaC	54	E2
*Cary	WkeC	55	B2
*Casar	ClvC	73	B1
Cash	ChfC	125	B2
Cash Corner	PamC	87	A7
Cashion Crossroads	CrkC	99	D1
Cashville	SptC	97	E6
Caskey	LtrC	101	D7
Cason Old Field	AnsC	103	D5
*Castalia	NshC	33	B4
Castle Heights	CckC	19	A7
Castle Heights	MkbC	11	C2
Castoria	GrnC	58	C6
Casville	CasC	8	B6
CASWELL CO	CasC	29	C1
*Caswell Beach	BwkC	146	D6
Catarrh	ChfC	124	A4
Cataska	MroC	65	D5
*Catawba	CwaC	48	E4
CATAWBA CO	CwaC	47	E6
Catchall	SmtC	139	D5
Cateechee	PckC	96	A6
Cates	PerC	9	D7
Catfish	CwaC	48	E4
Catherine Lake	OnsC	110	E4
Caton	SvrC	42	B3
Catons Grove	CckC	42	E3
Cat Square	LinC	47	E7
Causey	HryC	143	D1
Cauthens Crossroads	LtrC	122	E2
Cave	AlnC	161	B7
Ca-Vel	PerC	9	D5
*Cayce	LexC	137	E6
Cayton	CvnC	86	C3
Cedar Bay	BwkC	145	B6
Cedar Bluff	SvrC	42	B2
Cedar Bluff	WasC	1	D2
Cedar Cliff	TwnC	93	B3
Cedar Creek	CumC	107	C3
Cedar Creek	GreC	19	E5
Cedar Creek	RldC	137	D2
Cedar Creek	WmbC	166	A2
Cedar Falls	RndC	52	D3
Cedar Fork	DupC	110	C3
Cedar Grove	CtrC	21	B1
Cedar Grove	DavC	51	B4
Cedar Grove	HalC	9	E2
Cedar Grove	HryC	157	C1
Cedar Grove	MkbC	11	D1
Cedar Grove	RndC	52	B5
Cedar Hammock	ChtC	181	A5
Cedar Hill	AnsC	77	D7
Cedar Hill	BwkC	130	D7
*Cedar Point	CarC	112	B6
*Cedar Rock	CwlC	23	E7
Cedar Rock	PckC	96	C5
Cedar Springs	ChsC	172	E6
Cedar Swamp	WmbC	156	A4
Cedar Valley	CwlC	47	E1
Ceffo	PerC	9	C5
Celeste Hinkle	IrdC	49	A3
Celo	YanC	45	D2
Center	DveC	50	A1
Center	MroC	65	D1
Center	YadC	25	E4
Center Crossroads	GtnC	157	A3
Center Hill	ChwC	16	B7
Center Pigeon	HwdC	69	E1
Centerville	AndC	117	B4
Centerville	DilC	126	C5
*Centerville	FraC	33	A2
Centerville	GreC	20	C1
Central	CtrC	21	C1
Central	IrdC	25	A7
*Central	PckC	96	A7
Central Crossroads	ClnC	141	B7
*Central Pacolet	SptC	99	A4
Central-Shiloh	AbbC	134	B1
*Cerro Gordo	CbsC	128	A6
*Chadbourn	CbsC	128	B6
Chadwick Acres	OnsC	132	C2
Challedon	LexC	137	D5
Chalybeate Springs	HntC	55	B7
Champion	WksC	24	B4
Chanceytown	PolC	91	C1
Chandler	ChsC	173	E3
Chandlers	WmbC	156	C4
Chapanoke	PqmC	16	E7
*Chapel Hill	DurC	30	D7
Chapel Hill	MdnC	20	B7
*Chapel Hill	OrgC	30	C7
*Chapin	LexC	137	A3
Chapmans Crossroads	SalC	135	E4
*Chappells	NbrC	135	D3
Charity	BrkC	173	C1
Charity	DupC	109	E4
Charles	IrdC	49	C1
*Charleston	ChsC	173	B5
Charleston	HlfC	35	B3
CHARLESTON CO	ChsC	179	A1
Charleston Crossroads	AbbC	133	E4
*Charlotte	MklC	75	C6
CHATHAM CO	ChaC	53	C4
CHATHAM CO	ChtC	180	C5
Chatmoss	HenC	7	B2
Chauga Heights	OcnC	116	A1
Chavistown	MrlC	104	D7
Cheddar	AndC	117	E3
Cheeks	RndC	53	A6
Cheeks Crossroads	OrgC	30	A4
Chennault	LncC	133	C7
Cheoah	GhmC	67	B3
Cheohee	OcnC	95	B4
*Cheraw	ChfC	104	B7
CHEROKEE CO	CheC	65	E6
CHEROKEE CO	CrkC	98	E1
Cherokee Falls	CrkC	99	C1
Cherokee Forest	GrvC	97	B4
Cherokee Springs	SptC	98	D2
Cherry	WshC	37	E6
Cherry Crossroads	EdgC	34	B4
Cherryfield	TrnC	70	A6
Cherry Grove	CasC	8	B7
Cherry Grove	CbsC	143	E1
Cherry Hill	BrkC	165	B5
Cherry Hill	WmbC	166	B1
Cherry Lane	AlgC	4	A5
Cherry Point	CvnC	112	B2
Cherryvale	SmtC	139	D6
*Cherryville	GasC	74	A3
*Chesapeake		17	B1
*Chesnee	SptC	72	D7
*Chester	CstC	100	C7
CHESTER CO	CstC	100	C6
Chesterfield	BkeC	47	B3
*Chesterfield	ChfC	103	D7
CHESTERFIELD CO	ChfC	123	E1
Chestnut Crossroads	HryC	144	C6
Chestnut Dale	AvyC	22	B5
Chestnut Gap	FnnC	91	C4
Chestnut Grove	StkC	5	E7
Chestnut Hill	AshC	2	E5
Chestnut Hill	HdrC	71	B1
Chestnut Hills	GrvC	97	A6
Chestnut Knob	HenC	7	A2
Chestnut Ridge	GreC	20	B4
Chestnut Springs	GrvC	71	A6
Chestnut Valley	MroC	66	A2
Chestoa	UciC	21	A4
Chestuee	MroC	65	C1
Chick Springs	GrvC	97	C4
Chicod	PitC	59	D7
Chicora	BrkC	164	D4
Childsbury	BrkC	165	B7
*Chimney Rock	RthC	71	C2
*China Grove	RowC	50	B6
Chinners	HryC	143	C5
Chinquapin Falls	LexC	150	D2
Chip	CvnC	86	A4
Chip	MntC	78	B5
Chisman	StkC	6	D7
Chisolm	BftC	177	B3
*Chocowinity	BeaC	60	A6
Choestoe	UniC	92	E6
Chopped Oak	GilC	91	B6
Choppee	GtnC	156	E6
CHOWAN CO	ChwC	16	B7
Christie	HalC	10	A3
Chublake	PerC	9	D5
Church Hill	WrnC	12	B4
Churchland	DavC	50	D3
Cid	DavC	51	D4
City View	GrvC	97	A5
Clairmont	BwkC	146	D1
Clambank	GtnC	167	C3
*Claremont	CwaC	48	D4
Claremont	SmtC	139	C6
CLARENDON CO	ClnC	163	E1
Claresville	GsvC	13	E1
Clark	CvnC	85	E5
Clark	HwdC	69	B2
*Clarkesville	HabC	115	A2
Clarketown	CtrC	21	D3
Clarks Crossroads	BldC	129	A3
Clarks Crossroads	WmbC	155	C2
*Clarksville	MkbC	10	E2
*Clarkton	BldC	128	E3
Clatworthy Crossroads	AbbC	134	B5
Claussen	FloC	141	E3
Clay	GraC	31	E1
CLAY CO	ClyC	67	B7
Clayroot	PitC	85	D1
Clayton	FaiC	120	E4
*Clayton	JtnC	56	B4
*Clayton	RabC	94	B4
Clearbranch	UciC	20	E5
Clear Creek	MklC	76	B6
Clearmont	OcnC	116	B1
Clear Pond	BamC	162	A6
Clear Run	SamC	108	E6
Clearwater	AknC	149	D7
Cleland Crossroads	HmpC	169	E3
Clement	SamC	81	E6
*Clemmons	FsyC	26	E6
Clemmons Station	FsyC	26	E6
*Clemson	PckC	116	E1
Cleora	EgfC	149	A2
Clevedale	SptC	98	B4
*Cleveland	RowC	49	E4
CLEVELAND CO	ClvC	47	C7
Click Mill	CckC	43	C1
Cliffside	RthC	72	E5
Clifton	AshC	2	C6
Clifton	SptC	98	E3
Clifton Station	SptC	98	E3
Cliftonville	WlnC	57	D1
Climax	LexC	136	E4
Clingman	WksC	25	B3
*Clinton	LarC	119	D4
*Clinton	SamC	108	D2
*Clio	MrlC	126	B2
Clito Mill	GsnC	3	E1
Closs	LnrC	85	A3
*Clover	YorC	100	C1
Clover Garden	AlmC	29	B3
Clubhouse Crossroads	DorC	172	A3
Club House Crossroads	LexC	137	A6
Clyburn	KswC	123	B5
Clyde	DlgC	124	C6
*Clyde	HwdC	43	D7
Coachmans Corners	DorC	172	B2
Coakley	EdgC	35	A6
Coalville	CheC	66	E6
*Coats	HntC	81	D2
Coats Crossroad	LtrC	123	A4
Coats Crossroads	JtnC	56	A7
Cobbham	MdfC	148	A6
Cobbham Crossroads	MdfC	148	A6
Cobbs	WlnC	57	E1
Cobbs Crossroad	WlnC	57	E1
Cobb Town	EdgC	58	C3
Coburn	BcbC	44	A7
Cochrantown	HryC	143	D7
COCKE CO	CckC	19	B6
Cockrell Beach	BeaC	61	C7
Coddle Creek	CabC	75	E1
Coffee Ridge	UciC	20	E6
*Cofield	HtfC	15	C5
Coggins Mine	MntC	77	E1
Cog Hill	McmC	65	A4
Cognac	RchC	105	A3
Cokercreek	MroC	65	E5
Cokers Crossroads	WanC	84	A1
Cokesbury	GrwC	134	D1
Cokesbury	HntC	55	A7
Cokesbury	VncC	11	D6
Coldbrook	EffC	180	C1
Cold Point	LarC	119	A5
Cold Spring	JhnC	1	D4
Cold Spring	SulC	1	A3
Cold Springs	BkeC	22	D7
Cold Springs	BntC	41	A3
Cold Springs	CabC	76	C2
Cold Water	CabC	76	B2
Coleman	McdC	45	C5
Colemans Crossroads	SalC	135	E4
*Colerain	BrtC	36	E1
Coleridge	RndC	53	A5
Coles Crossing	FloC	141	D2
Coleville	StkC	6	B4
Colington	DarC	39	E3
College Acres	AknC	150	A7
College Park	CtrC	21	C1
Colleton	ColC	170	C1
COLLETON CO	ColC	169	E1
Colliers	EgfC	149	A4
Collins Creek	ChsC	166	E6
Collinstown	StkC	5	E4
Collinsville	PlkC	72	A6
Colly	BldC	129	E4
Colon	LeCo	54	B7
Colonial Heights	CumC	106	E3
Colonial Heights	WkeC	55	D4
Coltranes Mill	RndC	28	B7
*Columbia	TyrC	38	C5
COLUMBIA CO	ClbC	149	A6
*Columbus	PlkC	71	D5
COLUMBUS CO	CbsC	146	A1
Colwell	FnnC	91	B4
Combs Fork	JnsC	84	E7
Comet	AshC	2	C5
Comfort	JnsC	111	A1
Comingtee	BrkC	165	B7
*Como	HtfC	15	A3
Conasauga Mill	MroC	65	D4
Conch Creek	GtnC	157	B4
Concord	AndC	117	C3
*Concord	CabC	76	B2
Concord	DupC	109	B4
Concord	PerC	9	C5
Concord	RthC	72	E4
Concord	SamC	108	C2
Concord	YanC	45	B1
Concord	YorC	100	E2
Concord Crossroads	AlnC	168	E2
Coneross	OcnC	95	B7
Conestee	GrvC	97	B6
*Conetoe	EdgC	59	A1
Congaree	RldC	138	D7
Congleton	PitC	59	D2
Conklin	WsgC	20	E3
Connaritsa	BrtC	36	A1
*Connelly Springs	BkeC	47	D3
Connestee	TrnC	70	B6
Connestee Falls	TrnC	70	B7
Connor	OraC	163	E3
Connor	WlnC	57	A3
*Conover	CwaC	48	C5
Contentnea Junction	WlnC	57	D4
Converse	SptC	98	D3
*Conway	HryC	158	A2
*Conway	NhnC	14	C4
Cook	WmbC	156	C4
Cooke Crossroads	DorC	172	C3
Cooks Crossroads	LarC	97	E7
Cooksville	CwaC	47	E6
Cooktown	MhlC	21	E5
Cool Branch	FaiC	121	A3
*Cooleemee	DveC	50	B2
Cooleemee Junction	DveC	50	B2
Cooleys Crossroads	HlfC	12	D4
Cooley Springs	SptC	72	C7
Cool Run	BwkC	145	C6
Cool Spring	HryC	143	C5
Cool Springs	IrdC	49	E2
Coolvale	BwkC	146	D5
Cooper	SamC	81	E6
Cooper	WmbC	156	A6
Cooper Creek	FnnC	92	B7
Coosaw	BftC	176	E3
Coosawhatchie	JprC	176	C2
*Cope	OraC	162	A2
Copeland	SryC	5	A7
Copper Ford	HdrC	71	C3
*Copperhill	PolC	91	C2
Corbett	CasC	30	A1
*Cordova	OraC	162	C1
Core Creek	CarC	113	B3
Core Point	BeaC	60	E7
Coreys Crossroads	MtnC	60	A2
Corinth	ChaC	54	D6
Corinth	NshC	33	C5
Corinth	OcnC	95	D7
Corinth	RthC	72	E3
Cornatzer	DveC	26	C7
*Cornelia	HabC	115	A4
*Cornelius	MklC	75	C1
Cornwall	GraC	10	B4
Cornwell	CstC	121	D2
Coronaca	GrwC	135	A1
Correll Park	RowC	50	C6
Corriher Heights	RowC	50	A7
Costin	PdrC	130	C2
*Cottageville	ColC	171	D3
Cotton Grove	DavC	51	A4
Cotton Valley	DilC	127	A4
Cottonville	StnC	77	C6
Couchton	AknC	150	C6
Courtenay	OcnC	95	D7
Courtney	YadC	26	A5
Cove	HwdC	43	D5
*Cove City	CvnC	85	C5
Cove Creek	HwdC	43	C6
Cove Creek Cascades	SvrC	41	D3
Covington	CasC	8	D5
Covington	RchC	78	B7
Cowans Ford	MklC	75	B2
Cowan Springs	BntC	41	B3
Cowanstown	JhnC	22	C1
*Coward	FloC	141	D6
Cowarts	JakC	69	A4
Cowden	AknC	159	E4
Cowee	MacC	68	B5
*Cowpens	SptC	98	E2
Cox Mill	CabC	75	E2
Cox Mill	GsnC	4	B2
Coxs Crossroads	BeaC	86	C1
Coxville	PitC	85	C1
Cozads Mill	MacC	68	B7
Cozart	GraC	31	B4
Crab Point Village	CarC	113	B5
Crabtree	CtrC	22	A3
Crabtree	HwdC	43	D6
Craft Spring	GreC	20	A1
Craggy	BcbC	44	D6
Craig	HenC	6	D2
*Cramerton	GasC	74	E5
Cranberry	AvyC	22	B4
Cranberry Gap	AvyC	22	B4
Crandull	JhnC	1	C4
Crane Forest	RldC	138	A4
Craven	RowC	50	E5
CRAVEN CO	CvnC	112	C2
Craytonville	AndC	117	E5
Creeches Mill	JtnC	56	E7
*Creedmoor	GraC	31	C3
Creek	WrnC	12	B7
Creek Junction	WasC	2	B2
Creeksville	NhnC	14	B5
Cremo	BrtC	36	C1
Crescent	RowC	50	D6
Crescent	SptC	98	A6
Cresthill	ChtC	180	E5
Creston	ClhC	153	A5
Crestview	DlgC	141	D1
Crestwood	HdrC	70	E3
*Creswell	WshC	38	A6
Cribb Crossroads	GtnC	157	A4

*Indicates incorporated city

Community	County	Map#	Grid
Cribb Town	CbsC	144	C1
Cricket	WksC	24	C3
Crims Crossroads	FsyC	27	D2
Crisp	EdgC	58	D2
Croatan	CvnC	112	C1
Crockers Nub	JtnC	57	A3
Crocketts Crossroad	LtrC	122	D1
Crocketville	HmpC	169	E3
Croft	AknC	150	A5
Croft	MklC	75	D3
Cromer Crossroads	NbrC	120	B5
Crooked Oak	CrlC	5	A1
Crooked Oak	SryC	4	D4
Cross Anchor	GreC	20	A2
Cross Anchor	SptC	119	D2
*Cross Hill	LarC	119	B7
Cross Keys	ShmC	14	D1
Cross Keys	UnnC	119	E2
Cross Landing	TyrC	38	B6
*Crossnore	AvyC	22	C6
Cross Plains	GrvC	97	A1
Cross Roads	HarC	116	B6
Cross Roads	OcnC	116	C2
Crossway	SctC	105	B6
Crosswell	PckC	96	E5
Crowburg	ChfC	102	D6
Crowders	GasC	74	C6
Crowells Crossroads	HlfC	34	D1
Crumplers Crossroads	JtnC	56	E6
Cruso	HwdC	70	A2
Crutchfield	SryC	25	E1
Crutchfield Crossroads	ChaC	53	C2
Culberson	CheC	92	A2
Culbreth	GraC	31	C1
Cullasaja	MacC	68	C7
Cumberland	CumC	106	E2
Cumberland	GtnC	166	D2
CUMBERLAND CO	CumC	107	C3
Cummings	HmpC	170	B5
Cummings Heights	WasC	1	B1
Cumnock	LeCo	54	A6
Cunningham	PerC	9	B4
Cunningham	SptC	98	A3
CURRITUCK CO	CurC	17	D3
Currytown	DavC	51	A1
Curtis	FnnC	91	C4
Cusaac Crossroads	FloC	141	C5
Cusco Willa	MkbC	11	C2
Cusick	SvrC	41	D1
Cutcane	FnnC	91	E3
Cutshalltown	MdnC	20	B7
Cycle	YadC	25	C4
Cypress Creek	CbsC	144	E2
Cypress Creek	DupC	110	B5
Cypress Crossroads	LeeC	140	D2
Cypress Fork Crossroads	ClnC	154	E3
Cyrus	OnsC	110	E6
D			
Dabney	VncC	11	A7
Dacusville	PckC	96	D4
Daddysville	FraC	32	E7
Dahlia	GsvC	13	D2
Daisy	HryC	144	B5
Dale	BftC	176	E2
Dalewood	GrwC	134	D1
*Dallas	GasC	74	D4
Dalton	StkC	26	D1
Damascus	JhnC	1	D5
*Damascus	WasC	1	E2
Dana	HdrC	71	A4
*Danbury	StkC	6	B6
Daniel	BynC	180	B7
Daniels	LinC	74	B1
Danieltown	RthC	72	C4
Danripple	HalC	9	C2
Dan River Shores	StkC	6	A6
Dan Valley	RocC	7	A6
*Danville		8	C3
Danwood	FloC	141	D4
Darby	WksC	23	D4
Dardens	MtnC	36	E7
DARE CO	DarC	18	D7
Dark Ridge	AvyC	22	C3
*Darlington	DlgC	125	C7
Darlington	HlfC	13	B6
DARLINGTON CO	DlgC	141	B1
Darraugh	AbbC	134	C3
Daufuskie Landing	BftC	181	C3
Davenport Forks	WshC	37	E5
Davidson	HmpC	170	C7
*Davidson	MklC	75	D2
DAVIDSON CO	DavC	26	E7
Davidson River	TrnC	70	B5
DAVIE CO	DveC	26	B6
Davie Crossroads	DveC	50	C2
Davis	CarC	114	A4
Davis Crossroads	ClnC	154	A6
Davis Hill	ColC	171	C3
Davis Springs	UciC	21	C3
Davis Station	ClnC	154	B5
Davistown	EdgC	58	D1
Davistown	FloC	142	B5
Davistown	McdC	45	E7
Dawkins	FaiC	121	B6
Dawson	LnrC	84	D2
Dawson Crossroads	HlfC	34	E2
Day Book	YanC	21	C7
Days Crossroads	HlfC	13	C5
Dean	MacC	68	C6
Deans	AndC	117	B6
Deans Store	NshC	33	D7
Deas Mill	YorC	100	E5
Debruce	RmdC	159	A3
Deep Creek	AnsC	103	C5
Deerfield	JprC	175	E5
Dehart	WksC	24	D1
De Hart Mill	SwnC	68	A3
DeKalb	KswC	123	B6
Delhart	GsnC	4	A3
Delhi	WlkC	133	C7
Delight	ClvC	73	B1
Delila	HalC	9	B3
Dellaplane	WksC	25	A3
Dellwood	HwdC	43	C7
Delmar	HlfC	13	C7
Delmar	SptC	98	D4
Delmar	WasC	1	D2
De Loach	HmpC	175	D1
Delphia	YorC	100	C3
Delta	StkC	6	C5
Delta	UnnC	120	C3
Delway	SamC	109	A5
Democrat	BcbC	44	E3
Dendron	McdC	45	D5
*Denmark	BamC	161	D3
Dennis	FsyC	27	C2
Denniston	HalC	9	E2
Denny	SalC	136	A5
Denny	WksC	23	E5
Denny Store	PerC	10	A6
Denny Terrace	RldC	137	E5
Denton	CckC	42	E2
*Denton	DavC	51	D5
Dentons	GhmC	66	E5
Denver	AndC	117	B3
Deppe	OnsC	111	D4
Derby	RchC	78	E7
Derusk	GreC	19	E4
Dexter	GraC	11	A6
Dial	FnnC	92	A6
Dickerson	CvnC	86	C5
Dickerson	GraC	31	E1
Dickerson Mill	RabC	94	B3
Dicks Hill	HabC	115	B2
Diggs	RchC	104	B5
*Dillard	RabC	94	B3
Dillard	StkC	6	D6
Dillard Crossroads	SptC	98	A5
Dillingham	BcbC	45	A3
*Dillon	DilC	126	E5
DILLON CO	DilC	143	B1
Dillons Fork	HenC	6	E1
*Dillsboro	JakC	68	D3
Dimmette	WksC	25	B2
Dinber	CstC	100	C6
Dinkins Mill	SmtC	139	C5
Dixiana	LexC	137	E7
Dixie	MklC	75	B6
Dixie	WlnC	57	D4
Dixie Crossroads	JtnC	56	E3
Dixon	OnsC	132	A1
Dixon Crossroads	HabC	115	A2
Dixon Crossroads	OcnC	116	A2
Dobbersville	WanC	82	E5
*Dobbins Heights	RchC	104	E4
*Dobson	SryC	4	E6
Dobyns	PatC	5	E2
Dockery	WksC	24	E1
Dodd Hill	SptC	98	B2
Dodgetown	StkC	6	C6
Dodsons Crossroads	OrgC	30	B6
Doe Creek	BwkC	145	E5
Doeville	JhnC	1	B6
Dog Bluff	HryC	143	B6
Dogwood Acres	OrgC	54	C1
*Donalds	AbbC	118	B6
Dongola	HryC	157	B2
Donnaha	FsyC	26	D2
Doolie	IrdC	49	B6
Dora	LinC	73	E1
Dorange	DorC	163	A5
DORCHESTER CO	DorC	171	E4
Dorchester Estates	DorC	172	C2
Dort	GatC	15	C2
*Dortches	NshC	33	E5
Dosheno	AndC	118	A4
Dothan	CbsC	144	D4
Dotsontown	GreC	20	C2
Double Branches	LncC	148	B3
Double Island	YanC	21	D7
Double Shoals	ClvC	73	C3
Doughton	WksC	4	A7
Douglas	LtrC	122	D1
Douglas Crossroads	BeaC	60	C5
Douglass	FaiC	121	C5
Dover	ClvC	73	C4
*Dover	CvnC	85	B4
Dover	MreC	78	E1
Dovesville	DlgC	125	B5
Downs Siding	GrwC	134	D1
Doyle	HryC	143	C6
Draco	CwlC	24	A7
Drake	MrlC	125	E4
Drake	NshC	34	A4
Draughn	EdgC	34	D3
Drawdy	ColC	171	B4
Drayton	SptC	98	C3
Draytonville	CrkC	99	C2
Drenn	CrlC	4	D2
Dresden	AshC	2	C5
Drew	BrtC	35	E3
Drewry	VncC	11	C4
*Drexel	BkeC	47	C4
Drexel Lake Hills	RldC	138	C5
Drigger Crossroad	ColC	171	C3
Driggerstown	BrkC	172	E1
Drivers Store	WlnC	58	A3
Drowning Ford	WasC	1	D2
Drum Hill	GatC	15	E2
Drums Crossroads	CwaC	48	E6
Dry Branch	AknC	160	A1
Dry Creek	WsgC	21	A3
Dry Fork	SmyC	2	B1
Dry Hill	JhnC	22	C1
Dry Pond	PatC	5	E3
Drysdale Hills	HdrC	70	D4
Duan	CwaC	48	C6
Duart	BldC	107	B5
*Dublin	BldC	128	D1
Dubose	SmtC	140	A5
Dubose Crossroads	DlgC	141	A1
Dubose Crossroads	LeeC	140	A4
Du Bose Park	KswC	139	B1
Duck	DarC	39	D1
Duck Creek	OnsC	132	D1
*Ducktown	PolC	91	C2
Dudley	ChfC	102	D6
Dudley Shoals	CwlC	48	A1
*Due West	AbbC	118	A7
Duff Creek	DupC	109	C5
Duffies	HokC	106	A4
Duford	HryC	143	D2
Dukes	HmpC	169	C4
Dukes	NshC	33	C4
Dulah	CbsC	144	E4
Dulaney	GreC	19	E4
Dula Springs	BcbC	44	D4
Dunbar	GtnC	156	E6
Dunbar	MrlC	126	B3
Dunbarton	BrnC	160	D5
Duncan	HntC	55	A6
*Duncan	SptC	97	E4
Dundarrach	HokC	106	B3
Dunean	GrvC	97	A5
Dunlape Crossroads	LeeC	140	D4
Dunn	FnnC	91	C3
*Dunn	HntC	81	E3
Dunns Rock	TrnC	70	A6
Dunns Store	HlfC	34	E2
DUPLIN CO	DupC	109	C3
Du Pont	SvrC	41	C2
Dupont Springs	SvrC	41	C2
Dupree Crossroads	PitC	58	E3
Durant	ClnC	154	D1
*Durham	DurC	30	E6
*Durham	OrgC	30	D6
*Durham	WkeC	55	A1
DURHAM CO	DurC	30	D7
Dutchman	SptC	98	D7
Dwight Crossroads	LtrC	102	B7
Dysartsville	McdC	46	D6
Dyson	GrwC	135	C3
E			
Eadytown	BrkC	164	D2
Eagle Mills	IrdC	25	D6
Eagle Rock	WkeC	56	B2
Eagletown	NhnC	14	D7
Eakers Corner	ClvC	73	B1
*Earl	ClvC	73	D6
Earle	WmbC	156	A7
Earles Grove	OcnC	116	C3
Earleys	HtfC	15	A7
Earlwood Park	DlgC	125	B7
Earlys Crossroads	DlgC	125	A7
Earpsboro	JtnC	56	D2
*Easley	PckC	96	D6
Easonburg	NshC	33	E6
Easons Crossroads	GatC	16	A3
*East Arcadia	BldC	129	E5
Eastatoe	PckC	95	D3
*East Bend	YadC	26	C2
Eastbrook	BwkC	130	C7
*East Ellijay	GilC	91	B7
East Etowah	McmC	65	B3
East Fork	SvrC	42	B2
East Fork	TrnC	70	A7
East Franklin	MacC	68	C6
East Gaffney	CrkC	99	B1
East Gantt	GrvC	97	B6
East Lake	DarC	39	B6
East Laport	JakC	69	A4
East Millers Cove	BntC	41	A4
Eastmont	RldC	138	B6
Eastover	CumC	81	C7
*Eastover	RldC	153	A1
Eastport	CckC	19	A7
East Rockingham	RchC	104	C4
East Side Park	RobC	127	C3
East Spartanburg	SptC	98	D4
*East Spencer	RowC	50	D5
East Sumter	SmtC	140	A7
East View	GrvC	118	A2
East View	RmdC	159	C1
Eastwood	MreC	79	C5
Easy Hill	BwkC	146	D1
Ebbs Mill	MdnC	43	D2
Ebenezer	CheC	66	C7
Ebenezer	OcnC	95	C6
Echo	RobC	127	A3
Echo Heights	WkeC	55	D4
Eden	LarC	118	D3
*Eden	RocC	7	C4
Edenhouse Point	BrtC	37	A4
*Edenton	ChwC	37	B3
Edgar	RndC	52	A1
Edgecombe	PdrC	131	E3
EDGECOMBE CO	EdgC	33	E7
*Edgefield	EgfC	149	C2
EDGEFIELD CO	EgfC	148	E6
Edgemont	CwlC	22	E6
Edgewood Terrace	MreC	79	A5
Edinburgh	HokC	105	E4
Edisto	OraC	162	C1
*Edisto Beach	ColC	178	B3
Edisto Club	BamC	161	D2
Edmonds	AlgC	4	B3
Edmondson	JtnC	55	E6
Edmund	LexC	151	C1
Edmundson Crossroads	WanC	57	E7
Edneyville	HdrC	71	B3
Edwards	WmbC	155	A6
Edwards Crossroads	AlgC	3	E4
Edwards Crossroads	NhnC	14	B5
Edwards Crossroads	NshC	33	B5
Edwards Fork	HlfC	35	A3
Edwina	CckC	43	A1
EFFINGHAM CO	EffC	175	B5
*Ehrhardt	BamC	162	A7
Eison Crossroads	NbrC	120	B5
Ekom	LarC	118	E5
Ela	SwnC	68	B2
Elams	WrnC	12	C3
Elamtown	MkbC	11	D1
Elberon	WrnC	11	E7
ELBERT CO	ElbC	133	B4
Elberta	MreC	78	E4
Eldorado	MntC	77	E1
Eleanors Crossroads	GatC	15	E4
Elease	CumC	107	B4
Eleazer	RndC	52	A7
Elf	ClyC	93	B2
*Elgin	KswC	138	D3
Elgin	LtrC	122	E1
Eliah	BwkC	130	C7
Elim	FloC	141	D5
Eli Whitney	AlmC	29	E7
*Elizabeth City	CdnC	17	C6
*Elizabeth City	PsqC	17	C6
*Elizabethton	CtrC	21	C1
*Elizabethtown	BldC	128	E1
*Elkin	SryC	25	C2
*Elkin	WksC	25	C2
Elk Mills	CtrC	22	B1
Elkmont	SvrC	41	E5
*Elko	BrnC	161	A2
*Elk Park	AvyC	22	B4
Elk Shoal	YanC	21	A7
Elkton	BldC	128	E4
Elk Valley	AvyC	22	C3
Elkville	WksC	23	E5
Ellejoy	BntC	41	B2
*Ellenboro	RthC	72	E4
Ellendale	AlxC	24	B7
*Ellerbe	RchC	104	D1
Ellerbees Mill	SmtC	139	C4
Ellerbe Grove	RchC	104	D4
*Ellijay	GilC	91	B7
Ellijay	MacC	68	D6
Elliott	SamC	109	A2
Ellisboro	RocC	6	E7
Ellis Crossroads	RowC	50	D4
Ellis Mill	MroC	65	D2
Ellis Store	BrtC	36	D5
*Elloree	OraC	153	C7
Ellwood	BrkC	165	B7
*Elm City	WlnC	57	E1
Elm Grove	LnrC	84	E5
Elmira Crossroads	PitC	59	E7
Elmo	HalC	9	B1
Elmore	SctC	105	B6
Elmores Crossroads	GasC	74	E6
Elmwood	IrdC	49	D3
Elmwood Park	AknC	150	A7
*Elon College	AlmC	29	B4
Elrod	RobC	127	A2
Elrod Mill	FnnC	91	D4
Elroy	WanC	83	E2
Elsie	LexC	137	B7
Embree	BamC	162	C4
Embreeville	WsgC	21	A3
Embro	WrnC	12	A5
*Emerald Isle	CarC	112	C6
Emerald Village	WkeC	55	E3
Emerson	BldC	129	A4
Emery	MntC	78	D5
Emit	JtnC	56	E3
Emory	SalC	136	A6
*Enfield	HlfC	34	B2
*Englewood	McmC	65	B2
English	MdnC	20	E7
English Creek	CckC	42	E1
English Crossroads	LeeC	140	B3
Eno	OrgC	30	D5
Enochville	RowC	50	A7
Enola	SptC	98	D2
Enon	YadC	26	C4
Enos	LexC	152	A2
Enterprise	DavC	27	A7
Enterprise	WrnC	12	C4
Eona	CrlC	4	D1
Ephesus	DveC	50	B2
Epperson	MroC	65	D5
Eppes Fork	MkbC	11	C3
Epsom	FraC	32	C1
Epworth	GrwC	135	A4
Erastus	JakC	68	E6
Erect	RndC	52	E5
Ernestville	UciC	20	E5
Ervintown	OnsC	110	E3
*Erwin	HntC	81	D3
Erwin	LtrC	122	D1
*Erwin	UciC	21	A4
Eskota	YanC	45	C3
Essex	HlfC	33	C1
Estatoe	MhlC	45	E1
Estelle	CasC	8	E4
*Estill	HmpC	169	C6
Ether	MntC	78	C1
Ethon Crossroads	LexC	137	B7
Etna	MacC	68	A4
*Etowah	McmC	65	A3
Eubanks	OrgC	30	C6

*Indicates incorporated city

RAND McNALLY

Cities and Communities

Community	County	Map#	Grid
Eufola	IrdC	49	A4
Eulala	SalC	135	C5
Eulonia	MrnC	142	E5
Eureka	AknC	149	E4
Eureka	JhnC	1	E4
*Eureka	WanC	57	E6
Eutaw Springs	OraC	164	B2
*Eutawville	OraC	164	A2
*Evans	ClbC	148	E7
Evans	CstC	121	D1
Evansdale	WlnC	57	E4
Evans Mill	ChfC	102	E7
*Everetts	MtnC	35	E7
Everetts Crossroads	BeaC	60	E6
Everetts Mill	RchC	104	B5
Evergreen	CtrC	22	B3
Evergreen	FloC	141	E4
Evergreen Hills	AndC	117	B4
Evergreen Hills	WasC	1	A2
Everton	DupC	109	C1
Exley	EffC	180	C1
Exum	BwkC	145	C3
Exway	RchC	78	B6
Ezzelltown	SamC	109	A7
F			
Fain	UniC	92	E5
*Fair Bluff	CbsC	127	D7
*Fairfax	AlnC	169	C3
*Fairfax	HmpC	169	C3
Fairfax	SwnC	67	E1
Fairfield	UnoC	102	E1
FAIRFIELD CO	FaiC	137	D1
Fairfield Harbour	CvnC	86	C6
Fairfiled Terrace	RldC	138	A4
Fairforest	SptC	98	B3
Fairgrove	CwaC	48	B4
*Fairmont	RobC	127	C3
Fairmont	SptC	98	A4
Fairmont Mills	SptC	98	A4
Fairntosh	DurC	30	E2
Fairport	GraC	32	A1
Fairs Crossroads	AbbC	134	A1
Fairview	BftC	176	E2
Fairview	CtrC	21	D3
Fairview	FrkC	115	E6
Fairview	GreC	20	A2
Fairview	GrvC	97	C3
Fairview	MacC	67	D4
Fairview	McmC	65	A1
Fairview	NbrC	136	E3
Fairview	OcnC	95	C7
Fairview	RocC	7	C4
Fairview	SpnC	115	D3
Fairview	SryC	4	E7
*Fairview	UnoC	76	B7
Fairview	WsgC	20	D1
Fairview Crossroads	LexC	151	A3
Fairview Crossroads	SryC	4	E7
Fairview Park	AlxC	48	D1
Fairway Hills	HwdC	69	C1
Fairwood	GsnC	2	D1
*Faison	DupC	83	B6
Faisons	NhnC	14	B4
*Faith	RowC	50	D6
*Falcon	CumC	81	D5
*Falcon	SamC	81	E5
*Falkland	PitC	58	E3
Fallcliff	JakC	68	E5
Falling Creek	LnrC	84	C4
Falls	WkeC	31	E6
*Fallston	ClvC	73	D2
FANNIN CO	FnnC	92	A5
Farmdale	ScrC	168	C7
Farmer	RndC	51	E5
Farmer Mill	CtrC	22	B2
Farmington	DveC	26	C6
Farmville	ChaC	54	A6
*Farmville	PitC	58	D5
Farrell Crossroads	BamC	162	C5
Farrells Mill	BrnC	161	A3
Farrington	ChaC	54	D2
Faulkner Crossroads	VncC	11	C7
Faust	MdnC	44	E1
*Fayetteville	CumC	81	A7
Fearrington	ChaC	54	C2
Fearrington Village	ChaC	54	C2
Feasterville	FaiC	121	A4
Fechtig	HmpC	170	B6
Feezor	DavC	51	A4
Felder	OraC	162	D1
Felderville	OraC	163	C1
Feltonville	WkeC	55	A4
Fendall	FloC	141	E3
Fenix	CumC	106	D1
Fenwick Crossroads	ChsC	172	E6
Fenwick Hills	ChsC	172	E6
Fero	McdC	46	B6
Fersners	OraC	152	E6
Fields	LnrC	84	B3
Fieldsboro	GrnC	58	C5
Fields of the Wood	CheC	65	E7
Fig	AshC	2	C5
Fighting Pine	SpnC	115	D3
Filbert	YorC	100	C1
Fillmore	WlnC	57	C3
Finchley	MkbC	11	A1
Finch Mill	WlnC	57	C2
Fines Creek	HwdC	43	D5
Finger	StnC	76	E3
Fingerville	SptC	72	B7
Finklea	HryC	143	E3
Finland	BamC	161	E3
Finley	CwlC	23	B5
Finney Patch	CckC	43	A1
Fires Creek	ClyC	92	E1

Community	County	Map#	Grid
Fisher Creek	JakC	68	E2
Fisher Town	CabC	76	A1
Fish Springs	CtrC	22	A1
Fitch	CasC	8	D7
Fitzgerald	RocC	7	D4
Five Forks	AndC	117	B2
Five Forks	DilC	126	E4
Five Forks	GrvC	97	D6
Five Forks	MrlC	126	A3
Five Forks	PatC	6	A3
Five Forks	PckC	96	C6
Five Forks	PerC	9	C5
Five Forks	RobC	127	B4
Five Forks	RowC	50	A6
Five Forks	WrnC	12	B3
Five Points	BeaC	60	D5
Five Points	ClvC	73	B2
Five Points	FraC	32	D6
Five Points	HdrC	71	A5
Five Points	HokC	105	D2
Five Points	OcnC	95	A7
Five Points	RowC	50	A7
Flag Branch	GreC	19	E5
Flat Branch	GatC	16	A5
Flat Branch	GilC	91	B6
Flat Creek	BcbC	44	D3
Flat Gap	BkeC	47	C4
Flat Ridge	GsnC	3	A1
Flat Rock	AndC	117	C5
*Flat Rock	HdrC	71	A5
Flat Rock	KswC	123	A4
Flat Rock	SryC	5	B4
Flat Rock	StkC	5	D6
Flat Rock	VncC	11	C5
Flats	MacC	67	D5
Flat Shoals	HarC	116	C6
Flat Shoals	OcnC	95	C5
Flat Shoals	StkC	6	B7
Flat Springs	AvyC	22	C2
Flat Top	BcbC	45	B7
Flatwood	AshC	2	B4
Flay	LinC	73	E2
Fleet	FloC	142	B6
Fleming Crossroad	LtrC	122	E1
Flemingtown	FloC	142	E6
*Fletcher	HdrC	71	A2
Fletcher	MrlC	105	A7
Flinns Crossroads	DlgC	124	E7
Flint Hill	FaiC	122	B6
Flint Hill	MntC	78	A1
Flint Hill	RndC	52	A2
Flint Hill	YadC	26	C3
Floral College	RobC	105	E6
*Florence	FloC	141	D2
Florence	GlfC	28	A5
Florence	PamC	87	C5
FLORENCE CO	FloC	125	E7
Florence Town	AlmC	29	D4
Flowers	JtnC	56	C4
Flows Store	CabC	76	B4
Floyd	DlgC	125	B6
FLOYD CO	FydC	5	C1
Floydale	DilC	126	E7
Floyds Crossroads	HryC	143	C1
Floytan Crossroads	VncC	32	A1
Folkstone	OnsC	132	A2
Folly	GatC	16	B3
*Folly Beach	ChsC	173	B7
Fontaine	HenC	7	B2
Fontana Village	GhmC	67	A2
Fonville	HntC	81	C4
Footsville	YadC	25	E5
Forbush	YadC	26	B3
Forest	CvnC	86	B5
*Forest Acres	RldC	138	B5
Forestbrook	HryC	158	A3
*Forest City	RthC	72	D4
Forest Grove	WatC	22	E1
*Forest Hills	JakC	68	E4
Forest Lake	YorC	101	B1
Forest Oaks	GlfC	28	D6
Foreston	ClnC	154	E5
Forest View	GrvC	97	B4
Forge Mill	FnnC	91	E4
Fork	DveC	50	D1
Fork Hill Crossroads	LtrC	123	B1
Fork Shoals	GrvC	118	C2
Forks of Ivy	BcbC	44	D3
Forney	HryC	157	C1
FORSYTH CO	FsyC	26	D4
Fort Barnwell	CvnC	85	C3
Fort Caswell	BwkC	146	D6
Fort Defiance	CwlC	23	D6
Fort Fisher	NhrC	147	A5
Fort Fremont	BftC	177	D5
Fort Harry	SvrC	42	A5
Fort Landing	TyrC	38	E5
*Fort Lawn	CstC	122	C1
Fort McAllister	BynC	180	D7
*Fort Mill	YorC	101	B2
Fort Motte	ClhC	153	A3
Fortsonia	ElbC	133	A6
Foscoe	WatC	22	E3
Foster	JakC	68	E3
Foster Creek	MdnC	44	C1
Foster Mill	SptC	98	D6
Fosters Crossroads	LtrC	101	C6
Fountain	DupC	110	C4
*Fountain	PitC	58	C3
Fountain Hill	AnsC	103	A1
Fountain Hill	LnrC	84	E1
*Fountain Inn	GrvC	118	D1
*Fountain Inn	LarC	118	D1
Four Holes	OraC	163	E3
*Four Oaks	JtnC	82	B1
Fourway	GrnC	58	D7

Community	County	Map#	Grid
Fowler	WmbC	155	E3
Fowler Crossroads	UnoC	102	C2
Fowler Grove	CckC	19	A6
Fowlertown	SpnC	115	C3
Fox	GsnC	3	B3
Foxfire	MreC	79	A6
Fox Run	DurC	30	D3
Foxtown	AknC	150	C4
Foxville	SmtC	139	C7
Francisco	StkC	5	E4
Francktown	OnsC	111	A3
Frank	AvyC	22	B5
*Franklin	MacC	68	B6
Franklin	RowC	50	C4
FRANKLIN CO	FraC	33	A3
FRANKLIN CO	FrkC	115	D6
Franklin Grove	SwnC	68	A2
*Franklinton	FraC	32	B4
*Franklinville	RndC	52	D3
Fraserville	GtnC	167	C1
Frazier Crossroads	NshC	57	A1
Fraziers Crossroads	HtfC	15	A6
Fredonia	LexC	136	E7
Freedman	ChsC	178	B3
Freeland	BwkC	145	B3
Freeman	CbsC	129	E6
Freeman Mill	GlfC	28	B7
Freemont	HryC	144	D6
*Fremont	WanC	57	D6
French Broad	CckC	43	D1
Frieds Bay	HryC	144	C4
Friendfield	FloC	141	E6
Friendfield	GtnC	167	B3
Friendship	AndC	118	B4
Friendship	CheC	92	A1
Friendship	DupC	83	C6
Friendship	GrwC	135	C5
Friendship	MrnC	142	E6
Friendship	SulC	1	B4
Friendship	TwnC	93	B3
Friendship	WasC	2	A1
Friendship	WkeC	55	A4
Friendship	YadC	26	B2
Friendship	YorC	101	B4
*Fries	GsnC	4	A1
Fripp Landing	BftC	176	D6
Frisco	DarC	90	B2
Frog Level	PitC	59	A5
Frog Level	RthC	72	C4
Frogmore	BftC	177	C5
Frog Pond	StnC	77	A5
Frogsboro	CasC	9	A7
Fruit Hill	SalC	135	D7
Fruitland	HdrC	71	A3
Fruitland	RchC	104	E3
Fudges	CstC	101	C7
Fulcher Landing	OnsC	132	C1
Fulchertown	MacC	68	C7
Fulford	BwkC	145	E5
Fuller	JhnC	1	E4
Fuller Mill	RndC	51	E3
Fulp	StkC	27	C2
Fulton	MrlC	104	C6
Fulton Crossroads	SmtC	153	C3
Funston	BwkC	146	D3
*Fuquay-Varina	WkeC	55	B6
Furches	AlgC	3	B5
*Furman	HmpC	169	D7
G			
Gaddistown	UniC	92	C7
Gaddys Crossroads	DilC	127	A5
Gaddysville	RobC	127	B4
*Gaffney	CrkC	99	B1
Gaillard Crossroads	SmtC	139	D5
Gaines Crossroads	GrwC	135	D5
Galatia	NhnC	14	B3
Galavon	DilC	126	C4
*Galax		4	B2
Galloway	FnnC	91	C3
Galloway Crossroads	PitC	59	D5
Galloway Mill	FnnC	91	C4
*Gamewell	CwlC	47	C2
Gandy	DlgC	125	C5
Gantt	GrvC	97	A6
Gap	StkC	5	E6
Gap Creek	CtrC	21	D1
Gap Creek	GrvC	70	E7
Gapway	MrnC	143	A2
Garber	WsgC	21	A2
*Garden City	ChtC	180	E3
Garden City	HryC	157	E5
Garden City Beach	HryC	157	B7
Gardens Corner	BftC	176	E2
Gardner Crossroads	FloC	142	A4
Gardnerville	PitC	85	C1
*Garland	SamC	108	C5
Garlington	LarC	120	B4
*Garner	WkeC	55	D3
Garners Mill	GsvC	13	B2
Garren Hill	MreC	79	B6
Gary	NbrC	120	A7
*Garysburg	NhnC	13	D4
Gashes Creek	BcbC	44	E7
*Gaston	LexC	151	E2
*Gaston	NhnC	13	C3
GASTON CO	GasC	75	A5
*Gastonia	GasC	74	D5
Gastonia South	GasC	74	C6
Gaston Mill	KswC	123	B5
GATES CO	GatC	16	B4
*Gatesville	GatC	15	E4
Gatewood	CasC	8	C3
*Gatlinburg	SvrC	42	A4
Gause Landing	BwkC	145	C6
Gay	JakC	68	D4

Community	County	Map#	Grid
Gayle Mill	CstC	121	C1
Gaylord	BeaC	61	A4
Gaylords Crossroads	GrvC	97	D7
Gela	GraC	10	E5
Genlee	DurC	55	A1
Genoa	MrlC	126	A5
Genoa	WanC	83	C3
Gentry Store	PerC	9	E5
George	NhnC	14	C6
Georges Mill	StkC	6	A4
Georgetown	BcbC	44	C6
Georgetown	ChtC	180	C5
Georgetown	DavC	27	D6
*Georgetown	GtnC	167	A2
GEORGETOWN CO	GtnC	166	D3
Georgeville	CabC	76	D4
Georgieville	GtnC	157	D7
Germantown	ChsC	166	D5
Germantown	HydC	61	E7
Gethsemane	EdgC	34	C3
Gettysville	DorC	172	A3
Ghio	RchC	104	E5
Ghio Scholl Station	SctC	104	E5
Gholsonville	BrwC	12	D1
Giant	DorC	163	E5
Gibbs Crossroads	FloC	142	A5
Gibbton	PamC	87	B6
Gibson	ChsC	172	B7
*Gibson	SctC	105	A6
Gibson Mill	SctC	105	C5
Gibsontown	HwdC	43	E7
*Gibsonville	AlmC	29	B4
*Gibsonville	GlfC	29	A4
Giddensville	SamC	82	E6
*Gifford	HmpC	169	C4
*Gilbert	LexC	137	A7
Gilbert Crossroads	HryC	157	C3
Gilbert Mill	PatC	6	B2
Gilead	BeaC	60	C7
Gilkey	RthC	72	B2
Gill	LncC	133	C7
Gill	VncC	32	B1
Gillburg	VncC	11	C7
Gillespie	ChfC	125	A2
Gilliard	GtnC	157	B6
Gillisonville	JprC	176	B2
Gilmania	JprC	176	C2
GILMER CO	GilC	91	B6
Gilreath	WksC	24	E5
*Girard	BurC	168	A1
Givhans	DorC	172	A1
Gladesboro	CrlC	5	A2
Gladstone	WsgC	20	D3
Glady	BcbC	70	B1
Glassy	GrvC	71	C7
*Glen Alpine	BkeC	46	E4
Glen Ayre	MhlC	21	E5
Glencoe	AlmC	29	C3
Glendale	SptC	98	D3
Glendon	MreC	79	C1
Glenfield	GrnC	84	C1
Glenfield Crossroads	GrnC	84	D1
Glenlaurel	MhlC	45	E2
Glenn Springs	SptC	98	D6
Glenola	RndC	52	A1
Glen Raven	AlmC	29	B4
Glenview	HlfC	33	E1
Glenwood	McdC	46	B6
Glenwood	PckC	96	D5
Glenwood Crossroads	JtnC	82	C4
Gliden	ChwC	16	B6
Globe	CwlC	23	A5
Glovers Crossroads	BrtC	15	D7
Gloverville	ColC	171	D3
Gluck	AndC	117	C5
Glymphville	NbrC	120	E6
Gneiss	MacC	68	D7
Goat Neck	TyrC	38	E4
Godsey	GrwC	135	B3
*Godwin	CumC	81	D5
Gold	BkeC	46	E3
Golden	RthC	46	E7
Golden Grove	GrvC	97	A7
Gold Hill	HokC	106	B3
Gold Hill	RocC	28	A1
Gold Point	MtnC	35	D7
Gold Rock	NshC	34	A3
Gold Sand	FraC	32	E2
*Goldsboro	WanC	83	C2
*Goldston	ChaC	53	E6
Gold Valley Crossroads	NshC	33	A7
Golightly	SptC	98	D5
Goloid	ScrC	168	B7
Gooch Crossroad	LtrC	122	D1
Good Hope	GtnC	157	A4
Good Hope	SalC	135	D5
Goodluck	HdrC	71	A2
Good Springs	McmC	65	A3
Goodwin Hills	CarC	88	C7
Goodwins Crossroads	LarC	119	C3
*Goose Creek	BrkC	173	A2
Goose Hollow	CbsC	129	C6
Goose Island	GilC	91	C6
Gooseneck	CbsC	130	B6
Goose Pimple Junction	WasC	1	A3
Goose Pond	BrtC	36	E1
Gordonton	PerC	30	B1
Gordontown	DavC	51	D3
Gordonville	WmbC	156	D4
Goretown	HryC	144	C4
Gorman	DurC	31	A5
Goshen	ChsC	172	C6
Goshen	WksC	24	B4
Goshen Grove	GasC	74	E5
Goshen Hill	UnnC	120	C4
Goucher	CrkC	99	A3

*Indicates incorporated city

Community	County	Map#	Grid
Gourdin	WmbC	155	B7
*Govan	BamC	161	D5
Gowensville	GrvC	71	D7
Graball	LncC	133	D7
Grabtown	BrtC	36	B5
Grace	LtrC	101	C7
Grady	McmC	65	B3
Gradys	WanC	83	E5
Gragg	AvyC	22	E5
*Graham	AlmC	29	C4
GRAHAM CO	GhmC	66	E3
Graham Mill	WsgC	20	D3
Grahams Crossroads	HryC	144	C5
Grahamville	HryC	158	A1
Grahamville	JprC	176	B4
Graingers	LnrC	84	E2
Gramling	SptC	97	E1
*Grandfather Village	AvyC	22	D5
Grandin	CwlC	23	E5
Grandview	CheC	66	C6
Grandview	GreC	20	B2
Grandview	KnoC	41	A1
*Granite Falls	CwlC	48	A3
*Granite Quarry	RowC	50	D6
Grant	GsnC	2	E2
Grantham	WanC	83	A3
Granthams Crossroads	DlgC	124	D5
*Grantsboro	PamC	86	E5
GRANVILLE CO	GraC	11	A5
Grape Creek	CheC	66	B7
Graphite	McdC	45	C5
Grassy Creek	HenC	7	A2
Grassy Creek	MhlC	46	A1
Grassy Creek	PolC	91	C2
Grassy Fork	CckC	43	B2
Grassy Pond	CrkC	73	B7
Gravel Hill	OraC	162	B1
Gravel Hill	WsgC	20	D3
Gravelton	AnsC	104	A3
Graves	GtnC	167	A2
*Gray Court	LarC	118	E2
Grays	JprC	170	A7
Graysburg	GreC	20	B1
Grays Chapel	RndC	52	D2
Grays Creek	CumC	107	B3
Grays Hill	BftC	176	E3
Grayson	AshC	2	A4
GRAYSON CO	GsnC	2	D2
Great Branch	OraC	152	B7
*Great Falls	CstC	122	C3
Great Neck	CvnC	113	B2
Great Neck Landing	OnsC	112	A6
*Greeleyville	WmbC	155	A6
Green Acres	WkeC	55	D3
Green Bay	BrkC	173	E1
Green Bay	GtnC	166	C1
Greenbrier	SvrC	41	D5
Green Cove	WasC	2	B2
GREENE CO	GreC	19	D4
GREENE CO	GrnC	58	C6
Greene Cove	MhlC	21	E6
*Greenevers	DupC	109	E4
*Greeneville	GreC	20	A3
Greenfield	WasC	1	D1
Green Hill	ChfC	124	C4
Green Hill	DlgC	124	E4
Green Hill	RthC	72	A2
Greenlee	McdC	45	E5
*Green Level	AlmC	29	D4
Green Level	WkeC	54	E2
Green Pine	CtrC	21	C2
Green Pond	SctC	105	A6
Green River	PlkC	72	A6
*Greensboro	GlfC	28	C5
Greens Creek	JakC	68	D4
Greens Cut	BurC	159	B6
Greens Fork	GatC	16	C4
Greens Mill	FnnC	91	D5
Green Spring	WasC	1	B2
GREENSVILLE CO	GsvC	13	C2
Green Valley	AshC	2	A6
*Greenville	GrvC	97	A5
*Greenville	PitC	59	B6
GREENVILLE CO	GrvC	117	E1
*Greenwood	GrwC	134	E2
Greenwood	WsgC	21	A2
GREENWOOD CO	GrwC	118	D7
Greenwood Shores	GrwC	135	C3
*Greer	GrvC	97	D4
*Greer	SptC	97	D3
Greesons Crossroads	GlfC	28	E5
Gregg Camp	FloC	142	A2
Gregory	CurC	17	D4
Gregory Crossroads	OnsC	110	E3
Gregory Forks	OnsC	110	E3
Grenadier	LexC	137	D5
Gretna Green	HlfC	12	E5
Greystone	GreC	20	B4
Greystone	VncC	11	C6
Griffins Crossroads	AnsC	103	B2
Griffins Crossroads	ChaC	54	C3
*Grifton	LnrC	85	A2
*Grifton	PitC	85	A1
Grigsby	HawC	19	C1
Grimball Park	ChtC	181	A5
Grimesdale	HdrC	70	E3
*Grimesland	PitC	59	E5
Grimshawes	JakC	95	A1
Grissett	HryC	157	E1
Grissettown	BwkC	145	B6
Grissom	GraC	31	E4
Grist	CbsC	128	B6
Groometown	GlfC	28	B6
Grove Hall	BrkC	172	E1
Grove Hill	WrnC	12	C6
Grovemont	BcbC	45	A6

Community	County	Map#	Grid
Grove Point	ChtC	180	D6
*Grover	ClvC	73	E6
Grover	DorC	163	B7
Grubbs	ChtC	180	D5
Gudger	MroC	65	C1
Guide	CbsC	144	D4
Guideway	CbsC	144	C3
GUILFORD CO	GlfC	27	E7
Gulf	ChaC	53	E6
Gull Rock	HydC	62	E7
Gumberry	NhnC	13	E4
Gum Branch	OnsC	111	A3
Gumlog	FrkC	116	A4
Gum Neck	TyrC	62	D2
Gum Springs	ChaC	54	A3
Gumtree	DavC	27	B6
Guntertown	MdnC	44	B1
Gupton	FraC	33	A2
Gurley	HryC	143	E5
Guthrie	FsyC	27	C4
Guthries	YorC	100	C4
Guyton	BldC	128	C1
*Guyton	EffC	175	A6
H			
HABERSHAM CO	HabC	115	A2
Hackney	BeaC	60	A7
Hadden Crossroads	SptC	98	B4
Hadden Heights	SptC	98	B4
Haddock	OraC	162	C1
Haddocks Crossroads	PitC	59	B6
Haddonville	EffC	175	C5
Hagan	BrkC	173	C1
Hagood	MkbC	12	A1
Hagood	SmtC	139	C5
Hagoods Mill	BrnC	161	B5
Hairtown	HntC	80	E4
Hale	PckC	96	D5
Hale	WsgC	20	E1
Half Hell	BwkC	146	B4
Half Moon	OnsC	111	A4
*Halifax	HlfC	13	C6
HALIFAX CO	HalC	10	B2
HALIFAX CO	HlfC	13	C4
Halifax Crossing	NshC	33	E6
Halleytown	ClnC	154	B4
Halls	HtfC	15	B6
Halls Ferry Junction	StnC	77	B2
Halls Ford	SwnC	68	A3
Halls Mill	HmpC	169	D3
Halls Mills	WksC	24	C1
Halls Store	SamC	82	A7
HAMBLEN CO	HamC	19	A4
Hambright	PolC	65	A5
Hamer	CasC	8	E5
*Hamilton	MtnC	35	D6
Hamilton Crossroads	UnoC	102	E2
*Hamlet	RchC	104	E4
Hammetts Crossroads	LeeC	140	A3
Hammond	AndC	117	C3
Hammond	HryC	144	B6
Hammond	KswC	139	B3
Hammond Crossroads	ClhC	152	C4
Hammond Crossroads	RobC	127	A4
*Hampton	HmpC	169	E4
HAMPTON CO	HmpC	170	B5
Hampton Heights	GrvC	97	B4
Hampton Mill	GreC	20	B4
Hamrick	YanC	45	D3
Hams Crossroads	PitC	59	D6
*Hanahan	BrkC	173	A3
Hancock	ChwC	37	B2
Hancock	LtrC	101	D4
Hand	HryC	144	C7
Handy	DavC	51	D6
Hankins	McdC	46	B4
Hankinson	AknC	159	D3
Hannah	FloC	142	B7
Hanrahan	PitC	85	A1
Happy Acres	TrnC	70	B7
Happy Home	RocC	7	E4
Happy Valley	CwlC	23	C6
Harbuck	PolC	91	C1
Hardee Cross Roads	JtnC	81	E1
*Hardeeville	JprC	176	A7
Hardin	CheC	67	A5
Hardins	GasC	74	C3
Hare	AlgC	4	A5
Hares Crossroads	JtnC	56	E4
Hargetts Store	JnsC	110	D1
Hargrove Crossroads	SamC	82	E7
*Harkers Island	CarC	113	D5
Harley	WksC	23	E3
*Harleyville	DorC	163	E5
Harlowe	CarC	113	A3
Harmon	JhnC	1	C4
Harmony	EgfC	149	D2
Harmony	HalC	9	D3
*Harmony	IrdC	25	D7
Harmony	YorC	101	B5
Harmony Grove	CckC	43	C1
Harnett	HntC	81	B3
HARNETT CO	HntC	55	B7
Harper	JtnC	82	C4
Harper Crossroads	WmbC	156	B7
Harpers Crossroads	ChaC	53	C6
Harr	SulC	1	B4
Harrell Hill	MhlC	21	D5
*Harrells	DupC	109	A6
*Harrells	SamC	109	A6
*Harrellsville	HtfC	15	E6
Harrelsonville	CbsC	128	D7
Harrelsonville Crossroads	CbsC	128	D7
Harris	GrwC	134	D2
Harris	MreC	79	B4
Harris	RthC	72	D5

Community	County	Map#	Grid
*Harrisburg	CabC	76	A4
Harrisburg	SvrC	42	A1
Harris Crossroads	FraC	32	C6
Harris Crossroads	VncC	11	B5
Harris Mill	UciC	20	D6
Harrisons Crossroads	RocC	7	D6
Harris Springs	LarC	119	B7
Harristown	BrkC	165	C2
Harrisville	MntC	78	C5
Harrock Hall	ChtC	181	A5
HART CO	HarC	117	A7
Hartland	CwlC	47	B2
Hartsboro	EdgC	34	C6
Hartsease	EdgC	34	C6
Harts Store	StkC	6	A4
*Hartsville	DlgC	124	D6
*Hartwell	HarC	116	D7
Harvin	ClnC	154	B2
Haskell Heights	RldC	138	A4
Haslin Corners	BeaC	61	C5
*Hassell	MtnC	35	C6
Hastings Corner	CdnC	17	C4
Hasty	SctC	105	C7
Hatcher	SamC	83	A7
Hatchertown	SvrC	41	D4
Hattieville	BrnC	160	C7
*Havelock	CvnC	112	D2
Haw Branch	MreC	79	D1
Haw Branch	OnsC	110	D2
Hawfields	AlmC	29	E5
Hawk Branch	YanC	21	B7
HAWKINS CO	HawC	19	A1
Hawkins Landing	BeaC	60	E7
Hawra	WlnC	57	B4
*Haw River	AlmC	29	D4
Haws Run	OnsC	110	E6
Hawthorne	AknC	160	A3
Hayes Crossroads	AlnC	169	B1
*Hayesville	ClyC	93	A1
Hayesville	GreC	20	A6
Hayne	SamC	108	A2
Hayne Station	SptC	98	C3
Haywood	ChaC	54	C5
HAYWOOD CO	HwdC	70	A4
Hazel Farm	BftC	177	B5
Hazelton	GatC	16	A2
Hazelwood Acres	RldC	138	B6
Healing Springs	BrnC	161	C2
Healing Springs	DavC	51	C6
Heardmont	ElbC	133	B4
Heath	JhnC	1	E5
*Heath Springs	LtrC	123	A2
Heathsville	HlfC	13	A7
Heaton	AvyC	22	C3
Heatoncreek	CtrC	22	A4
Hebron	BnkC	115	B7
Hebron	GraC	10	C7
Hebron Crossroads	WmbC	155	B1
Hedrick Grove	DavC	51	C3
Heflin	JtnC	56	E3
Heineman	WmbC	155	B6
*Helen	WhtC	93	C7
Helena	NbrC	136	B1
Helens Crossroads	PitC	59	C7
Helton	AshC	2	D4
*Hemby Bridge	UnoC	102	A1
Hemby Bridge	UnoC	76	A7
*Hemingway	WmbC	156	D2
Hemlock	AshC	2	A5
Hemp	FnnC	92	A4
*Henderson	VncC	11	B7
HENDERSON CO	HdrC	71	A4
Hendersonville	ColC	171	A5
*Hendersonville	HdrC	71	A4
Hendricks	PckC	96	D4
Hendrix	WksC	23	E4
Henrietta	EdgC	34	D7
Henrietta	RthC	72	E5
Henry	LinC	47	E7
Henry	WmbC	156	C4
HENRY CO	HenC	7	B2
Henry River	BkeC	47	E4
Henrytown	BwkC	146	C2
Hepco	HwdC	43	C5
*Hephzibah	RmdC	159	A4
Herbert	UnnC	120	E4
Hermitage Mill	KswC	139	B1
Herrings Crossroads	DupC	83	E6
Herrings Crossroads	SamC	82	C5
*Hertford	PqmC	37	D1
HERTFORD CO	HtfC	16	A6
Hester	AbbC	133	D4
Hester	GraC	31	C2
Hesters Store	PerC	9	B7
Hestertown	RobC	127	E2
Hewitt	SwnC	67	D4
Hexlena	BrtC	36	A1
*Hiawassee	TwnC	93	B3
Hibernia	SalC	150	C1
Hickmans Crossroads	CbsC	128	B4
*Hickory	BkeC	48	A4
*Hickory	CwaC	48	B4
*Hickory	CwlC	48	A3
Hickory	NshC	34	A2
Hickory Crossroads	JtnC	57	B5
Hickory Crossroads	PqmC	16	C6
Hickory Flat	CrlC	4	B1
Hickory Grove	HokC	105	E3
Hickory Grove	HryC	143	E7
Hickory Grove	PlkC	71	E6
Hickory Grove	SalC	136	A4
*Hickory Grove	YorC	99	E3
Hickory Grove Crossroads	BldC	108	C6
Hickory Hill	ChsC	172	E6
Hickory Hill	ColC	171	B7
Hickory Knoll	MacC	94	B1

Community	County	Map#	Grid
Hickory Rock	FraC	33	A2
Hickory Tavern	LarC	118	D4
Hicks Crossroads	MklC	75	B2
Hicks Crossroads	VncC	11	A5
Hicks Store	OcnC	116	C2
Hicks Village	PerC	9	C6
Hidetown	GhmC	67	C3
Higdon	FnnC	91	B4
Higdonville	MacC	68	D6
Higgins	SalC	136	A4
Higgins	YanC	21	A7
Higgins Crossroads	CrlC	4	D2
High Bluff	KnoC	41	A1
High Crossroads	NshC	57	B1
Highfalls	MreC	79	B1
High Hampton	JakC	95	B1
High Hill	HalC	10	C1
High Hill Crossroads	DilC	127	B6
Highland	GrvC	97	B1
Highland Park	BrkC	173	A3
Highland Park	OraC	162	C1
Highland Park	RchC	104	E4
Highland Pines	RchC	104	D4
*Highlands	JakC	95	A1
*Highlands	MacC	94	E1
High Point	AndC	117	E4
High Point	CckC	19	A4
*High Point	DavC	27	D7
*High Point	GlfC	27	E7
*High Point	RndC	27	D7
High Rock	DavC	51	B6
*High Shoals	GasC	74	C3
Highsmith	PdrC	130	D3
Highsmiths	SamC	108	B3
Hightowers	CasC	8	E7
Hightsville	NhrC	130	E7
Hilander Park	WasC	1	A2
*Hilda	BrnC	161	C4
*Hildebran	BkeC	47	E4
Hillcrest	HokC	106	B2
Hill Crest	MreC	79	C4
Hillcrest	SmtC	139	D5
Hillgirt	HdrC	70	E3
Hilliardston	NshC	33	D3
Hills	StnC	77	A4
*Hillsborough	OrgC	30	C4
Hills Crossroads	DupC	83	D6
Hills Crossroads	HlfC	34	E1
Hillsdale	DveC	26	D6
Hillsdale	GlfC	28	B2
Hillside	DlgC	141	D1
Hills Store	BurC	168	C2
*Hilltonia	ScrC	168	B4
Hilltop	SptC	98	C3
Hilltown	GsnC	4	A1
Hilton	RldC	137	B3
*Hilton Head Island	BftC	181	E2
Hines Crossroads	WanC	83	E5
Hinnes Crossroads	HlfC	13	A5
Hinson	WshC	60	E1
Hinson Crossroads	CbsC	127	E7
Hitesburg	HalC	10	B2
Hiwassee	CheC	65	E7
Hiwassee Village	CheC	65	E6
Hobbs Crossroads	SmtC	141	A5
Hobbton	SamC	82	D6
Hobbyville	SptC	119	C1
*Hobgood	HlfC	35	A4
Hocutts Crossroads	JtnC	56	D3
*Hodges	GrwC	134	C1
*Hoffman	RchC	105	B1
Hoffmeyer Crossroads	FloC	141	C2
Hoflers Fork	GatC	16	B4
Hogetown	WatC	23	D3
Hogeye Crossroads	WmbC	155	C1
Hog Island	MreC	79	E6
Hoke	WshC	60	E2
HOKE CO	HokC	105	E2
*Holden Beach	BwkC	145	E6
Holdens Crossroads	WlnC	58	A3
Holland Mill	GreC	20	A1
Hollands	PitC	58	E3
Hollands Crossroads	WanC	57	B6
Holland Store	AndC	116	E6
Hollemans Crossroads	WkeC	54	E5
Hollis	RthC	73	A2
Hollman Crossroads	FloC	141	B4
Hollow Creek	AknC	159	E2
Hollow Creek	LexC	136	E6
Holly Grove	DavC	51	B2
Holly Grove	GatC	16	B2
Holly Hill	HdrC	70	E4
*Holly Hill	OraC	163	E3
Holly Ridge	ColC	171	E1
*Holly Ridge	OnsC	131	E3
Holly Springs	CarC	112	D4
Holly Springs	HdrC	70	C4
Holly Springs	MroC	65	C4
Holly Springs	OcnC	94	E7
Holly Springs	SptC	97	D3
*Holly Springs	WkeC	55	B4
Holly Vw Frst-Highlnd Pk	SryC	5	A5
Hollyville	PamC	87	B4
*Hollywood	ChsC	172	C6
Hollywood	HabC	115	A1
Hollywood Hills	RldC	138	A4
Holmesville	RobC	127	C6
Holston Valley	SulC	1	A4
Holtson Crossroads	SalC	136	C7
Holy Hill	JhnC	1	D5
Homeland Park	AndC	117	B5
*Homer	BnkC	115	A7
Homewood	HryC	143	D7
Hominy	BcbC	44	C7
*Honea Path	AbbC	118	B5
*Honea Path	AndC	118	A5

*Indicates incorporated city

Cities and Communities

Community	County	Map#	Grid
Honey Hill	BrkC	166	B5
Honey Hill	CbsC	128	E7
Honey Island	BwkC	145	D2
Honey Pond	BwkC	145	B4
Honolulu	CvnC	85	D2
Hood	UniC	92	E6
Hood Swamp	WanC	83	E1
Hoodtown	YorC	99	E4
Hooker	AlgC	3	E5
*Hookerton	GrnC	84	D1
Hooper Hill	BwkC	130	C6
Hootentown	BeaC	60	B5
*Hope Mills	CumC	106	E2
Hopewell	MklC	75	D1
Hopewell	RthC	73	A3
Hopewell	WanC	83	D4
Hopewell	WmbC	156	D4
Hopewell	YorC	99	E4
Hopkins	WkeC	32	C7
Hopson	CtrC	21	E2
Horace	HdrC	71	C3
Horatio	SmtC	139	C5
Hornet	SvrC	41	C3
Horneytown	FsyC	27	D6
Hornsboro	ChfC	103	A6
Horrell Hill	RldC	138	D6
Horry	HryC	143	C6
HORRY CO	HryC	142	E6
Horse Creek	GreC	20	C4
Horsegall	HmpC	170	A6
Horse Neck	RobC	107	A5
Horse Pasture	HenC	7	A2
Horseshoe	CdnC	17	A3
Hothouse	CheC	91	E2
Hothouse	FnnC	91	D3
*Hot Springs	MdnC	43	E1
Housley	CtrC	1	A6
Houston	UnoC	102	A3
Houstonville	IrdC	25	D6
Howard	HryC	144	B3
Howards Crossroads	DlgC	125	D7
Howe	FloC	141	D3
Howell	ClbC	148	B6
Howells	HryC	143	E5
Howellsville	RobC	107	A7
Hubbard	BntC	41	A3
*Hudson	CwlC	47	D2
Hudsons Mill	ColC	170	D3
Huets Crossroads	EgfC	149	D3
Huffmantown	OnsC	110	E2
Huggins Crossroads	GtnC	156	E3
Hughes	BamC	162	A6
Hugo	LnrC	84	D2
Hugo	ShmC	14	B2
Hull Mill	GreC	19	D2
Hulls Crossroads	LinC	73	E1
Hulls Island	HryC	144	C4
Humbert Woods	ChsC	172	D6
Huntdale	MhlC	21	C6
*Huntersville	MklC	75	D2
Hunting Creek	WksC	24	E4
Huntley	SamC	82	A7
Hunts	NshC	33	A5
Huntsboro	GraC	10	E7
Hunts Crossroads	DlgC	124	E5
Hunts Mill	ChfC	124	E1
Huntsville	YadC	26	C5
Hurricane	MdnC	44	A1
Hurst	FnnC	92	A5
Husk	AshC	2	C3
Hyatt Creek	HwdC	69	B1
HYDE CO	HydC	63	B5
Hydeland	HydC	62	C6
Hydro	MntC	77	D6
Hyman	FloC	142	A5
Hymans	CvnC	85	E5
I			
Icard	BkeC	47	D4
Icaria	ChwC	16	B6
Ida Mill	SctC	105	B5
Idlewild	AshC	23	E1
Ijames Crossroads	DveC	26	A7
*Independence	GsnC	3	D2
Independents	RldC	138	C6
Index	AshC	2	E6
India Hook	YorC	101	A2
*Indian Beach	CarC	112	E6
Indian Cave Park	HdrC	70	E4
Indian Hills	JakC	68	C1
Indian Springs	WanC	84	A4
Indiantown	CdnC	17	E5
Indiantown	WmbC	156	B3
*Indian Trail	UnoC	76	A7
Inez	WrnC	12	A7
Ingalls	AvyC	22	B7
Ingleside	FraC	32	D2
Ingleside	SptC	71	E7
Ingold	SamC	108	D4
Ingram	AnsC	103	E1
*Inman	SptC	98	A2
Inman Mills	SptC	98	A2
Institute	LnrC	84	B2
Intelligence	RocC	7	A6
Inverness	HokC	80	A6
Iotla	MacC	68	B5
Iredell	BwkC	145	A6
IREDELL CO	IrdC	25	C6
Irisburg	HenC	7	C2
Irish Cut	CckC	19	A7
*Irmo	LexC	137	D4
*Irmo	RldC	137	D4
Iron Crossroads	ColC	171	D4
Iron Duff	HwdC	43	C6
Ironhill	CbsC	144	C3
Ironsburg	MroC	65	D5
Irvines Landing	GrwC	135	A2
Irvings Crossroads	LnrC	84	D7
Irwin	LtrC	122	D1
Isabella	PolC	91	D2
Iseman Crossroads	DlgC	141	A1
Isenhour	StnC	77	C2
Isenhour Park	AlxC	48	C1
Island Ford	JakC	69	B5
Isle of Hope	ChtC	181	A5
*Isle of Palms	ChsC	173	D5
Ita	HlfC	33	D2
Italy	GtnC	166	C1
*Iva	AndC	117	C7
Ivey Crossroads	RobC	127	C5
Ivy	MdnC	44	E2
Ivy	MroC	65	C4
Ivy Hills	HwdC	43	C7
Ivylog	UniC	92	C3
Ivy Ridge	MdnC	44	D1
J			
Jaars	UnoC	101	E5
*Jackson	AknC	159	E3
Jackson	GtnC	157	B7
*Jackson	NhnC	14	A5
Jackson	UnoC	102	A5
JACKSON CO	JakC	42	E7
Jackson Creek	RndC	51	E3
Jackson Hamlet	MreC	79	C6
Jackson Hill	DavC	51	C6
Jackson Line	SwnC	68	A3
Jacksons Store	DupC	110	B3
Jacksontown	VncC	11	C5
Jacksonville	AknC	149	D7
*Jacksonville	OnsC	111	B5
Jacksonville	TwnC	93	A4
Jacktown	McdC	46	B5
Jakesville	DavC	51	A1
Jalapa	MroC	65	D3
Jalapa	NbrC	120	B7
Jaluco	HryC	158	A2
James Crossroads	ClnC	154	C5
*Jamestown	BrkC	165	E4
Jamestown	FloC	142	A1
*Jamestown	GlfC	28	A6
Jamestown	HryC	157	D1
*Jamesville	MtnC	60	D1
Jamison	OraC	152	D5
Janeiro	PamC	113	A1
Jarmantown	OnsC	110	D2
Jarrett	SpnC	115	D2
Jarrett Cove	MdnC	44	C1
Jason	GrnC	84	B2
Jasper	CvnC	85	E4
Jasper	JprC	176	C6
JASPER CO	JprC	180	E2
Jedburg	DorC	172	C1
*Jefferson	AshC	2	D6
*Jefferson	ChfC	123	E1
JEFFERSON CO	JfnC	42	C1
Jefferson Park	RchC	104	D4
Jeffress	MkbC	10	E1
Jenkins Meadow	GhmC	66	E2
Jenkins Mill	CckC	42	E3
Jennings	FaiC	137	D2
Jennings	IrdC	25	C6
Jenny Lind	LnrC	84	B4
Jennys	AlnC	169	E1
Jericho	CasC	29	D1
Jericho	ChsC	172	B6
Jernigan Crossroads	DlgC	141	A2
Jernigans Crossroads	HryC	144	A3
Jerome	BldC	107	C4
Jerry	TyrC	38	C6
Jerusalem	DveC	50	C2
Jessup Mill	StkC	5	E4
Jeter Mountain Terrace	HdrC	70	D5
Jewelville	BnkC	115	B6
Jinnys Branch	BwkC	145	D6
Jocassee	OcnC	95	D3
Jockey	GreC	20	C1
Joe	MdnC	43	E2
Johns	SctC	105	C7
Johns Mill	OcnC	116	A2
JOHNSON CO	JhnC	2	A4
Johnson City	SptC	98	B3
*Johnson City	WsgC	21	A1
Johnson Crossroads	AknC	160	B2
Johnson Crossroads	EgfC	149	A3
Johnson Crossroads	FloC	141	C5
Johnson Crossroads	JtnC	55	E7
Johnsons Mill	HokC	106	C1
Johnsons Mills	PitC	85	C1
Johnsonville	CheC	91	E2
*Johnsonville	FloC	156	D1
Johnsonville	HntC	80	C4
*Johnston	EgfC	149	E2
JOHNSTON CO	JtnC	83	A1
Johnstown	AknC	149	D7
Johnstown	LinC	74	A2
Jonas Ridge	BkeC	22	C7
Jonathan	HwdC	43	C7
Jones	CasC	8	C5
JONES CO	JnsC	110	D1
Jonesboro Crossing	CbsC	128	E6
*Jonesborough	WsgC	20	E1
Jones Cove	SvrC	42	C2
Jones Creek	UniC	92	B5
Jones Crossroads	AknC	150	D3
Jones Crossroads	FloC	141	C4
Jones Crossroads	HryC	143	B5
Jones Crossroads	LtrC	122	E1
Jones Crossroads	SalC	136	B6
Jones Mill	CheC	66	E7
Jones Mill	GilC	91	B6
Jonestown	HryC	143	B6
Jonestown	LnrC	84	D7
Jonesville	ColC	170	D6
*Jonesville	UnnC	99	B5
*Jonesville	YadC	25	C2
Joplor	MklC	75	D3
Joppa	GatC	16	C5
Jordan	ClnC	154	C5
Jordan	GrvC	97	C2
Jordan	JtnC	56	D4
Jordania	OcnC	116	D1
Jordan Mill	KswC	123	C5
Jordanville	HryC	143	B7
Joy	BkeC	46	E2
Joyce Mill	StkC	5	D4
Joyceville	BrwC	12	B2
Joyners Crossing	NshC	33	E7
Joynes	WksC	3	E7
Jubilee	DavC	50	D3
Judson	CumC	107	B2
Judson	GrvC	97	A5
Jugtown	BcbC	44	B7
Jugtown	MreC	52	E7
Juniper	WkeC	55	D5
Juniper Bay	HryC	143	C7
Juno	BcbC	44	C5
Jupiter	BcbC	44	D3
Just Crossroads	AlmC	29	E2
Justice	FraC	33	A4
K			
Kalmia	MhlC	22	B7
*Kannapolis	CabC	76	A1
*Kannapolis	MklC	75	D2
Kansas City	WsgC	20	E3
Kanuga Pines	HdrC	70	E5
Katesville	FraC	32	C4
Kathwood	AknC	159	D3
Kawana	AvyC	22	D7
Kearney	FraC	32	D1
Keats	MkbC	11	C3
Keener	SamC	82	D7
Keitts Crossroads	NbrC	120	D7
*Kelford	BrtC	35	D1
Kellehan Crossroads	WmbC	156	A5
Kellerville	WatC	22	C2
Kellogs Fork	GatC	16	B3
Kellum	OnsC	111	C4
Kellumtown	OnsC	111	D6
Kelly	UnnC	99	C6
Kellys Crossroads	VncC	11	A6
Kellytown	DlgC	124	D6
Kellytown	KswC	138	E1
Kelton	UnnC	99	C6
Kemper	DilC	127	B6
*Kenansville	DupC	109	D2
Kendall Chapel	BwkC	146	E3
*Kenly	JtnC	57	A5
Kennebec	WkeC	55	C6
Kennedy Crossroads	FloC	142	B4
Kennedy Mill	UnnC	98	E5
Kennel Beach	PamC	86	D7
Kenneytown	GreC	19	E2
Kensington	GtnC	167	A1
Kent	GtnC	166	C2
Kentuck	PtsC	8	D1
Keowee	AbbC	118	A6
Keowee	OcnC	116	E1
*Kernersville	FsyC	27	D4
Kerr	SamC	108	E7
*Kershaw	LtrC	123	B3
Kershaw	PamC	87	A7
KERSHAW CO	KswC	123	C5
Ketchuptown	HryC	143	C3
Keys Crossroads	GatC	16	C5
Keys Field	HryC	157	D2
*Kiawah Island	ChsC	178	D2
Kibler	NbrC	136	E2
Kibler	PatC	5	C2
Kiffs Crossroads	LeeC	140	D2
Kikers	AnsC	103	B1
Kilby	AlxC	24	C6
Kilby Mill	RabC	94	A3
Kilgore	SptC	119	B1
Kilkenny	TyrC	62	C3
Kilkenny Landing	TyrC	62	D1
*Kill Devil Hills	DarC	40	A3
Killian	RldC	138	B3
Killian Crossroads	CwaC	48	E7
Kimesville	GlfC	29	A7
Kindy Forest	HdrC	70	E4
*King	FsyC	26	E2
*King	StkC	26	E2
Kingdale	RobC	127	D3
Kingsboro	EdgC	34	C6
Kingsburg	FloC	142	D7
Kings Creek	CrkC	99	E1
Kings Creek	CwlC	23	E6
Kings Crossroads	PitC	58	E4
Kings Grant	NhrC	131	A7
Kings Landing	PdrC	131	D5
*Kings Mountain	ClvC	74	A5
*Kings Mountain	GasC	74	B6
*Kingstown	ClvC	73	B3
*Kingstree	WmbC	155	C4
Kings Wood	ChtC	180	E5
Kingville	RldC	153	A2
*Kinston	LnrC	84	D3
Kinton Fork	GraC	10	D6
Kipling	HntC	55	B7
Kirbys Crossing	WlnC	57	B4
Kirkland	KswC	123	B7
Kirkland	NhrC	131	B6
Kirkley Mill	KswC	123	C4
Kirkman Crossroad	GlfC	28	B6
Kirksey	GrwC	135	A5
Kitchings Mill	AknC	150	E6
Kittredge	BrkC	165	A7
*Kittrell	VncC	32	B1
Kitty Fork	SamC	82	C7
*Kitty Hawk	DarC	39	E2
*Kline	BrnC	161	B7
Klondike	HryC	157	D3
Kneece	LexC	150	D1
*Knightdale	WkeC	56	A2
Knightsville	DorC	172	C1
Knob Creek	ClvC	73	C1
Knob Creek	SvrC	41	C2
Knotts Crossroads	VncC	11	A5
Knotty Branch	HryC	143	C6
*Knox	CstC	100	E7
KNOX CO	KnoC	41	A1
*Knoxville	KnoC	41	A1
Koehler	HenC	7	A1
Kona	YanC	21	D7
Konig	HryC	158	A3
Konnarock	WasC	2	B2
Koonce	MrnC	143	A3
Kornegay	DupC	84	A7
Kress	JprC	176	C1
Kross Keys	PlkC	72	A5
Kuhns	CarC	112	A4
Kungsboro	EdgC	34	C6
*Kure Beach	NhrC	147	A4
Kyle	FnnC	91	C3
Kyle	MacC	67	D6
Kyles Crossroads	IrdC	49	B4
L			
Laboratory	LinC	74	B2
Lackey Hill	SwnC	68	B2
Lackey Store	StkC	6	B4
Ladonia	SryC	4	C4
*Ladson	ChsC	172	D2
La France	AndC	117	A2
Lagoon	BldC	129	C2
*La Grange	LnrC	84	A3
*Lake City	FloC	155	D1
Lake Forest	GrvC	97	B5
Lake Landing	HydC	62	E6
Lake Lanier	GrvC	71	D6
*Lake Lure	RthC	71	D2
Lakemont	GrvC	96	C1
Lake Murray Shores	SalC	136	D4
Lake Norman of Catawba	CwaC	49	B6
*Lake Park	UnoC	102	A1
Lake Secession	AbbC	133	D1
Lake Shores	GrwC	135	A1
Lakeside	GrvC	97	A6
Lakeside Park	ChtC	181	A5
Lake Taro	GrvC	97	C7
Lakeview	AlmC	29	C3
Lakeview	DavC	50	E4
*Lake View	DilC	127	B6
Lakeview	MreC	79	E5
Lakeview Estates	HdrC	71	A4
*Lake Waccamaw	CbsC	129	B6
Lakewood	GlfC	28	D3
Lakewood	HdrC	70	E4
Lakewood	HryC	158	A4
Lakewood	SmtC	154	A1
Lakewood	YorC	101	A2
Lake Wylie	YorC	101	A1
*Lamar	DlgC	140	E2
Lamarville	ChtC	180	D4
Lambert	GtnC	166	B3
Lambert	StnC	76	E4
Lambrick	OraC	162	E3
Lamm Crossroads	NshC	33	B6
Lamms Crossroads	WlnC	57	B4
Lancaster	EdgC	34	B7
*Lancaster	LtrC	122	E1
LANCASTER CO	LtrC	101	D7
Lancaster Mill	LtrC	101	D7
Lance Mill	UniC	92	B3
Lanceville	CckC	19	D7
*Landis	RowC	50	B7
Lando	CstC	101	A6
*Landrum	SptC	71	D6
Lands End	BftC	177	B7
Landsford	CstC	101	B6
Lane	CumC	81	B4
*Lane	WmbC	155	C7
Lanes Creek	GtnC	156	E7
Lanes Store	RthC	46	D7
Laney	ChfC	104	A6
Lanford	LarC	119	B2
Langfords Crossroads	RldC	138	C2
Langley	AknC	149	D7
Langley Crossroads	NshC	33	D7
Langston	WanC	83	D1
*Lansing	AshC	2	D5
Lanvale	BwkC	146	C1
*Lasker	NhnC	14	B6
Lassiter Crossroads	NhnC	14	B5
Latham	BeaC	59	E4
Latimer	AbbC	133	D3
*Latta	DilC	126	D6
*Lattimore	ClvC	73	B4
Lauada	SwnC	68	A3
Laughlin	MrnC	142	C2
Laurel	SvrC	42	B3
Laurel Bay	BftC	176	E4
Laureldale	WasC	1	E2
Laurel Fork	CtrC	22	B3
Laurel Grove	PtsC	9	A1
Laurel Hill	BcbC	70	B1
Laurel Hill	LinC	47	D7
Laurel Hill Plantation	ChsC	166	C7
*Laurel Park	HdrC	70	E4
Laurel Park	HenC	7	C1
Laurel Rock Acres	HdrC	70	E5
*Laurens	LarC	119	B4

*Indicates incorporated city

Community	County	Map#	Grid
LAURENS CO	LarC	135	A1
*Laurinburg	SctC	105	C6
*Lavonia	FrkC	116	A5
Law Chapel	BntC	41	A4
*Lawndale	ClvC	73	C2
Lawrence	EdgC	34	E4
Laws	OrgC	30	B2
Lawson	SptC	98	C3
Lawson Crossroad	BntC	41	B5
Lawsons Mill	LnrC	84	C6
Lawsonville	RocC	8	A6
Lawtonville Crossroads	HmpC	169	C6
Laxon	WatC	23	C2
Laytown	CwlC	23	E5
Leah	ClbC	148	B5
Leaksville Junction	PtsC	7	D3
Leander	WatC	22	D1
Leatherman	MacC	68	C4
Leathersville	LncC	148	A4
Leawood	GrvC	97	A4
Lebanon	AndC	117	B2
Lebanon	FaiC	121	C6
Ledbetter	RchC	104	E3
Ledger	MhlC	21	E7
LEE CO	LeCo	54	A7
LEE CO	LeeC	124	B7
Leechville	BeaC	61	D4
Lee Crossroads	FloC	142	A7
Leeds	CstC	121	A1
Lees	BamC	161	C3
Leesburg	WsgC	20	D1
Lees Crossroads	DlgC	124	D7
Lee's Mill	JtnC	82	C3
Legareville	ChsC	178	E1
Legerwood	CwlC	23	D6
*Leggett	EdgC	34	D5
Leggett Crossroads	RobC	127	D4
Leggetts Crossroads	BeaC	59	E2
*Leland	BwkC	130	D7
Lemon Springs	LeCo	80	B2
Lena	CumC	107	C3
Lena	HmpC	169	C6
Lennon Crossroads	BwkC	146	A5
Lennons Crossroads	CbsC	128	B4
*Lenoir	CwlC	47	D1
LENOIR CO	LnrC	110	C1
Lenoxville	CarC	113	C5
Leo	FloC	156	A1
Leon	DupC	110	A1
Lesslie	YorC	101	B4
Lester	MrlC	104	E7
Letitia	CheC	92	A1
Level Cross	RndC	52	C1
Level Cross	SryC	5	A7
Level Land	AbbC	117	E7
Levels	TyrC	38	C6
Levy	JprC	181	A1
Lewis	CstC	100	D6
Lewis	GraC	10	D6
Lewis	ScrC	168	B5
Lewisburg	YanC	21	B6
Lewis Crossroads	DlgC	125	A7
Lewis Crossroads	HlfC	13	A6
*Lewiston Woodville	BrtC	35	D3
*Lewisville	FsyC	26	D4
Lewner	UniC	92	A3
*Lexington	DavC	51	B2
*Lexington	LexC	137	C6
LEXINGTON CO	LexC	150	E1
Liberia	WrnC	12	A6
Liberty	CheC	65	E7
*Liberty	PckC	96	B6
*Liberty	RndC	53	A1
Liberty	RowC	51	A6
Liberty	WsgC	20	C4
LIBERTY CO	LbyC	180	A7
Liberty Hill	CckC	19	A5
Liberty Hill	GreC	20	B1
Liberty Hill	MccC	134	D7
Liberty Hill	McmC	65	B2
Liberty Hill	MntC	77	E4
Licklog	CckC	43	A2
Lickskillet	MacC	94	D2
Lickskillet	WrnC	32	D1
Lickville	GrvC	118	B2
Liddell	LnrC	84	A5
Light Oak	ClvC	73	D5
Liledoun	AlxC	48	C1
*Lilesville	AnsC	104	A3
*Lillington	HntC	81	B2
Lilly	CdnC	17	A3
Lillydale	UciC	21	A4
Lima	CvnC	86	A4
Lima	GrvC	97	A1
Limehouse	JprC	181	A1
Limehouse Station	ChsC	172	E6
Limerick	BrkC	165	D6
Limestone	EgfC	135	B7
Limestone Cove	UciC	21	C3
Limp	SalC	135	D6
Linberry	RndC	52	D1
LINCOLN CO	LinC	75	A1
LINCOLN CO	LncC	133	D7
Lincoln Park	MreC	79	C7
Lincoln Park	YanC	45	C1
Lincolnshire	RldC	138	A4
*Lincolnton	LinC	74	C1
*Lincolnville	ChsC	172	D1
Lindell	GrnC	58	A5
*Linden	CumC	81	C4
Lineberry	RndC	52	D1
Line Spring	SvrC	41	D4
Lingles Crossroads	LtrC	102	A7
Linsdale	PolC	65	A5
Linville	AvyC	22	D5
Linville Falls	BkeC	22	C7

Community	County	Map#	Grid
Lisbon	BldC	129	A3
Listening Rock	AshC	2	B4
Litchfield Beach	GtnC	157	D7
Little Africa	SptC	72	B7
Little Cherokee	WsgC	21	A2
Little Cove	SvrC	41	D3
Little Creek	MdnC	44	D1
Little Edisto	ChsC	178	A2
Littlefield	PitC	85	A1
Little Kelly	PdrC	130	E3
Little Milligan	CtrC	22	B1
Little Mountain	McdC	46	D4
*Little Mountain	NbrC	136	E2
Little Prong	BwkC	145	B3
Little Richmond	SryC	25	D1
Little River	AlxC	48	B1
Little River	TrnC	70	C5
Littles Mill	RchC	78	A6
Littles Quarters	AnsC	103	C5
Little Switzerland	McdC	46	A2
Little Texas	GrvC	97	A3
Little Texas	ShmC	14	B1
*Littleton	HlfC	12	D5
Littleton	RldC	137	D2
Little Town	HryC	144	D6
Live Oak	HryC	144	A4
*Livingston	OraC	151	E6
Livingstons Quarters	SctC	105	B6
Lizard Lick	WkeC	56	C1
Lizzie	GrnC	58	D6
Lloyd Crossroads	HtfC	15	E6
Loafers Glory	MhlC	21	E6
Lobeco	BftC	176	E2
*Lockhart	UnnC	99	E6
Lockhart Junction	UnnC	99	B6
Lockhart Oil Field	KswC	123	C5
*Locust	StnC	76	D5
Locust Hill	CasC	8	C7
Locust Hill	GrvC	97	B2
Locust Springs	GreC	20	A1
*Lodge	ColC	170	B1
Lodge Hall	GtnC	166	D3
Lodi	WasC	1	E1
Loftins Crossroads	LnrC	84	E5
Logan	RthC	72	C2
Lola	CarC	114	C1
Lomax	WksC	25	A1
London	CckC	43	C1
Lone Hickory	YadC	25	E5
Lone Oak	SptC	98	B3
Lone Star	ClhC	153	B5
Long Bay Estates	HryC	158	A4
Long Bottom Ford	OcnC	94	E4
Long Branch	BrnC	161	A3
Long Branch	LarC	119	D4
Long Creek	CckC	19	B7
Long Creek	PdrC	130	D4
Long Hill	SryC	5	B6
Long Island	CwaC	48	E5
Long Pine	AnsC	103	C5
Long Point	HryC	144	B5
Long Ridge	BrkC	164	D6
Long Ridge	MdnC	44	D3
Long Shoals	LinC	74	C2
Longshore	NbrC	136	A1
Longs Store	PerC	9	C5
Longtown	BkeC	46	C3
Longtown	FaiC	122	D7
Longtown	YadC	25	D4
*Long View	BkeC	47	E4
Long View	BldC	130	A3
*Long View	CwaC	48	A4
Longwood	BftC	177	B6
Lopers Crossroads	AlnC	169	C3
Loray	IrdC	49	A2
Lorenzo	EffC	175	A5
*Loris	HryC	144	B4
Lost Cove	YanC	21	A5
Lota	GrwC	135	A1
Lotts Crossroads	DorC	172	B1
*Louisburg	FraC	32	D4
Love Field	JakC	68	E3
Lovejoy	MntC	78	A2
Love Station	UciC	21	A4
*Love Valley	IrdC	25	A6
Lovill	WatC	23	A2
Loving	FnnC	92	A4
Lowe	RobC	127	C1
*Lowell	GasC	74	E5
Lowell Mill	JtnC	57	A6
Lower Elk Creek	GsnC	3	D1
Lowesville	LinC	75	A2
Low Gap	GsnC	4	B3
Lowndes Landing	ColC	171	E4
*Lowndesville	AbbC	133	C2
Lowrys	AnsC	103	C4
*Lowrys	CstC	100	C6
Luart	HntC	81	A2
*Lucama	WlnC	57	C4
Lucia	GasC	75	A3
Lucius	GilC	91	C6
Luck	MdnC	43	E7
Lucknow	LeeC	124	A4
Lukens	CarC	113	D1
*Lumber Bridge	RobC	106	D4
*Lumberton	RobC	127	D1
LUMPKIN CO	LmpC	93	A7
Lumptown	MdnC	44	B1
Lunday	YanC	21	D7
Lundy Crossroads	HryC	143	B7
Lunn	DlgC	125	A6
*Luray	HmpC	169	C5
Luther	BcbC	44	B7
Lydia	DlgC	124	D7
Lydia Mills	LarC	119	C5
Lykes	RldC	138	C7

Community	County	Map#	Grid
Lyman	DupC	110	B4
*Lyman	SptC	97	E3
Lynch Beach	PamC	87	B5
*Lynchburg	LeeC	140	E4
Lynches Mill	FloC	141	C5
Lynchs Corner	PsqC	16	E4
Lyndhurst	BrnC	161	A5
Lynn	PlkC	71	D6
Lynn Crossroads	DurC	31	B7
Lyons	GraC	31	C3
M			
Mabel	WatC	22	E1
MacArthurs Junction	AbbC	118	C5
Macbeth	BrkC	165	A4
*Macclesfield	EdgC	58	C2
Macedon	LexC	151	C2
Macedonia	CheC	92	B2
Macedonia	CrkC	98	E1
Macedonia	McmC	65	B3
Macedonia	NbrC	136	E4
Macedonia	TwnC	93	C4
Macedonia	WkeC	55	C3
Machpelah	LinC	74	E1
Mackeys	WshC	37	B5
Macks Village	WkeC	55	C5
Maco	BwkC	130	B7
*Macon	WrnC	12	B5
MACON CO	MacC	93	E1
Maddens	LarC	119	A5
Madison	AknC	149	E6
Madison	OcnC	115	E2
*Madison	RocC	6	E6
MADISON CO	MdnC	20	C7
*Madisonville	MroC	65	C1
Madola	FnnC	91	C3
Maggies Mill	PolC	65	B5
*Maggie Valley	HwdC	69	B1
*Magnolia	DupC	109	C3
*Maiden	CwaC	48	C6
Maine	DveC	26	B7
Makatoka	BwkC	145	C3
Mallory	DilC	126	C5
Malmo	BwkC	130	C7
Malonee Mill	MacC	68	B5
Malpass Corner	PdrC	130	C3
Malta	SmtC	153	C1
Maltby	CheC	66	D7
Mamers	HntC	80	E2
Mamie	CurC	39	C1
Manchester	CumC	80	D5
Mandale	AlmC	53	E1
Mangum	RchC	77	E7
Mangums	ChfC	103	A6
Manila	McmC	65	B1
Manly	MreC	79	D6
*Manning	ClnC	154	C4
Manning Crossroads	DilC	126	C4
*Manteo	DarC	40	A5
Manville	LeeC	140	A3
Maple Crossroads	HryC	143	E6
Maplecypress	CvnC	85	C2
Maple Grove	CwlC	23	A6
Maple Grove	FnnC	92	A4
Maple Springs	SwnC	67	E3
Maple Springs	WksC	24	A3
Mapleton	HtfC	15	A4
Mapleville	FraC	32	E4
Marbleton	UciC	21	B3
Maready	DupC	110	B4
Marengo	MkbC	12	A1
Maretts	HarC	116	C5
Margaret	FraC	32	E5
Margret	FnnC	92	A6
Maribel	PamC	87	B5
*Marietta	RobC	127	C6
Marines	OnsC	132	C1
*Marion	McdC	46	B5
*Marion	MrnC	142	D2
MARION CO	MrnC	127	A7
Mariposa	LinC	74	E2
Mark Pine	CbsC	144	E1
Marlboro	MrlC	125	D3
MARLBORO CO	MrlC	104	D6
Marler	YadC	25	C4
Marlow	EffC	175	A7
Mar-Mac	WanC	83	C3
Marmaduke	WrnC	12	B6
Marrowbone Heights	HenC	7	B2
Mars Bluff	FloC	142	A2
*Marshall	MdnC	44	B3
*Mars Hill	MdnC	44	D2
*Marshville	UnoC	102	E2
Martha	RndC	51	E6
*Martin	SpnC	115	E4
MARTIN CO	MtnC	60	C2
Martin Crossroads	LarC	119	B2
*Martinez	ClbC	149	A7
Martins Creek	CheC	92	C2
Martins Crossroads	LncC	148	B3
Martins Crossroads	WmbC	155	A4
*Martinsville		7	B1
Marvin	GreC	19	C2
*Marvin	LtrC	101	C2
*Marvin	UnoC	101	D3
Mary	HryC	143	D7
Mary Louise	SptC	98	D1
Marys Grove	ClvC	74	A4
Marysville	GtnC	167	C1
Mascot	SptC	97	E1
Mashburn	McmC	65	A2
Mashburn Mill	FnnC	92	B4
Mashoes	DarC	39	C4
Masonboro	NhrC	147	A1
Masons Cross Road	AndC	117	A3
Masons Crossroads	SctC	105	B7

Community	County	Map#	Grid
Mason Store	HntC	81	A3
Masontown	CarC	114	A2
Mast	WatC	22	E1
Mathews Heights	GrwC	134	E3
Mathis Corner	FloC	141	E4
Matkins	CasC	29	B1
Matney	WatC	22	E3
Matrimony	RocC	7	B4
*Matthews	MklC	75	E7
Matthews Crossroads	NshC	33	B4
*Mauldin	GrvC	97	C6
Maury	GrnC	58	D7
Max	CrlC	4	D3
Maxim	LncC	148	B2
*Maxton	RobC	105	E6
*Maxton	SctC	105	D6
Maxwell	FnnC	91	D5
Maybinton	NbrC	120	E5
Mayday	WsgC	20	E3
*Mayesville	SmtC	140	C6
Mayfield	RocC	8	A4
Mayhew	IrdC	49	B7
May Hilltop	DilC	127	B7
Mayo	HalC	9	E3
Mayo	SptC	98	D1
*Mayodan	RocC	6	E6
Mayo Mills	SptC	98	D1
Mayos Crossroads	EdgC	35	B7
Mays Crossroads	NshC	33	A5
Mayson Crossroads	EgfC	134	E7
Maysville	ChfC	103	B6
*Maysville	JnsC	111	E2
Mazeppa	IrdC	49	D5
*McAdenville	GasC	74	E5
McAllister Hill	PolC	91	D2
McArthur Crossroads	SctC	105	C7
McBean	RmdC	159	C5
*McBee	ChfC	124	B4
McCain	HokC	105	E1
McCaskill	KswC	139	A3
*McCaysville	FnnC	91	C2
*McClellanville	ChsC	166	D7
McClure Mill	MacC	94	B1
*McColl	MrlC	126	B1
McConnell	BeaC	60	B7
McConnell	MreC	79	B1
*McConnells	YorC	100	C5
McCookville	SvrC	42	A3
*McCormick	MccC	148	C1
MCCORMICK CO	MccC	148	C1
McCormick Crossroads	DilC	126	C4
McCray	AlmC	29	D3
McCullen	SamC	82	E7
McCullers	WkeC	55	C4
McCullers Crossroads	WkeC	55	C4
McCullough	FnnC	92	A3
McCutchens Crossroads	LeeC	140	B3
McDade	OrgC	30	B3
McDaniel	SamC	108	B4
*McDonald	RobC	127	B3
McDonald Mill	MacC	94	B1
MCDOWELL CO	McdC	22	C7
MCDUFFIE CO	MdfC	148	A6
*McFarlan	AnsC	104	A5
McFarland	HokC	105	D2
McFarland	PolC	65	C6
McGee Crossroads	JtnC	55	E7
McGee Mill	JtnC	55	E7
McGeetown	PolC	91	D2
McGehees Mill	PerC	9	C4
McGinnis Crossroads	PlkC	72	B6
McGuires	GhmC	66	D4
McHarg	PolC	91	C2
McKelvey Crossroads	GrvC	118	B2
McKennon	ChfC	124	D3
McKenzie Crossroads	FloC	141	B7
McKeown	CstC	121	D2
McKinney Cove	MhlC	21	E6
McKnights Mill	GsnC	4	B3
McKoy	JtnC	82	B4
McLamb Crossroads	SamC	82	C5
McLaughlin Crossroads	DlgC	140	E2
McMahan	SvrC	41	C1
McMillan	RobC	106	E4
MCMINN CO	McmC	65	B2
McPhersonville	HmpC	170	C7
McQueen Crossroads	HryC	143	C4
Meadow	JtnC	82	B3
Meadow Brook	DlgC	141	D1
Meadow Brook Village	CwaC	48	A5
Meadowfield	PatC	5	D3
Meadows	StkC	6	B7
Meadowview	DavC	51	A2
Mean Crossroads	UnnC	99	A6
Meat Camp	WatC	23	B2
*Mebane	AlmC	29	E4
*Mebane	OrgC	29	E4
Mecca	McmC	65	C3
Mechanic	RndC	52	A5
Mechanic Hill	RmdC	159	C4
Mechanicsville	DlgC	125	D6
Mechanicsville	LeeC	140	A4
MECKLENBURG CO	MkbC	12	A2
MECKLENBURG CO	MklC	101	D2
Medfield	WkeC	55	C2
Meeks	FloC	141	E2
Meeting Street	EgfC	135	C7
*Meggett	ChsC	172	C7
Melanchton	RndC	52	E1
Melrose	BntC	41	A3
Melrose	PlkC	71	B6
Melton	RmdC	159	A3
Melville	AlmC	29	D5
Menola	HtfC	14	E6
Mepkin	BrkC	165	B7
Mercer	EdgC	58	B1

*Indicates incorporated city

RAND McNALLY

PAGE AB

Cities and Communities

Community	County	Map#	Grid
Merchant	SalC	136	B5
Meriwether	MccC	148	E5
Merrimon	CarC	113	C1
Merry Oaks	ChaC	54	D5
*Mesic	PamC	87	C4
Metcalf	ClvC	73	C3
Mewborns Crossroads	LnrC	84	D2
Micaville	YanC	45	D1
Michfield	RndC	52	C6
*Micro	JtnC	56	E6
Middendorf	ChfC	124	C3
*Middleburg	VncC	11	C5
Middle Creek	SvrC	41	E2
Middle Fork	TrnC	69	E7
Middle River	BwkC	145	E4
*Middlesex	NshC	56	E2
*Middleton	ElbC	133	A4
Middletown	HydC	63	A6
*Midland	CabC	76	C5
Midland Valley	AknC	149	E6
Midpine	ClvC	74	A6
Midway	AlxC	48	D1
Midway	BamC	162	B4
Midway	BeaC	60	D6
Midway	CckC	43	C1
Midway	ClhC	153	B7
Midway	DavC	27	B7
Midway	HabC	115	B2
Midway	HalC	10	B1
Midway	JhnC	1	E6
Midway	LtrC	123	C2
Midway	MkbC	11	D1
Midway	RocC	28	C1
Midway Crossroads	GtnC	156	E3
Midway Crossroads	LtrC	123	C2
Midway Crossroads	WmbC	156	B2
Milburnie	WkeC	56	A2
Milburnton	GreC	20	C2
Mildred	EdgC	34	E7
Miles	OrgC	30	A4
Miles Crossroad	GlfC	28	B7
Milesville	CasC	8	C7
Milford	GrvC	97	C3
Milford	SmtC	153	C3
Millboro	RndC	52	D2
Mill Branch	BwkC	145	C4
Mill Branch	FloC	142	B4
Millbridge	RowC	50	C5
Mill Brook	WsgC	20	C2
Mill Creek	AshC	23	C1
Mill Creek	BwkC	146	C3
Mill Creek	CarC	113	B3
Mill Creek	GsnC	2	D3
Mill Creek	JhnC	1	D7
Miller Cove	BntC	41	A4
Miller Crossing	YorC	100	E3
Miller Crossroads	GtnC	157	A3
Miller Hill	ChsC	173	A6
Millers Crossroads	EgfC	149	A3
Millers Mill	AbbC	134	C2
Millersville	AlxC	48	C2
Millett	AlnC	160	D7
Millhaven	ScrC	168	B3
Millican Grove	SvrC	42	A1
Millingport	StnC	77	A3
Mill Neck	HtfC	15	B3
Mill Stone Landing	JprC	175	E7
*Milton	CasC	9	A3
Milton	LarC	119	D7
Milwaukee	NhnC	14	C5
Mimosa Shores	BeaC	60	B6
*Mineral Bluff	FnnC	91	E4
Mineral Springs	AnsC	103	B3
*Mineral Springs	UnoC	101	E3
Mingo	SamC	82	A6
*Minnesott Beach	PamC	112	E1
Minter	GrvC	97	B4
*Mint Hill	MklC	76	A6
*Mint Hill	UnoC	76	B7
Minton Mill	KswC	123	E4
Mintons Store	HtfC	14	D7
Mintonsville	GatC	16	B5
Mintz	SamC	108	B3
Miranda	RowC	50	A6
Misenheimer	StnC	77	A1
Mission	CheC	92	E1
MITCHELL CO	MhlC	21	D5
Mitchells Fork	GatC	16	B5
Mitchells Mill	GsvC	13	D2
Mitchellville	JprC	176	B4
Mitchiners Crossroads	FraC	32	B3
Mitford	FaiC	122	B4
Mixville	AknC	149	E7
Mize	SpnC	115	C4
Mock Mill	WasC	1	D1
*Mocksville	DveC	50	B1
Moffett	HalC	10	A1
Moffitt Hill	McdC	45	E6
Mohawk Crossroad	GreC	19	C2
Mollie	CbsC	144	D2
Moltonville	SamC	108	E2
*Momeyer	NshC	33	B6
Monaghan	GrvC	97	A5
Monarch	UnnC	99	C7
Monbo	CwaC	49	A5
*Moncks Corner	BrkC	165	A5
*Monetta	AknC	150	C1
*Monetta	SalC	150	C1
Monks Crossroads	SamC	82	D5
Monogram	BwkC	145	D6
*Monroe	UnoC	102	B2
MONROE CO	MroC	65	D3
Monroe Crossroads	MrlC	125	E3
Monroeton	RocC	28	D1
Montague	GrvC	97	A4
Montague	PdrC	130	C4

Community	County	Map#	Grid
Mont Clare	DlgC	125	C6
Monteith	ChtC	180	D2
Monterey Park	GasC	74	D4
Montezuma	AvyC	22	C5
Montgomery	ChtC	180	E6
Montgomery	RldC	137	D3
MONTGOMERY CO	MntC	79	A6
Monticello	FaiC	121	B7
Monticello	GlfC	28	D2
Montmorenci	AknC	150	B7
*Montreat	BcbC	45	C5
Montrose	ChfC	125	B1
Montrose	HokC	105	E1
Moody Cove	OcnC	95	B4
Moonville	GrvC	97	B7
MOORE CO	MreC	105	B1
Moore Crossroads	WmbC	155	C1
Moorefield	BrkC	164	D4
Moores Beach	BeaC	87	C1
*Mooresboro	ClvC	73	A4
Moores Chapel	JtnC	56	E4
Moores Corner	ChsC	166	D7
Moores Corner	PamC	87	B7
Moores Crossroads	AlnC	169	B2
Moores Crossroads	JtnC	57	A4
Moores Crossroads	WlnC	57	B4
Moores School House	JtnC	57	A4
Moores Springs	StkC	6	A6
*Mooresville	IrdC	49	D7
Mooretown	PdrC	131	B4
*Morehead City	CarC	113	C5
Moreland	BrkC	173	C1
Morgan	JprC	176	A7
Morgana	EgfC	149	A5
Morgan Ford	RowC	51	B6
Morgans Corners	PsqC	17	A4
*Morganton	BkeC	46	E4
*Morganton	FnnC	91	E4
Moriah	PerC	30	E1
Morningside	GrvC	97	B4
Morning Star	HwdC	70	A1
Morris Acres	ChsC	172	E6
*Morrisville	WkeC	55	A2
Morrisville	WmbC	156	C5
Mortimer	CwlC	22	E6
Morton Fork	OnsC	111	E4
*Morven	AnsC	103	E4
Moselle	ColC	170	A2
*Mosheim	GreC	19	D3
Moss Hill	LnrC	84	B5
Moss Neck	RobC	127	B1
Motleta	RndC	52	A3
Moulton	FraC	32	D2
Mountain Brook	RldC	138	C6
*Mountain City	JhnC	1	E5
*Mountain City	RabC	94	B4
Mountain Grove	MacC	68	D6
Mountain Home	HdrC	70	E3
Mountain Island	GasC	75	A4
Mountain Lake Camp	HdrC	70	E4
Mountain Lake Colony	GrvC	96	C1
Mountain Page	HdrC	71	B6
Mountain Park	SryC	4	C7
Mountain Scene	TwnC	93	C5
Mountain Valley	HdrC	70	E6
Mountain View	BcbC	70	E1
Mountain View	CwaC	48	A5
Mountain View	GasC	74	B5
Mountain View	OrgC	30	C4
Mountain View	SptC	98	C1
Mountain View	StkC	26	E1
*Mt Airy	HabC	115	A4
*Mt Airy	SryC	5	A5
Mt Beulah	AknC	160	D1
Mt Carmel	GreC	19	D2
Mt Carmel	WsgC	20	E3
*Mt Croghan	ChfC	103	B6
Mt Energy	GraC	31	D3
Mt Gallagher	LarC	118	D6
Mt Gilead	AvyC	22	C2
*Mt Gilead	MntC	77	E5
Mt Gould	BrtC	36	E2
Mt Hermon	PtsC	8	C1
*Mt Holly	GasC	75	A4
Mt Mitchell	CabC	76	B1
Mt Mourne	IrdC	49	C7
Mt Olive	BldC	129	A2
Mt Olive	CbsC	128	C4
Mt Olive	HdrC	70	E5
Mt Olive	HryC	143	D3
Mt Olive	StkC	5	E7
*Mt Olive	WanC	83	C5
Mt Olivet	HarC	116	C6
Mt Pilgrim	MtnC	35	B4
Mt Pisgah	KswC	123	D3
Mt Pleasant	AvyC	22	C5
Mt Pleasant	BnkC	115	A6
*Mt Pleasant	CabC	76	D2
*Mt Pleasant	ChsC	173	C5
Mt Pleasant	GreC	19	D3
Mt Pleasant	MreC	80	B5
Mt Pleasant	NshC	57	B1
Mt Pleasant	WkeC	55	D6
Mt Pleasant	WksC	24	A4
Mt Pleasant	YadC	26	A2
Mt Rena	GtnC	157	C6
Mt Sterling	HwdC	43	A3
Mt Tabor	UnnC	99	D6
Mt Tirzah	PerC	30	E1
Mt Valley	PlkC	71	C5
Mt Vernon	MroC	65	D2
Mt Vernon	RowC	50	B3
Mt Vernon	RthC	72	C2
Mt Vernon Springs	ChaC	53	C4
Mt View	GrvC	97	B2
Mt Willing	SalC	136	B6

Community	County	Map#	Grid
Mt Zion	FloC	142	B6
Mt Zion	WksC	23	E4
Mouzon	WmbC	155	B3
Moxley	WksC	3	E7
Moyd	GtnC	166	E2
Mud Castle	NhnC	13	D4
Muddy Creek	FsyC	26	E6
Muddy Cross	GatC	16	B5
Mudlick	NbrC	135	D1
Mulberry	CwlC	23	B6
Mulberry	SmtC	140	A6
Mulberry	WksC	24	C2
Mulberry Grove	ChtC	180	D2
Muldrow Mill	FloC	141	B2
*Mullins	MrnC	143	A2
Mullins Crossroads	HlfC	34	E3
Mundo Vista	RndC	52	A3
Munster	RldC	137	E5
Murad	JprC	176	D3
Murchison	YanC	45	C2
Murchisontown	HntC	80	B3
*Murfreesboro	HtfC	14	E4
Murphey	DupC	109	E5
*Murphy	CheC	66	C7
Murphy Junction	FnnC	91	D4
Murphys Estates	EgfC	149	C6
Murphytown	BldC	108	D7
Murray	LexC	136	E6
Murray Hill	BurC	168	A3
Murrays Hill	CwaC	48	E5
Murraysville	BrkC	164	E5
Murraysville	NhrC	131	A6
Murraytown	NshC	56	E1
Murray Town	PdrC	130	E1
Musgraves Crossroads	WanC	57	E7
*Myrtle Beach	HryC	158	B3
Myrtle Grove	BynC	180	C7
Myrtle Grove	NhrC	147	A2
Myrtle Grove Junction	NhrC	147	A2
Myrtle Head	BwkC	145	B2
Myrtle Island	BftC	181	D1
N			
*Nags Head	DarC	40	A5
Nahunta	WanC	57	B6
Nantahala	SwnC	67	D4
Naples	HdrC	70	E3
Narrow Ridge	MreC	79	A7
NASH CO	NshC	34	A7
*Nashville	NshC	33	D6
Nathans Creek	AshC	2	E5
Natural Bridge	CckC	19	B5
*Navassa	BwkC	130	D7
Nebo	YadC	26	A2
Nebraska	HydC	63	A6
Ned Swamp	HryC	143	C7
Needmore	CbsC	144	D2
Needmore	FraC	32	B3
Needmore	HamC	19	A1
Needmore	RowC	50	B3
Needmore	SwnC	67	E3
*Neeses	OraC	151	E7
Neff	WasC	1	D1
Neighbors Crossroads	LarC	119	E5
Nellie	HwdC	43	A6
Nelms	PamC	87	B6
Nelson	DurC	55	A1
Nettleridge	PatC	6	C3
Neubert	KnoC	41	A1
Neva	JhnC	1	D6
Nevadun	JprC	176	C4
Nevitt Forest	AndC	117	C4
New Belden	PitC	59	C4
*New Bern	CvnC	86	B6
*Newberry	NbrC	136	C1
NEWBERRY CO	NbrC	135	D2
New Bethel	McmC	65	A4
New Britton	BwkC	145	A3
New Candler	BcbC	44	B7
New Castle	WksC	25	B4
New Cut	LtrC	102	A6
Newdale	YanC	45	D1
Newell	MklC	75	E5
*New Ellenton	AknC	160	B2
Newell Station	SvrC	41	B1
New Era	SvrC	41	E2
Newfound	BcbC	44	B6
Newfoundland	TyrC	38	D5
New Gilead	CabC	76	B1
NEW HANOVER CO	NhrC	146	E3
New Haven	AlgC	3	D4
New Holland	AknC	150	D4
New Holland	HydC	62	D6
New Holland Crossroads	AknC	150	D4
New Home	ClvC	73	B1
New Hope	BwkC	146	B3
New Hope	FloC	141	D5
New Hope	FraC	32	C6
New Hope	GilC	91	A7
New Hope	GtnC	166	D2
New Hope	IrdC	25	B6
New Hope	LncC	148	B3
New Hope	OrgC	30	C5
New Hope	PqmC	38	A1
New Hope	RndC	51	E7
New Hope	SryC	4	E6
New Hope	WanC	83	E2
New Hope	WlnC	57	D2
New House	ClvC	73	A3
*Newland	AvyC	22	C5
Newland	BrkC	166	B5
New Life	CbsC	144	B3
Newlife	WksC	3	D7
New Light	AndC	117	A3
New Light	WkeC	31	E5
*New London	StnC	77	B2

Community	County	Map#	Grid
Newmansville	GreC	20	B1
New Market	DlgC	124	D6
New Market	RndC	52	B2
New Mt Cross	PtsC	8	B2
*Newport	CarC	112	E4
*Newport	CckC	19	A7
Newport	FnnC	91	E7
Newport	YorC	100	E3
New Prospect	SptC	72	A7
New Salem	UnoC	76	E7
News Ferry	HalC	9	C1
Newsom	DavC	51	C7
*Newsoms	ShmC	14	E1
New Switzerland	HabC	115	A3
*Newton	CwaC	48	C6
*Newton Grove	SamC	82	C4
Newtons Crossroads	SamC	109	B7
Newtonville	MrlC	105	A7
New Town	DilC	126	E5
New Victory	WsgC	20	D2
Neyles	ColC	171	C5
Niagara	MreC	79	D6
Nicanor	PqmC	16	C6
*Nichols	MrnC	143	C1
Nicholson Village	AknC	150	B6
Nimmons	PckC	95	E3
Nine Times	PckC	95	E4
*Ninety Six	GrwC	135	B3
Nixon	RmdC	159	C3
Nixons Crossroads	HryC	144	E7
Nixonton	PsqC	17	B7
Nixonville	HryC	158	B1
Nixville	HmpC	169	D6
Nobles Crossroads	LnrC	84	C6
Nobles Mill	LnrC	84	D6
Nonaburg	McmC	65	B2
Norfleet	HlfC	35	C2
*Norlina	WrnC	11	E4
*Norman	RchC	78	D6
Norman	WlkC	133	A6
Normanville	MhlC	21	E7
Norrington Crossroads	HntC	81	A3
*Norris	PckC	96	A6
*North	OraC	151	E5
NORTHAMPTON CO	NhnC	12	E3
North Asheboro	RndC	52	C3
*North Augusta	AknC	159	C1
*North Augusta	EgfC	149	B7
North Brevard	TrnC	70	B5
*North Charleston	ChsC	173	A4
North Cooleemee	DveC	50	B2
North Cove	McdC	46	B2
North Cove Crossing	McdC	46	B2
Northcutt	GilC	91	B7
North Fork	WatC	22	E1
North Gate	FloC	141	D1
North Harlowe	CvnC	113	A3
North Hartsville	DlgC	124	E6
North Henderson	VncC	11	B6
North Hickory	CwaC	48	A3
Northlake	AndC	117	B3
Northlakes	CwlC	48	A3
North Litchfield Beach	GtnC	157	D7
*North Myrtle Beach	HryC	158	E1
North Pacolet	SptC	72	A7
North River	CarC	113	C4
North Santee	GtnC	166	E4
North Side	GraC	31	C4
*North Topsail Beach	OnsC	132	B3
Northview	LeCo	54	B7
*Northwest	BwkC	130	B6
*North Wilkesboro	WksC	24	D3
Norton	JakC	69	A7
Norton	MacC	94	B2
Norvello	MkbC	11	C1
*Norway	OraC	161	E1
Norwood	RocC	7	D7
*Norwood	StnC	77	D5
Norwood Crossroad	SmtC	141	B6
Norwood Hollow	AvyC	22	D4
Nottely Orchards	UniC	92	D4
Notchy Creek	MroC	65	D1
Nough	CckC	43	C1
O			
*Oakboro	StnC	77	A5
*Oak City	MtnC	35	C5
Oakdale	FloC	141	B2
Oak Dale Crossroads	CbsC	128	B5
Oakey Bay	HryC	157	C1
Oak Forest	JtnC	82	B2
Oak Grove	AknC	150	D3
Oak Grove	BwkC	145	E5
Oak Grove	CheC	66	E6
Oakgrove	ChsC	178	C1
Oak Grove	ClhC	152	B2
Oak Grove	ClvC	73	E5
Oak Grove	CtrC	21	D1
Oak Grove	DilC	126	B6
Oak Grove	DurC	31	B6
Oak Grove	FloC	142	B3
Oak Grove	GtnC	166	D2
Oak Grove	JnsC	85	D7
Oak Grove	MacC	68	B5
Oak Grove	SryC	4	D5
Oak Grove	WatC	23	A2
Oak Grove Inn	JtnC	57	A6
Oak Hill	AknC	160	A1
Oak Hill	BkeC	46	E3
Oak Hill	CckC	19	C6
Oak Hill	CwlC	47	E1
Oak Hill	GraC	10	C5
Oak Hill	GsnC	3	A3
Oak Hill	HdrC	71	A3
Oak Hill	MacC	68	B6
Oak Hill	SctC	105	D3

*Indicates incorporated city

Community	County	Map#	Grid
Oak Hill Court	HdrC	70	D3
Oakhurst	LtrC	123	A3
*Oak Island	BwkC	146	B6
Oakland	NshC	33	B5
Oakland	RobC	106	E3
Oakland	SmtC	139	D6
Oakland	TrnC	69	C7
Oakland	WsgC	20	C2
Oakland Crossroads	DilC	126	D4
Oakley	BrkC	165	A6
Oakley	PitC	59	C2
Oak Park	BcbC	70	E2
Oak Park	CheC	65	E7
*Oak Ridge	GlfC	27	E3
Oak Ridge	PtsC	8	A3
Oak Ridge	StkC	6	C4
Oak Ridge Park	RchC	104	D4
Oaks	OrgC	29	E6
Oakton	RobC	127	D4
Oak View	BntC	41	A3
Oak Villa	HtfC	15	B5
Oakville	WrnC	12	A4
Oakway	OcnC	116	B2
Oakwood	AknC	150	C7
Oakwood Acres	DavC	51	B5
Oakwoods	WksC	24	D4
Oaky	EffC	175	A3
Oasis	FnnC	91	B4
Oatland	GtnC	156	E7
Oats	DlgC	140	E1
Obids	AshC	23	E1
Ocean	CarC	112	C6
*Ocean Isle Beach	BwkC	145	C7
Oceanview	ChsC	173	B6
Oceda	GtnC	166	D2
Oconaluftee Indian Village	SwnC	68	C1
OCONEE CO	OcnC	116	C1
O'Dell	WrnC	12	D5
Oden Mill	BeaC	60	E5
Odis Crossroads	BnkC	115	B6
Offset	SulC	1	C3
Ogburns Crossroads	GlfC	28	A2
Ogden	ClyC	92	E2
Ogden	NhrC	131	B7
Ogden	YorC	100	E5
OGLETHORPE CO	OgtC	133	A6
Ogreeta	CheC	66	B6
Oine	WrnC	11	D4
Okeewemee	MntC	78	B2
Okisko	PsqC	17	A6
Okolona	CtrC	21	C2
Ola	HwdC	43	B5
*Olanta	FloC	141	B6
*Olar	BamC	161	D6
Old Bethlehem	WrnC	12	C7
Old Cordesville	BrkC	165	B6
Old Dock	CbsC	145	A2
Old Ford	BeaC	60	A4
*Old Fort	McdC	45	D6
Old Gilreath	WksC	24	D5
Oldham	SvrC	42	A3
Old House	JprC	176	C4
Old Hundred	SctC	105	A5
Old Joe	BrkC	173	D1
Old Madison	OcnC	115	E2
Old Morrisville	WmbC	156	D5
Old Pickens	OcnC	95	D6
Olds	CurC	18	C7
Old Sparta	EdgC	58	D1
Old Town	BwkC	146	E2
Oldtown	CckC	19	A7
Oldtown	GsnC	4	A2
Oldtown	NbrC	135	E3
Old Trap	CdnC	17	E6
Olga	PckC	96	D2
Olin	GtnC	166	D1
Olive Branch	UnoC	77	A7
Olive Grove	ClvC	47	C7
Olive Hill	MacC	68	A6
Olive Hill	PerC	9	C5
Oliver	JtnC	56	E7
Oliver Crossroads	DilC	127	A5
Olivers	JnsC	111	D1
Olivers Crossroads	CwaC	48	D6
Olivers Crossroads	JnsC	85	C7
Olivet	JakC	68	D2
Olivette	CwlC	23	B7
Olympia	PamC	86	C5
Olympia	RldC	138	A6
Olyphic	CbsC	144	E5
Omega	HalC	10	A1
O'Neal	GrvC	97	C2
ONSLOW CO	OnsC	112	A6
Onvil	MntC	78	B4
Ophir	MntC	77	E1
Ora	ClvC	73	C4
Ora	LarC	119	B3
Orange	SamC	82	B6
ORANGE CO	OrgC	29	E4
*Orangeburg	OraC	152	C7
ORANGEBURG CO	OraC	151	D6
Orange Factory	DurC	31	A3
Orange Grove	OrgC	30	A6
Oregon Hill	RocC	7	E5
Ore Knob	AshC	3	A6
*Oriental	PamC	87	B7
Orion	AshC	2	E6
Orlando	MacC	94	B2
Ormondsville	GrnC	58	E7
Orrs	CstC	100	D7
*Orrum	RobC	127	E4
Orum	FloC	142	B4
Osborn	ChsC	172	A6
Osborn	TwnC	93	C4
Osborne	RchC	104	D5
Osborne Knob	McdC	45	E2
Osbornville	WksC	25	A5
Osceola	GlfC	28	E2
Osceola	WasC	1	D2
Osgood	LeCo	54	C7
Osmond	CasC	9	A5
Ossipee	AlmC	29	B3
Oswalt	IrdC	49	C5
Oswego	FraC	32	E3
Oswego	SmtC	140	B5
Otes	HawC	19	C1
Othello	AshC	2	E7
Ottanola	HdrC	71	C3
Ottinger	CckC	19	B5
Ottway	GreC	19	E1
Otway	CarC	113	D4
Outland	WmbC	156	D2
Outlaws Bridge	DupC	84	A6
Oval	AshC	23	D1
Overhills	HntC	80	D5
Overlook	HdrC	70	E4
Overshot	JtnC	82	C3
Owdoms	SalC	135	D6
Owens	GtnC	156	E3
Owens Crossroad	BrnC	161	A6
Owings	LarC	118	E2
Owltown	BcbC	44	B6
Owltown	UniC	92	E5
*Oxford	GraC	10	E7
Oxford Park	CwaC	48	D3
Oyster Point	ChsC	173	B6
P			
Paces	HalC	9	B1
*Pacolet	SptC	98	E4
*Pacolet Mills	SptC	99	A4
Pactolus	PitC	59	D4
Padena	FnnC	92	A5
Padgett	OnsC	110	E7
Padgett Mill	CckC	42	E2
Padgetts	ColC	170	C1
*Pageland	ChfC	102	E6
Painter Spring	SulC	1	A3
Painter Spring	WsgC	20	D4
Paint Fork	BcbC	44	E4
Paint Fork	MdnC	45	A2
Paint Gap	YanC	45	B1
Paint Hill	KswC	139	D4
Paint Rock	MdnC	19	D7
Paint Town	JakC	68	D1
Pala Alto	OnsC	111	E4
Palestine	StnC	77	B2
Palmer Crossroads	MkbC	11	E2
Palmer Springs	MkbC	11	D2
Palmerville	BrkC	166	A4
Palmerville	StnC	77	C2
Palmetto	DlgC	141	C1
Palmetto	PatC	6	B3
Palmetto Bluff	BftC	181	C1
Palmyra	HlfC	35	B3
Pamlico	PamC	87	C6
PAMLICO CO	PamC	112	E1
Pamlico Beach	BeaC	87	C1
*Pamplico	FloC	142	B5
Pandora	JhnC	1	C6
Pannill Fork	HenC	6	E1
Panola	ClnC	153	E4
*Pantego	BeaC	61	B4
Pantertown	FnnC	91	D2
Panther Creek	HwdC	43	C5
Paramount Park	GrvC	97	B6
Parhams	FrkC	115	D5
Paris	GrvC	97	B4
Parker	AshC	2	A5
Parker	GrvC	97	A5
Parker Crossroads	FloC	142	A2
Parkersburg	ChtC	181	A5
Parkersburg	SamC	108	C4
Parkers Ferry	ChsC	171	E6
Parkers Fork	GatC	16	B2
Parkersville	GtnC	157	D7
Parkertown	HarC	116	B5
Parkertown Mill	HarC	116	B5
Park Place	GrvC	97	A5
Parks Crossroads	RndC	52	E4
Park Settlement	SvrC	41	C4
Parks Mill	MccC	148	D1
Parks Mill	WasC	1	B2
Park Spring	CasC	8	C4
Parkstown	WanC	84	A2
*Parksville	MccC	148	D2
*Parkton	RobC	106	D3
Parktown	WrnC	12	A7
Parkville	PqmC	16	E6
Parkwood	MreC	79	B2
Parler	OraC	153	D7
*Parmele	MtnC	59	C1
Parr	FaiC	137	B1
Parrish Gap	MacC	68	A5
Parrot Point	ChsC	173	B6
Parrott Fork	LnrC	84	D4
*Parrottsville	CckC	19	B6
Parsonville	WksC	24	C3
Partersville	OraC	153	D7
Paschall	WrnC	11	E4
Pasley	DupC	109	E5
Pasquotank	PsqC	17	A6
PASQUOTANK CO	PsqC	16	E4
Pate Hill	GreC	19	B4
Pates	RobC	106	B7
Patetown	WanC	57	D1
*Patrick	ChfC	124	E2
PATRICK CO	PatC	6	B2
Patten	McdC	46	D5
Patterson	CwlC	23	C6
Patterson Mill	BrnC	160	E6
Patterson Mill	PolC	91	B2
*Patterson Springs	ClvC	73	D5
Pattons Ridge	WksC	23	E2
Pauls Crossing	StnC	77	A2
*Paxville	ClnC	154	A3
Payne	HenC	7	A1
Paynes Store	AlxC	48	D1
Paynes Tavern	PerC	9	D6
Peach	PqmC	16	C5
Peach Bottom	GsnC	3	E3
*Peachland	AnsC	103	B2
Peachtree	CheC	92	D1
Peacock Crossroads	WanC	57	C7
Peacocks Crossroads	JtnC	82	B3
Pea Hill	HlfC	13	D7
*Peak	NbrC	137	B2
Pearces	FraC	32	D7
Pea Ridge	PlkC	72	A4
Pea Ridge	YadC	25	C4
Pearl	ElbC	133	B4
Pecan Terrace	GrvC	97	A7
Peden	AlgC	3	B5
Pee Dee	AnsC	104	B3
Pee Dee	MntC	77	E5
Peedee	MrnC	142	B2
Pee Dee Crossroads	HryC	157	B1
Pekin	MntC	78	B6
*Peletier	CarC	112	B5
Pelham	SptC	97	D5
*Pelion	LexC	151	C3
*Pelzer	AndC	117	E2
*Pembroke	RobC	106	B7
Pender	HlfC	13	C6
PENDER CO	PdrC	110	B7
Penderlea	PdrC	109	E4
Penders Crossroads	WlnC	58	A2
*Pendleton	AndC	117	A1
Penelo	EdgC	34	C6
Peniel	PlkC	71	E5
Peniel Crossroads	FloC	141	C4
Penland	MhlC	21	E7
Penny Hill	PitC	58	E2
Pensacola	YanC	45	C2
Peoria	WatC	22	D2
Peppers	MhlC	21	D6
Percival Crossroads	OcnC	116	A1
Perfection	CvnC	85	D4
Perkins Crossroads	FloC	141	C4
Perkinsville	BkeC	47	A1
PERQUIMANS CO	PqmC	17	A7
Perrot	FloC	142	A5
*Perry	AknC	151	B5
Perrytown	BrtC	36	E2
Persimmon	RabC	93	E5
PERSON CO	PerC	10	A5
Peru	OnsC	132	C2
Petche Gap	BkeC	47	B4
Pet Crossroads	WkeC	56	A1
Petersburg	BkeC	47	B4
Petersburg	MdnC	44	C2
Petersburg	OnsC	110	E2
Petersburg Crossing	DupC	110	B2
Peters Creek	PatC	5	E3
Petersfield	GtnC	157	B4
Peterson	MhlC	21	B6
Petersville	DavC	50	D2
Petra Mills	CwlC	48	A2
Pharrs Mill	CabC	76	A4
Phil	RobC	106	B7
Philadelphia	RchC	104	D3
Philadelphia	WsgC	20	C3
Philadelphus	RobC	106	B6
Phillips Crossroads	EdgC	34	B5
Phillips Crossroads	JnsC	85	A6
Philson Crossroads	LarC	119	E3
Phinizy	ClbC	148	B5
Phinney	OcnC	95	C7
Phoenix	BwkC	130	C6
Phoenix	GrwC	134	E4
*Pickens	PckC	96	B4
PICKENS CO	PckC	116	E1
Picket Post	OcnC	95	B5
Piedmont Park	GrvC	97	B4
Pierce	CtrC	1	A7
Pierces Crossroads	HlfC	13	B6
Piercetown	AndC	117	D1
Pierceville	CdnC	17	A3
Pierceville	FnnC	91	C3
*Pigeon Forge	SvrC	41	E3
Pigeonroost	MhlC	21	C5
Pike City	CrlC	5	C1
Pike Crossroads	WanC	57	C7
Pike Road	BeaC	61	B2
*Pikeville	WanC	57	D7
Pilands Crossroads	HtfC	15	D6
Pilot	FraC	32	D7
Pilot Knob	GreC	19	C2
*Pilot Mountain	SryC	5	C6
Pimlico	BrkC	165	B7
Pinckney Colony	BftC	176	C7
Pinckney Crossroad	SmtC	139	D6
Pinckneyville	UnnC	99	D5
*Pinebluff	MreC	79	C7
Pine Crest	BeaC	61	B7
Pine Crest	CtrC	21	C1
Pinefield Crossroads	BnkC	115	A5
Pine Grove	BrkC	173	A1
Pine Harbor	MklC	75	A7
Pine Hill	HokC	105	D1
Pine Hill	SryC	5	B7
Pine House Crossroads	EgfC	149	D3
Pinehurst	GrwC	135	A2
Pinehurst	HdrC	70	E4
*Pinehurst	MreC	79	C6
Pine Hurst Park	WkeC	55	E4
Pine Island	HryC	158	A3
*Pine Knoll Shores	CarC	113	A6
Pineland	ChsC	174	B1
Pine Level	CbsC	144	D3
*Pine Level	JtnC	56	E7
Pinelog	ClyC	92	D2
Pine Log Village	ClyC	92	D2
Pine Mountain	RabC	94	E3
Pineola	AvyC	22	D6
*Pineora	EffC	175	A7
Pine Ridge	DlgC	124	C6
Pine Ridge	FraC	32	E7
*Pine Ridge	LexC	137	E7
Pine Ridge	MklC	76	A4
Pine Ridge	PolC	65	D7
Pine Ridge	SryC	4	E5
*Pinetops	EdgC	58	C1
Pine Tree	WlnC	58	A2
Pine Valley	NhrC	147	A1
Pineview	HntC	80	C4
*Pineville	MklC	101	C1
Pinewood	RldC	152	C1
*Pinewood	SmtC	153	D3
Piney	CwlC	47	A1
Piney Forest Crossroads	CbsC	128	B4
Piney Green	OnsC	111	D6
Piney Green	SamC	82	B7
Pineygrove	BeaC	60	B5
Piney Grove	BwkC	146	B4
Piney Grove	CtrC	21	D3
Piney Grove	EdgC	34	E6
Piney Grove	McmC	65	A2
Piney Grove	OrgC	30	C5
Piney Grove	RchC	104	C3
Piney Plains	WkeC	55	C3
Piney Ridge	SamC	108	D2
Piney Wood	PdrC	130	C2
Pin Hook	DupC	110	B5
*Pink Hill	LnrC	84	B7
Pinkney	WanC	57	B6
Pinkston	AnsC	103	D2
Pin Point	ChtC	180	E6
Pinson	RndC	51	E7
Pioneer Mills	CabC	76	B5
Pipers Gap	CrlC	4	C2
Pireway	CbsC	144	E4
Pisgah	RndC	52	B7
Pisgah	SmtC	139	D3
Pisgah Shadows	TrnC	70	C5
Pitmon Crossroad	LtrC	122	D3
PITT CO	PitC	60	A5
*Pittman Center	SvrC	42	B3
Pittman Corner	DilC	127	A6
*Pittsboro	ChaC	54	B3
Pittsburg	GrwC	135	B6
PITTSYLVANIA CO	PtsC	7	E2
Plainview	FrkC	115	C6
Plain View	RchC	78	D7
Plainview	RobC	126	E2
Plain View	SamC	82	A4
Plantersville	GtnC	157	B6
Plateau	CwaC	48	A6
Platt Spring	HryC	158	A4
Playcards	HryC	143	E4
Plear	PdrC	131	B1
Pleasant Gap	PtsC	8	B1
*Pleasant Garden	GlfC	28	C7
Pleasant Garden	UciC	21	C4
Pleasant Gardens	McdC	46	A5
Pleasant Grove	AlmC	29	D2
Pleasant Grove	BcbC	44	E5
Pleasant Grove	BkeC	47	C6
Pleasant Grove	CasC	8	E6
Pleasant Grove	CckC	42	E1
Pleasant Grove	DupC	84	A7
Pleasant Grove	GtnC	156	C7
Pleasant Grove	HenC	6	E1
Pleasant Grove	NhnC	14	A4
Pleasant Grove	UniC	92	C5
Pleasant Grove	WshC	37	C5
Pleasant Hill	AlmC	53	B1
Pleasant Hill	CheC	65	E6
Pleasant Hill	FnnC	91	E3
Pleasant Hill	GreC	20	C4
Pleasant Hill	GtnC	156	E4
Pleasant Hill	HawC	19	B1
Pleasant Hill	JnsC	84	D7
Pleasant Hill	LtrC	123	A2
Pleasant Hill	SvrC	41	D2
Pleasant Lane	EgfC	135	B7
Pleasant Plain	LtrC	123	B2
Pleasant Plains	HtfC	15	B5
Pleasant Ridge	WksC	25	B1
Pleasant Vale	GreC	20	B2
Pleasant Valley	CheC	66	C7
Pleasant Valley	GrvC	97	A6
Pleasant View	TyrC	38	C6
Pleasantville	MreC	79	C3
Pleasantville	RocC	7	B6
*Plum Branch	MccC	148	C1
Plyler	StnC	77	A3
*Plymouth	WshC	37	A7
Pocalla Springs	SmtC	154	A1
Pocomoke	FraC	31	E4
Pocotaligo	JprC	176	D1
Poga	CtrC	22	C2
Point Caswell	PdrC	130	B4
Point Pleasant	CckC	19	A4
Pole Creek	BcbC	44	B7
POLK CO	PlkC	71	D4
POLK CO	PolC	65	B6
*Polkton	AnsC	103	B2
*Polkville	ClvC	73	B2
Pollards Corner	ClbC	148	C5
Pollocks	JnsC	85	B6
*Pollocksville	JnsC	111	E1
Polson Crossroads	DlgC	124	E7
*Pomaria	NbrC	136	E1

*Indicates incorporated city

Cities and Communities

Community	County	Map#	Grid
Ponpon	ChsC	171	E6
Pontiac	RldC	138	C3
Ponzer	HydC	61	D4
*Pooler	ChtC	180	C3
Pooletown	RowC	51	B6
Poor Town	HtfC	15	A7
Pope Crossroads	GtnC	157	A3
Poplar	MhlC	21	B5
Poplar Forks	HryC	143	E6
Poplar Grove	FrkC	116	A4
Poplar Grove	PlkC	71	E3
Poplar Grove	SamC	83	A7
Poplar Grove	WatC	23	A3
Poplar Hill	HryC	143	D5
Poplar Hill	WmbC	156	D3
Poplar Springs	LarC	118	D5
Poplar Springs	SptC	98	A5
Poplar Springs	StkC	26	E1
Porter	StnC	77	C5
Porter Junction	BeaC	60	A6
Port Hill	GtnC	157	A3
*Port Royal	BftC	177	A5
Port Royal	BynC	180	C7
Portsmouth	CarC	114	B2
*Port Wentworth	ChtC	180	D3
Possum Corner	JprC	170	B7
Possumtrot	YanC	45	A1
Postell	CheC	91	E1
Postelle	PolC	91	C1
Poston	FloC	142	D7
Poston Crossroads	FloC	142	B7
Potecasi	NhnC	14	C5
Potters Curve	CbsC	128	C7
Potters Hill	DupC	110	C2
Pottertown	WatC	2	A7
Poverty Hill	EgfC	149	B6
Powderville	AndC	96	E6
Powell Crossroads	GatC	16	A5
Powells Crossing	CbsC	128	B6
Powells Store	RocC	7	E4
*Powellsville	BrtC	15	C7
Powelltown	TrnC	70	A7
Powers	RobC	106	E7
Powhatan	JtnC	56	B5
Pregnall	DorC	163	D6
Prentiss	MacC	68	C7
Prescott	BeaC	86	E3
Presley	TwnC	93	C4
Preston	HenC	6	E1
Preston Hills	WasC	1	A2
Prestonville	StkC	6	C5
Price	RocC	7	A4
Price Creek	YanC	45	B2
Price Crossroads	FloC	141	E2
Pricetown	WanC	83	E5
Priceville	LexC	137	A6
Primus	LtrC	123	A1
*Princeton	JtnC	57	A7
Princeton	LarC	118	C4
*Princeville	EdgC	34	E7
Princeville	HryC	144	A4
Pringle Bend	ColC	171	C4
Pringletown	BrkC	164	B6
Prioleau	BrkC	164	C2
Pritchard	BftC	181	B1
Pritchardville	BftC	181	B1
Privateer	SmtC	153	E1
Privetts	HryC	143	E6
Probst	PolC	65	B6
*Proctorville	RobC	127	D4
Progress	RndC	52	A1
Promised Land	GrwC	134	D3
Propst Crossroads	CwaC	48	A6
Prospect	BntC	41	B2
Prospect	BwkC	145	E4
Prospect	McmC	65	C3
Prospect	RobC	106	A6
Prospect Crossroads	FloC	156	B1
Prosper	CbsC	130	A7
*Prosperity	NbrC	136	D2
Providence	BntC	41	B2
Providence	GraC	31	D1
Providence	GsnC	4	A1
Providence	LexC	137	C5
Providence	McdC	46	A5
Pumpkin Center	LinC	48	D7
Pumpkin Center	OnsC	111	C4
Pumpkintown	JakC	68	D5
Pumpkintown	PckC	96	C2
Puncheon Creek	GtnC	166	C1
Pungo	BeaC	61	C3
Purley	CasC	8	D5
Purnell	WkeC	31	E5
Purvis	RobC	127	A2
Puryear Corner	MkbC	10	D2
Purysburgh	JprC	175	E7
Putnam	MreC	79	C1
Pyatte	AvyC	22	B6
Q			
Quail Ridge	LeCo	80	A2
Quail Roost	DurC	30	E2
Quaker Gap	StkC	6	A7
Qualla	JakC	68	C2
Quarantine	GtnC	167	B4
Quebec	TrnC	69	E7
Quick	CasC	8	B6
Quick Crossroads	MrlC	104	D7
*Quinby	FloC	141	D1
Quinerly	PitC	85	B2
Quinland	HwdC	69	C2
Quinns Crossroad	SmtC	140	A6
Quinns Store	DupC	110	C3
Quitsna	BrtC	36	A5
R			
Rabbit Hill	BynC	180	C7
Rabon Crossroads	HryC	157	E1
Rabon Crossroads	KswC	122	E7
Rabontown	BwkC	146	B2
RABUN CO	RabC	95	A3
Radford Crossroads	JtnC	57	B6
Radical	WksC	24	D1
*Raeford	HokC	106	A2
Raemon	RobC	126	E1
Rafter	MroC	66	B3
Rahns	EffC	175	C6
Rainbow Falls	AknC	149	D6
Rainbow Springs	MacC	93	E1
*Raleigh	DurC	31	B7
*Raleigh	WkeC	55	D2
*Ramseur	RndC	52	E3
Ramsey	BkeC	47	C6
Ramsey Grove	GtnC	157	A7
Ramseytown	YanC	21	B6
*Randleman	RndC	52	C2
RANDOLPH CO	RndC	28	C7
Rangeley	HenC	6	E1
Ranger	CheC	92	B2
Rangewood	WkeC	55	D3
*Ranlo	GasC	74	D4
Ransomville	BeaC	61	B7
Raven Branch	CckC	43	A2
*Ravenel	ChsC	172	C6
Ravensford	SwnC	68	D1
Ravenswood	JnsC	111	E1
Rawls	HntC	55	B6
Rayflin	LexC	150	E3
*Raynham	RobC	127	B2
Raynor	FraC	32	D5
Raynor Town	WanC	83	A2
Reads Chapel	BeaC	87	A2
Reavistown	GsnC	4	A2
Rebel City	SamC	82	A7
Reb Kee	PdrC	130	A1
Redallia	PitC	59	B7
Red Bank	BntC	41	B5
Red Bank	LexC	137	C7
Red Banks	RobC	106	A7
Red Bluff	MrlC	126	C2
Red Bluff Crossroads	HryC	144	B7
Red Brush	SryC	4	E5
Redbug	CbsC	128	E7
Redcross	RndC	52	D1
Red Cross	StnC	76	E5
Red Hill	BldC	129	C4
Red Hill	DupC	83	E7
Red Hill	EdgC	34	C3
Red Hill	FrkC	115	D5
Red Hill	GtnC	156	D6
Red Hill	HryC	143	A5
Red Hill	LeeC	139	E3
Red Hill	MhlC	21	D6
Red Hill	SamC	82	C6
Red House	CasC	9	A4
Redland	DveC	26	C6
Redlawn	MkbC	11	D1
Redmon	MdnC	44	B3
Red Mountain	DurC	30	E2
*Red Oak	NshC	33	D4
Red River	YorC	101	B3
*Red Springs	RobC	106	B5
Red Star	LexC	136	E5
Red Top	ChsC	172	D5
Redwine	CckC	19	A5
Redwood	DurC	31	B5
Reed Creek	HarC	116	B5
Reeds Crossroads	DavC	50	E2
Reedy Creek	DavC	26	E7
Reelsboro	PamC	86	D5
Reepsville	LinC	74	A1
Reese	WatC	22	E2
Reesetown	PolC	91	D1
Reeves	CbsC	144	E4
*Reevesville	DorC	163	B5
Refuge Mission	MntC	78	A2
Regal	CheC	66	D7
Regan	BwkC	145	A4
Register	DupC	109	D4
Register Crossroads	DlgC	140	D1
Rehobeth	HryC	143	B6
Rehoboth	NhnC	14	A6
Reid	TrnC	69	D7
*Reidsville	RocC	7	D7
Relief	MhlC	21	C6
Ren	WshC	60	E1
Rena	YadC	25	D3
Renfrew	GrvC	96	E3
*Rennert	RobC	106	C5
Renno	LarC	119	E5
Renston	PitC	59	A6
Republican	BrtC	35	E2
Rest Haven	BeaC	61	A7
Retreat	HwdC	69	D2
Retreat	OcnC	116	B2
Return	OcnC	116	C2
Revere	MdnC	44	B1
Rex	RobC	106	D4
Reynold	BrnC	161	B3
Reynolds Mill	PatC	6	D2
Reynoldson	GatC	15	C1
Rheasville	HlfC	13	B4
Rheatown	GreC	20	B2
Rhems	CvnC	85	E7
Rhems	WmbC	156	D5
Rhodes	BrtC	35	E2
Rhodes Crossroads	ColC	171	A2
Rhodes Crossroads	LeeC	140	C5
*Rhodhiss	BkeC	47	E4
*Rhodhiss	CwlC	47	E3
Rhodo	CheC	67	B6
Rhoney	CwaC	48	A6
Rhyne	MklC	75	A4
Rhyne Crossroads	PdrC	130	D2
Rice Bend	UciC	20	D7
Rice Crossroads	GtnC	157	B4
Ricefield	CbsC	129	C5
Rice Hope	BrkC	165	B7
Rice Mill	MdnC	44	C1
Ricetown	JprC	176	B3
Riceville	BcbC	44	E6
Richardson	BldC	128	B2
Richardson Cove	SvrC	42	B2
*Richburg	CstC	101	A7
*Richfield	StnC	77	B1
Rich Hill	AlgC	4	A5
Rich Hill Crossroads	LtrC	123	A1
Richland	CwlC	23	C5
Richland	OcnC	116	B1
Richland	SalC	136	A6
RICHLAND CO	RldC	138	C7
Richlands	MhlC	21	C5
*Richlands	OnsC	110	E3
Richmond	BrkC	165	C7
RICHMOND CO	RchC	103	E1
RICHMOND CO	RmdC	159	A4
*Richmond Hill	BynC	180	B6
Richmond Hill	YadC	26	A2
Richmond Hills	GrvC	96	E4
Richmond Mills	SctC	105	B5
Rich Mountain	JakC	69	B4
*Rich Square	NhnC	14	C7
Richtex	FaiC	137	D2
Rico	CbsC	128	E4
Riddle	CdnC	17	E6
Ridgecrest	AknC	150	A5
Ridgecrest	BcbC	45	C6
*Ridgeland	JprC	176	B4
Ridge Road Crossroads	LexC	136	E6
*Ridge Spring	SalC	150	B1
Ridgeville	CasC	9	A7
*Ridgeville	DorC	164	B7
*Ridgeway	FaiC	122	B7
*Ridgeway	HenC	7	B3
Ridgeway	WrnC	11	D5
Riley	ClhC	152	D5
Riley	FraC	32	C6
Riley Hill	WkeC	56	B1
Rimer	CabC	76	C1
Rimini	ClnC	153	E3
*Rincon	EffC	175	C7
Ringwood	HlfC	33	E1
Rion	FaiC	121	E7
Rio Vista	ChtC	180	E6
Rip Rap	HalC	10	B3
Ritter	ColC	171	B5
Rivelon	OraC	162	C1
River Acres	BeaC	60	C6
*River Bend	CvnC	86	A6
Riverdale	DilC	126	E5
Riverdale	HalC	9	E1
Riverdale	ShmC	15	B1
River Falls	GrvC	70	D7
River Haven	StnC	77	D4
River Hill	UciC	21	A4
Riverland	ChsC	173	B7
Rivermont	LnrC	84	D4
River Road	BeaC	60	C6
Riverside	ChtC	181	B4
Riverside	CvnC	85	C2
Riverside	GrvC	97	A5
Riverside	GsnC	4	A2
Riverside	HwdC	43	C6
Riverside	LtrC	101	C6
Riverside	MacC	94	B1
Riverside	YanC	45	B1
Riverview	CbsC	145	A2
Riverview	GrvC	96	D1
Riverview	UciC	21	A4
Riverview	YorC	101	A2
*Roanoke Rapids	HlfC	13	C4
Roaring Creek	AvyC	22	B5
Roaring Springs	GreC	20	A1
Robat	UnnC	99	D6
Robbins	BrnC	160	B6
*Robbins	MreC	79	A2
Robbins Neck	DlgC	125	C4
*Robbinsville	GhmC	67	A4
Roberdel	RchC	104	D3
Roberdo	MntC	78	A4
Roberson Store	MtnC	60	D1
*Robersonville	MtnC	59	D1
Robertstown	WhtC	93	B7
Robertville	JprC	175	D2
ROBESON CO	RobC	127	C3
Robinson Crossroad	LtrC	123	A4
Rock Bluff	WmbC	155	D5
Rock Branch	ElbC	133	A2
Rock Creek	AlmC	29	B7
Rock Fence Crossroads	BurC	168	C1
Rockfish	HokC	106	D2
Rockford	SryC	26	A1
Rock Hill	FaiC	137	C1
*Rock Hill	YorC	101	A4
*Rockingham	RchC	104	D3
ROCKINGHAM CO	RocC	27	E1
Rockland	ChsC	178	C1
Rock Ridge	WlnC	57	B3
Rock Springs	RthC	71	E2
Rockton	FaiC	121	E7
Rockview	BcbC	45	A3
*Rockville	ChsC	178	C2
*Rockwell	RowC	50	D7
Rockwood Hill	GreC	19	E4
Rocky Bluff Crossroads	SmtC	140	A6
Rocky Bottom	PckC	96	A2
Rocky Branch	BntC	41	A4
Rocky Cross	NshC	56	E1
Rocky Ford	FraC	32	C2
Rocky Fork	UciC	20	D6
Rocky Grove	SvrC	42	D3
Rocky Hill	TrnC	70	A6
Rockyhock	ChwC	37	A1
Rocky Knoll	DurC	31	A5
*Rocky Mount	EdgC	34	A6
*Rocky Mount	NshC	34	A5
Rocky River	AbbC	133	C3
Rocky River	CabC	76	B4
Rocky Spring	MroC	65	D1
Rocky Springs	AlxC	24	E7
Rodanthe	DarC	64	D3
Roddey	YorC	101	B5
Rodgers	ClnC	154	B6
Rodman	CstC	100	E6
Rodmans Quarter	BeaC	60	E5
Roduco	GatC	15	D3
Roe	CarC	88	C7
Roetown	WasC	1	D2
Rogers Crossroads	DlgC	141	B1
Rogers Crossroads	GtnC	156	E3
Rogers Crossroads	NshC	56	E2
*Rolesville	WkeC	32	A7
Rome	WmbC	156	D4
Romeo	GreC	19	D1
Rominger	WatC	22	D2
*Ronda	WksC	25	B2
Rooks	PdrC	130	B3
Roosevelt	GilC	91	A7
*Roper	WshC	37	B6
Ropers Crossroads	ClbC	148	D7
Ropers Crossroads	EgfC	149	B4
Roper Springs	HlfC	12	D4
Rosa Lees Crossroads	DlgC	124	E6
Rose Bay	HydC	62	A6
*Roseboro	SamC	108	A2
Roseborough	AvyC	22	E6
Rosebud	WlnC	57	E2
*Rose Hill	DupC	109	C4
Rose Hill	GtnC	156	D5
Rose Hill	WrnC	11	C3
Roseida	BftC	177	A4
Roseland	CbsC	144	B1
Roseland	LinC	74	B2
Roseland	MreC	79	B7
Rosemary	HlfC	13	B4
Rosemead	BrtC	36	D1
Rosemont	ClbC	148	D5
Rosemont	GtnC	167	A2
Roseneath	HlfC	34	E3
Roseville	PerC	9	C6
Rosewood	WanC	83	B1
Rosindale	BldC	129	B4
Rosin Hill	SamC	82	C5
Rosinville	DorC	163	C4
Roslin	CumC	106	E3
*Rosman	TrnC	69	E7
Rosser	LeCo	54	C6
Ross Store	StkC	6	B7
Rossville	CstC	122	A2
Rotalata	EgfC	149	D3
Roten	AshC	2	B5
Roughedge	UnoC	102	B4
Roundhill	SwnC	67	E2
Round Peak	SryC	4	D4
Roundtree	PitC	59	A7
Rouse	HmpC	169	C4
Rover	BeaC	86	B1
Rowan	BldC	129	E3
ROWAN CO	RowC	77	A1
Rowell	CstC	101	B6
Rowes Corner	CvnC	86	C5
*Rowesville	OraC	162	D2
*Rowland	RobC	127	A3
*Roxboro	PerC	9	D6
*Roxobel	BrtC	35	C1
Royal	BeaC	87	A2
Royal	FraC	32	C5
Royal Pines	BcbC	70	E1
*Royston	FrkC	116	A7
*Royston	HarC	116	A7
Rozier Siding	RobC	106	E6
*Ruby	ChfC	103	C7
Rubyatt	MntC	78	D5
Ruby City	JakC	69	A3
*Ruckersville	ElbC	133	A3
Rudd	GlfC	28	C3
Ruffin	ColC	170	E2
Rufus	CwlC	23	B6
Rugby	GsnC	2	B5
Rugby	HdrC	70	E3
Ruggles	HlfC	13	C7
Runion	MdnC	44	A1
Runnymede	ChsC	172	E4
*Rural Hall	FsyC	27	A2
Rural Vale	MroC	65	C4
Rushville	GrwC	134	E5
Rusk	SryC	25	D1
Ruskin	BldC	107	D7
Russell	OcnC	94	E4
Russell Crossroad	GreC	19	D4
Russells Creek	BwkC	146	C2
Russellville	AnsC	103	C2
Russellville	BrkC	165	A2
Russtown	BwkC	145	C5
Rust Hollow	WasC	1	A1
*Ruth	RthC	72	C3
RUTHERFORD CO	RthC	47	A7
*Rutherford College	BkeC	47	D4
*Rutherfordton	RthC	72	C3
Rutherwood	WatC	23	C2
Ryes	HntC	80	E1
Ryland	ChwC	16	B6
Rymers Ferry	GhmC	67	A2

*Indicates incorporated city

Community	County	Map#	Grid
S			
Saconon	HdrC	71	B4
Saddletree	RobC	106	D7
Sadie	CtrC	1	A6
Sadler	RocC	7	E6
St. Andrews	RldC	137	E5
St. Charles	LeeC	140	B4
*St. George	DorC	163	C6
*St. Helena	PdrC	130	E3
*St. James	BwkC	146	C6
St. James	GreC	19	D6
St. John	HtfC	15	A6
St. Johns	ChwC	37	D4
St. Lewis	EdgC	58	B2
*St. Matthews	ClhC	152	E4
St. Paul	ClnC	153	E6
Saint Pauls	GtnC	157	C5
*St. Pauls	RobC	106	E5
Saint Phillips	NbrC	120	D7
*St. Stephen	BrkC	165	B5
St. Stephens	CwaC	48	B3
Salak	GrwC	134	D3
Salem	BkeC	47	A4
Salem	CckC	19	B6
Salem	FloC	142	C7
Salem	LinC	74	C2
Salem	NshC	33	E3
*Salem	OcnC	95	C4
Salem	RndC	52	C2
Salem	SryC	5	A4
*Salemburg	SamC	108	B1
Salem Crossroads	FaiC	121	B5
Salem Crossroads	HryC	143	C6
Sales Ford	CheC	66	D7
*Salisbury	RowC	50	C5
Salkehatchie	ColC	170	D7
*Salley	AknC	151	B6
Salters Depot	WmbC	155	C5
*Saluda	HdrC	71	B5
*Saluda	PlkC	71	B5
*Saluda	SalC	135	E6
SALUDA CO	SalC	136	B5
Salvo	DarC	64	D4
Samarcand	MreC	78	D4
Samaria	LexC	150	E2
Samaria	NshC	33	A7
Sampit	GtnC	166	D2
SAMPSON CO	SamC	129	E1
Sanders Corner	SmtC	139	C5
Sandfly	ChtC	181	A5
Sandhill	PamC	86	E5
Sandridge	BrkC	164	A4
Sand Ridge	HryC	157	D1
Sands	WatC	23	B2
Sandy	ChsC	172	E5
Sandy	JhnC	1	E6
Sandy Bottom	LnrC	84	C5
Sandy Bottom	MdnC	44	A2
Sandy Bottoms	SctC	105	B6
*Sandy Creek	BwkC	130	B7
Sandy Cross	GatC	16	C5
Sandy Cross	NshC	33	D7
Sandy Cross	RocC	7	D6
*Sandyfield	CbsC	129	E5
Sandy Flat	GrvC	97	B3
Sandy Fork	MkbC	10	D2
Sandy Grove	DavC	51	B3
Sandy Grove	HokC	106	C3
Sandy Hill	BwkC	146	A5
Sandy Lane	MroC	65	E4
Sandy Level	HenC	7	D3
Sandymush	BcbC	44	A5
Sandy Mush	RthC	72	D4
Sandy Plain	CbsC	144	C3
Sandy Plain	WkeC	31	C4
Sandy Plains	ClvC	74	A5
Sandy Plains	PlkC	71	E5
Sandy Ridge	GlfC	27	E5
Sandy River	CstC	121	B1
Sandy Run	ClhC	152	B2
Sandy Run	OraC	163	A3
Sandy Springs	AndC	117	A2
*Sanford	LeCo	80	B1
Sansbury Crossroads	FloC	141	B4
Sans Souci	BrtC	36	E6
Sans Souci	GrvC	97	A5
Sans Souci Heights	GrvC	97	A4
Santaluca	GilC	91	B6
*Santee	OraC	153	D7
Santee Circle	BrkC	165	A4
*Santeetlah	GhmC	67	A3
Santuc	UnnC	120	D2
Sanville	HenC	6	D1
Sapps Crossroads	LtrC	102	A6
*Saratoga	WlnC	58	A4
Saratt	CrkC	99	D4
*Sardis	BurC	168	A2
Sardis	CckC	42	E1
Sardis	FloC	141	A5
Sarecta	DupC	110	A2
Sarem	GatC	15	D3
Sarvis Crossroads	HryC	144	A4
Sassers Mill	JnsC	85	A6
Satolah	RabC	94	E3
Satterwhite	GraC	10	C6
Saulston	WanC	83	E1
Saunook	HwdC	69	C2
Savage	GatC	16	B3
*Savannah	ChtC	180	E5
Savannah	JakC	68	D4
*Sawmills	CwlC	47	D3
Saxapahaw	AlmC	29	E7
Saxon	SptC	98	B3
Saylors Crossroads	AndC	117	E6
Scalesville	GlfC	28	B2
Scaly	MacC	94	E2
Schley	OrgC	30	C3
Schofield	BamC	161	D6
Scoot Mill	GreC	19	A4
Scotch Grove	SctC	105	C4
*Scotia	HmpC	169	C7
SCOTLAND CO	SctC	105	C5
*Scotland Neck	HlfC	35	A2
Scott	BftC	177	B6
Scott	MrlC	125	E3
Scotts	IrdC	48	E2
Scotts	WlnC	57	C4
Scotts Hill	PdrC	131	C6
Scotts Store	PamC	86	E5
Scottsville	SmtC	140	C6
*Scranton	FloC	141	D7
SCREVEN CO	ScrC	168	C5
Scuffleton	GrnC	59	A7
Scuppernong	WshC	37	E6
*Seaboard	NhnC	13	E3
Sea Breeze	NhrC	147	A3
Seabrook	ColC	177	E3
*Seabrook Island	ChsC	178	D2
Seaforth	ChaC	54	D3
Seagate	NhrC	147	B1
*Seagrove	RndC	52	C7
Seaton Spring	SvrC	42	A2
Secession	BwkC	145	E6
Secessionville	ChsC	173	B7
Sedalia	GlfC	28	E5
Sedalia	UnnC	120	A2
Sedgefield	GlfC	28	B6
Sedgefield Park	GlfC	28	B6
Seeshore	TrnC	70	B7
Sega Lake	TrnC	70	A6
Segars	DlgC	124	D6
Seiglers Crossroads	AknC	150	B5
Seigling	AlnC	169	B1
Seivern	AknC	151	A4
Selica	TrnC	70	A6
*Sellers	MrnC	126	C7
*Selma	JtnC	56	D6
Selwin	GatC	16	B5
Seminole	HntC	80	D1
*Seneca	OcnC	116	C1
Senter	HntC	81	B3
Servilla	PolC	65	B5
Seven Bridges	RobC	105	D7
Seven Creeks	CbsC	144	E3
*Seven Devils	AvyC	22	D4
*Seven Devils	WatC	22	E4
Seven Lakes	MreC	79	A4
Seven Oaks	LexC	137	D5
Seven Paths	FraC	33	A5
*Seven Springs	WanC	84	A4
*Severn	NhnC	14	D3
Sevier	McdC	46	B3
SEVIER CO	SvrC	41	E3
Sevier Home	KnoC	41	A1
*Sevierville	SvrC	41	E1
Seward	FsyC	26	E3
Sexton	MdnC	44	C3
Seymour Heights	SvrC	41	B1
Shacktown	YadC	26	B4
Shady Banks	BeaC	60	C6
Shady Forest	BwkC	145	B7
Shady Grove	HalC	10	A2
Shady Grove	JnsC	84	E6
Shady Grove	SvrC	42	B3
Shaken	PdrC	131	B1
*Shallotte	BwkC	145	D5
Shallow Ford	MacC	68	A4
Shallowford	UciC	20	E5
Shamokin	KswC	123	B7
Shanghai	SamC	109	A6
Shankle	StnC	77	D6
Shannon Hill	LeeC	140	C1
Shannon Hills	HenC	7	B2
Shannontown	SmtC	140	A7
Sharon	CdnC	17	A2
Sharon	IrdC	48	E3
Sharon	PtsC	8	A1
*Sharon	YorC	100	A3
Sharon Park	GrvC	97	A3
Sharp	RldC	138	B4
Sharpes Hill	LexC	151	D2
Sharp Point	PitC	58	D3
*Sharpsburg	EdgC	34	A7
*Sharpsburg	NshC	33	E7
Shatley Springs	AshC	2	E5
Shawnee	EffC	175	A4
Shawtown	HntC	81	B2
Sheffield	DveC	25	E7
*Shelby	ClvC	73	D5
Shell	HryC	144	A7
Shell Bluff	BurC	159	D6
Shell Creek	CtrC	22	A3
Shell Point	BftC	177	A5
Shelmerdine	PitC	59	D7
Shelter Neck	PdrC	131	A1
Shelton	CasC	8	B4
Shelton	FaiC	120	E4
Shelton Laurel	HwdC	43	C5
Shelton Store	StkC	6	C4
Shelton Town	SryC	5	B5
Shenandoah Heights	CtrC	21	C1
Shepard	KswC	123	C7
Shepherds	IrdC	49	C5
Sheppard Crossroads	GrwC	135	A6
Sherwood	WatC	22	E2
Sherwood Forest	FsyC	26	D3
Sherwood Forest	TrnC	70	B7
Sherwood Terrace	TrnC	70	B7
Shields Commissary	HlfC	35	B2
Shiloh	ChfC	124	D1
Shiloh	LtrC	101	D6
Shiloh	OcnC	116	D1
Shiloh	RocC	7	B5
Shiloh	RthC	72	C4
Shiloh	ShmC	14	D1
Shiloh	SmtC	140	E6
Shiloh Mills	EdgC	34	E5
Shine	GrnC	84	A1
Shines Crossroads	GrnC	84	A1
Shingle Hollow	RthC	72	A1
Shingletown	JhnC	1	E4
Shiny Rock	MkbC	10	D3
Shirley	HmpC	175	B1
Shirley Grove	HabC	115	B1
Shoal Creek	HarC	116	B5
Shoals	SryC	26	B1
Shoals Junction	GrwC	118	C7
Shoates	AnsC	103	C4
Shoe	WksC	24	A2
Sholars Crossroads	DupC	110	B5
Shoofly	GraC	31	C2
Shooks	KnoC	41	A1
Shooks Gap	BntC	41	B1
Shookville	MacC	68	E7
Shooting Creek	ClyC	93	D1
Shopton	MklC	75	B6
Shorts Mill	HabC	115	A3
Shotwell	WkeC	56	B3
Shoups Ford	BkeC	47	C6
Shuffletown	MklC	75	B4
Shuler	LexC	151	D1
Shulerville	BrkC	166	A5
Shulls Mill	WatC	23	A3
Shumont	BcbC	71	C1
Shupings Mill	RowC	50	C7
Siddon	MkbC	10	C3
Sidney	BeaC	61	B6
Sidney	CbsC	144	C2
Sidney	ColC	171	C2
Sidney Crossroads	BeaC	61	B6
Sigsbee	SptC	98	B3
*Siler City	ChaC	53	C4
Silk Hope	ChaC	53	D2
Silk Hope	ChtC	180	D4
Silver	ClnC	154	A4
Silver Bluff	HwdC	69	E1
Silver City	HamC	19	A2
Silver City	HokC	106	A2
Silverdale	OnsC	112	A5
Silver Hill	DavC	51	B4
Silver Hill	PamC	86	E5
Silver Hill	SctC	105	C4
Silver Lake	JhnC	1	E4
Silver Lake	NhrC	147	A2
Silver Spring	MreC	79	C7
Silverstone	WatC	22	E1
*Silverstreet	NbrC	136	A2
Silver Valley	DavC	51	D4
Simmons Bay	CbsC	144	E3
Simmonsville	BrkC	166	A4
Simmonsville	GtnC	167	C1
Simpson	FaiC	122	A7
*Simpson	PitC	59	C5
Simpson Crossing	BrkC	165	A4
*Simpsonville	GrvC	97	C7
*Sims	WlnC	57	B2
Sinclair Crossroads	DilC	126	C3
Singletary Forks	WmbC	165	E2
Singleton	ClhC	152	E4
Singleton Crossroads	HryC	157	B1
Sioux	YanC	21	B6
Sivey Town	BwkC	145	E5
Six Forks	PdrC	131	A1
Six Forks Crossroads	WkeC	56	A1
*Six Mile	PckC	95	E6
Sixty Six	OraC	162	D4
Skidaway Island	ChtC	181	A6
Skinner Crossroad	GreC	19	B3
Skinnersville	WshC	37	C5
Skippers Corner	NhrC	131	A5
Skyland	GrvC	97	C2
Skyline	MreC	79	E5
*Sky Valley	RabC	94	C3
Sladesville	HydC	61	E6
Slandsville	DorC	172	C2
Slater	GrvC	96	E2
Slates Corner	GsvC	13	B2
Slatestone	BeaC	60	C5
Slickrock Ford	MacC	67	E6
Slighs	NbrC	136	E2
Sligo	CurC	17	D3
Sloan	DupC	110	A5
Slocomb	CumC	81	A6
Sloop Point	PdrC	131	E4
Small	BeaC	86	E3
Smalls Crossroads	ChwC	16	B7
Smallwood	FaiC	122	B7
Smethport	AshC	2	D6
Smith	BwkC	146	C5
Smith	YorC	100	E5
Smithboro	DilC	127	A7
Smith Creek	NhrC	131	A7
Smith Crossing	CbsC	128	E6
Smith Crossroads	BldC	108	D7
*Smithfield	JtnC	56	C7
Smithfield	MroC	65	E4
Smith Ford	CrkC	99	D3
Smith Grove	DveC	26	C7
Smiths	RobC	128	B1
Smiths Crossroads	MkbC	11	E1
Smithtown	BeaC	61	B5
Smithtown	YadC	26	B2
Smithwick	MtnC	60	B2
*Smoaks	ColC	162	D7
Smokemont	SwnC	42	C7
*Smyrna	CrkC	99	E2
Smyrna	NbrC	136	A1
*Smyrna	YorC	99	E2
SMYTH CO	SmyC	2	C1
Snake Nation	FnnC	91	D5
Snead	ClbC	148	E6
Sneads Grove	SctC	105	C5
*Snelling	BrnC	160	E5
Sniders Crossroads	ColC	170	D4
Snoddy	SptC	98	A4
Snowden	CurC	17	D2
Snowhill	CbsC	144	D3
*Snow Hill	GrnC	84	C1
Snow Hill	PqmC	16	C6
Snow Hill	SamC	108	B2
Snow Hill	StkC	6	B5
Snow Hill	WrnC	11	E5
Snow Junction	WmbC	156	C4
Snow Town	WmbC	156	C5
Soapstone	PtsC	7	E1
Socastee	HryC	157	E3
Social Plains	FraC	56	E1
*Society Hill	DlgC	125	C4
Soda Hill	WatC	23	B1
Solo	WatC	23	B1
Solola Valley	SwnC	68	A1
Solomons Crossroads	AlnC	169	B5
Somers Crossroads	WksC	25	B5
Somerset	PerC	9	D6
Soudan	MkbC	10	E2
Soul City	WrnC	11	D5
Sound Side	TyrC	38	C4
SOUTHAMPTON CO	ShmC	13	E1
*South Boston	HalC	9	E1
*South Congaree	LexC	137	E7
*Southern Pines	MreC	79	D6
Southern Shops	SptC	98	B3
*Southern Shores	DarC	39	E1
South Forest Estates	GrvC	97	B6
South Gastonia	GasC	74	C6
South Hills	UnnC	120	C1
South Hominy	BcbC	70	B1
South Lynchburg	LeeC	140	E4
Southmont	DavC	51	A5
South of the Border	DilC	126	E4
*Southport	BwkC	146	D6
South River	CarC	113	D1
South Rosemary	HlfC	13	B4
South Santee	ChsC	166	D5
Southside	FloC	141	D3
Southside	LinC	74	C2
South Union	OcnC	116	B3
South Weldon	HlfC	13	C5
Southwood	LnrC	84	E4
Sparks Mill	FnnC	92	B4
*Sparta	AlgC	3	D4
*Spartanburg	SptC	98	C3
SPARTANBURG CO	SptC	119	C1
Speaks Mill	HmpC	169	E6
Spear	AvyC	22	B6
*Speed	EdgC	35	A5
Speedwell	JakC	68	E4
Speights Bridge	GrnC	58	B6
Speigner	SalC	136	A7
*Spencer	RowC	50	D4
*Spencer Mountain	GasC	74	E4
Spences Corner	CdnC	17	C4
Spiderweb	AknC	159	D2
Spies	MreC	78	E2
Spillcorn	MdnC	20	C7
Spilo	UniC	92	D3
Spilona	JtnC	56	B7
*Spindale	RthC	72	C3
Spiveys Corner	SamC	82	B5
Spot	CurC	39	C1
Spout Springs	HntC	80	D4
Spring Branch	MrnC	142	D1
Spring Creek	BeaC	87	B2
Spring Creek	MdnC	43	B6
Springdale	AknC	149	D5
Springdale	GasC	74	D4
*Springdale	LexC	137	E6
Springdale	LtrC	122	D1
Springdell	LtrC	101	C5
*Springfield	EffC	175	B6
*Springfield	OraC	151	B7
Springfield	WksC	3	C7
Springfield Mills	SctC	105	B6
Spring Garden	CvnC	85	E4
Spring Gully	GtnC	166	D2
Spring Hill	BwkC	146	C1
Spring Hill	HlfC	35	A1
Spring Hill	HryC	143	D6
Spring Hill	HwdC	69	E1
Spring Hill	LeeC	139	D3
Spring Hill	RldC	137	B3
Spring Hill	SctC	105	D4
Spring Hope	CvnC	86	C4
*Spring Hope	NshC	33	A6
*Spring Lake	CumC	80	E6
Springmaid Beach	HryC	158	A4
Springs Park	LtrC	122	C2
Spring Valley	GsnC	3	E1
Springwood	GasC	74	E5
*Spruce Pine	MhlC	22	A7
Spurgeon	WksC	25	A5
Squires	DilC	127	A7
Stacey	RocC	8	A5
Stackhouse	MdnC	44	A1
Stafford	HmpC	175	D1
Staffordtown	PolC	91	C2
Stag Park	PdrC	131	A2
Stakely Mill	MroC	65	D2
*Staley	RndC	53	A2
Staley Crossroads	ClhC	152	B4
*Stallings	UnoC	101	E1
Stallings Crossroads	BeaC	60	B3
Stallings Crossroads	FraC	33	A4
Stalvey	HryC	158	A3

*Indicates incorporated city

Cities and Communities

Community	County	Map#	Grid
Stamey Town	AvyC	22	C6
Stancils Chapel	JtnC	56	E4
*Stanfield	StnC	76	D5
Stanhope	NshC	33	B7
*Stanley	GasC	74	E3
Stanley Mill	GilC	91	D7
Stanleys Store	DveC	26	A6
STANLY CO	StnC	77	B4
*Stantonsburg	WlnC	58	A5
*Star	MntC	78	C2
Star Bluff Crossroads	HryC	144	D7
Starkeytown	SvrC	41	E4
Starlight	WanC	82	E4
Starling	OnsC	111	E6
Starlings Crossroads	HenC	7	D3
*Starr	AndC	117	B6
Startex	SptC	98	A4
Stateburg	SmtC	139	C6
*Statesville	IrdC	49	C3
Statesville	ShmC	15	A2
Statesville West	IrdC	49	B3
Staton	PitC	59	B3
Staunton Mill	GreC	19	E4
Stearns	PlkC	71	D5
Stecoah	GhmC	67	C3
*Stedman	CumC	107	D1
Steedman	LexC	150	E2
Steeds	MntC	78	C1
Steen Town	RchC	104	E4
Stella	PatC	6	C3
*Stem	GraC	31	C2
STEPHENS CO	SpnC	116	A3
Stephens Crossroads	RocC	7	E5
Stevens Creek	GsnC	4	A1
Stevens Mill	WanC	83	B3
Stewart Crossroads	LtrC	102	B6
Stewart Crossroads	RobC	127	A4
Stewart Hill	WsgC	20	E1
Stewart Mill	FnnC	91	D5
Stewarts Mill	GlfC	28	E5
Stiefeltown	AknC	149	E6
Stiles	MacC	68	A5
Still Bluff	PdrC	130	B4
Stilley	BeaC	86	D2
Stilleys Crossroads	JtnC	56	E3
Stillwell	EffC	175	C6
Stilton	OraC	152	D7
Stock Hill	FnnC	91	E7
Stocksville	BcbC	44	D4
Stockton	HenC	7	C1
Stokes	ColC	171	A3
Stokes	HmpC	175	D1
Stokes	SmtC	154	A2
STOKES CO	StkC	26	D1
*Stokesdale	GlfC	27	E2
Stokestown	PitC	59	C7
Stomp Springs	LarC	120	A5
Stoneboro	LtrC	122	E3
Stones Crossroads	MdfC	148	A7
Stone Station	SptC	98	C5
*Stoneville	RocC	7	A5
*Stonewall	PamC	87	A5
Stoney Hill	NbrC	136	C3
Stoney Knob	BcbC	44	D5
Stono Station	ChsC	172	E6
Stony Creek	CasC	29	C1
Stony Fork	BcbC	70	B1
Stony Fork	WatC	23	D3
Stony Hill	WkeC	31	D6
Stony Knoll	SryC	25	E1
Stony Mill	PtsC	8	A2
Stony Point	GrwC	134	E1
Storys	GatC	15	C4
*Stovall	GraC	10	E5
Stover	FaiC	122	A3
Strabane	LnrC	84	B5
Straits	CarC	113	D5
Stratford	AlgC	3	C4
Stratford Forest	GrvC	97	A4
Strawberry	BrkC	165	A7
Strawberry	GtnC	167	B3
Strawberry Ridge	MhlC	45	E2
Strickland Crossroads	JtnC	82	C2
Strickland Crossroads	NshC	57	C1
Strother	FaiC	121	A6
*Stuart	PatC	6	A2
Stubbs	ClvC	73	D4
*Stuckey	WmbC	156	C3
Stumptown	McdC	46	B5
Sturdivants Crossroads	UnoC	103	A4
Sturgills	AshC	2	D4
Suburb	BwkC	146	B4
*Suffolk		15	D1
Sugar Creek	FnnC	91	D4
Sugar Creek	JhnC	1	E3
Sugar Hill	McdC	46	A6
*Sugar Mountain	AvyC	22	D4
Sugar Town	AnsC	103	C1
Suggs Crossroads	DlgC	140	E1
Suit	CheC	92	A1
SULLIVAN CO	SulC	1	B4
Sullivan Crossroads	EgfC	134	E7
*Sullivans Island	ChsC	173	C6
Sulphur Springs	SryC	5	B3
*Summerfield	GlfC	28	A3
Summerhaven	BcbC	45	B5
Summerlins Crossroads	DupC	83	D7
*Summerton	ClnC	154	A5
*Summerville	BrkC	172	D1
*Summerville	DorC	172	D2
Summit	HawC	19	B1
Summit	HlfC	12	E4
*Summit	LexC	136	E7
Summit	WksC	23	E2
*Sumter	SmtC	153	E1
SUMTER CO	SmtC	139	E7

Community	County	Map#	Grid
Sumter Junction	SmtC	153	C1
Sunbeam	ShmC	15	A1
Sunburst	HwdC	69	D3
Sunny Brook	AknC	149	E4
Sunny Point	CheC	92	A2
Sunnyside	BkeC	47	B5
Sunnyside	GasC	74	B4
Sunnyside	GreC	20	A4
Sunny Side	GtnC	157	E5
Sunnyvale	McdC	45	E4
Sunny View	PlkC	71	D3
Sunrise Beach	CwaC	48	E3
*Sunset Beach	BwkC	145	B7
Sunset Harbor	BwkC	146	B6
Sunset Hills	RocC	7	B4
Sunshine	RthC	72	E2
*Surf City	OnsC	132	A3
*Surf City	PdrC	131	E4
*Surfside Beach	HryC	158	A5
Surl	PerC	9	E7
SURRY CO	SryC	26	B1
Sussex	AshC	2	E4
Sutherland	JhnC	1	E3
Sutherlands	AshC	2	A6
Sutphin	AlmC	53	D1
Suttentown	SamC	82	E5
Sutton	FraC	32	D6
Sutton Park	UnoC	102	C3
Suttons	WmbC	165	E2
Suttons Corner	BldC	129	A1
Suttontown	HwdC	43	B6
SWAIN CO	SwnC	42	C6
Swainsville	ClvC	73	B4
Swan	FnnC	92	A6
Swancreek	YadC	25	C3
Swann	CasC	8	B4
Swann	HntC	80	C2
Swannanoa Hills	BcbC	44	E6
Swan Quarter	HydC	62	B7
*Swansboro	OnsC	112	A6
*Swansea	LexC	151	E3
Sweden	BamC	161	E2
Sweet Gum	FnnC	92	A2
Sweetgum	GhmC	67	B4
Sweetwater	AknC	149	C6
Sweetwater	WatC	22	D1
*Swepsonville	AlmC	29	D5
Swindell	BeaC	61	B4
Swindell Fork	HydC	62	C6
Swiss	YanC	45	A1
Switzer	SptC	98	B6
Switzerland	JprC	176	B4
*Sycamore	AlnC	169	C1
*Sylva	JakC	68	D3
*Sylvania	ScrC	168	B6
Syracuse	DlgC	141	A1
T			
Tablerock	BkeC	46	E2
*Tabor City	CbsC	144	B2
Taft	WmbC	155	D7
Tahoma	RmdC	159	C3
Talatha	AknC	160	A2
Talc Mountain	SwnC	67	D4
Talleys Crossing	FsyC	27	C4
*Tallulah Falls	HabC	94	B7
*Tallulah Falls	RabC	94	B7
Tanglewood	GrvC	97	A5
Tants Crossroads	FraC	32	E7
Tapoco	GhmC	66	E2
*Tarboro	EdgC	34	D7
Tarboro	JprC	175	D3
Tar Corner	CdnC	17	A3
*Tar Heel	BldC	107	C6
Tarheel	GatC	15	D3
Tariffville	MroC	66	A1
Tar Landing	OnsC	111	A5
Tar River	GraC	31	D2
Tate City	TwnC	93	D4
*Tatum	MrlC	126	A1
Taxahaw	LtrC	123	C1
Taylor Crossroads	NshC	33	C7
Taylor Mill	WsgC	20	D1
Taylors Bridge	SamC	108	E4
Taylors Corner	JnsC	110	D1
Taylors Crossroads	NbrC	136	D1
Taylors Store	BrtC	36	E3
Taylors Store	NshC	33	C4
Taylors Valley	WasC	2	A3
*Taylorsville	AlxC	48	D1
Taylorsville Beach	AlxC	48	C2
*Taylortown	MreC	79	B5
*Teachey	DupC	109	D5
Teaguetown	FsyC	27	D5
Teer	OrgC	30	A6
*Tega Cay	YorC	101	A2
Telfair Woods	BurC	159	E7
Tellico	MacC	67	E5
*Tellico Plains	MroC	65	E3
Temperance Hill	MrnC	126	D7
Ten Mile	ChsC	173	E3
Ten Mile Fork	JnsC	85	E7
Teresita	MacC	94	B1
Terra Ceia	BeaC	61	A4
Terrell Crossroad	WmbC	155	C1
Terrells	ChaC	54	A2
Terry Creek	GrvC	71	A7
Terry Fork	MdnC	45	A2
Testo	LexC	151	C2
Texaco Beach	CdnC	17	C5
Thankful	WksC	24	B5
Thayer	ColC	171	B4
The Borough	PdrC	130	C4
The Farms	BrkC	173	A3
The Hollow	PatC	5	B3
Thelma	HlfC	12	E4

Community	County	Map#	Grid
Thermal City	RthC	72	B1
Thicketty	CrkC	99	A2
Thomasboro Crossroads	BwkC	145	A6
Thomas Crossroads	MreC	79	B4
Thomas Landing	OnsC	132	B3
Thomas Mill	UnlC	92	B3
*Thomasville	DavC	51	D1
*Thomasville	RndC	51	D1
Thor	LexC	151	C4
Three Forks	RabC	94	E3
Three Mile	AvyC	22	B7
Thula	GreC	19	B3
*Thunderbolt	ChtC	181	A5
Thursa	LeeC	140	A1
Tibwin	ChsC	166	C7
*Tiger	RabC	94	B5
Tiger Valley	CtrC	21	D2
Tigerville	GrvC	97	B1
Tillery	HlfC	13	E7
Timberland	HokC	105	E2
Timber Ridge	GreC	19	D4
*Timmonsville	FloC	141	A3
Timothy	SamC	82	B5
Tina	ClhC	153	B5
Tindall	SmtC	154	A2
Tipton Hill	MhlC	21	C6
Tirzah	YorC	100	D2
Tisdale	WmbC	156	A7
Titus	TwnC	93	D3
*Tobaccoville	FsyC	26	E2
Tobermory	BldC	107	A5
Tobys Bluff	ColC	170	B3
*Toccoa	SpnC	115	C3
Todds Crossroads	BrtC	36	D3
Toddville	HryC	157	D2
Toddy	PitC	58	C4
Toecane	MhlC	21	D6
Tokeena Crossroads	OcnC	116	D2
Tolarsville	RobC	107	A5
Toledo	YanC	21	C7
Toliver	AshC	2	C7
Tolley Town	CtrC	21	D3
Toluca	LinC	47	D7
Tomahawk	SamC	108	D6
Tomotla	CheC	66	D7
Tomotley	BftC	176	D1
Tompkins	HryC	143	B6
Toms Creek	McdC	46	A4
Toms Creek	SpnC	115	D4
Tom Town	CckC	43	C2
Toney Creek	AndC	118	A3
Topia	AlgC	3	B4
Topnot	CasC	8	E6
Topsail	PdrC	131	D5
*Topsail Beach	PdrC	131	D5
Topsy	GatC	15	C3
Totness	ClhC	152	D3
Towee	PolC	65	B5
Town Creek	BwkC	146	C2
Town Creek	UniC	92	E5
Town Creek	WlnC	58	A1
Town Forest	HdrC	70	E4
TOWNS CO	TwnC	93	C4
*Townsend	BntC	41	B5
Townsend Mill	TwnC	93	A4
Tradesville	LtrC	102	C6
Trading Ford	RowC	50	E4
Tramway	LeCo	80	A1
Transou	AshC	3	B6
TRANSYLVANIA CO	TrnC	69	B6
Trap	BrtC	36	D1
*Travelers Rest	GrvC	97	A3
Travis	TyrC	38	B6
Tree Top	AshC	2	D6
Tremont	BntC	41	C6
*Trenton	EgfC	149	D4
*Trenton	JnsC	85	C7
*Trent Woods	CvnC	86	A6
*Trent Woods	JnsC	86	A6
Triangle	LinC	75	A1
Trinity	NbrC	136	A1
*Trinity	RndC	51	E1
Trinity	UnoC	102	C5
Trio	WmbC	155	E7
Triple Springs	PerC	10	A4
Triplet	BrwC	12	E2
Triplett	WatC	23	C3
Trotville	GatC	16	B5
Trout	AshC	2	B6
*Troutdale	GsnC	2	E1
*Troutman	IrdC	49	C4
Troxlers Mill	GlfC	28	D5
*Troy	GrwC	134	C6
*Troy	MntC	78	B3
Trundle Crossroad	SvrC	41	C1
Trust	MdnC	43	E3
Tryon	GasC	74	B4
*Tryon	PlkC	71	D6
Tuckerdale	AshC	2	C4
Tuckertown	UnnC	120	D4
Tugtown	OraC	164	A3
Tugwell	PitC	58	D4
Tulls Creek	CurC	17	C2
Tulls Mill	LnrC	84	B5
Tulula	GhmC	67	B5
Tumblerville	MacC	68	C7
Tungsten	VncC	11	B4
Tunis	HtfC	15	C5
*Turbeville	ClnC	141	A7
Turbeville	HalC	9	C2
*Turkey	SamC	109	A1
Turkey Ford	SryC	5	A6
Turkey Pond	BrkC	166	A4
Turlington	HntC	81	D2
Turnage	EdgC	58	C3
Turners Crossroads	GsvC	13	C2

Community	County	Map#	Grid
Turners Crossroads	NhnC	14	B3
Turners Rock	ChtC	181	B5
Turnerville	HabC	115	B1
Turnpike	BcbC	44	A7
Tuscarora	CvnC	85	E5
Tuscola Park	HwdC	43	C7
*Tusculum	GreC	20	B3
Tusk	CarC	113	E5
Tuskeegee	GhmC	67	C2
Tuxedo	HdrC	71	A6
Twelvemile	HryC	157	B1
Twin Lakes	HntC	80	E5
Twin Oak	PdrC	131	A3
Twin Oaks	AlgC	3	D4
Twin Oaks	SulC	1	B3
*Tybee Island	ChtC	181	D5
Tyger	SptC	97	D4
Tyler Crossroads	GtnC	157	A4
Tylersville	LarC	119	C3
Tyro	DavC	50	E2
TYRRELL CO	TyrC	62	C2
U			
Ulah	RndC	52	C5
*Ulmer	AlnC	161	D7
Una	LeeC	140	D1
Una	SptC	98	B3
Unahala	SwnC	68	B3
Unaka	CheC	66	B6
Unaka Springs	UciC	21	A5
UNICOI CO	UciC	21	B3
Union	FnnC	91	D3
Union	HtfC	15	A6
Union	LtrC	102	B7
Union	MacC	68	B7
Union	NbrC	136	D1
Union	RthC	72	B4
Union	TrnC	95	C1
*Union	UnnC	99	B7
Union	UnoC	101	E3
UNION CO	UniC	92	C5
UNION CO	UnnC	119	E2
UNION CO	UnoC	101	E4
Union Cross	FsyC	27	C5
Union Crossroads	ClnC	155	A2
Union Crossroads	WmbC	156	D4
Union Grove	BeaC	61	C3
Union Grove	YadC	26	A3
Union Hill	HdrC	71	B3
Union Hill	SpnC	115	D4
Union Hill	YadC	26	C2
Union Hope	NshC	56	E1
Union Point	CarC	112	E4
Union Ridge	AlmC	29	C2
Union Temple	GreC	20	B1
*Unionville	UnoC	102	C1
Unity	FrkC	115	C6
Unity	LtrC	101	E6
University Estates	RocC	7	D6
U-No	HdrC	71	A3
Upchurch	GreC	20	A2
Upper Peachtree	CheC	66	E7
Upper Pigeonroost	MhlC	21	C5
Upper Poplar	MhlC	21	C4
Upper Shady	JhnC	1	C5
Upper Shell Creek	CtrC	22	B3
Upton	CwlC	23	A5
Upward	HdrC	71	B4
Uree	RthC	71	E2
Utica	OcnC	116	D1
Uwharrie	MntC	77	E2
V			
Vade Mecum	StkC	6	A6
Vails Mill	WasC	1	E2
*Valdese	BkeC	47	C4
Vale	AvyC	22	C5
Valentine	HmpC	169	C5
Valhalla	ChwC	37	B2
Valhalla	PlkC	71	C6
Valle Crucis	WatC	22	E3
Valley	AvyC	22	B5
Valley Falls	SptC	98	B2
Valley Forge	CtrC	21	D1
Valleytown	CheC	67	A6
*Vance	OraC	163	E1
Vance	PtsC	8	A1
VANCE CO	VncC	11	B5
*Vanceboro	CvnC	85	E3
Vandalia	GlfC	28	C6
*Vandemere	PamC	87	B4
Vander	CumC	107	B1
Vandiver	FrkC	115	D6
Vann Crossroads	SamC	82	C5
Vannoy	WksC	24	C1
*Varnamtown	BwkC	146	A6
*Varnville	HmpC	169	E4
Vashti	AlxC	24	E6
*Vass	MreC	79	E4
Vaucluse	AknC	149	E5
Vaughan	WrnC	12	C5
Vaughans Crossroads	DlgC	140	D2
Vaughanville	NbrC	135	C2
Vein Mountain	McdC	46	C7
Venable	BcbC	44	C7
Venters	FloC	156	D2
Venters	PitC	59	B7
Verdery	GrwC	134	C4
*Vernonburg	ChtC	180	E6
Vernon View	ChtC	180	E6
Verona	OnsC	111	A7
Vesta	PatC	5	E1
Vests	CheC	66	A7
Vicksboro	WrnC	11	E7
Vienna	FsyC	26	D4
Villa Heights	HenC	7	A1

*Indicates incorporated city

Community	County	Map#	Grid
Vinegar Hill	CbsC	144	B2
Vinegar Hill	SulC	1	A4
Vinton Woods	GasC	74	D4
Violet	CheC	66	A6
*Virgilina	HalC	10	B3
*Virginia Beach		17	E1
Vista	PdrC	131	D4
Vixen	YanC	45	C1
Volney	GsnC	2	E2
Volunteer	StkC	5	D7
Vultare	NhnC	13	A3
W			
*Waco	ClvC	73	E3
*Wade	CumC	81	C6
Wade Hampton	GrvC	97	B4
*Wadesboro	AnsC	103	E3
Wades Point	BeaC	61	C7
Wadeville	MntC	78	A4
Wadsworth	SptC	98	B3
*Wagener	AknC	151	A5
Wagoner	AshC	3	A6
Wagoner	YadC	25	D3
*Wagram	SctC	105	D4
WAKE CO	WkeC	32	A6
*Wake Forest	FraC	32	A5
*Wake Forest	WkeC	32	A6
Wakelon	BrtC	36	D2
Wakulla	RobC	106	B5
*Walhalla	OcnC	95	B6
Walker	BrnC	161	B2
Walkers	PdrC	130	E2
Walkers Crossroads	WkeC	32	A7
Walkertown	BcbC	45	B5
*Walkertown	FsyC	27	C3
Walkertown	GreC	20	B2
Walkertown	HntC	81	B4
Walkinshaw	RmdC	159	C4
*Wallace	DupC	109	D6
Wallace Mill	CasC	8	D3
Walla Watta	BeaC	60	E5
Wallburg	DavC	27	C6
Walnut	MdnC	44	B2
*Walnut Cove	StkC	27	C1
*Walnut Creek	WanC	83	E3
Walnut Grove	JhnC	1	E6
Walnut Grove	SptC	98	C7
Walnut Grove	SvrC	42	C1
Walser	DavC	51	C3
Walsh	WksC	23	E2
*Walstonburg	GrnC	58	C5
*Walterboro	ColC	171	A3
Walter Crossroad	GreC	19	D4
Waltons Store	OnsC	111	A5
Wampee	BrkC	165	A4
Wampee	HryC	144	D7
Wando	BrkC	173	D3
Wappoola	BrkC	165	A7
*Ward	SalC	150	A1
Wards	CbsC	128	C7
Wards Corner	PdrC	130	C2
Wardville	GatC	16	B4
Ware Place	GrvC	118	A2
*Ware Shoals	AbbC	118	C6
*Ware Shoals	GrwC	118	D6
WARREN CO	WrnC	11	D5
Warren Crossroads	ChsC	172	B5
Warren Crossroads	KswC	122	D7
Warren Plains	WrnC	12	A5
Warrensburg	GreC	19	B4
*Warrenton	WrnC	12	A5
Warrior	CwlC	23	C7
*Warsaw	DupC	109	B1
Warsaw	WmbC	156	B7
Washburn	ClvC	73	B4
Washburn	RthC	72	E3
*Washington	BeaC	60	B5
Washington	BrkC	166	A4
WASHINGTON CO	WasC	1	C2
WASHINGTON CO	WsgC	20	E1
WASHINGTON CO	WshC	37	C6
Washington College	WsgC	20	D2
*Washington Park	BeaC	60	B5
Wasp	CckC	43	D2
Watauga	WasC	1	C1
WATAUGA CO	WatC	2	A7
Wateree	RldC	153	B2
Water Fork Mill	GreC	20	B4
Waterlily	CurC	18	B4
*Waterloo	LarC	119	A7
Watertown	BntC	41	B4
Waterville	HwdC	43	B3
Watery Branch	WanC	58	A5
*Watha	PdrC	109	D7
Watkins	VncC	11	A7
Watkins Mill	MacC	94	C2
Watson	UnoC	102	D1
Watson Crossroads	WanC	57	C5
Watts	AbbC	133	E4
Watts Crossroads	CabC	76	D1
Watts Landing	PdrC	131	E3
Wattsville	LarC	119	B4
Waucheesi	MroC	66	B3
Waverly	MdnC	45	A2
Waverly Mills	GtnC	167	C1
Waves	DarC	64	D3
*Waxhaw	UnoC	101	E4
Wayah Depot	MacC	68	A7
Waycross	SamC	109	A4
WAYNE CO	WanC	82	E4
*Waynesboro	BurC	159	B7
*Waynesville	HwdC	69	C1
Wayside	HokC	106	B2
Wear Valley	SvrC	41	D4
Weaver	DurC	31	A5

Community	County	Map#	Grid
Weavers Ford	AshC	2	E3
*Weaverville	BcbC	44	D5
Webb	MhlC	21	C6
Webbs	LinC	49	A7
*Webster	JakC	68	E3
Weddell	RldC	138	B4
*Weddington	UnoC	101	E2
Wedgewood	SmtC	153	C1
Weeks	ColC	171	B1
Weeksville	PsqC	17	D7
Wehutty	CheC	91	D1
Welch	ChwC	16	B6
Welcome	AndC	117	B3
Welcome	DavC	51	A1
Welcome	GrvC	97	A5
*Weldon	HlfC	13	C4
Weldons Mill	VncC	11	C7
*Wellford	SptC	97	E3
Wells	OraC	163	D2
Wells Crossroads	LeeC	140	C4
*Wendell	WkeC	56	C2
Wenona	WshC	61	B2
Wentworth	RocC	7	C6
Wertz Crossroads	ClhC	152	D5
Wesleyanna	McmC	65	A3
*Wesley Chapel	UnoC	102	A3
Wesser	SwnC	67	E4
West Anderson	AndC	117	B4
West Bend	FsyC	26	C4
Westbourne	MklC	75	B4
Westbrook	BldC	129	C3
West Canton	HwdC	43	E7
Westcliffe	GrvC	96	E5
*West Columbia	LexC	137	E6
West Cramerton	GasC	74	E5
Western Prong	CbsC	128	D4
West Fork	PtsC	7	E2
West Gantt	GrvC	97	A6
West Gastonia	GasC	74	C5
West Greenville	GrvC	97	A5
West Haven	BcbC	70	D1
*West Jefferson	AshC	2	D6
West Marion	McdC	46	B5
West Marion	MrnC	142	D2
West Miller Cove	BntC	41	A4
*Westminster	OcnC	116	A1
Westminster	RthC	72	D2
Westmore	MreC	78	E1
Westmoreland	MklC	75	A5
West Myers	CckC	19	B7
Weston	RldC	152	D1
West Onslow Beach	OnsC	132	A3
Westover	RmdC	159	B2
Westover	WshC	37	B6
*West Pelzer	AndC	117	E2
West Philadelphia	MreC	78	E3
Westport	LinC	75	A1
Westry	NshC	33	D5
Wests Mill	MacC	68	A4
West Springs	UnnC	98	E6
West Statesville	IrdC	49	B3
West Store Crossroads	EgfC	149	A3
*West Union	OcnC	95	B7
West View	SptC	98	B4
Westville	GrvC	97	A5
West Yanceyville	CasC	8	C6
Wetmore	PolC	65	A5
Whaley	AvyC	22	C2
Whaley	BrnC	161	B1
Wharton	BeaC	60	A4
Wheeland	NbrC	136	E3
Whetsell	OraC	163	B3
Whetstone	OcnC	94	E5
Whichard	PitC	59	D3
Whichard Beach	BeaC	60	B6
*Whispering Pines	MreC	79	D5
*Whitakers	EdgC	34	B3
*Whitakers	NshC	34	B3
WHITE CO	WhtC	93	B7
White Bluff Corssroads	LtrC	123	B1
White Cross	OrgC	30	B7
White Hall	ColC	171	A7
Whitehall	GrwC	134	D4
Whitehall	LexC	137	D5
Whitehall Terrace	ChsC	173	E4
Whitehead	AlgC	3	D5
Whitehead Hill	CtrC	21	E2
White Hill	LeCo	80	A2
White Hill	ScrC	168	C7
White Horn	HawC	19	B1
White Horse	GrvC	97	A6
White Horse Heights	GrvC	96	E5
Whitehouse	RthC	46	A7
Whitehurst	PitC	59	C2
*White Lake	BldC	129	B1
White Level	FraC	33	B3
Whitemarsh Island	ChtC	181	B5
White Oak	FaiC	121	E4
White Oak	GatC	15	E4
White Oak	HlfC	33	E2
White Oak	NshC	33	B6
Whiteoak Flats	YanC	21	B6
White Path	GilC	91	C7
White Plains	AndC	117	D1
White Plains	CrkC	99	A3
White Plains	SryC	5	A5
White Plains Crossroad	LarC	119	C7
White Pond	AknC	160	D1
White Pond	HryC	144	A3
White Pond	RobC	127	B5
Whitepost	BeaC	60	D6
White Rock	CtrC	21	E2
Whiterock	MdnC	20	B7
White Rock	RldC	137	B3
Whitesand	GreC	20	A4

Community	County	Map#	Grid
Whites Chapel	RndC	52	E3
Whites Crossroads	BrtC	36	D2
Whites Crossroads	DlgC	140	E3
Whites Pond Crossroad	SmtC	140	A6
White Stocking	PdrC	131	A1
White Stone	SptC	98	E4
White Store	AnsC	103	B4
Whitesville	BrkC	164	E6
Whitetown	CasC	8	B3
Whitetown	MccC	148	D1
*Whiteville	CbsC	128	D6
Whitfield Crossroads	LnrC	84	A4
Whitley Heights	JtnC	56	C6
Whitmell	PtsC	8	A1
*Whitmire	NbrC	120	B4
Whitney	SptC	98	C3
Whitney	StnC	77	C1
Whitney Heights	SptC	98	C3
*Whitsett	GlfC	29	A4
Whitson	MhlC	21	C5
Whitt Town	PerC	9	D6
Whitworth	FrkC	116	A4
Whortonville	PamC	87	C6
Whynot	RndC	52	D7
Wiggins	ColC	177	C1
Wiggins Crossroads	EdgC	58	C1
Wiggins Crossroads	GatC	16	B2
Wilbanks	WlnC	58	A2
Wilbar	WksC	24	B2
Wilbourns	GraC	10	B4
Wildacres	McdC	45	E2
Wilder	BrkC	165	B3
Wildwood	BntC	41	A3
Wildwood	CarC	112	E5
Wiles Crossroads	ClhC	153	A3
Wiley	RabC	94	B6
Wilkerson Crossroads	WlnC	57	B3
WILKES CO	WksC	23	E5
WILKES CO	WlkC	133	B7
*Wilkesboro	WksC	24	D4
Wilkes Crossroads	DlgC	140	E2
Wilkins	BftC	177	B4
Wilkinson	BeaC	61	B4
Wilkinson Heights	OraC	152	D7
Wilkinsville	CrkC	99	D3
Wilksburg	CstC	100	A7
*Willard	PdrC	109	D6
Willeyton	GatC	15	E3
Williams	CbsC	144	C1
*Williams	ColC	170	D1
Williams	WanC	83	D5
Williamsboro	VncC	11	B5
Williamsburg	IrdC	25	D6
Williamsburg	McmC	65	A3
Williamsburg	RocC	29	A1
WILLIAMSBURG CO	WmbC	166	A1
Williams Crossroads	WkeC	55	D4
Williams Hill	GtnC	157	A3
Williamson Crossroads	CbsC	128	A6
*Williamston	AndC	117	E2
*Williamston	MtnC	36	A7
Willington	MccC	133	E6
Willis Landing	OnsC	111	E7
*Williston	BrnC	160	E2
Williston	CarC	113	E4
Willits	JakC	69	A3
Willits-Ochre Hill	JakC	69	A2
Willow	GatC	16	A5
Willow Creek	GrnC	58	E6
Willow Creek Siding	FloC	142	A4
Willow Green	GrnC	58	E7
Willow Springs	JtnC	56	A6
Willow Springs	WkeC	55	C5
Willow Springs Park	AknC	149	C7
Wills	JhnC	1	E4
Willtown Bluff	ChsC	171	E7
Wilmar	BeaC	85	E1
*Wilmington	NhrC	146	E1
Wilmington Beach	NhrC	147	A4
Wilmington Park	ChtC	181	B5
Wilmot	JakC	68	C2
Wilson	BcbC	45	A6
Wilson	ClnC	154	D4
*Wilson	WlnC	57	D3
WILSON CO	WlnC	34	A7
Wilson Crossroads	DlgC	141	B2
Wilson Mill	FnnC	91	E7
*Wilson's Mills	JtnC	56	C5
Wilson Station	MroC	65	D2
Wilsonville	ChaC	54	D3
Wilton	GraC	31	E3
Wilton Springs	CckC	42	E1
Wind Blow	MntC	78	E6
Windemere	NhrC	131	A7
Windhams Crossroads	DlgC	140	E2
Windom	YanC	45	C1
*Windsor	AknC	160	D1
*Windsor	BrtC	36	C4
Windsor Estates	RldC	138	B4
Windsors Crossroads	YadC	25	C5
Windy Gap	WksC	25	A4
Windy Ridge	FnnC	91	E4
Wineberg Crossroads	DlgC	141	D1
*Winfall	PqmC	16	D7
Winfield	ClbC	148	A5
Winfield Hill	ClbC	148	A5
Wing	MhlC	21	E7
*Wingate	UnoC	102	D3
*Winnsboro	FaiC	121	E6
Winnsboro Mills	FaiC	121	E6
Winona	FloC	142	A2
Winstead Crossroads	NshC	57	D1
Winsteadville	BeaC	61	C6
*Winston-Salem	FsyC	27	B4
Winterseat	MccC	134	D6

Community	County	Map#	Grid
*Winterville	PitC	59	B6
*Winton	HtfC	15	C5
Wisacky	LeeC	140	C3
Wise	WrnC	11	E4
Wise Forks	JnsC	84	E4
Wisemans View	BkeC	46	C1
Witherbee	BrkC	165	C6
Witherspoon Crossroad	CwaC	48	D5
Wittys Crossroads	RocC	28	B1
Wolf Creek	CckC	43	D1
Wolf Creek	CheC	91	D2
Wolf Ford	TrnC	70	B4
Wolf Glade	CrlC	4	C1
Wolf Mountain	JakC	69	B5
Wolfton	OraC	152	B6
Wood	FraC	33	B2
Woodard	BrtC	36	D6
Woodbury	MrnC	157	B2
Woodby Hill	UciC	21	D3
Woodcliff	ScrC	168	A6
Woodfield Park	KnoC	41	A1
Woodfields	GrvC	97	B6
*Woodfin	BcbC	44	D5
Woodford	AshC	2	C7
*Woodford	OraC	151	E4
Woodington	LnrC	84	D5
Woodland	BrkC	173	C1
*Woodland	NhnC	14	D6
Woodland Hills	HdrC	70	D3
Woodland Hills	LexC	137	E5
Woodlawn	AlmC	29	E4
Woodlawn	GasC	74	E4
Woodlawn	GreC	19	E1
Woodlawn	LncC	148	A4
Woodlawn	MccC	148	E5
Woodlawn	McdC	46	A3
Woodlawn	WsgC	20	E2
Woodleigh	CurC	18	A1
Woodley	TyrC	38	A6
Woodrow	HwdC	69	E1
Woodrow	LeeC	139	E4
*Woodruff	SptC	98	B7
Woods Crossroads	AlnC	169	A2
Woods Crossroads	JtnC	82	A3
Woodsdale	PerC	9	D4
Woodside	GrvC	97	A5
Woodside	PdrC	131	D4
Woodside Hills	BcbC	44	C7
Woodville	CheC	66	E6
Woodville	ChsC	173	E3
Woodville	GrvC	118	A1
Woodville	PqmC	17	A7
Woodville	SryC	5	C4
Woodward	FaiC	121	D4
Woodworth	VncC	11	B3
Wootens Crossroads	CbsC	128	C4
Wootens Crossroads	GrnC	58	C6
Wootens Crossroads	LnrC	84	D2
Workman	WmbC	155	A3
Worley	MdnC	44	A3
Wormsloe	ChtC	181	A5
Worry	BkeC	47	A2
Worthams Ferry	HryC	144	E6
Wrendale	EdgC	34	C5
Wright Mill	FnnC	92	A4
Wrightsboro	NhrC	130	E6
*Wrightsville Beach	NhrC	131	B7
Wyatts Crossroads	CbsC	128	B5
Wyche	BrwC	12	E1
Wymberly	ChtC	181	A5
Wyndale	WasC	1	A1
Y			
Yadkin	RowC	50	D4
YADKIN CO	YadC	26	B3
Yadkin College	DavC	50	E1
Yadkin Valley	CwlC	23	D6
*Yadkinville	YadC	26	A4
Yamacraw	PdrC	130	B3
YANCEY CO	YanC	21	B6
*Yanceyville	CasC	8	D6
Yarborough Crossroads	DlgC	140	E1
Yates	AshC	23	E1
Yates Hill	RchC	104	C3
Yauhannah	GtnC	157	C4
Yeatesville	BeaC	61	A5
Yellow Creek	GhmC	67	A2
Yellow Gap	BkeC	47	B5
*Yemassee	BftC	170	D7
*Yemassee	HmpC	170	D7
Yenome	BrnC	161	B6
Yeopim	ChwC	37	D3
York	RabC	94	B3
*York	YorC	100	C3
YORK CO	YorC	101	A4
Youngcane	UniC	92	B5
*Young Harris	TwnC	93	A3
Youngs	LarC	119	A1
Youngstown	UniC	92	D4
*Youngsville	FraC	32	A5
Yow Mill	RndC	52	D7
Z			
Zara	BldC	129	D4
*Zebulon	WkeC	56	D1
Zeigler	ScrC	168	A6
Zemp	LeeC	140	A1
Zephyr	SryC	4	C7
Zion	MrnC	142	E1
Zion Grove	MreC	79	A3
Zion Grove	SvrC	42	B3
Zion Hill	McmC	65	B2
Zion Hill	SptC	98	D3

*Indicates incorporated city

MAP

1

REGIONAL MAP

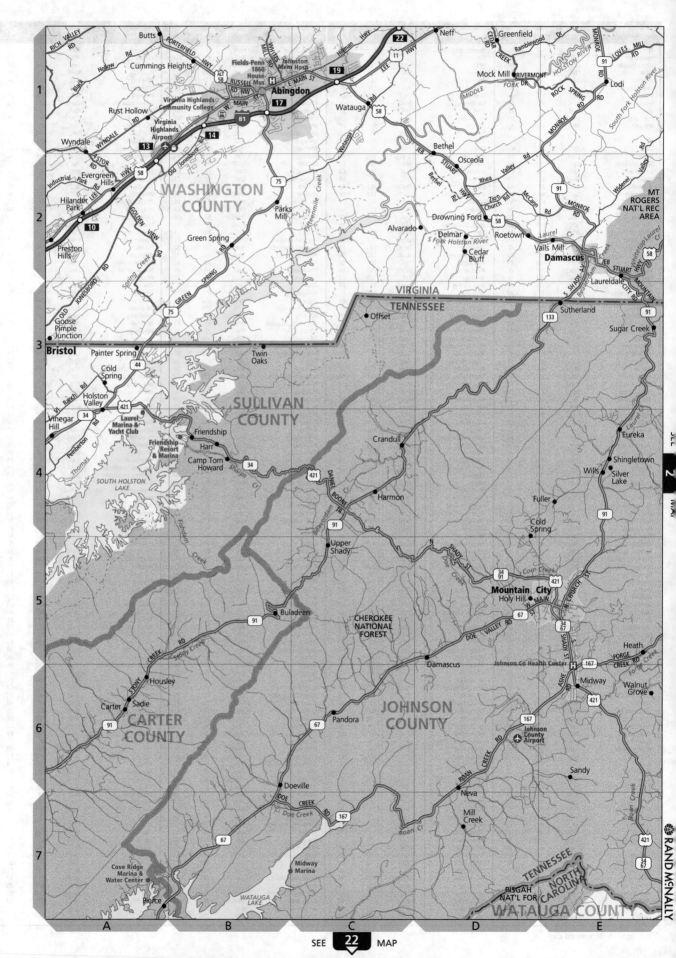

1:190,080
1 in. = 3 mi.

0   2   4
miles

N

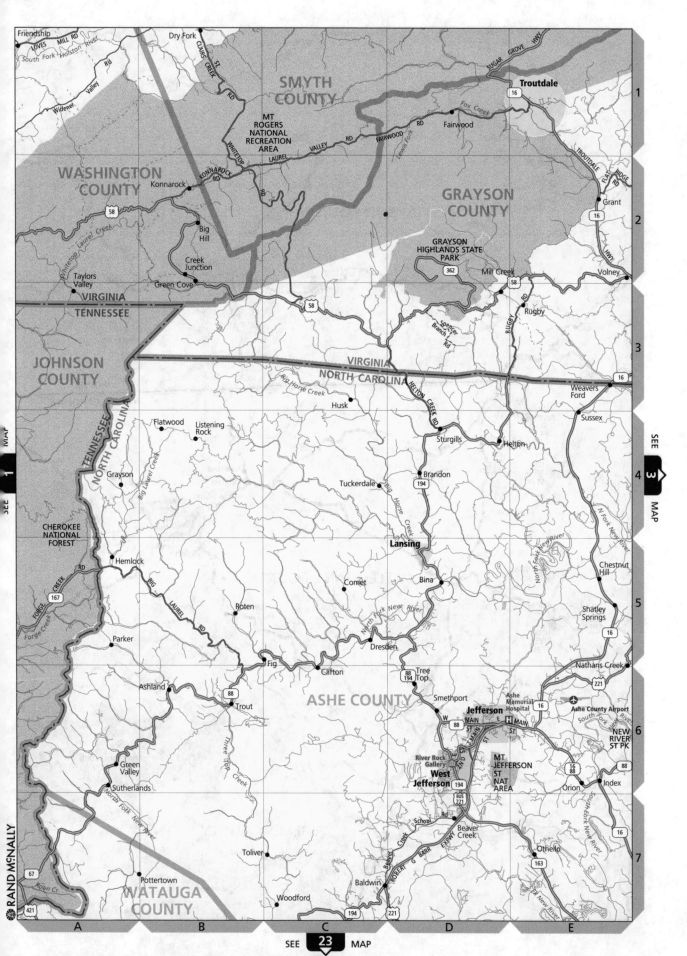

MAP
2

1:190,080
1 in. = 3 mi.

0   2   4
miles

Friendship
LOVES MILL RD
South Fork Holston River
Dry Fork
Widener
Valley

SMYTH COUNTY

MT ROGERS NATIONAL RECREATION AREA

Troutdale
SUGAR GROVE HWY
16

Fox Creek
FAIRWOOD RD
Fairwood

WASHINGTON COUNTY

Konnarock
KONNAROCK RD
WHITETOP
LAUREL
VALLEY RD

58

Big Hill

Creek Junction

Taylors Valley
VIRGINIA
TENNESSEE
Green Cove

58

GRAYSON COUNTY

GRAYSON HIGHLANDS STATE PARK
362

Mill Creek
58
RUGBY RD
Rugby

Spencer Branch Rd

Grant
16
TROUTDALE FLAT RIDGE RD
HWY

Volney
16

JOHNSON COUNTY

TENNESSEE
NORTH CAROLINA

VIRGINIA
NORTH CAROLINA

HELTON CREEK RD

Weavers Ford
16

Sussex

Big Horse Creek
Husk

Flatwood
Listening Rock

Sturgills
Helton

Grayson

Big Laurel Creek

Brandon
194
Tuckerdale

Big Horse Creek

CHEROKEE NATIONAL FOREST

FORGE CREEK RD
167

Hemlock

BIG LAUREL RD

Lansing

Comet
Bina

Chestnut Hill

N Fork New River

Shatley Springs
16

Forge Creek

Parker

Roten

North Fork New River

Dresden

Nathans Creek
221

Ashland

Fig
Clifton

88
Trout

88 194
Tree Top

ASHE COUNTY

Smethport

Ashe Memorial Hospital
Jefferson
W 88 MAIN ST E
MAIN ST
16
Ashe County Airport

NEW RIVER ST PK

Green Valley

Sutherlands

Three Top Creek

River Rock Gallery
West Jefferson
194
BUS 221

MT JEFFERSON ST NAT AREA

Orion

16 88

Index
88

16

North Fork New River

67

Toliver

Beaver Creek
School Rd
ROBERT G BARR EXPWY
Beaver Creek

Othello
163

South Fork New River

421

Pottertown

WATAUGA COUNTY

Baldwin
Woodford
194
221

New River

A   B   C   D   E

1   2   3   4   5   6   7

SEE 3 MAP

SEE 1 MAP

MAP

3

REGIONAL MAP

1:190,080
1 in. = 3 mi.

0   2   4
miles

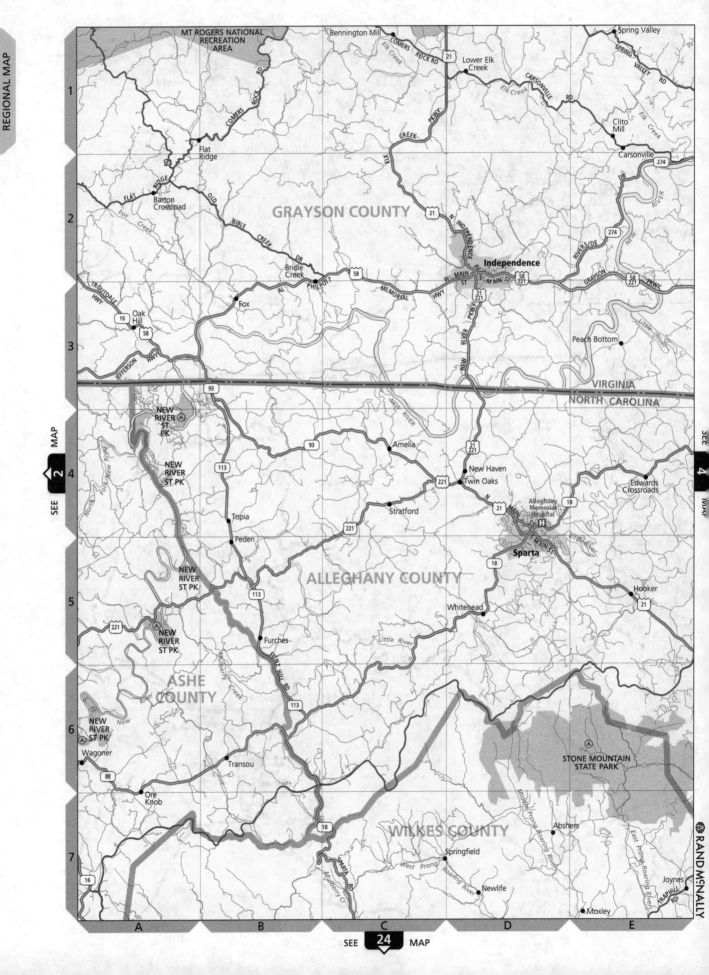

MAP
4

REGIONAL MAP

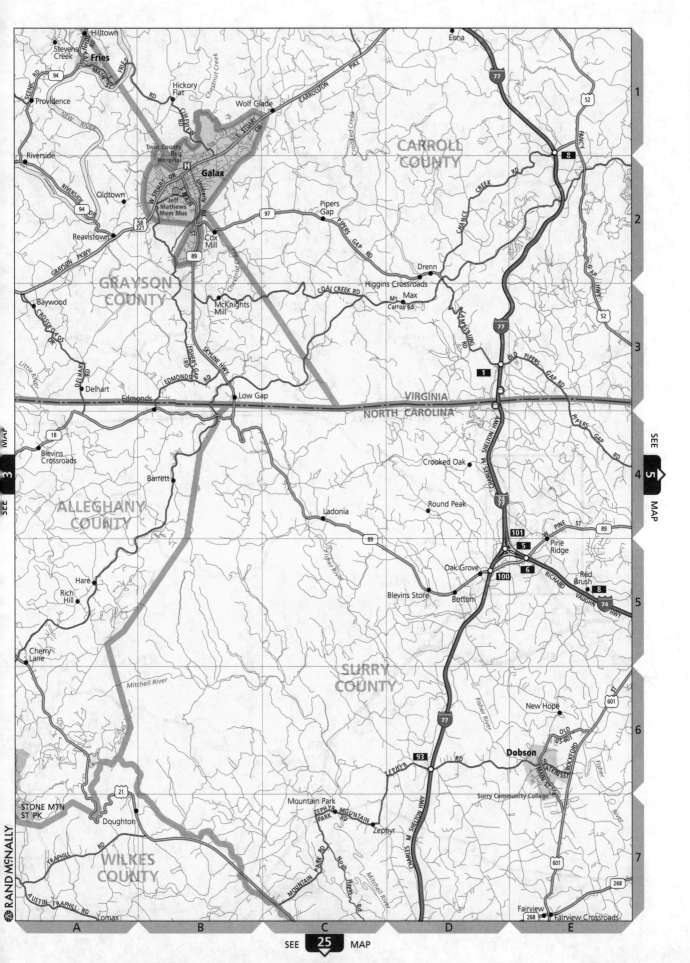

MAP
5

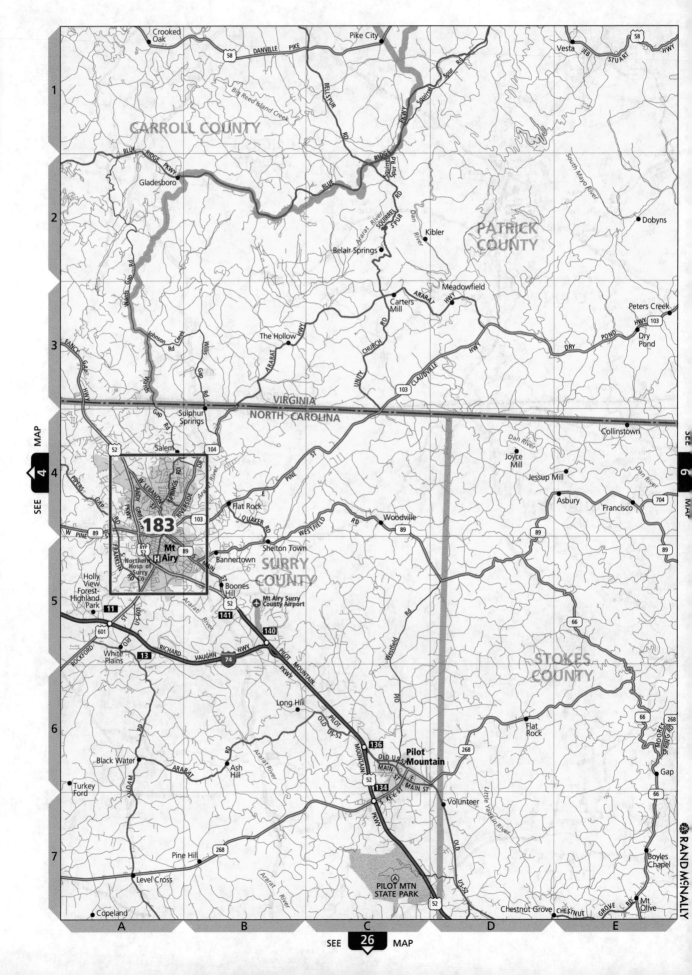

1:190,080
1 in. = 3 mi.

0   2   4
miles

CARROLL COUNTY

Crooked
Oak

Pike City

DANVILLE   PIKE

58

Vesta

JEB STUART HWY

58

Big Reed Island Creek

BELLSPUR   RD

Squirrel Spur Rd

South Mayo River

Dobyns

1

BLUE   RIDGE   PKWY

Gladesboro

BLUE   RIDGE   PKWY

SQUIRREL   SPUR   RD

Ararat River

Dan River

Kibler

PATRICK
COUNTY

2

Belair Springs

Meadowfield

ARARAT   HWY

Peters Creek

HWY 103

Johnson Creek

The Hollow

ARARAT   HWY

Carters
Mill

UNITY   CHURCH   RD

CLAUDVILLE   HWY

103

DRY   POND

Dry
Pond

FANCY   GAP   HWY

Willis   Gap

3

GAP   RD

VIRGINIA
NORTH CAROLINA

Collinstown

Dan River

SEE   MAP   4

Sulphur
Springs

52

Salem

104

PINE   ST

Dan River

Joyce
Mill

Jessup Mill

Asbury

Francisco

704

SEE   MAP   6

W. LEBANON

SPRINGS   RD

RIVERSIDE   DR

Ararat River

E

103

Flat Rock

QUAKER   RD

WESTFIELD   RD

Woodville

89

ANDY   GRIFFITH   PKWY

PIPERS   GAP   RD

W   PINE   ST

89

4

183

Mt
Airy

89

Shelton Town

89

89

FRANKLIN   RD

BYP
52

Northern
Hosp of
Surry
Co

Bannertown

SURRY
COUNTY

Westfield   Rd

S   MAIN   ST

Holly
View
Forest-
Highland
Park

11

Boones
Hill

52

141

Mt Airy Surry
County Airport

66

5

601

13

RICHARD   VAUGHN   HWY

140

PILOT   MOUNTAIN   PKWY

STOKES
COUNTY

White
Plains

ROCKFORD   RD

Ararat River

74

6

Long Hill

PILOT   MOUNTAIN   OLD   US-52

136

OLD   US-52

268

66

268

Flat
Rock

66

Black Water

ARARAT   RD

Ash
Hill

52

Pilot
Mountain

E   MAIN   ST

MOORES   SPRING   RD

Turkey
Ford

SWAMPS   RD

Ararat River

134

MAIN   ST

Volunteer

Little Yadkin River

Gap

66

7

Pine Hill

268

S   KEY   ST   PKWY

OLD   US-52

Boyles
Chapel

Level Cross

Ararat River

PILOT MTN
STATE PARK

52

Chestnut Grove

CHESTNUT   GROVE   RD

Mt
Olive

Copeland

A   B   C   D   E

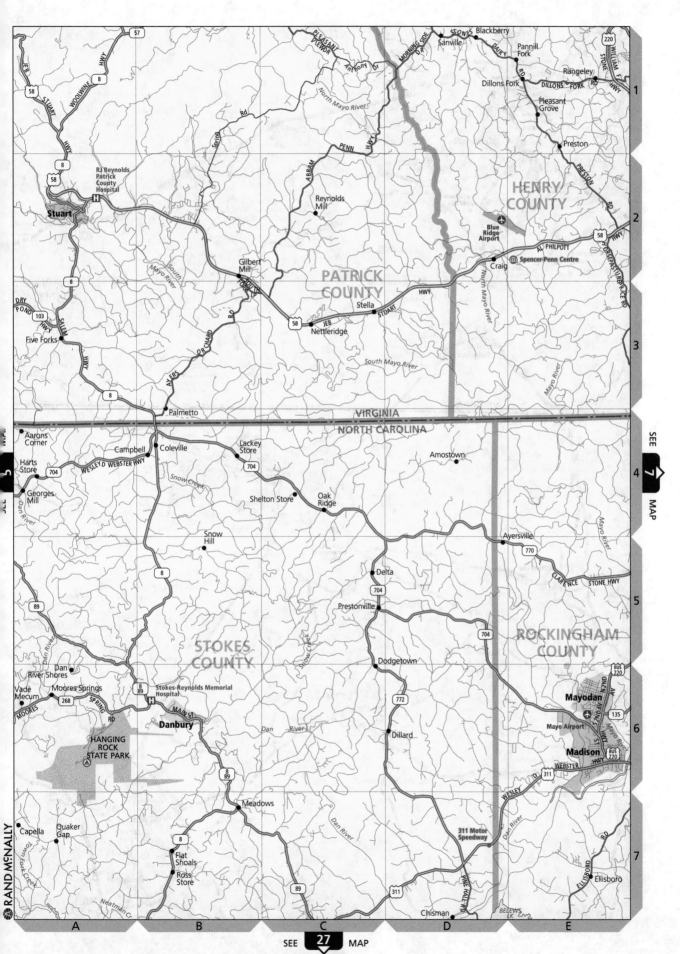

MAP
6

REGIONAL MAP

1:190,080
1 in. = 3 mi.

0   2   4

miles

57

JEB
WOOLWINE
HWY
8
58
STUART
HWY

PENN
HWY

ABRAM
RD

Spring
Rd

North Mayo River

PLEASANT
MANOR

Anthony
Dr

MORNING SIDE
DR

STONES
Blackberry
Sanville
DAIRY
Pannill
Fork
RD
DILLONS
FORK
RD
Dillons Fork
Rangeley
220
WILLIAM F
STONE
HWY

Pleasant
Grove

PRESTON
RD

Preston

**HENRY
COUNTY**

8
58
RJ Reynolds
Patrick
County
Hospital
H
Stuart

Reynolds
Mill

South
Mayo
River

Gilbert
Mill

SOUTH
FORK
RD

58
JEB
Nettleridge

HWY
Stella
STUART

**PATRICK
COUNTY**

Blue
Ridge
Airport

Al PHILPOTT
Craig
Spencer-Penn Centre

58
HWY
HORSEPASTURE RD

North Mayo River

Mayo River

8
DRY
POND
HWY
103
SALEM
HWY

Five Forks

AYERS
RD

ORCHARD
RD

South Mayo River

8

Palmetto

SEE
7
MAP

VIRGINIA
NORTH CAROLINA

Aarons
Corner

Harts
Store
704
WESLEY D WEBSTER HWY
Campbell
Coleville
Lackey
Store
704

Amostown

Georges
Mill
Dan River
Snow Creek

Shelton Store
Oak
Ridge

Ayersville
770
Mayo River

CLARENCE
STONE HWY

Snow
Hill

8

89

Dan River

Delta
704
Prestonville
704

**ROCKINGHAM
COUNTY**

BUS
220
N 2ND AV

**STOKES
COUNTY**

Snow Creek

Dodgetown

Mayodan
S 2ND AV
Mayo River
135
Mayo Airport

Dan
River Shores

Moores Springs
8
89
Stokes-Reynolds Memorial
Hospital
H
MAIN ST
Danbury

772

Dillard

Madison
BUS
220
WEBSTER
HWY
311

Vade
Mecum
268
MOORES
SPRING
RD

**HANGING
ROCK
STATE PARK**

Dan   River

8
89

Snow Creek

WESLEY D

Dan River

Capella
Quaker
Gap
Town Fork Creek

8
Meadows

Dan River

311 Motor
Speedway

PINE HALL RD

Flat
Shoals
Ross
Store

89
311
Chisman
BELEWS
LK

Ellisboro
Ellisboro

Nootman Cr

A   B   C   D   E

MAP
7

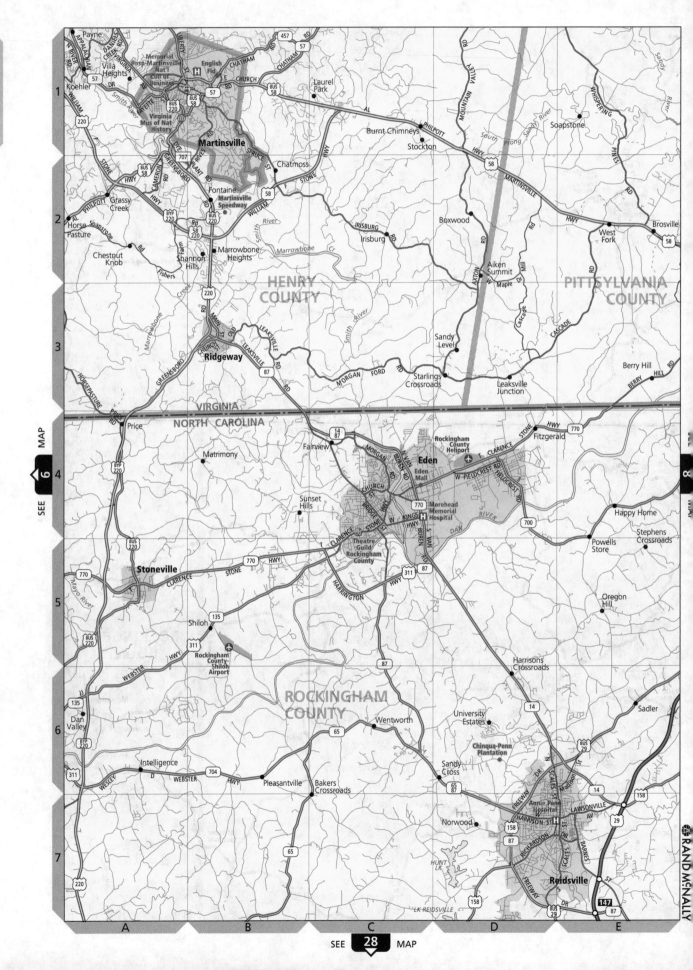

1:190,080
1 in. = 3 mi.

0   2   4
miles

SEE MAP 6

SEE 8 MAP

HENRY COUNTY

PITTSYLVANIA COUNTY

Martinsville

VIRGINIA
NORTH CAROLINA

Eden

ROCKINGHAM COUNTY

Stoneville

Reidsville

RAND MCNALLY

SEE 28 MAP

A   B   C   D   E

MAP
8

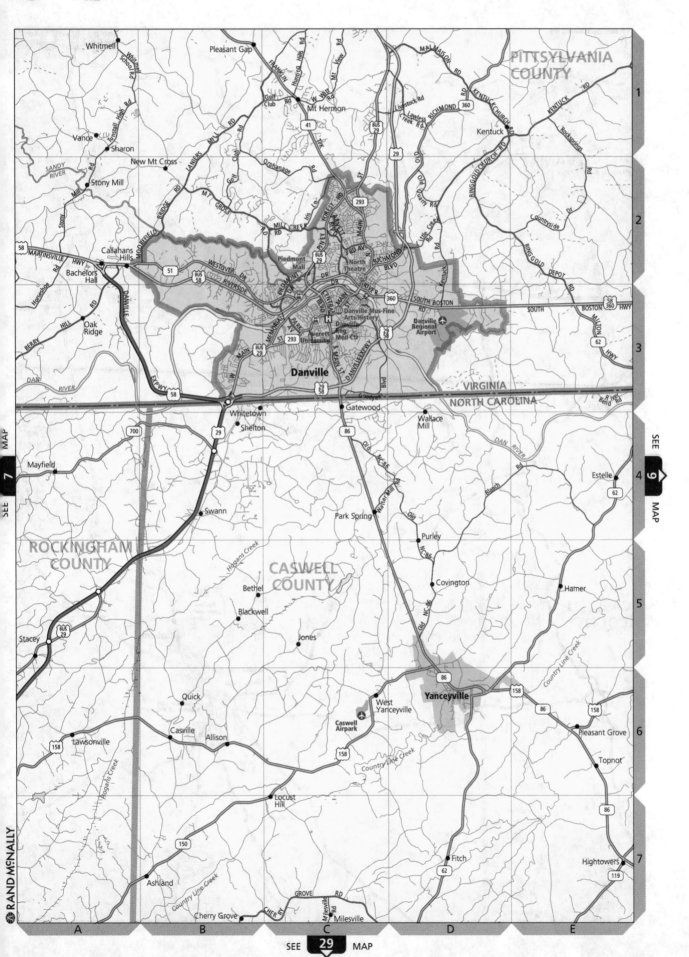

1:190,080
1 in. = 3 mi.

0   2   4
miles

PITTSYLVANIA COUNTY

Whitmell

Pleasant Gap

Vance

Sharon

New Mt Cross

Stony Mill

Mt Hermon

Kentuck

SANDY RIVER

Callahans Hills

Bachelors Hall

MARTINSVILLE HWY

Oak Ridge

Piedmont Mall

North Theatre

Danville Mus-Fine Arts/History

Averett University

Danville Reg Med Ctr

Danville

Danville Regional Airport

SOUTH BOSTON

VIRGINIA
NORTH CAROLINA

DAN RIVER

Whitetown

Gatewood

Wallace Mill

Shelton

Mayfield

Estelle

Swann

ROCKINGHAM COUNTY

Park Spring

Purley

Covington

Hamer

CASWELL COUNTY

Bethel

Blackwell

Jones

Stacey

Quick

Casville

Allison

West Yanceyville

Yanceyville

Pleasant Grove

Lawsonville

Caswell Airpark

Topnot

Country Line Creek

Locust Hill

Hogans Creek

Fitch

Hightowers

Ashland

Cherry Grove

Milesville

SEE 7 MAP
SEE 9 MAP
SEE 29 MAP

A   B   C   D   E

1 2 3 4 5 6 7

MAP
9

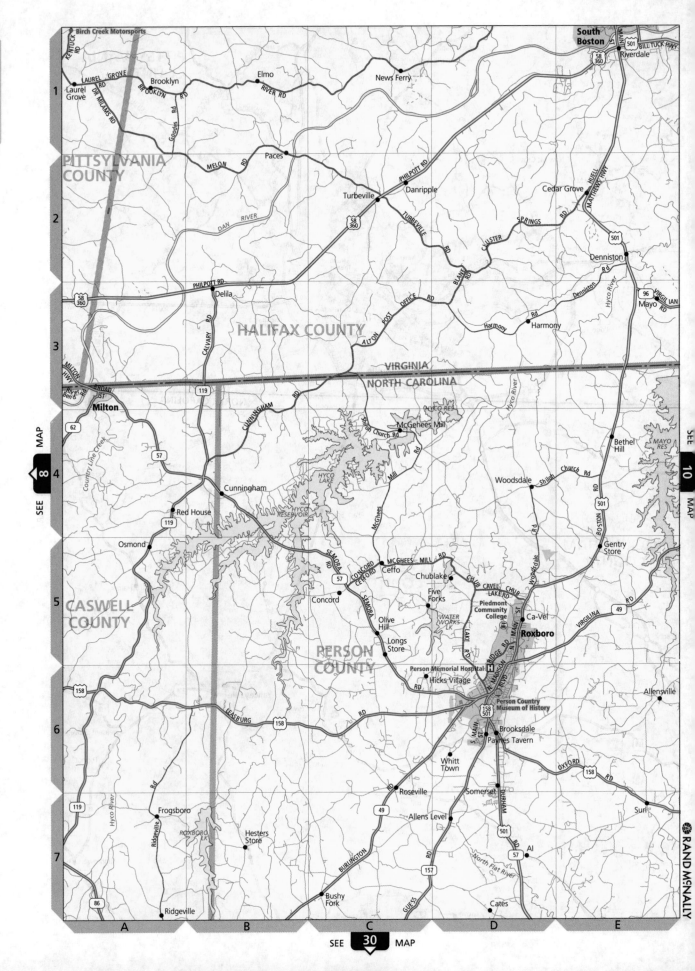

1:190,080
1 in. = 3 mi.
0   2   4
miles

Birch Creek Motorsports

PITTSYLVANIA COUNTY

Laurel Grove
Brooklyn
Elmo
News Ferry

South Boston
Riverdale
BILL TUCK HWY

Paces
Turbeville
Danripple
Cedar Grove
Denniston
Mayo

HALIFAX COUNTY

Delila
Harmony
Harmony

VIRGINIA
NORTH CAROLINA

Milton
McGehees Mill
Bethel Hill

MAP 8
SEE

Cunningham
HYCO LAKE
Woodsdale
Gentry Store

Red House
Osmond
HYCO RESERVOIR

Concord
Ceffo
Chublake
Ca-Vel

CASWELL COUNTY

Concord
Five Forks
Piedmont Community College
Roxboro

Olive Hill
WATER WORKS LK
Person Memorial Hospital

Longs Store
Hicks Village

PERSON COUNTY

Person Country Museum of History

Brooksdale
Paynes Tavern

Whitt Town

Roseville
Somerset
Allensville
Surl

Frogsboro
Allens Level
Al

ROXBORO LK
Hesters Store

Ridgeville

Bushy Fork
Cates

Ridgeville

MAP 10
SEE

RAND McNALLY

A   B   C   D   E

SEE 30 MAP

MAP
10

REGIONAL MAP

1:190,080
1 in. = 3 mi.

0   2   4
miles

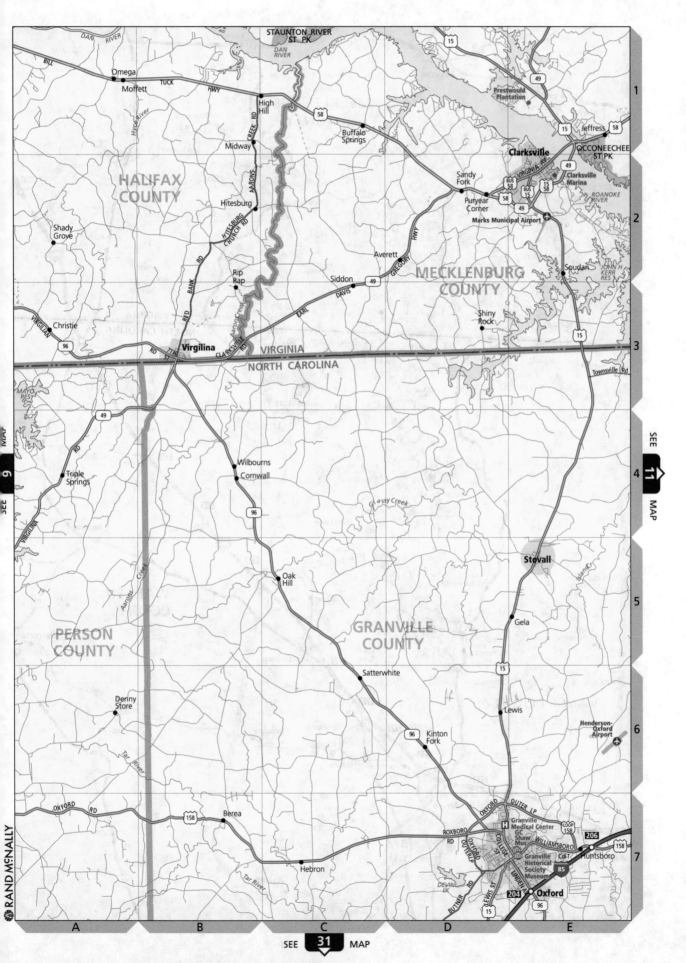

STAUNTON RIVER
ST. PK.

DAN RIVER

15

BILL

DAN RIVER

Omega

Moffett

TUCK

HWY

High Hill

58

Buffalo Springs

Prestwould Plantation

49

Jeffress

58

15

OCCONEECHEE
ST. PK.

Midway

Clarksville

VIRGINIA AVE.

49

Clarksville Marina

HALIFAX COUNTY

Shady Grove

Hitesburg

AARONS

Sandy Fork

BUS
58

BUS
15

15
58

ROANOKE RIVER

HITESBURG CHURCH RD

RD

Puryear Corner

58

49

Marks Municipal Airport

Rip Rap

BANK

RED

Averett

GREGORY

HWY

MECKLENBURG COUNTY

Soudan

JOHN H KERR RES.

Christie

96

Siddon

DAVIS

49

EARL

Shiny Rock

15

VIRGILIAN

7TH ST

RD

Virgilina

CLARKSVILLE RD

Aaron Creek

VIRGINIA

NORTH CAROLINA

Townsville Rd

MAYO RES.

49

RD

Wilbourns

Cornwall

Grassy Creek

SEE
11
MAP

SEE
9
MAP

VIRGILINA

Triple Springs

96

Stovall

Oak Hill

Island

PERSON COUNTY

Aarons Creek

GRANVILLE COUNTY

Gela

15

Satterwhite

Denny Store

Tar River

Lewis

Henderson-Oxford Airport

96

Kinton Fork

158

Berea

OXFORD   RD

ROXBORO

RD

OXFORD

OUTER LP

Oxford

WILLIAMSBORO

Granville Medical Center

GC
Shaw Mus

LOOP
158

206

158

Hebron

Tar River

OXFORD

OUTER LP

COLLEGE

ST

Granville Historical Society Museum

85

CoT

Huntsboro

158

DEVIN
LK

LINDEN

ST

204

Oxford

96

BUTNER

RD

LEWIS

ST

15

A   B   C   D   E

MAP
11

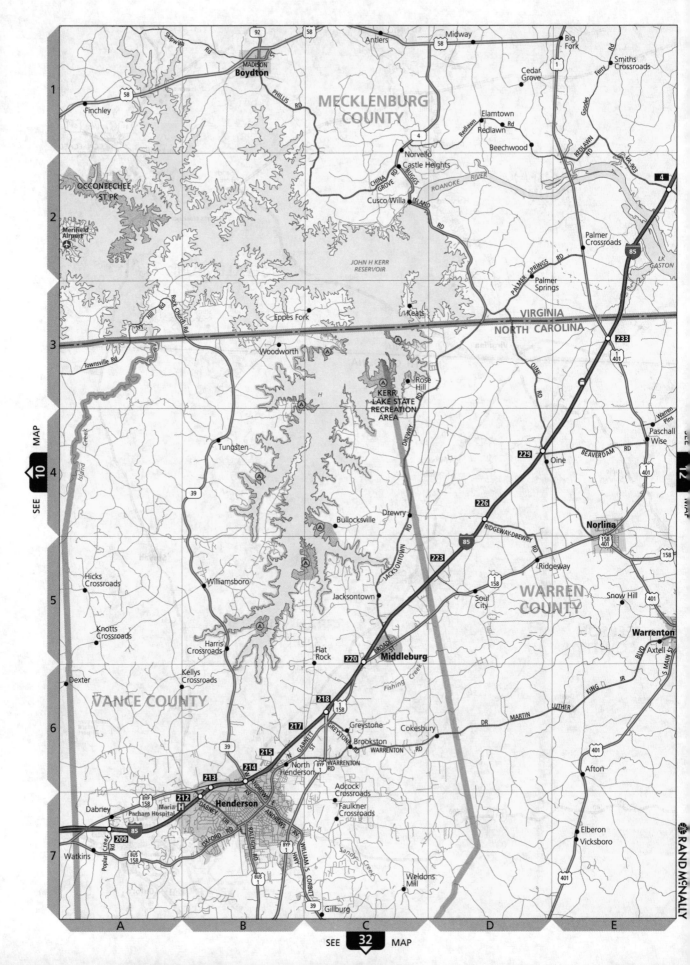

1:190,080
1 in. = 3 mi.

0   2   4
miles

Skipwith Rd

92   58   Antlers   58   Midway   Big Fork   Rd   Smiths Crossroads

MADISON
Boydton   PHILLIS   RD   Cedar Grove   1

58   Finchley   **MECKLENBURG COUNTY**   Elamtown   Redlawn   Redlawn Rd   Beechwood   REDLAWN RD   VA 903   4

4   Norvello   Castle Heights   BUGGS   RD   ROANOKE RIVER   Palmer Crossroads   85   LK GASTON

OCCONEECHEE ST PK   CHINA GROVE RD   Cusco Willa   ISLAND   Palmer Springs RD   Palmer Springs

Merrifield Airport   JOHN H KERR RESERVOIR   Eppes Fork   Keats   **VIRGINIA**   **NORTH CAROLINA**   233   401

Rock Church Rd   Woodworth   PINE RD   233

Townsville Rd   KERR LAKE STATE RECREATION AREA   Rose Hill   DREWRY RD   Paschall   Wise   401

SEE   **10**   MAP

Island Creek   Tungsten   Drewry   229   Oine   BEAVERDAM RD   401

39   Bullocksville   226   RIDGEWAY-DREWRY   RD   **Norlina**   158

Hicks Crossroads   Williamsboro   JACKSONTOWN RD   85   Ridgeway   158   401   Snow Hill

Knotts Crossroads   Jacksontown   223   158   Soul City   **WARREN COUNTY**   Warren Plns

Harris Crossroads   Flat Rock   220   BROAD ST   **Middleburg**   **Warrenton**   Axtell   S MAIN ST

Dexter   Kellys Crossroads   Fishing Creek   BLVD   KING JR   LUTHER   DR   MARTIN

VANCE COUNTY   218   158   Greystone   Cokesbury   401

217   GARRETT ST   GREYSTONE RD   Brookston   WARRENTON RD   Afton

39   215   N ANDREWS   WARRENTON RD   North Henderson   BYP   Adcock Crossroads

214   Faulkner Crossroads   Elberon

213   AV   Vicksboro

BYP 158   212   Maria Parham Hospital   H   **Henderson**   DABNEY DR   ANDREWS AV   WILLIAM S CORBITT HWY

Dabney   OXFORD RD   RALEIGH RD

85   209   BYP   Weldons Mill

Watkins   BUS 158   Poplar Creek Rd   Sandy Creek   BUS 1   401

39   Gillburg

1   2   3   4   5   6   7

MAP   SEE   **12**   MAP

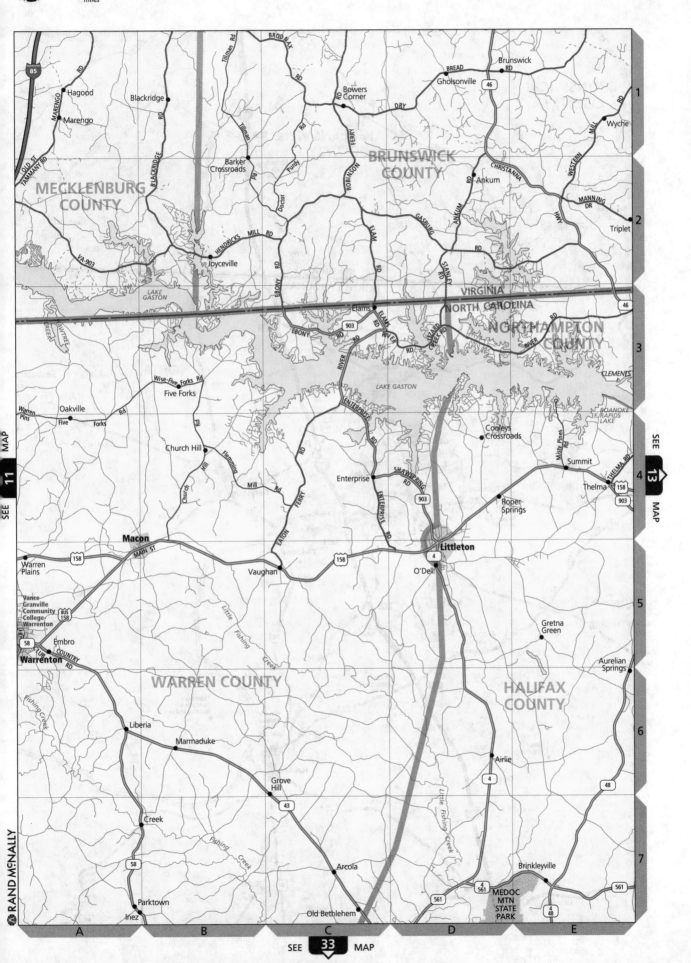

MAP
12

REGIONAL MAP

1:190,080
1 in. = 3 mi.

0   2   4
miles

85

MARENGO RD
Hagood
Marengo
Marengo

BRODNAX
Blackridge

Tillman Rd

BREAD
Gholsonville
Brunswick RD
46

BOWERS
Corner

Wyche

DRY

BLACKRIDGE RD

OLD ST TAMMANY RD

MECKLENBURG COUNTY

Barker Crossroads

Tillman

Purdy Rd

Rd

ROBINSON FERRY

BRUNSWICK COUNTY

CHRISTANNA

Ankum
Ankum RD

MANNING DR

WESTERN HWY

Triplet

VA-903

Doctor Rd

HENDRICKS MILL RD

Joyceville

FLAM

GASBURG

STANLEY RD

ANKUM RD

RD

MILL RD

LAKE GASTON

EBONY RD

Elams

VIRGINIA
NORTH CAROLINA

NORTHAMPTON COUNTY

46

MAP
11
SEE

EBONY

903

ELAMS RD

RIVER

LIZARD CREEK RD

RIVER

CLEMENTS

ROANOKE RAPIDS LAKE

SEE
13
MAP

Wise-Five Forks Rd
Five Forks

Warren Plns
Oakville
Five   Forks

RIVER RD

ENTERPRISE RD

LAKE GASTON

Cooleys Crossroads

Misty Pines Rd

THELMA RD

Church Hill

FLEMMING

Enterprise

SHAWSPRING RD

Summit

Thelma
158
903

CHURCH HILL PR

MILL RD

EATON FERRY RD

ENTERPRISE RD

903

Roper Springs

Macon
158
MAIN ST

EBONY FERRY RD

158

Littleton
4

Warren Plains

Vaughan

O'Dell

Gretna Green

Vance Granville Community College Warrenton
BUS 158

Little Fishing Creek

Aurelian Springs

58
Embro
COUNTRY RD

Warrenton

WARREN COUNTY

HALIFAX COUNTY

Liberia

Marmaduke

Airlie
4

48

Grove Hill
43

Fishing Creek

Little Fishing Creek

Creek

Brinkleyville
561

58

Arcola

561

4 561

561

4 48

Parktown
Inez

Old Bethlehem

MEDOC MTN STATE PARK

® RAND McNALLY

MAP
13

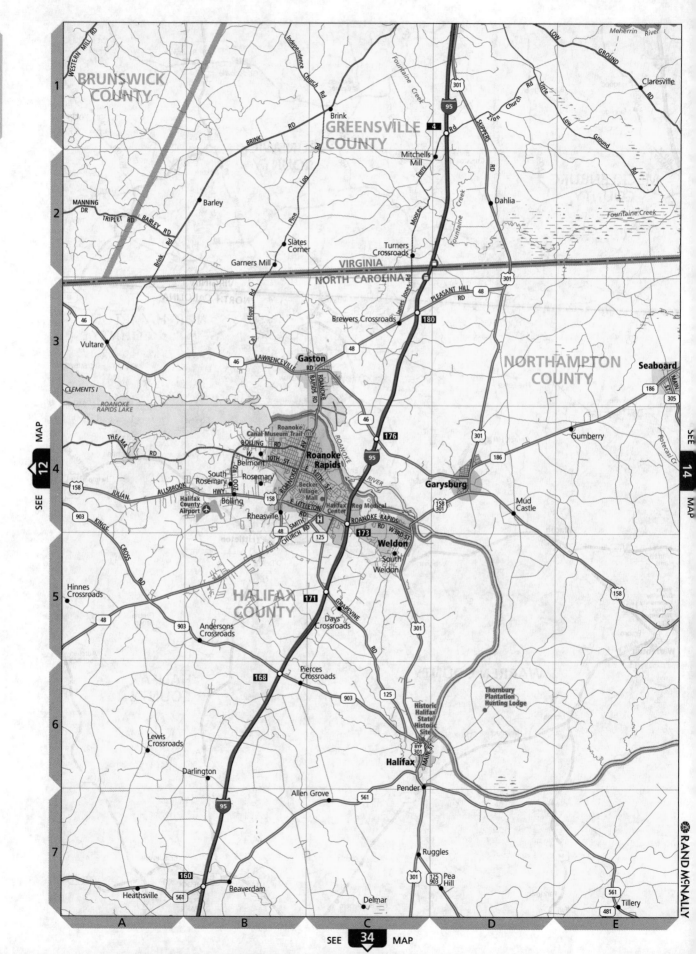

1:190,080
1 in. = 3 mi.

0   2   4
miles

BRUNSWICK
COUNTY

Meherrin River

LOW GROUND

Claresville

Little Low Ground RD

Zion Church RD

Brink

GREENSVILLE
COUNTY

SHIPPERS RD

Independence Church RD

Mitchells Mill

Dahlia

Fountaine Creek

MANNING DR

Barley

TRIPLET RD

BARLEY RD

BRINK RD

Brink RD

Pine Log RD

Slates Corner

Turners Crossroads

Moores RD

Ferry RD

Fountaine Creek

Garners Mill

VIRGINIA

NORTH CAROLINA

VIRGINIA

46

Cal Floyd RD

Vultare

Brewers Crossroads

James Jones RD

PLEASANT HILL RD

48

301

180

Pea Hill RD

46

LAWRENCEVILLE

Gaston

48

NORTHAMPTON
COUNTY

Seaboard

MAIN ST

186

305

CLEMENTS I

ROANOKE RAPIDS LAKE

ROANOKE RAPIDS RD

46

176

Roanoke Canal Museum Trail

THELMA RD

BOLLING RD

95

301

186

Gumberry

Potecasi Cr

SEE 12 MAP

ROANOKE AVE

Roanoke Rapids

ROANOKE RIVER

Garysburg

SEE 14 MAP

158

South Rosemary

Belmont

10TH ST

W

Rosemary

E 10TH ST

JULIAN RD

ALLSBROOK

ZOO RD

Becker Village Mall

Mud Castle

158

Halifax County Airport

Bolling

158

E LITTLETON RD

Halifax Center

Reg Medical

158 301

903

KINGS CROSS RD

Rheasville

SMITH RD

CHURCH RD

48

125

H

ROANOKE RAPIDS RD

W 3RD ST

173

Weldon

Hinnes Crossroads

HALIFAX
COUNTY

171

GRAPEVINE RD

South Weldon

158

48

903

Andersons Crossroads

Days Crossroads

301

168

Pierces Crossroads

903

125

Thornbury Plantation Hunting Lodge

Lewis Crossroads

Historic Halifax State Historic Site

Darlington

BYP 301

Halifax

MAIN ST

Allen Grove

561

Pender

Ruggles

95

160

561

Heathsville

Beaverdam

Delmar

301

125 903

Pea Hill

561

Tillery

481

A   B   C   D   E

MAP
14

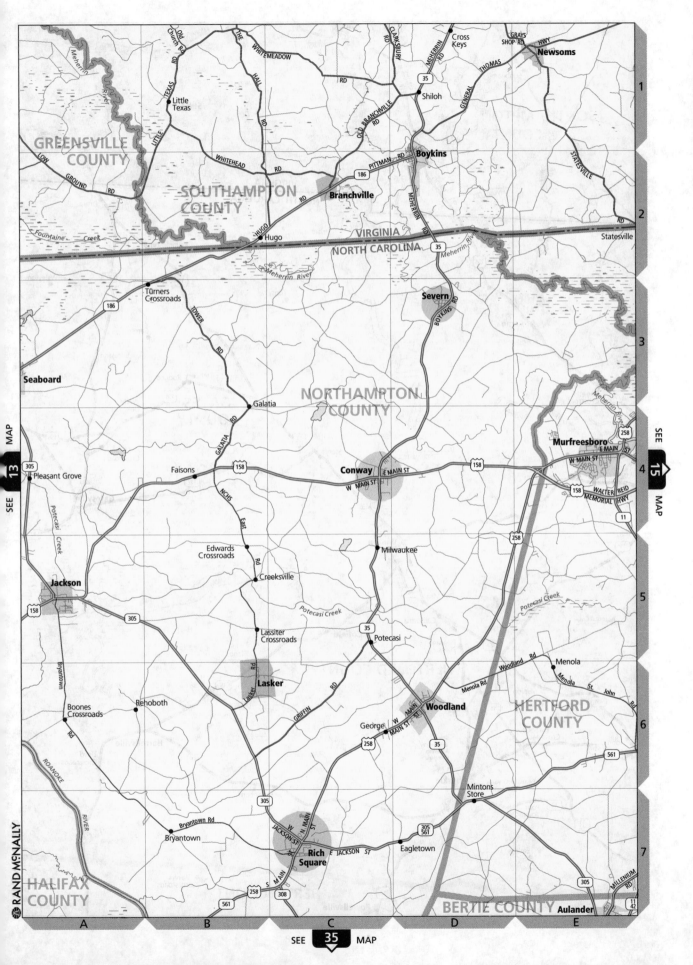

1:190,080
1 in. = 3 mi.

0   2   4
miles

SEE 13 MAP

SEE 15 MAP

SEE 35 MAP

RAND McNALLY

GREENSVILLE COUNTY

SOUTHAMPTON COUNTY

Little Texas

Boykins

Branchville

Hugo

Cross Keys

Newsoms

Shiloh

VIRGINIA
NORTH CAROLINA

Statesville

Turners Crossroads

Severn

Seaboard

NORTHAMPTON COUNTY

Galatia

Pleasant Grove

Faisons

Conway

Murfreesboro

Milwaukee

Jackson

Edwards Crossroads

Creeksville

Lassiter Crossroads

Potecasi

Menola

Boones Crossroads

Rehoboth

Lasker

Woodland

George

HERTFORD COUNTY

Mintons Store

Bryantown

Rich Square

Eagletown

HALIFAX COUNTY

BERTIE COUNTY   Aulander

A   B   C   D   E

MAP
15

REGIONAL MAP

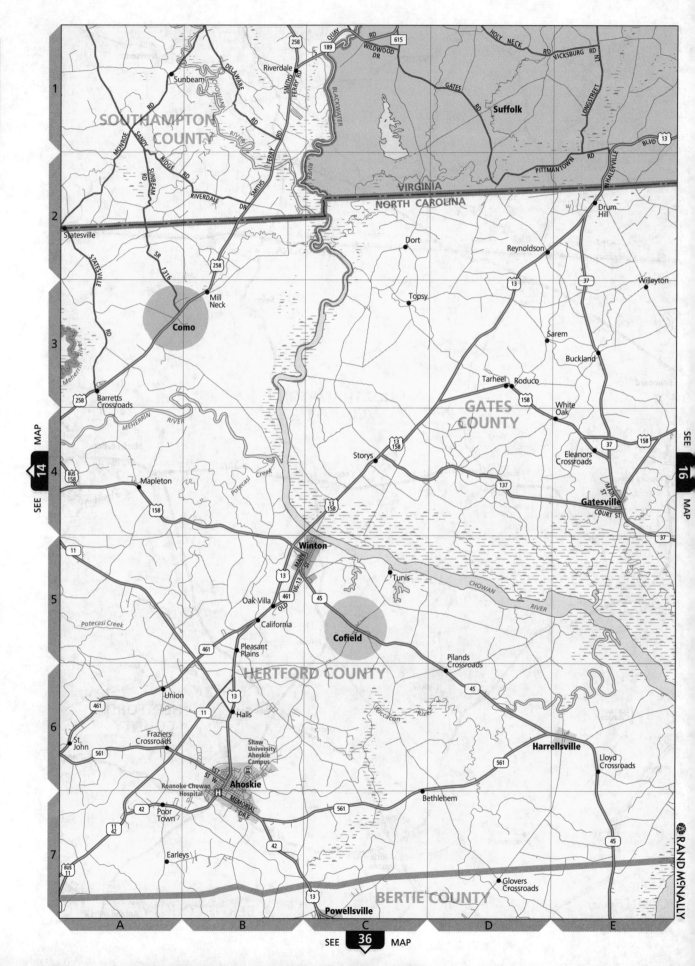

1:190,080
1 in. = 3 mi.

0   2   4

miles

N

MAP 15

SUNBEAM

Riverdale

SOUTHAMPTON COUNTY

Suffolk

Statesville

VIRGINIA
NORTH CAROLINA

Drum Hill

Dort

Reynoldson

Willeyton

Mill Neck

Topsy

Como

Sarem

Buckland

Tarheel · Roduco

GATES COUNTY

Barretts Crossroads

White Oak

MEHERRIN RIVER

Storys

Eleanors Crossroads

Mapleton

SEE MAP 14

SEE MAP 16

Gatesville

Winton

Tunis

CHOWAN RIVER

Oak Villa

California

Cofield

Pleasant Plains

Pilands Crossroads

HERTFORD COUNTY

Union

Halls

Waccamaw River

St. John

Fraziers Crossroads

Harrellsville

Lloyd Crossroads

Shaw University Ahoskie Campus

Roanoke Chowan Hospital

Ahoskie

Poor Town

Bethlehem

Earleys

Glovers Crossroads

BERTIE COUNTY

Powellsville

A   B   C   D   E

SEE 36 MAP

RAND McNALLY

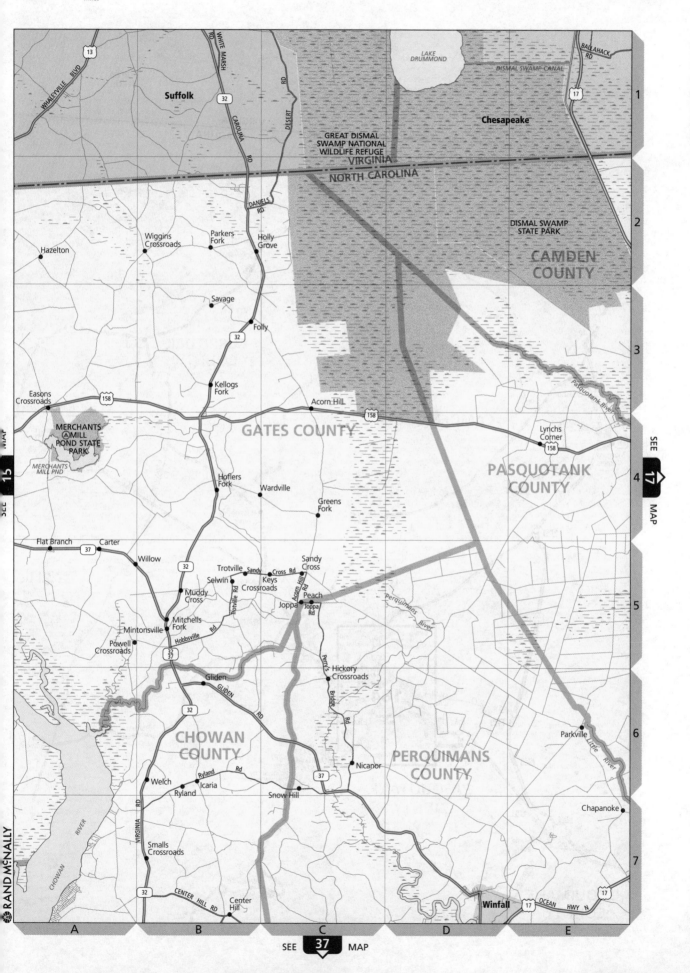

MAP
16

1:190,080
1 in. = 3 mi.

0   2   4
miles

N

Whaleville Blvd

13

Suffolk

White Marsh Rd

32

Carolina Rd

Desert Rd

Lake Drummond

Dismal Swamp Canal

Ballahack Rd

17

1

Great Dismal Swamp National Wildlife Refuge

Chesapeake

VIRGINIA
NORTH CAROLINA

Dismal Swamp State Park

CAMDEN COUNTY

2

Hazelton

Wiggins Crossroads

Parkers Fork

Holly Grove

Daniels Rd

Savage

Folly

32

Pasquotank River

3

Easons Crossroads

158

Kellogs Fork

Acorn Hill

158

Lynchs Corner

158

GATES COUNTY

MERCHANTS MILL POND STATE PARK

MERCHANTS MILL PND

Hoflers Fork

Wardville

Greens Fork

PASQUOTANK COUNTY

4

SEE 15 MAP

Flat Branch

Carter

37

Willow

32

Trotville

Selwin

Muddy Cross

Mitchells Fork

Mintonsville

Hobbsville Rd

Trotville Rd

Sandy Cross Rd

Keys Crossroads

Sandy Cross

Acorn Hill Rd

Peach

Joppa

Joppa Rd

Perquimans River

SEE 17 MAP

5

Powell Crossroads

32
37

Gliden

Gliden Rd

Perr's Bridge Rd

Hickory Crossroads

CHOWAN COUNTY

32

PERQUIMANS COUNTY

Parkville

Little River

6

Welch

Ryland Rd

Icaria

Ryland

37

Nicanor

Snow Hill

Chapanoke

Virginia Rd

Chowan River

Smalls Crossroads

7

32

Center Hill Rd

Center Hill

Winfall

17

Ocean Hwy N

17

A   B   C   D   E

SEE 37 MAP

MAP
17

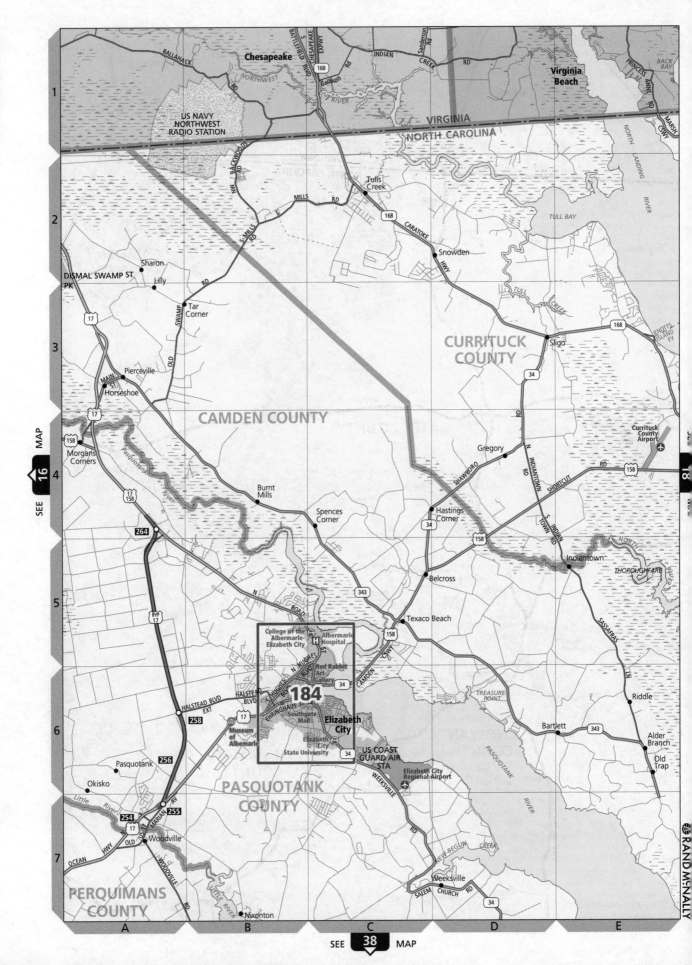

1:190,080
1 in. = 3 mi.

0   2   4
miles

SEE **16** MAP

SEE **38** MAP

RAND McNALLY

Chesapeake

Virginia Beach

VIRGINIA
NORTH CAROLINA

US NAVY NORTHWEST RADIO STATION

Tulls Creek

Snowden

Sharon
Lilly

DISMAL SWAMP ST PK

Tar Corner

CURRITUCK COUNTY

Sligo

Pierceville
Horseshoe

CAMDEN COUNTY

Gregory

Currituck County Airport

Morgans Corners

Burnt Mills

Spences Corner

Hastings Corner

Indiantown

Belcross

Texaco Beach

184

College of the Albemarle- Elizabeth City
Albermarle Hospital
Red Rabbit Art Gallery

Riddle

Halstead Blvd Ext
Southgate Mall

Bartlett

Elizabeth City

Museum of Albemarle

Alder Branch
Old Trap

Pasquotank
Elizabeth City State University

US COAST GUARD AIR STA

Okisko

Elizabeth City Regional Airport

PASQUOTANK COUNTY

Woodville

Weeksville

PERQUIMANS COUNTY

Nixonton

A   B   C   D   E

MAP
18

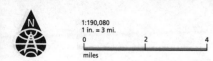

1:190,080
1 in. = 3 mi.

0   2   4
miles

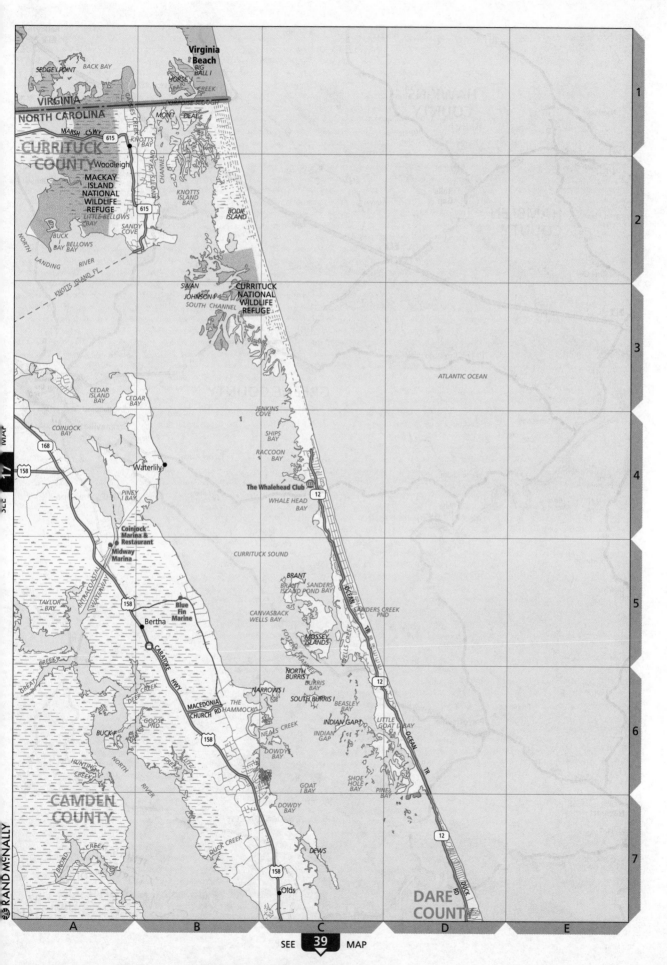

Virginia
Beach
BIG
BALL I
HORSE I
MONT   DEAL

VIRGINIA
NORTH CAROLINA
MARSH CSWY
615
CURRITUCK
COUNTY   Woodleigh
MACKAY
ISLAND
NATIONAL
WILDLIFE
REFUGE
LITTLE BELLOWS
615
SANDY
COVE
BUCK
BAY   BELLOWS
BAY
NORTH
LANDING   RIVER
KNOTTS ISLAND FY

KNOTTS
BAY
KNOTTS ISLAND CHANNEL
KNOTTS
ISLAND
BAY
BODIE
ISLAND

BACK BAY
SEDGE POINT

SWAN
JOHNSON I
SOUTH CHANNEL
CURRITUCK
NATIONAL
WILDLIFE
REFUGE

ATLANTIC OCEAN

CEDAR
ISLAND
BAY   CEDAR
BAY

JENKINS
COVE

SHIPS
BAY

RACCOON
BAY

COINJOCK
BAY
168
158
Waterlily

The Whalehead Club
12
WHALE HEAD
BAY

PINEY
I BAY

Coinjock
Marina &
Restaurant
Midway
Marina

CURRITUCK SOUND

BRANT
BRANT   SANDERS
ISLAND POND BAY

SANDERS CREEK
PND

TAYLOR
BAY
158
Blue
Fin
Marine
Bertha

INTRACOASTAL WATERWAY

CARATOKE HWY

CANVASBACK
WELLS BAY

MOSSEY
ISLANDS

WELLS CREEK

OCEAN TR

12

NORTH
BURRIS I
BURRIS
BAY

NARROWS I
MACEDONIA
CHURCH RD
THE
HAMMOCK
SOUTH BURRIS I
BEASLEY
BAY

BUCK I
GOOSE
PND

NEALS CREEK
INDIAN GAP I
INDIAN
GAP
LITTLE
GOAT I BAY

HUNTING
CREEK
NORTH
RIVER
158

DOWDY
BAY
SHOE
HOLE
BAY   PINE
BAY

GOAT
I BAY

DEEP CREEK

KNOTTS CREEK

DUCK CREEK
DEWS
DOWDY
BAY

12

BROAD CREEK

CAMDEN
COUNTY

158
Olds

DARE
COUNT

DUCK RD

A   B   C   D   E

SEE   39   MAP

MAP
19

REGIONAL MAP

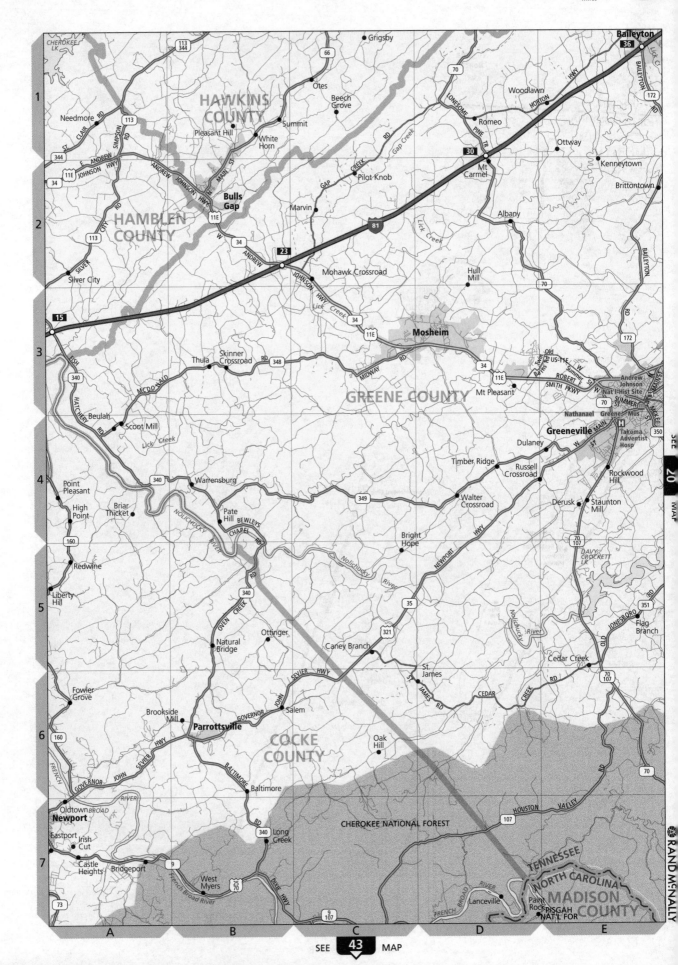

1:190,080
1 in. = 3 mi.

0   2   4
miles

MAP
20

REGIONAL MAP

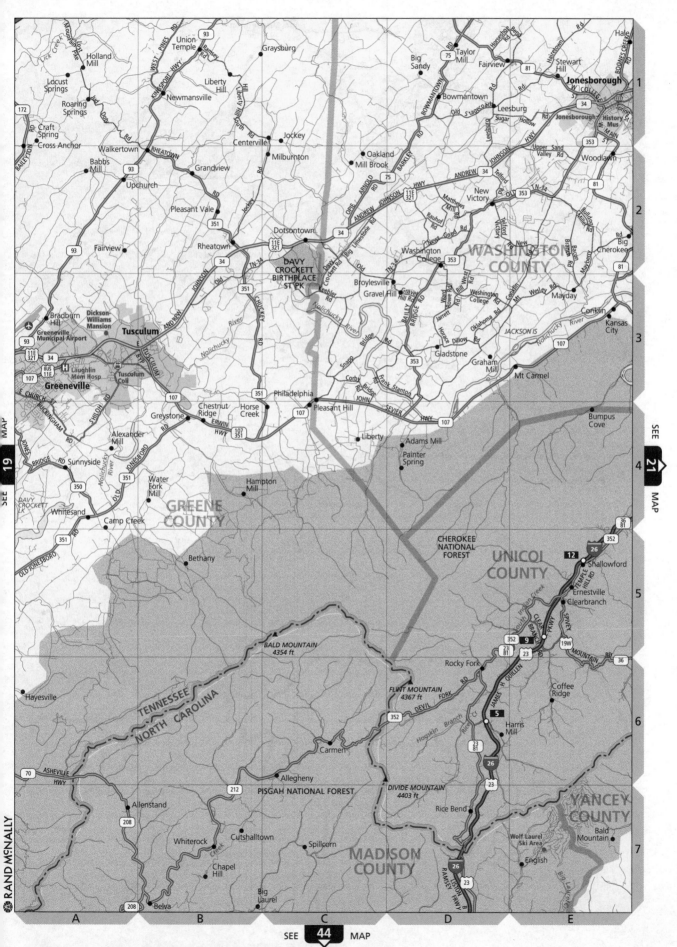

1:190,080
1 in. = 3 mi.

0   2   4
miles

A   B   C   D   E

SEE **44** MAP

SEE **19** MAP

SEE **21** MAP

MAP
21

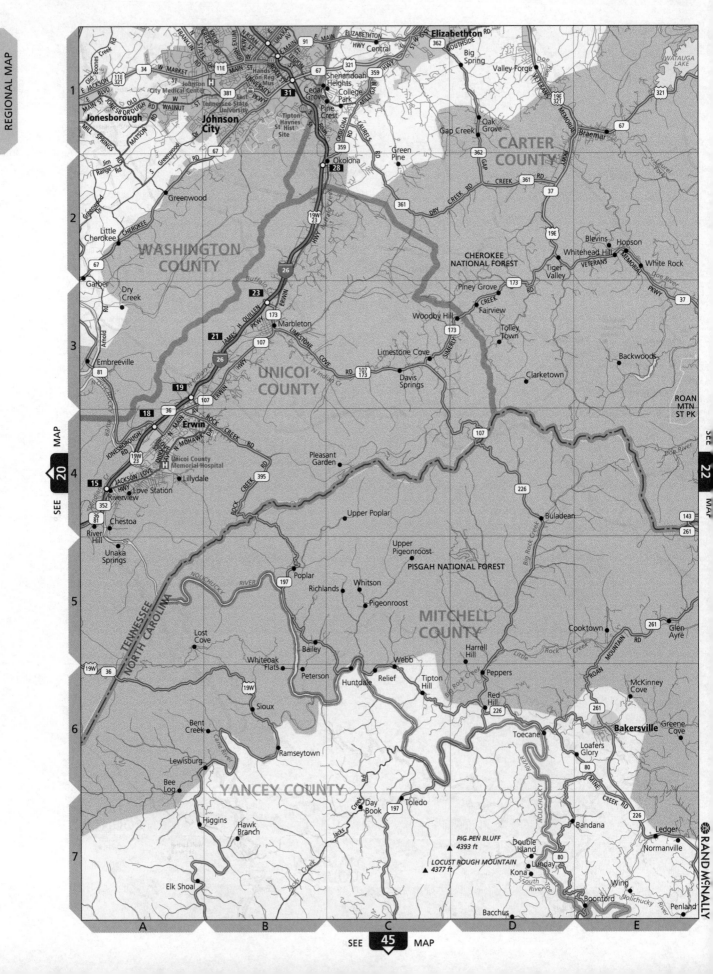

1:190,080
1 in. = 3 mi.

0   2   4
miles

N

Elizabethton

CARTER COUNTY

WASHINGTON COUNTY

Jonesborough

Johnson City

CHEROKEE NATIONAL FOREST

UNICOI COUNTY

Erwin

Unicoi County Memorial Hospital

ROAN MTN ST PK

PISGAH NATIONAL FOREST

MITCHELL COUNTY

Bakersville

TENNESSEE
NORTH CAROLINA

YANCEY COUNTY

PIG PEN BLUFF 4393 ft

LOCUST ROUGH MOUNTAIN 4377 ft

SEE MAP 20
SEE MAP 22
SEE 45 MAP

RAND McNALLY

A   B   C   D   E

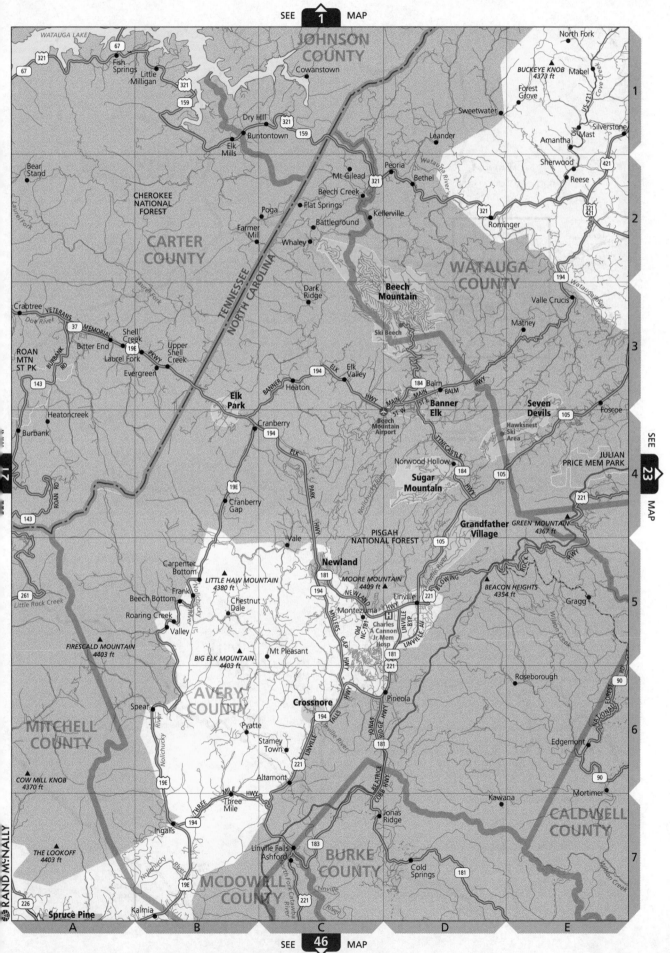

MAP
22

REGIONAL MAP

1:190,080
1 in. = 3 mi.
0   2   4
miles

SEE MAP 1

SEE 23 MAP

SEE 46 MAP

WATAUGA LAKE

67
321
67
Fish Springs
Little Milligan
321
159
321
159
Dry Hill
Buntontown
Elk Mills
Bear Stand

JOHNSON COUNTY
Cowanstown

North Fork
Mabel
BUCKEYE KNOB 4373 ft
Forest Grove
Sweetwater
Amantha
Mast
Silverstone
US-421
Cove Creek

CHEROKEE NATIONAL FOREST

CARTER COUNTY

Mt Gilead
Beech Creek
Flat Springs
Poga
Battleground
Farmer Mill
Whaley
Peoria
Bethel
Kellerville

321
321
Sherwood
Reese
Rominger
Leander
321
321 421
421
194
Watauga River

WATAUGA COUNTY

Dark Ridge
Beech Mountain
Valle Crucis
Matney

Laurel Fork
Doe River
Crabtree
VETERANS MEMORIAL
37
Shell Creek
Bitter End
19E
Laurel Fork
Upper Shell Creek
Evergreen
ROAN MTN ST PK
143
Heatoncreek
Burbank

BURBANK RD
ROAN RD

Ski Beech
Elk Valley
194
ELK HWY
Heaton
BANNER
Elk Park
Cranberry
194
184
Balm
BALM
Banner Elk
MAIN ST W
MAIN ST E
Beech Mountain Airport
Seven Devils
Hawksnest Ski Area
105
Foscoe
JULIAN PRICE MEM PARK

143
261
Little Rock Creek
Carpenter Bottom
Frank
Beech Bottom
Roaring Creek
Valley
FIRESCALD MOUNTAIN 4403 ft

ELK
PARK HWY

Vale
LITTLE HAW MOUNTAIN 4380 ft
Chestnut Dale
Big Elk Mountain 4403 ft
Mt Pleasant

AVERY COUNTY

Norwood Hollow
Sugar Mountain
184
TYNECASTLE
105
105
Grandfather Village
GREEN MOUNTAIN 4367 ft
221
BEACON HEIGHTS 4354 ft
Gragg

PISGAH NATIONAL FOREST

Newland
181
194
MOORE MOUNTAIN 4409 ft
NEWLAND
Linville
Montezuma
MILLERS GAP HWY
Old NC-181
Charles A Cannon Jr Mem Hosp
LINVILLE BYP
LINVILLE AV
221
Linville River
BLOWING ROCK HWY

Roseborough
90

MITCHELL COUNTY
COW MILL KNOB 4370 ft

Spear
Pyatte
Stamey Town
19E
221
Crossnore
194
Altamont
THREE MILE HWY
Ingalls
Three Mile
MILE HWY
194

LINVILLE FALLS HWY
181
221
Pineola
Kawana
Edgemont
90
Mortimer

BEATRICE COBB HWY

Jonas Ridge

CALDWELL COUNTY

THE LOOKOFF 4403 ft
19E
226
Spruce Pine
Kalmia
183
Linville Falls
Ashford

BURKE COUNTY
Cold Springs
181

MCDOWELL COUNTY
221
North Fork Catawba River
Linville River

TENNESSEE
NORTH CAROLINA

Wilson Creek
NATIONAL FOREST RD

1
2
3
4
5
6
7

A   B   C   D   E

RAND MCNALLY

MAP
23

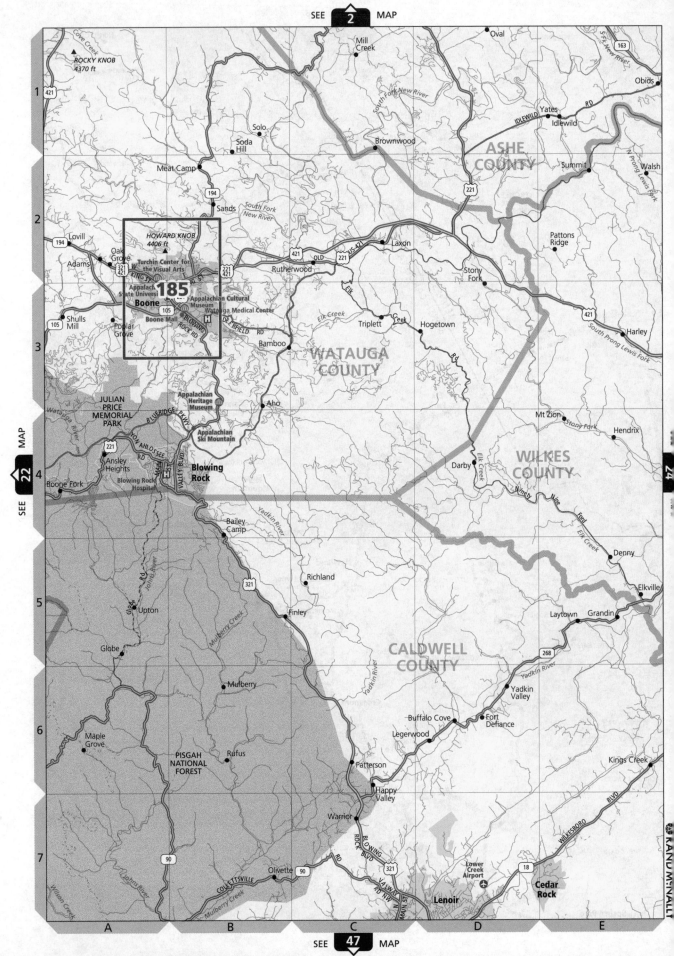

1:190,080
1 in. = 3 mi.

0   2   4
miles

SEE MAP **2**

SEE MAP **22**

SEE MAP **47**

RAND McNALLY

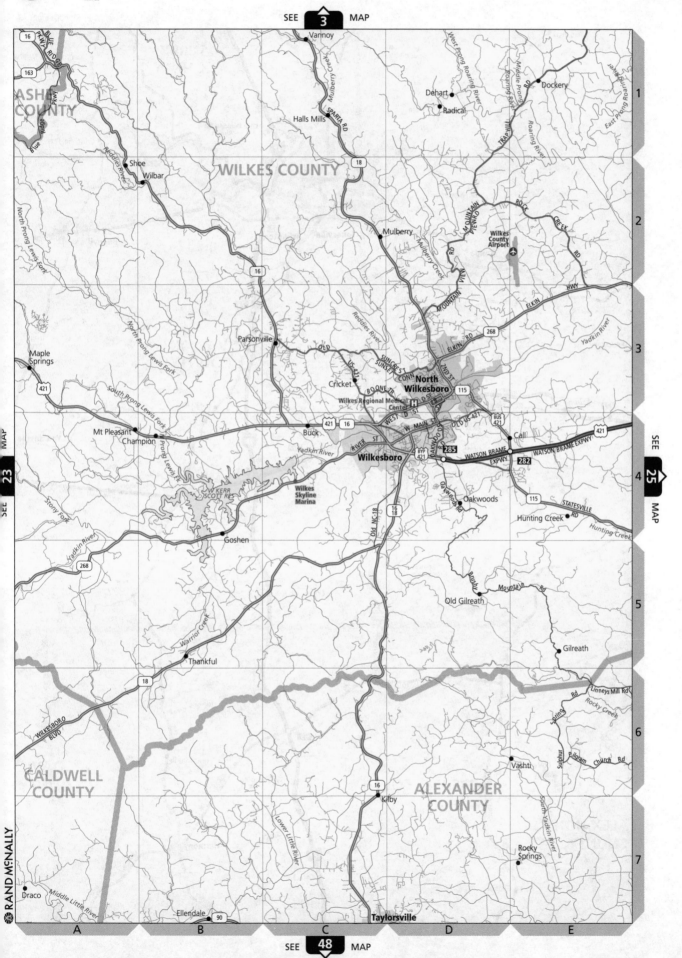

MAP
24

1:190,080
1 in. = 3 mi.
0   2   4
miles

SEE   MAP
3

Vannoy

16
163

West Prong Roaring River

Dockery

Dehart
Radical

ASHE
COUNTY

Halls Mills

SPARTA RD

Roaring River

Middle Prong Roaring River

East Prong Roaring River

1

Blue Ridge Pkwy

BLUE RIDGE PKWY

Reddies River

Shoe
Wilbar

WILKES COUNTY

18

Mulberry Creek

Mulberry

MOUNTAIN VIEW RD

Wilkes County Airport

ROCK CREEK RD

2

North Prong Lewis Fork

16

Reddies River

Mulberry Creek

MOUNTAIN VIEW RD

ELKIN HWY

268

Yadkin River

ELKIN RD

Maple Springs

South Prong Lewis Fork

Parsonville

OLD US-421

SUNCRE ST
SUNSET
CONN

North Wilkesboro

2ND ST

115

3

421

North Prong Lewis Fork

Cricket

BOONE TR

D ST

Wilkes Regional Medical Center

BUS 421

421

SEE
MAP
23

Mt Pleasant
Champion

Prong Lewis Fk

421
16

Buck

WEST D ST
RIVER ST
W MAIN ST

OAKWOOD RD

OLD US 421

Call

WATSON BRAME EXPWY

421

SEE
25
MAP

Stony Fork

Yadkin River

Wilkesboro

BYP 421

285

282

WATSON BRAME EXPWY

4

W KERR SCOTT RES

Wilkes Skyline Marina

Yadkin River

Oakwoods

115

STATESVILLE RD

Hunting Creek

268

Goshen

Old NC 18

GLENWOOD RD

Hunting Creek

5

Warrior Creek

Old Gilreath

Bushy Mountain Rd

Gilreath

Linneys Mill Rd

Spring Rd

Rocky Creek

18

Thankful

WILKESBORO BLVD

6

Sulphur Springs

Pilgram Church Rd

Vashti

South Yadkin River

CALDWELL COUNTY

16

ALEXANDER COUNTY

Kilby

Lower Little River

Rocky Springs

7

Draco

Middle Little River

Ellendale

90

RAND MCNALLY

SEE MAP

Taylorsville

A   B   C   D   E

SEE   **48**   MAP

MAP
25

REGIONAL MAP

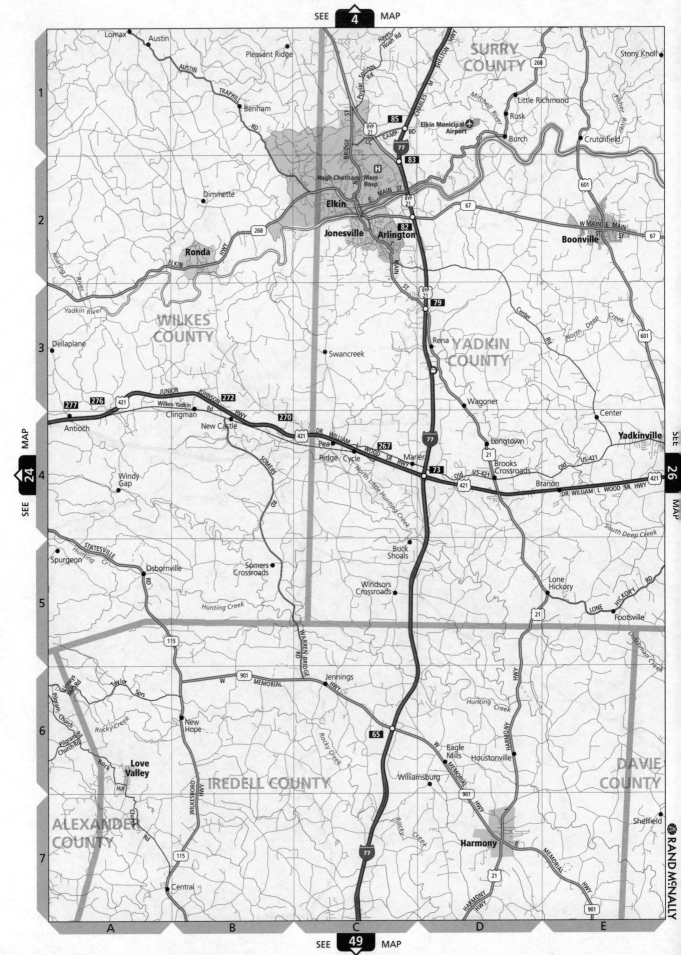

1:190,080
1 in. = 3 mi.

0   2   4
miles

SEE 4 MAP

SEE 24 MAP

SEE 26 MAP

SEE 49 MAP

RAND McNALLY

Lomax
Austin
Pleasant Ridge
Stony Knoll
AUSTIN
TRAPHILL
Benham
RD
SURRY COUNTY
268
Hayes Noah Rd
Mitchell River
Little Richmond
Rusk
Burch
Crutchfield
Popular Springs Rd
BRIDGE ST
CHARLES M SHELTON HWY
BYP 21
CAMP
CC
85
83
H
Hugh Chatham Mem Hosp
Elkin Municipal Airport
77
601
Dimmette
Elkin
E MAIN ST
BYP 21
82
67
W MAIN E MAIN ST
Boonville
67
Jonesville
Arlington
268
ELKIN
HWY
Ronda
MAIN ST
BYP 21
79
Riverlog River
Yadkin River
WILKES COUNTY
YADKIN COUNTY
Rena
Center Rd
North Deep Creek
601
Dellaplane
Swancreek
Wagoner
Center
Yadkinville
277 276
421
JUNIOR
JOHNSON
272
Wilkes-Yadkin Rd
HWY
270
421
DR WILLIAM L WOOD SR HWY
267
77
21
US-421
US-421
Old
421
Antioch
Clingman
New Castle
Pea Ridge
Cycle
Marler
73
Brooks Crossroads
Branon
DR WILLIAM L WOOD SR HWY
421
North Little Hunting Creek
SOMERS RD
Windy Gap
South Deep Creek
Spurgeon
Hunting Cr
STATESVILLE
Osbornville
Somers Crossroads
Buck Shoals
Lone Hickory
LONE HICKORY RD
Footsville
Dutchman Creek
Hunting Creek
RD
Windsors Crossroads
21
WARREN BRIDGE RD
115
W 901 MEMORIAL
Jennings HWY
Hunting Creek
HARMONY HWY
Cheers Mill Rd
Taylor Sprs
Pilgram Church
Pilgrant Church Rd
Rocky Creek
New Hope
65
Eagle Mills
W MEMORIAL
Houstonville
DAVIE COUNTY
Rocky Creek
Rock
Hill
Love Valley
WILKESBORO HWY
IREDELL COUNTY
Williamsburg
901
Sheffield
ALEXANDER COUNTY
Church Rd
77
Harmony
MEMORIAL HWY
115
21
HARMONY HWY
901
Central

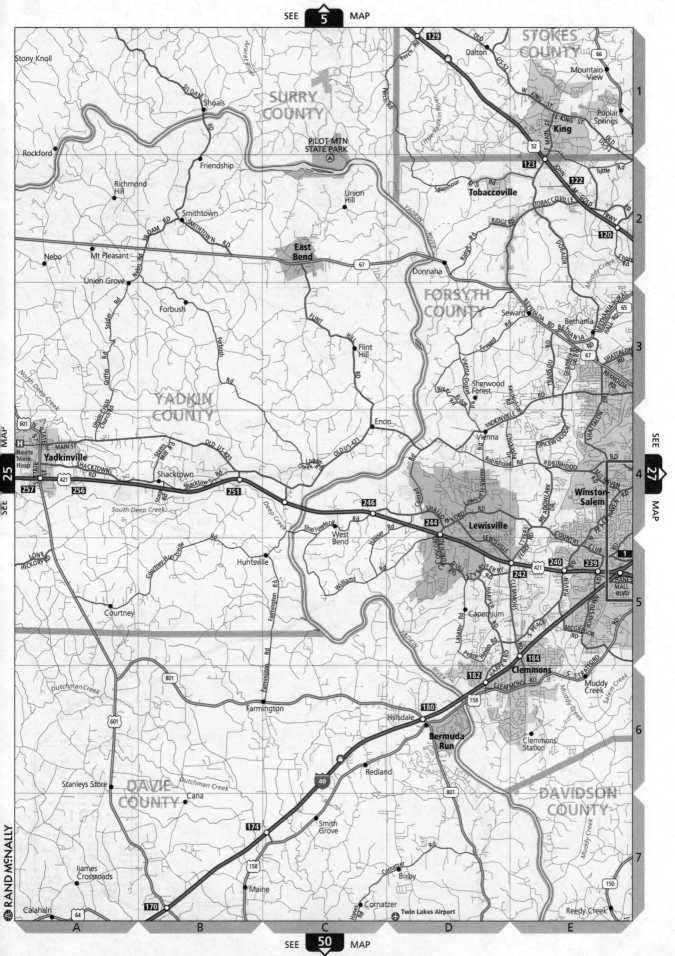

MAP
26

REGIONAL MAP

1:190,080
1 in. = 3 mi.

0   2   4
miles

SEE 5 MAP

SEE 25 MAP

SEE 27 MAP

SEE 50 MAP

RAND McNALLY

STOKES COUNTY

SURRY COUNTY

FORSYTH COUNTY

YADKIN COUNTY

DAVIE COUNTY

DAVIDSON COUNTY

Stony Knoll
Shoals
Rockford
Richmond Hill
Friendship
Nebo
Mt Pleasant
Union Grove
Forbush
Smithtown
PILOT MTN STATE PARK
Union Hill
East Bend
Donnaha
Dalton
Mountain View
Poplar Springs
King
Tobaccoville
Bethania
Seward
Sherwood Forest
Vienna
Yadkinville
Hoots Mem Hosp
Shacktown
Courtney
Huntsville
West Bend
Enon
Flint Hill
Lewisville
Winston-Salem
Clemmons
Capernium
Hillsdale
Bermuda Run
Clemmons Station
Muddy Creek
Stanleys Store
Cana
Farmington
Redland
Smith Grove
Ijames Crossroads
Maine
Calahaln
Bixby
Cornatzer
Twin Lakes Airport
Reedy Creek

A   B   C   D   E

1 2 3 4 5 6 7

MAP
27

REGIONAL MAP

1:190,080
1 in. = 3 mi.

0   2   4
miles

N

SEE **6** MAP

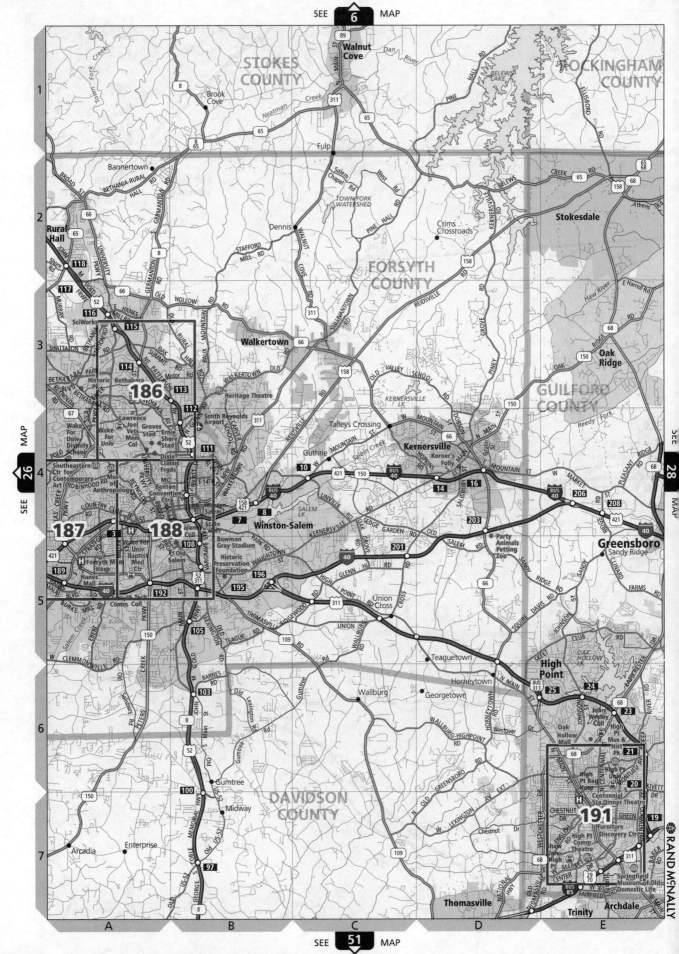

SEE **26** MAP

SEE **28** MAP

SEE **51** MAP

RAND M°NALLY

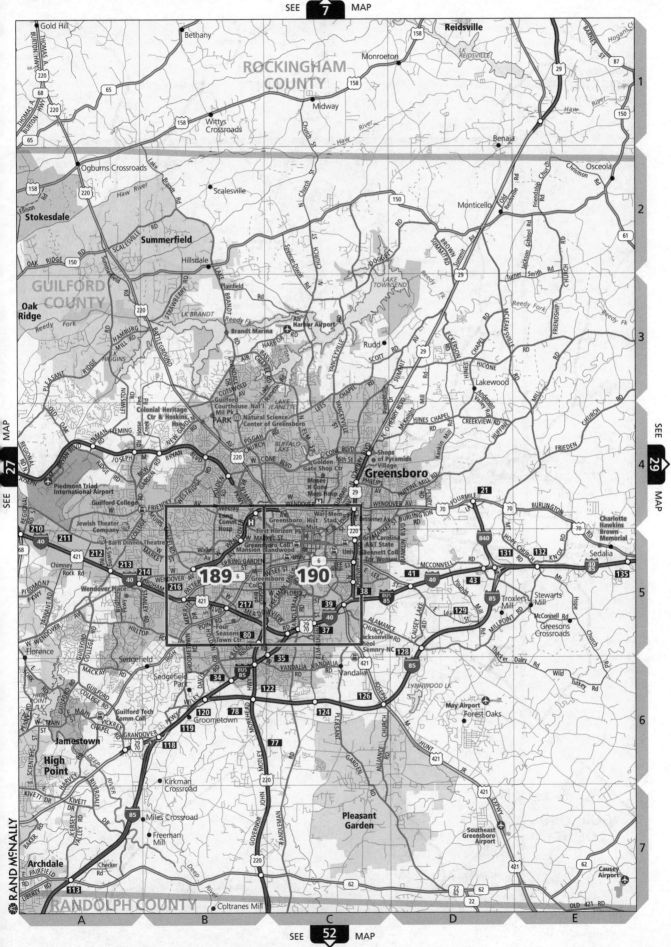

MAP
28

REGIONAL MAP

1:190,080
1 in. = 3 mi.

0   2   4
miles

N

Gold Hill

Bethany

Reidsville

158

Monroeton

LK REIDSVILLE

158

87

ROCKINGHAM COUNTY

29

150

Midway

1

BURTON HWY
THOMAS A RD
220

68

220

65

65

158

Wittys Crossroads

Church St

Haw River

Benaja

Osceola

Chrisman Rd

Ogburns Crossroads

Scalesville

Monticello

150

61

2

158

220

220

Stokesdale

Haw River

Ellison Rd

OAK RIDGE RD

150

Reedy Fork

Summerfield

Hillsdale

Plainfield

N CHURCH ST

DOGGETT

LAKE TOWNSEND

BROWN SUMMIT RD

SUMMIT AV

Reedy Fk

OLD REIDSVILLE RD

Jackson School Rd

FRIENDSHIP CHURCH RD

3

GUILFORD COUNTY

Oak Ridge

Reedy Fork

SCALESVILLE RD

STRAWBERRY RD

LK BRANDT

Air Harbor Airport

Brandt Marina

Rudd

29

SCOTT RD

ECKERSON RD

MCLEANSVILLE RD

Reedy Fk

220

BATTLEGROUND

HAMBURG MILL RD

HIGGINS

LEWISTON RD

AIR HARBOR RD

HARBOR

LAKE JEANETTE

LEES CHAPEL

N ELM

N O'HENRY BLVD

HINES CHAPEL RD

HICONE

Lakewood

Anderson Valley Rd

CREEKVIEW RD

HINES CHAPEL RD

RANKIN MILL RD

HUFFINE

FRIEDEN

4

SEE **27** MAP

PLEASANT RIDGE RD

OLD OAK RIDGE RD

INMAN FLEMING

JOSEPH M BRYAN

NEW GARDEN RD

Colonial Heritage Ctr & Hoskins Hse

Guilford Courthouse Nat'l Mil Pk

PARK

Natural Science Center of Greensboro

PISGAH CHURCH

COTSWOLD AV

BUFFALO LAKE

16th St

W CONE BLVD

E CONE BLVD

Golden Gate Shop Ctr

Moses H Cone Mem Hosp

29

Shops of Pyramids Village

Greensboro

Phillips

HUFFINE MILL RD

FOURMILE

21

70

BURLINGTON

Charlotte Hawkins Brown Memorial

840

Piedmont Triad International Airport

REGIONAL RD

JOSEPH

210

40

211

68

421

212

Chimney Rock Rd

213

214

40

Guilford College

Jewish Theater Company

Barn Dinner Theatre

FRIENDLY AV

W MARKET ST

MARKET ST

Walker Av

SPRING GARDEN

Wesley Long Comm Hosp

H

Greensboro Coll

Greensboro Hist Mus

First Horizon Pk

Blandwood

Mansion

UNCG

War Mem'l Stad

Bennett Coll for Women

6

38

BESSEMER AV

E MARKET ST

N C A&T State Univ

BUS 85

E LEE ST

FRANKLIN BLVD

BURLINGTON RD

70

MCCONNELL

131

132

Sedalia

189 6

190

220

216

WENDOVER

GUILFORD COLLEGE RD

HOLDEN RD

B MARTIN

GROOMETOWN RD

417

STANLEY RD

HILLTOP

PATTERSON

421

40

MERR

MEADOWVIEW

Four Seasons Town Ctr

80

217

37

40

39

PLEASANT GARDEN

29 70

LEE ST

RANDLEMAN RD

S ELM EUGENE ST

S FLORIDA ST

ALAMANCE CHURCH RD

128

85

41

MCCONNELL RD

43

129

LEE

Troxlers Mill

Stewarts Mill

McConnell Rd

Greesons Crossroads

135

MILLPOINT

Jacksonville RD

Semnry-NC

CAUSEY LAKE

HOPE RD

YOUNGS

5

Wendover Place

PIEDMONT PKWY

TARRANT RD

W WENDOVER AV

Florence

Sedgefield

Sedgefield Park

HIGH POINT RD

WILEY DAVIS RD

NORWOOD RD

34

BUS 85

122

35

VANDALIA RD

Nandalia RD

Vandalia

421

126

LYNWOOD LK

May Airport

Forest Oaks

JOSEPH M HUNT JR

6

COLLEGE RD

GUILFORD COLLEGE RD

Guilford Tech Comm Coll

W MAIN

VICKREY CHAPEL RD

120

78

124

77

MOTLEY RD

PLEASANT GARDEN RD

ALLIANCE CHURCH RD

421

Jamestown

29 70

118

119

Groometown

High Point

Kirkman Crossroad

220

Pleasant Garden

421

85

Miles Crossroad

Freeman Mill

GOVERNOR JOHN MOTLEY

RANDLEMAN RD

Deep River

220

62

421

EXPY

Southeast Greensboro Airport

7

S SCIENTIFIC ST
W MAIN ST

PENNY RD

S MAIN ST

PIEDMONT PKWY

KIVETT DR

DEEP RIVER

Archdale

E FAIRFIELD RD

Checker Rd

Coltranes Mill

62

62

22 62

Causey Airport

62

22

OLD 421 RD

RANDOLPH COUNTY

113

BAKER RD
LIBERTY RD
BARVEY

KIVETT DR
KERSEY
VALLEY RD

A   B   C   D   E

MAP
29

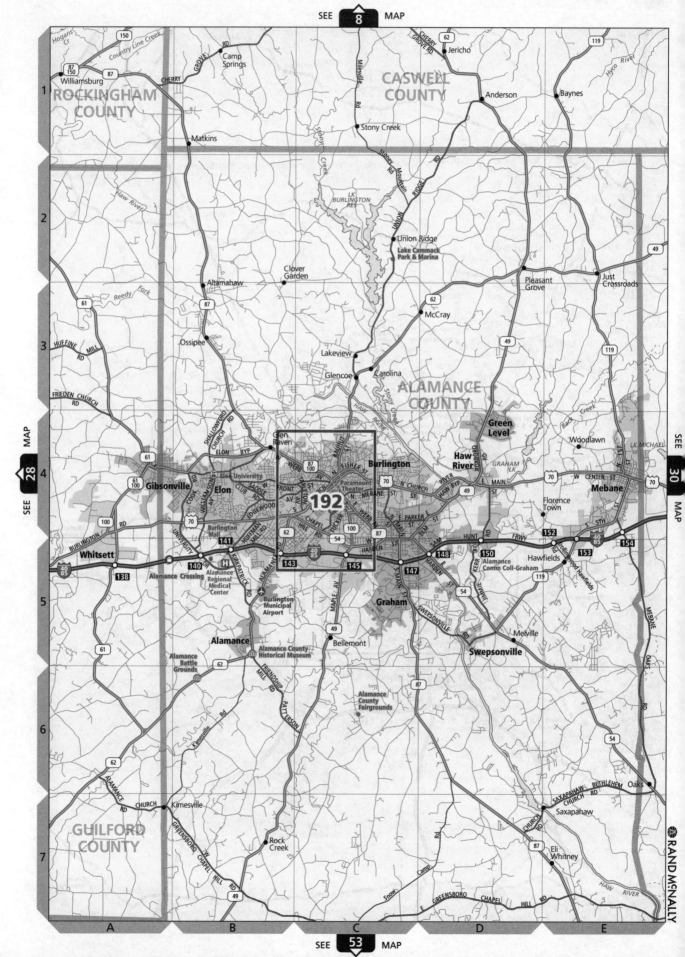

1:190,080
1 in. = 3 mi.

0   2   4
miles

SEE **8** MAP

ROCKINGHAM COUNTY

CASWELL COUNTY

ALAMANCE COUNTY

GUILFORD COUNTY

SEE **28** MAP

SEE **30** MAP

SEE **53** MAP

RAND McNALLY

MAP
30

1:190,080
1 in. = 3 mi.

miles

SEE **9** MAP

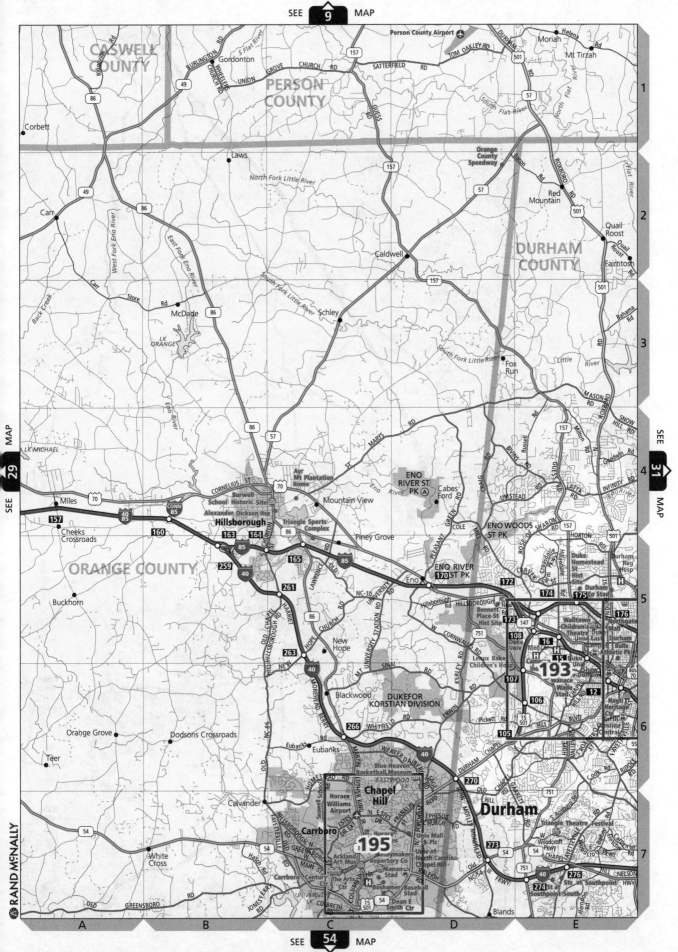

SEE **29** MAP

SEE **31** MAP

SEE **54** MAP

RAND McNALLY

MAP
31

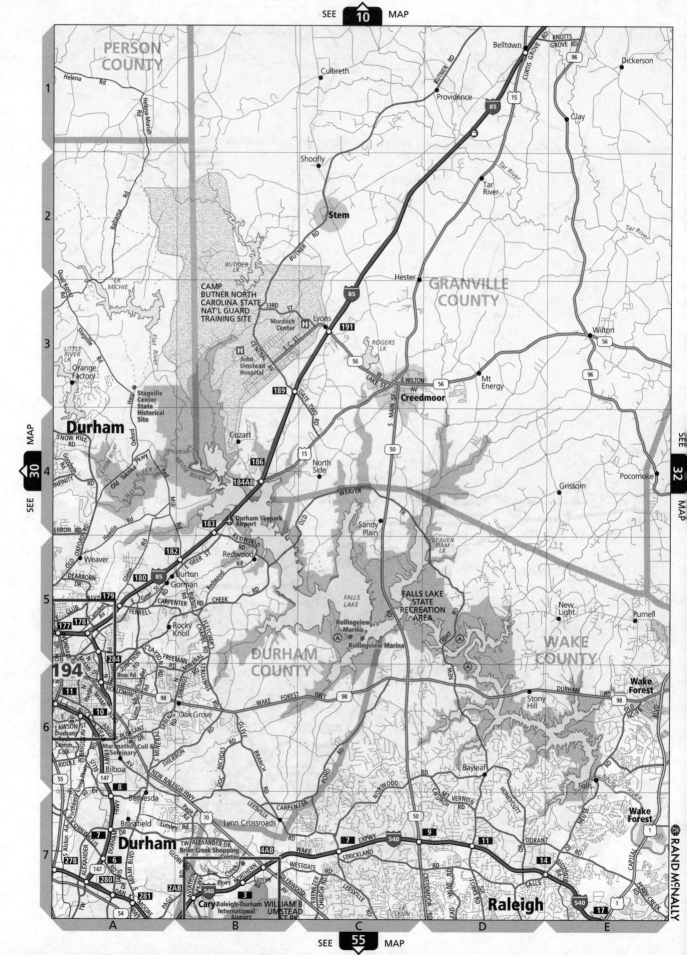

1:190,080
1 in. = 3 mi.

0   2   4
miles

N

REGIONAL MAP

SEE **30** MAP

SEE **32** MAP

SEE **55** MAP

RAND M°NALLY

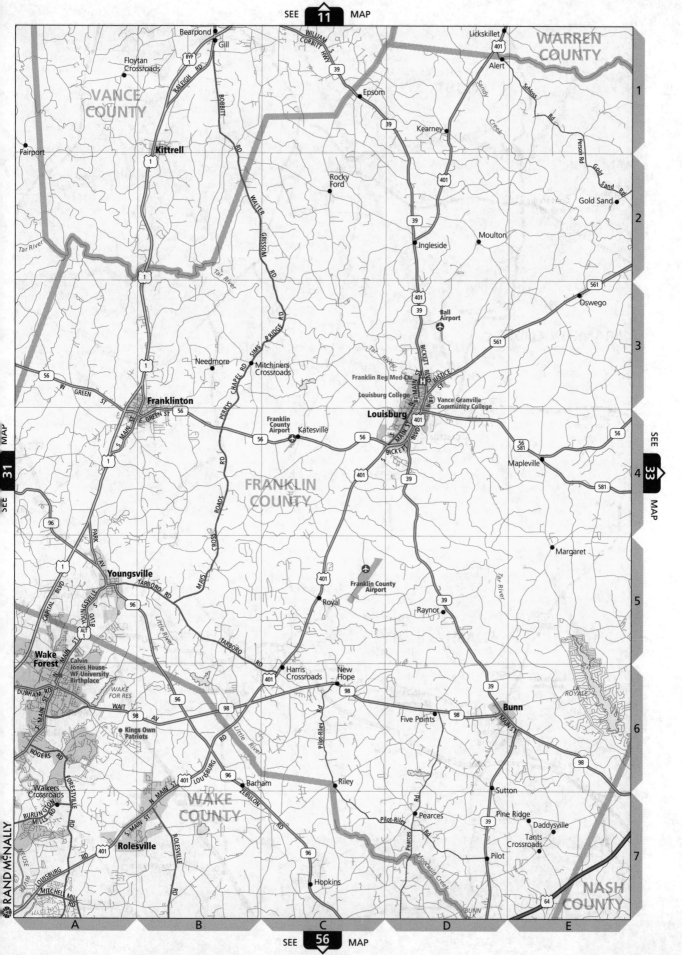

MAP
32

REGIONAL MAP

1:190,080
1 in. = 3 mi.

0   2   4
miles

SEE 11 MAP

WARREN COUNTY

Lickskillet

VANCE COUNTY

Floytan Crossroads

Bearpond

Gill

Alert

BYP 1

RALEIGH RD

1

Fairport

Kittrell

1

BOBBITT RD

WALTER GRISSOM RD

WILLIAM CORBITT HWY

Epsom

39

Kearney

Sandy Creek

Schloss Rd

Person Rd

Gold Sand Rd

2

Gold Sand

Rocky Ford

401

39

Moulton

Ingleside

561

Oswego

56

W GREEN ST

GREEN ST

Needmore

SIMS BRIDGE RD

CHAPEL RD

Mitchiners Crossroads

PERRYS

Tar River

BICKETT BLVD

JUSTICE

Franklin Reg Med Ctr.

Louisburg College

N MAIN ST

Vance Granville Community College

561

3

Franklinton

56

Louisburg

401

56 581

56

SEE 33 MAP

1

Franklin County Airport

Katesville

56

BICKETT

S MAIN ST

BLVD

401

39

Mapleville

56

581

4

CROSS ROADS RD

MAYS RD

FRANKLIN COUNTY

401

Franklin County Airport

39

Margaret

96

1

PARK AV

YOUNGSVILLE BLVD S

Youngsville

TARBORO RD

96

Little River

TARBORO RD

Royal

401

Raynor

39

Tar River

LK ROYALE

5

ALT 1

MAIN ST

Wake Forest

Calvin Jones House-WF University Birthplace

WAKE FOR RES

98

WAIT AV

Kings Own Patriots

96

98

Harris Crossroads

401

New Hope

98

PILOT-RILEY RD

Five Points

98

98

Bunn

MAIN S

6

ROGERS RD

DURHAM RD

S MAIN ST

FORESTVILLE RD

LOUISBURG RD

Little River

96

Barham

ZEBULON RD

Riley

Pilot-Riley

Sutton

98

7

BURLINGTON MILLS RD

Walkers Crossroads

401

Rolesville

N MAIN ST

ROLESVILLE RD

ROLESVILLE RD

401

WAKE COUNTY

96

Pearces

Pearces Rd

39

Pilot-Riley Rd

Pilot

Pine Ridge

Daddysville

Tants Crossroads

LOUISBURG RD

MITCHELL MILL RD

Hopkins

96

Moccasin Creek

BUNN BLK

64

NASH COUNTY

RAND McNALLY

SEE 56 MAP

A   B   C   D   E

MAP
33

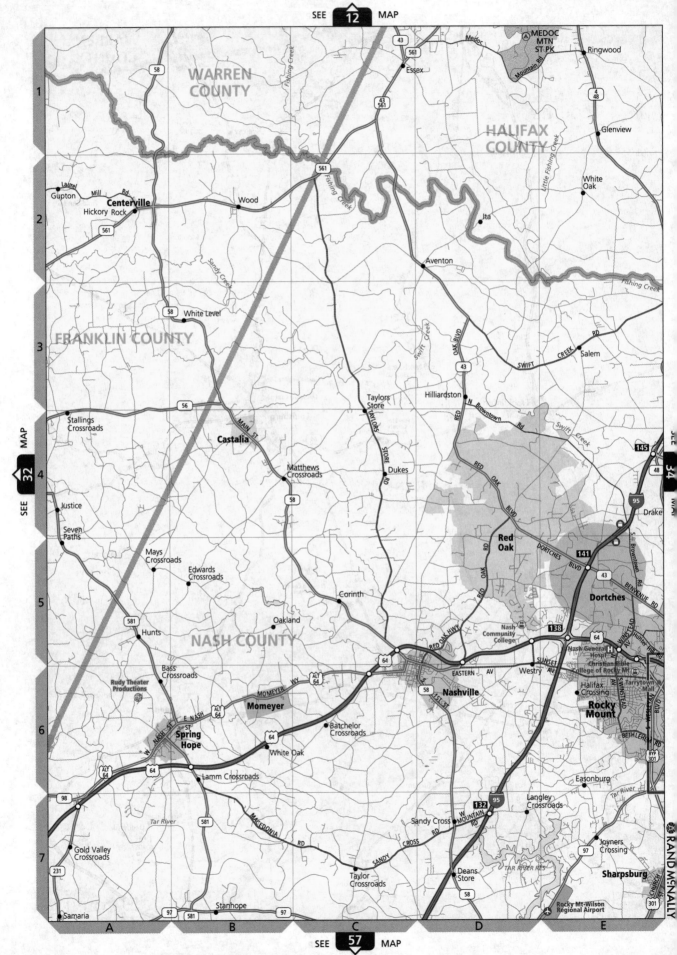

1:190,080
1 in. = 3 mi.

0   2   4
miles

WARREN COUNTY

HALIFAX COUNTY

FRANKLIN COUNTY

NASH COUNTY

SEE 32 MAP

SEE 34 MAP

MEDOC MTN ST PK

Ringwood
Essex
Glenview
White Oak
Ita
Aventon
Salem
Hilliardston
Taylors Store
Dukes
Red Oak
Dortches
Drake
Corinth
Oakland
Nash Community College
Nash General Hosp.
Christian Bible College of Rocky Mt
Westry
Rocky Mount
Halifax Crossing
Tarrytown Mall
Nashville
Batchelor Crossroads
White Oak
Momeyer
Spring Hope
Lamm Crossroads
Bass Crossroads
Rudy Theater Productions
Edwards Crossroads
Mays Crossroads
Hunts
Seven Paths
Justice
Stallings Crossroads
Castalia
Matthews Crossroads
White Level
Wood
Centerville
Hickory Rock
Gupton
Laurel Mill Rd
Sandy Cross
Deans Store
Langley Crossroads
Easonburg
Joyners Crossing
Sharpsburg
Rocky Mt-Wilson Regional Airport
Taylor Crossroads
Gold Valley Crossroads
Samaria
Stanhope

RAND McNALLY

A   B   C   D   E

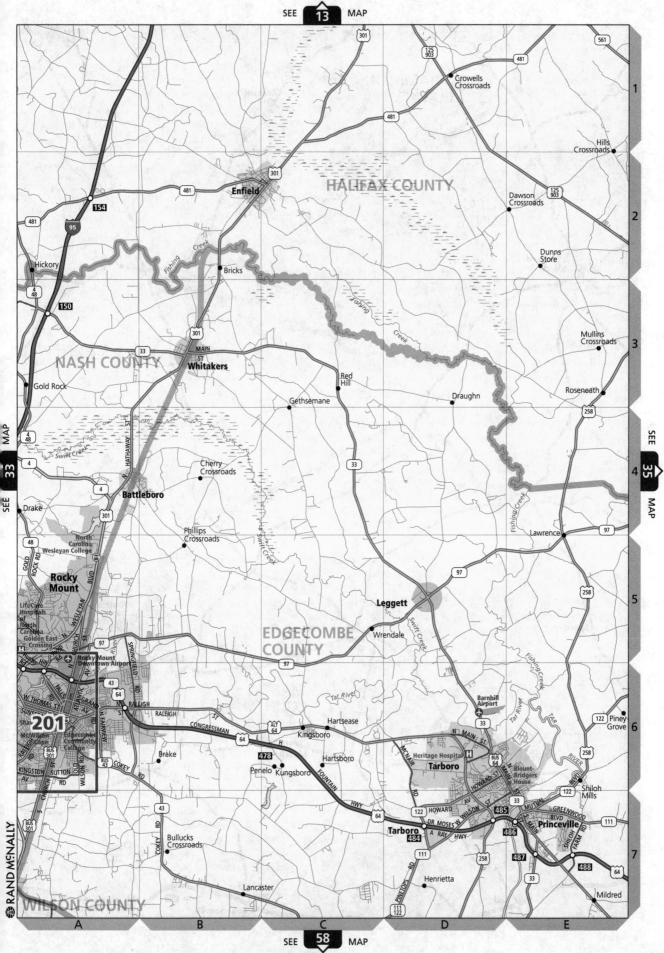

MAP
34
REGIONAL MAP

1:190,080
1 in. = 3 mi.

miles
0   2   4

SEE 13 MAP

561
301
301
125
903
481

Crowells
Crossroads

481

Hills
Crossroads

1

481

154
481

HALIFAX COUNTY

Enfield

301

Dawson
Crossroads

125
903

2

95

Dunns
Store

Hickory

Bricks

Fishing   Creek

150

4
48

Fishing   Creek

301

33

MAIN
ST

Mullins
Crossroads

NASH COUNTY

Whitakers

3

Gold Rock

Red
Hill

Roseneath

Gethsemane

Draughn

258

SEE 35 MAP

4
48

4

Cherry
Crossroads

33

Swift Creek

HATHAWAY ST

4

Battleboro

Drake

301

Phillips
Crossroads

Lawrence

97

48

North
Carolina
Wesleyan College

97

258

GOLD ROCK RD

Rocky
Mount

Swift   Creek

Leggett

5

LifeCare
Hospitals
of North
Carolina
Golden East
Crossing

97

EDGECOMBE
COUNTY

Wrendale

Fishing Creek

CHURCH ST

WESLEYAN

Rocky Mount
Downtown Airport

97

Tar River

Barnhill
Airport

SPRINGFIELD RD

43

Tar River

122 Piney
Grove

64

N RALEIGH

33

6

W THOMAS ST

N FAIRVIEW

RALEIGH   ST

CONGRESSMAN

ALT
64

Hartsease

N MAIN ST

258

201

ATLANTIC AV

LA GRANGE

64

L

Kingsboro

McNAIR RD

Heritage Hospital H

BUS
64

Blount-
Bridgers House

Mt Wilson

Edgecombe
Community
College

BUS
43

H

Brake

478

Hartsboro

FOUNTAIN

Tarboro

122

Shiloh
Mills

RALEIGH
KINGSTON
AV

OLD WILSON RD

COKEY RD

Penelo   Kungsboro

HOWARD ST

33

485

GREENWOOD
BLVD

111

BUS
301

SUTTON
RD

43

COKEY RD

64

122 HOWARD

DR MOSES W WILSON ST

486

Princeville

Bullucks
Crossroads

Tarboro

484

A RAY HWY

258

SHILOH FARM RD

7

BUS
301

111

PINETOPS RD

Henrietta

487

33

488

64

Lancaster

111
122

Mildred

WILSON COUNTY

A   B   C   D   E

SEE 58 MAP

MAP
35

REGIONAL MAP

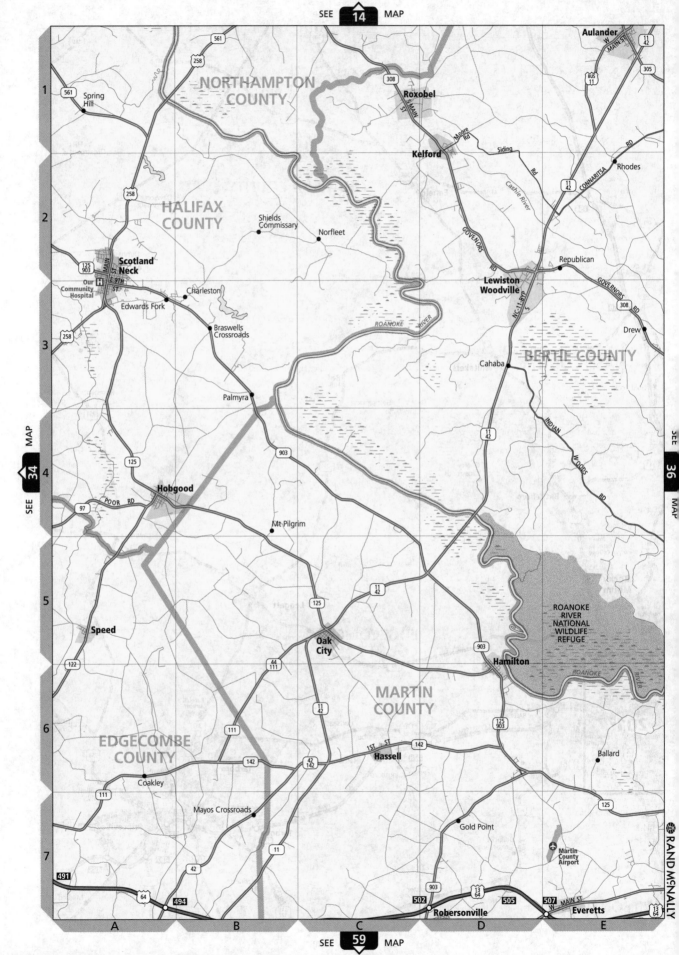

1:190,080
1 in. = 3 mi.

0   2   4
miles

SEE 14 MAP

SEE 34 MAP

SEE 36 MAP

SEE 59 MAP

RAND McNALLY

NORTHAMPTON COUNTY

HALIFAX COUNTY

BERTIE COUNTY

MARTIN COUNTY

EDGECOMBE COUNTY

ROANOKE RIVER NATIONAL WILDLIFE REFUGE

561
258
308
11 42
305
BUS 11

Spring Hill
Aulander
Roxobel
Kelford
Rhodes

258
Shields Commissary
Norfleet
Siding
11 42
CONNARITSA

Scotland Neck
Our Community Hospital
Charleston
Edwards Fork
Braswells Crossroads
Lewiston Woodville
Republican
308
GOVERNORS RD
Drew

125 903
258
Palmyra
Cahaba
11 42
INDIAN WOODS RD

125
Hobgood
97
POOR RD
903
Mt Pilgrim

Speed
125
11 42
903
Hamilton
ROANOKE RIVER

122
Oak City
44 111
MARTIN COUNTY
125 903
Ballard

111
42 142
Hassell
1ST ST
142
125

Coakley
142
Gold Point
Mayos Crossroads

11
42
Martin County Airport

491
64
494
502
903
13 64
505
507
W MAIN ST
Everetts
13 64

Robersonville

A   B   C   D   E

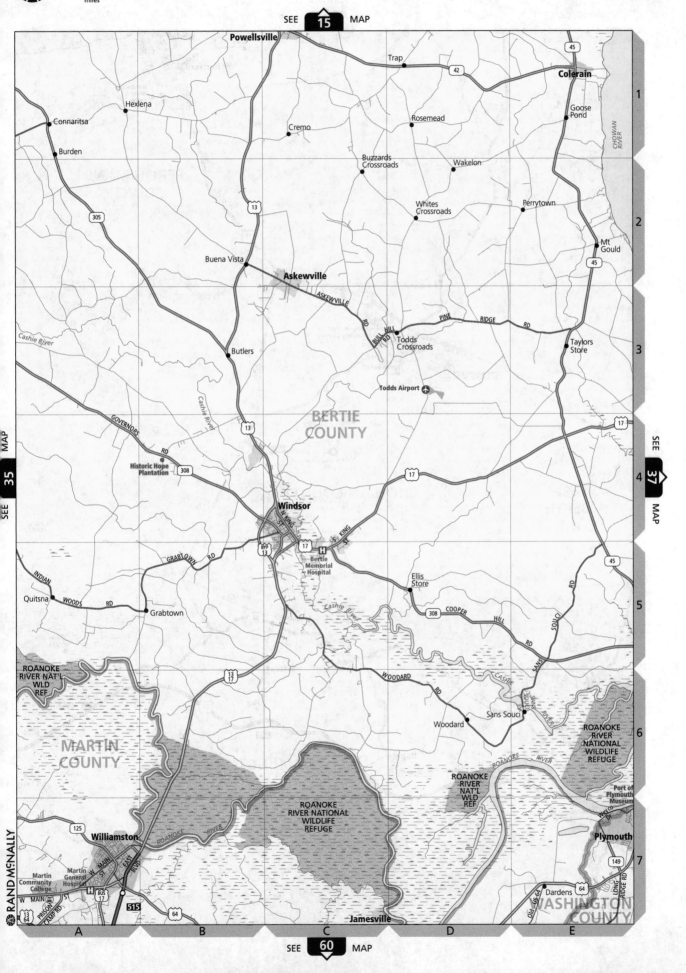

MAP
36

REGIONAL MAP

1:190,080
1 in. = 3 mi.

0   2   4
miles

SEE 15 MAP

Powellsville

Trap

Colerain

45

42

Hexlena

Goose
Pond

1

Connaritsa

Cremo

Rosemead

Burden

Buzzards
Crossroads

Wakelon

305

Whites
Crossroads

Perrytown

2

13

Mt
Gould

Buena Vista

45

Askewville

ASKEWVILLE

RD

PINE   RIDGE   RD

BULL HILL RD

Todds
Crossroads

Taylors
Store

3

Butlers

CHOWAN RIVER

Cashie River

Cashie River

Todds Airport

BERTIE
COUNTY

17

GOVERNORS

17

SEE 37 MAP

RD

308

Historic Hope
Plantation

13

17

4

SEE 35 MAP

Windsor

N KING ST

S. KING ST

BYP
13

17

H

Bertie
Memorial
Hospital

45

GRABTOWN   RD

Ellis
Store

INDIAN

Quitsna

WOODS   RD

Grabtown

Cashie River

308

COOPER   HILL

RD

SANS SOUCI RD

5

ROANOKE
RIVER NAT'L
WLD
REF

WOODARD

RD

CASHIE

Sans Souci

SANS SOUCI RIVER

13
17

MARTIN
COUNTY

Woodard

ROANOKE
RIVER
NATIONAL
WILDLIFE
REFUGE

6

ROANOKE
RIVER
NAT'L
WLD
REF

ROANOKE   RIVER

Port of
Plymouth
Museum

125

Williamston

ROANOKE   RIVER

ROANOKE
RIVER NATIONAL
WILDLIFE
REFUGE

Plymouth

WCo Dr.

Martin
Community
College

Martin
General
Hospital

H

W. MAIN ST

EAST   BLVD

BUS
17

149

7

13
64

W MAIN ST

PRISON CAMP RD

515

64

Old US 64

Dardens

64

LONG RIDGE RD

WASHINGTON
COUNTY

Jamesville

A   B   C   D   E

SEE 60 MAP

MAP
37

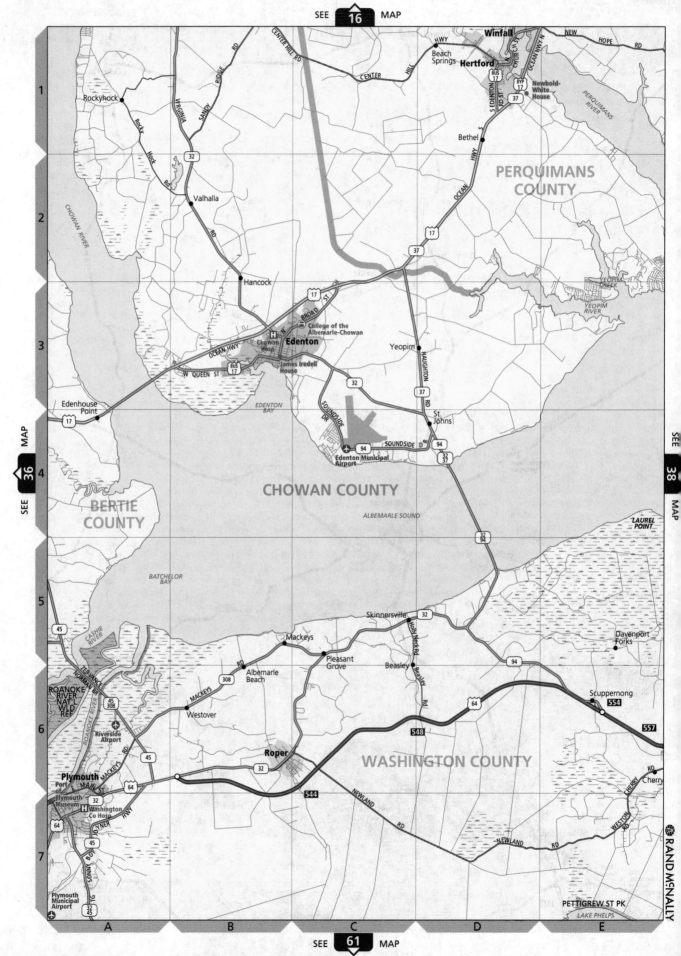

1:190,080
1 in. = 3 mi.

0   2   4
miles

SEE **16** MAP

Winfall
Hertford
Beach Springs
Newbold-White House
NEW HOPE RD
CTR CH ST
OCEAN HWY N
BUS 17
BYP 17
37
S EDENTON RD ST

Rockyhock

CENTER HILL RD
CENTER HILL RD
CENTER
VIRGINIA
SANDY RIDGE RD
ROCKY HOCK RD

32

Valhalla

Bethel
OCEAN HWY S

PERQUIMANS COUNTY

CHOWAN RIVER

Hancock

17

17
37

YEOPIM CREEK
YEOPIM RIVER

BROAD ST
College of the Albemarle-Chowan
Chowan Hosp.
Edenton
James Iredell House
OCEAN HWY
BUS 17
W QUEEN ST

Yeopim

HAUGHTON RD
37

Edenhouse Point
17

EDENTON BAY

SOUNDSIDE DR

St. Johns
94
SOUNDSIDE DR
32 37

SEE **36** MAP

BERTIE COUNTY

CHOWAN COUNTY

ALBEMARLE SOUND

Edenton Municipal Airport
94

32 94

LAUREL POINT

SEE **38** MAP

BATCHELOR BAY

45

CASHIE RIVER

Skinnersville
32

Mackeys
Pleasant Grove
Beasley
HOLLY NECK RD
BEASLEY RD

94

Davenport Forks

ZEB VANCE
NORMAN BR
ROANOKE RIVER NAT'L WLD REF
45 308
MACKEYS RD
Albemarle Beach
308
MACKEYS
Westover

Scuppernong
554

64
548

557

Riverside Airport
45
Roper
32

WASHINGTON COUNTY

557

Plymouth
Port of Plymouth Museum
MAIN ST
MACKEYS
64
45
32
Washington Co Hosp
JOYNER HWY
64
45
SONNY RD

544
NEWLAND RD

NEWLAND RD

CHERRY RD
Cherry
WESTON RD

Plymouth Municipal Airport
32 45

PETTIGREW ST PK
LAKE PHELPS

RAND MCNALLY

A   B   C   D   E

SEE **61** MAP

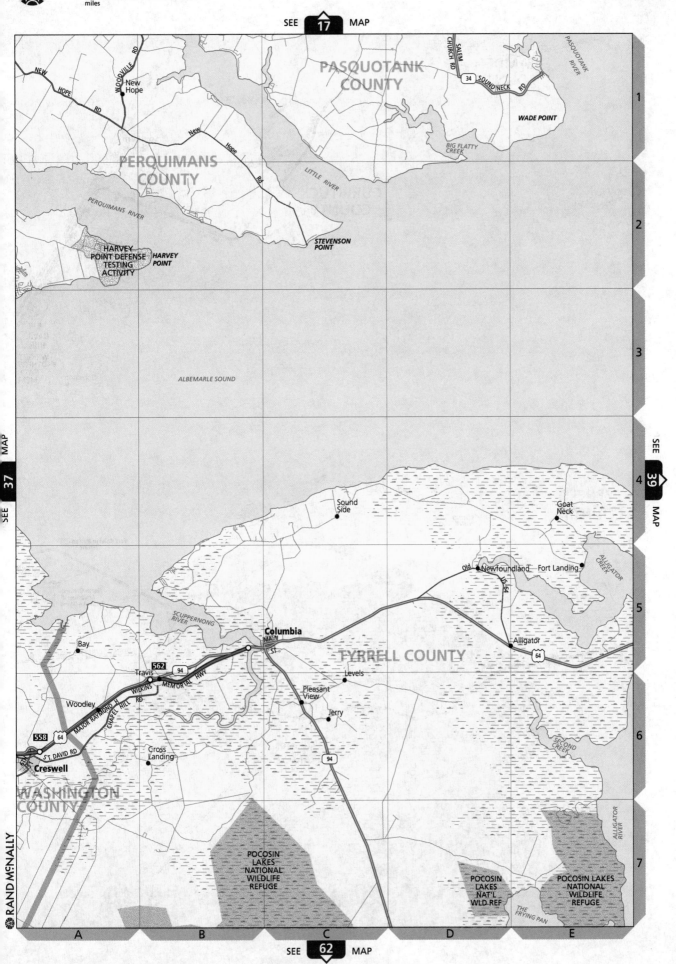

MAP
38

REGIONAL MAP

1:190,080
1 in. = 3 mi.

0   2   4
miles

SEE **17** MAP

SEE **37** MAP

SEE **39** MAP

SEE **62** MAP

PASQUOTANK COUNTY

WOODVILLE RD

NEW HOPE RD

New Hope

New Hope Rd

SALEM CHURCH RD

34 SOUND NECK RD

PASQUOTANK RIVER

WADE POINT

BIG FLATTY CREEK

PERQUIMANS COUNTY

PERQUIMANS RIVER

LITTLE RIVER

STEVENSON POINT

HARVEY POINT DEFENSE TESTING ACTIVITY

HARVEY POINT

ALBEMARLE SOUND

Sound Side

Goat Neck

ALLIGATOR CREEK

Old Newfoundland Fort Landing

US 64

SCUPPERNONG RIVER

Bay

Columbia
MAIN ST

TYRRELL COUNTY

Alligator
64

562
94
Travis

Levels

Pleasant View

Jerry

SECOND CREEK

Woodley

MAJOR RAYMOND H MEMORIAL HWY

WILKINS RD

CHAPEL HILL RD

558
64
ST. DAVID RD

Creswell

Cross Landing

94

WASHINGTON COUNTY

POCOSIN LAKES NATIONAL WILDLIFE REFUGE

POCOSIN LAKES NAT'L WLD. REF.

POCOSIN LAKES NATIONAL WILDLIFE REFUGE

THE FRYING PAN

ALLIGATOR RIVER

RAND M°NALLY

A   B   C   D   E

MAP
39

1:190,080
1 in. = 3 mi.

0   2   4
miles

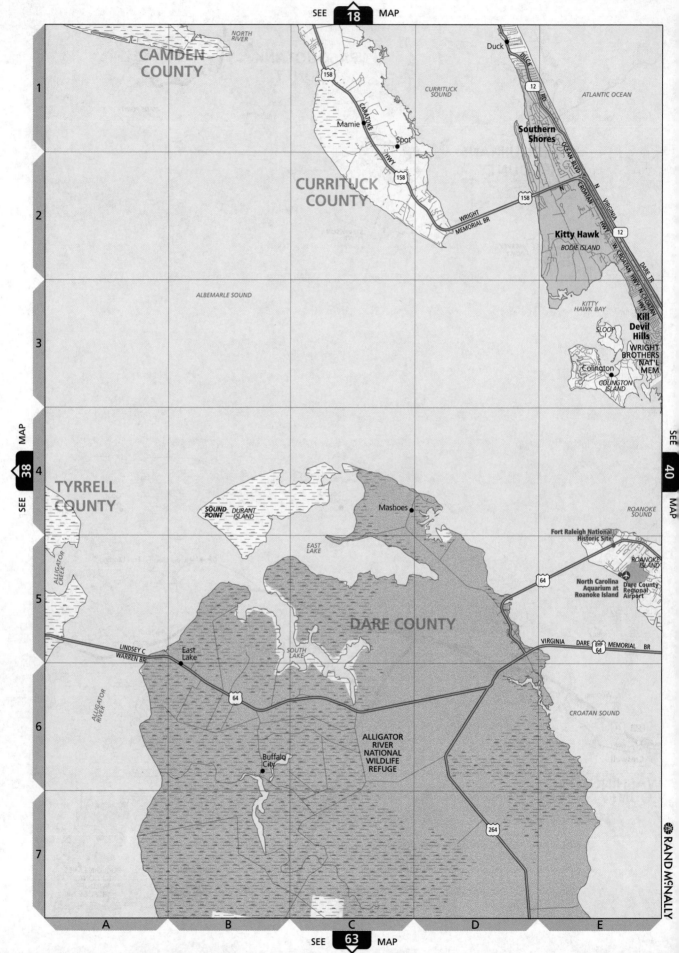

SEE 18 MAP

N

CAMDEN
COUNTY

NORTH
RIVER

Duck

CURRITUCK
SOUND

ATLANTIC OCEAN

12

Mamie

Spot

Southern
Shores

CURRITUCK
COUNTY

158

WRIGHT
MEMORIAL BR

OCEAN BLVD

N. CROATAN HWY

N. VIRGINIA DARE TR

Kitty Hawk

BODIE ISLAND

12

W. CROATAN HWY

ALBEMARLE SOUND

KITTY
HAWK BAY

SLOOP

Kill
Devil
Hills

WRIGHT
BROTHERS
NAT'L
MEM

Colington

COLINGTON
ISLAND

SEE 38 MAP

TYRRELL
COUNTY

SOUND
POINT

DURANT
ISLAND

EAST
LAKE

Mashoes

ROANOKE
SOUND

Fort Raleigh National
Historic Site

ROANOKE
ISLAND

SEE 40 MAP

ALLIGATOR
CREEK

DARE COUNTY

North Carolina
Aquarium at
Roanoke Island

Dare County
Regional
Airport

64

LINDSEY C
WARREN BR

East
Lake

SOUTH
LAKE

VIRGINIA DARE BYP 64 MEMORIAL BR

CROATAN SOUND

64

ALLIGATOR
RIVER

ALLIGATOR
RIVER
NATIONAL
WILDLIFE
REFUGE

Buffalo
City

264

RAND MCNALLY

A   B   C   D   E

1

2

3

4

5

6

7

MAP
40

1:190,080
1 in. = 3 mi.

0   2   4
miles

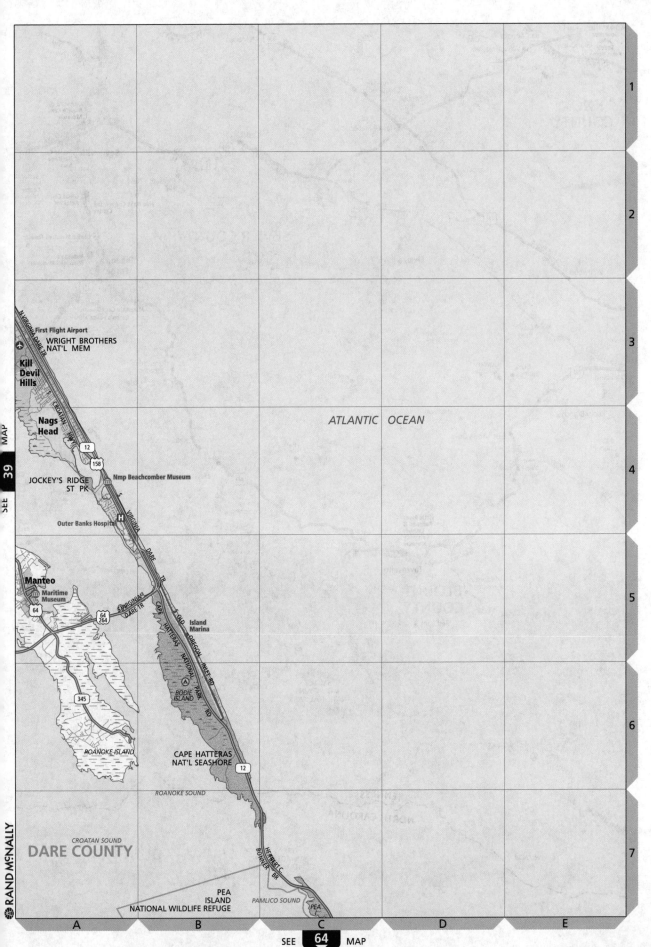

1

2

3

First Flight Airport
**WRIGHT BROTHERS
NAT'L MEM**

**Kill
Devil
Hills**

ATLANTIC   OCEAN

**Nags
Head**

12

158

**JOCKEY'S RIDGE
ST PK**

Nmp Beachcomber Museum

4

Outer Banks Hospital   H

VIRGINIA DARE TR

Manteo

Maritime
Museum

64

64
264

S VIRGINIA
DARE TR

Island
Marina

5

345

CAPE HATTERAS NATIONAL PARK RD

OLD OREGON INLET RD

BODIE
ISLAND

6

ROANOKE ISLAND

**CAPE HATTERAS
NAT'L SEASHORE**

12

ROANOKE SOUND

CROATAN SOUND
DARE COUNTY

HERBERT C.
BONNER BR

7

**PEA
ISLAND
NATIONAL WILDLIFE REFUGE**

PAMLICO SOUND

PEA
I.

A   B   C   D   E

SEE **64** MAP

SEE MAP **39**

RAND McNALLY

MAP
41

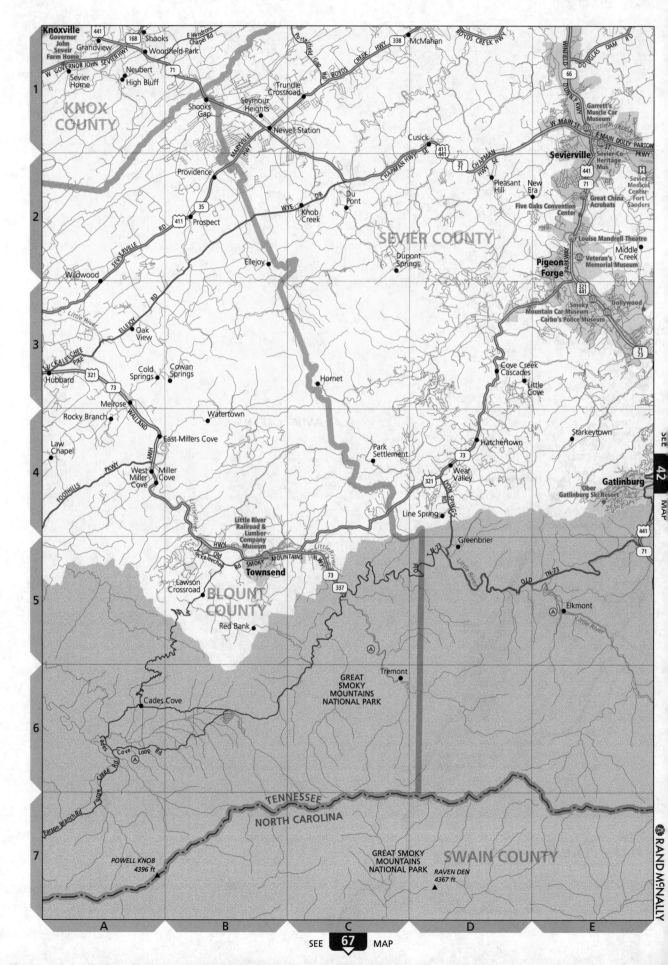

1:190,080
1 in. = 3 mi.

0   2   4
miles

KNOX COUNTY

Knoxville
Governor John Sevier Farm Home
441
168 Shooks
Grandview
E Hendrons Chapel Rd
Woodfield Park
W GOVERNOR JOHN SEVIER HWY
71
Neubert
Sevier Home
High Bluff
Shooks Gap
Seymour Heights
Trundle Crossroad
Portefield Gap Rd
BOYDS CREEK HWY
338 McMahan
BOYDS CREEK HWY
WINFIELD
DOUGLAS DAM RD
66
Garrett's Muscle Car Museum
W MAIN ST
E MAIN DOLLY PARTON
Sevierville
Newell Station
Cusick
411 441
35 71
CHAPMAN HWY SE
441
71
Sevier Co. Heritage Mus
Great China Acrobats
H Sevier Medical Center-Fort Sanders

Providence
Pleasant Hill
New Era
Five Oaks Convention Center
Louise Mandrell Theatre
Middle Creek
Pigeon Forge
Veteran's Memorial Museum
35
411 Prospect
WYE DR
Knob Creek
Du Pont
SEVIER COUNTY
Dupont Springs
321 441
Smoky Mountain Car Museum
Carbo's Police Museum
Dollywood
71 73

Wildwood
Ellejoy
Little River
SEVIERVILLE RD
ELLEJOY RD
Oak View
Cove Creek Cascades
Little Cove
TUCKALEECHEE PIKE
321 Hubbard
73
Cold Springs
Cowan Springs
Hornet
Melrose
Watertown
Starkeytown
Rocky Branch
WALLAND HWY
Law Chapel
East Millers Cove
Park Settlement
Hatchertown
73
FOOTHILLS PKWY
West Miller Cove
Miller Cove
321
Wear Valley
VOLES SPRINGS RD
Line Spring
Ober Gatlinburg Ski Resort
Gatlinburg
441
71
Little River Railroad & Lumber Company Museum
Little River HWY
Greenbrier
Little River
OLD TN-73
Elkmont
A
Little River
Old Tuckaleechee Rd
SMOKY MOUNTAINS HWY
Townsend
73
TN-73
337
BLOUNT COUNTY
Lawson Crossroad
Red Bank
A
SEE 42 MAP
RAND McNALLY

Tremont
GREAT SMOKY MOUNTAINS NATIONAL PARK
Cades Cove
Cove Loop Rd
A
COVE CREEK RD
TENNESSEE
NORTH CAROLINA
Parson Branch Rd
POWELL KNOB 4396 ft
GREAT SMOKY MOUNTAINS NATIONAL PARK
RAVEN DEN 4367 ft
SWAIN COUNTY

A   B   C   D   E

SEE 67 MAP

1 2 3 4 5 6 7

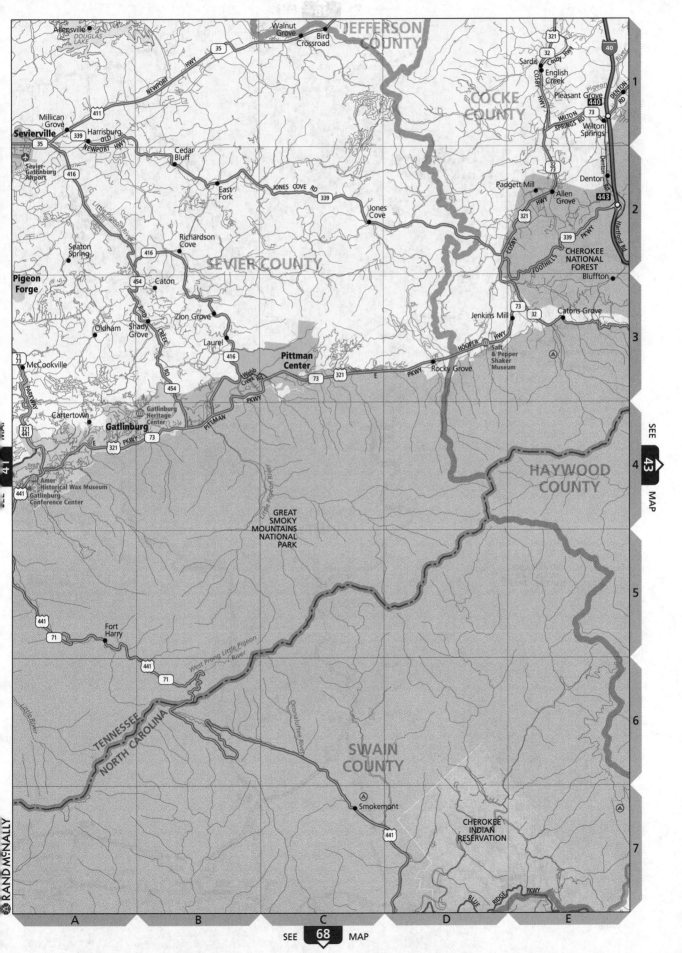

MAP
42

REGIONAL MAP

1:190,080
1 in. = 3 mi.

0   2   4
miles

N

SEE
43
MAP

RAND MºNALLY

Allensville

DOUGLAS
LAKE

Walnut
Grove

Bird
Crossroad

**JEFFERSON
COUNTY**

321

32

40

Sardis

English
Creek

COSBY HWY

**COCKE
COUNTY**

Pleasant Grove

440
73

Pigeon

DENTON RD

1

Millican
Grove

Sevierville

339

Harrisburg
OLD

411

35

NEWPORT HWY

Cedar
Bluff

WILTON
SPRINGS RD

Wilton
Springs

32
73

Denton RD

Denton

443

Hartford Rd

NEWPORT

416

Sevier-
Gatlinburg
Airport

Seaton
Spring

416

East
Fork

JONES COVE RD

339

Jones
Cove

Padgett Mill

321

Allen
Grove

COSBY HWY

339

PKWY

2

**Pigeon
Forge**

454   Caton

Richardson
Cove

SEVIER COUNTY

FOOTHILLS

**CHEROKEE
NATIONAL
FOREST**

Bluffton

Oldham

Shady
Grove

BIRD CREEK RD

Zion Grove

Laurel

416

Jenkins Mill

73

32

Catons Grove

71
73

McCookville

**Pittman
Center**

454

73

321

HOOPER HWY

Salt
& Pepper
Shaker
Museum

Rocky Grove

3

PARKWAY

Cartertown

Webb
Creek Rd

PKWY

Gatlinburg
Heritage
Center

E

PKWY

PITTMAN

321
441

Gatlinburg

321

73

E

Little Pigeon River

**HAYWOOD
COUNTY**

4

441

Amer
Historical Wax Museum
Gatlinburg
Conference Center

**GREAT
SMOKY
MOUNTAINS
NATIONAL
PARK**

Little Pigeon River

5

441

71

Fort
Harry

441

71

West Prong Little Pigeon River

Oconaluftee River

6

Little River

**TENNESSEE
NORTH CAROLINA**

**SWAIN
COUNTY**

Smokemont

**CHEROKEE
INDIAN
RESERVATION**

7

441

BLUE RIDGE PKWY

A   B   C   D   E

MAP
43

REGIONAL MAP

SEE **19** MAP

1:190,080
1 in. = 3 mi.

0   2   4
miles

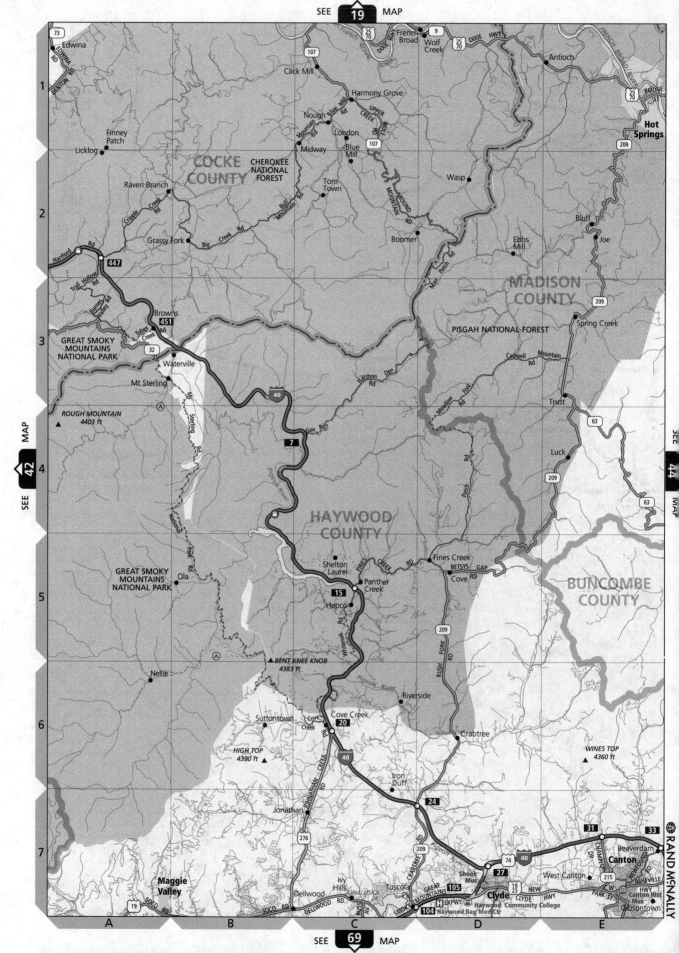

SEE **42** MAP

SEE **444** MAP

RAND MCNALLY

A   B   C   D   E

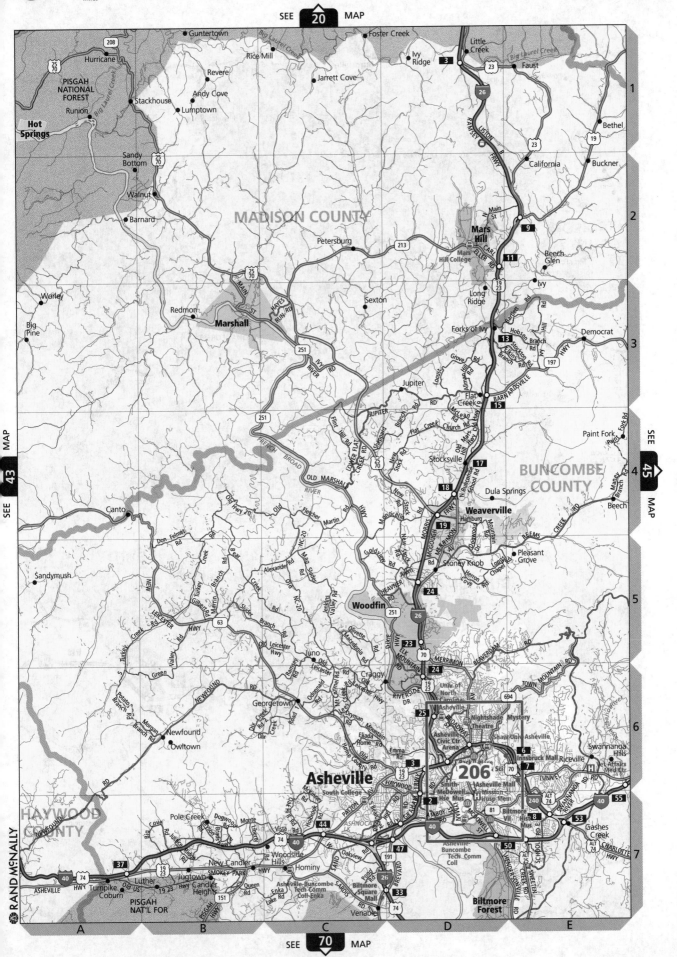

MAP
44

1:190,080
1 in. = 3 mi.

0   2   4

miles

SEE 20 MAP

PISGAH
NATIONAL
FOREST

Hot
Springs

MADISON COUNTY

Runion

Hurricane

Stackhouse

Sandy
Bottom

Walnut

Barnard

Worley

Big
Pine

Guntertown

Rice Mill

Revere

Andy Cove

Lumptown

Redmon

Marshall

Petersburg

Sexton

Foster Creek

Little
Creek

Ivy
Ridge

Jarrett Cove

Mars
Hill

Mars
Hill College

Faust

California

Bethel

Buckner

Beech
Glen

Ivy

Long
Ridge

Forks of Ivy

Democrat

Paint Fork

SEE 43 MAP

SEE 45 MAP

Jupiter

Flat
Creek

Stocksville

BUNCOMBE
COUNTY

Dula Springs

Beech

Canto

Sandymush

Weaverville

Hamburg

Stoney Knob

Pleasant
Grove

Woodfin

Georgetown

Newfound

Owltown

Craggy

Univ. of
North
Carolina

Asheville

Nightshade Mystery
Theatre

Shaw Univ Asheville

Asheville Civic Ctr
Arena

Innsbruck Mall

Riceville

Swannanoa
Hills

Asheville

South College

Smith
McDowell
Hse Mus

Asheville Mall

Mission
Hosp Mem

Biltmore
Vil.

Biltmore
Hm
Mus

Gashes
Creek

HAYWOOD
COUNTY

Pole Creek

New Candler

Woodside
Hills

Hominy

Luther

Coburn

Turnpike

Candler
Heights

Jugtown

Asheville-Buncombe
Tech Comm
Coll-Enka

Woodside
Hills

Biltmore
Square
Mall

Asheville-
Buncombe
Tech. Comm.
Coll

Venable

Biltmore
Forest

PISGAH
NAT'L FOR

ASHEVILLE

SEE 70 MAP

A   B   C   D   E

MAP
45

REGIONAL MAP

1:190,080
1 in. = 3 mi.

0   2   4
miles

N

SEE ⬆ **21** MAP

MITCHELL COUNTY

Swiss
Bald Creek
Cane River
19W
Old US-19E
Cane River
Lincoln Park
197
W MAIN ST E MAIN ST
Windom
80
Paint Gap
19
Riverside
19E
Burnsville
19E
Micaville
Newdale
19E
Estatoe
Possumtrot
Cane

1

Bowlens Creek
Vixen
Bowditch
Blue Rock

Price Creek
Concord
CALLAWAY MOUNTAIN 4403 ft
YANCEY COUNTY
80
Celo

Waverly
Paint Fork

2

MADISON COUNTY
Pensacola
197
Emerald Village
Strawberry Ridge
Osborne Knob
Glenlaurel

Terry Fork
Murchison
Wildacres

Hamrick

N FORK RD

197
Rockview
SHEEPWALLOW KNOB 4363 ft
Eskota
PISGAH NATIONAL FOREST
80

3

DILLINGHAM RD
Paint Fork Rd
Dillingham
MT MITCHELL ST PK Ⓐ
Busick

CRAGGY GDNS

SEE ⬆ **44** MAP

JESS KNOB 4357 ft
Craggy Gdns
128
BUCK CREEK RD
Sunnyvale
80

SEE **46** MAP

4

Blackberry Inn
MCDOWELL COUNTY

South Toe River

5

BUNCOMBE COUNTY
BURNETTE RES
Graphite
Coleman
Dendron
70
Greenlee

Walkertown
75

Summerhaven
Old Fort
MAIN
40

70
40
72
MAIN ST
Moffitt Hill
73

6

Grovemont
Swannanoa Valley Mus
E STATE ST
65
66
Montreat Montreat College
BLUE STAR MEMORIAL HWY Ridgecrest
70
OLD FORT RD
SUGAR HILL RD

Swannanoa River
TOMAHAWK
70 W STATE ST
64 **Black Mountain**
Catawba River

BLACK MOUNTAIN HWY
40
59
Wilson
BLUE RIDGE RD
Oakey Gap Rd

CAVE
BAT

7

CHARLOTTE HWY
JESSES HIGH TOP 4350 ft
Flat Top
Chestnut Hill Rd
9
Davistown

Old Fort Rd
Flat Creek River
Broad River
OLD FORT RD

Blue Ridge Forest
Garren Creek Rd
Garren Creek Rd

A   B   C   D   E

SEE **71** MAP

RAND MCNALLY

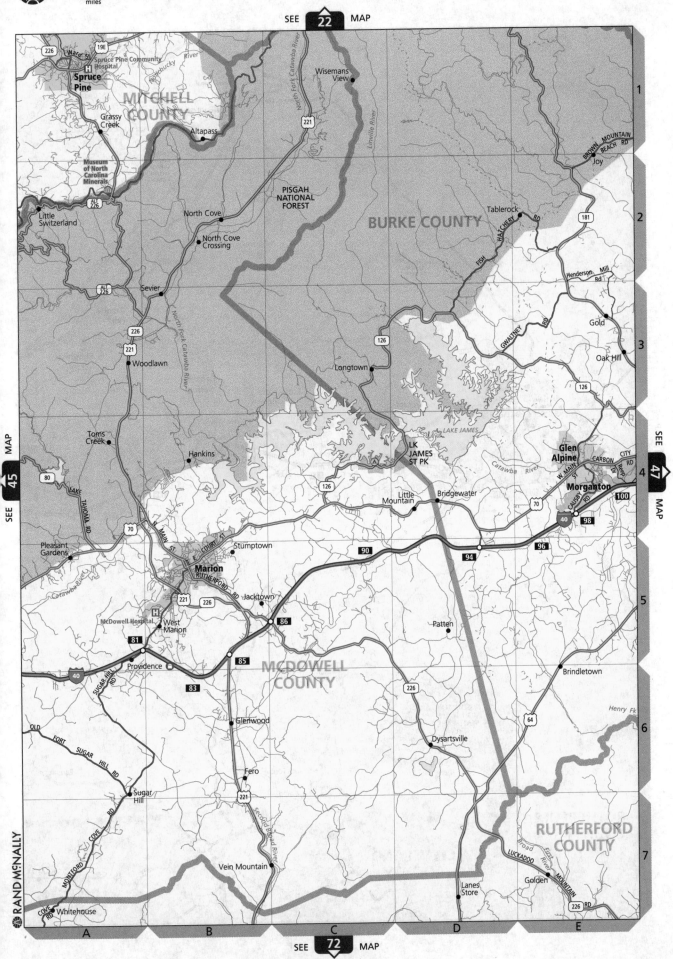

MAP
46

REGIONAL MAP

SEE 22 MAP

1:190,080
1 in. = 3 mi.

0   2   4
miles

226   Wafer St   19E
Spruce Pine Community
Hospital
H
**Spruce
Pine**

Toecane River

**MITCHELL
COUNTY**

Grassy
Creek

Altapass

Museum
of North
Carolina
Minerals

ALT 226

Little
Switzerland

North Cove

North Cove
Crossing

North Fork Catawba River

Sevier

ALT
226

226

221

Woodlawn

North Fork Catawba River

Wisemans
View

221

Linville River

**PISGAH
NATIONAL
FOREST**

BURKE COUNTY

126

Longtown

BROWN MOUNTAIN
BEACH RD

Joy

Tablerock   RD

181

HATCHERY

FISH

Henderson   Mill
Rd

GWALTNEY   RD

Gold

126

Oak Hill

126

LAKE JAMES

*LK
JAMES
ST PK*

Glen
Alpine

CITY
RD

CARBON

Morganton

SEE

45

MAP

80

LAKE
TAHOMA RD

Toms
Creek

Hankins

126

126

Little
Mountain

Bridgewater

Catawba   River

W. MAIN   ST

CAUSBY   RD

70

40

98

100

SEE

47

MAP

70

N. MAIN ST

E. COURT ST

Stumptown

90

94

96

Pleasant
Gardens

Catawba River

Marion

RUTHERFORD   RD

Jacktown

221

226

H
McDowell Hospital

West
Marion

81

40

Providence

SUGAR HILL RD

85

83

86

Patten

**McDOWELL
COUNTY**

226

Brindletown

64

Henry   Fk

OLD

FORT

SUGAR   HILL   RD

Glenwood

Fero

Dysartsville

221

Second Broad River

Sugar
Hill

**RUTHERFORD
COUNTY**

MONTFORD   COVE   RD

Vein Mountain

LUCKADOO   RD

Broad   River

FLINT   MOUNTAIN

Lanes
Store

Golden

226   RD

CONE   RD   Whitehouse

A   B   C   D   E

SEE 72 MAP

MAP
47

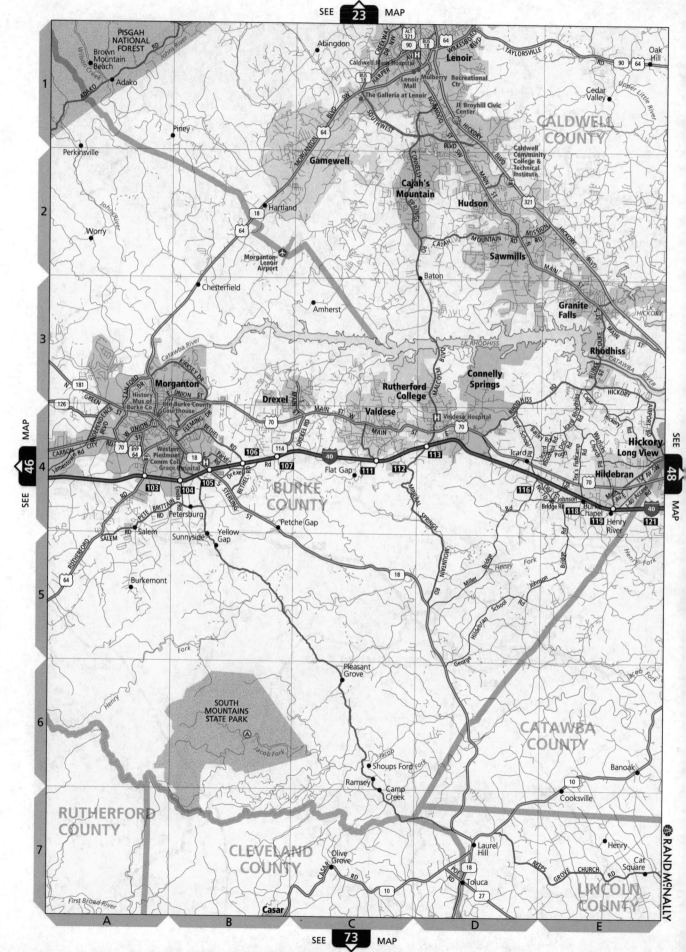

1:190,080
1 in. = 3 mi.

0 2 4
miles

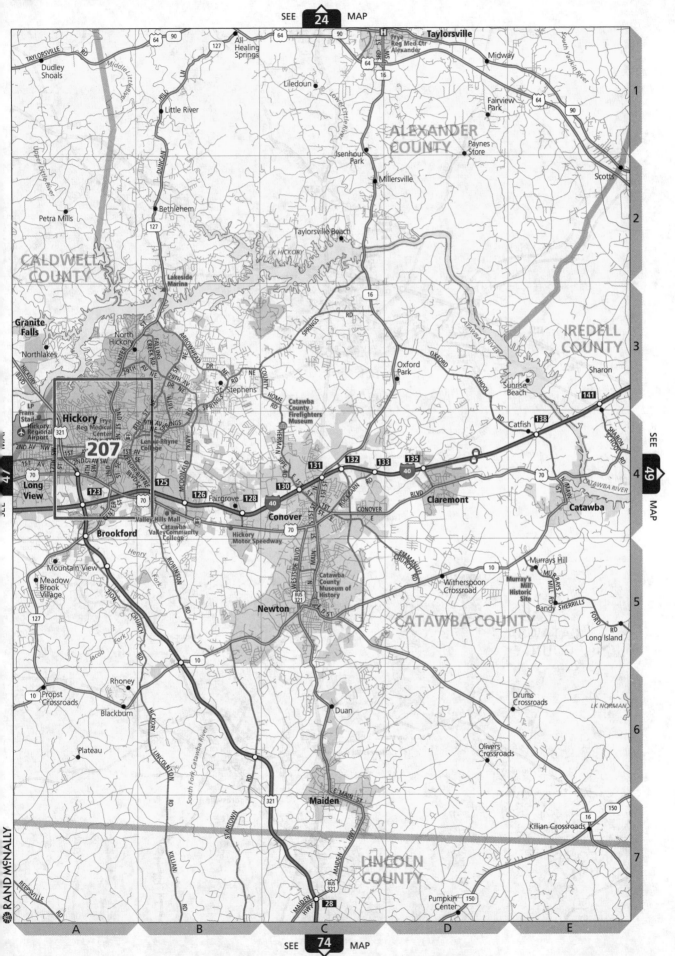

MAP
48

REGIONAL MAP

1:190,080
1 in. = 3 mi.

0   2   4
miles

SEE 24 MAP

Taylorsville

Frye Reg Med Ctr Alexander

Midway

All Healing Springs

Liledoun

Fairview Park

Dudley Shoals

TAYLORSVILLE RD

Little River

Scotts

ALEXANDER COUNTY

Paynes Store

Isenhour Park

Millersville

Petra Mills

Bethlehem

Taylorsville Beach

LK HICKORY

IREDELL COUNTY

CALDWELL COUNTY

Lakeside Marina

Sharon

Granite Falls

North Hickory

Oxford Park

Sunrise Beach

Northlakes

St. Stephens

Catawba County Firefighters Museum

Catfish

141

138

LP Frans Stad

Hickory Regional Airport

Hickory

Frye Reg Medical Center

207

Lenoir-Rhyne College

131   132   133   135

40

Catawba River

SEE 49 MAP

Long View

123

125

126   128   130

Fairgrove

Conover

Claremont

Catawba

Brookford

Catawba Valley Community College

Hickory Motor Speedway

Mountain View

Murrays Hill

Murray's Mill Historic Site

Meadow Brook Village

Catawba County Museum of History

Newton

CATAWBA COUNTY

Witherspoon Crossroad

Bandy   Sherrills

127

10

Long Island

Propst Crossroads

Rhoney

10

Drums Crossroads

LK NORMAN

Blackburn

Duan

Olivers Crossroads

Plateau

Maiden

Killian Crossroads

16   150

LINCOLN COUNTY

Pumpkin Center   150

SEE 74 MAP

A   B   C   D   E

RAND MCNALLY

MAP
49

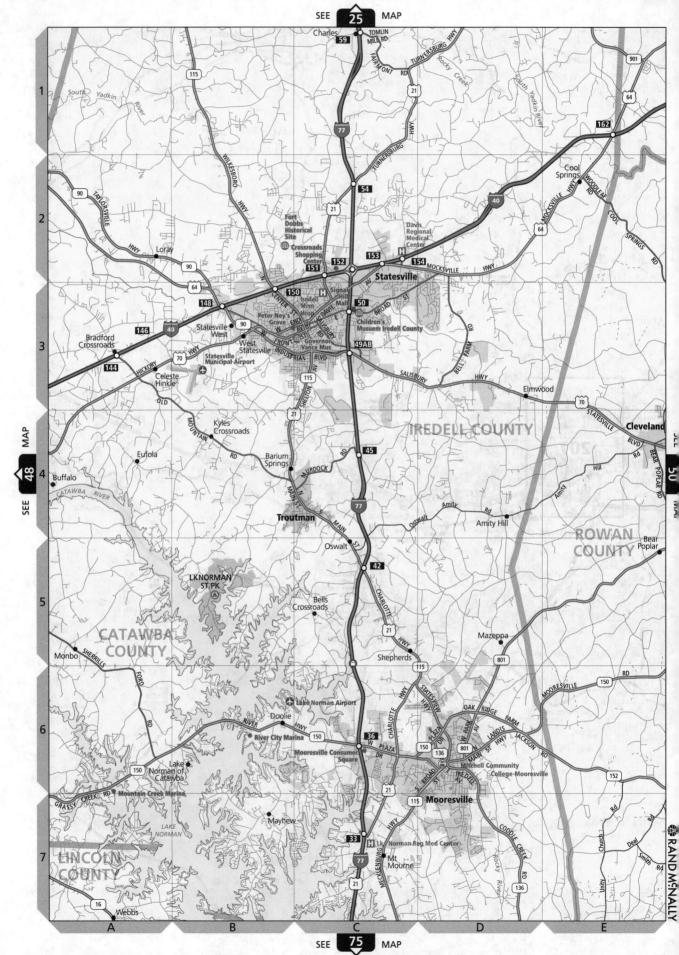

1:190,080
1 in. = 3 mi.

0   2   4
miles

SEE [25] MAP

Charles
59
TOMLIN MILL RD
FAIRMONT RD
TURNERSBURG HWY
Rocky Creek
South Yadkin River
901

115

1

21
64

162

90
TAYLORSVILLE HWY
WILKESBORO HWY
54
40
Cool Springs
WOODLEAF RD
COOL SPRINGS RD

2

Loray
90
21
Fort Dobbs Historical Site
Crossroads Shopping Center
152
151
153
Statesville
154 MOCKSVILLE HWY
Davis Regional Medical Center
64
MOCKSVILLE HWY

64
148
150
Iredell Mem Hosp
Signal Hill Mall
DAVIE AV
50
BROAD ST
Children's Musuem Iredell County

146
40
Statesville West
90
Peter Ney's Grave
W FRONT ST
SALISBURY
INDUSTRIAL
Governor Vance Mus
BLVD
49AB
SALISBURY HWY
BELLS FARM RD
Elmwood
70
STATESVILLE BLVD

3

Bradford Crossroads
144
70 HWY
HICKORY
Celeste Hinkle
Statesville Municipal Airport
West Statesville
SHELTON AV
115
21
IREDELL COUNTY
Cleveland

OLD
MOUNTAIN RD
Kyles Crossroads
45
BEAR POPLAR RD
Hill
Amity Rd

4

Buffalo
CATAWBA RIVER
Eufola
Barium Springs
MURDOCK RD
MAIN ST
77
Amity Rd
Amity Hill
ROWAN COUNTY
Bear Poplar
50

SEE [48] MAP

Troutman
Oswalt
Ostwalt
42

5

LK NORMAN ST PK
Bells Crossroads
CHARLOTTE HWY
21 HWY
Mazeppa
801
150

Monbo
SHERRILLS FORD RD
CATAWBA COUNTY
Shepherds
115
MOORESVILLE RD

6

Lake Norman Airport
River City Marina
Doolie
RIVER HWY
150
36
Mooresville Consumer Square
W PLAZA DR
STATESVIEW HWY
CHARLOTTE HWY
150
136
801
OAK RIDGE FARM RD
MAIN ST
IREDELL AV
LANDIS HWY
JACKSON RD
152
Mitchell Community College-Mooresville

Lake Norman of Catawba
150
Mountain Creek Marina
GRASSY CREEK RD
21
115 Mooresville
BROAD ST
CODDLE CREEK
Church RD
Deal Rd

LAKE NORMAN
Mayhew
33
77
Norman Reg Med Center
Mt Mourne
MECKLENBURG HWY
21
136
Rocky River RD
Smith Rd
Unity

7

LINCOLN COUNTY
16
Webbs

A   B   C   D   E

SEE [75] MAP

MAP
50

REGIONAL MAP

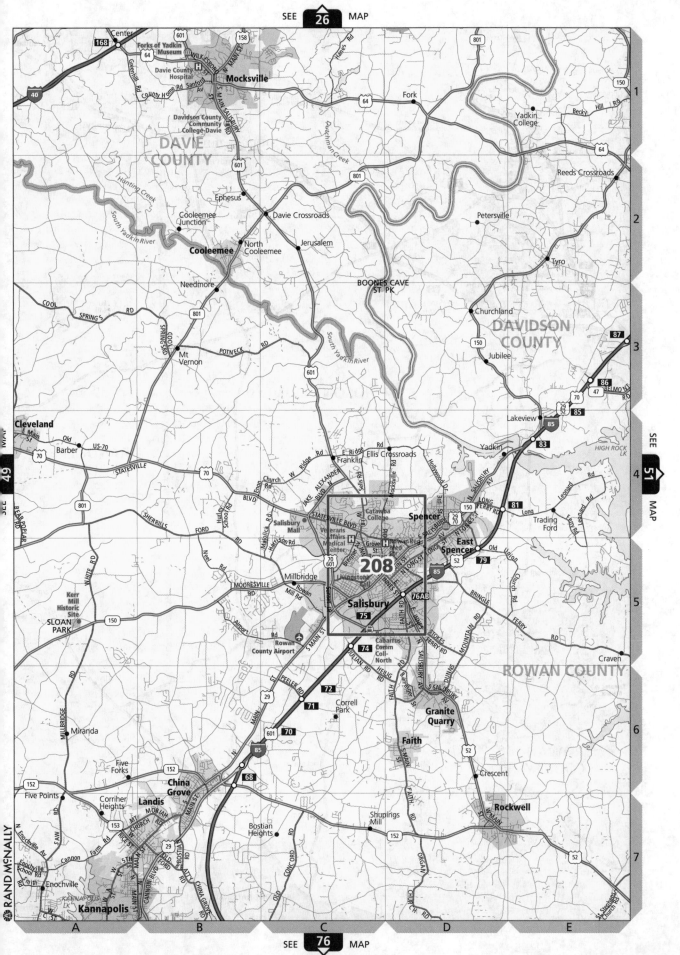

1:190,080
1 in. = 3 mi.

0   2   4
miles

N

168
Center

40

64
Greenhill Rd
County Home Rd
Sanford Av
158
601

Forks of Yadkin Museum

Davie County Hospital

H
Mocksville

801
Hanes Rd

Fork
64

150

Davidson County Community College-Davie

601

1

DAVIE COUNTY

Yadkin College

Becky Hill Rd

Hunting Creek

Duchman Creek

64

Reeds Crossroads

Ephesus

801

Davie Crossroads

Petersville

2

South Yadkin River

Cooleemee Junction

North Cooleemee

Jerusalem

Tyro

Cooleemee

Needmore

BOONES CAVE ST PK

DAVIDSON COUNTY

Churchland

150

87

801

Mt Vernon

POTNECK RD

601

South Yadkin River

Jubilee

86
47
BELMONT RD

29
52
70

3

COOL SPRINGS RD

COOL SPRINGS RD

85

85

HIGH ROCK LK

Cleveland

E Main St

Barber
US-70

STATESVILLE

70

801

70

Church Rd

W Ridge Rd

JAKE ALEXANDER BLVD

E Ridge Rd

Ellis Crossroads

Franklin

Sells Rd

Mocksville Rd

Hollywood Dr

N Salisbury

Lakeview

Yadkin

83

150

LONG FERRY RD

81
Long

Leonard Rd

Rd

Trading Ford

SEE 51 MAP

4

SEE 49 MAP

SHERRILLS FORD

WHITE RD

Henry School Rd

Mallard Rd

Halton Rd

Neel Rd

Salisbury Mall

STATESVILLE BLVD

Catawba College

Grove St

Brenner

Main St

3rd St

29
70

Spencer

150

Long

79
81

52

Kerr Mill Historic Site

SLOAN PARK

150

Millbridge

MOORESVILLE RD

Rowan Mill Rd

Sunset Dr

Veterans Affairs Medical Center

H
70
601

H

208

N Long St

Salisbury Av

East Spencer

85
52

79

Old

Union Church Rd

FERRY RD

5

Airport Rd

Rowan County Airport

S Main St

Julian Rd

74

Cabarrus Comm Coll-North

Livingstone Coll

Miles St

Faith Rd

Salisbury

75

76AB

BRINGLE

STOKES FERRY RD

MOUNTAIN RD

Craven

ROWAN COUNTY

MILLBRIDGE RD

Miranda

PEELER RD

29

72

71

Correll Park

601
70

Granite Quarry

52

SALISBURY AV

S SALISBURY AV

Barringer Rd

Faith

S MAIN ST

6

Five Forks

152

85

68

China Grove

MT MORIAH CHURCH RD

Crescent

Five Points
152

Corriher Heights

Landis

153

Bostian Heights

Shupings Mill

152

ORGAN CHURCH RD

W MAIN ST

Rockwell

52

FAITH RD

N Enochville Av

SAW RD

RICE RD

Bostian Rd

MT CHURCH RD

N MAIN ST

OLD CHINA GROVE RD

CANNON BLVD

29

CONCORD RD

OLD CONCORD RD

S Stemberg Rd

St Stephens Church Rd

52

7

RAND McNALLY

Enochville School Rd

Cannon

Enochville

5TH ST

N MAIN ST

W C ST

KANNAPOLIS LK

Kannapolis

A   B   C   D   E

MAP
51

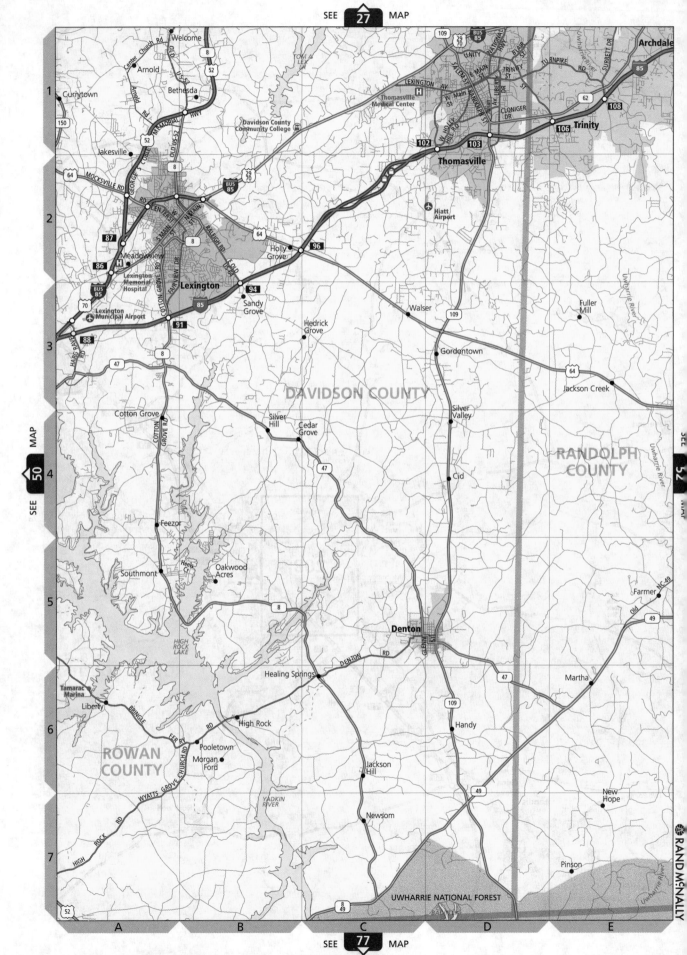

1:190,080
1 in. = 3 mi.
0   2   4
miles

SEE 27 MAP

N

Archdale

Welcome
Arnold
Bethesda
Currytown
Jakesville
Thomasville
Medical Center
Davidson County
Community College
LEXINGTON
Trinity
Thomasville
Hiatt
Airport
Meadowview
Lexington
Memorial
Hospital
Lexington
Municipal Airport
Lexington
Holly
Grove
Sandy
Grove
Hedrick
Grove
Walser
Gordontown
Silver
Valley
Jackson Creek
Fuller
Mill
DAVIDSON COUNTY
RANDOLPH COUNTY
Cotton Grove
Silver
Hill
Cedar
Grove
Cid
Feezor
Heels
Cr.
Oakwood
Acres
Southmont
Farmer
HIGH
ROCK
LAKE
Denton
Martha
Tamarac
Marina
Healing Springs
Liberty
Handy
High Rock
**ROWAN
COUNTY**
Pooletown
Morgan
Ford
Jackson
Hill
New
Hope
YADKIN
RIVER
Newsom
Pinson
UWHARRIE NATIONAL FOREST

SEE 50 MAP

SEE 52 MAP

RAND McNALLY

SEE 77 MAP

1   2   3   4   5   6   7

A   B   C   D   E

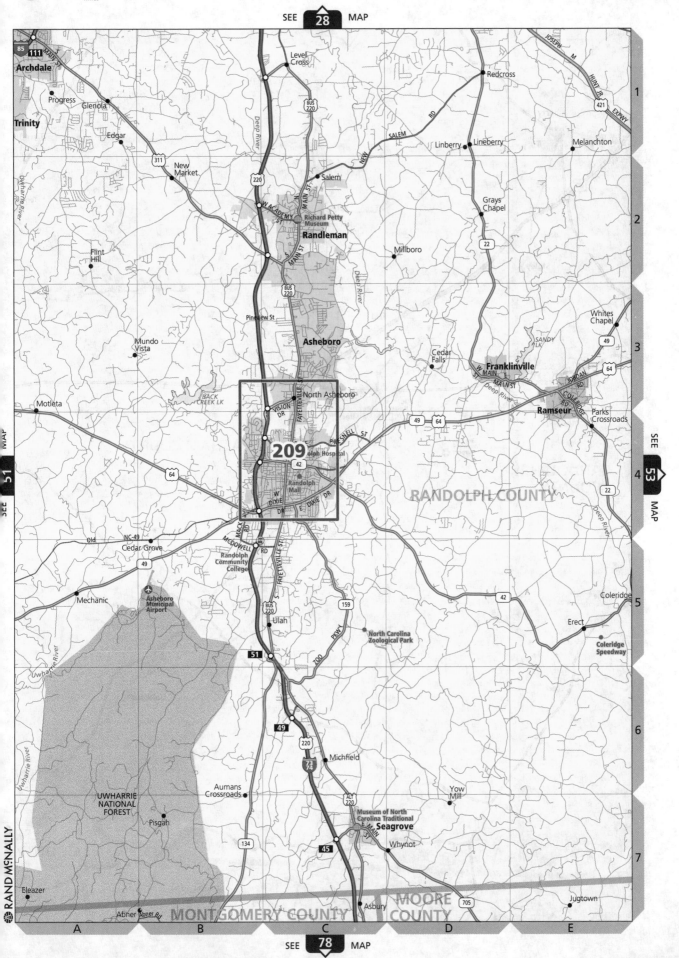

MAP
52

REGIONAL MAP

1:190,080
1 in. = 3 mi.

0   2   4
miles

SEE [28] MAP

85 [111]
Archdale
Trinity
Progress
Glenola
Edgar
311
New Market
Flint Hill
Mundo Vista
Motieta
64
Old NC-49
Cedar Grove
49
Mechanic
Asheboro Municipal Airport
UWHARRIE NATIONAL FOREST
Pisgah
Eleazer

Level Cross
Redcross
BUS 220
Deep River
NEW SALEM RD
Linberry
Lineberry
Melanchton
220
Salem
W ACADEMY ST
Richard Petty Museum
Randleman
MAIN ST
Millboro
Grays Chapel
22
BUS 220
Pineview St
Asheboro
Deep River
Cedar Falls
Franklinville
W MAIN ST
Whites Chapel
49
64
SANDY LK
JORDAN RD
Ramseur
COLERIDGE RD
Parks Crossroads
BACK CREEK LK
North Asheboro
VISION DR
FAYETTEVILLE
209
PRESNELL ST
olph Hospital
42
Randolph Mall
W DIXIE DR
E DIXIE DR
49
64
RANDOLPH COUNTY
22
Coleridge
Erect
Coleridge Speedway

MACK RD
MCDOWELL RD
Randolph Community College
FAYETTEVILLE ST
BUS 220
Ulah
51
159
700 PKWY
North Carolina Zoological Park
42
45

49
220
I 73 74
Michfield
ALT 220
Aumans Crossroads
134
Museum of North Carolina Traditional
E MAIN ST
Seagrove
Whynot
Yow Mill

MONTGOMERY COUNTY
MOORE COUNTY
Asbury
705
Jugtown

SEE [78] MAP

A   B   C   D   E

1 2 3 4 5 6 7

RAND MCNALLY

SEE 51 MAP

SEE [53] MAP

MAP
53

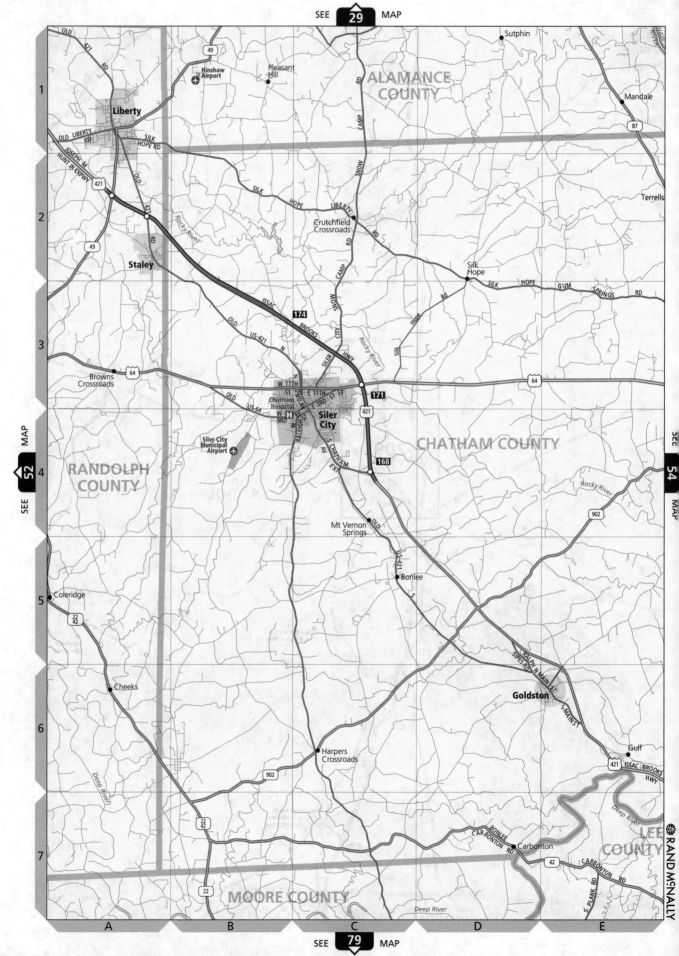

REGIONAL MAP

1:190,080
1 in. = 3 mi.

0   2   4
miles

SEE **29** MAP

OLD 421 RD

49

Hinshaw Airport

Pleasant Hill

Sutphin

ALAMANCE COUNTY

Mandale

87

Terrells

1

Liberty

OLD LIBERTY RD

SILK HOPE RD

JOSEPH M HUNT JR EXPWY

421

Rocky River

SILK HOPE RD

LIBERTY RD

Crutchfield Crossroads

SNOW CAMP RD

Silk Hope

SILK HOPE RD

GUM SPRINGS RD

2

49

Staley

OLD US-421 N

ISSAC BROOKS

174

SILER CITY HWY

SNOW CAMP RD

Rocky River

Silk Hope Rd

3

64

Browns Crossroads

OLD US-64

W 11TH ST

N 2ND

E 11TH ST

E 3RD ST ST

Chatham Hospital

W 3RD

Siler City

171

421

64

CHATHAM COUNTY

SEE **54** MAP

SEE **52** MAP

4

RANDOLPH COUNTY

Siler City Municipal Airport

S CHATHAM AV EXT

168

902

Rocky River

5

Coleridge

22 42

Mt Vernon Springs

OLD US-421 S

Bonlee

RALPH N MAIN ST

STIPES RD

6

Cheeks

Harpers Crossroads

902

Goldston

S MAIN ST

Gulf

421

ISSAC BROOKS HWY

Deep River

7

22 42

BONLEE CARBONTON RD

Carbonton

42

CARBONTON RD

Deep River

S PLANK RD

LEE COUNTY

Deep River

MOORE COUNTY

22

SEE **79** MAP

A   B   C   D   E

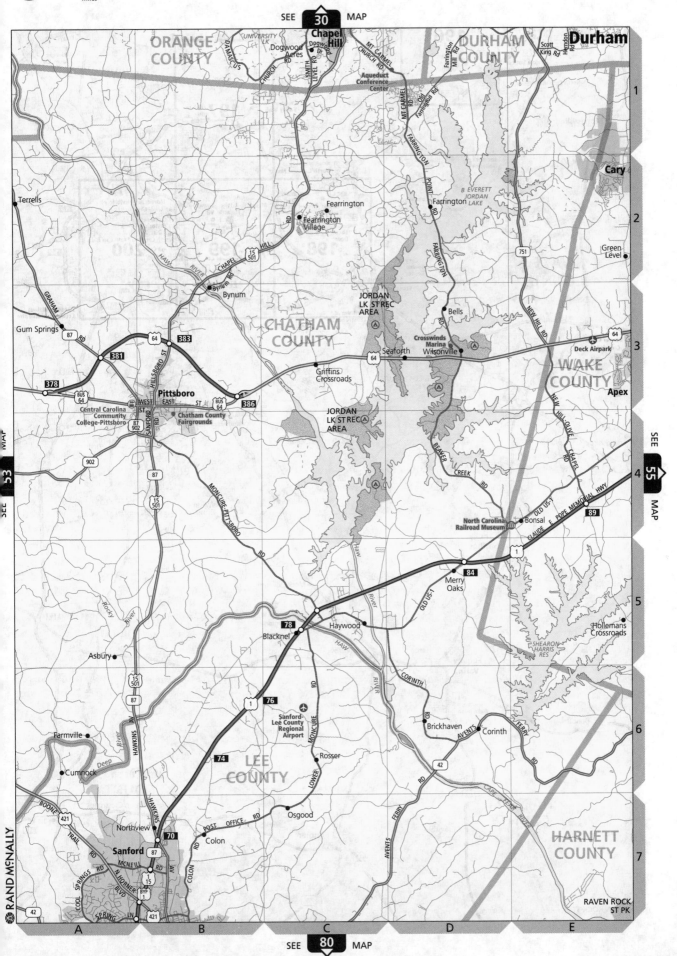

MAP
54

REGIONAL MAP

1:190,080
1 in. = 3 mi.

miles
0   2   4

SEE 30 MAP

ORANGE COUNTY

DURHAM COUNTY

Durham

Chapel Hill

Dogwood Acres RD

Aqueduct Conference Center

Cary

Terrells

Fearrington

Farrington

Green Level

Fearrington Village

Bynum

Bynum

JORDAN LK ST REC AREA

Bells

CHATHAM COUNTY

Gum Springs

87

381

64

383

386

Crosswinds Marina

Seaforth

Wilsonville

Deck Airpark

64

WAKE COUNTY

Apex

378

BUS 64

Central Carolina Community College-Pittsboro

Pittsboro

WEST   EAST   ST

BUS 64

Griffins Crossroads

JORDAN LK ST REC AREA

87 902

Chatham County Fairgrounds

902

87

15 501

North Carolina Railroad Museum

Bonsal

89

SEE 55 MAP

SEE 53 MAP

Merry Oaks

84

Haywood

78

Blacknel

Hollemans Crossroads

SHEARON HARRIS RES

Asbury

Sanford-Lee County Regional Airport

76

Brickhaven

Corinth

74

LEE COUNTY

Rosser

42

Farmville

Cumnock

421

Osgood

HARNETT COUNTY

Northview

70

Colon

Sanford

87

1

15

BYP 1

421

42

RAVEN ROCK ST PK

SEE 80 MAP

A   B   C   D   E

RAND MCNALLY

MAP
55

REGIONAL MAP

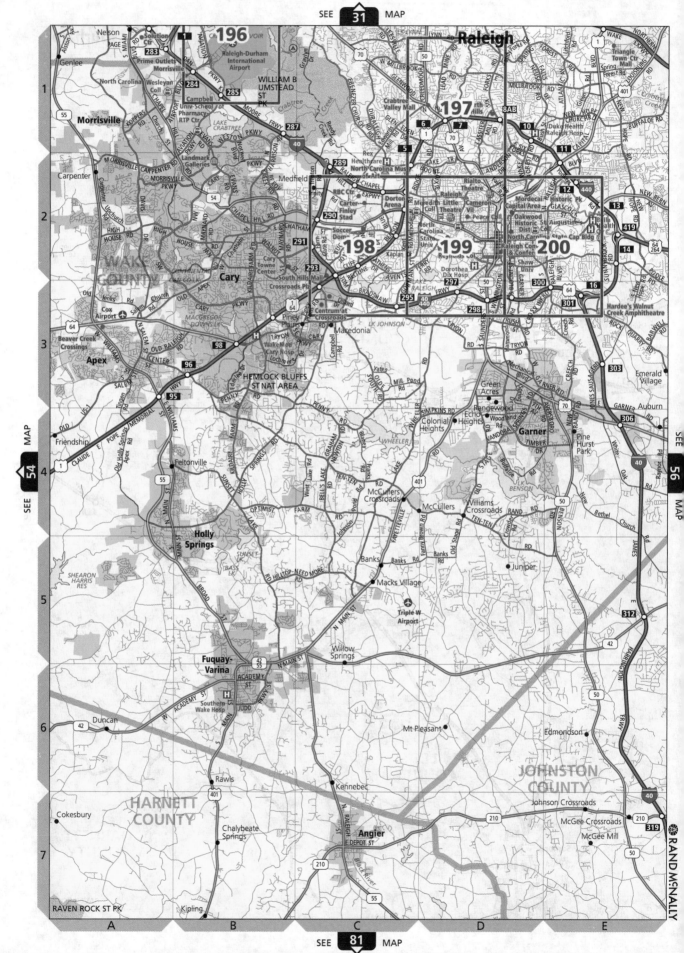

MAP
56

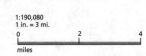

1:190,080
1 in. = 3 mi.

0   2   4
miles

SEE [32] MAP

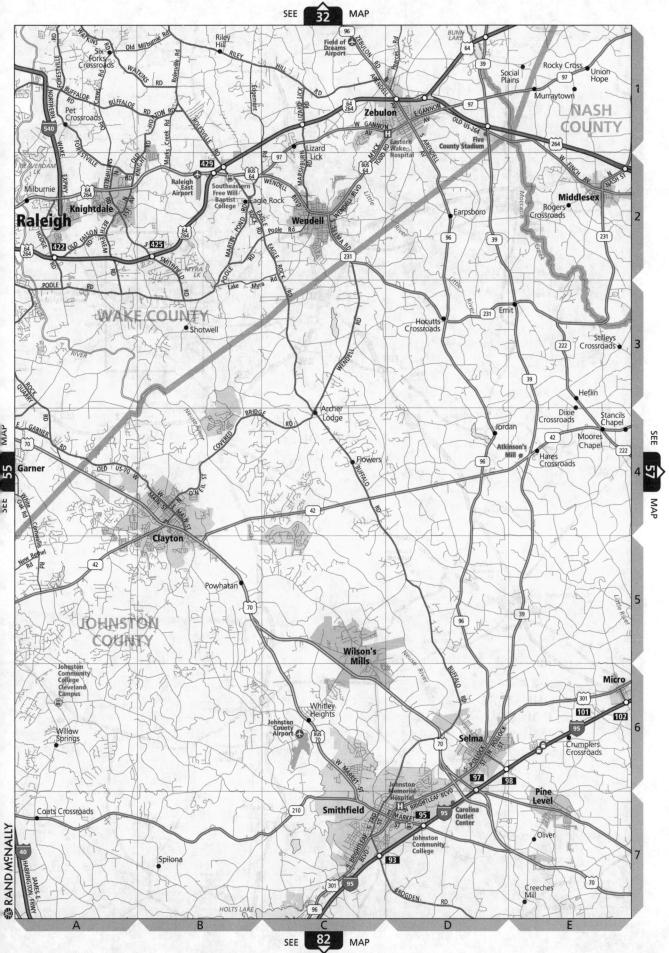

SEE [82] MAP

RAND MCNALLY

MAP
57

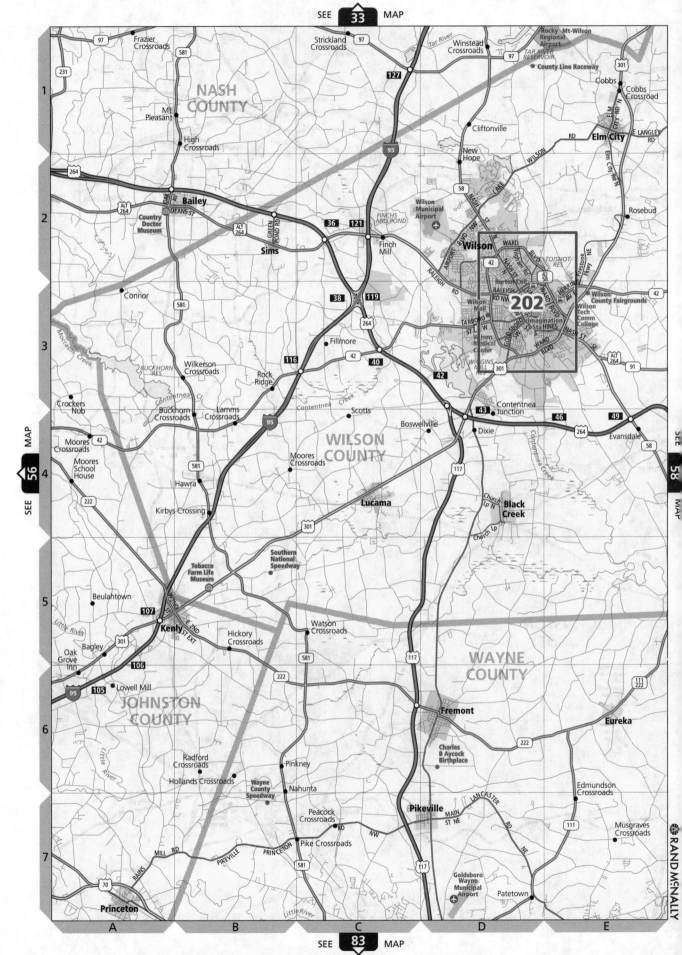

1:190,080
1 in. = 3 mi.
0   2   4
miles

SEE 33 MAP

SEE 56 MAP

SEE 58 MAP

SEE 83 MAP

NASH COUNTY

WILSON COUNTY

WAYNE COUNTY

JOHNSTON COUNTY

RAND McNALLY

MAP
58

REGIONAL MAP

1:190,080
1 in. = 3 mi.

miles
0   2   4

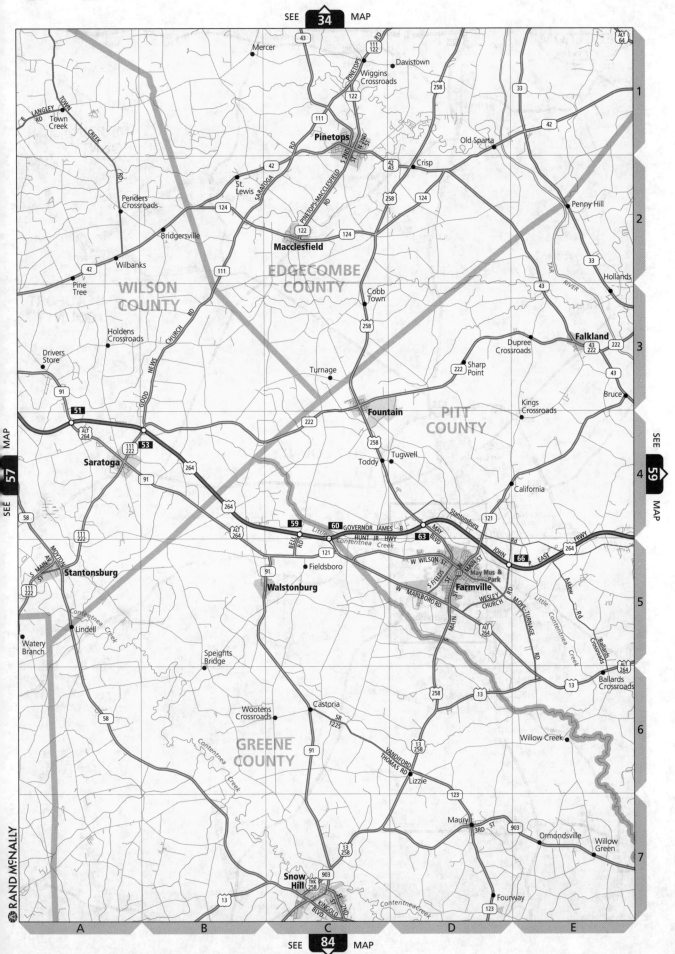

Mercer

Davistown

Wiggins
Crossroads

Old Sparta

Crisp

Penny Hill

Town Creek
LANGLEY RD

St. Lewis

Pinetops

Penders
Crossroads

Bridgersville

Macclesfield

Wilbanks

Pine Tree

WILSON COUNTY

EDGECOMBE COUNTY

Cobb Town

Hollands

Falkland

Holdens
Crossroads

Turnage

Dupree
Crossroads

Sharp Point

Drivers Store

Fountain

PITT COUNTY

Kings Crossroads

Bruce

Saratoga

Toddy

Tugwell

California

Stantonsburg

GOVERNOR JAMES B
HUNT JR HWY

Fieldsboro

Walstonburg

W WILSON ST

Farmville

May Mus & Park

W MARLBORO RD

Lindell

Watery Branch

Speights
Bridge

Ballards
Crossroads

Ballards
Crossroads

Castoria

Willow Creek

Wootens
Crossroads

GREENE COUNTY

Vandiford
Thomas Rd

Lizzie

Maury

3RD ST

Ormondsville

Willow Green

Snow
Hill

Fourway

Contentnea Creek

A   B   C   D   E

RAND MCNALLY

MAP
59

1:190,080
1 in. = 3 mi.

0   2   4
miles

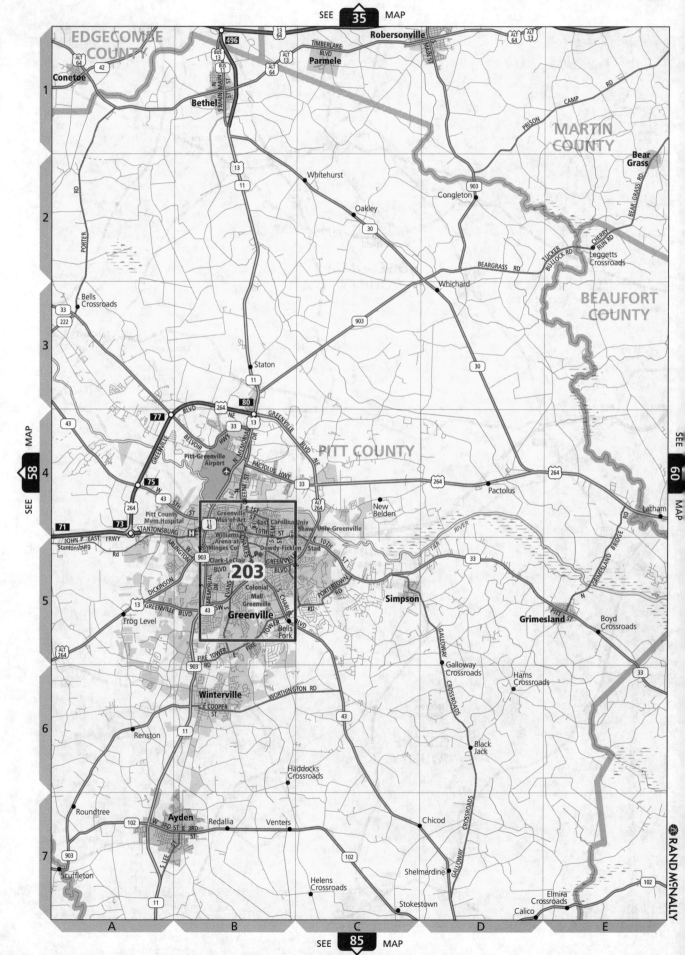

EDGECOMBE
COUNTY

Conetoe

Robersonville

Parmele

Bethel

Whitehurst

MARTIN
COUNTY

Bear
Grass

Oakley

Congleton

Whichard

Leggetts
Crossroads

Bells
Crossroads

BEAUFORT
COUNTY

Staton

PITT COUNTY

Pitt-Greenville
Airport

Pactolus

New
Belden

Pitt County
Mem Hospital
STANTONSBURG
Stantonsburg
Rd

Greenville
Mus of Art
Williams
Arena at
Minges Col
Clark-LeClair

East Carolina Univ
Shaw Univ-Greenville
Dowdy-Ficklen
Stad

Simpson

203
Colonial
Mall
Greenville
Greenville

Grimesland

Boyd
Crossroads

Bells
Fork

Frog Level

Galloway
Crossroads

Harris
Crossroads

Winterville

Black
Jack

Renston

Haddocks
Crossroads

Roundtree

Ayden

Redallia

Venters

Chicod

Shelmerdine

Scuffleton

Helens
Crossroads

Stokestown

Elmira
Crossroads

Calico

A   B   C   D   E

REGIONAL MAP

MAP
60

REGIONAL MAP

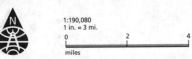

1:190,080
1 in. = 3 mi.

0   2   4
miles

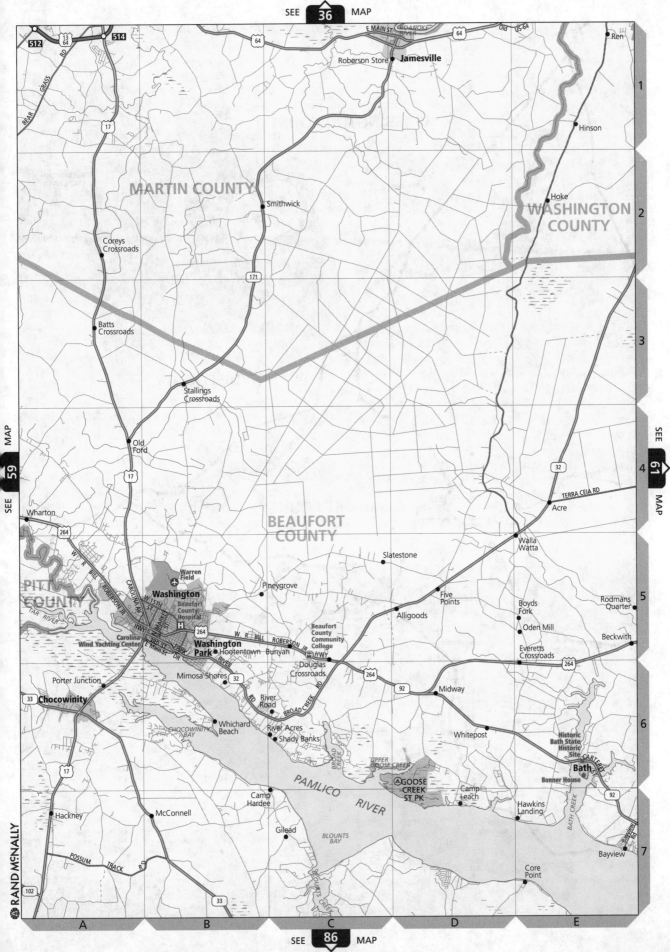

SEE **36** MAP

SEE **59** MAP

SEE **61** MAP

SEE **86** MAP

RAND MCNALLY

512
514
64
13 64 RD

E MAIN ST
ROANOKE RIVER
64
Old US-64
Ren

Roberson Store **Jamesville**

1

Hinson

MARTIN COUNTY

Smithwick

Hoke

WASHINGTON COUNTY

2

Coreys Crossroads

171

Batts Crossroads

3

Stallings Crossroads

32

Old Ford

TERRA CEIA RD

4

17

Acre

Wharton

264

Walla Watta

BEAUFORT COUNTY

Slatestone

Rodmans Quarter

5

WARREN FIELD
Pineygrove

Five Points

Boyds Fork

Washington
Beaufort County Hospital

Alligoods

Oden Mill

Beckwith

CAROLINA AV
ROBERSON JR
W 15TH ST
MARKET
264
W. R. BILL ROBERSON JR HWY

Beaufort County Community College

Everetts Crossroads

264

Carolina Wind Yachting Center
3RD ST
E MAIN ST
PARK DR

Washington Park
Hootentown Bunyan

Douglas Crossroads

264

92

Porter Junction

32

Mimosa Shores

River Road

Midway

33 Chocowinity

Whichard Beach

River Acres

Whitepost

6

CHOCOWINITY BAY

Shady Banks

BROAD CREEK RD

UPPER GOOSE CREEK

Historic Bath State Historic Site

Bath
Bonner House

17

PAMLICO RIVER

GOOSE CREEK ST PK

Camp Leach

CARTERET

92

Hackney

Camp Hardee

McConnell

Hawkins Landing

BATH CREEK

Gilead

BLOUNTS BAY

Bayview

7

102

POSSUM TRACK RD

33

Core Point

BLOUNTS CREEK

A   B   C   D   E

MAP
61

REGIONAL MAP

1:190,080
1 in. = 3 mi.
0   2   4
miles

SEE 37 MAP

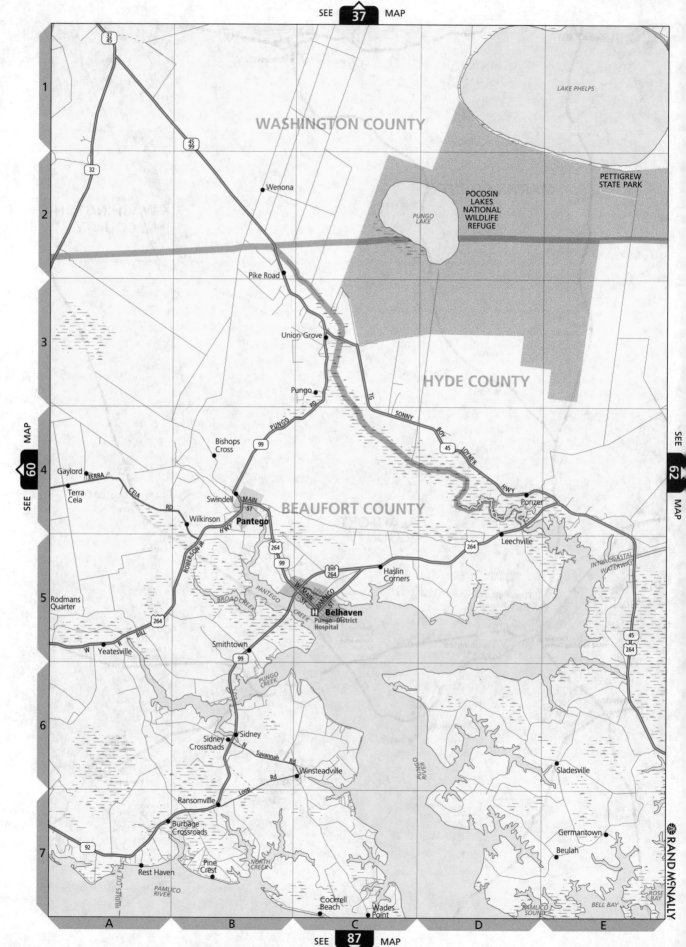

WASHINGTON COUNTY

LAKE PHELPS

32
45

45
99

32

Wenona

PETTIGREW
STATE PARK

POCOSIN
LAKES
NATIONAL
WILDLIFE
REFUGE

PUNGO
LAKE

Pike Road

Union Grove

HYDE COUNTY

Pungo

TG

SONNY BOY

JOYNER HWY

45

SEE 60 MAP

SEE 62 MAP

Bishops
Cross

99

PUNGO RD

Gaylord

TERRA P

Terra
Ceia

CEIA RD

Swindell

MAIN ST

BEAUFORT COUNTY

Ponzer

HWY

Wilkinson

Pantego

264

ROBERSON JR HWY

99

BYP
264

Haslin
Corners

264

Leechville

Rodmans
Quarter

BROAD CREEK

PANTEGO CREEK

WIL MAIN ST

PAMLICO ST

H Belhaven
Pungo District
Hospital

INTRACOASTAL WATERWAY

45
264

264

BILL

Yeatesville

W R

Smithtown

99

PUNGO CREEK

Sidney
Crossroads

Sidney

N

Savannah Rd

PUNGO RIVER

Sladesville

Rd

Winsteadville

Loop

Ransomville

Burbage
Crossroads

Germantown

92

Beulah

HUDDLES CUT PT

Rest Haven

Pine
Crest

NORTH CREEK

PAMLICO
RIVER

Cockrell
Beach

Wades
Point

PAMLICO
SOUND

BELL BAY

ROSE
BAY

RAND McNALLY

A   B   C   D   E

SEE 87 MAP

1

2

3

4

5

6

7

MAP
62

REGIONAL MAP

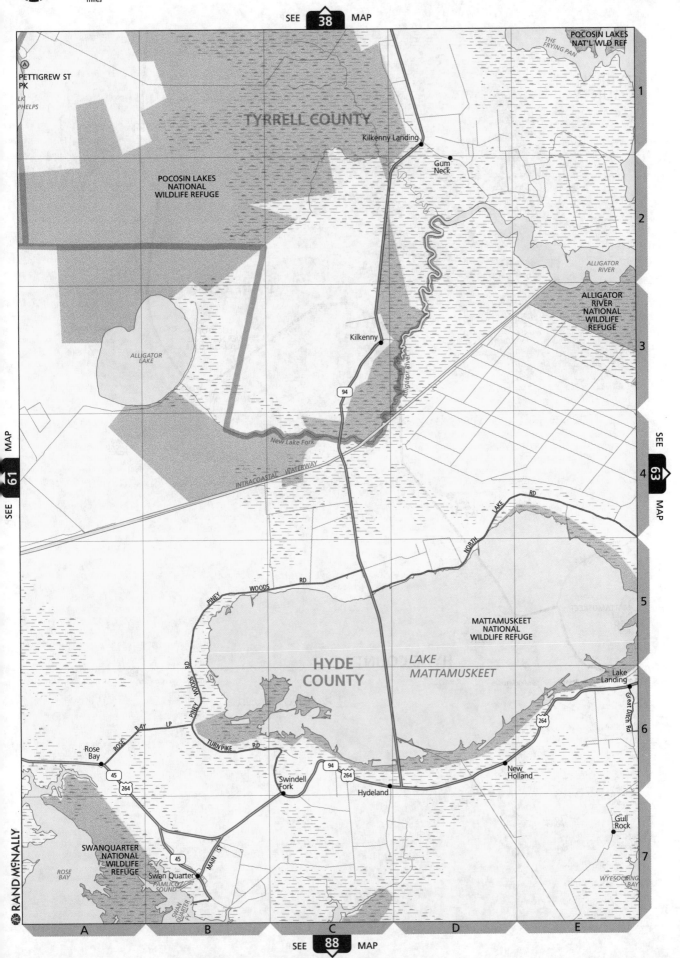

1:190,080
1 in. = 3 mi.

0   2   4
miles

N

POCOSIN LAKES
NAT'L WLD REF

THE
FRYING PAN

PETTIGREW ST
PK

LK
PHELPS

TYRRELL COUNTY

Kilkenny Landing

Gum
Neck

POCOSIN LAKES
NATIONAL
WILDLIFE REFUGE

ALLIGATOR
RIVER

ALLIGATOR
RIVER
NATIONAL
WILDLIFE
REFUGE

ALLIGATOR
LAKE

Kilkenny

Alligator River

94

SEE [61] MAP

SEE [63] MAP

New Lake Fork

INTRACOASTAL WATERWAY

RD

LAKE

NORTH

PINEY   WOODS   RD

PINEY

MATTAMUSKEET
NATIONAL
WILDLIFE REFUGE

HYDE
COUNTY

LAKE
MATTAMUSKEET

Lake
Landing

Great Ditch Rd

ROSE   BAY   LP

PINEY WOODS RD

TURNPIKE   RD

264

Rose
Bay

45

264

94

264

New
Holland

Swindell
Fork

Hydeland

Gull
Rock

ROSE
BAY

SWANQUARTER
NATIONAL
WILDLIFE
REFUGE

45

MAIN ST

Swan Quarter

PAMLICO
SOUND

SWAN
QUARTER FY

WYESOCKING
BAY

A   B   C   D   E

1
2
3
4
5
6
7

MAP

63

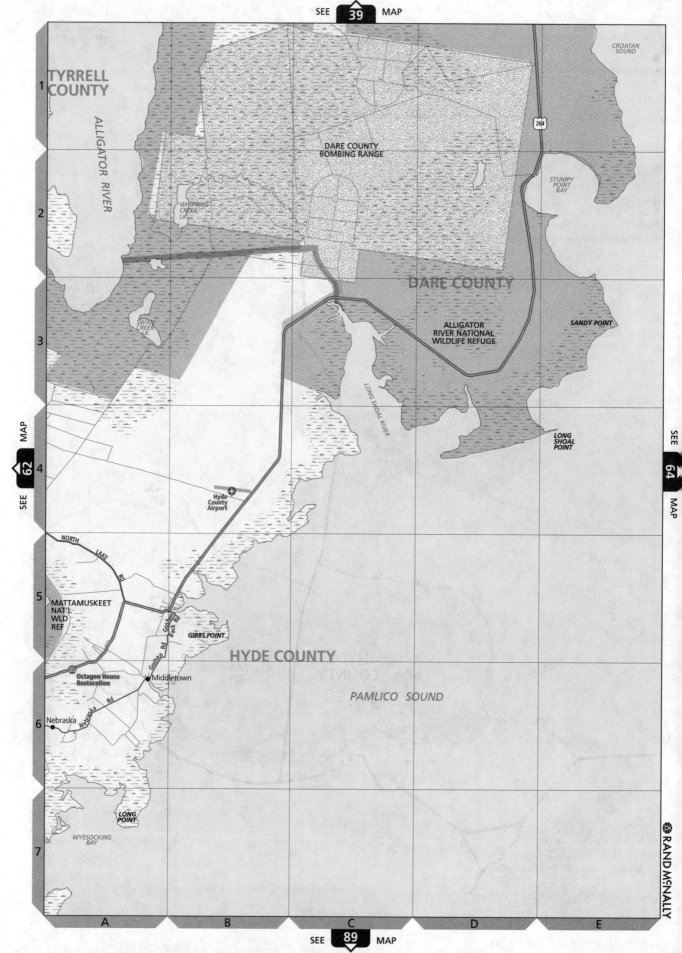

SEE **39** MAP

TYRRELL
COUNTY

1

ALLIGATOR RIVER

WHIPPING
CREEK
LK.

DARE COUNTY
BOMBING RANGE

264

CROATAN
SOUND

STUMPY
POINT
BAY

2

DARE COUNTY

SWAN
CREEK
LK.

ALLIGATOR
RIVER NATIONAL
WILDLIFE REFUGE

SANDY POINT

3

LONG SHOAL RIVER

LONG
SHOAL
POINT

MAP
62
SEE

4

Hyde
County
Airport

SEE
64
MAP

NORTH
LAKE
RD.

5

MATTAMUSKEET
NAT'L
WLD
REF

Goshen Back Rd

GIBBS POINT

HYDE COUNTY

PAMLICO SOUND

Goshen Rd

Octagon House
Restoration

Middletown

Nebraska Rd

6

Nebraska

LONG
POINT

WYESOCKING
BAY

7

A   B   C   D   E

SEE **89** MAP

MAP

64

1:190,080
1 in. = 3 mi.

0   2   4

miles

SEE **40** MAP

CROATAN SOUND

PEA ISLAND

PEA ISLAND
NATIONAL WILDLIFE
REFUGE

1

2

3

Rodanthe

Waves

DARE COUNTY

PAMLICO SOUND

Salvo

4

ATLANTIC OCEAN

HATTERAS I.

CAPE HATTERAS
NAT'L SEASHORE

5

12

6

7

Avon

A   B   C   D   E

SEE **90** MAP

MAP

65

REGIONAL MAP

1:190,080
1 in. = 3 mi.

0   2   4
miles

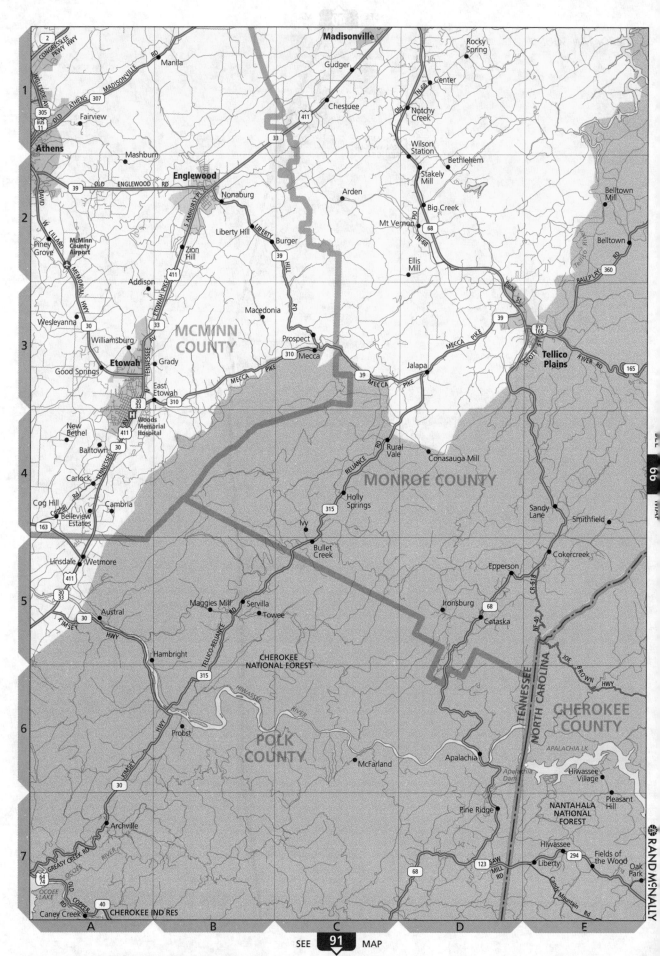

MAP 66

Madisonville

Rocky Spring

Manila

Gudger

Center

Chestuee

Old TN-68

Notchy Creek

Fairview

411

33

Mashburn

Wilson Station

Bethlehem

Englewood

Stakely Mill

Belltown Mill

Nonaburg

Arden

Mt Vernon

Big Creek

68

Belltown

Liberty Hill

Burger

Ellis Mill

Belltown RD

360

Zion Hill

39

Piney Grove

McMinn County Airport

411

Addison

Macedonia

39

165

Tellico Plains

Wesleyanna

30

McMINN COUNTY

Prospect

Jalapa

Mecca Pike

River RD

165

Williamsburg

310

Mecca

39

Etowah

Grady

Mecca Pike

Good Springs

East Etowah

310

New Bethel

Woods Memorial Hospital

411

Balltown

30

Rural Vale

Conasauga Mill

MONROE COUNTY

Carlock

Sandy Lane

Smithfield

Cog Hill

Cambria

Holly Springs

Belleview Estates

163

Ivy

315

Cokercreek

Linsdale

Wetmore

Bullet Creek

Epperson

CR-618

411

30 33

Maggies Mill

Servilla

Ironsburg

68

Austral

30

Towee

Cataska

NF-40

KIMSEY HWY

Hambright

315

CHEROKEE NATIONAL FOREST

JOE BROWN HWY

CHEROKEE COUNTY

HIWASSEE RIVER

POLK COUNTY

APALACHIA LK

Probst

McFarland

Apalachia

Apalachia Dam

Hiwassee Village

30

Pine Ridge

NANTAHALA NATIONAL FOREST

Pleasant Hill

Archville

Hiwassee

Fields of the Wood

GREASY CREEK RD

OCOEE RIVER

123

SAW MILL RD

Liberty

294

Oak Park

64 74

OCOEE LAKE

OLD COPPER RD

68

Canoe Mountain Rd

40

Caney Creek

CHEROKEE IND RES

A   B   C   D   E

RAND MCNALLY

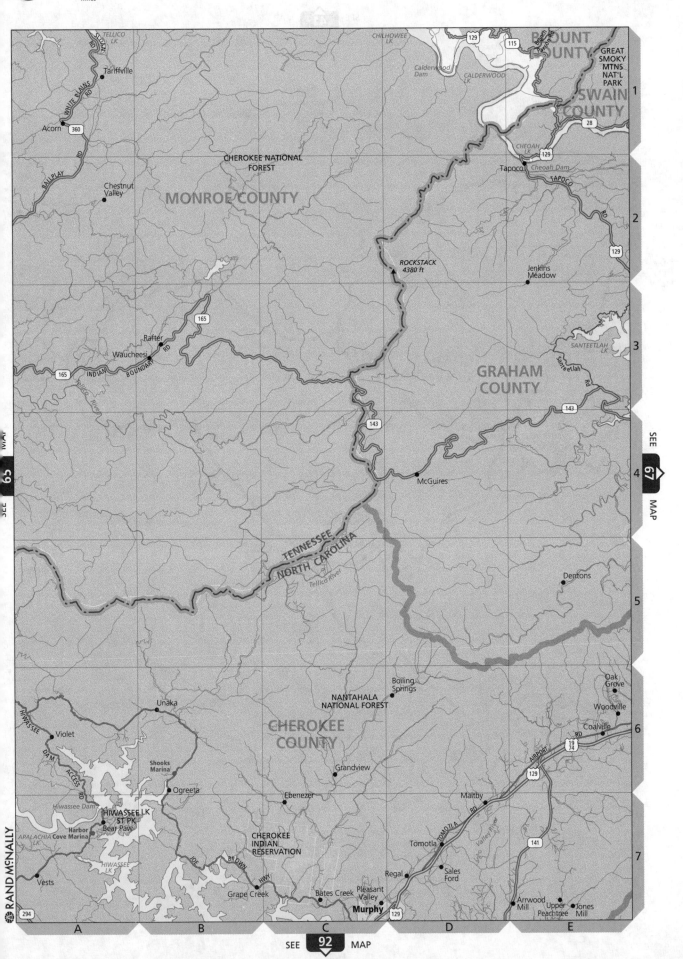

MAP
66

REGIONAL MAP

1:190,080
1 in. = 3 mi.

0   2   4
miles

N

RAND McNALLY

SEE 65 MAP

SEE 67 MAP

TELLICO LK

STECOAH RD

WHITE PLAINS RD

Tariffville

Acorn 360

BALLPLAY RD

Chestnut Valley

CHEROKEE NATIONAL FOREST

MONROE COUNTY

CHILHOWEE LK

129

115

Calderwood Dam

CALDERWOOD LK

BLOUNT COUNTY

GREAT SMOKY MTNS NAT'L PARK

SWAIN COUNTY

28

CHEOAH LK

129

Tapoco Cheoah Dam

TAPOCO

RD

129

1

2

ROCKSTACK 4380 ft

Jenkins Meadow

165

Rafter

Waucheesi

165 INDIAN BOUNDARY RD

Telico River

SANTEETLAH LK

GRAHAM COUNTY

Santeetlah Rd

143

143

3

143

McGuires

Dentons

TENNESSEE

NORTH CAROLINA

Tellico River

4

5

HIWASSEE

Violet

HIWASSEE DAM ACCESS RD

Hiwassee Dam

APALACHIA LK

Harbor Cove Marina

HIWASSEE LK ST PK
Bear Paw

HIWASSEE LK

Vests

294

Unaka

Shooks Marina

Ogreeta

JOE BROWN HWY

Grape Creek

CHEROKEE COUNTY

Boiling Springs

NANTAHALA NATIONAL FOREST

Grandview

Ebenezer

CHEROKEE INDIAN RESERVATION

Bates Creek

Pleasant Valley

Murphy

129

Oak Grove

Woodville

Coalville

19 74 RD

AIRPORT RD

129

Maltby

TOMOTLA RD

Tomotla

Valley River

Regal

Sales Ford

141

Arrwood Mill

Upper Peachtree

Jones Mill

6

7

A   B   C   D   E

MAP
67

REGIONAL MAP

1:190,080
1 in. = 3 mi.

0   2   4
miles

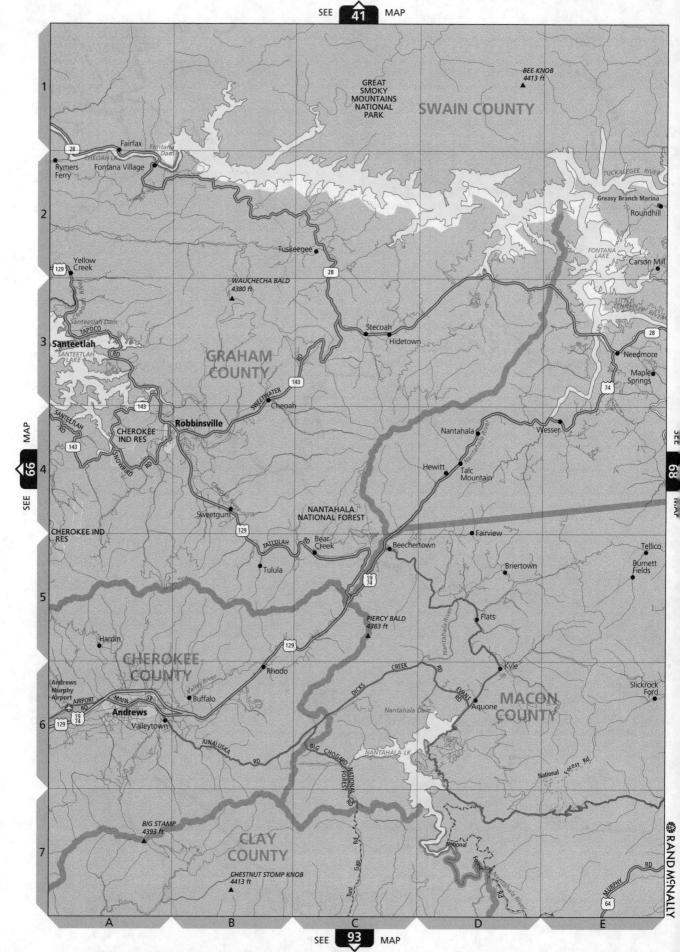

SEE **41** MAP

GREAT
SMOKY
MOUNTAINS
NATIONAL
PARK

SWAIN COUNTY

BEE KNOB
4413 ft ▲

1

28 Fairfax
Fontana Dam

Rymers
Ferry   Fontana Village   CHEOAH LK

TUCKALEGEE RIVER

Greasy Branch Marina
Roundhill

2

129 Yellow
Creek

Cheoah RIver

Tuskeegee   **28**

WAUCHECHA BALD
4380 ft ▲

FONTANA
LAKE

Carson Mill

Santeetlah Dam
TAPOCO

Stecoah
Hidetown

LITTLE
TENNESSEE
RIVER

3

Santeetlah
SANTEETLAH
LAKE
RD

GRAHAM
COUNTY

143

74

Needmore

Maple
Springs

28

SANTEETLAH
RD

143

SWEETWATER

143   Cheoah

Robbinsville

CHEROKEE
IND RES

SNOWBIRD   RD

Nantahala Mountain

Nantahala   Wesser

SEE **66** MAP

4

CHEROKEE IND
RES

Cheoah River

Sweetgum

Hewitt
Talc
Mountain

NANTAHALA
NATIONAL FOREST

129

TALLULAH

Bear
Creek

Beechertown

Fairview

Nantahala River

Tellico

Briertown

Burnett
Fields

SEE **68** MAP

5

Tulula

19
74

Hardin

129

PIERCY BALD
4383 ft

Flats

Nantahala River

CHEROKEE
COUNTY

Valley River

Rhodo

CREEK

Kyle

Slickrock
Ford

Andrews
Murphy
AIRPORT
RD

6

AIRPORT
RD

MAIN   ST

Andrews

Buffalo

DICKS

EVANS
RD

Aquone

MACON
COUNTY

129

19
74

Valleytown

JUNALUSKA

RD

BIG CHOGARD

Nantahala Dam

NANTAHALA LK

NATIONAL
FOREST
RD

National Forest Rd

National

7

BIG STAMP
4393 ft ▲

CLAY
COUNTY

Tuni Gap Rd

Forest

Nantahala River

MURPHY   RD

CHESTNUT STOMP KNOB
4413 ft ▲

64

A   B   C   D   E

SEE **93** MAP

RAND M?NALLY

MAP
68

REGIONAL MAP

1:190,080
1 in. = 3 mi.

0   2   4
miles

SEE 42 MAP

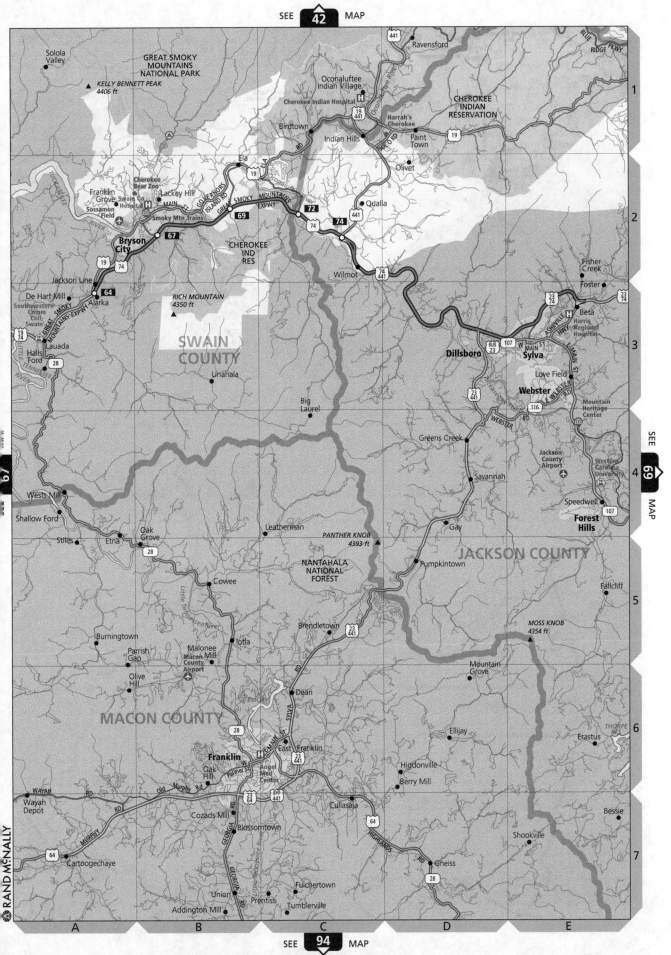

441
Ravensford

GREAT SMOKY
MOUNTAINS
NATIONAL PARK

BLUE RIDGE PKWY

Solola
Valley

▲ KELLY BENNETT PEAK
4406 ft

Oconaluftee
Indian Village

Cherokee Indian Hospital ⊞
19 441

Harrah's
Cherokee

CHEROKEE
INDIAN
RESERVATION

Birdtown

Indian Hills

441

Paint
Town

19

Ela
19

Olivet

Cherokee
Bear Zoo

Lackey Hill

GOVERNORS ISLAND RD

Franklin
Grove
Swain Co.
Hospital ⊞
Sossamon
Field

MAIN

GREAT SMOKY MOUNTAINS EXPWY

69

72

74

441

Qualla

Smoky Mtn Trains

Bryson
City

67

74

441

19

74

Fisher
Creek

Wilmot

74 441

Foster

23 74

23 74

Jackson Line

64

CHEROKEE
IND
RES

De Hart Mill

Alarka

ASHVILLE HWY

Beta ⊞

Harris
Regional
Hospital

Southwestern
Comm
Coll-
Swain

GREAT SMOKY MOUNTAINS EXPWY

RICH MOUNTAIN
4350 ft ▲

BUS
23

107

W MAIN ST

Dillsboro

Sylva

19 74

Halls
Ford

Lauada

28

SWAIN
COUNTY

Love Field

Webster

E MAIN ST

E WEBSTER RD

LITTLE TENNESSEE RIVER

TUCKASEGEE RIVER

Unahala

23
441

116

Mountain
Heritage
Center

Big
Laurel

WEBSTER RD

Greens Creek

Jackson
County
Airport

Western
Carolina
University

SEE 69 MAP

Wests Mill

Savannah

Speedwell

107

Forest
Hills

Shallow Ford

Stiles

Etna

Oak
Grove

28

Leatherman

PANTHER KNOB
4393 ft ▲

Gay

JACKSON COUNTY

Fallcliff

Burningtown

Little Tennessee River

Cowee

NANTAHALA
NATIONAL
FOREST

Pumpkintown

MOSS KNOB
4354 ft ▲

Parrish
Gap

Malonee
Mill

Iotla

Brendletown

23
441

Macon
County
Airport

Mountain
Grove

Olive
Hill

EMORY

Dean

SYLVA RD

Ellijay

Erastus

THORPE RES

MACON COUNTY

28

East Franklin

Franklin

23
441

Higdonville

Oak
Hill

Palmer St

Angel
Med
Center

Berry Mill

E MAIN ST

BYP 441

WAYAH RD

Old Murphy Rd

23
64

Cullasaja

64

Bessie

Wayah
Depot

MURPHY RD

Cozads Mill

GEORGIA RD

Blossomtown

HIGHLANDS RD

Shookville

64

Cartoogechaye

GEORGIA RD

Little Tennessee River

Gneiss

Fulchertown

28

Union

Prentiss

Tumblerville

Addington Mill

1   2   3   4   5   6   7

MAP
69

REGIONAL MAP

1:190,080
1 in. = 3 mi.

0 ··· 2 ··· 4
miles

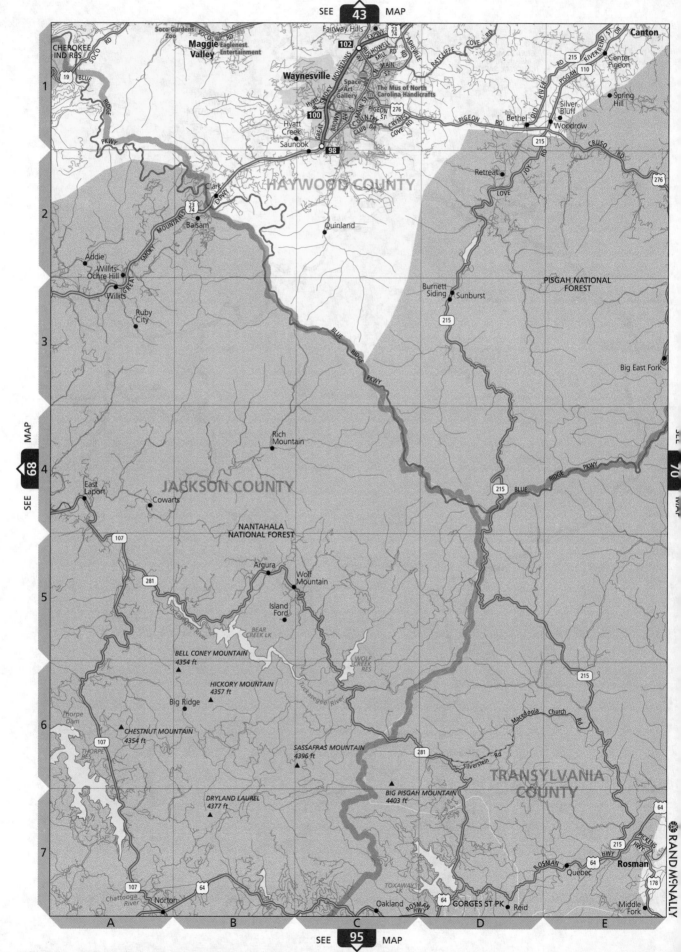

SEE **43** MAP

CHEROKEE
IND RES

Soco Gardens
Zoo

**Maggie
Valley**

Eaglenest
Entertainment

Fairway Hills

Canton

Center
Pigeon

Waynesville

Space
Art
Gallery

The Mus of North
Carolina Handicrafts

Bethel

Silver
Bluff

Spring
Hill

1

19

BLUE

RIDGE

PKWY

Hyatt
Creek

Saunook

98

Woodrow

100

Clark

HAYWOOD COUNTY

Retreat

2

23
74

Balsam

Quinland

LOVE

Addie

Willits
Ochre Hill

Willits

**PISGAH NATIONAL
FOREST**

Ruby
City

Burnett
Siding

Sunburst

3

215

BLUE

RIDGE

PKWY

Big East Fork

East
Laport

Rich
Mountain

4

JACKSON COUNTY

Cowarts

215

BLUE

RIDGE

PKWY

107

**NANTAHALA
NATIONAL FOREST**

281

Argura

Wolf
Mountain

5

Island
Ford

BEAR
CREEK LK

Tuckasegee River

WOLF
CREEK
RES

BELL CONEY MOUNTAIN
4354 ft
▲

215

Thorpe
Dam

HICKORY MOUNTAIN
4357 ft
▲

Big Ridge

Tuckasegee River

6

107

▲ **CHESTNUT MOUNTAIN**
4354 ft

THORPE
RES

SASSAFRAS MOUNTAIN
4396 ft
▲

281

Macedonia
Church
Rd

Silverstein Rd

**TRANSYLVANIA
COUNTY**

DRYLAND LAUREL
4377 ft
▲

BIG PISGAH MOUNTAIN
4403 ft
▲

64

215

7

107

64

TOXAWAY
LK

215

PICKENS
HWY

Rosman
Hwy

Quebec

Rosman

178

Chattooga
River

Norton

Oakland

ROSMAN
HWY

64

GORGES ST PK

Reid

Middle
Fork

SEE **68** MAP

SEE **70** MAP

A   B   C   D   E

SEE **95** MAP

RAND M\^cNALLY

MAP
70

REGIONAL MAP

1:190,080
1 in. = 3 mi.

0   2   4
miles

SEE 44 MAP

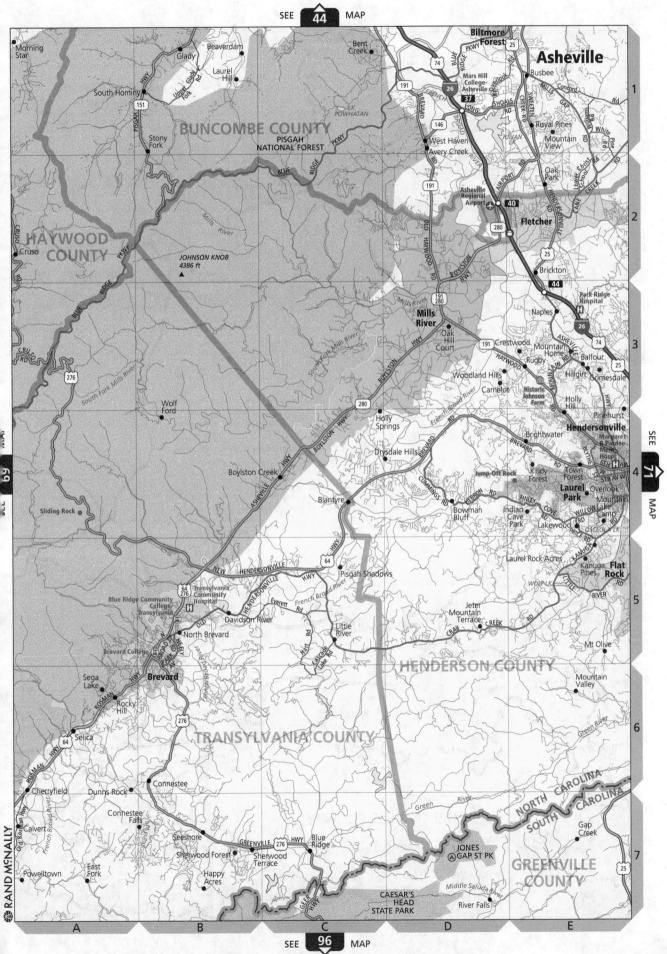

SEE 69 MAP

SEE 71 MAP

SEE 96 MAP

RAND MCNALLY

MAP
71

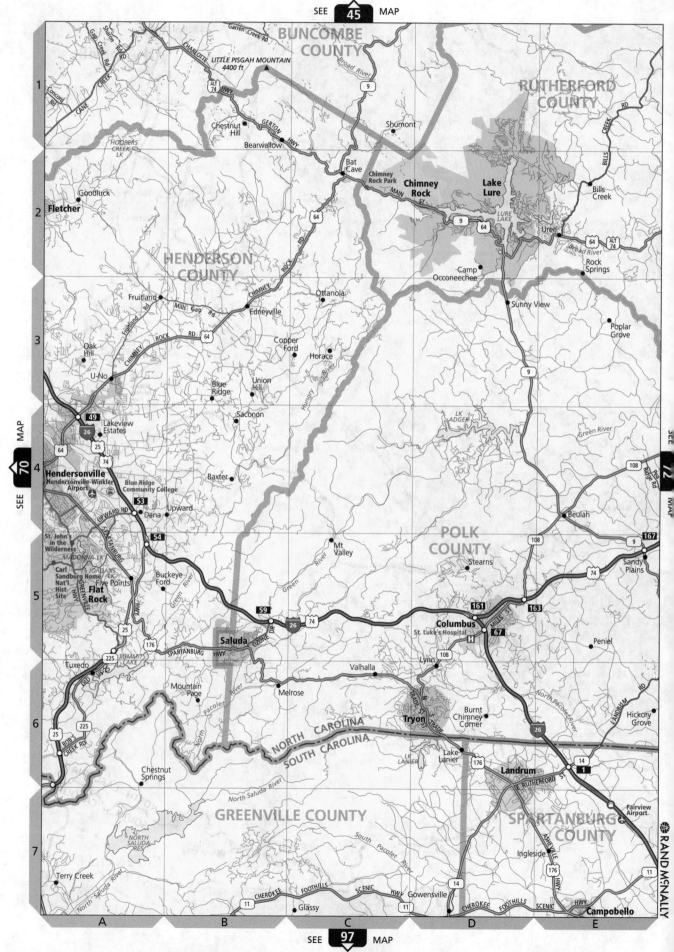

1:190,080
1 in. = 3 mi.

0   2   4
miles

SEE 45 MAP

BUNCOMBE COUNTY

RUTHERFORD COUNTY

Garren Creek Rd

Broad River

CHARLOTTE

LITTLE PISGAH MOUNTAIN
4400 ft

ALT 74 HWY

9

Shumont

Bills Creek RD

Chestnut Hill

GERTON HWY

Bearwallow

Bat Cave

Chimney Rock Park

Chimney Rock

Lake Lure

Bills Creek

CANE CREEK

Sharon RD
Gap Creek Rd

Concord RD

HOOPERS CREEK LK

Goodluck

Fletcher

HENDERSON COUNTY

CHIMNEY ROCK RD

64

MAIN ST

LURE LAKE

Uree

64
ALT 74

Broad River

Rock Springs

Fruitland

Mills Gap Rd

Edneyville

Ottanola

Camp Occoneechee

Sunny View

Poplar Grove

Fruitland Rd

CHIMNEY ROCK RD

64

Copper Ford

Horace

Oak Hill

U-No

Blue Ridge

Union Hill

Hungry River

9

LK ADGER

Green River

49

26

Lakeview Estates

Saconon

25

64

74

Hendersonville

53

Baxter

Mt Valley

POLK COUNTY

108

Beulah

108

167

108

SEE 72 MAP

Hendersonville-Winkler Airport

Blue Ridge Community College

HOWARD RD

Dana

Upward

9

163

Sandy Plains

St. John's in the Wilderness

54

Green River

74

St. Luke's Hospital

MADONNA LK

SPARTANBURG

JORDANS LK

Buckeye Ford

Stearns

161

Columbus

67

Peniel

Carl Sandburg Home Nat'l Hist Site

Five Points

GREENVILLE HWY

Flat Rock

Green River

59

26

74

DZONE DR

H

108

Lynn

25

AMH

176

SPARTANBURG HWY

Saluda

Valhalla

Trade St

N TRADE

Burnt Chimney Corner

Hickory Grove

North Pacolet River

LANDRUM RD

Tuxedo

225

SUMMIT LAKE

Mountain Page

Pacolet River

Melrose

Tryon

26

14

25

225

BOB CREEK RD

North Pacolet River

NORTH CAROLINA

SOUTH CAROLINA

LK LANIER

Lake Lanier

176

1

Landrum

Chestnut Springs

North Saluda River

E. RUTHERFORD ST

Fairview Airport

GREENVILLE COUNTY

SPARTANBURG COUNTY

NORTH SALUDA RES

South Pacolet River

Ingleside

ASHEVILLE HWY

176 HWY

Terry Creek

North Saluda River

CHEROKEE FOOTHILLS SCENIC HWY

11

14

Gowensville

176

CHEROKEE FOOTHILLS SCENIC HWY

11

Campobello

11

Glassy

11

A   B   C   D   E

SEE 97 MAP

SEE 70 MAP

MAP
72

REGIONAL MAP

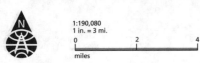

1:190,080
1 in. = 3 mi.
0   2   4
miles

SEE 46 MAP

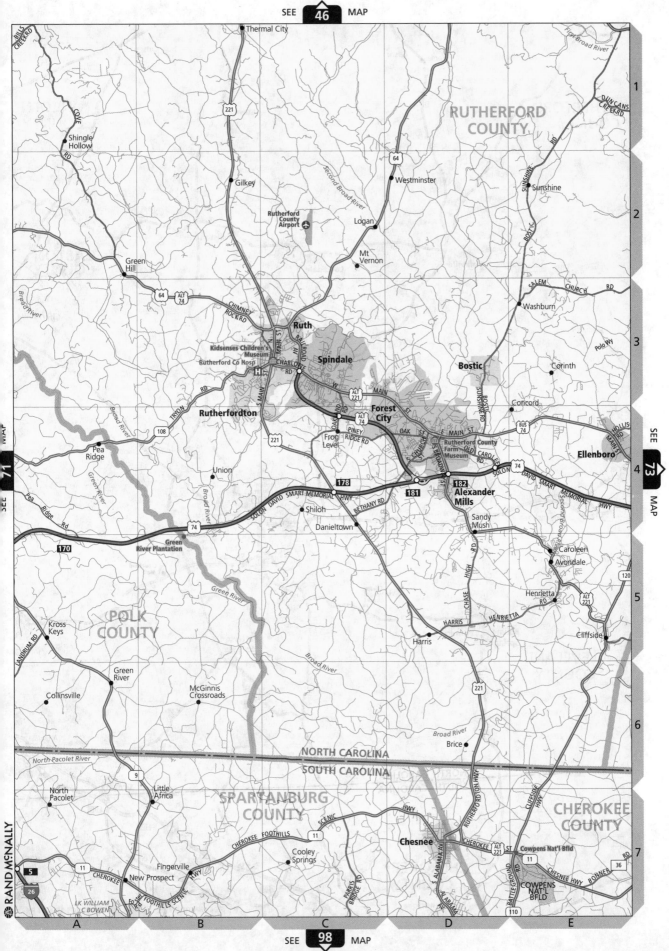

Thermal City

RUTHERFORD COUNTY

DUNCANS CREEK RD

Gilkey

Westminster

Sunshine

Logan

Rutherford County Airport

Mt Vernon

Washburn

SALEM CHURCH RD

Green Hill

CHIMNEY ROCK RD

Ruth

Kidsenses Children's Museum
Rutherford Co Hosp

Spindale

Bostic

Corinth

Polo Wy

Rutherfordton

Concord

Forest City

Frog Level

PINEY RIDGE RD

Rutherford County Farm Museum

Ellenboro

Pea Ridge

Union

SOLON DAVID SMART MEMORIAL HWY

Alexander Mills

Shiloh

Sandy Mush

Danieltown

BETHANY RD

Green River Plantation

Caroleen

Avondale

Henrietta

Kross Keys

POLK COUNTY

Harris

Cliffside

Green River

McGinnis Crossroads

Collinsville

Broad River

NORTH CAROLINA
SOUTH CAROLINA

Brice

North Pacolet River

SEE 71 MAP

SEE 73 MAP

North Pacolet

Little Africa

SPARTANBURG COUNTY

CHEROKEE COUNTY

CHEROKEE FOOTHILLS SCENIC HWY

Chesnee

Cowpens Nat'l Bfld

Fingerville

Cooley Springs

New Prospect

LK WILLIAM C BOWEN

COWPENS NAT'L BFLD

RAND McNALLY

A   B   C   D   E

MAP
73

REGIONAL MAP

1:190,080
1 in. = 3 mi.

0   2   4
miles

N

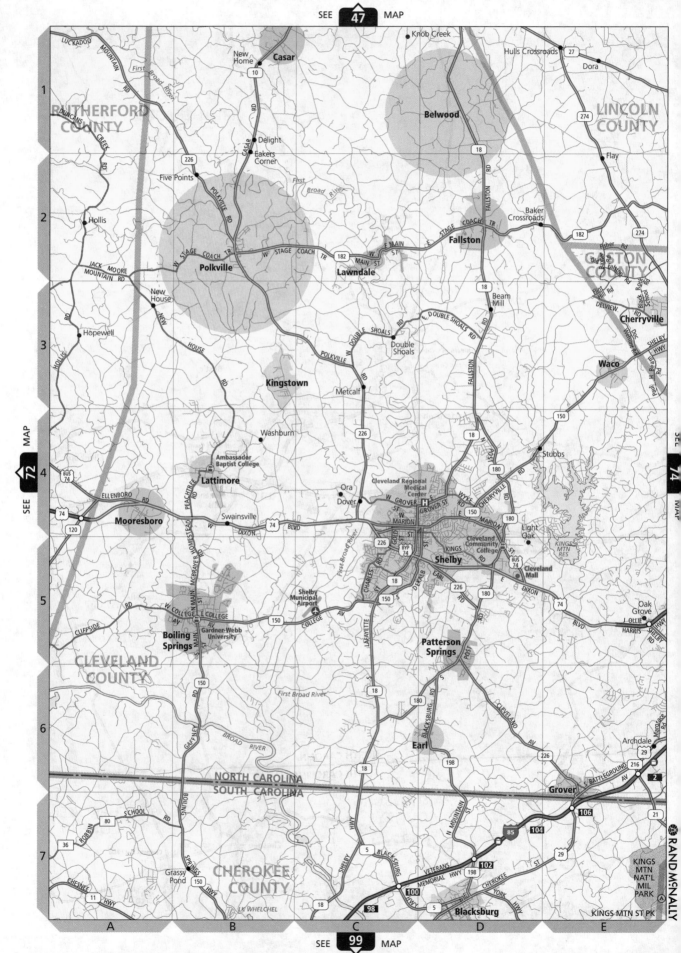

SEE **47** MAP

SEE **72** MAP

SEE **74** MAP

RUTHERFORD COUNTY

LINCOLN COUNTY

GASTON COUNTY

CLEVELAND COUNTY

CHEROKEE COUNTY

Knob Creek

Casar

New Home

Delight

Eakers Corner

Five Points

Hollis

Polkville

New House

Hopewell

Kingstown

Washburn

Ambassador Baptist College

Lattimore

New Home

Belwood

Hulls Crossroads

Dora

Flay

Fallston

Baker Crossroads

Lawndale

Double Shoals

Metcalf

Beam Mill

Cherryville

Waco

Stubbs

Cleveland Regional Medical Center

Ora
Dover

Mooresboro

Swainsville

Boiling Springs

Gardner-Webb University

Shelby Municipal Airport

Shelby

Kings

Cleveland Community College

Light Oak

KINGS MTN RES

Cleveland Mall

Oak Grove

Patterson Springs

First Broad River

Earl

Grover

Archdale

NORTH CAROLINA
SOUTH CAROLINA

Grassy Pond

Blacksburg

LK WHELCHEL

KINGS MTN NAT'L MIL PARK

KINGS MTN ST PK

RAND M^{c}NALLY

MAP
74

REGIONAL MAP

1:190,080
1 in. = 3 mi.
0   2   4
miles

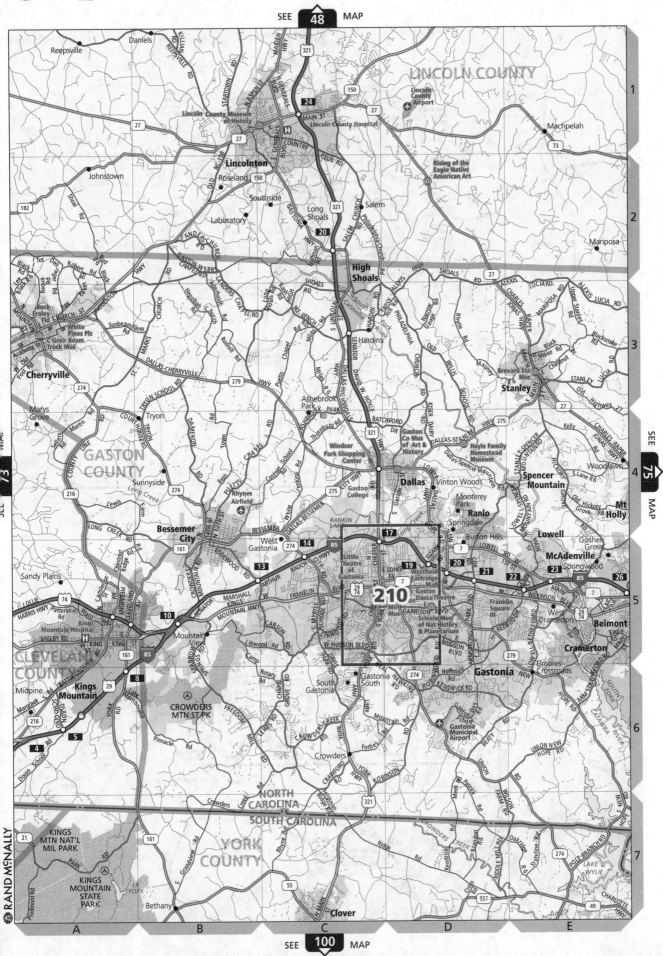

SEE 48 MAP
SEE 75 MAP
SEE 73 MAP
SEE 100 MAP

RAND McNALLY

MAP
75

REGIONAL MAP

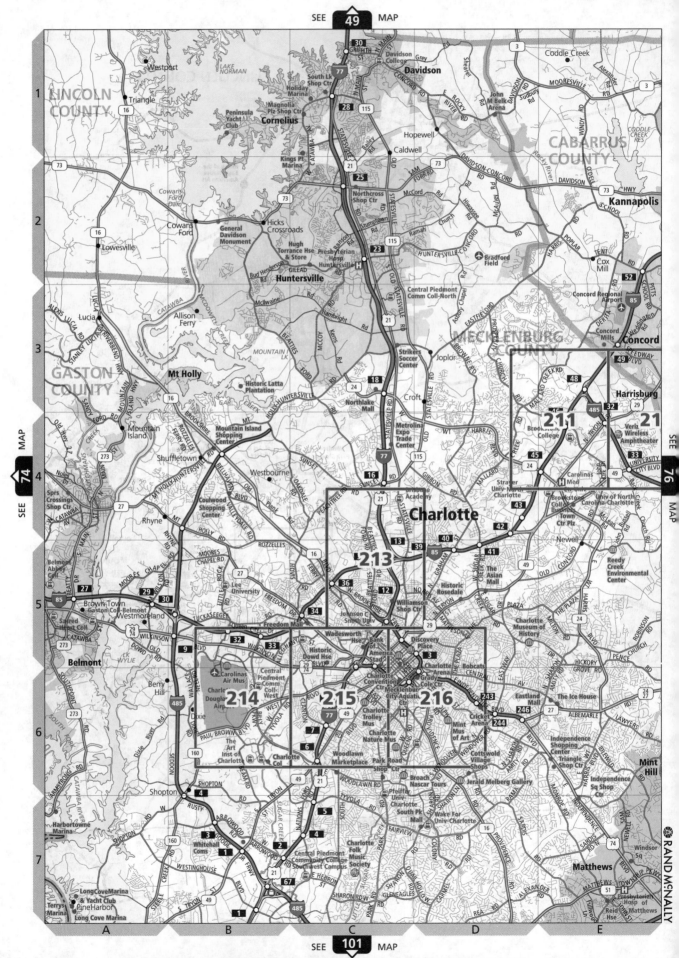

1:190,080
1 in. = 3 mi.

0   2   4
miles

SEE [101] MAP

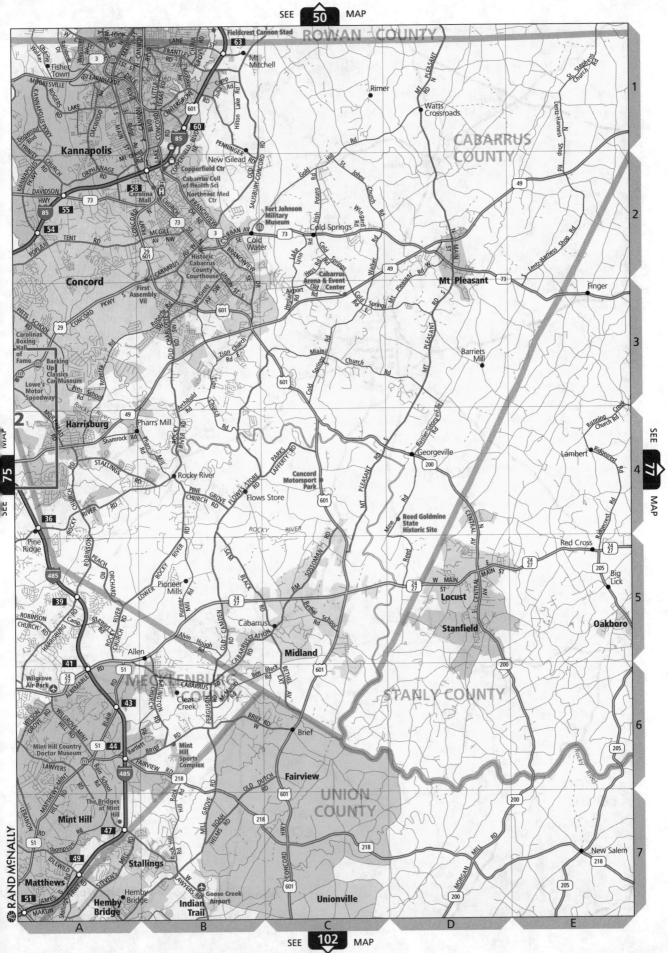

MAP
76
REGIONAL MAP

N

1:190,080
1 in. = 3 mi.

0   2   4
miles

SEE 50 MAP

ROWAN COUNTY

Fieldcrest Cannon Stad
63

Mt Mitchell

Rimer

Watts Crossroads

CABARRUS COUNTY

1

49

Lentz-Harness Shop Rd

St. Stephens Church Rd

Kannapolis

New Gilead

Penninger Rd

Copperfield Ctr
Cabarrus Coll of Health Sci
Northeast Med Ctr

Old Salisbury-Concord Rd

Fort Johnson Military Museum

Cold Springs

73

49

Mt Pleasant

73

Finger

2

Carolina Mall

Davidson
HWY
85
55
54

TENT

Concord

First Assembly Vil

Historic Cabarrus County Courthouse

Cold Water

Corban Av

Cabarrus Arena & Event Center

Airport Rd

Miami Church Rd

Barriers Mill

3

Carolinas Boxing Hall of Fame

Backing Up Classics Car Museum

Lowe's Motor Speedway

29

49

Pharrs Mill

Harrisburg

Shamrock Rd

Zion Church Rd

601

Cold Springs Rd

Georgeville

200

Lambert

Ridgecrest Rd

Running Creek
Church Rd

4

SEE 77 MAP

SEE 75 MAP

36

Pine Ridge

Rocky River

Flows Store

Concord Motorsport Park

601

Reed Goldmine State Historic Site

Red Cross
24 27

205

Big Lick

485

39

Pioneer Mills

24
27

Cabarrus

24
27

Locust

W MAIN ST

MAIN ST

Stanfield

200

Oakboro

5

ROBINSON CHURCH RD

41

Wilgrove Air Park

24
27

Allen

Cabarrus Station

Midland

601

STANLY COUNTY

43

Clear Creek

Mint Hill Country Doctor Museum

44

Mint Hill Sports Complex

485

Brief

Brief Rd W

6

Fairview

601

UNION COUNTY

200

205

Mint Hill

51

47

218

218

200

New Salem
218

7

Matthews

49

Stallings

Hemby Bridge

Indian Trail

Goose Creek Airport

Unionville

205

SEE 102 MAP

A   B   C   D   E

MAP
77

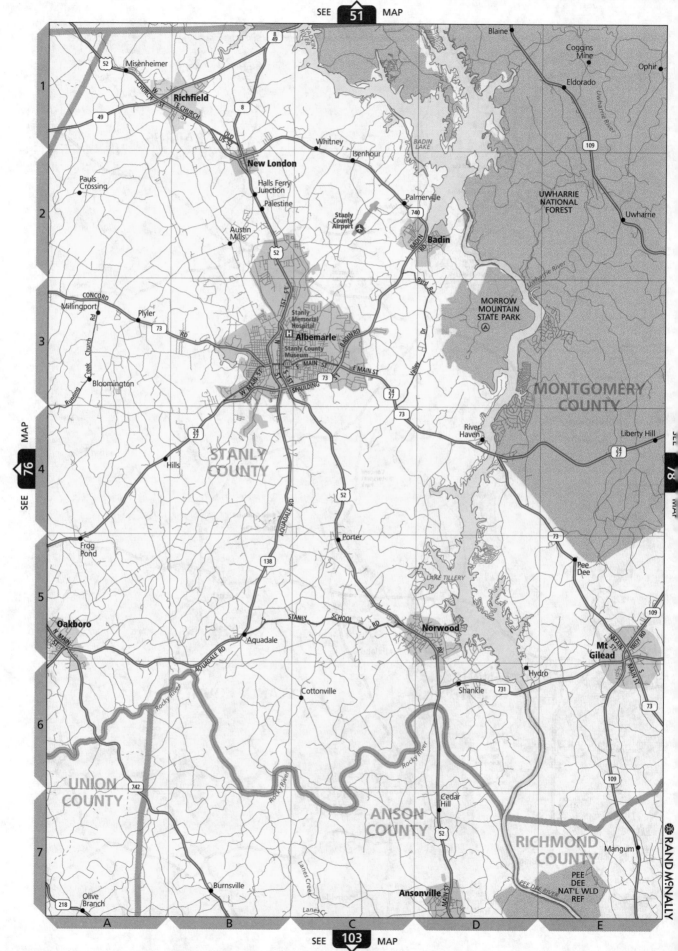

1:190,080
1 in. = 3 mi.

0   2   4
miles

N

SEE **51** MAP

SEE **76** MAP

SEE **78** MAP

SEE **103** MAP

Blaine

Coggins
Mine

Ophir

Eldorado

52 Misenheimer

UWHARRIE
NATIONAL
FOREST

Uwharrie

109

Richfield

8
49

49

52

YADKIN RIVER

Whitney   Isenhour

New London

Palmerville

740

BADIN
LAKE

Pauls
Crossing

Halls Ferry
Junction

Palestine

Badin

Austin
Mills

Stanly
County
Airport

52

BADIN RD

MORROW
MOUNTAIN
STATE PARK

CONCORD

Byrd Rd

Millingport

Plyler

73   RD

Stanly
Memorial
Hospital

Albemarle

Stanly County
Museum

1ST ST

BADIN RD

**MONTGOMERY
COUNTY**

Running Creek Church

Bloomington

S 3RD ST

E MAIN ST

Valley Dr

24
27

73

River
Haven

Liberty Hill

24
27

W MAIN ST   SPAULDING

73

**STANLY
COUNTY**

24
27

Hills

AQUADALE RD

52

Porter

73

Pee
Dee

109

Frog
Pond

138

LAKE TILLERY

Oakboro

N MAIN ST

STANLY   SCHOOL   RD

Aquadale

Norwood

N 2ND ST

**Mt
Gilead**

N MAIN ST   TROY RD

AQUADALE RD

Hydro

Cottonville

731

Shankle

73

**UNION
COUNTY**

742

Rocky River

Rocky River

Cedar
Hill

**ANSON
COUNTY**

52

109

**RICHMOND
COUNTY**

Mangum

Olive
Branch

218

Burnsville

Lanes Creek

Ansonville

N MAIN ST

PEE DEE RIVER

PEE
DEE
NAT'L WLD
REF

RAND McNALLY

A   B   C   D   E

1

2

3

4

5

6

7

MAP
78

REGIONAL MAP

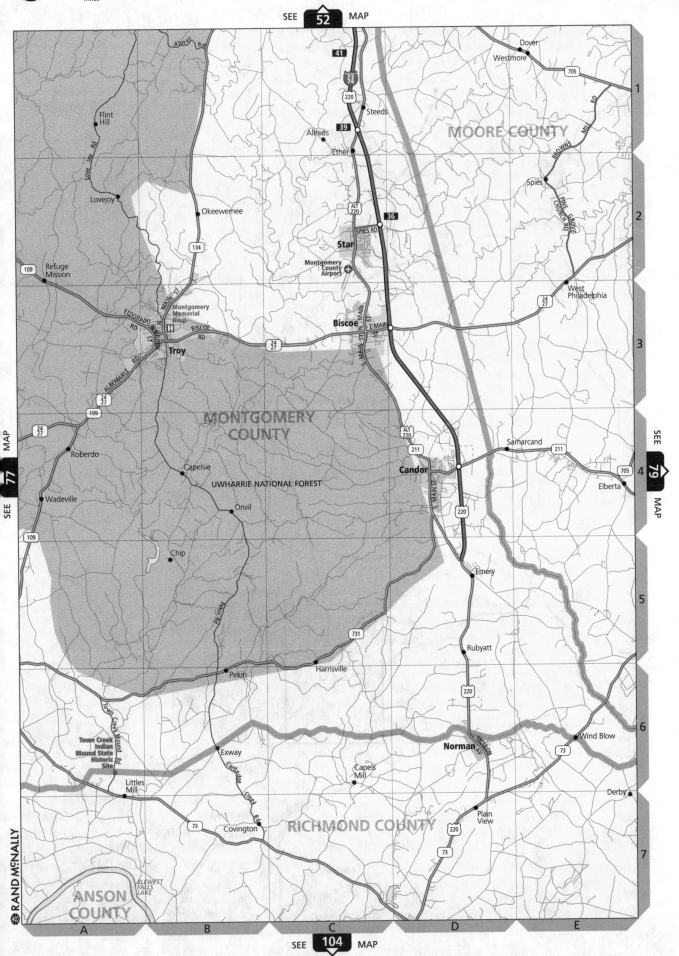

1:190,080
1 in. = 3 mi.

0   2   4
miles

SEE 52 MAP

SEE 77 MAP

SEE 79 MAP

SEE 104 MAP

MOORE COUNTY

MONTGOMERY COUNTY

UWHARRIE NATIONAL FOREST

RICHMOND COUNTY

ANSON COUNTY

Dover
Westmore
Flint Hill
Steeds
Allreds
Ether
Spies
Okeewemee
Star
Montgomery County Airport
West Philadelphia
Refuge Mission
Montgomery Memorial Hosp
Biscoe
Troy
Roberdo
Capelsie
Candor
Samarcand
Elberta
Wadeville
Onvil
Chip
Emery
Rubyatt
Pekin
Harrisville
Wind Blow
Town Creek Indian Mound State Historic Site
Exway
Capels Mill
Norman
Derby
Littles Mill
Covington
Plain View
BLEWETT FALLS LAKE

RAND McNALLY

MAP

79

REGIONAL MAP

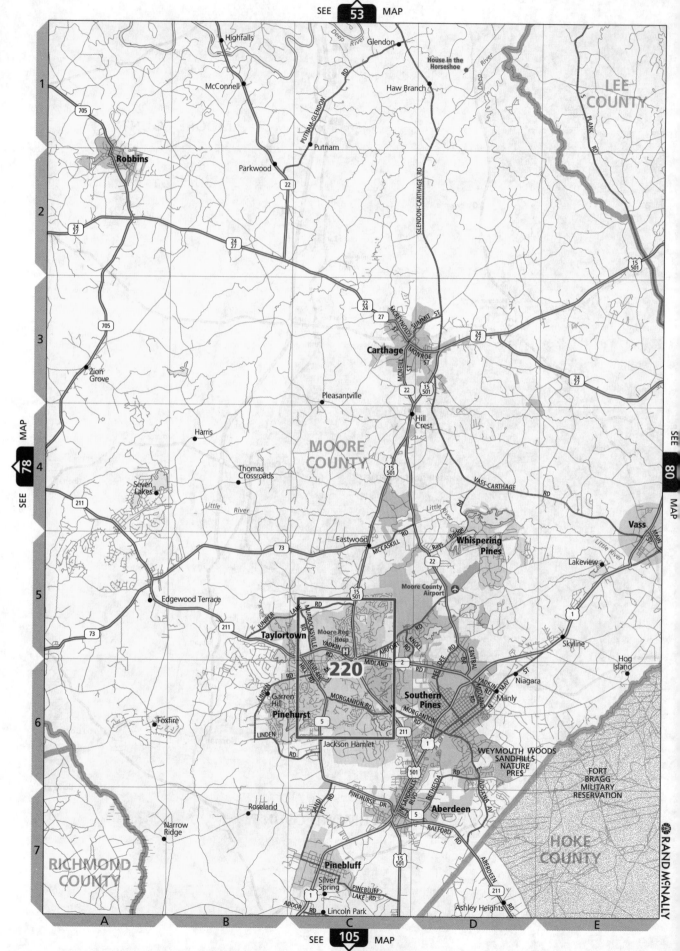

SEE **53** MAP

SEE MAP **78**

SEE **80** MAP

SEE **105** MAP

RAND McNALLY

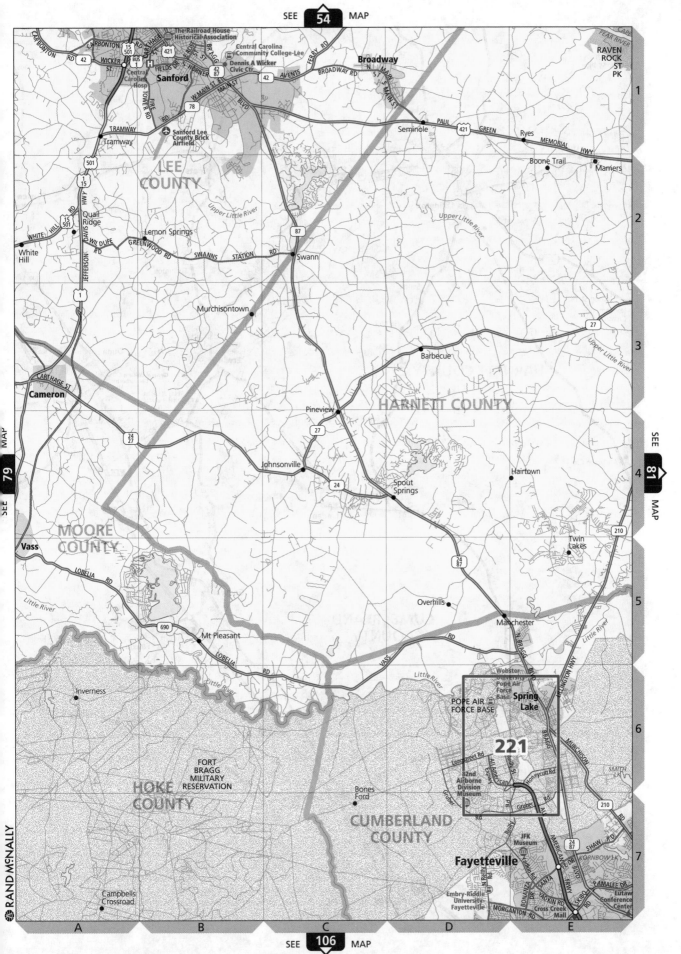

MAP
80

REGIONAL MAP

1:190,080
1 in. = 3 mi.

0   2   4
miles

SEE **54** MAP

The Railroad House
Historical Association

Central Carolina
Community College-Lee

RAVEN
ROCK
ST
PK

Broadway

Dennis A Wicker
Civic Ctr

CARBONTON RD

42

CARBONTON RD

15
501

BUS
1

421

Sanford

Central
Carolina
Hosp

FIELDS DR

S HORNER

42
87

BROADWAY RD

N ST S MAIN ST

W MAIN ST

MAIN ST

AVENTS

FERRY RD

78

BLVD

42

FIRE

TOWER RD

Seminole

PAUL

421

GREEN

Ryes

MEMORIAL

Boone Trail

HWY

Mamers

TRAMWAY

Sanford Lee
County Brick
Airfield

Tramway

1

501

LEE
COUNTY

Upper Little River

15
501

HWY

RD

15
15

Quail
Ridge

Upper Little River

2

WHITE
HILL

15
501

JEFFERSON

DAVIS

WIL DLIFE RD

Lemon Springs

87

White
Hill

GREENWOOD RD

SWANNS

STATION

RD

Swann

1

27

Murchisontown

Upper Little River

3

Barbecue

HARNETT COUNTY

CARTHAGE ST

Cameron

Pineview

Hairtown

SEE **81** MAP

4

27

24
27

Johnsonville

24

Spout
Springs

210

Twin
Lakes

MOORE
COUNTY

LOBELIA

RD

24
87

Little River

Vass

Overhills

Little River

Manchester

5

690

Mt Pleasant

LOBELIA

RD

VASS

RD

N BRAGG BLVD

ELLINGTON HWY

RD

Little River

Inverness

Little River

Webster

University

Pope Air
Force Base

**Spring
Lake**

BRAGG

MURCHISON

SMITH

6

FORT
BRAGG
MILITARY
RESERVATION

POPE AIR
FORCE BASE

221

Longstreet Rd

All American Expwy

Reilly St

Honeycutt Rd

210

RD

HOKE
COUNTY

Bones
Ford

82nd
Airborne
Division
Museum

Gruber

Rd

Gruber

Rd

American

Reilly

JFK
Museum

24
87

SHAW RD

KORNBOW LK

RAMALEE DR

CUMBERLAND
COUNTY

Fayetteville

Morganton Rd

Cedar Creek

BRAGG BLVD

BONANZA

SANTA

YADKIN RD

SK800

MORGANTON

Eutaw
Conference
Center

7

Campbells
Crossroad

Embry-Riddle
University-
Fayetteville

Cross Creek
Mall

RAND MᶜNALLY

SEE 79 MAP

MAP
81

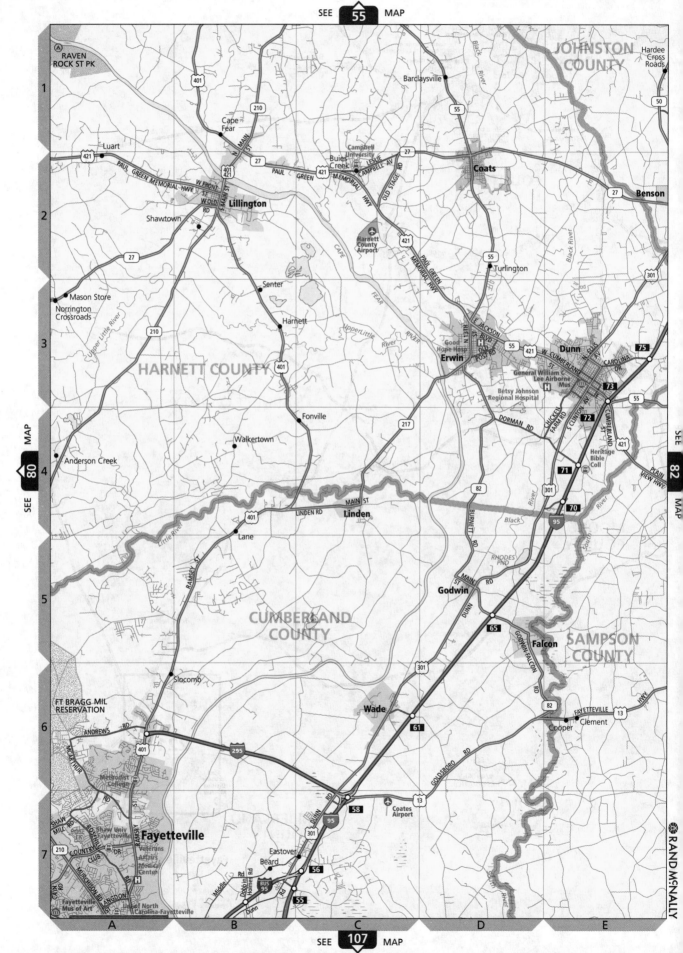

1:190,080
1 in. = 3 mi.
0   2   4
miles

SEE 55 MAP

JOHNSTON COUNTY

Hardee Cross Roads

RAVEN ROCK ST PK

Barclaysville

Cape Fear

Luart

Campbell University
Buies Creek

Coats

Benson

Lillington

Shawtown

Turlington

Mason Store
Norrington Crossroads

Senter

Harnett

Dunn

Erwin

Good Hope Hosp

General William C Lee Airborne Mus

Betsy Johnson Regional Hospital

HARNETT COUNTY

Fonville

Walkertown

Anderson Creek

SEE 80 MAP

Heritage Bible Coll

SEE 82 MAP

Linden

Lane

Black

CUMBERLAND COUNTY

Godwin

Falcon

SAMPSON COUNTY

Slocomb

FT BRAGG MIL RESERVATION

Andrews

Metrodist College

Wade

Cooper   Clement

Fayetteville

Coates Airport

Shaw Univ Fayetteville

Veterans Affairs Medical Center

Eastover
Beard

Fayetteville Mus of Art

Univ of North Carolina-Fayetteville

A   B   C   D   E

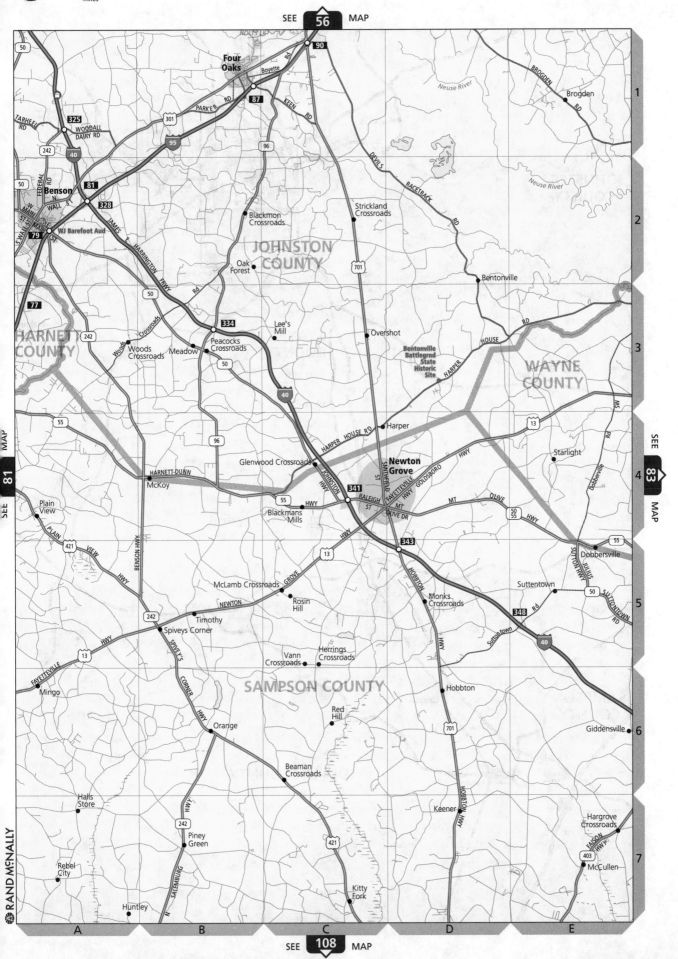

MAP
82

REGIONAL MAP

1:190,080
1 in. = 3 mi.

0   2   4
miles

SEE 56 MAP

1

2

3

4

5

6

7

SEE 81 MAP

SEE 83 MAP

RAND McNALLY

90

Four
Oaks

Boyette

87
KEEN RD

PARKER RD

301

95

96

50

325

WOODALL
DAIRY RD

242

40

77

50

FEDERAL RD

Benson

81

328

79

WJ Barefoot Aud

W MAIN ST
W WALL ST
S MAIN ST
JAMES E. HARRINGTON FRWY

Blackmon
Crossroads

JOHNSTON
COUNTY

Oak
Forest

50

334

Lee's
Mill

Peacocks
Crossroads

50

40

Woods
Crossroads

Meadow

242

Woods
Crossroads

55

96

Glenwood Crossroads

HARNETT-DUNN

McKoy

Plain
View

PLAIN VIEW HWY

421

BENSON HWY

Blackmans
Mills

55

HWY

JOHNSTON HWY

341

RALEIGH ST
SMITHFIELD ST
FAYETTEVILLE

Newton
Grove

MT OLIVE DR

343

13

McLamb Crossroads

NEWTON
GROVE

Rosin
Hill

242

Timothy

Spiveys Corner

SPIVEY'S CORNER HWY

13

FAYETTEVILLE HWY

Mingo

Vann
Crossroads

Herrings
Crossroads

SAMPSON COUNTY

Orange

Red
Hill

Beaman
Crossroads

Halls
Store

242

N SALEMBURG HWY

Piney
Green

421

Rebel
City

Huntley

Kitty
Fork

Strickland
Crossroads

DEVILS RACETRACK RD

701

Neuse River

Neuse River

BROGDEN RD

Brogden

Bentonville

HOUSE RD

HARPER

Bentonville
Battlegrnd
State
Historic
Site

Harper

HARPER HOUSE RD

WAYNE
COUNTY

13

Starlight

GOLDSBORO HWY

MT OLIVE HWY

50 55 HWY

Dobbersville

55

50

SUTTON HWY
JULIUS RD

Suttentown

HOBBTON HWY

Monks
Crossroads

348 RD

40

Suttontown

Hobbton

701

HOBBTON HWY

Keener

McCullen

403

Giddensville

Hargrove
Crossroads

EASON HWY

HARNETT
COUNTY

SEE 108 MAP

A   B   C   D   E

MAP
83

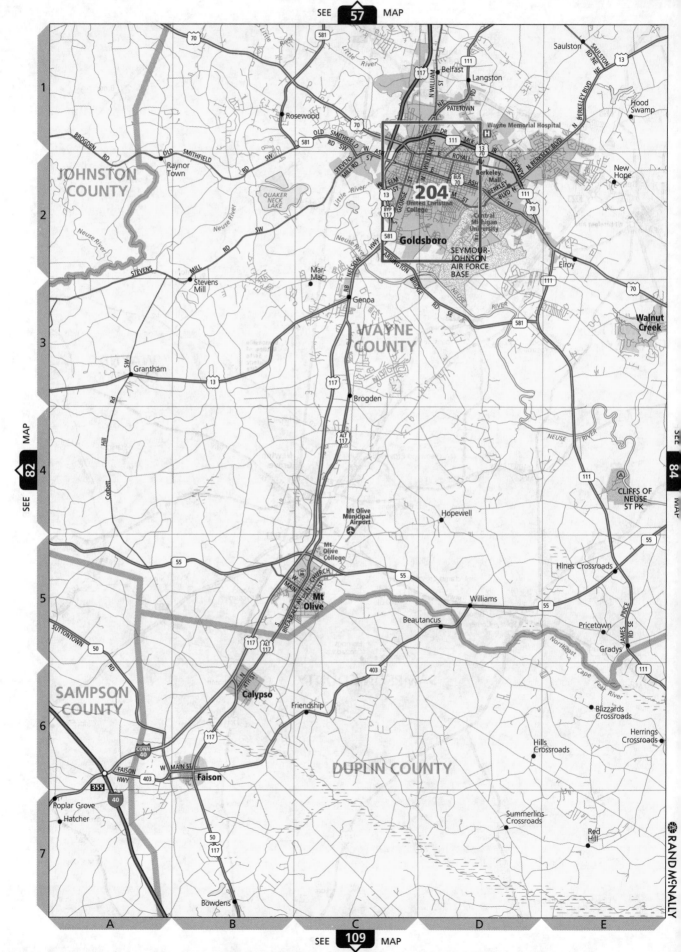

1:190,080
1 in. = 3 mi.

0   2   4
miles

SEE 57 MAP

SEE 82 MAP

SEE 84 MAP

SEE 109 MAP

RAND MCNALLY

JOHNSTON COUNTY
WAYNE COUNTY
SAMPSON COUNTY
DUPLIN COUNTY

Saulston
Belfast
Langston
Hood Swamp
Rosewood
PATETOWN
Wayne Memorial Hospital
New Hope
Raynor Town
QUAKER NECK LAKE
204
Goldsboro
United Christian College
Central Michigan University
Berkeley Mall
Elroy
Stevens Mill
Mar-Mac
Genoa
Walnut Creek
SEYMOUR-JOHNSON AIR FORCE BASE
Grantham
Brogden
Hopewell
Mt Olive Municipal Airport
Mt Olive College
CLIFFS OF NEUSE ST PK
Hines Crossroads
Mt Olive
Williams
Beautancus
Pricetown
Gradys
Calypso
Friendship
Blizzards Crossroads
Herrings Crossroads
Hills Crossroads
Faison
Poplar Grove
Hatcher
Summerlins Crossroads
Red Hill
Bowdens
NEUSE RIVER
Cape Fear River

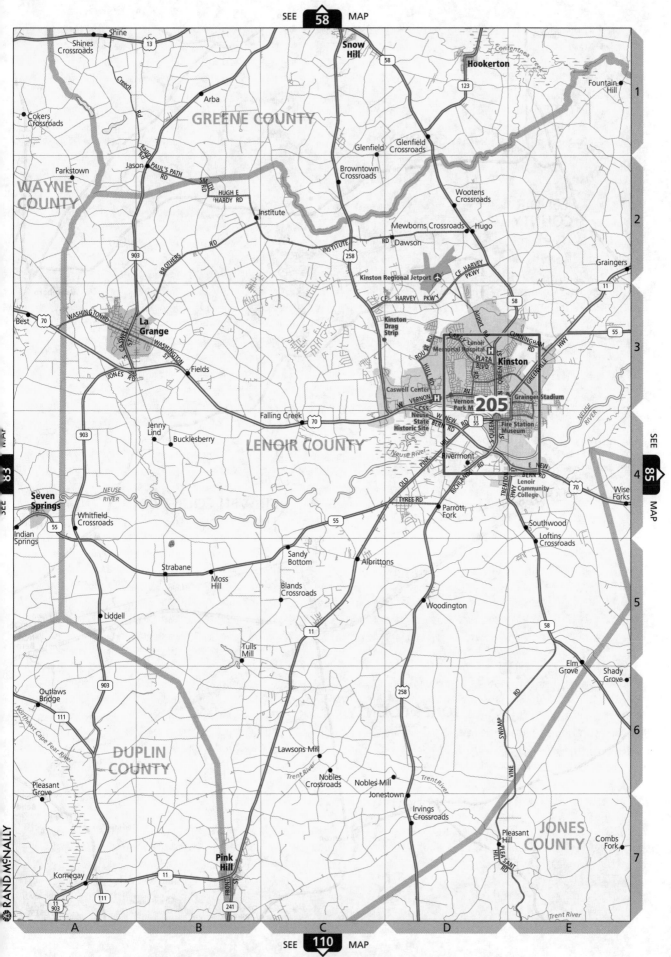

MAP
84

REGIONAL MAP

1:190,080
1 in. = 3 mi.

0   2   4
miles

Shine

Shines
Crossroads

Cokers
Crossroads

Arba

GREENE COUNTY

Parkstown

Jason

PAUL'S PATH RD

**WAYNE
COUNTY**

HUGH E
HARDY RD

Institute

Glenfield

Glenfield
Crossroads

Browntown
Crossroads

Wootens
Crossroads

Mewborns Crossroads

Hugo

Dawson

Snow
Hill

Hookerton

Fountain
Hill

1

123

58

13

Creech Rd

SM RD

903

BROTHERS RD

INSTITUTE RD

RD

258

Kinston Regional Jetport

CF HARVEY PKWY

CF HARVEY PKWY

Graingers

2

11

55

58

Best

70

La
Grange

WASHINGTON RD

CASWELL ST

WASHINGTON ST

JONES RD

Fields

Kinston
Drag
Strip

Caswell Center

VERNON AV

CCS

Neuse
State
Historic Site

HULL RD

ROUSE RD

PLAZA
BLVD

Lenoir
Memorial Hospital

Vernon
Park M

QUEEN ST

Kinston

CUNNINGHAM RD

GREENVILLE HWY

Grainger Stadium

205

Fire Station
Museum

NEUSE RIVER

SEE **85** MAP

3

903

Falling Creek

70

Jenny
Lind

Bucklesberry

LENOIR COUNTY

Neuse River

NEW BERN RD

NEW BERN RD

Rivermont

PINK HILL RD

OLD RICHLANDS RD

Lenoir
Community
College

TRENTON HWY

E NEW
BERN RD

Wise
Forks

70

4

Seven
Springs

Indian
Springs

NEUSE
RIVER

55

Whitfield
Crossroads

Strabane

Moss
Hill

Sandy
Bottom

Blands
Crossroads

Albrittons

TYREE RD

55

Parrott
Fork

Woodington

Southwood

Loftins
Crossroads

5

Liddell

Tulls
Mill

11

258

58

Elm
Grove

Shady
Grove

6

903

Outlaws
Bridge

111

Northeast Cape Fear River

**DUPLIN
COUNTY**

Lawsons Mill

Trent River

Nobles
Crossroads

Nobles Mill

Jonestown

Trent River

Irvings
Crossroads

SWAMP RD

VINE

Pleasant
Hill

PLEASANT RD

**JONES
COUNTY**

Combs
Fork

7

Pleasant
Grove

Kornegay

11
903

111

**Pink
Hill**

FRONT ST

11

241

Trent River

A   B   C   D   E

MAP
85

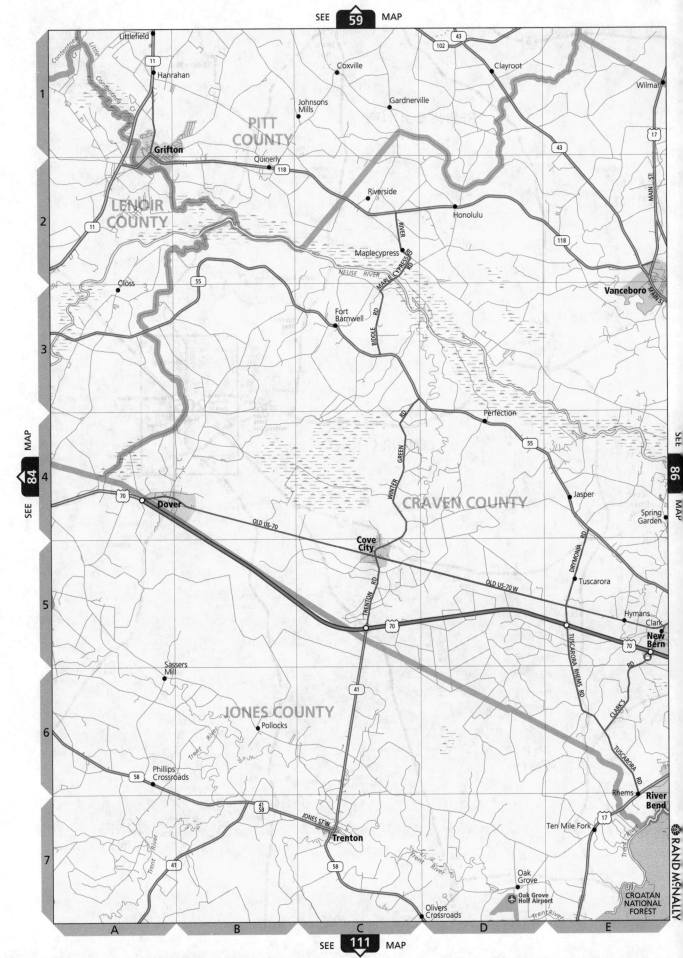

REGIONAL MAP

1:190,080
1 in. = 3 mi.
0   2   4
miles

Littlefield

11

Hanrahan

Coxville

Clayroot

102

43

Gardnerville

Wilman

17

PITT
COUNTY

Johnsons
Mills

43

Grifton

Quinerly

118

Riverside

Honolulu

LENOIR
COUNTY

11

118

Maplecypress

NEUSE RIVER

MARTIN CYPRESS RD

Vanceboro

MAIN ST

Closs

55

Fort
Barnwell

BIDDLE RD

RD

Perfection

55

WINTER GREEN RD

CRAVEN COUNTY

Jasper

DRYMONIA RD

Spring
Garden

MAP 84

SEE

70

Dover

OLD US-70

Cove
City

OLD US-70 W

Tuscarora

TRENTON RD

SEE 86 MAP

70

New
Bern

Hymans
Clark

TUSCARORA RHEMS RD

70

41

Sassers
Mill

JONES COUNTY

CLARK'S RD

Pollocks

Trent River

TUSCARORA RD

Phillips
Crossroads

58

41
58

Rhems

River
Bend

JONES ST W

Trenton

Ten Mile Fork

17

41

58

Trent River

Oak
Grove

Oak Grove
Holf Airport

CROATAN
NATIONAL
FOREST

RAND M^cNALLY

Olivers
Crossroads

Trent River

A   B   C   D   E

MAP
86

REGIONAL MAP

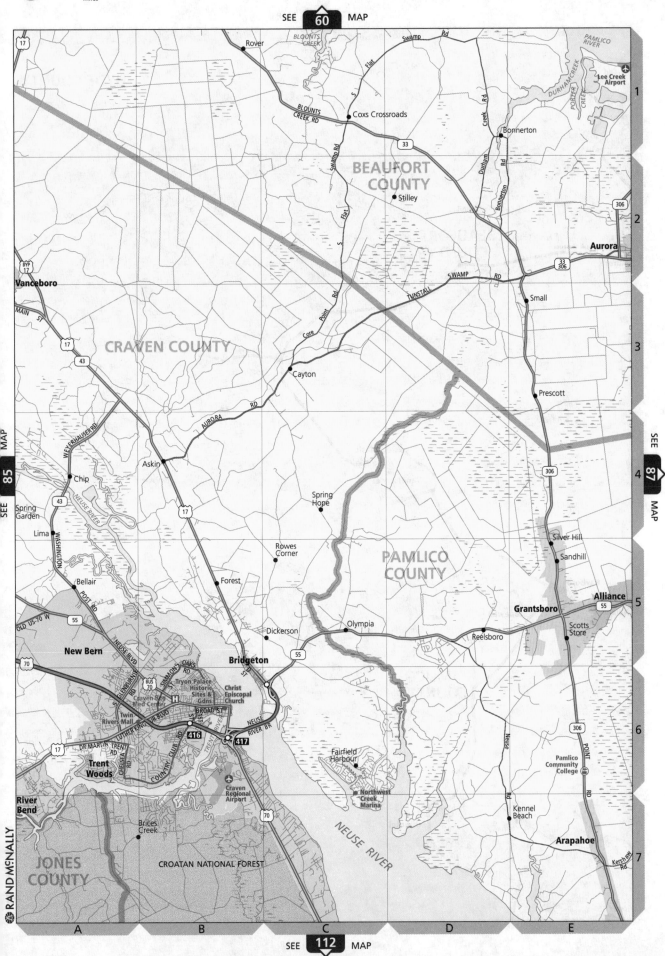

1:190,080
1 in. = 3 mi.

0   2   4
miles

SEE **60** MAP

Rover

BLOUNTS CREEK

Swamp Rd

PAMLICO RIVER

Lee Creek Airport

1

BLOUNTS CREEK RD

Coxs Crossroads

Flat

S

Swamp Rd

Creek Rd

DURHAM CREEK

PORTER CREEK

Bonnerton

33

BEAUFORT COUNTY

Stilley

Durham Rd

Bonnerton Rd

306

2

Vanceboro

BYP 17

17

MAIN ST

SWAMP   RD

TUNSTALL

Aurora

33 306

Small

CRAVEN COUNTY

43

17

Point Rd

Core

Cayton

AURORA RD

Prescott

3

SEE **87** MAP

306

4

Askin

Chip

43

Spring Garden

NEUSE RIVER

WEYERHAUSER RD

WASHINGTON

Lima

Spring Hope

Silver Hill

Sandhill

Bellair

POST RD

17

Rowes Corner

PAMLICO COUNTY

Forest

Alliance

55

5

Grantsboro

New Bern

55

OLD US-70 W

Dickerson

Olympia

55

Reelsboro

Scotts Store

70

NEUSE BLVD

ELENBURG RD

SIMMONS

OAKS RD

BUS 70

Tryon Palace Historic Sites & Gdns

Bridgeton

TRENT RIVER

Christ Episcopal Church

NEUSE RIVER BR

Neuse Rd

Pamlico Community College

306

POINT RD

Craven Reg Med Center

H

Twin Rivers Mall

S FRONT ST

BROAD ST

416

417

Fairfield Harbour

6

17

DR MARTIN LUTHER KING JR BLVD

TRENT RD

CHELSEA RD

COUNTRY CLUB RD

Kennel Beach

Trent Woods

Brices Creek

Craven Regional Airport

Northwest Creek Marina

River Bend

70

NEUSE RIVER

Arapahoe

Kershaw Rd

7

JONES COUNTY

CROATAN NATIONAL FOREST

A   B   C   D   E

SEE **112** MAP

SEE **85** MAP

MAP
87

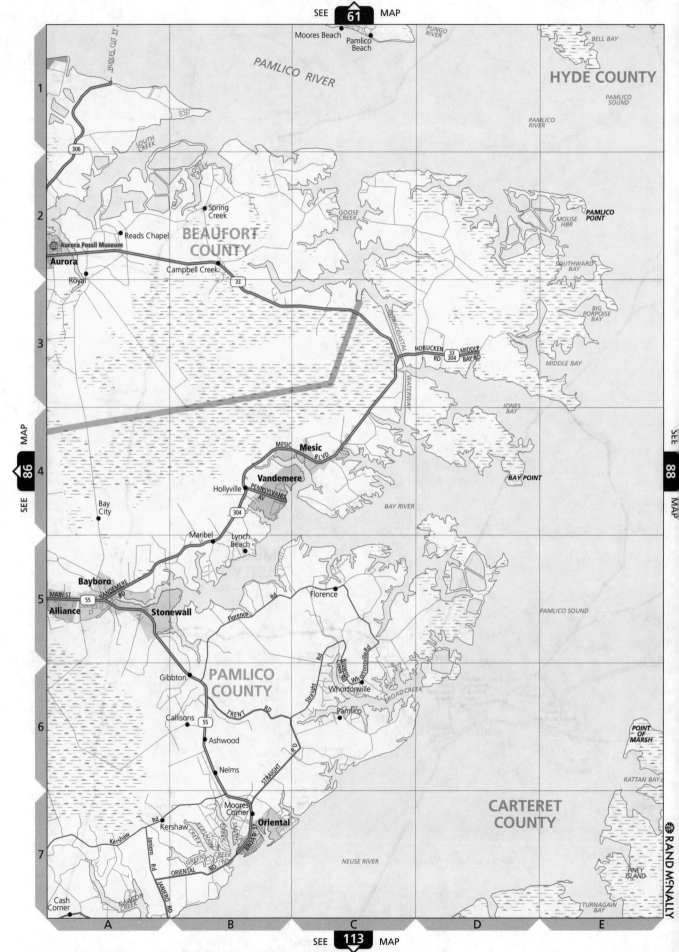

1:190,080
1 in. = 3 mi.
0   2   4
miles

SEE 61 MAP

Moores Beach
Pamlico Beach

PUNGO RIVER

BELL BAY

PAMLICO RIVER

HYDE COUNTY

PAMLICO SOUND

1

306

SOUTH CREEK

BOND CREEK

PAMLICO RIVER

MOUSE HBR

PAMLICO POINT

2

Spring Creek

Reads Chapel

GOOSE CREEK

BEAUFORT COUNTY

SOUTHWARD BAY

Aurora Fossil Museum
Aurora
Royal

Campbell Creek
33

BIG PORPOISE BAY

3

INTRACOASTAL WATERWAY

HOBUCKEN RD
33 304
MIDDLE BAY RD

MIDDLE BAY

SEE 86 MAP

WATERWAY

JONES BAY

MESIC
Mesic
BLVD

4

Vandemere
Hollyville
PENNSYLVANIA AV

BAY POINT

SEE 88 MAP

Bay City

304

Maribel

Lynch Beach

BAY RIVER

5

Bayboro
VANDEMERE RD
MAIN ST
55
Alliance   Stonewall

Florence
RD

Florence

Florence

PAMLICO SOUND

Gibbton

PAMLICO COUNTY

RD

Straight

Browns Creek Rd
Whortonville Rd
Whortonville

BROAD CREEK

POINT OF MARSH

6

Callisons
55
Ashwood

TRENT RD

RD

Pamlico

RATTAN BAY

Nelms

STRAIGHT

CARTERET COUNTY

Rd
Kershaw
KERSHAW CREEK
Moores Corner
Oriental
BROAD ST

7

Kershaw
Janiero Rd
GREENS CREEK
SMITH CREEK
ORIENTAL RD

NEUSE RIVER

PINEY ISLAND

Cash Corner
DAWSON CREEK
JANIERO RD

TURNAGAIN BAY

A   B   C   D   E

SEE 113 MAP

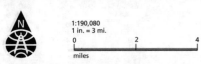

1:190,080
1 in. = 3 mi.

0   2   4
miles

MAP
88

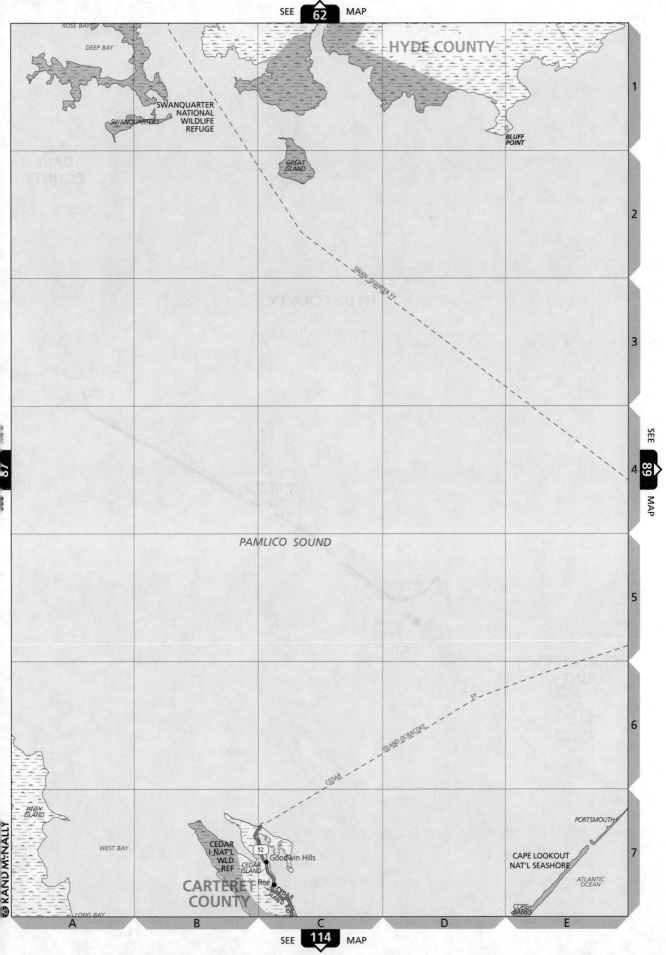

SEE **62** MAP

HYDE COUNTY

ROSE BAY

DEEP BAY

SWANQUARTER NATIONAL WILDLIFE REFUGE

SWANQUARTER

BLUFF POINT

GREAT ISLAND

SWAN QUARTER FY

HYDE COUNTY

SEE **89** MAP

PAMLICO SOUND

CEDAR ISLAND-OCRACOKE FY

PINEY ISLAND

WEST BAY

PORTSMOUTH

CEDAR I NAT'L WLD REF

CEDAR ISLAND

12

Goodwin Hills

CAPE LOOKOUT NAT'L SEASHORE

ATLANTIC OCEAN

CARTERET COUNTY

Roe

CEDAR ISLAND RD

CORE BANKS

LONG BAY

A   B   C   D   E

SEE **114** MAP

MAP
89

REGIONAL MAP

1:190,080
1 in. = 3 mi.

0   2   4
miles

SEE **63** MAP

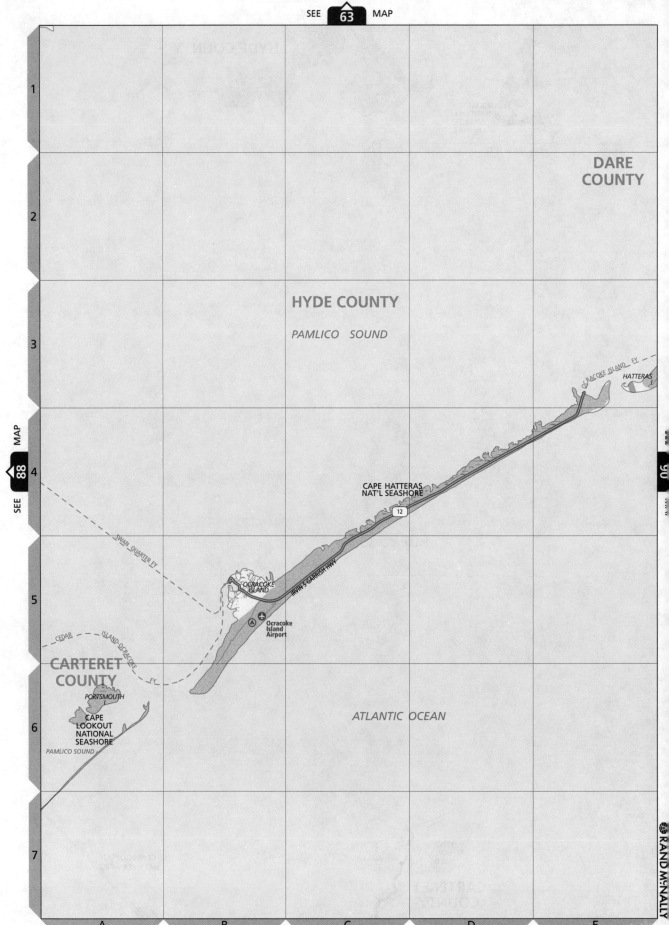

DARE
COUNTY

HYDE COUNTY

PAMLICO SOUND

OCRACOKE ISLAND FY

HATTERAS

MAP
88
SEE

90

CAPE HATTERAS
NAT'L SEASHORE

12

SWAN QUARTER FY

*OCRACOKE
ISLAND*

IRVIN S GARRISH HWY

Ocracoke
Island
Airport

CEDAR ISLAND-OCRACOKE FY

CARTERET
COUNTY

PORTSMOUTH

CAPE
LOOKOUT
NATIONAL
SEASHORE

PAMLICO SOUND

ATLANTIC OCEAN

RAND M NALLY

A   B   C   D   E

MAP
90

1:190,080
1 in. = 3 mi.

0   2   4
miles

SEE **64** MAP

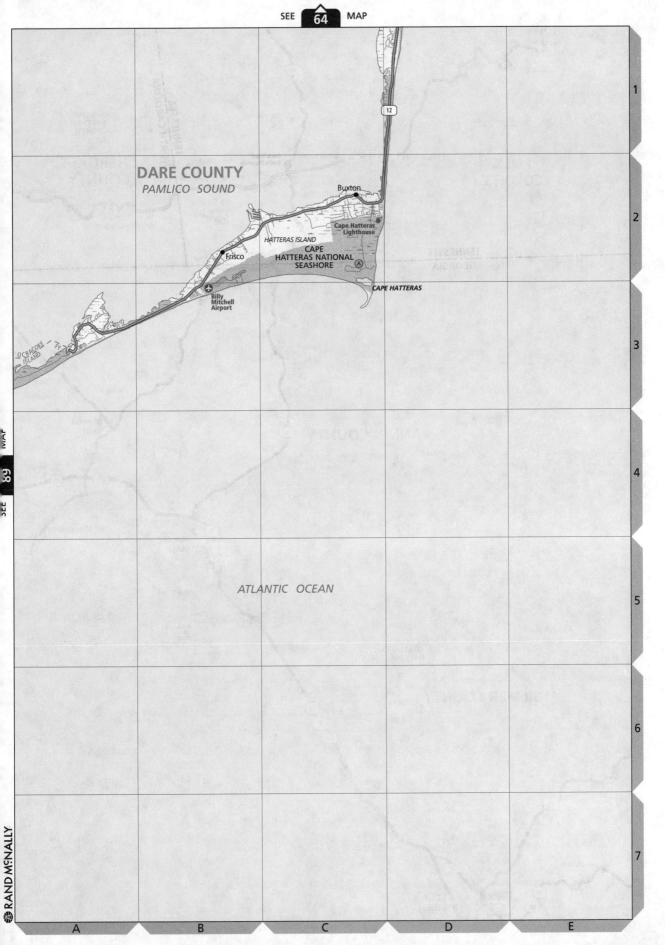

DARE COUNTY
PAMLICO SOUND

Buxton

Cape Hatteras
Lighthouse

HATTERAS ISLAND

CAPE
HATTERAS NATIONAL
SEASHORE

Frisco

CAPE HATTERAS

Billy
Mitchell
Airport

*OCRACOKE
ISLAND*

12

1

2

3

4

5

6

7

ATLANTIC OCEAN

A   B   C   D   E

SEE 89 MAP

MAP

91

REGIONAL MAP

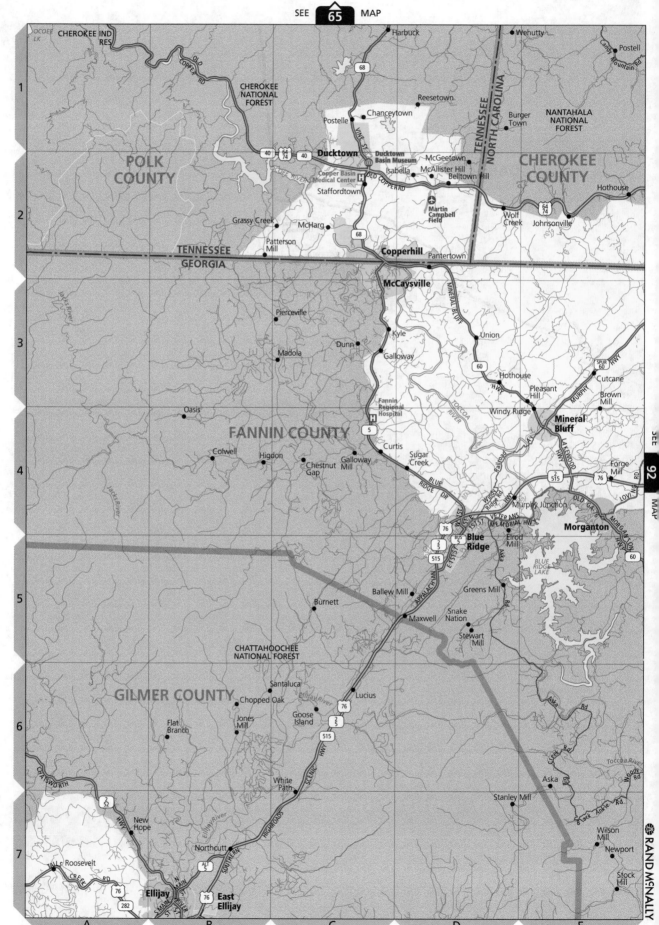

1:190,080
1 in. = 3 mi.

0   2   4
miles

N

SEE 65 MAP

CHEROKEE IND
RES

OCOEE
LK

OLD COPPER RD

CHEROKEE
NATIONAL
FOREST

68

Harbuck

Wehutty

Candy
Mountain Rd

Postell

Reesetown

TENNESSEE
NORTH CAROLINA

NANTAHALA
NATIONAL
FOREST

Postelle

Chanceytown

Burger
Town

VINE ST

POLK
COUNTY

40 64
    74 40

Ducktown

Ducktown
Basin Museum

McGeetown

CHEROKEE
COUNTY

Copper Basin
Medical Center H

Isabella

McAllister Hill

Belltown Hill

OLD COPPER RD

64
74

Hothouse

Staffordtown

Martin
Campbell
Field

Wolf
Creek

Johnsonville

Grassy Creek

McHarg

68

TENNESSEE
GEORGIA

Patterson
Mill

Copperhill

Pantertown

McCaysville

MINERAL BLUFF

Pierceville

Kyle

Union

60

SPUR
60

Dunn

Galloway

Hothouse

HWY

Cutcane

Madola

TOCCOA RIVER

Pleasant
Hill

MURPHY

Brown
Mill

Oasis

Fannin
Regional
Hospital H

Windy Ridge

Mineral
Bluff

FANNIN COUNTY

5

HWY

SEE 92 MAP

Colwell

Higdon

Chestnut
Gap

Galloway
Mill

Curtis

Sugar
Creek

Forge
Mill

Jacks River

BLUE RIDGE DR

Windy
Ridge Rd

2
515

76

Murphy Junction

OLD GA 76

Morganton

76

VETERANS
MEMORIAL HW

Elrod
Mill

BUS
5

Blue
Ridge

Aska Rd

BLUE
RIDGE LAKE

60

MORGANTON HWY

515

E 1ST ST
W 1ST ST

Greens Mill

Ballew Mill

APPALACHIAN

Snake
Nation

Burnett

Maxwell

Aska Rd

Stewart
Mill

CHATTAHOOCHEE
NATIONAL FOREST

Toccoa River

GILMER COUNTY

Santaluca

Lucius

Chopped Oak

Ellijay River

76

Aska

Woody Rd

Flat
Branch

Jones
Mill

Goose
Island

2
5

Big Creek Rd

CHATSWORTH

515

White
Path

SCENIC HWY

Stanley Mill

Black Ankle Rd

2
52

New
Hope

Elliay River

HIGHROADS

Wilson
Mill

Newport

Roosevelt

Northcutt

ALT
5

SOUTHERN

CREEK RD

76

Ellijay

282

N MAIN

S MAIN

River St

76

East
Ellijay

Stock
Hill

RAND McNALLY

A   B   C   D   E

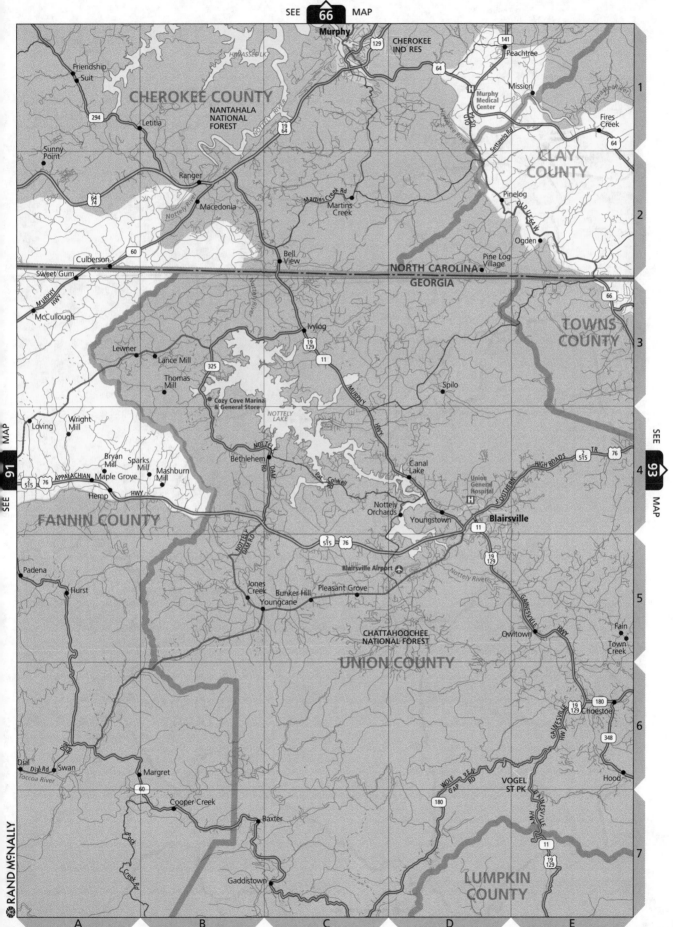

MAP
92

REGIONAL MAP

1:190,080
1 in. = 3 mi.

0   2   4
miles

SEE **66** MAP

Murphy

CHEROKEE
IND RES

Peachtree

141

64

Murphy
Medical
Center

Mission

CHEROKEE COUNTY

NANTAHALA
NATIONAL
FOREST

Friendship
Suit

294

Letitia

Sunny
Point

64
74

Ranger

Macedonia

19
64

Fires
Creek

64

**CLAY
COUNTY**

Pinelog

OLD USBAW

Ogden

Martins Creek Rd

Martins
Creek

60

Culberson

Bell
View

Sweet Gum

NORTH CAROLINA

GEORGIA

Pine Log
Village

66

MURPHY HWY

McCullough

Lewner

Lance Mill

Thomas
Mill

325

11

Ivylog

19
129

MURPHY HWY

**TOWNS
COUNTY**

Spilo

Cozy Cove Marina
& General Store

NOTTELY
LAKE

SEE **91** MAP

Loving

Wright
Mill

Bryan
Mill

Sparks
Mill

Mashburn
Mill

2
515

76

APPALACHIAN

Maple Grove

Hemp

HWY

FANNIN COUNTY

Bethlehem

NOTTELY RD

DAM

Colwell RD

Canal
Lake

Nottely
Orchards

Youngstown

HIGH ROADS

2
515

TR

76

Union
General
Hospital

Blairsville

11

SEE **93** MAP

515

76

NOTTELY DAM RD

Blairsville Airport

Nottely River

19
129

Padena

Hurst

Jones
Creek

Bunker Hill

Pleasant Grove

Youngcane

GAINESVILLE HWY

Owltown

Fain

Town
Creek

**CHATTAHOOCHEE
NATIONAL FOREST**

UNION COUNTY

19
129

Choestoe

180

Dial
Dial Rd
Swan

Toccoa River

Margret

60

Cooper Creek

WOLF GAP RD

180

**VOGEL
ST PK**

GAINESVILLE HWY

348

Hood

Baxter

11

Gaddistown

19
129

**LUMPKIN
COUNTY**

A   B   C   D   E

1 2 3 4 5 6 7

MAP
93

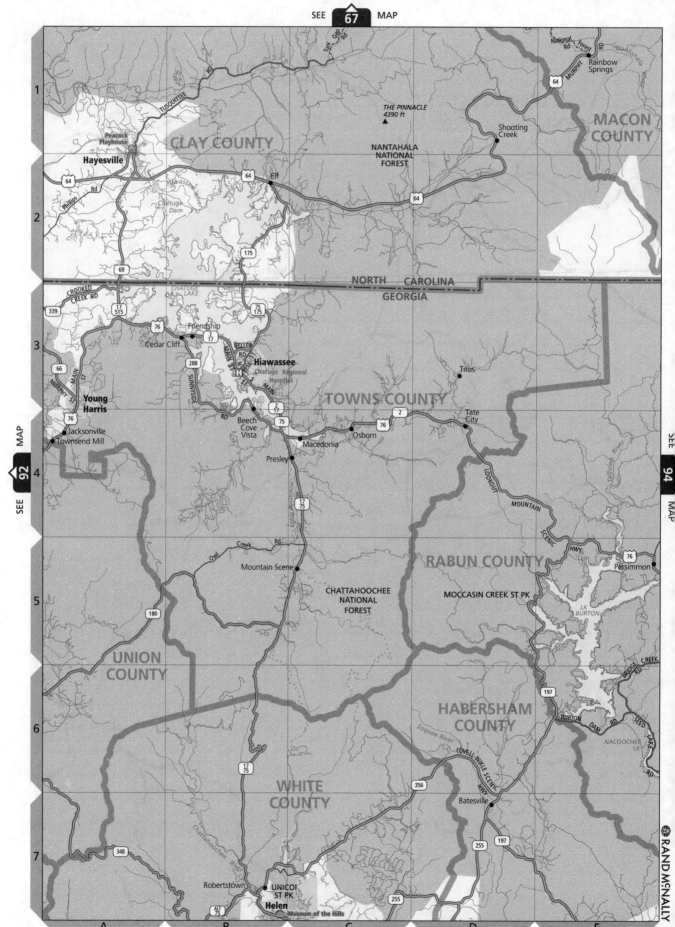

1:190,080
1 in. = 3 mi.

0   2   4
miles

REGISTRAL MAP

REGIONAL MAP

SEE 92 MAP

SEE 94 MAP

RAND McNALLY

Tusquitee Rd

MACON COUNTY

National Rd / Murphy Rd / National Forest / Nantahala River

64 Rainbow Springs

Shooting Creek

THE PINNACLE
4390 ft

CLAY COUNTY

NANTAHALA NATIONAL FOREST

Peacock Playhouse

Hayesville

64   Elf

64

64 Rd

Phillips Rd

Chatuge Dam

Hiawassee River

175

69

CHATUGE LAKE

NORTH CAROLINA
GEORGIA

CROOKED CREEK RD

339   17 515

75 175

76   Friendship
2 17

288   Cedar Cliff

66   MAIN ST   BELLER RD

MURPHY ST   **Hiawassee**
Chatuge Regional Hospital

Young Harris   MAIN ST

76   SUNNYSIDE RD   2 17

Jacksonville   Beech Cove Vista   75

Townsend Mill   Macedonia

Presley

TOWNS COUNTY

Titus

2

76   Tate City

Osborn

LOOKOUT MOUNTAIN

RABUN COUNTY

17 75

Hiawassee River

Creek Rd

Owl Creek

Mountain Scene

CHATTAHOOCHEE NATIONAL FOREST

MOCCASIN CREEK ST PK

SCENIC HWY

76   Persimmon

LK BURTON

180

UNION COUNTY

BRIDGE RD / CREEK

197

HABERSHAM COUNTY

BURTON DAM RD   SEED TICK RD

NACOOCHEE LK

Soquee River

17 75

LOVELL WILEY SCENIC HWY

WHITE COUNTY

356   Batesville

255   197

348

255

Robertstown   UNICOI ST PK

ALT 75   **Helen**   Museum of the Hills

A   B   C   D   E

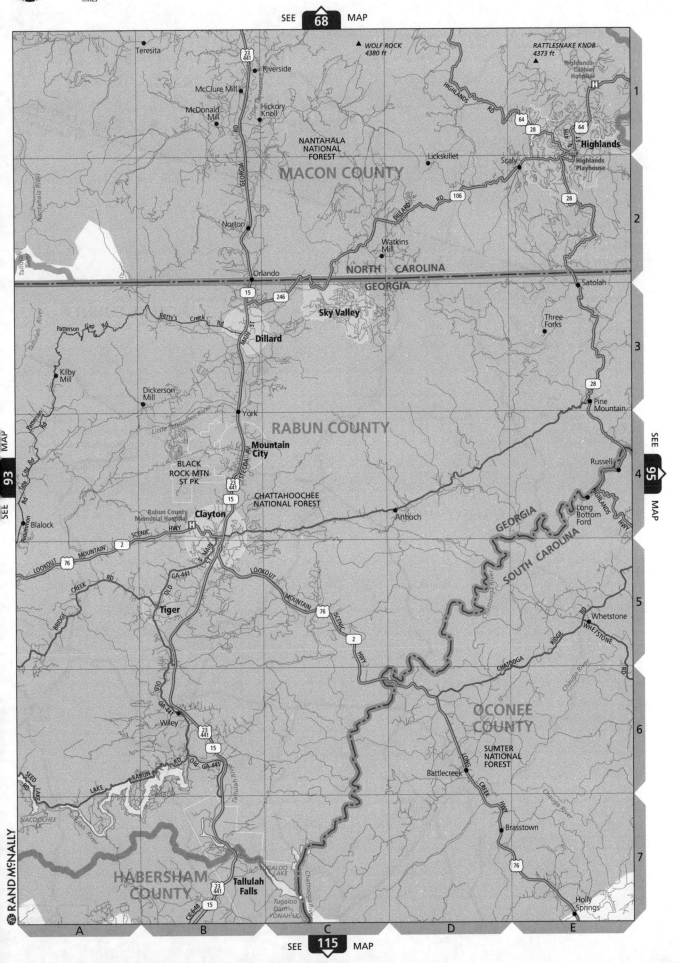

MAP
94

1:190,080
1 in. = 3 mi.
0   2   4
miles

SEE 68 MAP

Teresita

▲ WOLF ROCK
4380 ft

▲ RATTLESNAKE KNOB
4373 ft

Highlands-
Cashiers
Hospital

H

Riverside

McClure Mill

HIGHLANDS RD

64

28

64

N. 4TH ST

Highlands

McDonald
Mill

Hickory
Knoll

NANTAHALA
NATIONAL
FOREST

Lickskillet

Scaly

Highlands
Playhouse

23
441

GEORGIA RD

MACON COUNTY

RD

106

28

Norton

DILLARD RD

Watkins
Mill

NORTH   CAROLINA

Satolah

15

246

GEORGIA

MAIN ST

Sky Valley

Three
Forks

Betty's Creek Rd

Patterson Gap Rd

Dillard

28

Tallulah River

Kilby
Mill

Pine
Mountain

Dickerson
Mill

Patterson Rd

York

RABUN COUNTY

Little Tennessee River

Russell

SEE 93 MAP

SEE 95 MAP

**Mountain
City**

STEEKOA AV

BLACK
ROCK MTN
ST PK

23
441

15

CHATTAHOOCHEE
NATIONAL
FOREST

Antioch

Long
Bottom
Ford

HIGHLANDS HWY

Chattooga River

GEORGIA

Rabun County
Memorial Hospital

Clayton

H

Blalock

SCENIC   HWY

2

Tate City Rd

Redmon Rd

SOUTH CAROLINA

S MAIN ST

LOOKOUT   MOUNTAIN

76

GA-441

OLD

LOOKOUT   MOUNTAIN

76

2

SCENIC   HWY

Whetstone

WHETSTONE RD

CREEK   RD

CHATOOGA RIDGE

Tiger

BRIDGE

OLD
GA-441

Wiley

23
441

15

OLD GA-441

TALLULAH RD

**OCONEE
COUNTY**

Chauga River

Chattooga River

SEED
LAKE
RD

LAKE   RABUN

LAKE RABUN

NACOOCHEE

Tallulah River

SUMTER
NATIONAL
FOREST

Battlecreek

LONG   CREEK   HWY

Brasstown

Tugaloo
Lake

**HABERSHAM
COUNTY**

23
441

**Tallulah
Falls**

CR 648

15

Chattooga River

Tugaloo
Dam
YONAH LK.

76

Holly
Springs

A   B   C   D   E

SEE 115 MAP

1   2   3   4   5   6   7

MAP
95

REGIONAL MAP

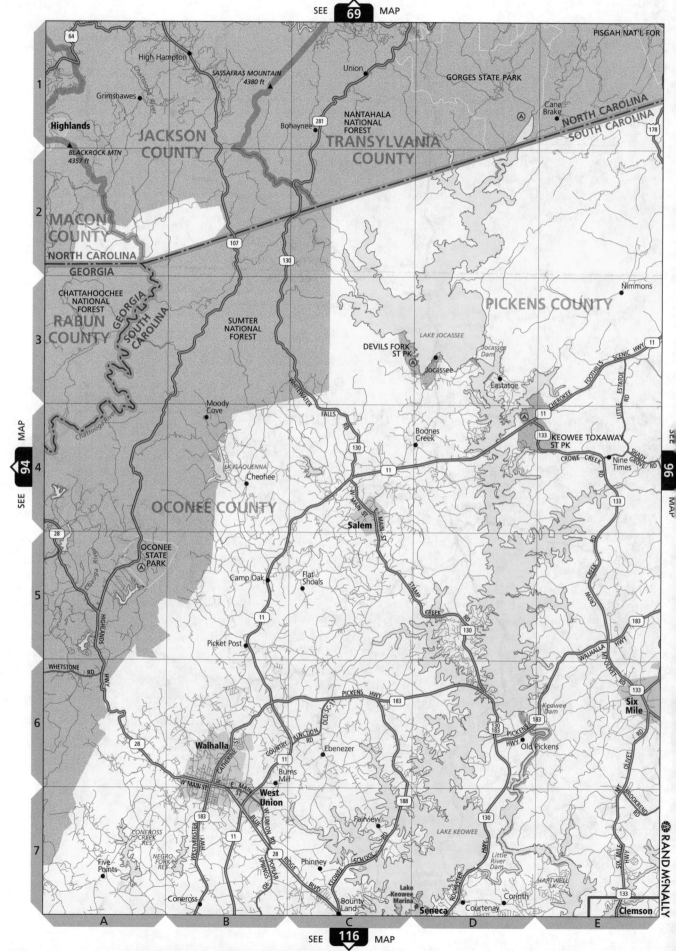

1:190,080
1 in. = 3 mi.

0   2   4
miles

PISGAH NAT'L FOR

64

High Hampton

SASSAFRAS MOUNTAIN
4380 ft

Union

GORGES STATE PARK

Grimshawes

Cane
Brake

NORTH CAROLINA

SOUTH CAROLINA

Highlands

NANTAHALA
NATIONAL
FOREST

281

Bohaynee

178

BLACKROCK MTN
4357 ft

JACKSON
COUNTY

TRANSYLVANIA
COUNTY

MACON
COUNTY

107

NORTH CAROLINA

GEORGIA

130

PICKENS COUNTY

Nimmons

CHATTAHOOCHEE
NATIONAL
FOREST

GEORGIA

SOUTH CAROLINA

SUMTER
NATIONAL
FOREST

LAKE JOCASSEE

11

RABUN
COUNTY

DEVILS FORK
ST PK

Jocassee
Dam

Jocassee

FOOTHILLS SCENIC HWY

LITTLE ESTATGE RD

Moody
Cove

WHITEWATER

Eastage

CHEROKEE

11

Chattooga River

FALLS
RD

Boones
Creek

11

133 KEOWEE TOXAWAY
ST PK

SEE 96 MAP

SEE 94 MAP

LK ISAQUENNA

130

CROWE CREEK

Nine
Times

SHADY GROVE RD

28

Cheohee

11

133

OCONEE COUNTY

W MAIN ST

E MAIN ST

Salem

OCONEE
STATE
PARK

Camp Oak

Flat
Shoals

STAMP

CREEK

CROW CREEK RD

183

11

CREEK

130

WALHALLA HWY

MT OLIVET RD

**Six
Mile**

Picket Post

130

133

WHETSTONE RD

HWY

PICKENS HWY

Keowee
Dam

HIGHLANDS

JUNCTION RD

OLD SC 11

183

130
183

PICKENS

28

JUNCTION
RD

Ebenezer

130
183

HWY

Old Pickens

MT OLIVET RD

Walhalla

COUNTRY RD

11

Burns
Mill

BROOKBEND RD

W MAIN ST

N CATHERINE ST

E MAIN ST

**West
Union**

188

183

WESTMINSTER HWY

BLUE RIDGE HWY

W UNION RD

Fairview

130

LAKE KEOWEE

Little
River
Dam

CONEROSS
CREEK
RES

11

POPLAR SPRINGS RD

28

Phinney

KEOWEE SCHOOL RD

HWY

SIX MILE RD

HARTWELL
LK

Five
Points

NEGRO
FORK
RES

ROCHESTER RD

Corinth

133

Coneross

Bounty
Land

Lake
Keowee
Marina

Seneca

Courtenay

Clemson

A   B   C   D   E

RAND MÇNALLY

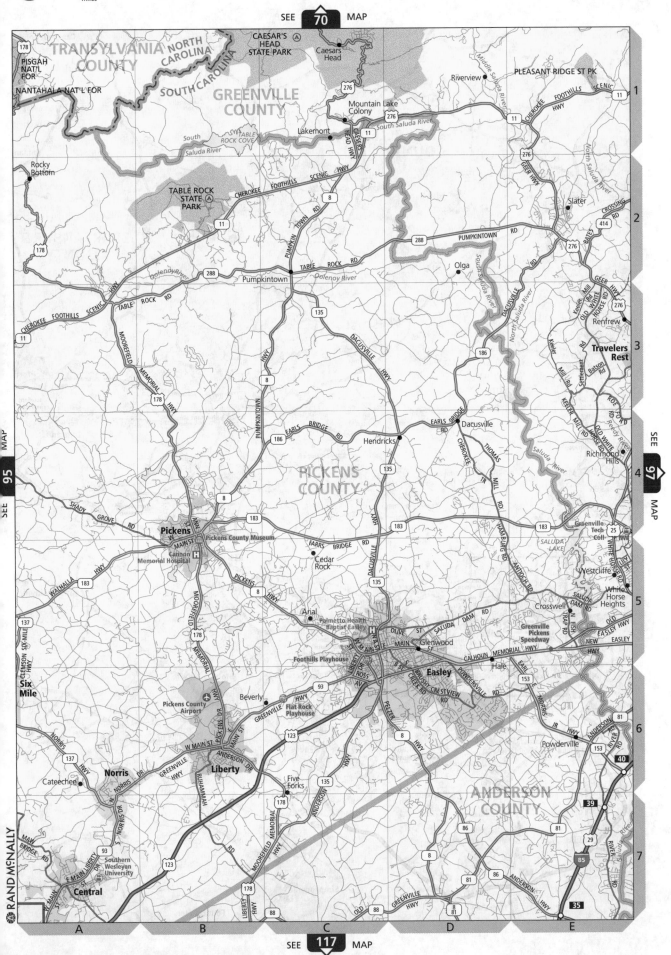

MAP
96

REGIONAL MAP

1:190,080
1 in. = 3 mi.

0   2   4
miles

SEE 70 MAP

TRANSYLVANIA COUNTY
NORTH CAROLINA

PISGAH NAT'L FOR
NANTAHALA NAT'L FOR

SOUTH CAROLINA

CAESAR'S HEAD STATE PARK
Caesars Head

Riverview

PLEASANT RIDGE ST PK

GREENVILLE COUNTY

178

276

Mountain Lake Colony

11

SCENIC 11

CHEROKEE FOOTHILLS HWY

1

Rocky Bottom

South Saluda River
TABLE ROCK COVE
SYLVIA

Lakemont

HEAD HWY

CHESEES

11

South Saluda River

11

276

GEER HWY

Middle Saluda River

North Saluda River

178

TABLE ROCK STATE PARK

CHEROKEE FOOTHILLS SCENIC HWY

8

PUMPKIN TOWN RD

Slater

414

BATES RD

CROSSING RD

2

11

288

TABLE ROCK RD

Pumpkintown

Oolenoy River

Oolenoy River

TABLE ROCK RD

288

PUMPKINTOWN RD

Olga

North Saluda River

DACUSVILLE

276

GEER HWY

Keeler Mill Rd

OLD WHITE HORSE RD

276

Renfrew

3

178

CHEROKEE FOOTHILLS SCENIC HWY

TABLE ROCK RD

MOOREFIELD MEMORIAL HWY

135

8

DACUSVILLE HWY

186

North Saluda River

Keeler Mill Rd

Settlement Rd

Batson Rd

Travelers Rest

SEE 97 MAP

178

PUMPKINTOWN HWY

186

EARLS BRIDGE RD

Hendricks

135

EARLS BRIDGE RD

Dacusville

CHEROKEE TR

THOMAS MILL RD

Saluda River

KEELER MILL RD

ROE FTON RD

OLD WHITE HORSE RD

Beechy River

Richmond Hills

4

8

SHADY GROVE RD

Pickens

ANNE ST

Pickens County Museum

FARRS BRIDGE RD

183

183

DACUSVILLE HWY

135

183

HAMBURG RD

ANTIOCH RD

Greenville Tech Coll

25

SW

SALUDA LAKE

WHITE HORSE RD LIST

Westcliffe

5

WALHALLA HWY

183

MAIN ST

Cannon Memorial Hospital

MOOREFIELD MEMORIAL

8

PICKENS HWY

Cedar Rock

8 HWY

Arial

Palmetto Health Baptist Easley

DACUSVILLE

135

SALUDA DAM RD

Crosswell

SALUDA DAM RD

N FISH TRAP RD

EASLEY HWY

White Horse Heights

137

CLEMSON SIX-MILE HWY

178

MOOREFIELD MEMORIAL HWY

OLIVE ST

SALUDA

MAIN

Glenwood ST

Greenville Pickens Speedway

CALHOUN MEMORIAL HWY

NEW EASLEY HWY

Six Mile

Pickens County Airport

Beverly

GREENVILLE ST

MAIN ST

93 HWY

Flat Rock Playhouse

Foothills Playhouse

W MAIN ST

LIBERTY ST

ROSS AV

B ST

Easley

CRESTVIEW

BRUSHY CREEK RD

POWDERSVILLE RD

Hale

153

CALHOUN MEMORIAL HWY

EARL E MORRIS HWY

81

6

137

NORRIS HWY

PICKENS DR

123

W MAIN ST

ANDERSON DR

RUHAMAH

PELZER

8 HWY

153

Powderville

JR HWY

ANDERSON RIVER RD

40

Norris

Cateechee

GREENVILLE HWY

Liberty

Five Forks

135

ANDERSON COUNTY

39

29

MAW BRIDGE RD

93

E MAIN LIBERTY

S NORRIS DR

Southern Wesleyan University

123

MOOREFIELD MEMORIAL HWY

178

ANDERSON

86

81

85

7

RAND MCNALLY

Central

E MAIN ST

LIBERTY HWY

88

88

OLD

GREENVILLE HWY

8
81

81

86

ANDERSON

85

35

A   B   C   D   E

SEE 117 MAP

SEE 95 MAP

MAP
97

REGIONAL MAP

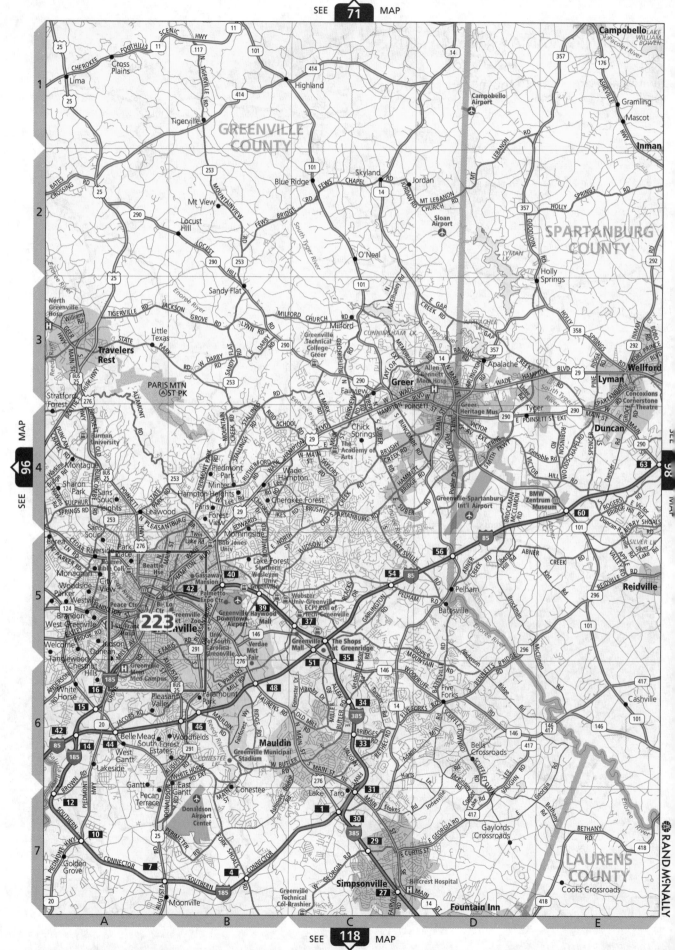

1:190,080
1 in. = 3 mi.

0   2   4
miles

RAND McNALLY

MAP
98
REGIONAL MAP

1:190,080
1 in. = 3 mi.
0   2   4
miles

SEE 72 MAP

N

RAND M°NALLY

SEE 97 MAP

SEE 99 MAP

SEE 119 MAP

Counties: CHEROKEE COUNTY · SPARTANBURG COUNTY · UNION COUNTY

Places:
Buckcreek Speedway · Mary Louise · Mayo Mills · Mayo · Macedonia · Mountain View · Carlisle · Cherokee Springs · Enola · Cowpens · Inman · Inman Mills · Campton · Dodd Hill · Valley Falls · Griffin · Whitney · Converse · Clifton Station · Clifton · Cunningham · Slosbee · Lone Oak · Lawsons · Zion Hill · Drayton · Glendale · Wellford · Fairforest · Una · Arcadia · Johnson City · Drayton · Hillcrest Shopping Center · Ben Avon · Arcadia Heights · Wadsworth · Calvert · Clevedale · Snoddy · Startex · Fairmont Mills · Hadden Heights · Hadden Crossroads · Westgate Mall · West View · Spartanburg · East Spartanburg · Southport · Delmar · Pacolet Mills · Central Pacolet · Pacolet · Fairmont · Camp Croft · White Stone · Calico · Poplar Springs · Reidville · Croft State Natural Area · Golightly · Dillard Crossroads · Stone Station · Walnut Grove Plantation · Switzer · Crescent · Glenn Springs · Foster Mill · West Springs · Thomas Price House · Walnut Grove · Dutchman · Woodruff · B J Workman Memorial Hospital · Brannon

Features/landmarks:
WILLIAM BOWEN · Sherman College Straight Chiropractic · Univ of South Carolina Upstate · Southern Shops · Spartanburg Tech Coll · Mary Black Hosp · Gibbs Stad · Spartanburg Reg Med Ctr · Wofford Coll · Piedmont Interstate Frgds · Converse Reg Mus of Spartanburg Co · Spartanburg Co Mus of Art · Seay House · Dorman Ctr · Spartanburg Downtown Mem Arpt · LK COOLEY · LK CRAIG

Rivers: Pacolet River · South Pacolet River · Tyger River · South Tyger River · Enoree River · RIVER RES NO 1

Roads/Highways (selected): 26 · 10 · 292 · 9 · 15 · 16 · 17 · 70 · 68 · 1 · 66 · 29 · 85 · 290 · 296 · 417 · 418 · 101 · 146 · 221 · 295 · 22 · 215 · 28 · 35 · 72 · 75 · 22 · 176 · 5 · 6 · 7 · 3 · 25 · 56 · 77 · 78 · 80 · 82 · 83 · 85 · 87 · 110 · 224 · 129 · 150 · 9 · Asheville Hwy · Blackstock Rd · Veterans Memorial Hwy · Charlotte Hwy · Old Georgia Hwy · Mayo Hwy · Gossett Rd · Warren H Abernathy Hwy · Buffalo-West Springs Hwy · Walnut Grove Rd · S J Workman Hwy · Fountain Inn Rd · Cross Anchor Hwy · Canaan Rd

Kennedy Mill

MAP
99

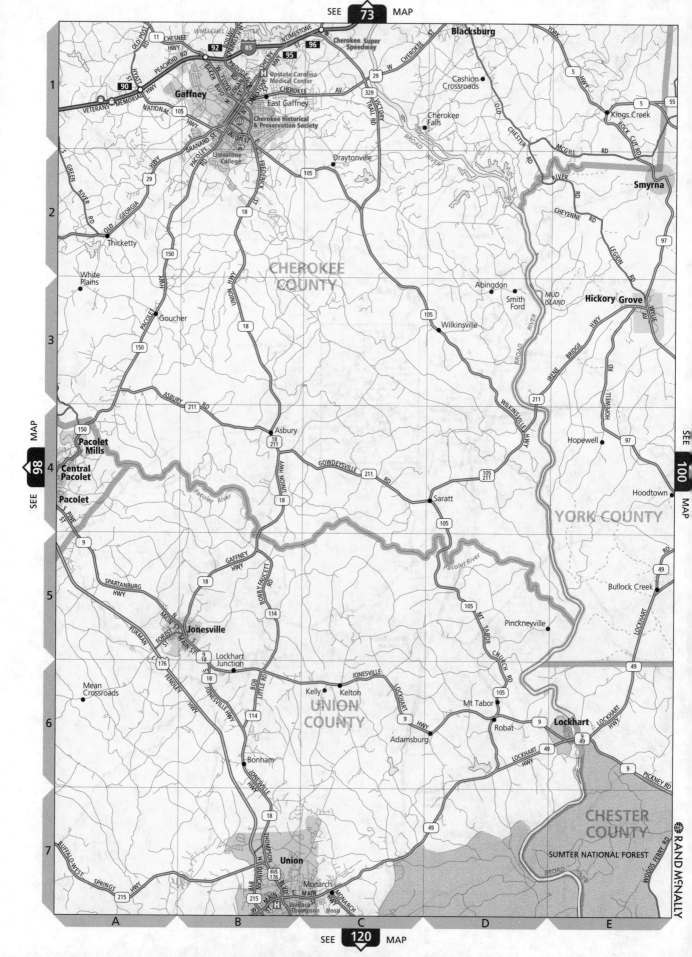

1:190,080
1 in. = 3 mi.

0   2   4
miles

SEE **73** MAP

SEE **98** MAP

SEE **100** MAP

SEE **120** MAP

RAND MCNALLY

MAP
100

REGIONAL MAP

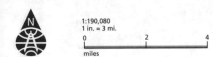

1:190,080
1 in. = 3 mi.

0   2   4
miles

SEE **74** MAP

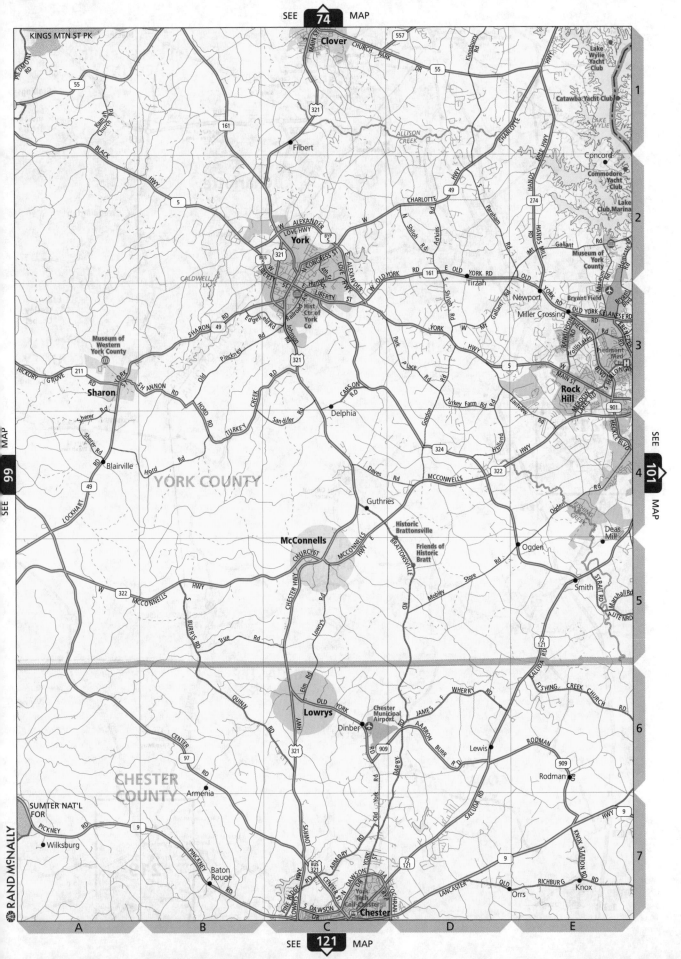

SEE **99** MAP

SEE **101** MAP

SEE **121** MAP

KINGS MTN ST PK

Clover

Catawba Yacht Club
Lake Wylie Yacht Club

Filbert

Concord

Commodore Yacht Club
Lake Club Marina

York

Museum of York County

Tirzah
Newport
Miller Crossing
Bryant Field
CELANESE

Museum of Western York County

Rock Hill

Sharon

Delphia

Blairville

YORK COUNTY

Guthries

Deas Mill

Historic Brattonsville
Friends of Historic Bratt

McConnells

Ogden

Smith

Lowrys

Dinber

Chester Municipal Airport

Lewis

Rodman

Armenia

CHESTER COUNTY

SUMTER NAT'L FOR

Wilksburg

Baton Rouge

Richburg
Knox
Orrs

York Tech Coll-Chester

Chester

RAND M°NALLY

A   B   C   D   E

1 2 3 4 5 6 7

MAP
101

REGIONAL MAP

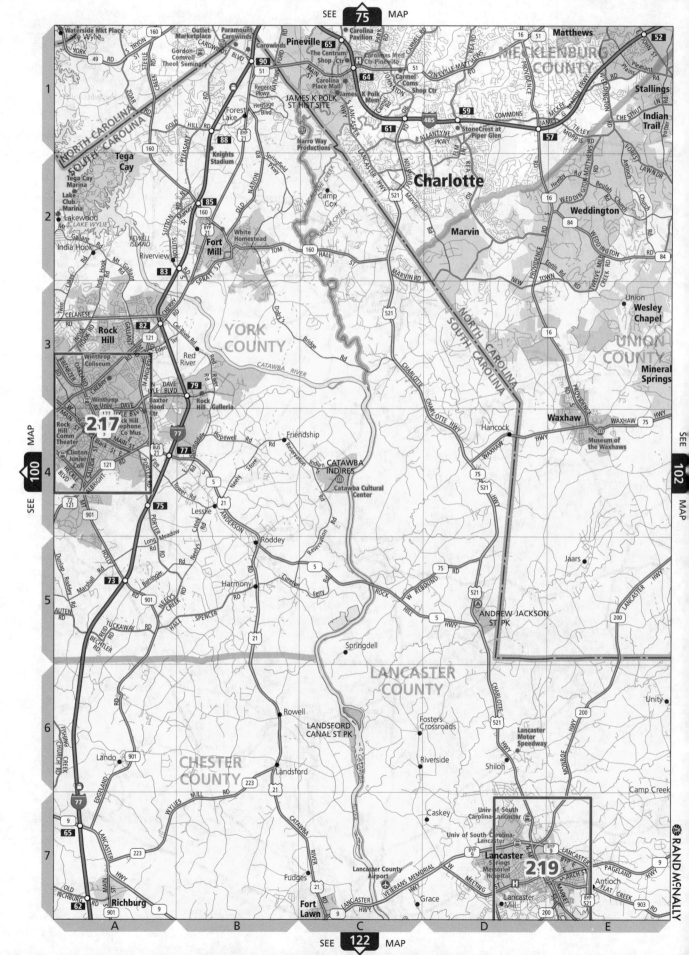

SEE 75 MAP

1:190,080
1 in. = 3 mi.

0   2   4
miles

N

SEE 100 MAP

SEE 102 MAP

SEE 122 MAP

RAND MCNALLY

MAP
102

REGIONAL MAP

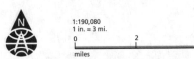

1:190,080
1 in. = 3 mi.

0   2   4
miles

SEE [76] MAP
SEE [101] MAP
SEE [103] MAP
SEE [123] MAP

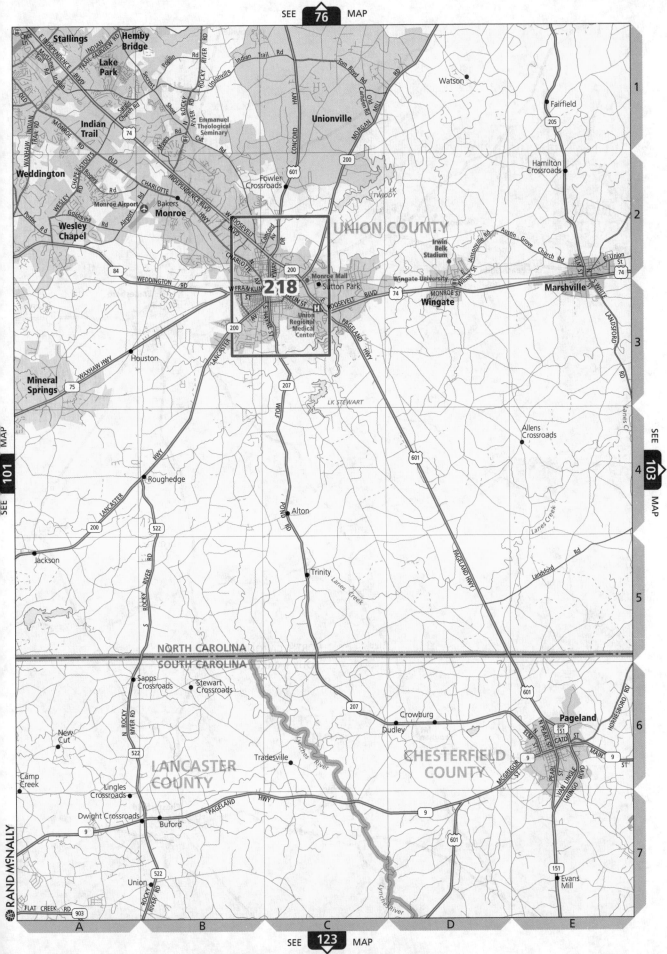

Stallings
Hemby Bridge
Lake Park
Indian Trail
Weddington
Monroe Airport
Bakers
Monroe
Wesley Chapel
Mineral Springs
Houston
Emmanuel Theological Seminary
Fowler Crossroads
Unionville
Watson
Fairfield
Hamilton Crossroads
UNION COUNTY
LK TWIDDY
Irwin Belk Stadium
Monroe Mall
Sutton Park
Wingate University
Wingate
Marshville
218
Union Regional Medical Center
Roughedge
LK STEWART
Alton
Allens Crossroads
Jackson
Trinity
Lanes Creek
NORTH CAROLINA
SOUTH CAROLINA
Sapps Crossroads
Stewart Crossroads
Crowburg
Dudley
Pageland
New Cut
Tradesville
CHESTERFIELD COUNTY
Lynches River
Camp Creek
LANCASTER COUNTY
Lingles Crossroads
Dwight Crossroads
Buford
Union
Evans Mill

RAND McNALLY

MAP
103

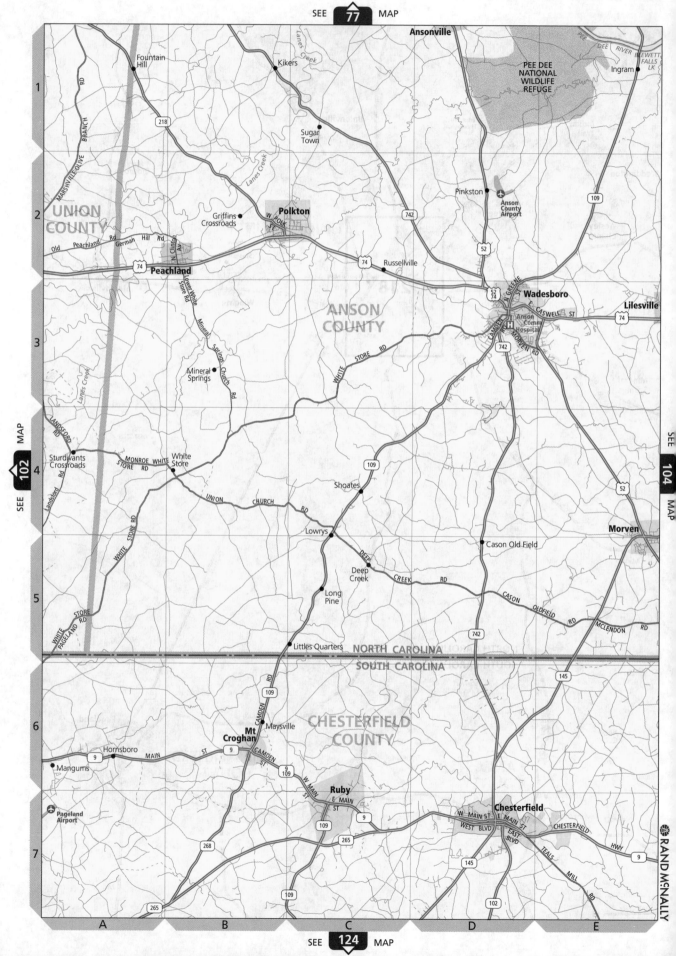

1:190,080
1 in. = 3 mi.

0   2   4
miles

SEE 77 MAP

Ansonville

Fountain Hill

Kikers

PEE DEE
NATIONAL
WILDLIFE
REFUGE

Ingram

PEE DEE RIVER BLEWETT FALLS LK

218

Sugar Town

MARSHVILLE-OLIVE BRANCH

UNION COUNTY

Pinkston

Anson County Airport

109

Griffins Crossroads

W POLK ST

Polkton

52

Old Peachland Rd   German Hill Rd

N CLINTON AV

74

Peachland

742

74   Russellville

52 74   Wadesboro

E CASWELL ST

Lilesville

74

ANSON COUNTY

Lower White Store Rd

Mineral Springs Church Rd

WHITE   STORE   RD

N GREENE ST

CAMDEN

Anson Comm Hospital

742

MORVEN RD

3

Mineral Springs

SEE 102 MAP

LANDSFORD RD

Sturdivants Crossroads

MONROE WHITE STORE RD

White Store

109

52

SEE 104 MAP

Landsford Rd

Lanes Creek

UNION   CHURCH   RD

Shoates

Morven

4

WHITE STORE RD

Lowrys

DEEP

Cason Old Field

CASON OLDFIELD RD

MCLENDON RD

Deep Creek

CREEK   RD

Long Pine

742

5

WHITE STORE RD

PAGELAND

Littles Quarters

NORTH CAROLINA
SOUTH CAROLINA

145

CAMDEN RD

109

CHESTERFIELD COUNTY

Maysville

Mt Croghan

6

Hornsboro

MAIN   ST

9

CAMDEN ST

9

9 109

W MAIN ST

Mangums

9

Ruby

E MAIN ST

9

Pageland Airport

109

265

Chesterfield

W MAIN ST   E MAIN ST

WEST BLVD   EAST BLVD

CHESTERFIELD

TEALS MILL RD

HWY

9

7

268

145

102

265

109

N

RAND MCNALLY

A   B   C   D   E

SEE 124 MAP

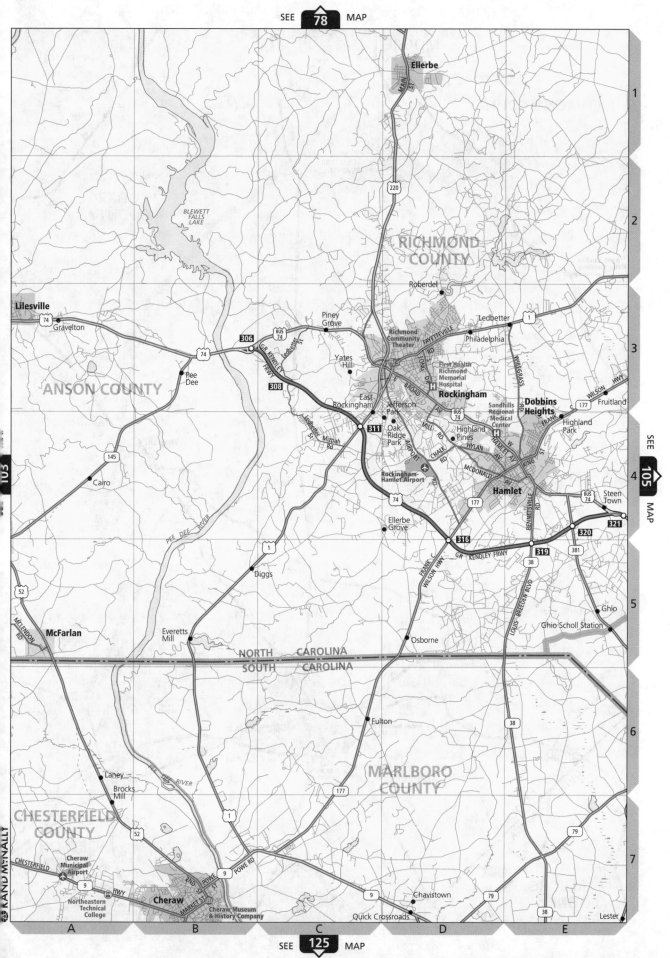

MAP
104

REGIONAL MAP

1:190,080
1 in. = 3 mi.

0   2   4
miles

Ellerbe

220

RICHMOND
COUNTY

BLEWETT
FALLS
LAKE

Roberdel

Lilesville

74

Gravelton

Piney
Grove

Ledbetter

1

Philadelphia

306

BUS
74

GR KENDLEY HWY

Ledbetter St

Yates
Hill

Richmond
Community
Theater

FAYETTEVILLE RD

LONG DR

First Health
Richmond
Memorial
Hospital

WIREGRASS

ANSON COUNTY

Pee
Dee

308

East
Rockingham

BROAD

AV

Rockingham

Sandhills
Regional
Medical
Center

Dobbins
Heights

177

Fruitland

Wilson Hwy

311

Ledbetter St

Mizpah
Rd

Jefferson
Park

Oak
Ridge
Park

MILL RD

Highland
Pines

FRANK

HAMLET AV

Highland
Park

145

CHALK RD

HYLAN

W

KING ST

Cairo

Rockingham-
Hamlet Airport

AIRPORT RD

McDONALD AV

BENNETTSVILLE RD

Ellerbe
Grove

177

Hamlet

BUS
74

Steen
Town

320

321

1

Diggs

316

GR KENDLEY FRWY

319

381

38

LOUIS BREEDEN BLVD

Ghio

52

FRANK C

WILSON HWY

Osborne

Ghio Scholl Station

McFarlan

McLENDON RD

Everetts
Mill

NORTH   CAROLINA

SOUTH   CAROLINA

Fulton

38

MARLBORO
COUNTY

177

Laney

Brocks
Mill

PEE DEE RIVER

79

CHESTERFIELD
COUNTY

52

1

CHESTERFIELD

Cheraw
Municipal
Airport

9

POWE RD

9

9

Chavistown

79

38

Lester

9

2ND ST

POWE ST

MARKET ST

HWY

Cheraw

Northeastern
Technical
College

Cheraw Museum
& History Company

Quick Crossroads

A   B   C   D   E

103

RAND MCNALLY

MAP
105

REGIONAL MAP

1:190,080
1 in. = 3 mi.

0   2   4

miles

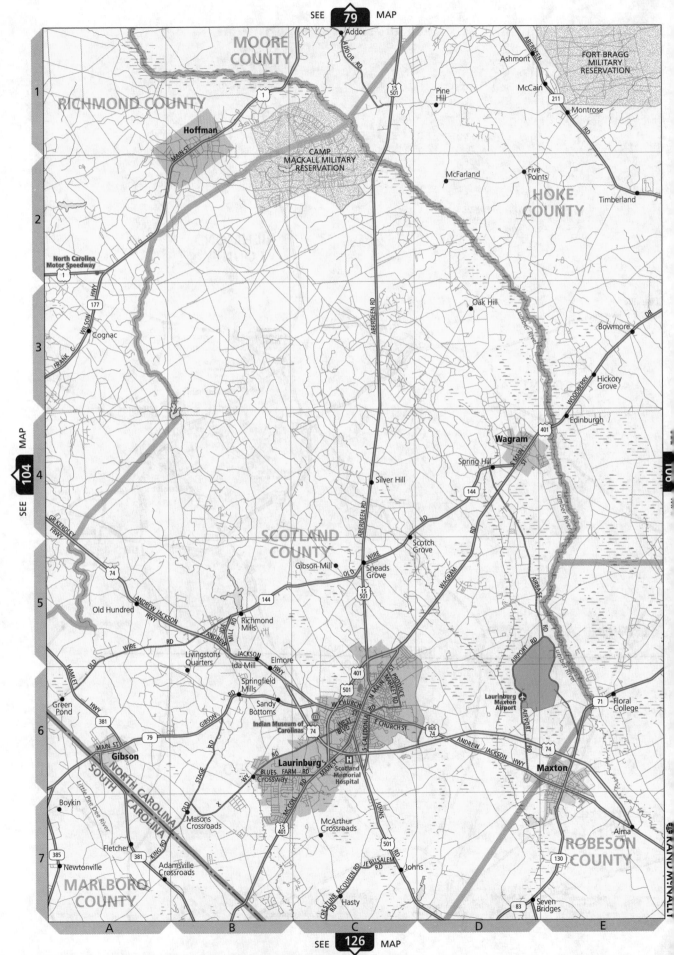

SEE **79** MAP

MOORE COUNTY

Addor

ADDOR RD

ABERDEEN

FORT BRAGG MILITARY RESERVATION

Ashmont

RICHMOND COUNTY

Hoffman

MAIN ST

1

15
501

Pine Hill

McCain

211

Montrose

RD

CAMP MACKALL MILITARY RESERVATION

McFarland

Five Points

HOKE COUNTY

Timberland

North Carolina Motor Speedway

1

177

Cognac

WILSON HWY

FRANK C

ABERDEEN RD

Oak Hill

Lumber River

Bowmore

DR

WOODBERRY

Hickory Grove

Edinburgh

401

Wagram

S MAIN ST

SEE **104** MAP

Spring Hill

Silver Hill

144

RD

Lumber River

GILKENDLEY FRWY

74

Old Hundred

ANDREW JACKSON HWY

SCOTLAND COUNTY

WIRE

Scotch Grove

WAGRAM

AIRBASE RD

Gibson Mill

OLD

Sneads Grove

15
501

RD

AIRPORT RD

Richmond Mills

144

IDA MILL RD

ANDREW

JACKSON

Elmore

HWY

Lumber River

Laurinburg Maxton Airport

71

Floral College

Livingstons Quarters

Ida Mill

Springfield Mills

RD

WIRE

RD

OLD

HAMLET

HWY

GIBSON

Sandy Bottoms

Indian Museum of Carolinas

74

WEST BLVD

S CALEDONIA RD

N MAIN ST

PRODUCE MARKET RD

W CHURCH ST

E CHURCH ST

BUS
74

ANDREW JACKSON HWY

RD

74

Maxton

Green Pond

381

MAIN ST

79

Gibson

NORTH CAROLINA

SOUTH CAROLINA

Little Pee Dee River

OLD STAGE RD

BLUES FARM RD

Crossway

Laurinburg

H

Scotland Memorial Hospital

MAIN ST

LINCOLN RD

501

401

McArthur Crossroads

501

RD

JERUSALEM RD

Johns

130

ROBESON COUNTY

Alma

Boykin

Masons Crossroads

15
401

Fletcher

385

381

KING RD

Adamsville Crossroads

CRESTLINE MCQUEEN RD

Hasty

83

Seven Bridges

Newtonville

MARLBORO COUNTY

A   B   C   D   E

RAND MCNALLY

106

MAP
106

REGIONAL MAP

1:190,080
1 in. = 3 mi.

0 2 4
miles

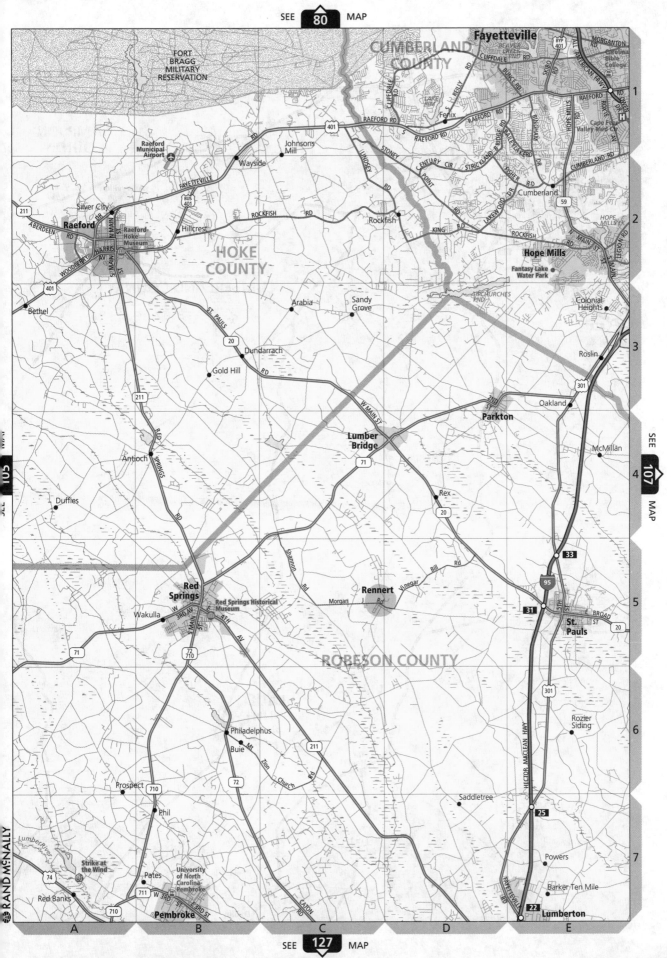

SEE **80** MAP

Fayetteville

CUMBERLAND COUNTY

BYP 401

Carolina Bible College

BEAVER CREEK RD
CLIFFDALE RD
BUNCE RD
SKIBO RD
MORGANTON RD
AMERICAN FRWY
RAEFORD RD
ROXIE AV
H

Cape Fear Valley Med Ctr

401

CLIFFDALE RD
RAEFORD RD
Fenix
RAEFORD RD
BINGHAM
HOPE MILLS RD
BRIDGE RD
BATTLEFIELD RD
FISHER RD
CUMBERLAND RD

Johnsons Mill

Wayside

Raeford Municipal Airport

LINDSEY RD
STONEY POINT RD
CENTURY CIR
STRICKLAND
KING RD

FAYETTEVILLE RD
BUS 401

Cumberland

59

HOPE MILLS

211
Silver City
ABERDEEN RD
Raeford
Raeford Hoke Museum
Hillcrest
ROCKFISH RD
Rockfish
ROCKFISH
N MAIN ST
LEGION RD
2

Hope Mills

Fantasy Lake Water Park

WOODBERRY
401
MARRIS AV
MAIN ST
N MAIN ST

HOKE COUNTY

Bethel

Arabia
Sandy Grove

UPCHURCHES PND

Colonial Heights

ST PAULS RD
20
Dundarrach
Gold Hill
RD

Roslin

211

301

RED SPRINGS RD
W MAIN ST

2ND ST
Oakland

Parkton

McMillan

Antioch

Duffies

Lumber Bridge

71

SEE **107** MAP

Rex
20

33

95

RD
Shannon RD
Bill RD
Vinegar
Morgan RD
Rennert

31

St. Pauls
5TH ST
E BROAD ST
20

Red Springs
Wakulla
W 3RD AV
S MAIN ST
4TH AV
Red Springs Historical Museum

71
72 710

ROBESON COUNTY

301

Philadelphus
Buie
Mt Zion Church Rd
211

HECTOR MACLEAN HWY

Saddletree

Prospect
710
72

Phil

25

LumberRiver

Strike at the Wind

Pates
University of North Carolina-Pembroke

Powers

74
711 W 3RD ST
E 3RD ST
CADEN RD

Barker Ten Mile

Red Banks

710
Pembroke

22
Lumberton
FAYETTEVILLE RD

A B C D E

SEE **127** MAP

MAP
107

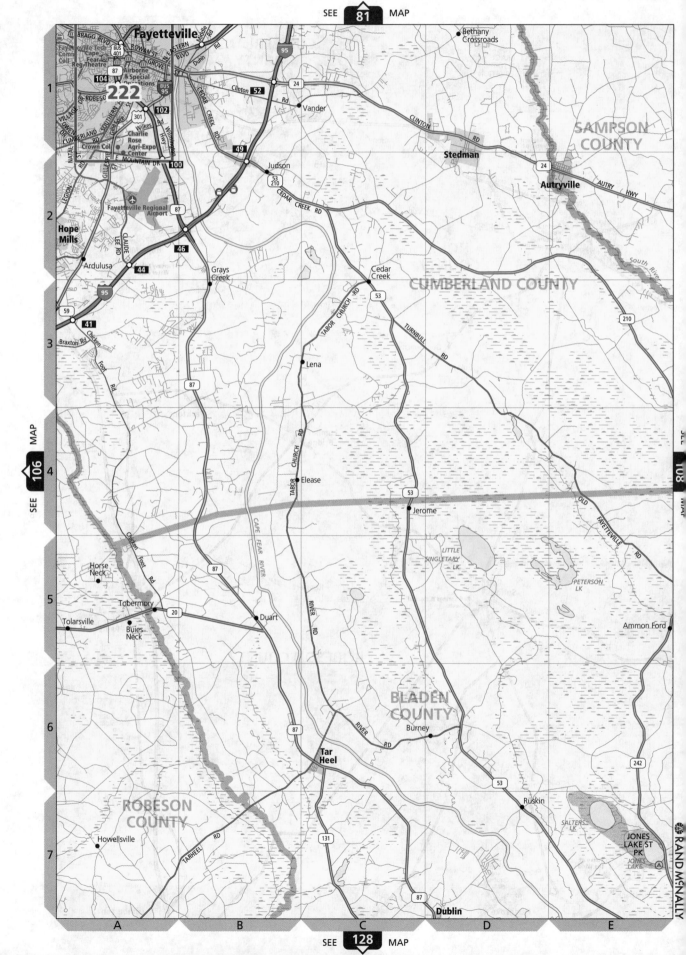

SEE **81** MAP

1:190,080
1 in. = 3 mi.

0   2   4
miles

Fayetteville

BRAGG BLVD
Fayetteville Tech Comm Coll
Cape Fear Reg Theatre
Airborne & Special Operations
222
104
87
BUS 401
ROWAN ST
GROVE ST
N EASTERN BLVD
Middle RD
Dunn Rd
CEDAR CREEK RD
BUS 95
102
301
Wilkes Rd
Charlie Rose Agri-Expo Center
E MOUNTAIN DR
100
Crown Coll
Gillespie St
CUMBERLAND RD
SOUTHERN
VILLAGE DR
OWEN DR
NATAL ST
ROBESON

Bethany Crossroads

SAMPSON COUNTY

95

24

Clinton 52

Vander

CLINTON RD

Stedman

24

AUTRY HWY

Autryville

49

Judson

53 210

CEDAR CREEK RD

87

Fayetteville Regional Airport

CLAUDE
LEE RD

Hope Mills

46

Ardulusa

44

95

59

41

Braxton Rd

Chicken Foot Rd

Grays Creek

Cedar Creek

CUMBERLAND COUNTY

53

TABOR CHURCH RD

TURNBULL RD

South River

210

87

Lena

TABOR CHURCH Rd

Elease

53

Jerome

OLD FAYETTEVILLE RD

LITTLE SINGLETARY LK

PETERSON LK

CAPE FEAR RIVER

SEE **106** MAP

SEE **108** MAP

Horse Neck

Tobermory

20

Tolarsville

Buies Neck

Duart

RIVER RD

Ammon Ford

BLADEN COUNTY

87

Burney

RIVER RD

53

Ruskin

242

SALTERS LK

ROBESON COUNTY

Tar Heel

Howellsville

TARHEEL RD

131

87

JONES LAKE ST PK

JONES LAKE

53

Dublin

RAND MCNALLY

A   B   C   D   E

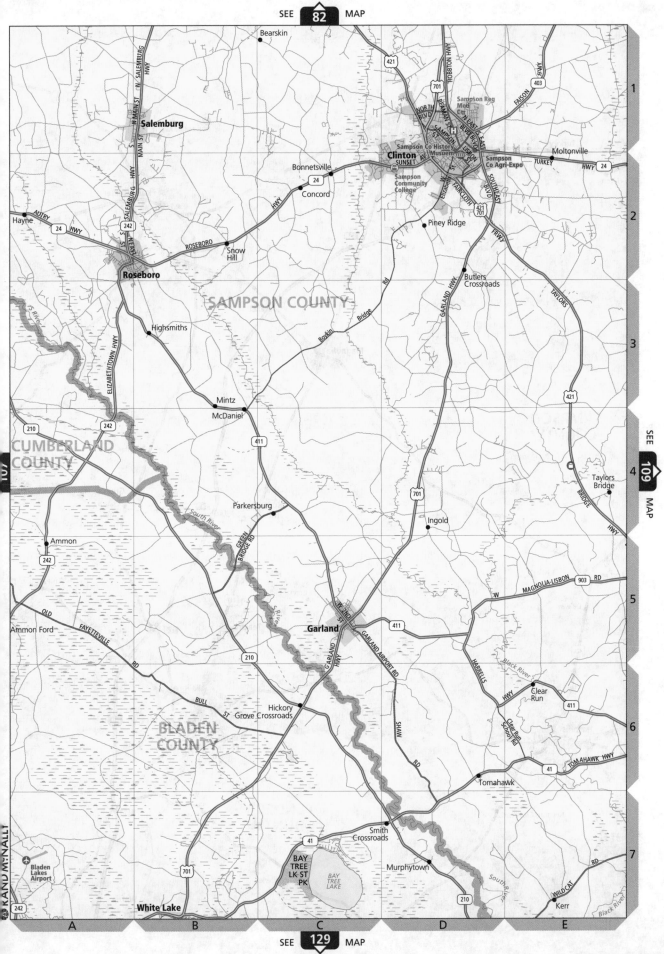

MAP
108

REGIONAL MAP

N

1:190,080
1 in. = 3 mi.
0   2   4
miles

SEE 82 MAP

Bearskin

Salemburg

Sampson Reg Med Ctr
Sampson Co History Musuem
Clinton
SUNSET AV
Sampson Co Agri-Expo
Moltonville
TURKEY HWY 24

Bonnetsville
Sampson Community College

Concord

Hayne

AUTRY HWY
24 HWY

242

ROSEBORO

Snow Hill

Roseboro

Piney Ridge

Butlers Crossroads

SAMPSON COUNTY

TAYLORS

Highsmiths

421

Mintz
McDaniel

411

210

242

SEE 109 MAP

Taylors Bridge

CUMBERLAND COUNTY

701

Parkersburg

Ingold

Ammon

242

MAGNOLIA-LISBON 903 RD

411

Ammon Ford

OLD FAYETTEVILLE RD

Garland

411

Clear Run
411

Hickory Grove Crossroads

BLADEN COUNTY

Tomahawk

41 TOMAHAWK HWY

Bladen Lakes Airport

242

210

BAY TREE LK-ST PK

41

Smith Crossroads

BAY TREE LAKE

Murphytown

210

Kerr

White Lake

701

A   B   C   D   E

SEE 129 MAP

1   2   3   4   5   6   7

RAND McNALLY

MAP
109

REGIONAL MAP

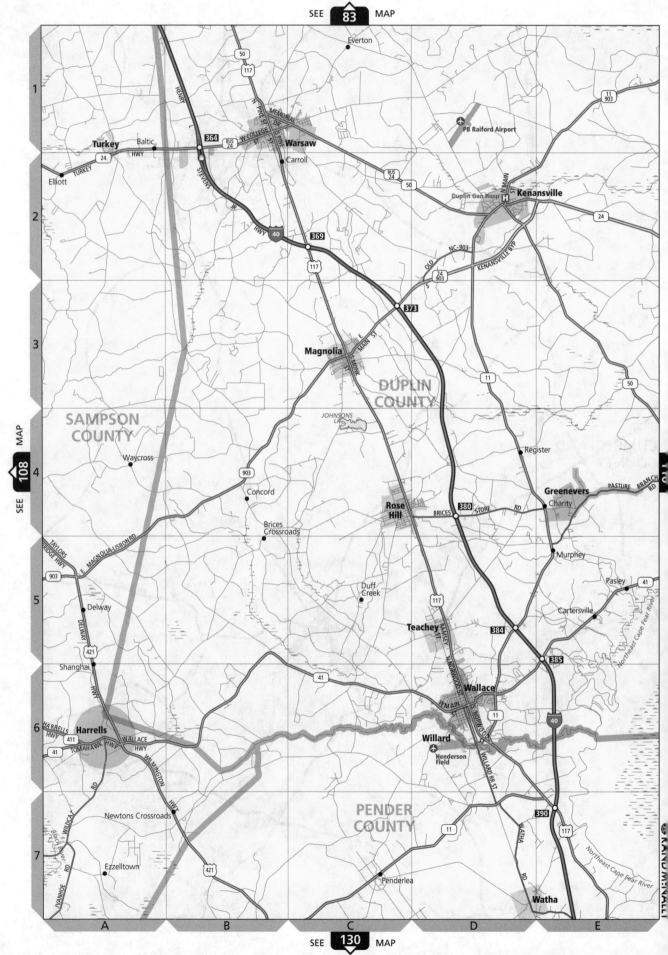

Everton

50
117

Turkey   Baltic   364   BUS   MEMORIAL   Warsaw   PB Raiford Airport
          HWY   24   DK   Carroll
24   BUS
Elliott   24   50   Duplin Gen Hosp   Kenansville
TURKEY   24

2   369
                                                                            117   OLD   NC-903   KENANSVILLE BYP

                                                                                                   24
                                                                                                   903   373

3   E
                                    Magnolia   MAIN ST   11
                                    S MONK ST   50
                                              DUPLIN
                                              COUNTY
SAMPSON   JOHNSONS
COUNTY   LK   Register

Waycross   Greenevers   PASTURE   BRANCH RD

4   903   380   STORE   RD   Charity
                          Concord   Rose   BRICES
                                                                     Hill
                          Brices   Murphey
                          Crossroads   Pasley   41

                                              Duff   Cartersville
                                              Creek   117
5   Delway   384
                                                                     Teachey
         DELWAY   385
                                                                     RAMSEY ST
         421   N NORWOOD
         Shanghai   41   Wallace
                                                                                W M AIN   40
TAYLORS   S NORWOOD
BRIDGE HWY   E MAGNOLIA-LISBON RD   11
903   Willard
HARRELLS   Harrells   WALLACE   Henderson
HWY   411   HWY   Field
6   41   TOMAHAWK   HWY   390
                                                                                WATHA   117
         RD   WILMINGTON   WILLARD RR ST

                                    Newtons Crossroads   11
7   IVANHOE RD   WILDCAT RD   Northeast Cape Fear River
         Ezzelltown   PENDER
                                    421   COUNTY
                                              Penderlea   Watha

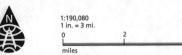

1:190,080
1 in. = 3 mi.

miles
0   2   4

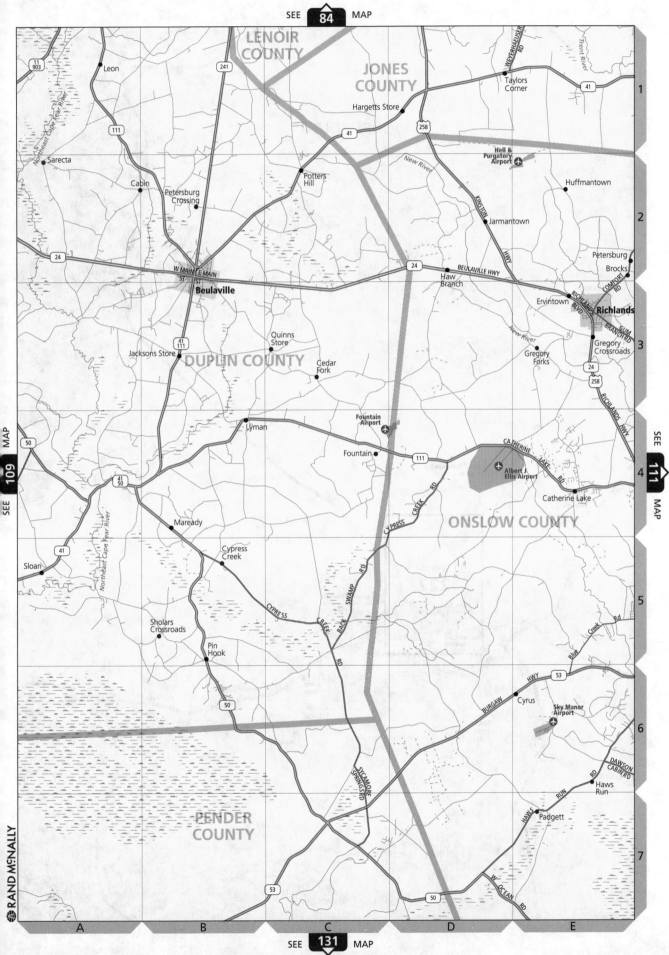

MAP
110

REGIONAL MAP

SEE 84 MAP

LENOIR COUNTY

JONES COUNTY

Leon

11 903

Sarecta

111

Cabin

Petersburg Crossing

241

Potters Hill

Hargetts Store

41

258

WEYERHAEUSER RD

Taylors Corner

41

Trent River

Hell & Purgatory Airport

Huffmantown

Jarmantown

KINSTON HWY

New River

24

24

Beulaville Hwy

Haw Branch

Petersburg

Brocks

W MAIN E MAIN ST ST

Beulaville

Ervintown

RICHLANDS BLVD

COMFORT RD

Richlands

GUM BRANCH RD

Quinns Store

41 111

DUPLIN COUNTY

Jacksons Store

Cedar Fork

New River

Gregory Forks

Gregory Crossroads

24

258

RICHLANDS HWY

SEE 111 MAP

Lyman

Fountain Airport

CATHERINE LAKE RD

Fountain

111

Albert J Ellis Airport

Catherine Lake

50

Maready

ONSLOW COUNTY

41 50

CYPRESS CREEK RD

BACK SWAMP RD

Sloan

41

Cypress Creek

Blue Creek Rd

Sholars Crossroads

CYPRESS CREEK RD

Pin Hook

BURGAW HWY

53

Cyrus

Sky Manor Airport

50

DAWSON CABIN RD

HAWS RUN RD

Haws Run

SYCAMORE SPRINGS RD

PENDER COUNTY

Padgett

HAWS

53

50

W OCEAN RD

Northeast Cape Fear River

SEE 109 MAP

50

SEE 131 MAP

A   B   C   D   E

1   2   3   4   5   6   7

RAND MCNALLY

MAP
111

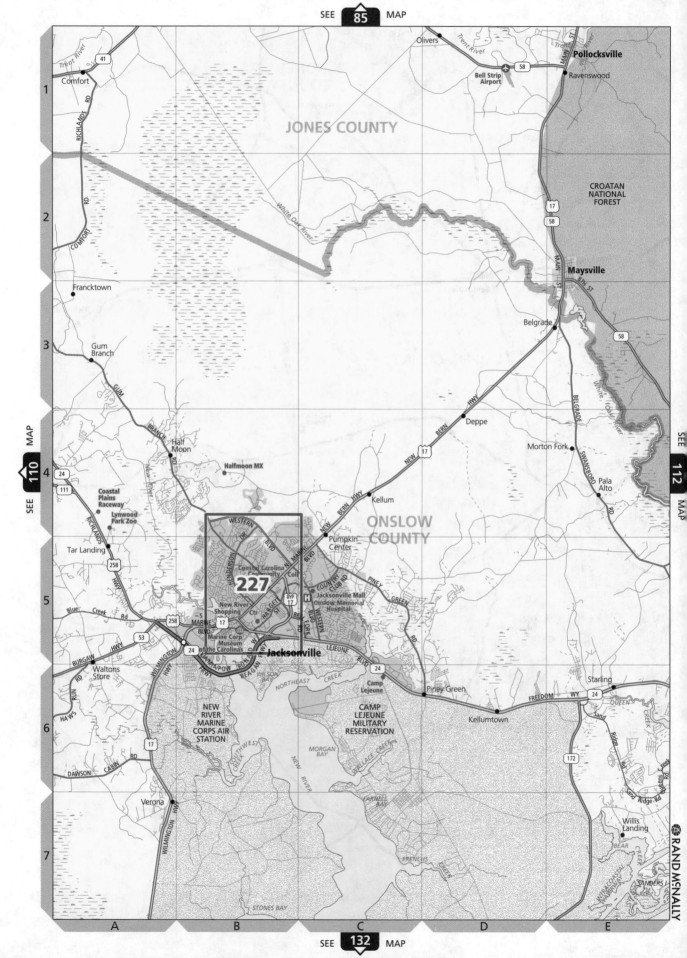

1:190,080
1 in. = 3 mi.

0   2   4
miles

SEE 85 MAP

JONES COUNTY

Comfort

Trent River

41

RICHLANDS RD

COMFORT RD

Francktown

Gum Branch

GUM

BRANCH

RD

Half Moon

Halfmoon MX

NEW RIVER RD

Coastal Plains Raceway

Lynwood Park Zoo

RICHLANDS HWY

Tar Landing

258

Blue   Creek   Rd

258

53

BURGAW RD

HAWS RUN RD

Waltons Store

17

DAWSON CABIN RD

Verona

WILMINGTON HWY

SWANNAHPOW HWY

24

WESTERN DR

HENDERSON DR

WESTERN BLVD

NEW BERN BLVD

S MARINE BLVD

227

Coastal Carolina Community Coll.

New River Shopping Ctr

Marine Corp Museum of the Carolinas

HERGETT ST

BYP 17

17

H

Jacksonville Mall

Onslow Memorial Hospital

Jacksonville

PLEASANT HWY

IRON RD

WILSON BAY

NORTHEAST   CREEK

NEW RIVER MARINE CORPS AIR STATION

SOUTHWEST CREEK

MORGAN BAY

STONES BAY

NEW RIVER

Pumpkin Center

ONSLOW COUNTY

Kellum

NEW BERN HWY

17

Deppe

NEW BERN HWY

COUNTRY CLUB RD

PINEY GREEN RD

WESTERN BLVD

BELL FORK RD

LEJEUNE BLVD

24

Camp Lejeune

CAMP LEJEUNE MILITARY RESERVATION

WALLACE CREEK

FARNELL BAY

FRENCHS   CREEK

Piney Green

Kellumtown

172

Olivers

Trent River

Bell Strip Airport

58

Pollocksville

Ravenswood

MAIN ST

17

58

CROATAN NATIONAL FOREST

Maysville

8TH ST

MAIN ST

Belgrade

58

White Oak River

BELGRADE

SWANSBORO RD

Morton Fork

Pala Alto

SEE 112 MAP

Starling

FREEDOM WY

24

QUEEN CREEK

Sand Ridge Rd

Sand Ridge Rd

Willis Landing

BEAR   CREEK

SANDERS L

INTRACOASTAL WATERWAY

SEE 110 MAP

24

111

SEE 132 MAP

A   B   C   D   E

White Oak River

RAND MCNALLY

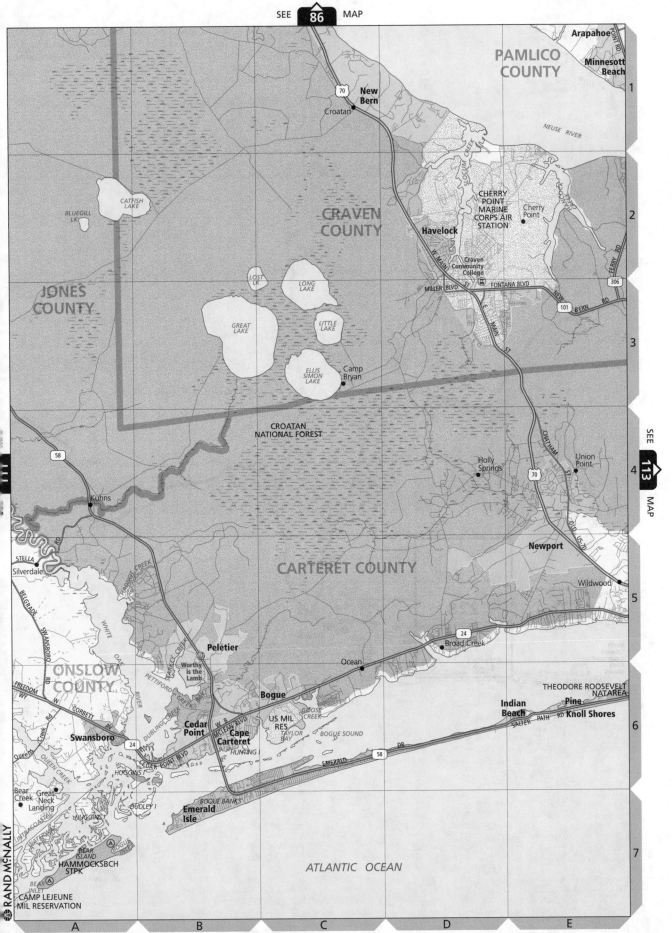

MAP
112

REGIONAL MAP

1:190,080
1 in. = 3 mi.

0   2   4
miles

SEE ◇86 MAP

PAMLICO COUNTY

Arapahoe

Minnesott Beach

POINT RD

NEUSE RIVER

1

New Bern

70

Croatan

SLOCUM CREEK

CRAVEN COUNTY

CHERRY POINT MARINE CORPS AIR STATION

Cherry Point

FERRY RD

2

Havelock

W. MAIN

E. MAIN ST

Craven Community College

MILLER BLVD   FONTANA BLVD

NEW BERN RD

306

101

JONES COUNTY

LOST LK

LONG LAKE

GREAT LAKE

LITTLE LAKE

3

ELLIS SIMON LAKE

Camp Bryan

CROATAN NATIONAL FOREST

CHATHAM ST

SEE ◇113 MAP

58

Holly Springs

Union Point

4

Kuhns

70

STELLA

Silverdale

Newport

Wildwood

BELGRADE

SWANSBORO RD

WHITE OAK

RIVER

HADNOT CREEK

CARTERET COUNTY

5

TURKEY CREEK

24

Broad Creek

Peletier

Worthy is the Lamb

Ocean

THEODORE ROOSEVELT NATAREA

ONSLOW COUNTY

FREEDOM WY

CORBETT AV

PETTIFORD CREEK

DUBLING CREEK

Bogue

GOOSE CREEK

US MIL RES

TAYLOR BAY

BOGUE SOUND

Indian Beach

Pine Knoll Shores

SALTER PATH RD

6

Swansboro

24

Cedar Point

W. B. MCLEAN BLVD

Cape Carteret

HUNTING I

CEDAR POINT BLVD

58

EMERALD

DR

Queens Creek RD

HUGGINS

Bear Creek

Great Neck Landing

DUDLEY I

HUGGINS

BOGUE BANKS

Emerald Isle

7

INTRACOASTAL WATERWAY

BEAR ISLAND

BOGUE

HAMMOCKS BCH STPK

BEAR INLET

ATLANTIC OCEAN

CAMP LEJEUNE MIL RESERVATION

RAND MCNALLY

A   B   C   D   E

MAP
113

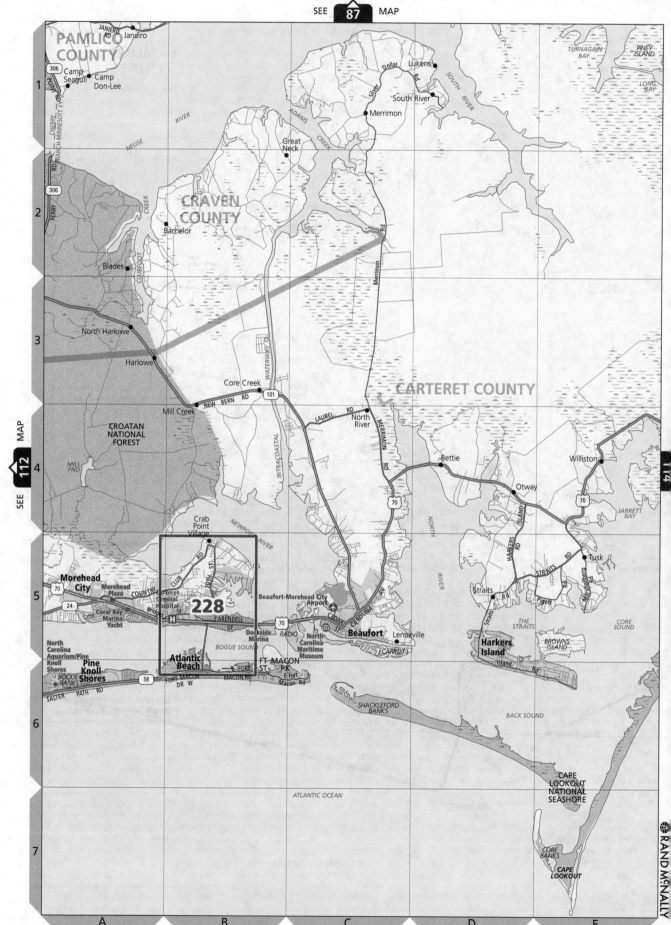

REGIONAL MAP

1:190,080
1 in. = 3 mi.

0 2 4
miles

SEE 87 MAP

N

PAMLICO COUNTY

JANIERO RD
Janeiro

306 Camp Seagull
Camp Don-Lee

CHERRY BRANCH-MINNESOTT FY
306
FERRY RD

NEUSE RIVER

CLUBFOOT CREEK

CRAVEN COUNTY

Bachelor

Blades

North Harlowe

Harlowe

CROATAN NATIONAL FOREST

MILL PND

SEE 112 MAP

Core Creek
101
NEW BERN RD
Mill Creek

WATERWAY ST

INTRACOASTAL

Great Neck

ADAMS CREEK

SOUTH RIVER

Dollar Rd
Lukens
South River
Silver Rd
Merrimon

TURNAGAIN BAY

PINEY ISLAND

LONG BAY

MERRIMON RD

CARTERET COUNTY

LAUREL RD
North River

Bettie
70
Otway
70

Williston

HARKERS ISLAND RD

STRAITS RD
Tusk

MARSHALLBERG RD

I 14

JARRETT BAY

NEWPORT RIVER

Crab Point Village

Morehead City
70
Morehead Plaza
24
Coral Bay Marina Yacht
COUNTRY CLUB RD
Carteret General Hospital
Bridges
20TH ST
H
ARENDELL ST
228
Dockside Marina
BOGUE SOUND

Beaufort-Morehead City Airport

North Carolina Maritime Museum

CEDAR ST
CAROLINA AV
RADIO
70
Beaufort
CARROT
Lenoxville

NORTH RIVER

Straits
Straits Rd
Pigott
THE STRAITS
Harkers Island
Island Rd

BROWNS ISLAND

CORE SOUND

North Carolina Aquarium/Pine Knoll Shores
Pine Knoll Shores
BOGUE BANKS
58
SALTER PATH RD

Atlantic Beach
FORT MACON DR W
FT MACON PK
E FORT MACON RD
MACON RD

SHACKLEFORD BANKS

BACK SOUND

CAPE LOOKOUT NATIONAL SEASHORE

ATLANTIC OCEAN

CORE BANKS

CAPE LOOKOUT

RAND McNALLY

A   B   C   D   E

MAP
114

1:190,080
1 in. = 3 mi.

0   2   4

miles

SEE **88** MAP

PINEY ISLAND

LONG BAY

WEST BAY

Lola

PAMLICO SOUND

CEDAR ISLAND NATIONAL WILDLIFE REFUGE

CEDAR ISLAND

12

THOROFARE BAY

CORE BANKS

CARTERET COUNTY

CEDAR ISLAND RD

OLD CEDAR ISLAND RD

Masontown

SHELL RD

CAPE

70

SEASHORE DR

Portsmouth

LOOKOUT FY

1

2

3

NELSON BAY

CORE SOUND

70

CAPE LOOKOUT NAT'L SEASHORE

Davis

CORE BANKS

ATLANTIC OCEAN

4

5

6

7

A   B   C   D   E

MAP
115

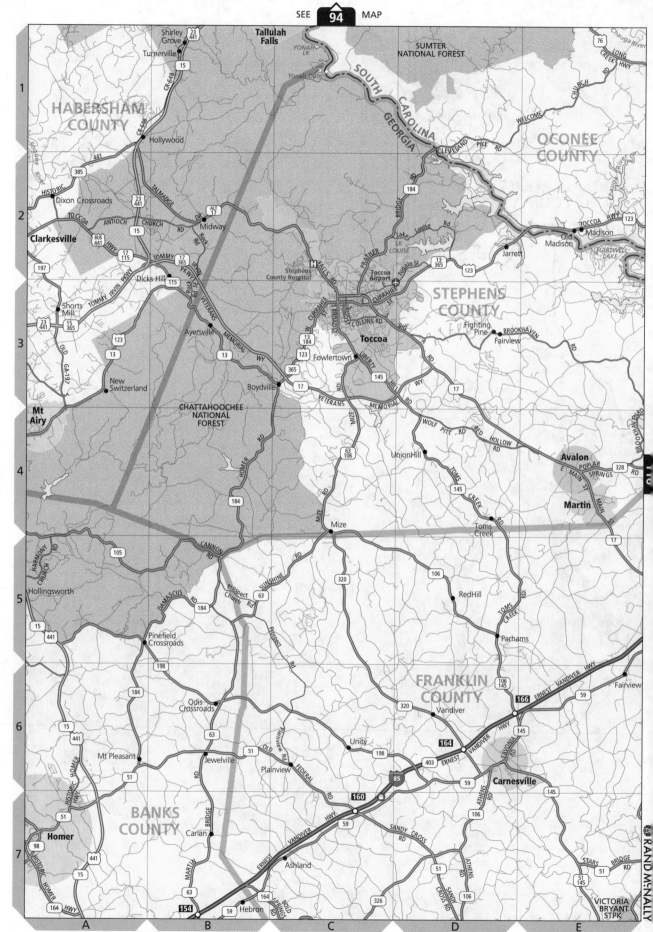

SEE **94** MAP

1:190,080
1 in. = 3 mi.

0   2   4
miles

N

MAP
116

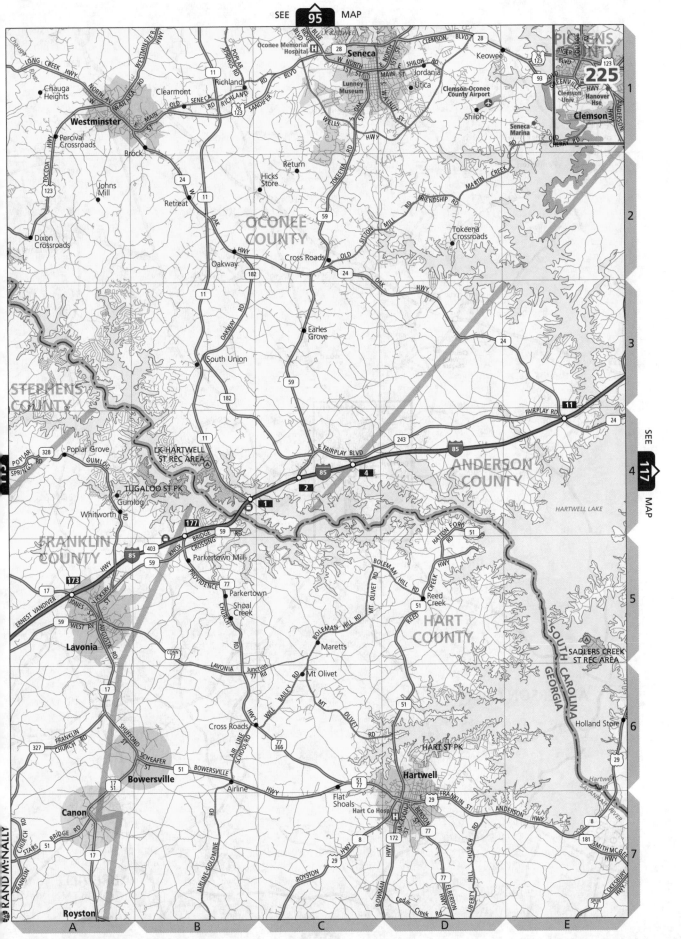

1:190,080
1 in. = 3 mi.

miles
0   2   4

SEE 117 ▶ MAP

RAND MCNALLY

MAP
117

1:190,080
1 in. = 3 mi.

0   2   4
miles

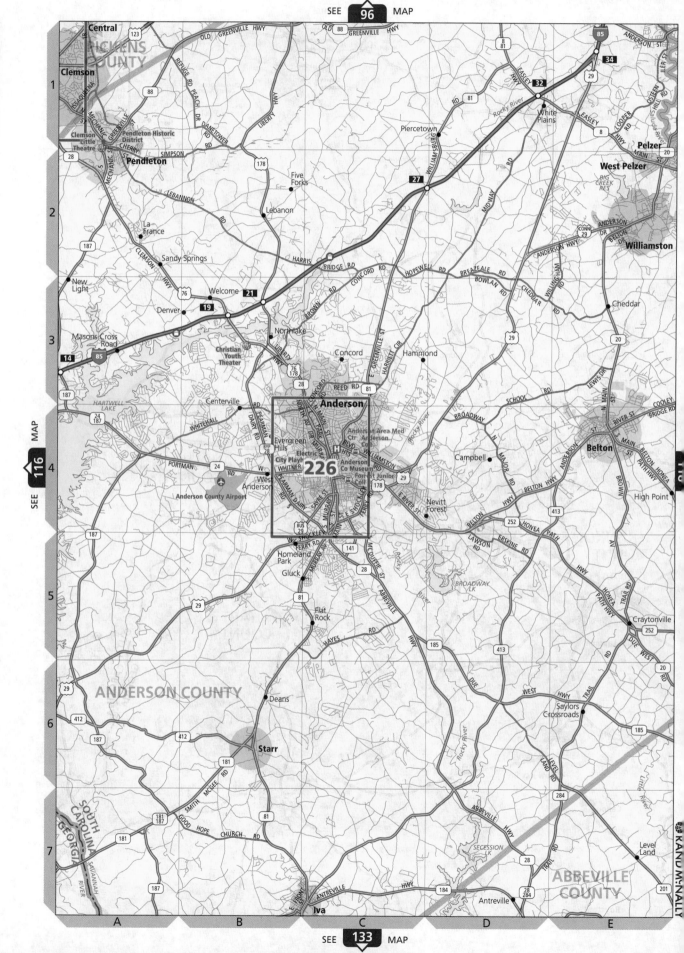

SEE **96** MAP

SEE **116** MAP

SEE **133** MAP

RAND McNALLY

Central
Clemson
PICKENS COUNTY
Pendleton Historic District
Clemson Little Theatre
Pendleton
La France
Sandy Springs
New Light
Denver
Masons Cross Road
Welcome
Northlake
Christian Youth Theater
Centerville
HARTWELL LAKE
Five Forks
Lebanon
Concord
Hammond
Piercetown
White Plains
West Pelzer
Williamston
Pelzer
Cheddar
Evergreen Hills
Electric City Playh
WHITNER
West Anderson
Anderson County Airport
PORTMAN
Anderson
Anderson Area Med Ctr
Anderson Co Museum
Anderson Col
Forrest Junior Coll
226
Campbell
Nevitt Forest
Belton
High Point
Homeland Park
Gluck
Flat Rock
Deans
BROADWAY LK
Craytonville
Saylors Crossroads
ANDERSON COUNTY
Starr
SOUTH CAROLINA
GEORGIA
SAVANNAH RIVER
SECESSION LK
Level Land
ABBEVILLE COUNTY
Iva
Antreville

A   B   C   D   E
1   2   3   4   5   6   7

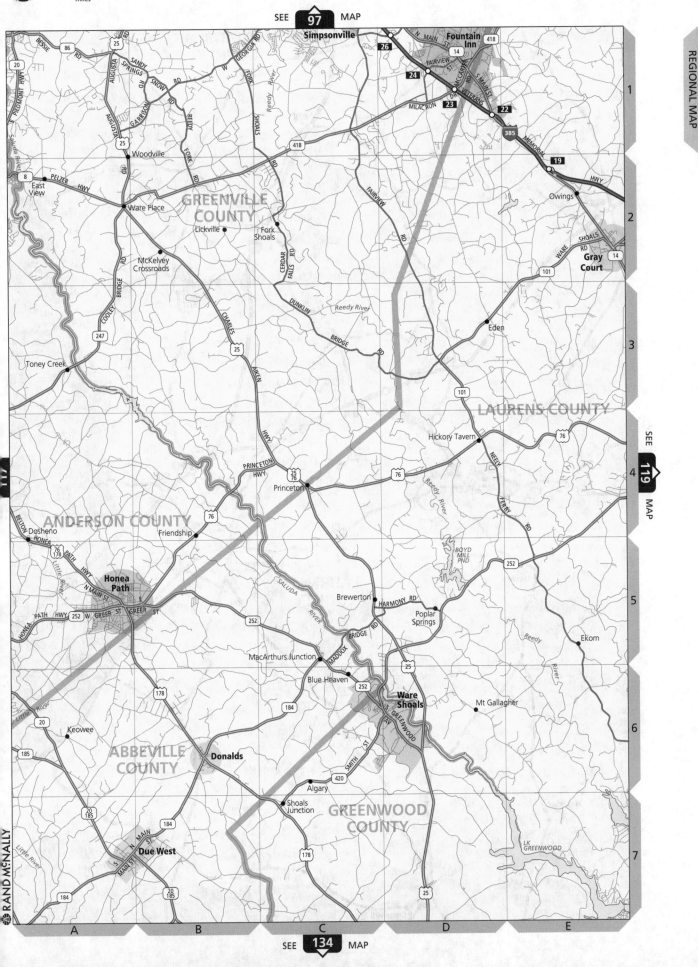

MAP
118

REGIONAL MAP

1:190,080
1 in. = 3 mi.

miles

SEE 97 MAP

Simpsonville

Fountain Inn

N MAIN ST

FAIRVIEW

14

S MAIN ST

418

26

24

MILACRON

23

VETERANS DR

22

385

MEMORIAL HWY

19

8

PELZER HWY

S PIEDMONT HWY

BESSIE RD

86 RD

25 RD

SANDY SPRINGS RD

SNOW RD

GARRISON RD

AUGUSTA RD

GEORGIA RD

W GEORGIA RD

SHOALS RD

REEDY FORK RD

REEDY River

Reedy River

20

25

Woodville

418

East View

Saluda River

Ware Place

GREENVILLE COUNTY

Lickville

Fork Shoals

CERDAR FALLS RD

FAIRVIEW RD

Owings

WARE SHOALS RD

101

Gray Court

14

McKelvey Crossroads

COOLEY BRIDGE RD

CHARLES RD

DUNKLIN BRIDGE RD

Reedy River

Eden

101

247

25

AIKEN RD

HWY

Toney Creek

LAURENS COUNTY

Hickory Tavern

76

SEE 119 MAP

117

PRINCETON HWY

25 76

Princeton

76

NEELY FERRY RD

252

BOYD MILL PND

ANDERSON COUNTY

Dosheno

Belton

76 178

HONEA PATH HWY

Little River

Friendship

SALUDA RIVER

Brewerton

HARMONY RD

Poplar Springs

Reedy River

Ekom

Honea Path

N MAIN ST

HONEA PATH HWY

252

GREER ST W

GREER ST

252

MacArthurs Junction

MADDOX RD

BRIDGE RD

25

Blue Heaven

252

Ware Shoals

Mt Gallagher

Keowee

178

184

S GREENWOOD AV

20

185

Little River

ABBEVILLE COUNTY

Donalds

SMITH ST

Algary

420

GREENWOOD COUNTY

LK GREENWOOD

20 185

184

S MAIN ST

Shoals Junction

178

Due West

184

20 185

25

SEE 134 MAP

RAND McNALLY

A   B   C   D   E

MAP
119

REGIONAL MAP

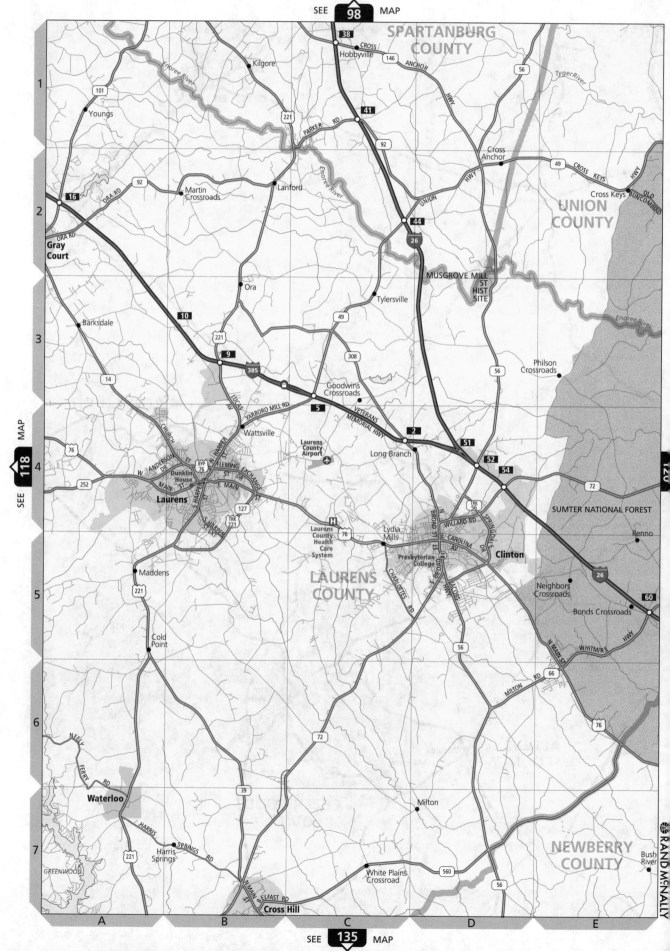

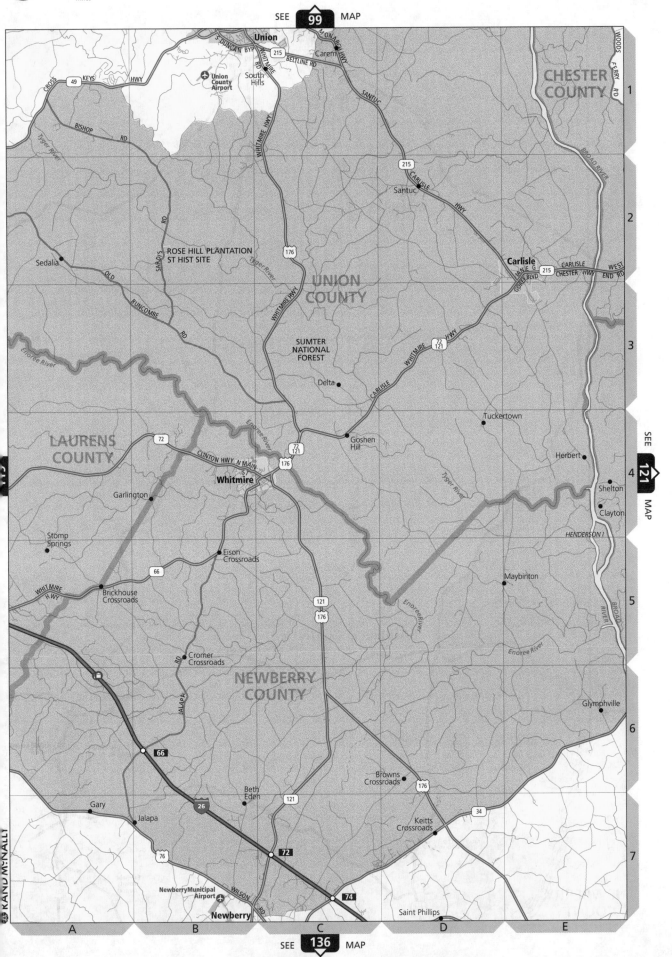

MAP
120

REGIONAL MAP

1:190,080
1 in. = 3 mi.

0   2   4
miles

SEE [99] MAP

Union

S. DUNCAN BYP
Carem
BELTLINE RD
215
MONARCHY HWY

KEYS
49
HWY
South
Hills
Union
County
Airport

CHESTER
COUNTY

WOODS FERRY RD

CROSS
BISHOP   RD
Tyger River

WHITMIRE HWY
RD

SANTUC

BROAD RIVER

215
CARLISLE
Santuc

2

SARDIS   RD

ROSE HILL PLANTATION
ST HIST SITE

176

Tiger River

UNION
COUNTY

HWY

Carlisle
NNIE G
GOREE BLVD
215
CARLISLE
CHESTER HWY
WEST
END RD

Sedalia
OLD
BUNCOMBE
RD

WHITMIRE HWY

SUMTER
NATIONAL
FOREST

CARLISLE
WHITMIRE
72
121
HWY

3

Enoree River

Delta

Tuckertown

LAURENS
COUNTY

72
CLINTON HWY N MAIN
ST
72
121
176
Whitmire

Enoree River

Goshen
Hill

Tyger River

Herbert

SEE
[121]
MAP

Garlington

Shelton
Clayton

HENDERSON I

Stomp
Springs

66

Eison
Crossroads

Maybinton

4

WHITMIRE HWY

Brickhouse
Crossroads

121
176

Enoree River

BROAD
RIVER

5

RD
Cromer
Crossroads

JALAPA
RD

NEWBERRY
COUNTY

Enoree River

Glymphville

6

66

Browns
Crossroads
176

Beth
Eden
121

34

Gary
Jalapa

26

Keitts
Crossroads

76

72

Newberry Municipal
Airport

WILSON RD

74

Saint Phillips

7

Newberry

A   B   C   D   E

SEE [136] MAP

RAND MCNALLY

MAP
121

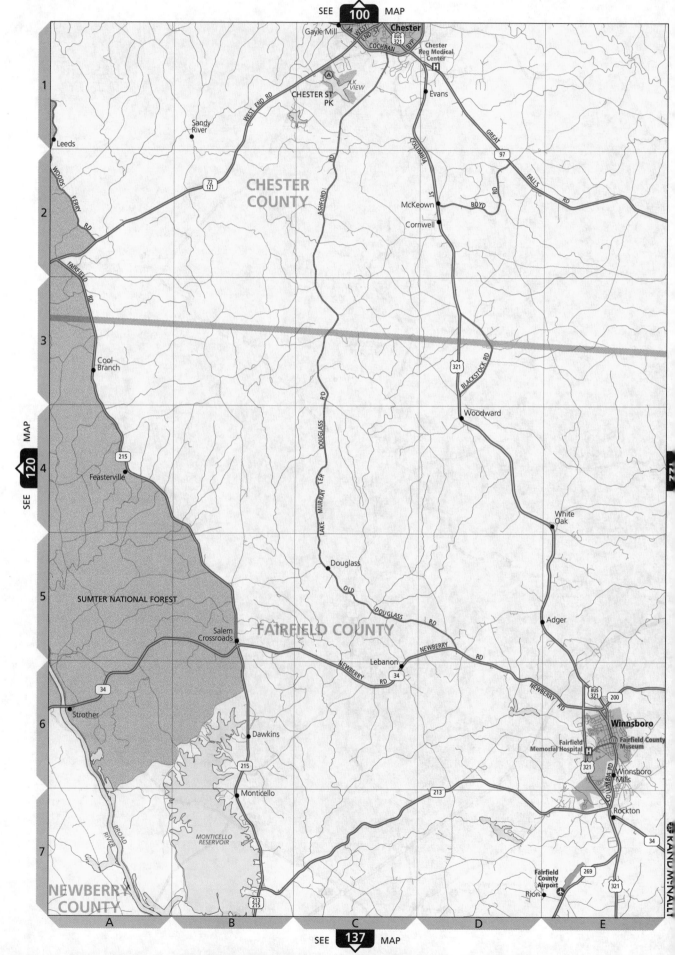

1:190,080
1 in. = 3 mi.
0   2   4
miles

N

SEE 100 MAP

Gayle Mill

Chester
BUS 321 BYP

Chester
Reg Medical
Center

WEST END ST
COCHRAN

1

Evans

CHESTER ST PK

LK VIEW

WEST END RD

Sandy
River

COLUMBIA

GREAT

FALLS

97

Leeds

72
121

CHESTER
COUNTY

WOODS FERRY RD

ASHFORD

RD

2

McKeown

BOYD

RD

RD

ST

Cornwell

FAIRFIELD RD

3

321

BLACKSTOCK RD

Cool
Branch

DOUGLASS

RD

SEE 120 MAP

121

Woodward

215

4

Feasterville

LAKE MURRAY TER

White
Oak

5

SUMTER NATIONAL FOREST

Douglass

OLD

DOUGLASS

RD

Adger

FAIRFIELD COUNTY

Salem
Crossroads

NEWBERRY

RD

NEWBERRY

RD

34

Lebanon

NEWBERRY

BUS
321

200

34

RD

Strother

6

Dawkins

215

Winnsboro

Fairfield
Memorial Hospital

Fairfield County
Museum

321

COLUMBIA RD

Winnsboro
Mills

Monticello

213

Rockton

34

BROAD

RIVER

7

MONTICELLO
RESERVOIR

Fairfield
County
Airport

269

Rion

321

NEWBERRY
COUNTY

213
215

RAND McNALLY

A   B   C   D   E

SEE 137 MAP

MAP
122

REGIONAL MAP

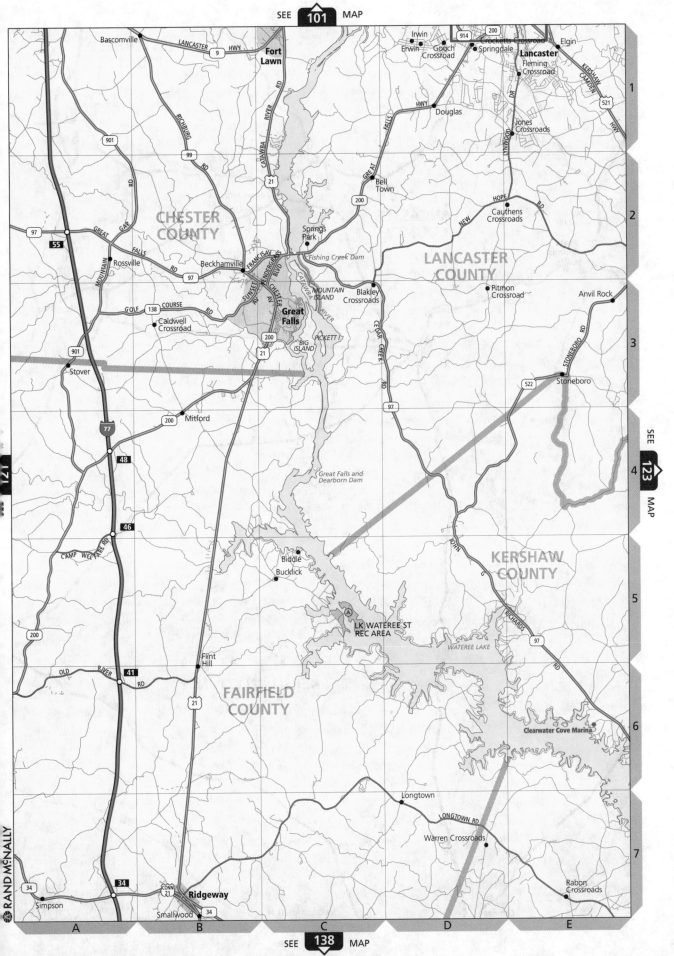

1:190,080
1 in. = 3 mi.

0   2   4
miles

SEE 101 MAP

SEE 123 MAP

SEE 138 MAP

Bascomville

LANCASTER HWY 9

Fort Lawn

Irwin
Erwin
Gooch Crossroad
Springdale
Crocketts Crossroad
Elgin
Lancaster
Fleming Crossroad

901

RICHBURG RD

99 RD

CATAWBA RIVER RD

21

FALLS HWY

Douglas

Jones Crossroads

KERSHAW CAMDEN HWY

521

LINWOOD DR

97

55

GREAT GAP RD

MOUNTAIN FALLS RD

Rossville

Beckhamville

FRANCIS AV
HENDERGRASS
SUNSET AV
CHESTER AV

Springs Park

GREAT

Bell Town

200

NEW HOPE RD

Cauthens Crossroads

CHESTER COUNTY

LANCASTER COUNTY

97

GOLF COURSE RD

138

Caldwell Crossroad

Great Falls

MOUNTAIN ISLAND

Fishing Creek Dam

Blakley Crossroads

CATAWBA RIVER

PICKETT

BIG ISLAND

CEDAR CREEK RD

Pitmon Crossroad

Anvil Rock

STONEBORO RD

901

Stover

200

21

97

522

Stoneboro

77

200

Mitford

48

Great Falls and Dearborn Dam

46

CAMP WELFARE RD

Biddle
Bucklick

JOHN

KERSHAW COUNTY

RICHARDS RD

200

OLD RIVER RD

41

Flint Hill

21

FAIRFIELD COUNTY

LK WATEREE ST REC AREA

WATEREE LAKE

97

Clearwater Cove Marina

Longtown

LONGTOWN RD

Warren Crossroads

34

34

CONN 21

Ridgeway

Smallwood

34

Simpson

Rabon Crossroads

RAND McNALLY

A   B   C   D   E

1 2 3 4 5 6 7

MAP
123

REGIONAL MAP

1:190,080
1 in. = 3 mi.

0   2   4
miles

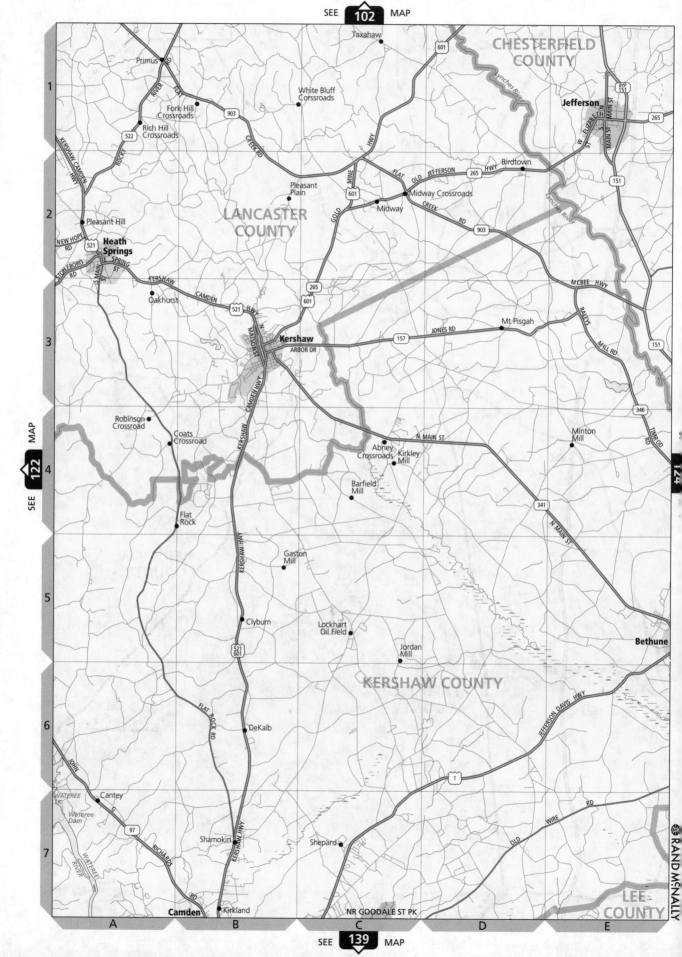

SEE ◇ 102 MAP

CHESTERFIELD
COUNTY

Taxahaw

601

Jefferson

BYP
151

Primus

RIVER

FLAT

903

Fork Hill
Crossroads

White Bluff
Corssroads

HWY

265

Birdtown

151

265

Rich Hill
Crossroads

522

CREEK RD

MINE

265

Lynches River

KERSHAW CAMDEN HWY

ROCKY

Pleasant
Plain

601

GOLD

Midway Crossroads

CREEK

RD

LANCASTER
COUNTY

Midway

903

MCBEE HWY

Pleasant Hill

265

RALEY'S

NEW HOPE
RD

521

Heath
Springs

SPRING
ST

S MAIN ST

STONEBORO RD

601

MILL RD

151

KERSHAW

CAMDEN

521

HWY

Oakhurst

MT Pisgah

JONES RD

157

MAIN ST

Kershaw

ARBOR DR

346

Robinson
Crossroad

Coats
Crossroad

N MAIN ST

Minton
Mill

Abney
Crossroads

Kirkley
Mill

KERSHAW HWY

CAMDEN HWY

Barfield
Mill

341

SEE ◇ 122 MAP

Flat
Rock

N MAIN ST

Gaston
Mill

Clyburn

Lockhart
Oil Field

521
601

Jordan
Mill

Bethune

KERSHAW COUNTY

FLAT ROCK RD

DeKalb

JEFFERSON DAVIS HWY

1

JOHN G

WATEREE
LK

Cantey

Wateree
Dam

97

RD

WIRE

KERSHAW HWY

OLD

Shamokin

RICHARDS

Shepard

WATEREE RIVER

RD

Camden

Kirkland

NR GOODALE ST PK

LEE
COUNTY

RAND McNALLY

A   B   C   D   E

SEE ◇ 139 MAP

124

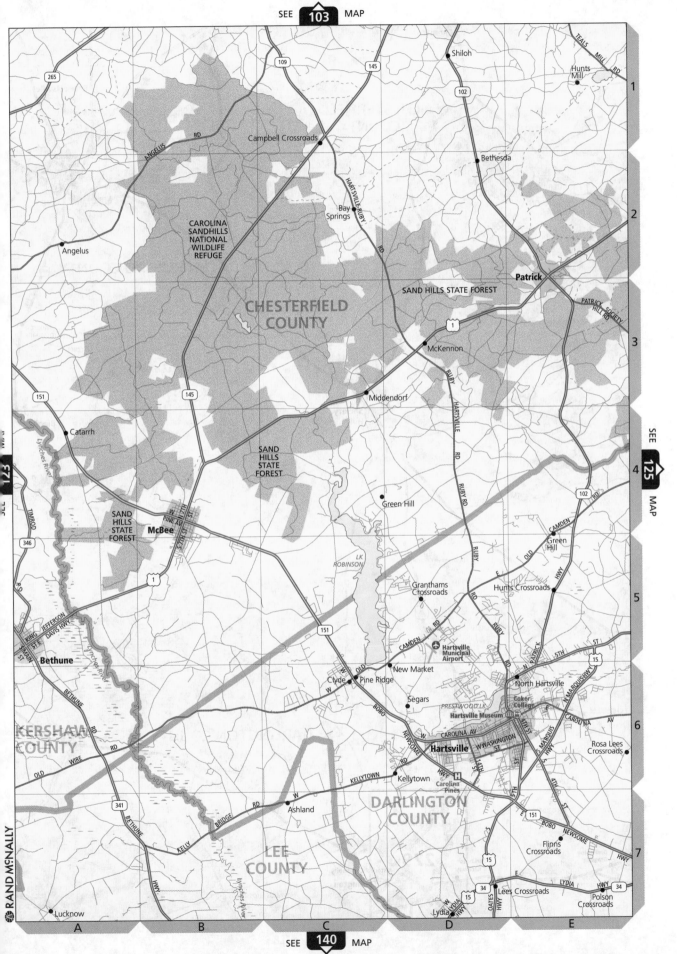

MAP
124

1:190,080
1 in. = 3 mi.
0   2   4
miles

SEE **103** MAP

265

109   145

Shiloh

Hunts
Mill

102

Campbell Crossroads

Bethesda

Angelus

ANGELUS   RD

CAROLINA
SANDHILLS
NATIONAL
WILDLIFE
REFUGE

HARTSVILLE-RUBY

Bay
Springs

SAND HILLS STATE FOREST

Patrick

PATRICK SOCIETY
HILL RD

151

CHESTERFIELD
COUNTY

1

McKennon

RUBY

3

145

Middendorf

HARTSVILLE

RD

SEE
125
MAP

Catarrh

SAND
HILLS
STATE
FOREST

RUBY RD

102   RD

Green Hill

4

Lynches River

TIMROD

346

SAND
HILLS
STATE
FOREST

W PINE AV

W 7TH

S 7TH ST

McBee

1

Green
Hill

CAMDEN

OLD   HWY

LK
ROBINSON

Granthams
Crossroads

Hunts Crossroads

RUBY

5

151

RD

RUBY   RD

N PATRICK

5TH   ST

15

KING
ST E
JEFFERSON
DAVIS HWY

MAIN   ST
STATE

Bethune

CAMDEN

Hartsville
Municipal
Airport

New Market

North Hartsville

N MARQUIS HWY

KERSHAW
COUNTY

Lynches River

RD

BETHUNE

RD

OLD   WIRE   RD

Clyde
W   Pine Ridge

Segars

BOBO

PRESTWOOD LK

Coker
College

Hartsville Museum

CAROLINA   AV

Rosa Lees
Crossroads

CAROLINA   AV

6

341

NEWSOME

KELLYTOWN

Kellytown

Hartsville

W WASHINGTON
ST

14TH   ST

5TH   ST

S MARQUIS HWY

4TH ST

BETHUNE

KELLY

BRIDGE   RD

Ashland

**DARLINGTON
COUNTY**

Carolina
Pines

151

BOBO   NEWSOME
HWY

Flinns
Crossroads

7

**LEE
COUNTY**

Lynches River

15

34   Lees Crossroads   LYDIA   HWY   34

Lucknow

15   Lydia
W LYDIA HWY

OATES HWY

Polson
Crossroads

A   B   C   D   E

SEE **140** MAP

SEE **123** MAP

MAP
125

REGIONAL MAP

1:190,080
1 in. = 3 mi.

0   2   4

miles

N

SEE [104] MAP

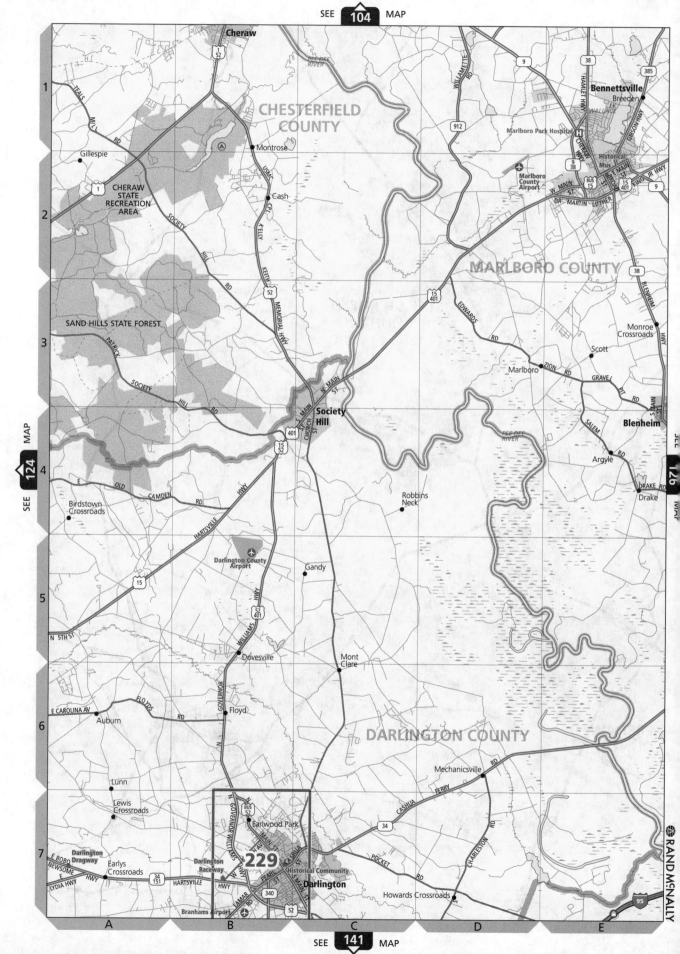

Cheraw

CHESTERFIELD COUNTY

Bennettsville

Breeden

WALLACE

Marlboro Park Hospital

Historical Mus.

1

Gillespie

Montrose

CHERAW STATE RECREATION AREA

2

Cash

Marlboro County Airport

MARLBORO COUNTY

SAND HILLS STATE FOREST

3

Monroe Crossroads

Scott

Marlboro

Blenheim

Society Hill

Argyle

DRAKE

Drake

SEE [124] MAP

SEE [126] MAP

4

Birdstown Crossroads

Robbins Neck

Darlington County Airport

Gandy

5

N 5TH ST

Dovesville

Mont Clare

E CAROLINA AV

Auburn

Floyd

DARLINGTON COUNTY

6

Mechanicsville

Lunn

Lewis Crossroads

Earlwood Park

229

7

Darlington Dragway

Earlys Crossroads

Darlington Raceway

Historical Community

Howards Crossroads

Darlington

Branhams Airport

A   B   C   D   E

SEE [141] MAP

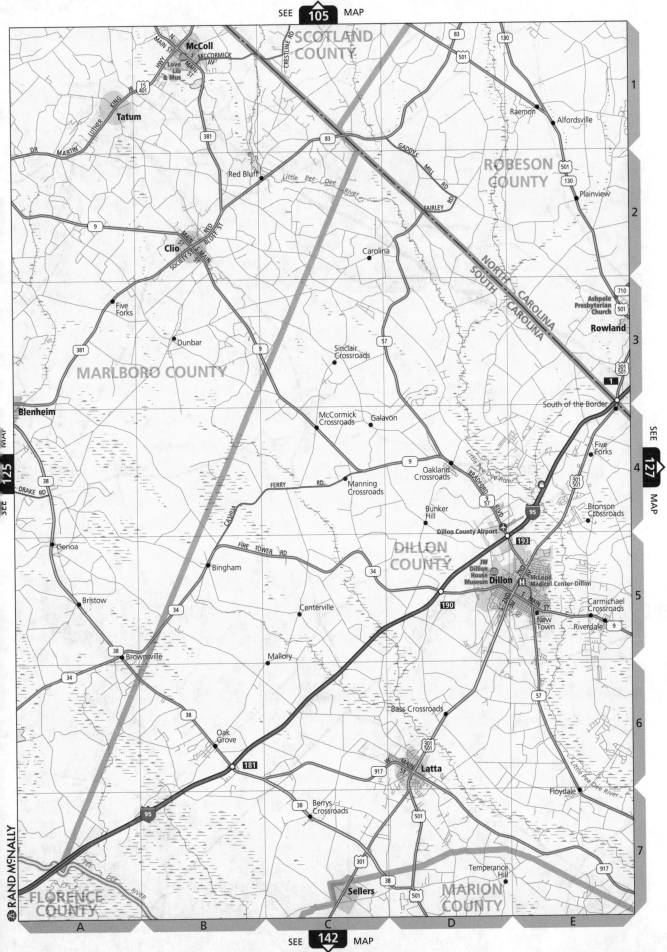

MAP
126

REGIONAL MAP

1:190,080
1 in. = 3 mi.

miles
0   2   4

SCOTLAND COUNTY

McColl
MCCORMICK AV
Love Lib & Mus
Tatum

Red Bluff

Little Pee Dee River

GADDY'S MILL RD

Raemon
Alfordsville

ROBESON COUNTY

Plainview

FAIRLEY RD

9

Clio

Carolina

NORTH CAROLINA
SOUTH CAROLINA

Ashpole Presbyterian Church

Rowland

Five Forks

Dunbar

Sinclair Crossroads

57

MARLBORO COUNTY

South of the Border

Blenheim

McCormick Crossroads

Galavon

9

Five Forks

Oakland Crossroads

Bronson Crossroads

FERRY RD

Manning Crossroads

Little Pee Dee River

BRADFORD BLVD

Genoa

Bunker Hill

Dillon County Airport

193

DILLON COUNTY

JW Dillon House Museum

Dillon

McLeod Medical Center-Dillon

Bingham

FIRE TOWER RD

34

Bristow

Centerville

190

New Town

Carmichael Crossroads

Riverdale

9

Brownsville

Mallory

57

Oak Grove

181

Bass Crossroads

917

W MAIN ST
Latta

Floydale

Little Pee Dee River

95

Berrys Crossroads

501

301

Temperance Hill

917

Sellers

501

MARION COUNTY

FLORENCE COUNTY

RAND MCNALLY

A   B   C   D   E

1   2   3   4   5   6   7

MAP
127

1:190,080
1 in. = 3 mi.

0   2   4
miles

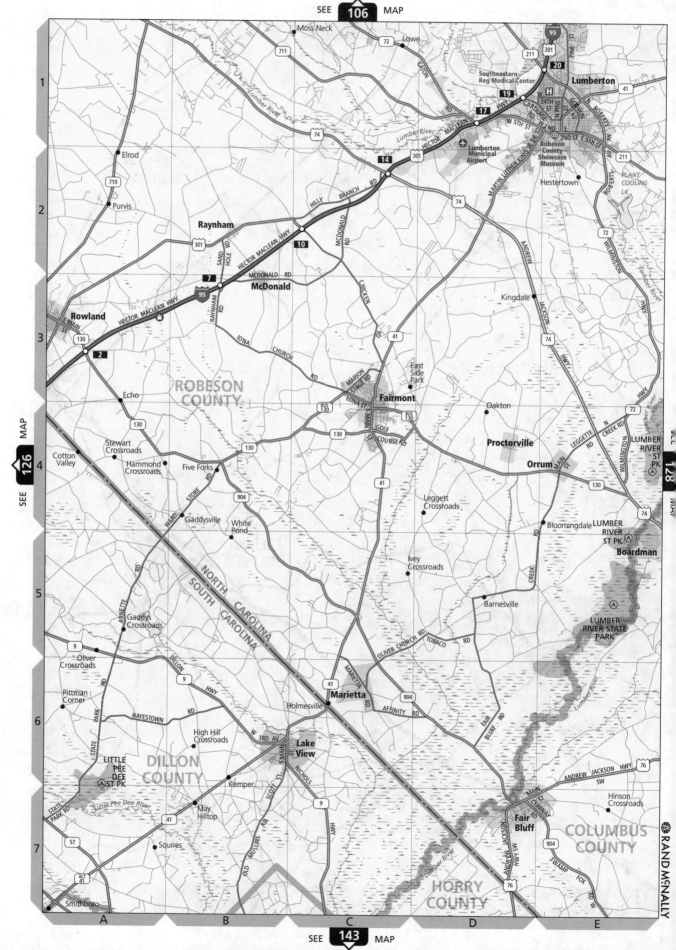

SEE **106** MAP

Moss Neck

711

72   Lowe

211
95   301
20

Southeastern
Reg Medical Center   Lumberton

19   24TH
ST   41

17   HWY

H
CARTHAGE RD

Lumber River

Elrod   HECTOR   MACLEAN   14   301   Lumberton
Municipal   Robeson County
Airport   Showcase
Museum

710   74

Purvis   Hestertown   211

BRANCH RD
HILLY

Raynham   PLANT
COOLING
LK

301   MCDONALD   74   72
SAND HOLE RD
10
RD

ANDREW
MCDONALD   RD

7   MCDONALD   Kingdale

95   RAYNHAM RD   JACKSON
HWY   74

CHICKEN

HECTOR MACLEAN HWY
Rowland

E MAIN ST
IONA
130   41

2   CHURCH   East
Side
Park   Oakton   LUMBER
RIVER
ST PK

Echo   MARION STAGE RD   Proctorville

ROBESON
COUNTY   LONA ST S MAIN   Fairmont   Orrum
130
130   LEGGETTE RD   130
Stewart   BUS
Crossroads   130

Cotton
Valley   Hammond   Five Forks   GOLF COURSE RD
Crossroads   Bloomingdale   LUMBER
RIVER
904   41   ST PK
WARD RD
STORE RD

Gaddysville   White
Pond   Leggett
Crossroads   Boardman

NORTH CAROLINA
SOUTH CAROLINA   Ivey
Crossroads

CREEK

Gaddys
Crossroads   Barnesville   LUMBER
RIVER STATE
PARK
9

Oliver
Crossroads   DILLON HWY   OLIVER CHURCH RD   TOBACO RD
9

Pittman
Corner   MARIETTA RD
HAYESTOWN   RD   41   904

State Park Rd   High Hill   Marietta   AFFINITY RD   FAIR BLUFF RD   76
Crossroads   W 3RD AV
Holmesville
DILLON
COUNTY   Lake   ANDREW   JACKSON   HWY
LITTLE   SCOTT ST S MAIN   View   SW   Hinson
PEE   Kemper   NICHOLS   MAIN ST CONWAY   Crossroads
DEE   ST
ST PK   May   9   Fair
Little Pee Dee River   Hilltop   Bluff
ANDREW JACKSON HWY SW   COLUMBUS
41   904   COUNTY

57
Squires   SWAMP FOX RD

ALT
41   76   HORRY
Smithboro   COUNTY

A   B   C   D   E

SEE **143** MAP

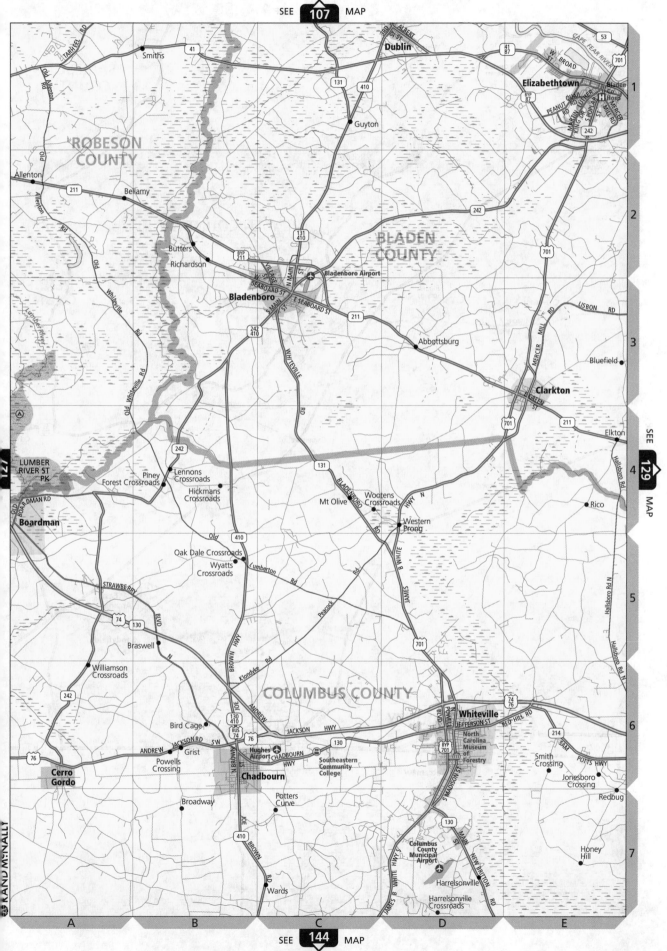

MAP
128

REGIONAL MAP

1:190,080
1 in. = 3 mi.

0   2   4
miles

SEE **107** MAP

Smiths

41

Dublin

131
410

Guyton

360 ST
ALBERT ST

41
87

701

53

W BROAD
ST

Elizabethtown

BYP
87

Bladen
Co Hosp

H

PEANUT
RD

QUAIL
RD

MARTIN RD

S SDAR ST

KING RD

OTHER

MILL RD

242

ROBESON
COUNTY

Allenton

211

Bellamy

Old
Allenton
Rd

Old
Allenton
Rd

131
410

242

BLADEN
COUNTY

701

Butters

BYP
211

Richardson

VILLAGE
RD

W STAGE

SEABOARD ST

N MAIN ST

ST ST

Bladenboro Airport

MERCER
MILL RD

LISBON RD

Whiteville
Rd

Old Whiteville Rd

Whiteville Rd

Bladenboro

S MAIN
ST

E SEABOARD ST

211

Abbottsburg

Bluefield

242
410

WHITEVILLE
RD

Clarkton

B GREEN
ST

701

211

Elkton

Hallsboro Rd

LUMBER
RIVER ST
PK

242

Lennons
Crossroads

Piney
Forest Crossroads

131

BLADENBORO RD

Wootens
Crossroads

HWY N

Rico

SEE **129** MAP

BOARDMAN RD

Boardman

Hickmans
Crossroads

Mt Olive

Western
Prong

Hallsboro Rd N

Old
410

Oak Dale Crossroads

Wyatts
Crossroads

Lumberton Rd

B WHITE

JAMES

701

Peacock Rd

STRAWBERRY

74

130

BLVD

Braswell

N

Williamson
Crossroads

242

COLUMBUS COUNTY

Whiteville

JEFFERSON ST

74
76

214

Klondyke Rd

JOE

BROWN
HWY

ANDREW

Bird Cage

130
410

BUS
74

JACKSON HWY

76

130

POWELL
BLVD

North
Carolina
Museum
of Forestry

RED HILL RD

SAM POTTS HWY

Smith
Crossing

JACKSON RD

ANDREW

SW

Grist

Hughes
Airport

CHADBOURN
HWY

BYP
701

Jonesboro
Crossing

76

Powells
Crossing

Southeastern
Community
College

S MADISON ST

Redbug

Cerro
Gordo

Broadway

Chadbourn

Potters
Curve

JOE

410

BROWN
RD

130

Columbus
County
Municipal
Airport

MAIN ST S

NEW BRITON RD

Honey
Hill

JAMES B WHITE HWY S

Harrelsonville

Wards

Harrelsonville
Crossroads

RAND McNALLY

A   B   C   D   E

SEE **144** MAP

1
2
3
4
5
6
7

MAP
129

REGIONAL MAP

SEE 108 MAP

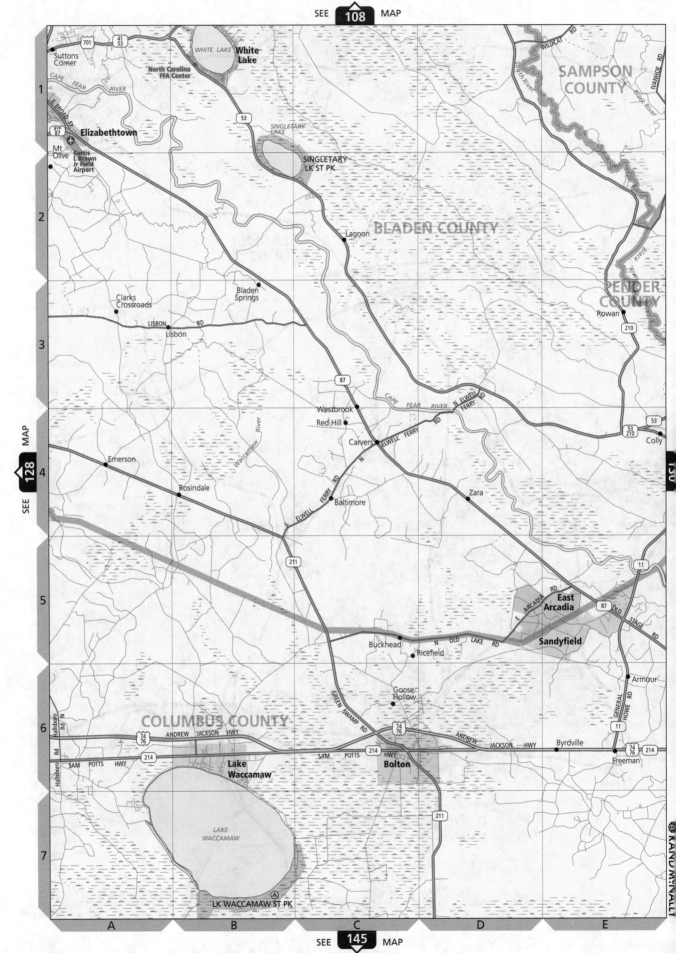

Suttons Corner

White Lake

WHITE LAKE

North Carolina FFA Center

CAPE FEAR RIVER

701

41 53

53

BYP 87

Elizabethtown

E BROAD ST

Mt Olive

Curtis L Brown Jr Field Airport

SINGLETARY LAKE

SINGLETARY LK ST PK

BLADEN COUNTY

SAMPSON COUNTY

WILDCAT RD

South River

Black River

IVANHOE RD

Lagoon

PENDER COUNTY

Rowan

210

Clarks Crossroads

Bladen Springs

LISBON RD

Lisbon

87

Waccamaw River

CAPE FEAR RIVER

N ELWELL FERRY RD

53 210

53

Colly

Westbrook

Red Hill

Carvers

ELWELL FERRY RD

ELWELL FERRY RD

N

Emerson

Rosindale

Baltimore

Zara

11

SEE 128 MAP

128

130

211

East Arcadia

E ARCADIA RD

87

OLD STAGE RD

Sandyfield

Buckhead

Ricefield

N OLD LAKE RD

Armour

Goose Hollow

GREEN SWAMP RD

74 76

GENERAL HOWE RD

11

COLUMBUS COUNTY

Halsboro Rd N

74 76

ANDREW JACKSON HWY

214

SAM POTTS HWY

SAM POTTS HWY

214

Bolton

ANDREW JACKSON HWY

Byrdville

74 76

214

Freeman

Halsboro Rd

Lake Waccamaw

LAKE WACCAMAW

211

LK WACCAMAW ST PK

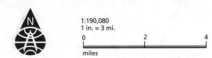

MAP
130

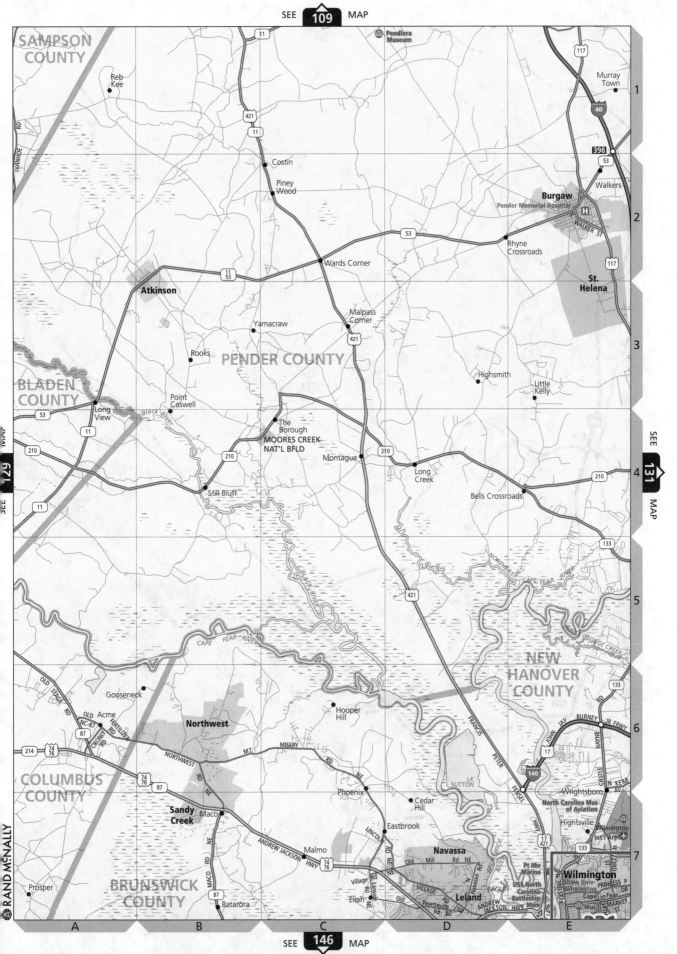

1:190,080
1 in. = 3 mi.

0   2   4
miles

SEE 109 MAP

SAMPSON
COUNTY

Reb
Kee

Costin

Piney
Wood

Burgaw
Pender Memorial Hospital

Murray
Town

Walkers

Rhyne
Crossroads

St.
Helena

Wards Corner

Atkinson

Malpass
Corner

Yamacraw

PENDER COUNTY

Rooks

Highsmith

Little
Kelly

BLADEN
COUNTY

Point
Caswell

Long
View

Black River

The
Borough
MOORES CREEK
NAT'L BFLD

Montague

Long
Creek

Bells Crossroads

SEE 131 MAP

Still Bluff

Pendlera
Museum

CAPE FEAR RIVER

NORTHEAST CAPE FEAR RIVER

GEORGE CREEK

NEW
HANOVER
COUNTY

Gooseneck

Acme
Old

Northwest

Hooper
Hill

Francis

BURNEY

JR FRWY

JOHN JAY

HAYNE

N KERR
AV

CASTLE

Wrightsboro

North Carolina Mus
of Aviation

COLUMBUS
COUNTY

Phoenix

Cedar
Hill

LK
SUTTON

Hightsville

Wilmington
Int'l Arpt

Sandy
Creek

Maco

Malmo

Eastbrook

ANDREW JACKSON HWY

Navassa

Pt Hbr
Marina

USS North
Carolina
Battleship
Mem

Wilmington
Shaw Univ
Cape Fear
Mus

Prosper

BRUNSWICK
COUNTY

Batarora

Village Rd

Elijah

Old

VILLAGE

Fayetteville

Leland

ANDREW
JACKSON HWY

PRINCESS P
DR
MARKET ST

A   B   C   D   E

1   2   3   4   5   6   7

SEE 146 MAP

MAP
131

REGIONAL MAP

1:190,080
1 in. = 3 mi.

0   2   4
miles

SEE **110** MAP

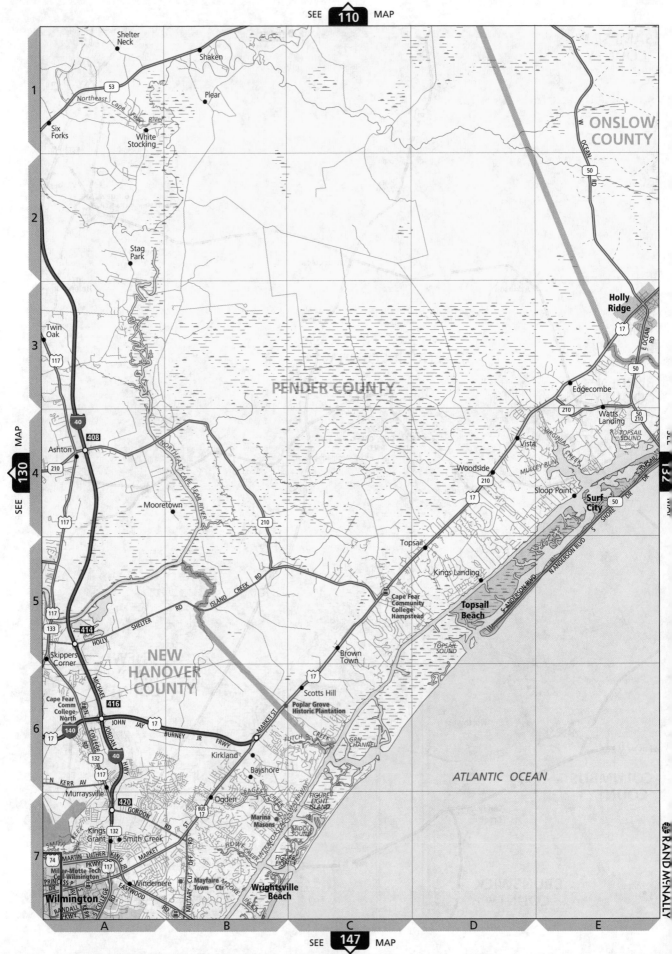

SEE **130** MAP

SEE **132** MAP

SEE **147** MAP

RAND M\u0107NALLY

MAP
132

REGIONAL MAP

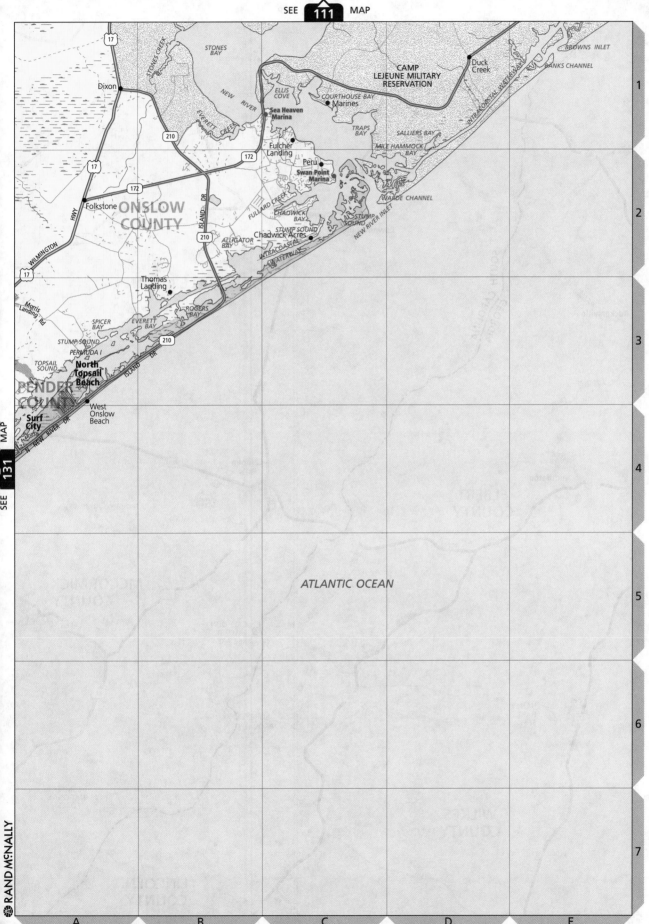

1:190,080
1 in. = 3 mi.

0   2   4
miles

SEE **111** MAP

STONES CREEK

STONES
BAY

17

Dixon

210

EVERETT CREEK

NEW RIVER

CAMP
LEJEUNE MILITARY
RESERVATION

Duck
Creek

BROWNS INLET

BANKS CHANNEL

INTRACOASTAL WATERWAY

1

ELLIS
COVE

COURTHOUSE BAY

Marines

Sea Heaven
Marina

TRAPS
BAY

SALLIERS BAY

MILE HAMMOCK
BAY

172

Fulcher
Landing

Peru

Folkstone

ONSLOW
COUNTY

17

172

Swan Point
Marina

ISLAND DR

FULLARD CREEK

WARDE CHANNEL

210

CHADWICK
BAY

STUMP
SOUND

NEW RIVER INLET

2

ALLIGATOR
BAY

Chadwick Acres

STUMP SOUND

INTRACOASTAL
WATERWAY

WILMINGTON HWY

17

Thomas
Landing

ROGERS
BAY

3

Morris
Landing Rd

SPICER
BAY

EVERETT
BAY

210

ISLAND DR

STUMP SOUND

PERMUDA I

TOPSAIL
SOUND

North
Topsail
Beach

PENDER
COUNTY

West
Onslow
Beach

Surf
City

N NEW RIVER DR

4

SEE **131** MAP

ATLANTIC OCEAN

5

6

7

A   B   C   D   E

MAP
133

REGIONAL MAP

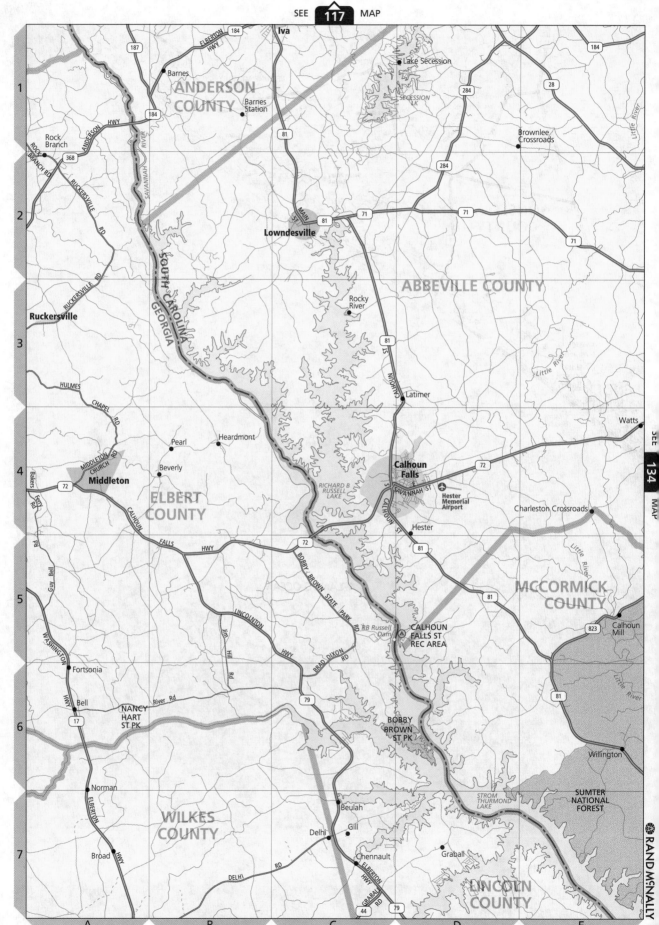

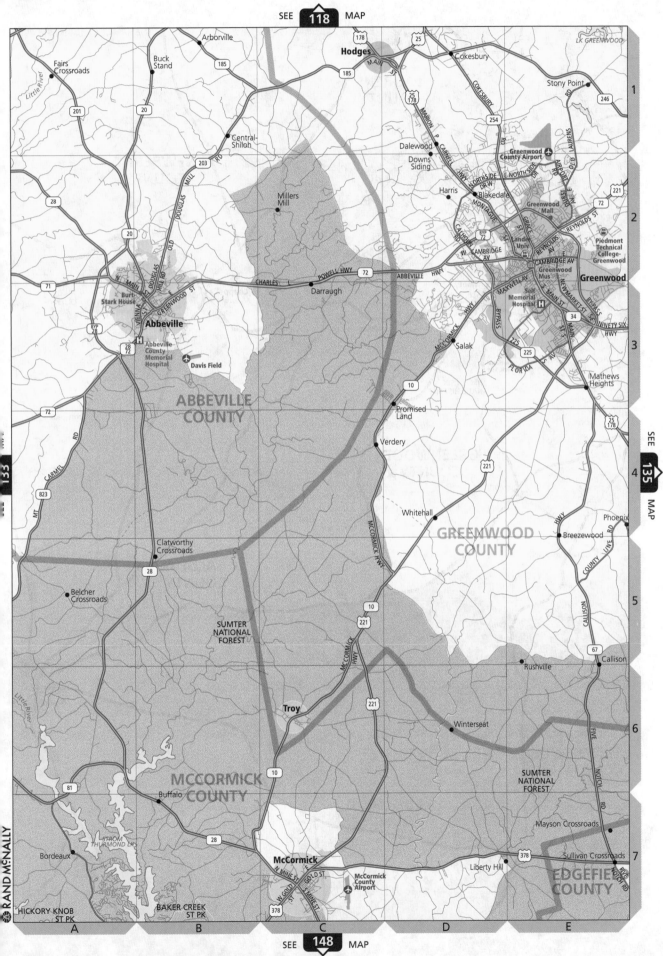

MAP
134

REGIONAL MAP

1:190,080
1 in. = 3 mi.

0   2   4
miles

SEE **118** MAP

SEE **135** MAP

SEE **148** MAP

Fairs
Crossroads

Arborville

Buck
Stand

Hodges

Cokesbury

Stony Point

Lk Greenwood

Little River

201

20

185

178

25

246

28

Central-
Shiloh

203

Dalewood

Downs
Siding

Greenwood
County Airport

254

221

72

20

Millers
Mill

Harris

Blakedale

NORTHSIDE
DR W

E NORTHSIDE

Greenwood
Mall

Piedmont
Technical
College-
Greenwood

71

POWELL HWY

CHARLES

Darraugh

ABBEVILLE HWY

72

MONTAGUE

CALHOUN
RD

W. CAMBRIDGE
AV

Landr
Univ

Greenwood
Mus

CAMBRIDGE AV

Greenwood

28

Burt
Stark
House

N MAIN ST

VIENNA ST

GREENWOOD ST

MAXWELL AV

Self
Memorial
Hospital

S MAIN ST

NEWMARKET ST

NINETY SIX
HWY

BYP
28

Abbeville

MT CARMEL RD

DOUGLAS HILL RD

OLD DOUGLAS MILL RD

Salak

McCORMICK
HWY

225

FLORIDA

34

Mathews
Heights

28
72

Abbeville
County
Memorial
Hospital

Davis Field

225

25
178

72

**ABBEVILLE
COUNTY**

10

Promised
Land

Verdery

221

Whitehall

**GREENWOOD
COUNTY**

Phoenix

Breezewood

COUNTY LINE RD

823

Clatworthy
Crossroads

28

Belcher
Crossroads

**SUMTER
NATIONAL
FOREST**

10

221

McCORMICK HWY

Rushville

CALLISON

67

Callison

81

Little River

Buffalo

**MCCORMICK
COUNTY**

10

28

Troy

221

Winterseat

**SUMTER
NATIONAL
FOREST**

FIVE NOTCH RD

Mayson Crossroads

Bordeaux

*J STROM
THURMOND LK*

**HICKORY KNOB
ST PK**

**BAKER CREEK
ST PK**

McCormick

N MINE ST

GOLD ST

W GOLD ST

S MINE ST

378

McCormick
County
Airport

Liberty Hill

378

Sullivan Crossroads

378

**EDGEFIELD
COUNTY**

A   B   C   D   E

1   2   3   4   5   6   7

MAP
135

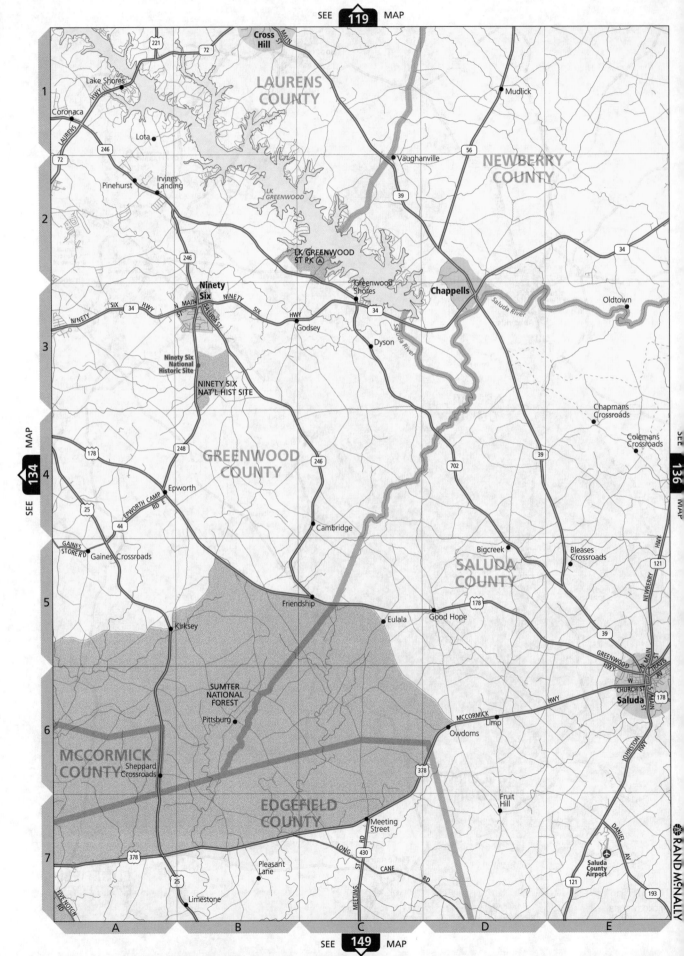

1:190,080
1 in. = 3 mi.

0   2   4
miles

Cross
Hill

LAURENS
COUNTY

Mudlick

Lake Shores

Coronaca

Lota

Vaughanville

NEWBERRY
COUNTY

Pinehurst

Irvines
Landing

LK
GREENWOOD

246

LK GREENWOOD
ST PK

34

Greenwood
Shores

Chappells

Oldtown

Saluda River

Ninety
Six

NINETY SIX HWY

N MAIN ST

SALUDA ST

34

Godsey

Dyson

Saluda River

Ninety Six
National
Historic Site

NINETY SIX
NAT'L HIST SITE

Chapmans
Crossroads

SEE MAP 134

178

248

GREENWOOD
COUNTY

246

39

702

Colemans
Crossroads

SEE 136 MAP

25

Epworth

EPWORTH CAMP RD E

44

Cambridge

Bigcreek

SALUDA
COUNTY

Bleases
Crossroads

121

GAINES
STORE RD

Gaines Crossroads

NEWBERRY HWY

Friendship

Eulala

Good Hope

178

39

GREENWOOD HWY

Kirksey

SUMTER
NATIONAL
FOREST

Pittsburg

MCCORMICK
Owdoms

Limp

Saluda

CHURCH ST

N MAIN ST

S MAIN ST

178

JOHNSTON HWY

MCCORMICK
COUNTY

Sheppard
Crossroads

378

Fruit
Hill

DANIEL AV

EDGEFIELD
COUNTY

Meeting
Street

Saluda
County
Airport

RAND McNALLY

378

25

Pleasant
Lane

LONG ST

MEETING ST

430

CANE RD

121

193

Limestone

FIVE NOTCH RD

A   B   C   D   E

MAP
136

REGIONAL MAP

1:190,080
1 in. = 3 mi.

0   2   4
miles

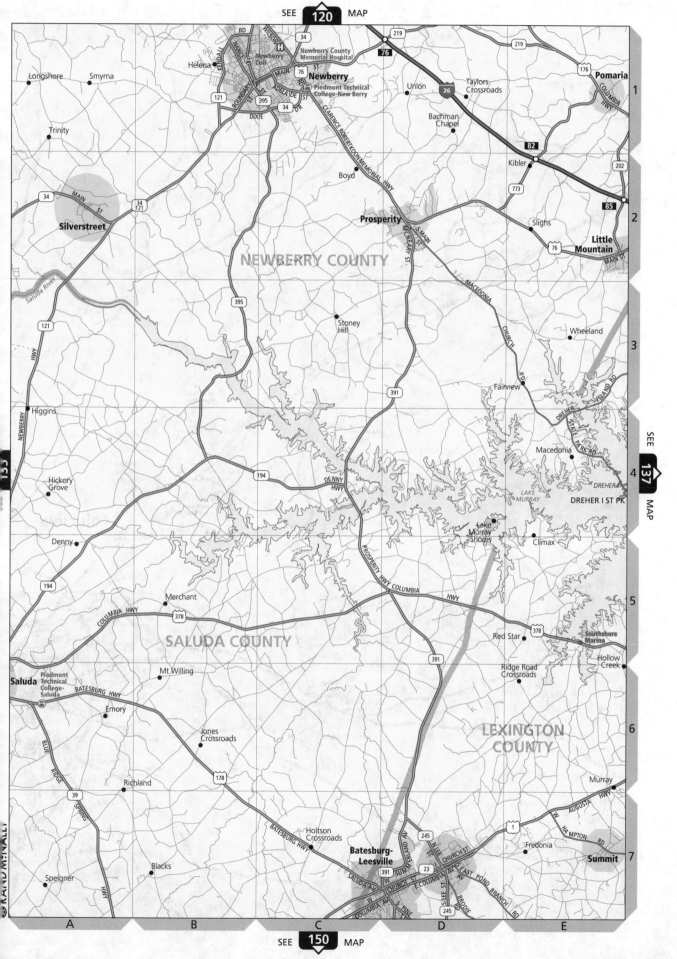

SEE **120** MAP

SEE **137** MAP

SEE **150** MAP

Longshore
Smyrna

Helena
Newberry Coll
Newberry County Memorial Hospital
Newberry
Piedmont Technical College-New Berry

Pomaria

Trinity

Union
Taylors Crossroads

Bachman Chapel

Kibler

Boyd

Silverstreet

Prosperity

Slighs

Little Mountain

NEWBERRY COUNTY

Saluda River

Stoney Hill

Wheeland

Fairview

Higgins

Macedonia

Hickory Grove

DREHER

Denny

Lake Murray Shores

Climax

DREHER I ST PK

LAKE MURRAY

SALUDA COUNTY

Merchant

Red Star

Southshore Marina

Hollow Creek

Mt Willing

Ridge Road Crossroads

Saluda
Piedmont Technical College-Saluda

LEXINGTON COUNTY

Emory

Jones Crossroads

Murray

Richland

Holtson Crossroads

Fredonia

Blacks

Batesburg-Leesville

Summit

Speigner

A   B   C   D   E

1   2   3   4   5   6   7

MAP
137

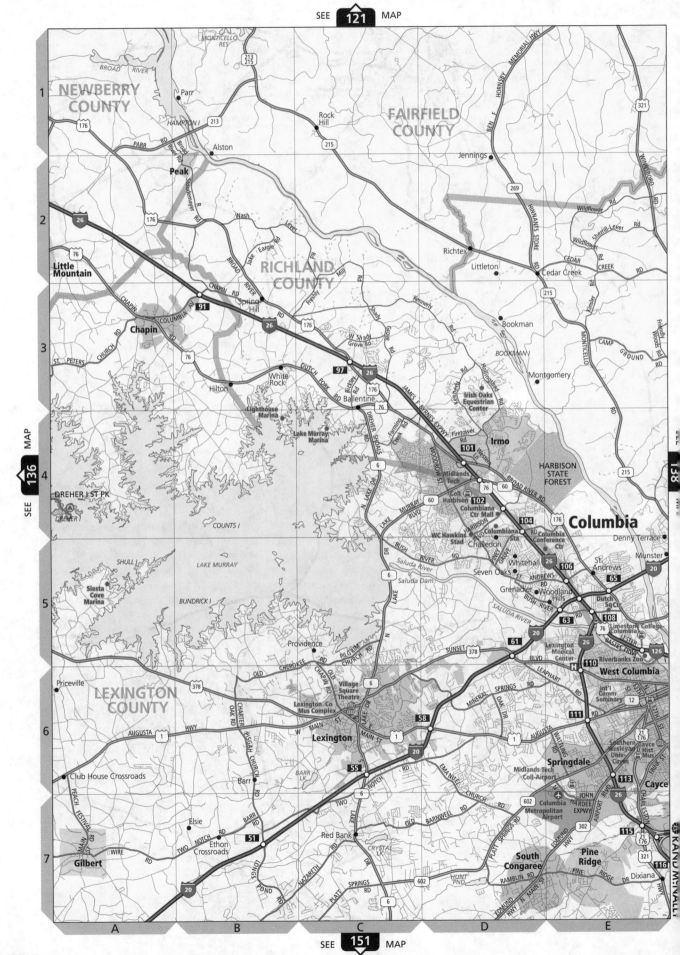

SEE **121** MAP

SEE **151** MAP

SEE **136** MAP

138

RAND MCNALLY

NEWBERRY COUNTY

FAIRFIELD COUNTY

RICHLAND COUNTY

LEXINGTON COUNTY

Parr

Rock Hill

Jennings

Alston

Peak

Little Mountain

Richtex

Littleton

Cedar Creek

Chapin

Spring Hill

Bookman

Montgomery

Irish Oaks Equestrian Center

White Rock

Hilton

Ballentine

Irmo

Lighthouse Marina

Lake Murray Marina

HARBISON STATE FOREST

DREHER I ST PK

Columbia

Midlands Tech Coll-Harbison

Columbiana Ctr Mall

Denny Terrace

Munster

LAKE MURRAY

Siesta Cove Marina

Columbia Conference Ctr

WC Hawkins Stad

Columbiana Sta

Challedon

St Andrews

Whitehall

Seven Oaks

Woodland Hills

Grenadier

Dutch Sq Ctr

Limestone College Columbia

Providence

Lexington Medical Center

Riverbanks Zoo

West Columbia

Priceville

Village Square Theatre

Lexington Co Mus Complex

Int'l Comm Seminary

Club House Crossroads

Lexington

Southern Wesleyan Univ-Cayce

Cayce Hist Mus

Springdale

Barr

Midlands Tech Coll-Airport

Cayce

Elsie

Ethon Crossroads

Red Bank

Columbia Metropolitan Airport

Gilbert

South Congaree

Pine Ridge

Dixiana

MAP
138

REGIONAL MAP

1:190,080
1 in. = 3 mi.

0   2   4
miles

SEE ◈ 122 ◈ MAP

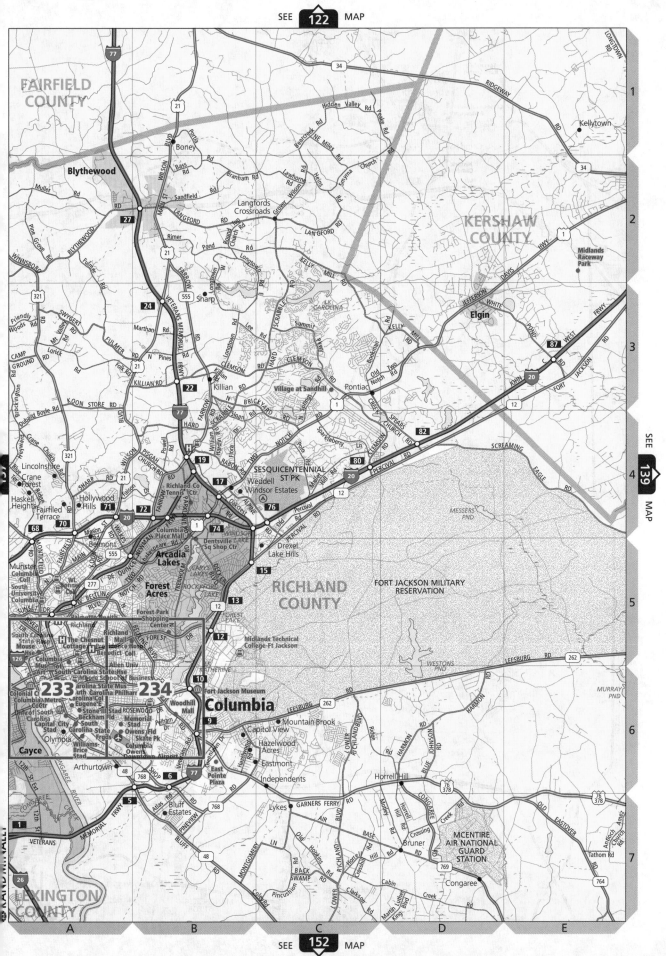

SEE
◄ 139 ►
MAP

SEE 152 MAP

FAIRFIELD COUNTY

KERSHAW COUNTY

Kellytown

Blythewood

Midlands Raceway Park

Elgin

Langfords Crossroads

Sharp

Village at Sandhill

Killian

Pontiac

SESQUICENTENNIAL ST PK

Weddell
Windsor Estates

SCREAMING EAGLE

RICHLAND COUNTY

MESSERS PND

FORT JACKSON MILITARY RESERVATION

Hollywood Hills

Haskell Heights
Fairfiled Terrace

Lincolnshire
Crane Forest

Blue Crane Ter

Munster

Columbia Coll
South University Columbia

Richland Co Tennis Ctr

Columbia Place Mall
Dentsville Sq Shop Ctr

Arcadia Lakes

Drexel
Lake Hills

Forest Acres

Forest Park Shopping Center

Forest Lake

WESTONS PND

MURRAY PND

Midlands Technical College–Ft Jackson

233

234

Richland Mall

Providence Hosp

Allen Univ

Fort Jackson Museum

Columbia

Woodhill Mall

Mountain Brook

Capitol View

Hazelwood Acres

Cayce

Williams Brice Stad

Columbia Owens Downtown Airport

Olympia

Arthurtown

East Pointe Plaza

Eastmont

Independents

Horrell Hill

Bluff Estates

Lykes

Bruner

MCENTIRE AIR NATIONAL GUARD STATION

Congaree

LEXINGTON COUNTY

A   B   C   D   E

MAP
139

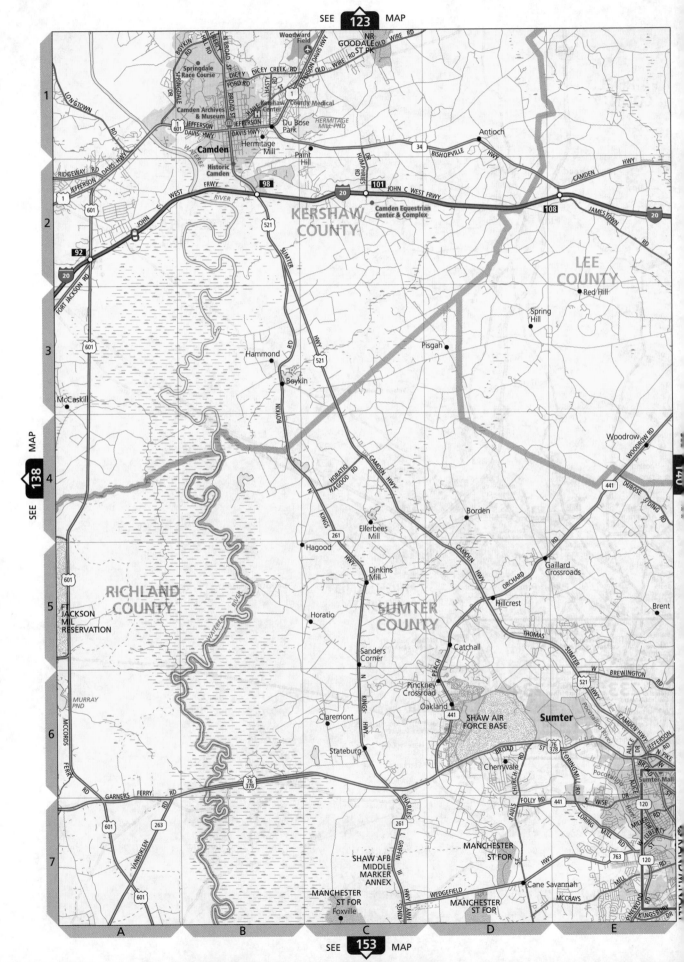

1:190,080
1 in. = 3 mi.

0 2 4
miles

SEE 123 MAP

MAP
SEE 138

140

SEE 153 MAP

A   B   C   D   E

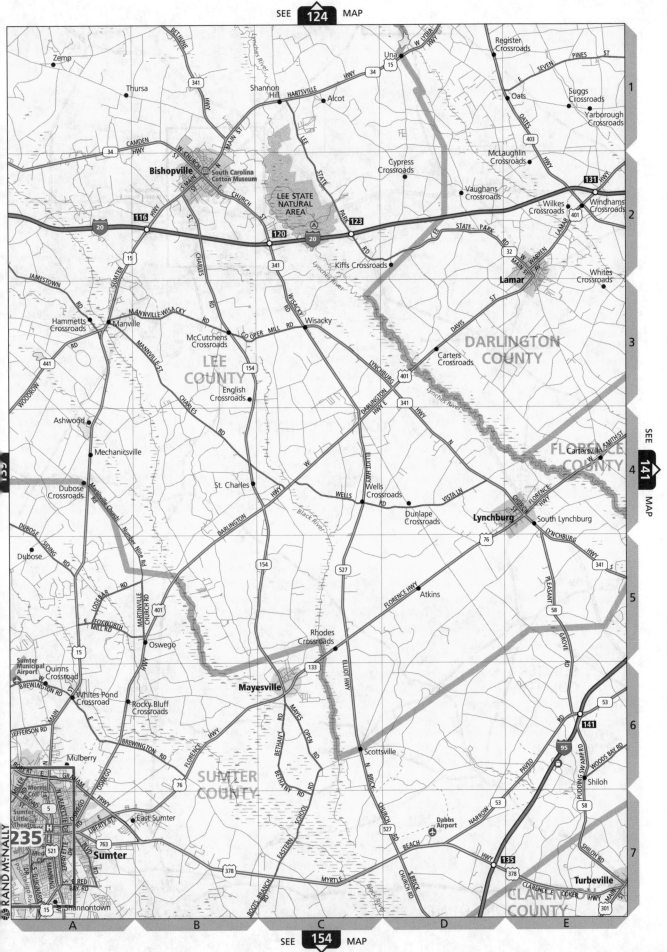

MAP
140
REGIONAL MAP

N

1:190,080
1 in. = 3 mi.

0   2   4
miles

SEE 124 MAP

Zemp

Thursa

Shannon Hill

Alcot

Una
15

34

W. LYDIA HWY

Register Crossroads

SEVEN PINES ST

E

341

BETHUNE

Lynches River

HARTSVILLE

Oats

Suggs Crossroads

Yarborough Crossroads

403

OATS HWY

CAMDEN HWY

34

Bishopville

W. CHURCH ST

S MAIN ST

N MAIN ST

S CHURCH ST

South Carolina Cotton Museum

LEE STATE NATURAL AREA

Cypress Crossroads

McLaughlin Crossroads

Vaughans Crossroads

131

Wilkes Crossroads

Windhams Crossroads

401

116 HWY

20

120

123

20

PARK RD

LEE STATE PARK

LEE STATE PARK RD

32

W. WARREN

Lamar

W MAIN ST-HWY

Whites Crossroads

15

CHARLES RD

341

Kiffs Crossroads

Lynches River

SUMTER

WISACKY RD

JAMESTOWN RD

Hammetts Crossroads

Manville

MANNVILLE-WISACKY RD

McCutchens Crossroads

COOPER MILL RD

Wisacky

DAVIS

DARLINGTON COUNTY

Carters Crossroads

441

MANNVILLE-ST. CHARLES RD

LEE COUNTY

154

English Crossroads

LYNCHBURG

401

341

Ashwood

CHARLES RD

DARLINGTON HWY E

FLORENCE COUNTY

Cartersville

W SMITH ST

SEE 141 MAP

135

Mechanicsville

ELLIOT HWY

Wells Crossroads

WELLS RD

VISTA LN

CHURCH ST

FLORENCE HWY

Dubose Crossroads

Martinville Church Number Nine Rd

St. Charles

W HWY

Wells

Dunlape Crossroads

Lynchburg

South Lynchburg

LYNCHBURG HWY

DUBOSE E SIDING RD

Dubose

DARLINGTON RD

Black River

76

PLEASANT HWY

341 S

154

527

Atkins

FLORENCE HWY

58

GROVE RD

LODEBAR RD

MARTINVILLE CHURCH RD

401

Rhodes Crossroads

ELLIOT HWY

E FOXWORTH MILL RD

Oswego

133

15

Sumter Municipal Airport

Quinns Crossroad

BREWINGTON RD

Whites Pond Crossroad

Rocky Bluff Crossroads

Mayesville

BETHANY RD

MAYES RD

OPEN RD

C BRICK

141

95

PUDDING SWAMP RD

WOODS BAY RD

53

Shiloh

JEFFERSON RD

N MAIN E

BREWINGTON RD

FLORENCE HWY

SUMTER COUNTY

Scottsville

SCHOOL RD

BETHANY RD

Dabbs Airport

53

PAVED

58

Mulberry

76

East Sumter

235

Sumter

ROBERT E LEE

GRAHAM

N LAFAYETTE DR

LIBERTY ST

763

521

MANNING

S GUIGNARD

RED BAY RD

US 15

Shannontown

378

EASTERN

BOOTS BRANCH RD

S BRICK CHURCH RD

MYRTLE

Black River

527

S BRICK CHURCH RD

BEACH

WARROW RD

135

378

Turbeville

301

CLARENDON COUNTY

COKER

N MAIN ST

RAND MC-NALLY

A   B   C   D   E

1   2   3   4   5   6   7

MAP
141

REGIONAL MAP

1:190,080
1 in. = 3 mi.

0   2   4
miles

N

SEE 125 MAP

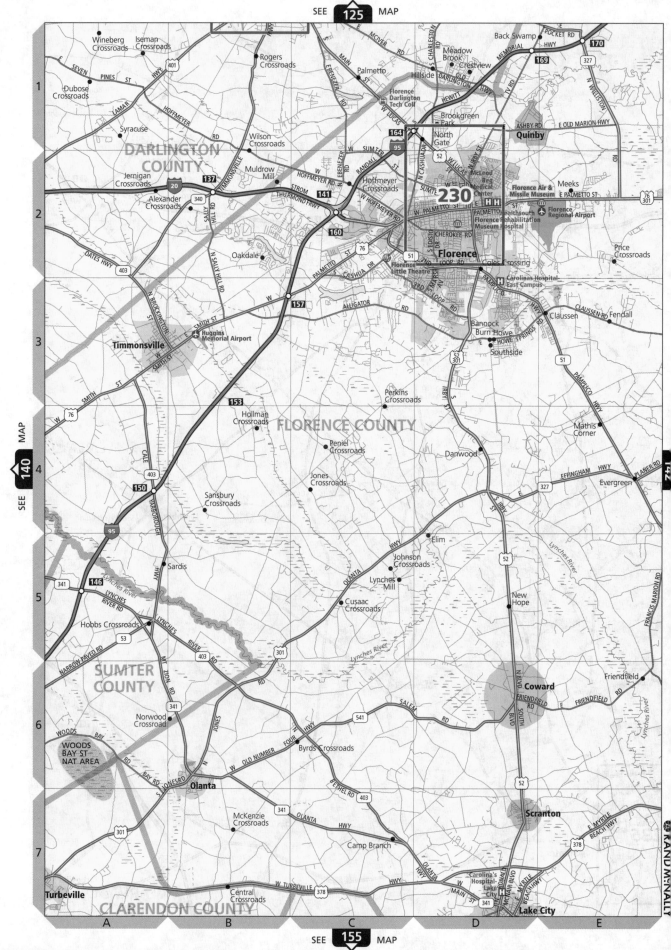

Wineberg Crossroads
Iseman Crossroads
Rogers Crossroads
Palmetto
Back Swamp
POCKET RD
170
169
327
MCIVER
Meadow Brook
Crestview
MEMORIAL HWY
N CHARLESTON
Hillside
Florence Darlington Tech Coll

SEVEN PINES ST
Dubose Crossroads
LAMAR
Syracuse
Wilson Crossroads
Brookgreen Park
North Gate
Quinby
ASHBY RD
E Old Marion Hwy
1

DARLINGTON COUNTY
Jernigan Crossroads
Alexander Crossroads
137
Muldrow Mill
Hoffmeyer Crossroads
164
95
McLeod Reg Medical Center
Florence Air & Missile Museum
Meeks
E PALMETTO ST
76 301
20
340
STROM THURMOND FRWY
141
160
HOFFMEYER RD
W HOFFMEYER RD
230
H H
Healthsouth Florence Rehabilitation Hospital
Florence Regional Airport
2

OATES HWY
403
Oakdale
76
Florence
Price Crossroads
N SALLY HILL RD
PALMETTO ST
CASHUA DR
157
ALLIGATOR
Florence Little Theatre
Coles Crossing
Carolinas Hospital East Campus

Huggins Memorial Airport
SMITH ST
153
Hollman Crossroads
Perkins Crossroads
Bannock
Burn Howe
HOWE SPRINGS RD
Claussen
CLAUSSEN RD
Fendall
Timmonsville
Southside
51
3

SMITH ST
76
W
CALE
Peniel Crossroads
Danwood
Mathis Corner
403
150
Sansbury Crossroads
Jones Crossroads
327
Evergreen
PLANER RD
95
EFFINGHAM HWY
4

YARBOROUGH
Sardis
Elim
Johnson Crossroads
Lynches Mill
New Hope
52
141
341
146
Lynches River
Hobbs Crossroads
Cusaac Crossroads
FRANCIS MARION RD
53
301
5

NARROW PAVED RD
SUMTER COUNTY
MT ZION RD
403 RD
301
Lynches River
Coward
Friendfield
FRIENDFIELD RD
E FRIENDFIELD RD
341
SALEM
N BLVD
6

WOODS BAY
Norwood Crossroad
JONES RD
541
Byrds Crossroads
52
WOODS BAY ST NAT AREA
S BAY RD
JONES RD
W OLD NUMBER FOUR HWY
BETHEL RD
403
Scranton
301
Olanta
McKenzie Crossroads
341
OLANTA HWY
Camp Branch
378
E MYRTLE BEACH HWY
7

Turbeville
Central Crossroads
W TURBEVILLE RD
378
Carolina's Hospital-Lake City
MCNAIR BLVD
341
Lake City
CLARENDON COUNTY

A   B   C   D   E

RAND McNALLY

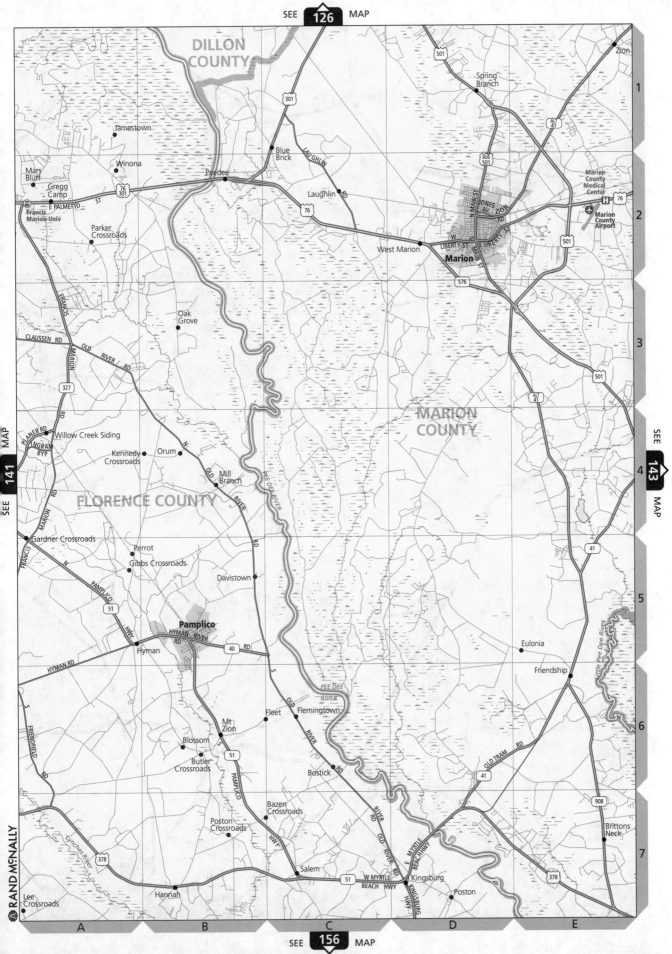

MAP
142

REGIONAL MAP

1:190,080
1 in. = 3 mi.

0   2   4
miles

SEE 126 MAP

DILLON
COUNTY

Zion

501

Spring
Branch

ALT
41

BUS
501

Jamestown

301

Marion
County
Medical
Center

Blue
Brick

LAUGHLIN

Mars
Bluff

Winona

Peedee

76
301

Laughlin RD

H

76

Marion
County
Airport

Gregg
Camp

E PALMETTO
ST

Francis
Marion Univ

76

Laughlin

501

Parker
Crossroads

West Marion

Marion

LIBERTY ST   E LIBERTY ST

JONES AV   ZION

W   MAIN ST

N MAIN ST

FRANCIS

CLAUSSEN RD

OLD   RIVER   RD

MARION

Oak
Grove

576

327

MARION
COUNTY

501

ALT
41

PLANER RD

Willow Creek Siding

INGRAM
BYP

Kennedy
Crossroads

Orum

N

SEE 143 MAP

MARION RD

OLD   RIVER   RD

Mill
Branch

PEE DEE RIVER

41

FLORENCE COUNTY

FRANCIS

Gardner Crossroads

N

Perrot

Gibbs Crossroads

Davistown

RD

41

PAMPLICO

51

HYMAN RD

HWY

Pamplico

HYMAN   RIVER

RD

40   RD

Eulonia

Hyman

S

Friendship

HYMAN RD

PEE DEE
RIVER

FRIENDFIELD

Fleet

Flemingtown

OLD

RIVER

RD

Mt
Zion

Blossom

51

Butler
Crossroads

PAMPLICO

Bostick

Little Pee Dee River

OLD TRAM   RD

41

Bazen
Crossroads

RIVER   RD

908

Poston
Crossroads

HWY

OLD   RIVER   RD

Brittons
Neck

Lynches River

378

Salem

51

E MYRTLE   BEACH HWY

Kingsburg

Poston

378

Lee
Crossroads

Hannah

W MYRTLE   BEACH   HWY

KINGSBURG   HWY

A   B   C   D   E

SEE 156 MAP

RAND McNALLY

1
2
3
4
5
6
7

MAP
143

REGIONAL MAP

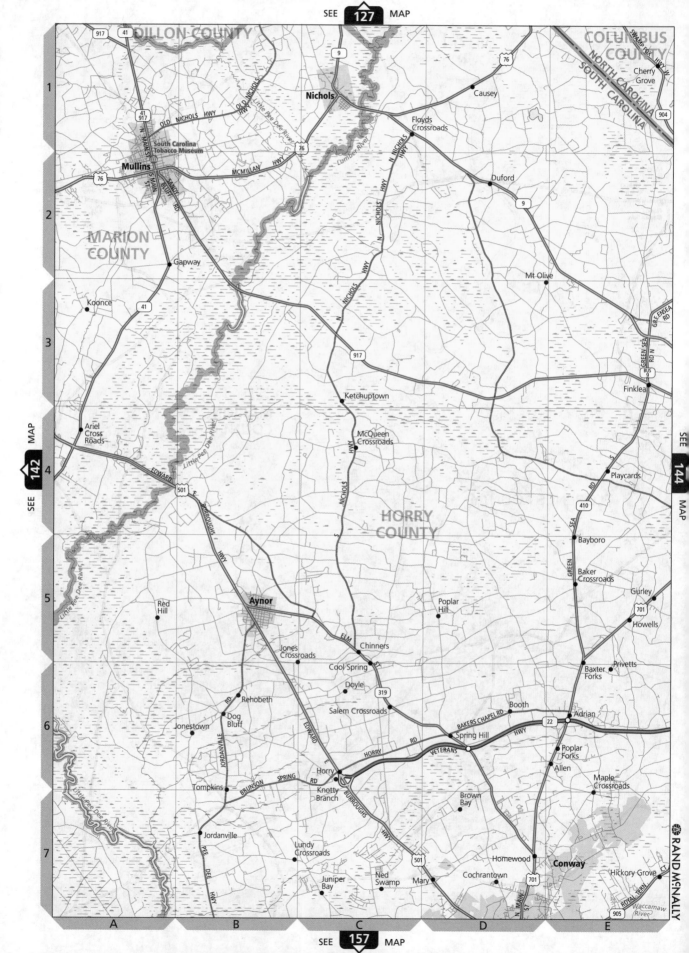

1:190,080
1 in. = 3 mi.

0   2   4
miles

SEE 127 MAP

SEE 142 MAP

SEE 144 MAP

SEE 157 MAP

DILLON COUNTY

COLUMBUS COUNTY

NORTH CAROLINA
SOUTH CAROLINA

Cherry Grove

917 41

Nichols

Causey

Floyds Crossroads

Duford

76

9

904

MARION COUNTY

Mullins

South Carolina Tobacco Museum

OLD NICHOLS HWY

McMILLAN HWY

Gapway

Koonce

41

Mt Olive

Ketchuptown

917

McQueen Crossroads

Finklea

Ariel Cross Roads

Playcards

501

410

Bayboro

HORRY COUNTY

Baker Crossroads

Gurley

701

Howells

Red Hill

Aynor

Poplar Hill

Chinners

Cool Spring

Privetts

Baxter Forks

Jones Crossroads

Doyle

319

Salem Crossroads

Booth

Adrian

Rehobeth

22

Spring Hill

Poplar Forks

Jonestown

Dog Bluff

VETERANS

Allen

Maple Crossroads

Tompkins

Horry

Knotty Branch

Brown Bay

Jordanville

Lundy Crossroads

Homewood

Conway

Hickory Grove

Juniper Bay

Ned Swamp

Mary

Cochrantown

701

905

Waccamaw River

Little Pee Dee River

Lumber River

RAND McNALLY

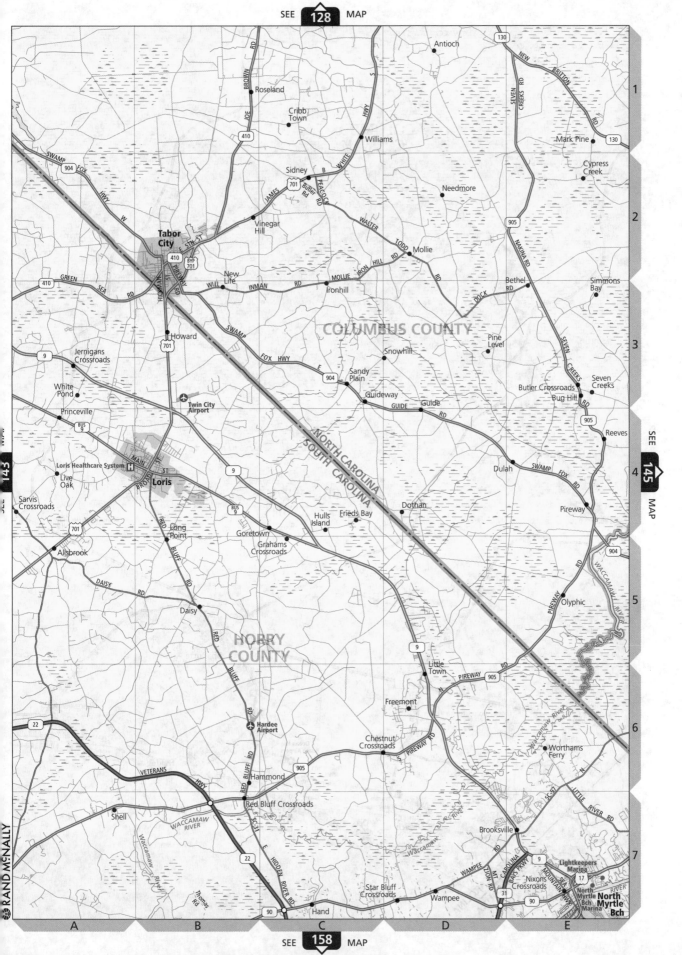

MAP
144

REGIONAL MAP

1:190,080
1 in. = 3 mi.

0   2   4
miles

SEE 128 MAP

Antioch

130

NEW BRITTON RD

Roseland

Cribb Town

Williams

Mark Pine

130

Cypress Creek

SWAMP FOX HWY
904

Sidney

Needmore

905

Vinegar Hill

Tabor City
410
BYP 701

New Life

Mollie

Bethel RD

Simmons Bay

Ironhill

COLUMBUS COUNTY

Howard
701

Snowhill

Pine Level

Seven Creeks

Jernigans Crossroads

SWAMP

FOX HWY
904

Sandy Plain

Butler Crossroads
Bug Hill

905

White Pond

Twin City Airport

Guideway

Guide

Reeves

Princeville
BUS 9

NORTH CAROLINA
SOUTH CAROLINA

Dulah

SWAMP FOX RD

SEE
145
MAP

Sarvis Crossroads

Loris Healthcare System

Loris

9

Dothan

Pireway

904

Live Oak

701

Long Point

Goretown

Hulls Island

Frieds Bay

Olyphic

Daisy

Grahams Crossroads

Allsbrook

DAISY RD

HOBRY COUNTY

9

Little Town

Freemont

Pireway
905

22

Hardee Airport

Chestnut Crossroads

PIREWAY RD

Worthams Ferry

VETERANS HWY

Hammond
905

Shell

Red Bluff Crossroads

Brooksville

WACCAMAW RIVER

22

Star Bluff Crossroads

Wampee

Nixons Crossroads

Lightkeepers Marina

17

North Myrtle Bch

Thomas Rd

90

Hand

90

A   B   C   D   E

MAP
145

REGIONAL MAP

1:190,080
1 in. = 3 mi.

0   2   4
miles

SEE **129** MAP

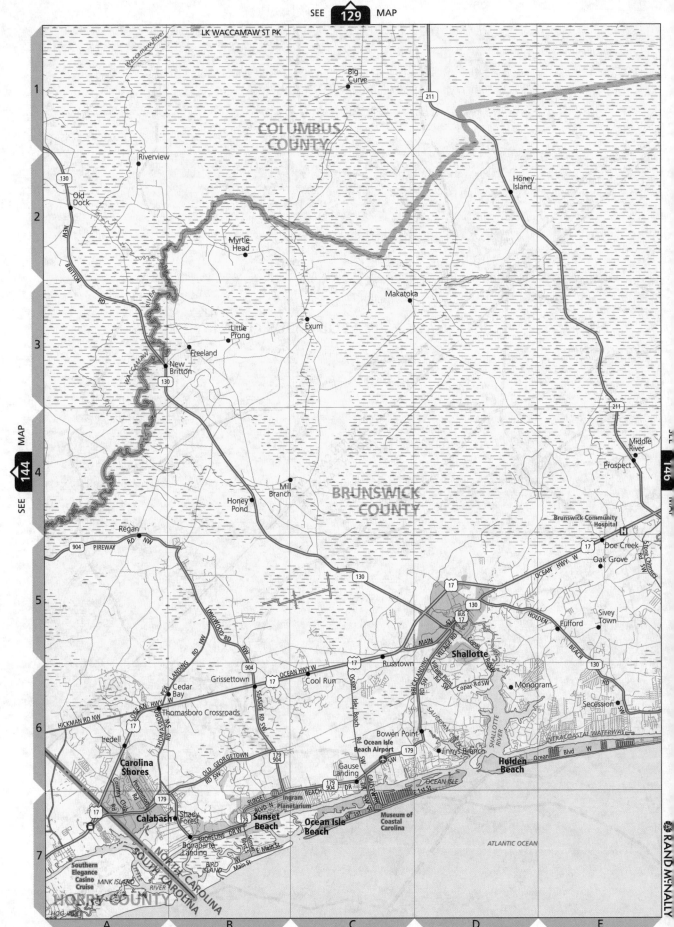

LK WACCAMAW ST PK

COLUMBUS COUNTY

Big Curve

211

Riverview

130

Old Dock

NEW BRITTON RD

Honey Island

Myrtle Head

WACCAMAW RIVER

Makatoka

Little Prong

Exum

Freeland

New Britton

130

211

Middle River

Prospect

SEE MAP 144

SEE MAP 146

Mill Branch

BRUNSWICK COUNTY

Honey Pond

Brunswick Community Hospital

Regan

904 PIREWAY RD NW

Doe Creek

17

Oak Grove

OCEAN HWY W

Stone Chimney Rd SW

130

17

130

BUS 17

HOLDEN BEACH RD SW

Fulford

Sivey Town

LONGWOOD RD NW

PEN LANDING RD NW

Shallotte

VILLAGE POINT RD SW

Copas Rd SW

130

904

OCEAN HWY W

17

Russtown

BRICK LANDING RD SW

Copas Rd SW

Monogram

SEASIDE RD SW

Grissettown

17

Cool Run

Ocean Isle Beach Rd SW

SAUCEPAN CREEK

SHALLOTTE RIVER

Secession

RD SW

Cedar Bay

OCEAN HWY

Thomasboro Crossroads

Bowen Point

Ocean Isle Beach Airport

Jinny's Branch

INTRACOASTAL WATERWAY

HICKMAN RD NW

17

THOMASBORO RD SW

OLD GEORGETOWN RD SW

179

Gause Landing

179 904

Ocean Blvd W

Holden Beach

Iredell

Carolina Shores

Country Club Rd

Persimmon

179 904

179 904 DR

GAUSE BLVD SW

E 1st St

OCEAN ISLE

Museum of Coastal Carolina

179

17

Calabash

BUS 179

Shady Forest

SUNSET BLVD N

Ingram Planetarium

Sunset Beach

W 1st St

Ocean Isle Beach

SHORELINE DR W

Bonaparte Landing

SUNSET BLVD

SOUTH CAROLINA

BIRD ISLAND

E Main St

ATLANTIC OCEAN

Southern Elegance Casino Cruise

MINK ISLAND

LITTLE RIVER

HORRY COUNTY

RAND McNALLY

A   B   C   D   E

1
2
3
4
5
6
7

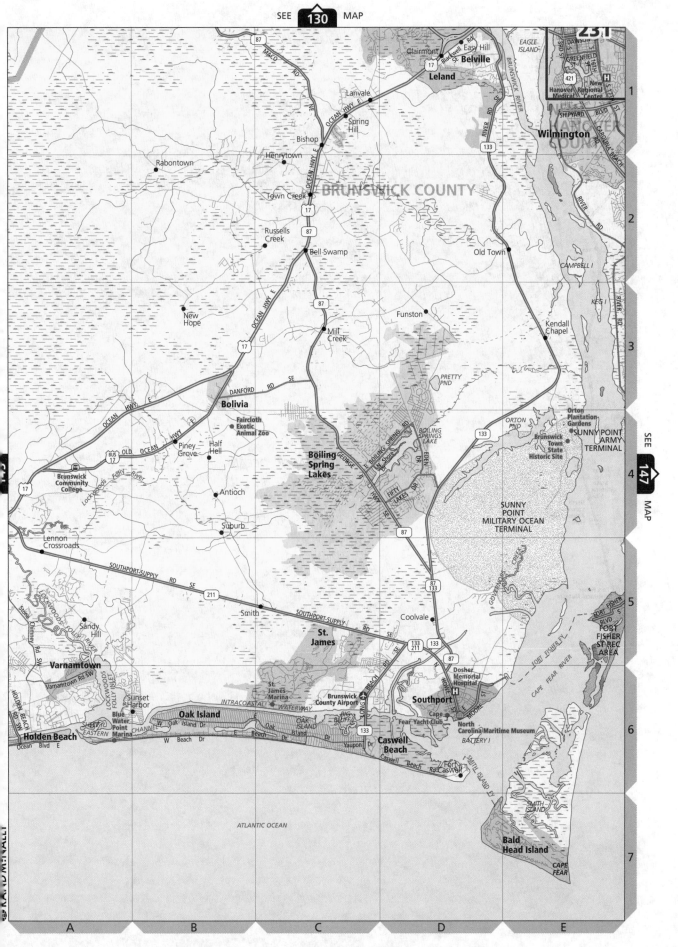

MAP
146
REGIONAL MAP

SEE 130 MAP

231

SEE 147 MAP

BRUNSWICK COUNTY

Wilmington

Belville
Leland
Clairmont
Easy Hill
Lanvale
Spring Hill
Bishop
Henrytown
Rabontown
Town Creek
Russells Creek
Bell Swamp
New Hope
Mill Creek
Funston
Old Town
Kendall Chapel
CAMPBELL I
KEG I

Orton Plantation Gardens
SUNNY POINT ARMY TERMINAL
Brunswick Town State Historic Site
ORTON PND
PRETTY PND

BOILING SPRINGS LAKE
Boiling Spring Lakes

Bolivia
Faircloth Exotic Animal Zoo
Piney Grove
Half Hell
Antioch
Suburb
Brunswick Community College

Lennon Crossroads

SOUTHPORT-SUPPLY RD SE

SUNNY POINT MILITARY OCEAN TERMINAL

Smith
Coolvale

St. James
St. James Marina
Brunswick County Airport
Southport
Dosher Memorial Hospital
Cape Fear Yacht Club
North Carolina Maritime Museum
BATTERY I

FORT FISHER
FORT FISHER ST REC AREA

Sandy Hill
Varnamtown
Sunset Harbor
Blue Water Point Marina
Holden Beach
Oak Island
Caswell Beach
Fort Caswell

INTRACOASTAL WATERWAY

ATLANTIC OCEAN

Bald Head Island
SMITH ISLAND
CAPE FEAR

A   B   C   D   E
1   2   3   4   5   6   7

MAP
147

REGIONAL MAP

SEE 131 MAP

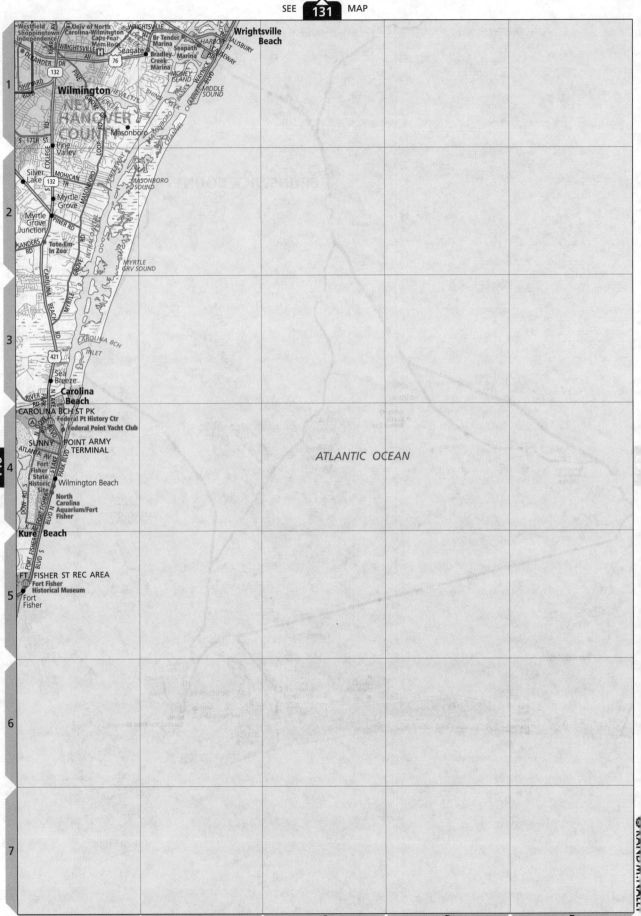

Westfield
Shoppingtown
Independence

Univ of North
Carolina-Wilmington
Cape Fear
Mem Hosp

WRIGHTSVILLE

Br Tender
Marina

Seapath
Marina

Wrightsville
Beach

OLEANDER DR

Seagate

76

Bradley
Creek
Marina

HARBOR ST

SALISBURY

CAUSEWAY

132

Wilmington

MONEY
ISLAND

MIDDLE
SOUND

1

NEW
HANOVER
COUNTY

HEWLETTS CREEK

Masonboro

S 17TH ST

COLLEGE RD

Pine
Valley

Silver
Lake

MOHICAN
TR

132

MASONBORO SOUND

2

Myrtle
Grove

Myrtle
Grove
Junction

PINER RD

Tote-Em-
In Zoo

SANDERS
RD

CAROLINA BEACH RD

MYRTLE GROVE RD

INTRACOASTAL

MYRTLE
GRV SOUND

CAROLINA BCH

3

421

CAROLINA BCH
INLET

Sea
Breeze

Carolina
Beach

RIVER RD

PARK RD

CAROLINA BCH ST PK

Federal Pt History Ctr

Federal Point Yacht Club

SUNNY
POINT ARMY
TERMINAL

ATLANTA AV

Fort
Fisher
State
Historic
Site

DOW RD S

FORT FISHER BLVD N

PARK BLVD

Wilmington Beach

North
Carolina
Aquarium/Fort
Fisher

4

ATLANTIC OCEAN

Kure Beach

K AV

FORT FISHER BLVD S

FT FISHER ST REC AREA

Fort Fisher
Historical Museum

Fort
Fisher

5

SEE 146 MAP

6

7

A   B   C   D   E

RAND MCNALLY

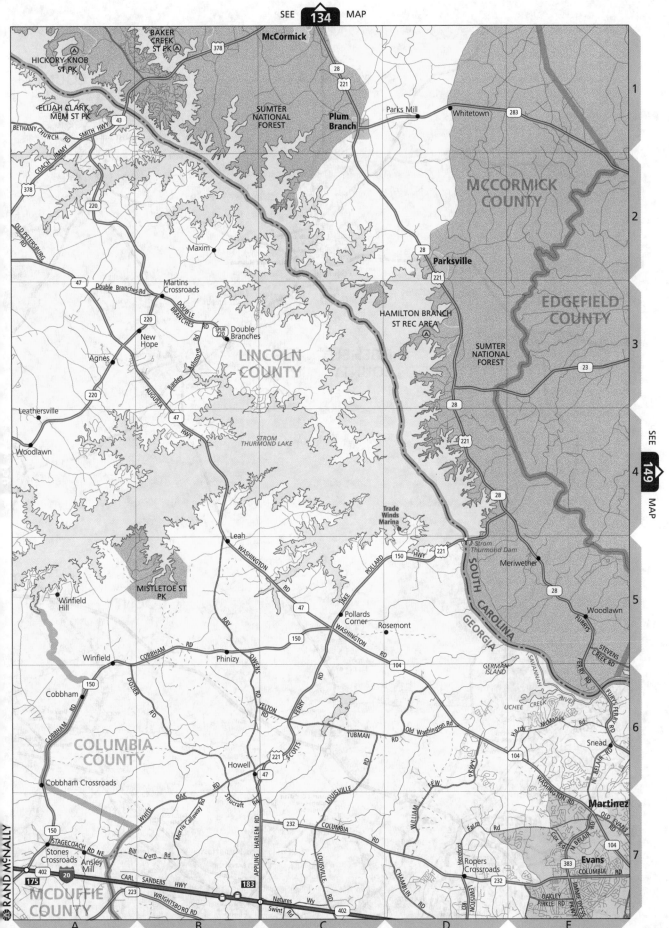

MAP
148

REGIONAL MAP

1:190,080
1 in. = 3 mi.

0   2   4
miles

SEE ⌃ 134 MAP

McCormick

HICKORY KNOB
ST PK

ELIJAH CLARK
MEM ST PK

BETHANY CHURCH RD

COACH JIMMY
SMITH HWY

378

220

OLD PETERSBURG RD

Maxim

SUMTER
NATIONAL
FOREST

Plum
Branch

Parks Mill

Whitetown

283

MCCORMICK
COUNTY

47

Double Branches Rd

Martins
Crossroads

DOUBLE BRANCHES RD

220

SPUR
220

New
Hope

Double
Branches

Agnes

AUGUSTA HWY

BARDEN

WASHMORE RD

LINCOLN
COUNTY

28

Parksville

221

HAMILTON BRANCH
ST REC AREA

EDGEFIELD
COUNTY

SUMTER
NATIONAL
FOREST

23

Leathersville

220

47

STROM
THURMOND LAKE

28

Woodlawn

221

Winfield
Hill

MISTLETOE ST
PK

RAY RD

WASHINGTON RD

Leah

47

150

Trade
Winds
Marina

LAKE POLLARD RD

150 HWY

221

Strom
Thurmond Dam

Meriwether

SOUTH CAROLINA
GEORGIA

28

SEE ⌃ 149 MAP

Woodlawn

FURYS

STEVENS
CREEK RD

Winfield

COBBHAM RD

Phinizy

OWENS RD

150

WASHINGTON RD

104

Pollards
Corner

Rosemont

GERMAN
ISLAND

FURYS FERRY RD

Cobbham

COBBHAM RD

DOVER RD

YELTON RD

FERRY RD

UCHEE CREEK

Hardy Rd

McManus Rd

SAVANNAH RIVER

Snead

104

N BELAIR RD

COLUMBIA
COUNTY

Cobbham Crossroads

Howell

221

SCOTTS RD

47

TUBMAN RD

Old Washington Rd

P SWY

FEW

WILLIAM

Martinez

WASHINGTON RD

OLD EVANS RD

OAK RD

WHITE RD

Morris Callaway Rd

Shucraft Rd

APPLING HARLEM RD

LOUISVILLE RD

232

COLUMBIA RD

LOUISVILLE RD

CHAMBLIN RD

Hereford Rd

Farm Rd

Ropers
Crossroads

232

383

COLUMBIA RD

104

N BELAIR RD

Cox Rd

Evans

150

STAGECOACH RD NE

Stones
Crossroads

Ansley
Mill

Bill Dom Rd

CARL SANDERS HWY

175

402

20

MCDUFFIE
COUNTY

223

WRIGHTSBORO RD

183

Natures Wy

Swint Rd

402

LEWISTON RD

OAKLEY
PIRKLE RD

JIMMIE DYESS PKWY

RAND MCNALLY

A   B   C   D   E

1   2   3   4   5   6   7

MAP
149

REGIONAL MAP

1:190,080
1 in. = 3 mi.

0   2   4
miles

SEE ⌃ 135 MAP

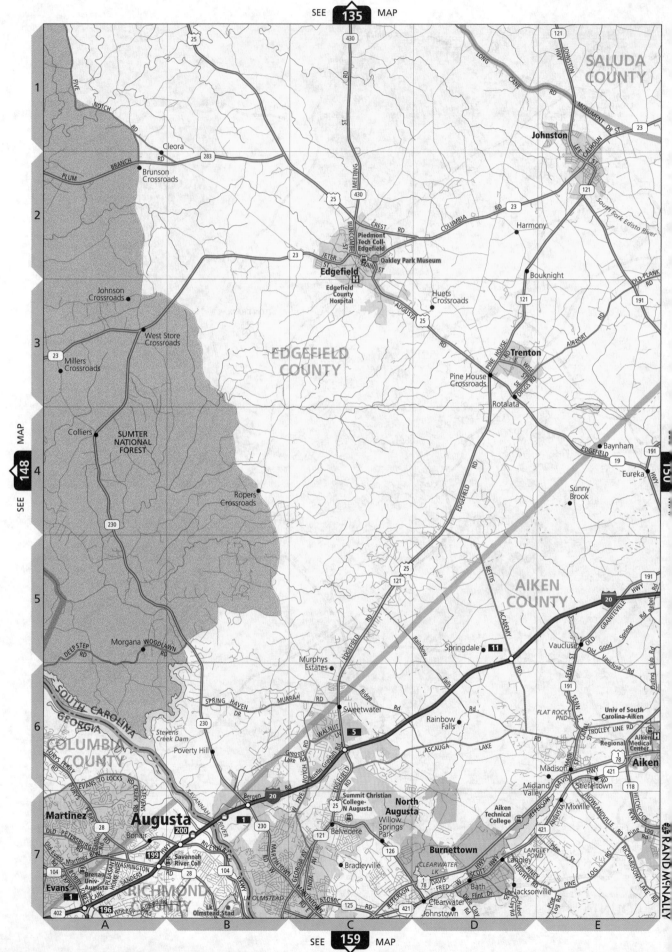

SEE ◁ 148 MAP

150

RAND McNALLY

SEE ⌄ 159 MAP

SALUDA COUNTY

Johnston

Harmony

Bouknight

Piedmont Tech Coll-Edgefield

Oakley Park Museum

Edgefield

Edgefield County Hospital

Huets Crossroads

Trenton

Pine House Crossroads

Rotalata

Baynham

Eureka

Sunny Brook

EDGEFIELD COUNTY

Johnson Crossroads

West Store Crossroads

Millers Crossroads

SUMTER NATIONAL FOREST

Colliers

Ropers Crossroads

Cleora

Brunson Crossroads

Morgana   WOODLAWN

Murphys Estates

Springdale

Vaucluse

AIKEN COUNTY

Rainbow Falls

Sweetwater

Univ of South Carolina-Aiken

Madison

Aiken

Aiken Regional Medical Center

SOUTH CAROLINA

GEORGIA

COLUMBIA COUNTY

Stevens Creek Dam

Poverty Hill

Bergen

Martinez

Augusta

Bonair

Summit Christian College-N Augusta

Belvedere

Willow Springs Park

North Augusta

Midland Valley

Stiefeltown

Mixville

Aiken Technical College

Burnettown

Langley

Savannah River Coll

Bradleyville

Evans

Drenau Home-Augusta

RICHMOND COUNTY

Lk Olmstead Stad

Clearwater

Johnstown

Bath

Nacksonville

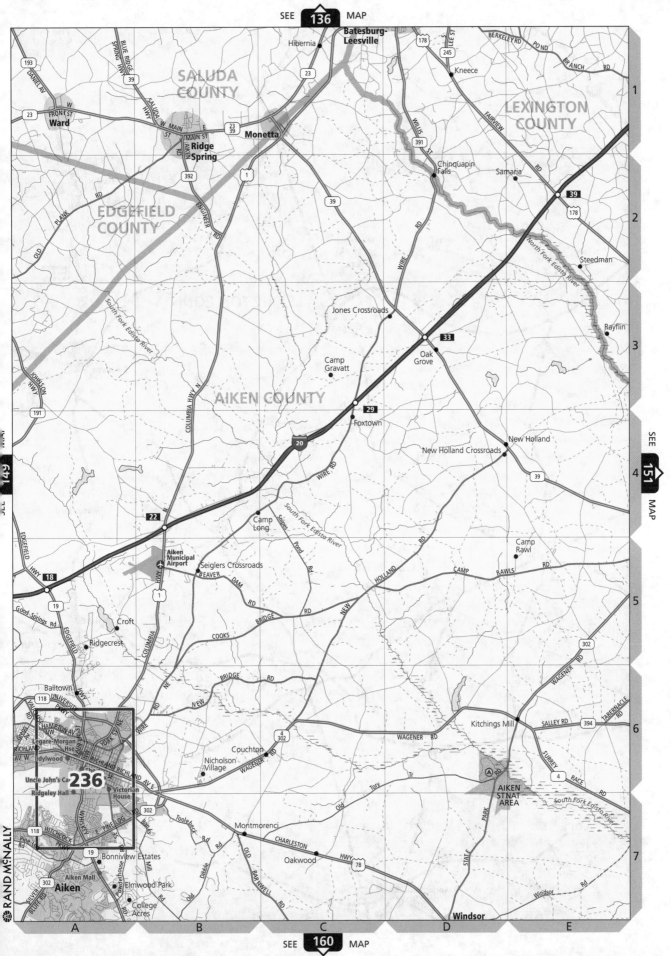

MAP
150

REGIONAL MAP

1:190,080
1 in. = 3 mi.

0   2   4
miles

SEE **136** MAP

Batesburg-
Leesville

Hibernia

178

245

BERKELEY RD

POND

BRANCH   RD

Kneece

193

DANIEL AV

SPRING HWY   BLUE RIDGE

SALUDA   HWY   39

**SALUDA
COUNTY**

LEE ST

LEXINGTON
COUNTY

FAIRVIEW   RD

23

FRONT ST
W
Ward

E
MAIN ST W   MAIN ST

23
39

Monetta

23
39

**Ridge
Spring**

391   WILLIS ST

Chinquapin
Falls

Samaria

39

178

PLANK RD   OLD

392

ENGINEER   RD

1

**EDGEFIELD
COUNTY**

39

WIRE   RD

North Fork Edisto River

Steedman

JOHNSON   HWY

South Fork Edisto River

Jones Crossroads

Rayflin

191

Camp
Gravatt

AIKEN COUNTY

Oak
Grove

33

COLUMBIA HWY N

29

Foxtown

20

New Holland

New Holland Crossroads

39

SEE **151** MAP

WIRE   RD

Camp
Rawl

22

Aiken
Municipal
Airport

Camp
Long

Saline

South Fork Edisto River

Pond   RD

NEW   HOLLAND   RD

CAMP   RAWLS   RD

EDGEFIELD HWY

18

COLUMBIA HWY   1

Seiglers Crossroads

BEAVER

DAM   RD

BRIDGE   RD

19

Good Springs Rd

Croft

COOKS

NEW

302

WAGENER   RD

Ridgecrest

EDGEFIELD HWY

BRIDGE   RD

394

SALLEY RD

TABERNACLE

Balltown

118

UNIVERSITY PKWY

YORK ST NE

NEW   RD

302

WAGENER   RD

Kitchings Mill

WAGENER   RD

SURREY   RD

4

RACE

HAMPTON AV NW

Legare-Morgan
Hse

Idylwood

RICHLAND   AV   W

RICHLAND

RICHLAND AV E

236

Couchton

Nicholson
Village

Uncle John's Ca
Victorian
House

Tory   Tr

STATE   PARK   RD

**AIKEN
ST NAT
AREA**

South Fork Edisto River

Ridgeley Hall

302

PINE LOG

118

HITCHCOCK   PKWY

302

PINE LOG ST

Tooleber   Rd

Backs   Rd

Montmorenci

CHARLESTON

4

Windsor   Rd

19

Bonniview Estates

Oakwood

HWY   78

302   SILVER BLUFF RD

Aiken Mall

Aiken

Cowdenhouse

Elmwood Park

College
Acres

Dribble   Rd

OLD   BARNWELL   RD

Windsor

SEE **160** MAP

A   B   C   D   E

RAND MCNALLY

SEE 149

MAP
151

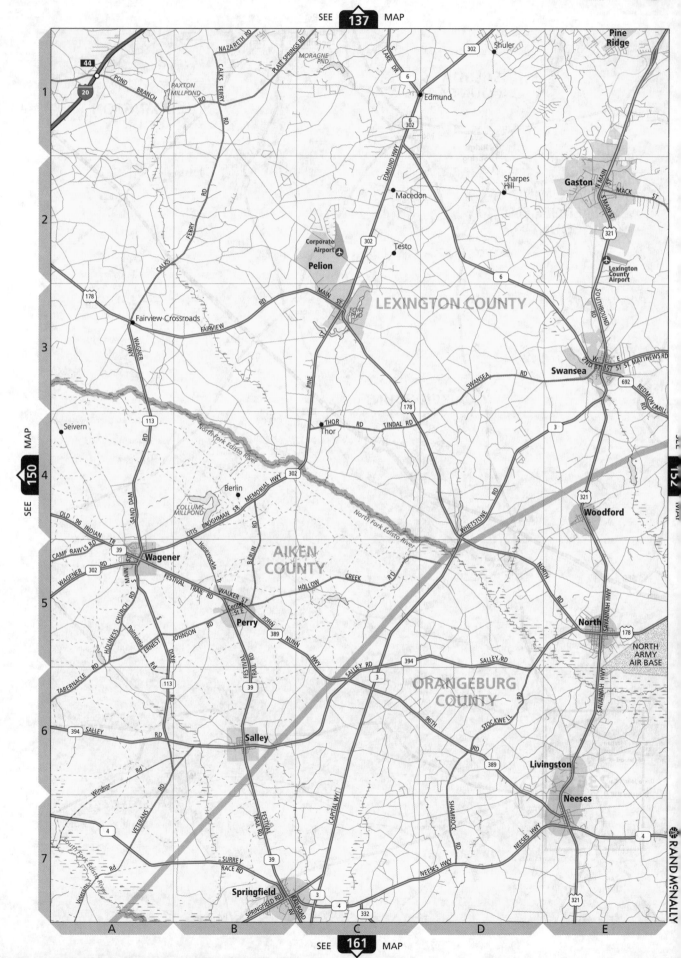

1:190,080
1 in. = 3 mi.

0   2   4
miles

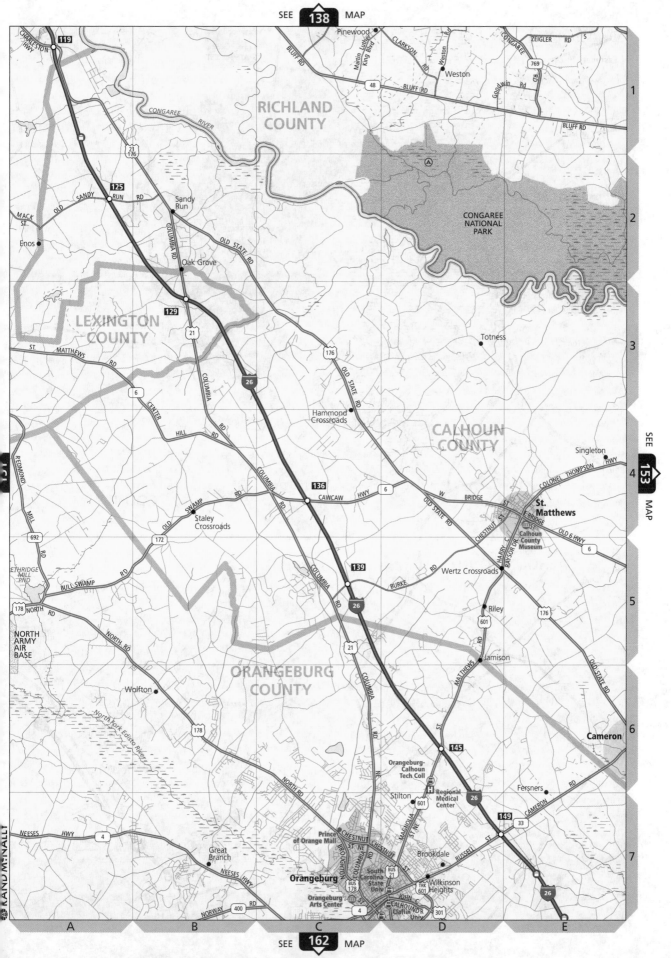

MAP
152

REGIONAL MAP

1:190,080
1 in. = 3 mi.

0   2   4
miles

SEE 138 MAP

119

Pinewood

CLARKSON RD

Martin Luther King Blvd

Weston

Wreston

Goodwin Rd

ZEIGLER RD

769

CONGAREE

48

BLUFF RD

BLUFF RD

RICHLAND COUNTY

CONGAREE RIVER

A

CONGAREE NATIONAL PARK

1

2

21 176

MACK ST.

OLD SANDY RUN RD

125

Sandy Run

COLUMBIA RD

Enos

Oak Grove

OLD STATE RD

129

LEXINGTON COUNTY

21

176

Totness

CALHOUN COUNTY

3

ST. MATTHEWS RD

6

COLUMBIA RD

26

Hammond Crossroads

OLD STATE RD

Singleton

HWY

COLONEL THOMPSON

SEE 153 MAP

4

CENTER

HILL

RD

136

CAWCAW HWY

6

W BRIDGE

St. Matthews

Chestnut ST

E BRIDGE

Calhoun County Museum

OLD 6 HWY

6

REDMOND

692 RD

MILL RD

OLD SWAMP RD

Staley Crossroads

172

COLUMBIA RD

OLD STATE RD

HARRY C RAYSOR DR

ETHRIDGE MILL POND

BULL SWAMP RD

178 NORTH RD

139

COLUMBIA RD

26

BURKE RD

Wertz Crossroads

Riley

601

176

5

NORTH ARMY AIR BASE

NORTH RD

21

MATTHEWS

RD

Jamison

ORANGEBURG COUNTY

OLD STATE RD

Wolfton

178

Cameron

6

NORTH RD

145

26

Orangeburg-Calhoun Tech Coll

Fersners

RD

NEESES HWY

4

Great Branch

NEESES HWY

NORWAY

400 RD

Prince of Orange Mall

CHESTNUT ST NE

CHESTNUT

BROUGHTON

COLUMBIA

MAGNOLIA ST NE

H Regional Medical Center

Stilton

601

Brookdale

RUSSELL ST

CAMERON RD

149

33

7

Orangeburg

BUS 178

South Carolina State Univ

Orangeburg Arts Center

ST

4

JOHN C CALHOUN DR

Wilkinson Heights

TRK 601

301

Claflin Univ

26

A   B   C   D   E

RAND McNALLY

MAP
153

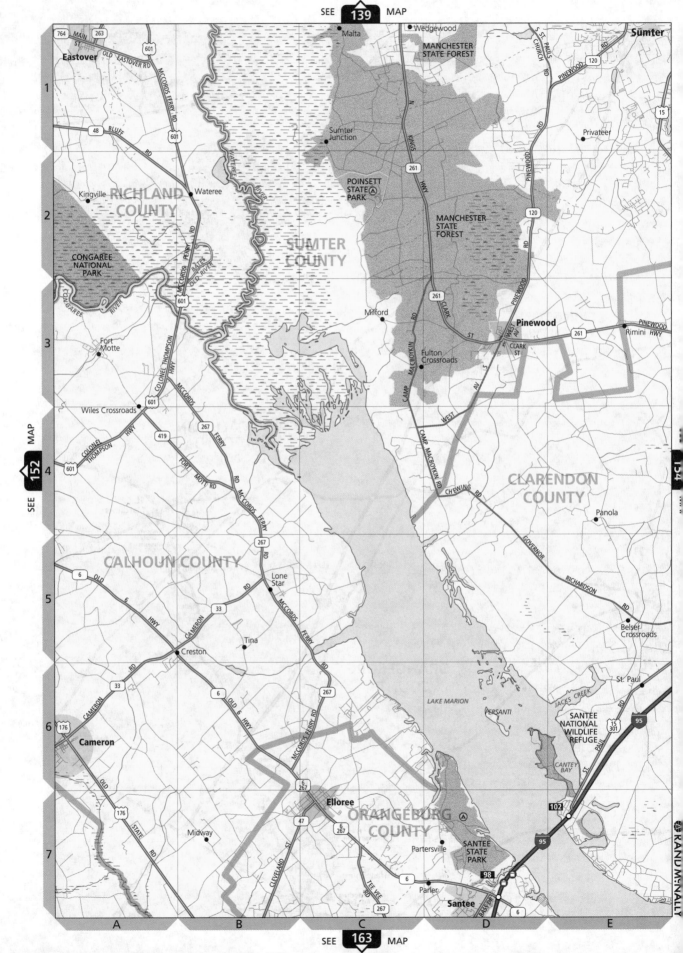

MAP 153

1:190,080
1 in. = 3 mi.

0   2   4
miles

Sumter

Eastover

Wedgewood

Malta

MANCHESTER STATE FOREST

764 MAIN ST
263
601

48 BLUFF RD
601

MCCORDS FERRY RD

Sumter Junction

KINGS HWY

261

S ST PAULS CHURCH RD

PINEWOOD RD

120

15

Privateer

1

RICHLAND COUNTY

Kingville

Wateree

WATEREE RIVER

SUMTER COUNTY

POINSETT STATE PARK

MANCHESTER STATE FOREST

261

120

PINEWOOD RD

2

CONGAREE NATIONAL PARK

CONGAREE RIVER

BATES OLD RIVER

601

Milford

261

CLARK ST

PINEWOOD

Pinewood

PINEWOOD HWY

Rimini

3

Fort Motte

COLONEL THOMPSON HWY

601

MCCORDS FERRY RD

Fulton Crossroads

CAMP MACBOYKIN RD

WEST AV

CLARK ST

WEST AV S

261

SEE MAP 152

Wiles Crossroads

COLONEL THOMPSON HWY

601

419

267

FORT MOTT RD

MCCORDS FERRY RD

WEST

CAMP MACBOYKIN RD

CLARENDON COUNTY

154

4

CHEWING RD

Panola

CALHOUN COUNTY

6 OLD

6 HWY

33

CAMERON RD

Lone Star

Tina

MCCORDS FERRY RD

267

GOVERNOR RICHARDSON RD

Belser Crossroads

5

Creston

33

6 OLD 6 HWY

267

LAKE MARION

PERSANTI

JACKS CREEK

St. Paul

SANTEE NATIONAL WILDLIFE REFUGE

15 301

95

6

CAMERON RD

176

Cameron

OLD STATE RD

6 267

Elloree

ST PAUL RD

CANTEY BAY

102

95

Midway

47

CLEVELAND ST

6 267

ORANGEBURG COUNTY

Partersville

SANTEE STATE PARK

98

RAND MCNALLY

7

176

TEE VEE RD

6

Parler

Santee

BASS DR

6

267

95

A   B   C   D   E

MAP
154

REGIONAL MAP

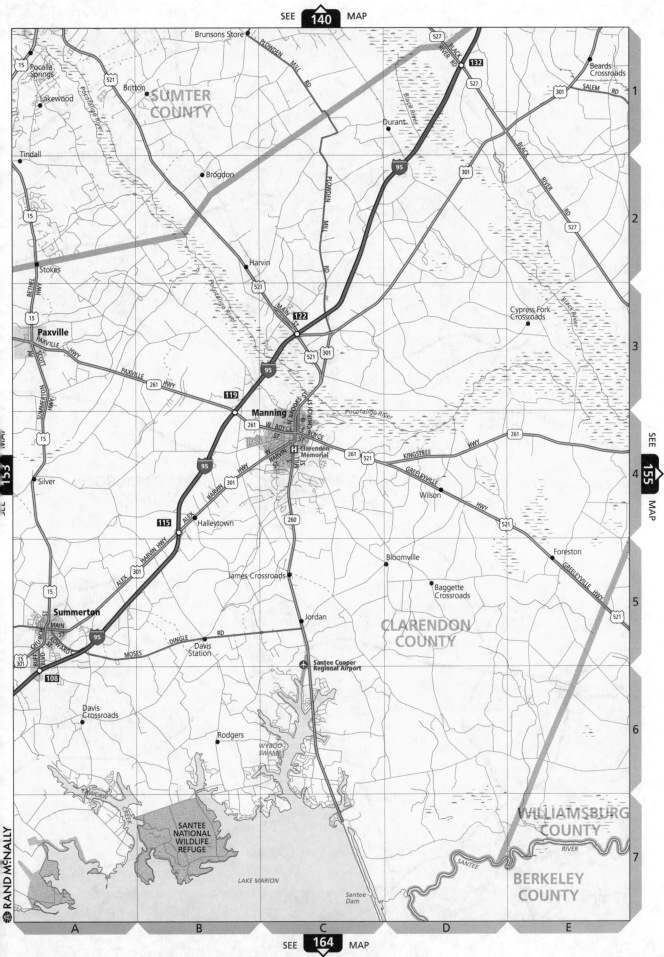

1:190,080
1 in. = 3 mi.

0   2   4
miles

SEE **140** MAP

Brunsons Store

527

132

Beards
Crossroads

301   SALEM RD

Pocalla
Springs

521

Britton

**SUMTER
COUNTY**

Durant

301   527

15

Lakewood

Pocotaligo River

95

Black River

1

Tindall

Brogdon

Black River RD

2

15

Stokes

BETHEL HWY

521

Harvin

301

527

Cypress Fork
Crossroads

Black River

15

Paxville

PAXVILLE HWY

Pocotaligo River

521

MAIN ST

122

301

3

PAXVILLE HWY

SUMMERTON HWY

261 HWY

119

95

521

Manning

N BROOKS ST
N HUGHR ST

Pocotaligo River

261

SEE
155
MAP

261

W BOYCE ST
N E BOYCE

W
ST

Clarendon
Memorial

261   521

KINGSTREE HWY

261

4

Silver

95

W
ST
HARVIN
MILL ST

GREELEYVILLE

15

HARVIN
ALEX

301

115

Halleytown

260

Wilson

GREELEYVILLE HWY

521

HARVIN HWY

James Crossroads

Bloomville

Foreston

5

15

ALEX
301

Jordan

Baggette
Crossroads

**CLARENDON
COUNTY**

521

Summerton

MAIN ST

DINGLE   RD

Davis
Station

Santee Cooper
Regional Airport

CHURCH ST
EDWARDS
BLUFF BLVD

MOSES

15
301

108

Davis
Crossroads

Rodgers

WYBOO
SWAMP

6

WATEREE CREEK

**SANTEE
NATIONAL
WILDLIFE
REFUGE**

**WILLIAMSBURG
COUNTY**

RIVER

7

SANTEE

LAKE MARION

Santee
Dam

**BERKELEY
COUNTY**

RAND MCNALLY

A   B   C   D   E

SEE **164** MAP

SEE
153
MAP

MAP
155

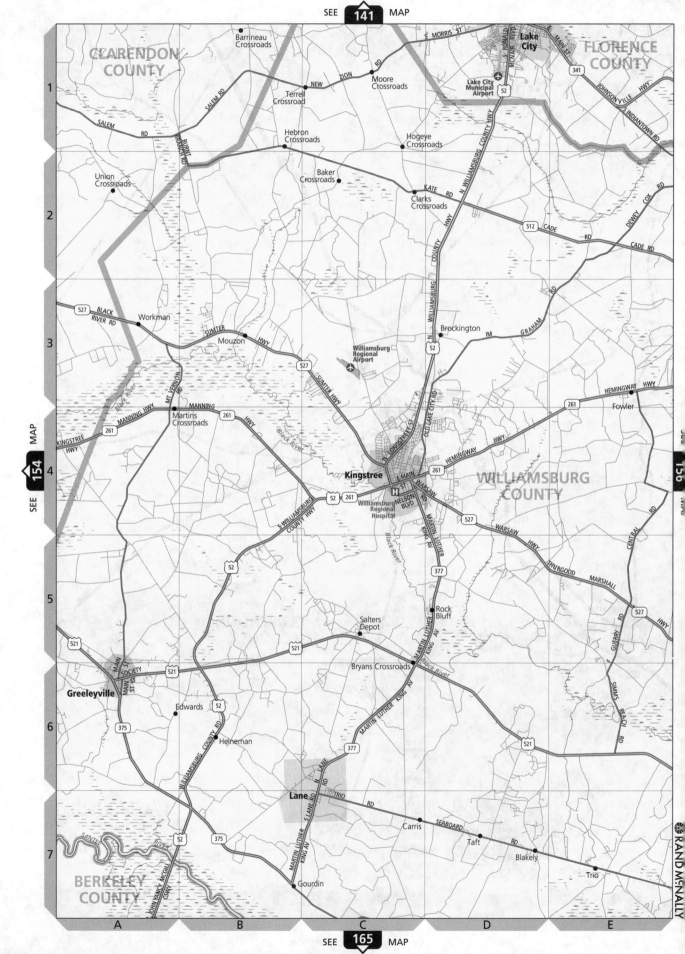

1:190,080
1 in. = 3 mi.

0   2   4
miles

N

SEE **141** MAP

CLARENDON COUNTY

FLORENCE COUNTY

WILLIAMSBURG COUNTY

BERKELEY COUNTY

SEE **154** MAP

SEE **156**

SEE **165** MAP

RAND McNALLY

Barrineau Crossroads
Moore Crossroads
Terrell Crossroad
Hebron Crossroads
Union Crossroads
Baker Crossroads
Hogeye Crossroads
Clarks Crossroads
Workman
Mouzon
Brockington
Martins Crossroads
Fowler
Kingstree
Salters Depot
Rock Bluff
Bryans Crossroads
Greeleyville
Edwards
Heineman
Lane
Carris
Taft
Blakely
Trio
Gourdin
Lake City
Lake City Municipal Airport
Williamsburg Regional Airport
Williamsburg Regional Hospital

MAP
156

REGIONAL MAP

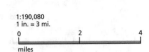

1:190,080
1 in. = 3 mi.

0   2   4
miles

SEE 142 MAP

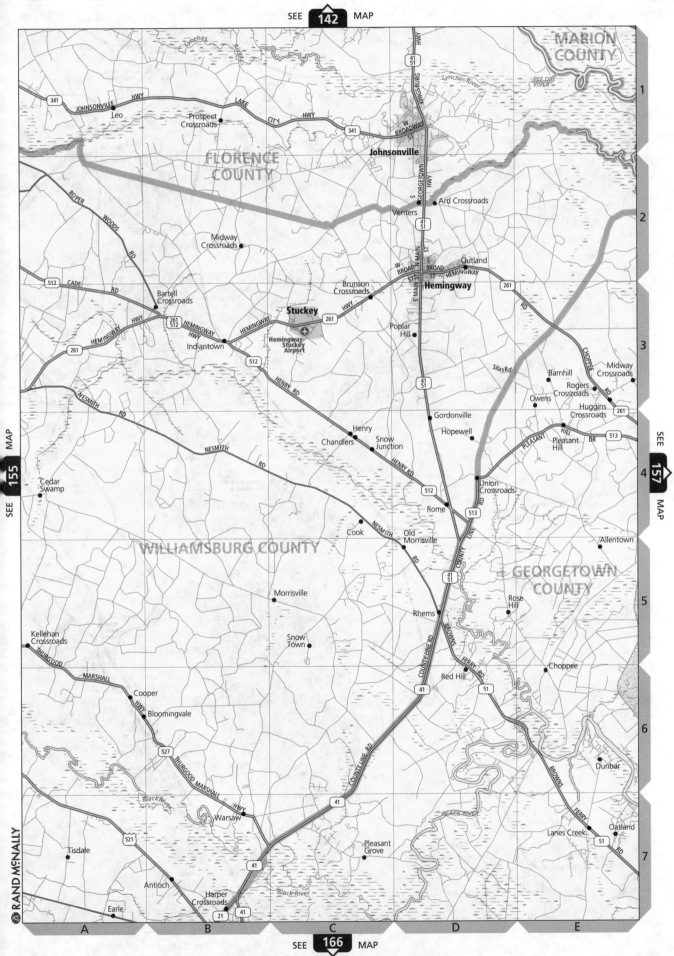

MARION COUNTY

PEE DEE RIVER

341 JOHNSONVILLE HWY

Leo

Prospect Crossroads

LAKE CITY HWY

341

FLORENCE COUNTY

Lynches River

W BROADWAY ST

Johnsonville

S GEORGETOWN HWY

KINGSBURG HWY

41 51

Ard Crossroads

Venters

41 51

ROPER WOODS RD

Midway Crossroads

512 CADE RD

Bartell Crossroads

HEMINGWAY HWY

261 512

261

HEMINGWAY HWY

Indiantown

512

W BROAD ST

S MAIN ST

BROAD ST

HEMINGWAY

Outland

HEMINGWAY

261

RD

CHOPPEE RD

Barnhill

Silas Rd

Owens

Rogers Crossroads

Midway Crossroads

261

Huggins Crossroads

Brunson Crossroads

Stuckey

261

HWY

Hemingway-Stuckey Airport

HENRY RD

Poplar Hill

41 51

Gordonville

Hopewell

PLEASANT HILL RD

Pleasant Hill

HILL DR

513

NESMITH RD

Henry

Chandlers

Snow Junction

HENRY RD

512

Union Crossroads

513

SEE 157 MAP

Cedar Swamp

NESMITH RD

Rome

COUNTY LINE RD

41 51

Allentown

WILLIAMSBURG COUNTY

Cook

NESMITH RD

Old Morrisville

GEORGETOWN COUNTY

Rose Hill

Morrisville

Rhems

Kellehan Crossroads

THURGOOD MARSHALL HWY

Snow Town

COUNTY LINE RD

BROWNS FERRY RD

Red Hill

51

Choppee

Cooper

Bloomingvale

527

THURGOOD MARSHALL HWY

41

Dunbar

Black River

Warsaw

BROWNS FERRY RD

521

Tisdale

41

Pleasant Grove

Lanes Creek

51

Oatland

Antioch

Harper Crossroads

21   41

Black River

Earle

A   B   C   D   E

1   2   3   4   5   6   7

SEE 166 MAP

MAP
157

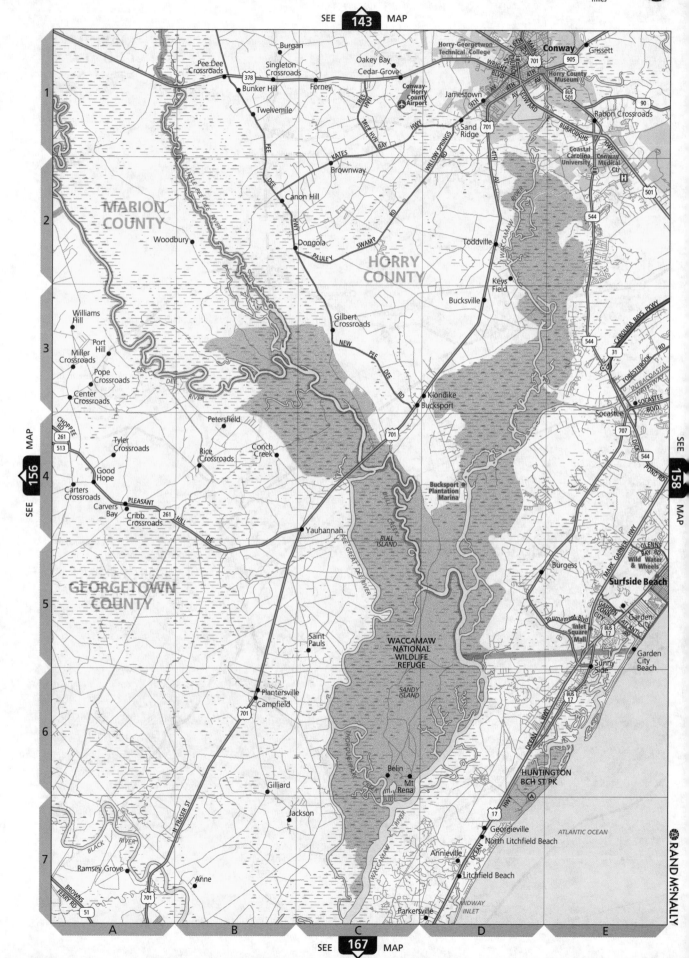

1:190,080
1 in. = 3 mi.

0   2   4
miles

SEE **143** MAP

SEE **156** MAP

SEE **158** MAP

SEE **167** MAP

RAND McNALLY

MARION COUNTY

HORRY COUNTY

GEORGETOWN COUNTY

Conway

Burgan
Oakey Bay
Cedar Grove
Singleton Crossroads
Pee Dee Crossroads
Bunker Hill
Forney
Twelvemile
Brownway
Canon Hill
Woodbury
Dongola
Toddville
Keys Field
Bucksville
Gilbert Crossroads
Williams Hill
Port Hill
Miller Crossroads
Pope Crossroads
Center Crossroads
Klondike
Bucksport
Petersfield
Tyler Crossroads
Rice Crossroads
Conch Creek
Good Hope
Carters Crossroads
Carvers Bay
Cribb Crossroads
Yauhannah
Bucksport Plantation Marina
Burgess
Surfside Beach
Garden City
Garden City Beach
Sunny Side
WACCAMAW NATIONAL WILDLIFE REFUGE
BULL ISLAND
SANDY ISLAND
Saint Pauls
Plantersville
Campfield
Gilliard
Jackson
Belin
Mt Rena
HUNTINGTON BCH ST PK
Georgieville
North Litchfield Beach
Annieville
Litchfield Beach
Ramsey Grove
Anne
Parkersville
ATLANTIC OCEAN
MIDWAY INLET
Grissett
Horry-Georgetown Technical College
Horry County Museum
Jamestown
Rabon Crossroads
Sand Ridge
Coastal Carolina University
Conway Medical Ctr
Socastee
Inlet Square Mall
Wild Water & Wheels

MAP
158

REGIONAL MAP

1:190,080
1 in. = 3 mi.

0   2   4
miles

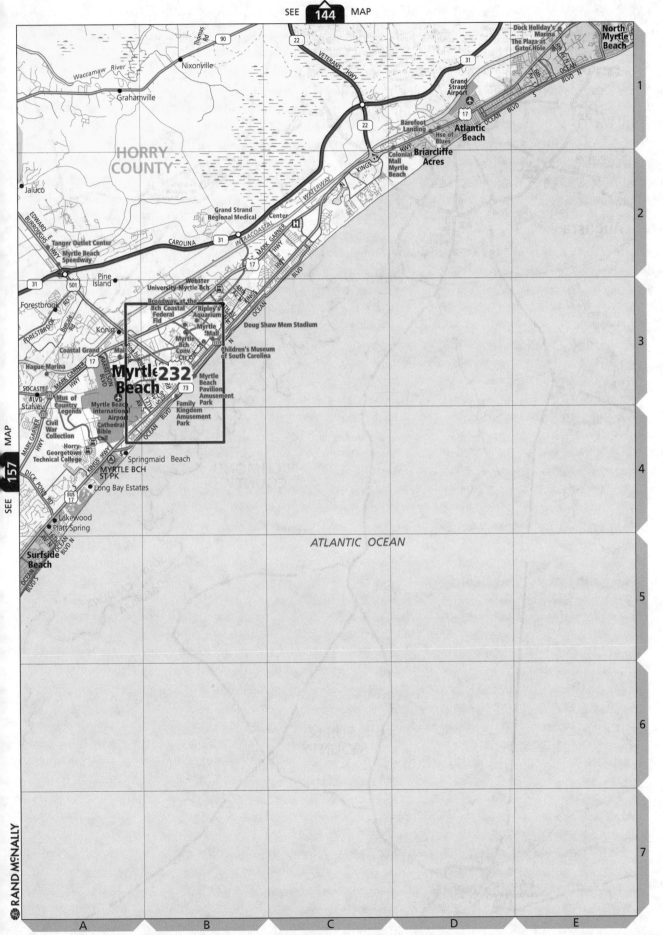

SEE [144] MAP

North Myrtle Beach

Dock Holiday's Marina
The Plaza at Gator Hole

Grand Strand Airport

Barefoot Landing

Hse of Blues

Atlantic Beach

Colonial Mall Myrtle Beach

Briarcliffe Acres

HORRY COUNTY

Waccamaw River

Nixonville

Grahamville

Jaluco

EDWARD E BURROUGHS HWY

Tanger Outlet Center

Myrtle Beach Speedway

Grand Strand Regional Medical Center

Pine Island

Forestbrook

Konig

Webster University-Myrtle Bch

Broadway at the Bch Coastal Federal Fld

Ripley's Aquarium

Myrtle Mall

Doug Shaw Mem Stadium

Coastal Grand Mall

Myrtle Bch Conv Ctr Cplx

Children's Museum of South Carolina

Myrtle Beach 232

73

Myrtle Beach Pavilion Amusement Park

Hague Marina

SOCASTEE

Stalvey

Mus of Country Legends

Myrtle Beach International Airport

Cathedral Bible Coll

Family Kingdom Amusement Park

Civil War Collection

Horry-Georgetown Technical College

Springmaid Beach

MYRTLE BCH ST PK

Long Bay Estates

Lakewood

Platt Spring

Surfside Beach

ATLANTIC OCEAN

SEE **157** MAP

RAND MCNALLY

A   B   C   D   E

1   2   3   4   5   6   7

MAP
159

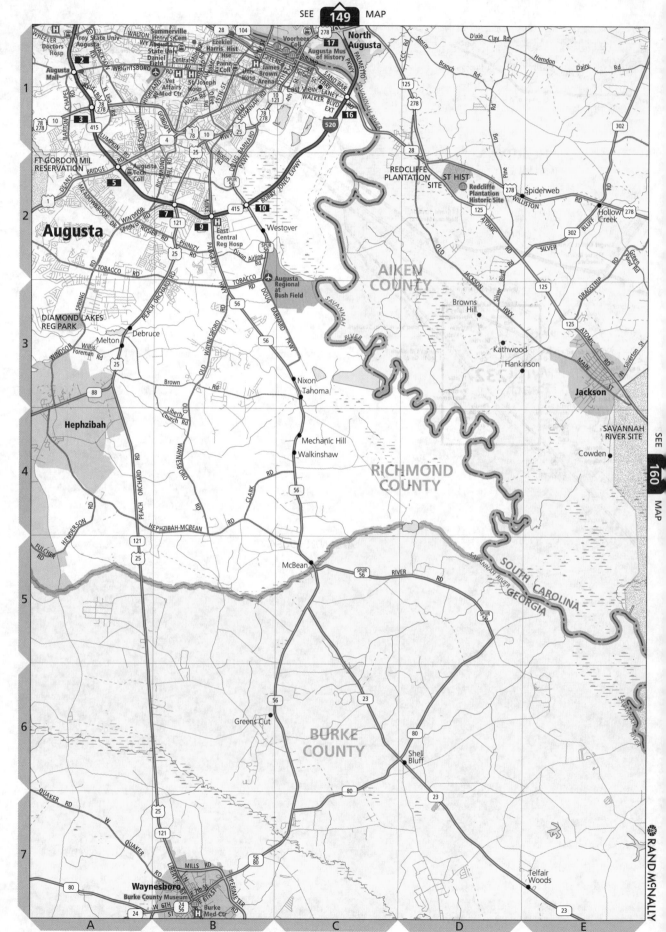

1:190,080
1 in. = 3 mi.

0   2   4
miles

SEE MAP
149

17
North
Augusta

16

WHEELER RD
Troy State Univ
Augusta
WY Aquah
State Univ
Daniel Field
Summerville
Henry St Cem
WALTON
28 104
Voorhees
Coll
278
Augusta Mus
of History

Doctors Hosp

Augusta
Mall
2

3

415

Ezekiel
Harris Hist
Hse
Central
Paine
Coll
James
Brown
Arena
Telfair
East View
WALKER
LANEY

St Joseph
Hosp
Univ
Hosp
White RD

Vet
Affairs
Med Ctr

78
278
10

10
121

520

FT GORDON MIL
RESERVATION

Augusta
Tech
Coll

5

BRIDGE

1

4

25

SPUR
56

125

28

REDCLIFFE
PLANTATION
ST HIST
SITE

Redcliffe
Plantation
Historic Site

278

Spiderweb

Williston

Hollow
Creek

278

302

125

Dixie Clay Rd

Storm
Branch

Herndon
RD
Dairy

AIKEN
COUNTY

Browns
Hill

302

SILVER

125

Green
Pond Rd

DRAGSTRIP

ATOMIC

2

1

Augusta

WINDSOR
SPRING RD
ROSIER RD
PHINIZY
PEACH ORCHARD RD
7
121
9
H
East
Central
Reg Hosp
Westover
415
10
SPUR
56
Dixon Airline Rd

TOBACCO RD

TOBACCO RD

56

Augusta
Regional
at Bush Field

OLD JACKSON

SILVER BLUFF

OLD

SAVANNAH

RIVER

2

DIAMOND LAKES
REG PARK

Melton

Debruce

Willis
Foreman
Rd

WINDSOR

25

88

56

56

OLD WAYNESBORO

Brown

Rd

Liberty
Church Rd

Nixon
Tahoma

Kathwood

Hankinson

Browns
Hill

Jackson

SAVANNAH
RIVER SITE

3

Hephzibah

WAYNESBORO

Mechanic Hill
Walkinshaw

RICHMOND
COUNTY

Cowden

SEE
160
MAP

4

HENDERSON RD

FULCHER
RD

PEACH ORCHARD RD

121
25

HEPHZIBAH-McBEAN RD

CLARK

56

McBean

SPUR
56

RIVER

RD

SOUTH CAROLINA
GEORGIA

SAVANNAH RIVER

5

QUAKER RD

25

121

56

23

Greens Cut

56
80

80

SPUR
56

SAVANNAH RIVER

6

BURKE
COUNTY

Shell
Bluff

80

23

7

QUAKER

W

80

MILLS RD

121

LIBERTY

56
80

Waynesboro
Burke County Museum
E 7th St
24
56
W 6TH
6TH ST
PERIMETER RD
Burke
Med Ctr

24

Telfair
Woods

23

RAND MCNALLY

A   B   C   D   E

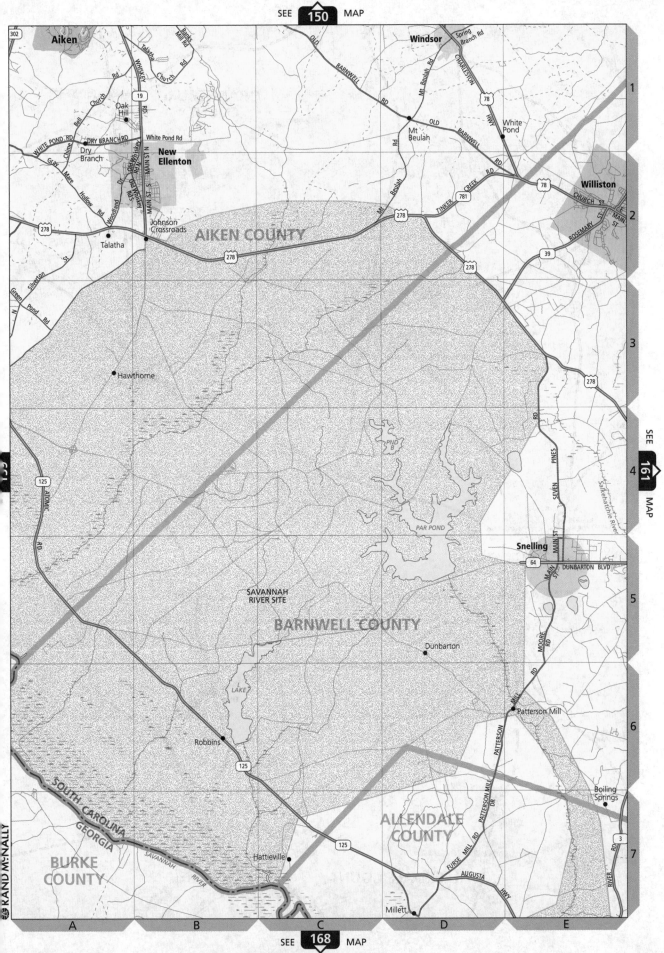

MAP
160

REGIONAL MAP

1:190,080
1 in. = 3 mi.

miles
0   2   4

SEE 150 MAP

Aiken

302

Windsor

Spring Branch Rd

19

Oak Hill

Church Rd

Talatha Church Rd

Banks Mill Rd

WHISKEY RD

Dry Branch

DRY BRANCH RD

White Pond Rd

New Ellenton

WHITE POND RD

Chime

Gray Mare

Hollow Rd

Woodland Dr

OLD WHISKEY RD

MAIN ST S

N NINTH ST

Johnson Crossroads

278

Talatha

Silverton

Green Pond Rd

Bell Rd

OLD BARNWELL RD

Mt Beulah Rd

Mt Beulah

CHARLESTON HWY

78

White Pond

OLD BARNWELL RD

Mt Beulah Rd

TINKER CREEK RD

781

278

Williston

CHURCH ST

ROSEMARY ST

E MAIN ST

78

39

AIKEN COUNTY

278

278

3

278

Hawthorne

ATOMIC RD

125

SEVEN PINES RD

MOORE RD

SEE 161 MAP

4

PND B

PAR POND

Salkehatchie River

Snelling

MAIN ST

64

DUNBARTON BLVD

SAVANNAH RIVER SITE

BARNWELL COUNTY

Dunbarton

5

LAKE

Robbins

125

MOORE RD

PATTERSON MILL RD

Patterson Mill

6

SOUTH CAROLINA

GEORGIA

SAVANNAH RIVER

125

ALLENDALE COUNTY

FURSE MILL RD

PATTERSON MILL DR

Boiling Springs

3

RIVER RD

7

BURKE COUNTY

Hattieville

125

AUGUSTA HWY

Millett

RAND MCNALLY

A   B   C   D   E

SEE 168 MAP

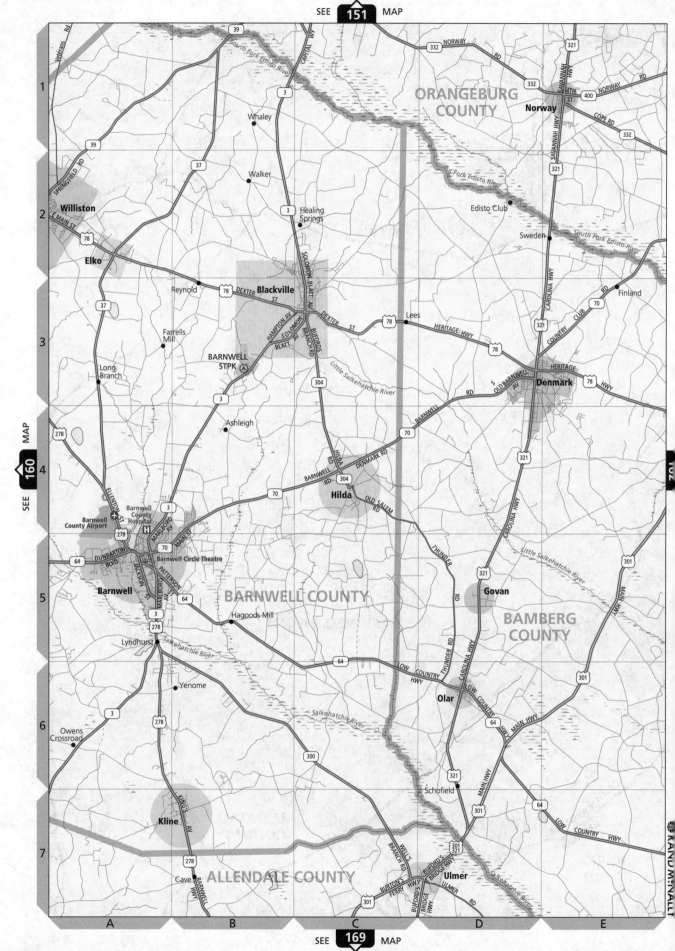

MAP
161

REGIONAL MAP

1:190,080
1 in. = 3 mi.

0   2   4
miles

SEE **151** MAP

Veterans Rd

39

South Fork Edisto River

332   NORWAY   RD

321

ORANGEBURG COUNTY

332

332

SAVANNAH ST

400

Norway

4TH ST

COPE RD

332

Whaley

3

321

E. Fork Edisto River

39

Williston

37

Walker

3

Edisto Club

Carolina Hwy

South Fork Edisto River

E MAIN ST

78

3   Healing Springs

Sweden

Elko

SOLOMON BLATT AV

CAPITAL WY

DEXTER ST

70   Finland

Reynolds

78   DEXTER   **Blackville**

78   Lees

HERITAGE HWY

321   COUNTRY CLUB RD

37

HAMPTON AV

SOLOMON BLATT AV

BUFORDS BRANCH RD

78

Farrells Mill

BLATT

304

Little Salkehatchie River

HERITAGE

78 HWY

Long Branch

BARNWELL STPK A

3

OLD BARNWELL AV

Denmark

78

278

3

Ashleigh

BARNWELL RD

70

321

SEE **160** MAP

HILDA RD

DENMARK RD

321

ELLENTON ST

Barnwell County Hospital H

Barnwell County Airport

3

BARNWELL RD   304

Hilda

OLD SALEM RD

Little Salkehatchie River

301

278

MARLBORO AV

MAIN ST

70

THUNDER RD

64   DUNBARTON BLVD

Barnwell Circle Theatre

PATTERSON

321

Govan

BAMBERG COUNTY

Barnwell

JACKSON ST

MARLBORO AV

64

BARNWELL COUNTY

Carolina Hwy

301

3   Hagoods Mill

278

Lyndhurst   Salkehatchie River

64

LOW COUNTRY HWY

301

THUNDER RD

Yenome

Salkehatchie River

Olar

CAROLINA HWY

3

64

MAIN HWY

278

Owens Crossroad

300

321

MAIN HWY

Schofield

LOW COUNTRY HWY

301

301

64

KING'S AV

Kline

WELLS BRANCH RD

301 321

278

ALLENDALE COUNTY

BURTON'S FERRY HWY

BUFORD'S BRIDGE HWY

Ulmer

ULMER RD

Salkehatchie River

Cave

BARNWELL HWY

301

RAND MCNALLY

A   B   C   D   E

SEE **169** MAP

MAP
162

REGIONAL MAP

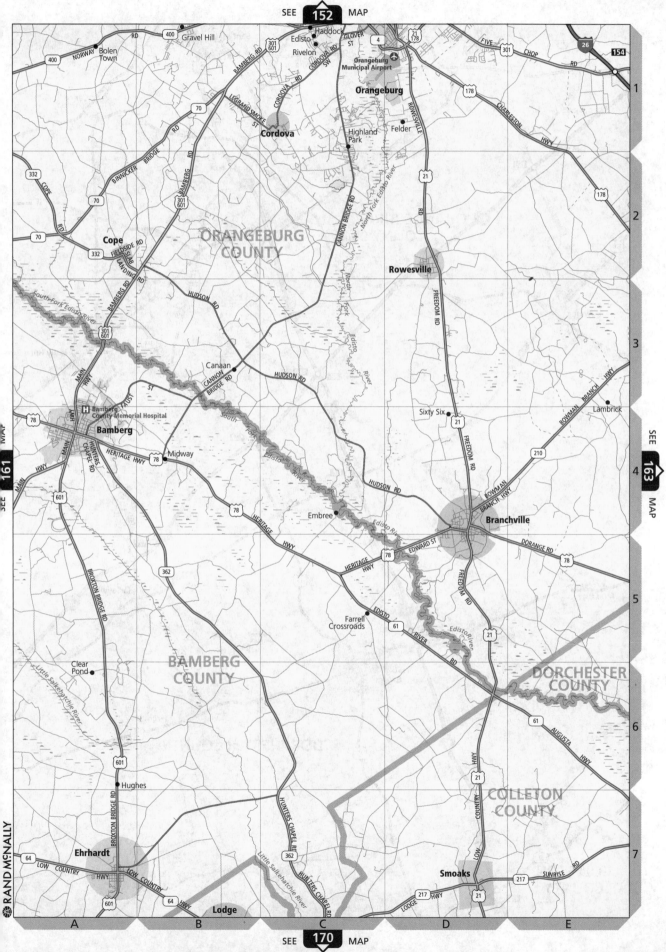

1:190,080
1 in. = 3 mi.

0   2   4
miles

SEE 152 MAP

26
154

400   NORWAY RD   Bolen Town   Gravel Hill
400   RD

301 601   Edisto   Haddock
Rivelon   GLOVER ST
CORDOVA RD SW
CORDOVA RD
4
21 178
FIVE CHOP RD
301

178

Orangeburg Municipal Airport
Orangeburg

1

70
LEGRAND SMOKE ST
Cordova
Highland Park
Felder
ROWESVILLE RD
178
21

CHARLESTON HWY

332   BINNICKER BRIDGE   COPE RD
70
BAMBERG RD
301 601

CANNON BRIDGE RD
North Fork Edisto River

178

2

70   RD
70

Cope   FIELDSIDE RD   ORANGEBURG COUNTY
332   SLAB LANDING RD
BAMBERG RD
HUDSON RD
North Fork
Rowesville
FREEDOM RD

3

South Fork Edisto River
301 601
Canaan
CANNON BRIDGE RD
HUDSON RD
Edisto River

BOWMAN BRANCH HWY
Lambrick

H Bamberg County Memorial Hospital
78   MAIN   FAUST ST
Bamberg
Sixty Six
21
FREEDOM RD

SEE 163 MAP

78   HUNTERS CHAPEL RD   HERITAGE HWY   Midway
78
South Fork Edisto River
210
Branchville

4

601
362
78
HERITAGE HWY
Embree
HUDSON RD
Edisto River
EDWARD ST
78
DORANGE RD
78

BROXTON BRIDGE RD
362
Farrell Crossroads
61
Edisto River

BOWMAN BRANCH BWY
FREEDOM RD

5

Little Salkehatchie River
Clear Pond
BAMBERG COUNTY
River
DORCHESTER COUNTY
61   AUGUSTA HWY

6

601
Hughes

21

COLLETON COUNTY

HUNTERS CHAPEL RD
362
Little Salkehatchie River
HUNTERS CHAPEL RD

7

64   LOW COUNTRY HWY   Ehrhardt
64 HWY
601   64 HWY
Lodge
LODGE HWY
217 HWY
Smoaks
21
217
SUNRISE

A   B   C   D   E

SEE 161 MAP

MAP
163

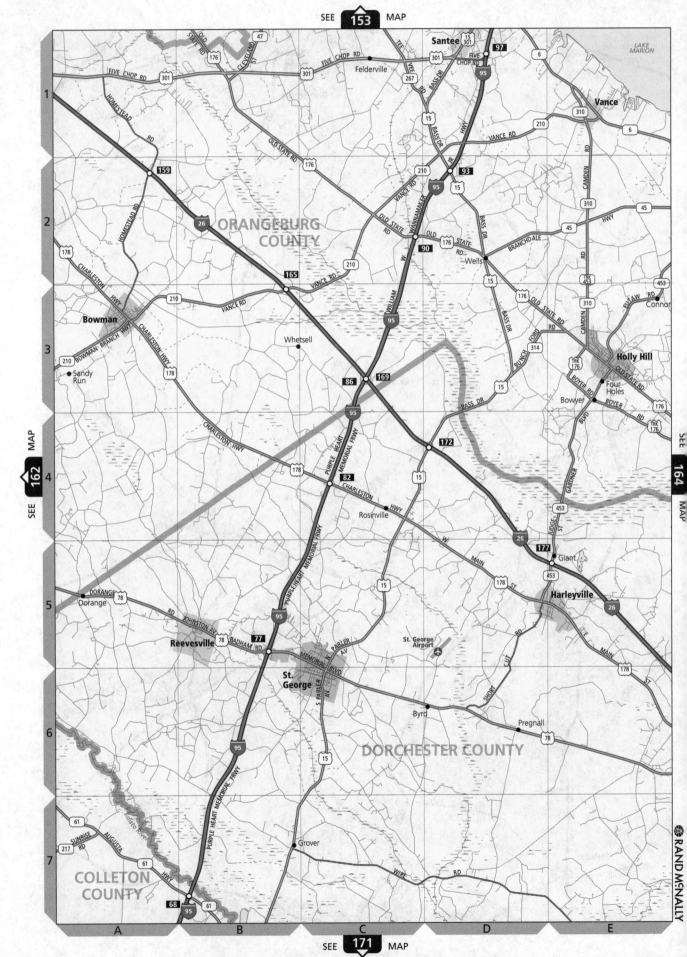

1:190,080
1 in. = 3 mi.

0   2   4
miles

SEE 153 MAP

Santee

Vance

ORANGEBURG
COUNTY

Felderville

Wells

Bowman

Whetsell

Sandy
Run

Holly Hill

Four
Holes

Bowyer

SEE 162 MAP

SEE 164 MAP

Rosinville

Giant

Harleyville

Dorange
Dorange

Reevesville

St. George
Airport

St.
George

Byrd

Pregnall

DORCHESTER COUNTY

Grover

COLLETON
COUNTY

SEE 171 MAP

RAND McNALLY

A   B   C   D   E

MAP
164

REGIONAL MAP

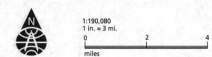

1:190,080
1 in. = 3 mi.

0   2   4
miles

SEE 154 MAP

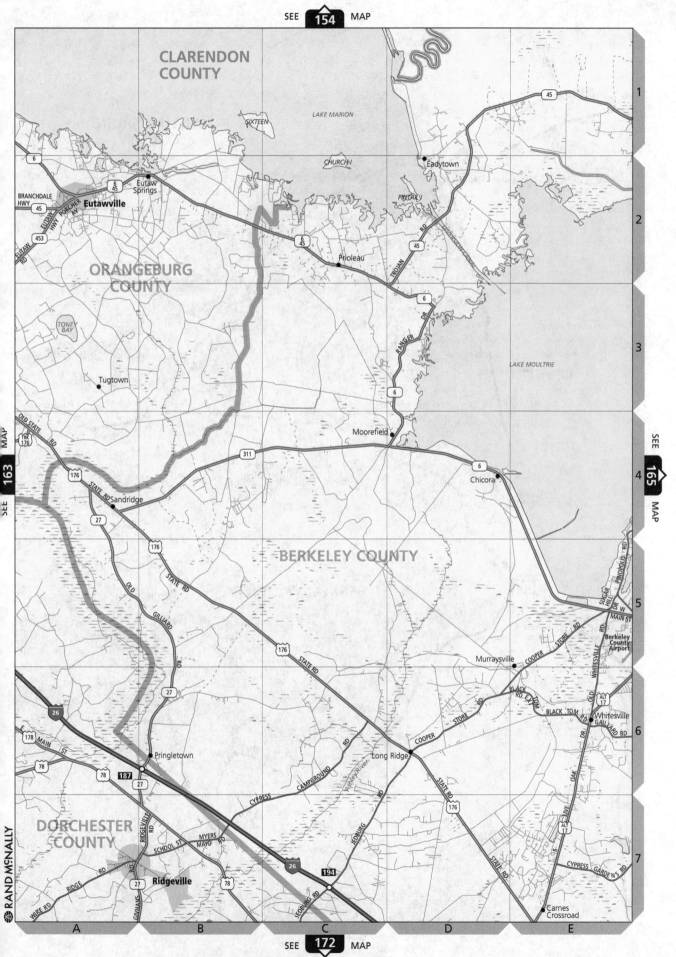

CLARENDON
COUNTY

LAKE MARION

SIXTEEN

CHURCH-I

Eadytown

45

6

6
45

Eutaw
Springs

PINTAIL

BRANCHDALE
HWY

45

Eutawville

EUTAW HWY PORCHER AV

453

45

5
45

Prioleau

TROJAN

6

EUTAW RD

**ORANGEBURG
COUNTY**

TONEY
BAY

RANGER DR

6

LAKE MOULTRIE

Tugtown

OLD STATE RD

SEE 163 MAP

TRK
176

Moorefield

311

6

176

State Rd Sandridge

SEE 165 MAP

Chicora

27

176

BERKELEY COUNTY

STATE RD

PINOPOLIS RD

OLD GILLIARD RD

SUGAR HILL DR W

MAIN ST

5

176

STATE RD

WHITESVILLE RD

**Berkeley
County
Airport**

COOPER STORE RD

27

Murraysville

COOPER STORE RD

26

BLACK TOM RD EXTN

OLD ALT 17

178

E MAIN ST

STORE RD

BLACK TOM RD

Whitesville

GAILLARD RD

6

78

Pringletown

COOPER RD

Long Ridge

OAK DR

187

27

CAMPGROUND RD

RIDGEVILLE RD

JEDBURG RD

STATE RD

176

ALT 17

**DORCHESTER
COUNTY**

CYPRESS

MYERS

SCHOOL ST

MAYO RD

7

26

194

CYPRESS GARDENS RD

RIDGE RD

WIRE RD

GIVHANS RD

27

Ridgeville

78

JEDBURG RD

Carnes
Crossroad

A   B   C   D   E

SEE 172 MAP

MAP
165

REGIONAL MAP

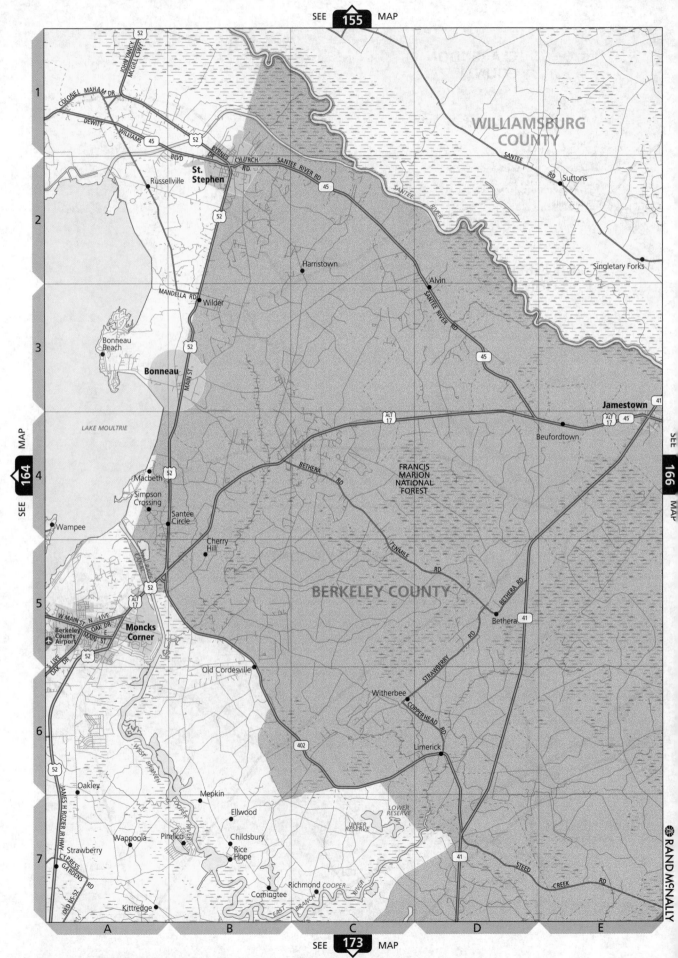

1:190,080
1 in. = 3 mi.

0   2   4
miles

SEE 155 MAP

SEE 164 MAP

SEE 166 MAP

SEE 173 MAP

WILLIAMSBURG COUNTY

BERKELEY COUNTY

FRANCIS MARION NATIONAL FOREST

LAKE MOULTRIE

St. Stephen
Russellville
Bonneau Beach
Bonneau
Wilder
Harristown
Alvin
Suttons
Singletary Forks
Jamestown
Beufordtown
Macbeth
Simpson Crossing
Santee Circle
Wampee
Cherry Hill
Moncks Corner
Berkeley County Airport
Old Cordesville
Bethera
Witherbee
Limerick
Oakley
Mepkin
Ellwood
Wappoola
Pimlico
Childsbury
Rice Hope
Strawberry
Richmond
Comingtee
Kittredge
Lower Reserve
Upper Reserve

COOPER RIVER
EAST BRANCH
WEST BRANCH

SANTEE RIVER

RAND McNALLY

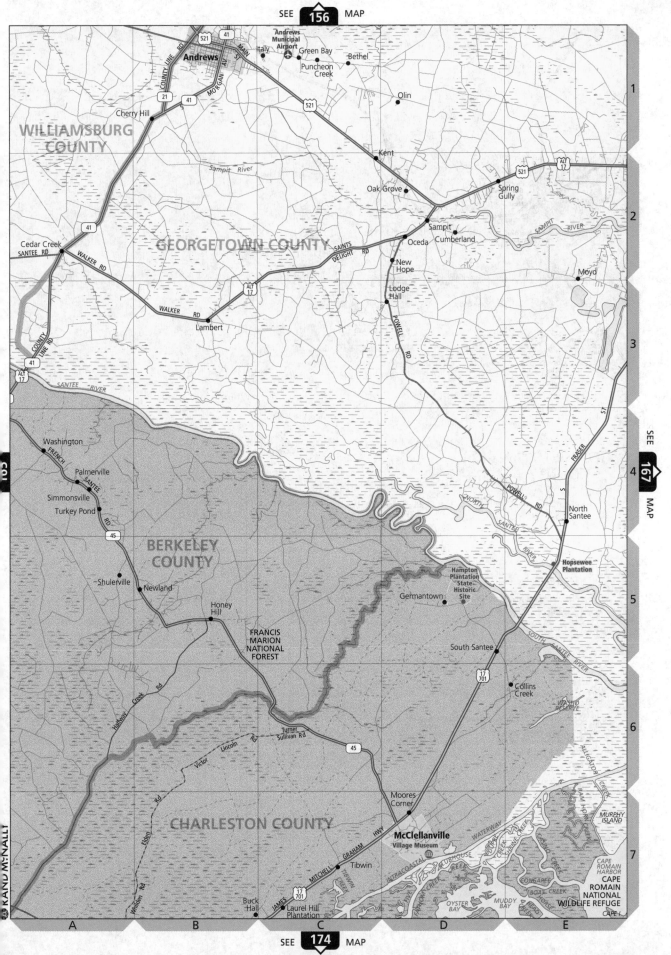

MAP
166

1:190,080
1 in. = 3 mi.
0   2   4
miles

SEE 156 MAP

1

521
41
Andrews
Municipal
Airport
Italy
Green Bay
Bethel
Puncheon
Creek
Olin

WILLIAMSBURG
COUNTY

Andrews
521
41
21
41

Cherry Hill

Kent

ALT 17
521

Oak Grove
Spring
Gully

2

Sampit River

41

GEORGETOWN COUNTY
SAINTS
DELIGHT RD

Sampit
Oceda
Cumberland

SAMPIT RIVER

Cedar Creek
SANTEE RD
WALKER RD

New
Hope

Moyd

ALT
17

Lodge
Hall

3

WALKER RD

Lambert

POWELL RD

COUNTY LINE RD

41
ALT
17

SANTEE RIVER

FRASER ST

SEE
167
MAP

Washington
FRENCH

POWELL RD

4

Palmerville
SANTEE

North
Santee

NORTH
SANTEE RIVER

Simmonsville
Turkey Pond
RD

North
Santee

45

Hopsewee
Plantation

BERKELEY
COUNTY

Shulerville
Newland

Hampton
Plantation
State
Historic
Site

Germantown

5

Honey
Hill

FRANCIS
MARION
NATIONAL
FOREST

South Santee

SOUTH SANTEE RIVER

Halfway Creek Rd

Turner
Rd
Sullivan Rd

45

17
701

Collins
Creek

WASHO
RESERVE

6

Lincoln
Rd

Victor

Rd

Elder
Rd

Moores
Corner

ALLIGATOR CREEK

MURPHY
ISLAND

CHARLESTON COUNTY

GRAHAM HWY

McClellanville
Village Museum

INTRACOASTAL WATERWAY

RAM HORN CREEK

CLUBHOUSE
CREEK

7

MITCHELL

Tibwin

TIBWIN CREEK

CONGAREE
BOAT CREEK

CAPE
ROMAIN
HARBOR

CAPE
ROMAIN
NATIONAL
WILDLIFE REFUGE

Whilden Rd

Buck
Hall

17
701
JAMES

Laurel Hill
Plantation

OYSTER
BAY

MUDDY
BAY

HORSE CREEK

CAPE I

RAND MCNALLY

A   B   C   D   E

SEE 174 MAP

MAP
167

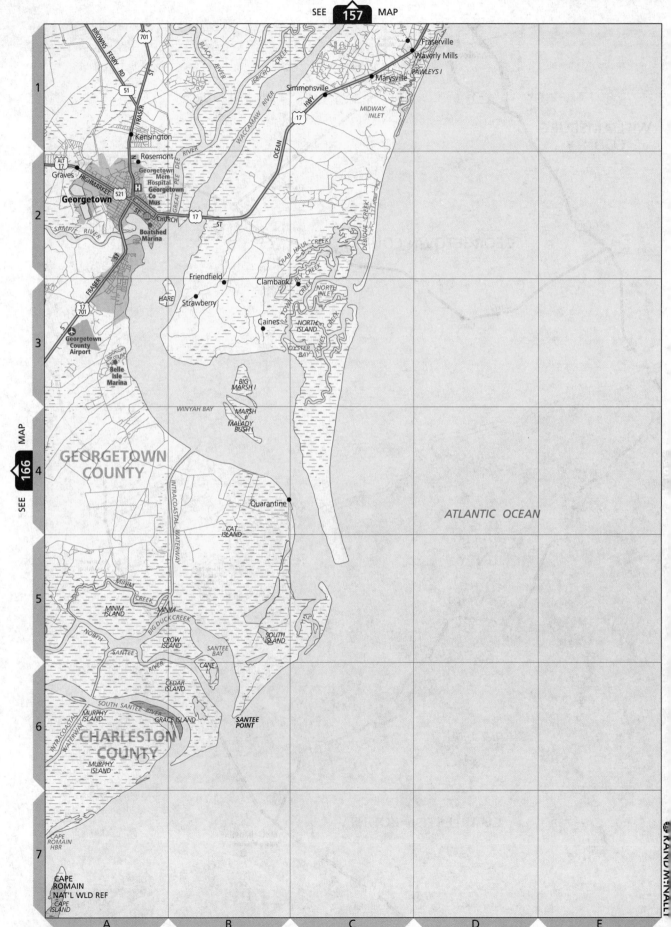

1:190,080
1 in. = 3 mi.

0   2   4
miles

N

SEE **166** **MAP**

701

51

FRASER ST

BROWNS FERRY RD

Kensington

Rosemont

ALT 17

Graves

HIGHMARKET

521

Georgetown

H

Georgetown
Mem
Hospital
Georgetown
Co
Mus

CHURCH ST

Boatshed
Marina

SAMPIT RIVER

FRASER ST

17
701

Georgetown
County
Airport

Belle
Isle
Marina

HARE I

Friendfield

Strawberry

Caines

WINYAH BAY

BIG
MARSH I

MARSH
I
MALADY
BUSH I

**GEORGETOWN
COUNTY**

INTRACOASTAL WATERWAY

Quarantine

CAT
ISLAND

BLACK RIVER

JERICHO CREEK

WACCAMAW RIVER

GREAT PEE DEE RIVER

OCEAN

Simmonsville

17

HWY

MIDWAY
INLET

Marysville

Fraserville

Waverly Mills

PAWLEYS I

CRAB HAUL CREEK

DEBIDUE CREEK

TOWN CREEK

BLY CREEK

Clambank

NORTH
INLET

NORTH
ISLAND

OYSTER
BAY

JONES CREEK

ATLANTIC   OCEAN

MINIM
CREEK

MINIM
ISLAND

MINIM

NORTH SANTEE

BIG DUCK CREEK

CROW
ISLAND

SANTEE
BAY

SOUTH
ISLAND

SANTEE RIVER

CANE I

CEDAR
ISLAND

SOUTH SANTEE RIVER

MURPHY
ISLAND

GRACE ISLAND

SANTEE
POINT

**CHARLESTON
COUNTY**

INTRACOASTAL WATERWAY

MURPHY
ISLAND

CAPE
ROMAIN
HBR

CAPE
ROMAIN
NAT'L WLD REF

CAPE
ISLAND

1

2

3

4

5

6

7

A   B   C   D   E

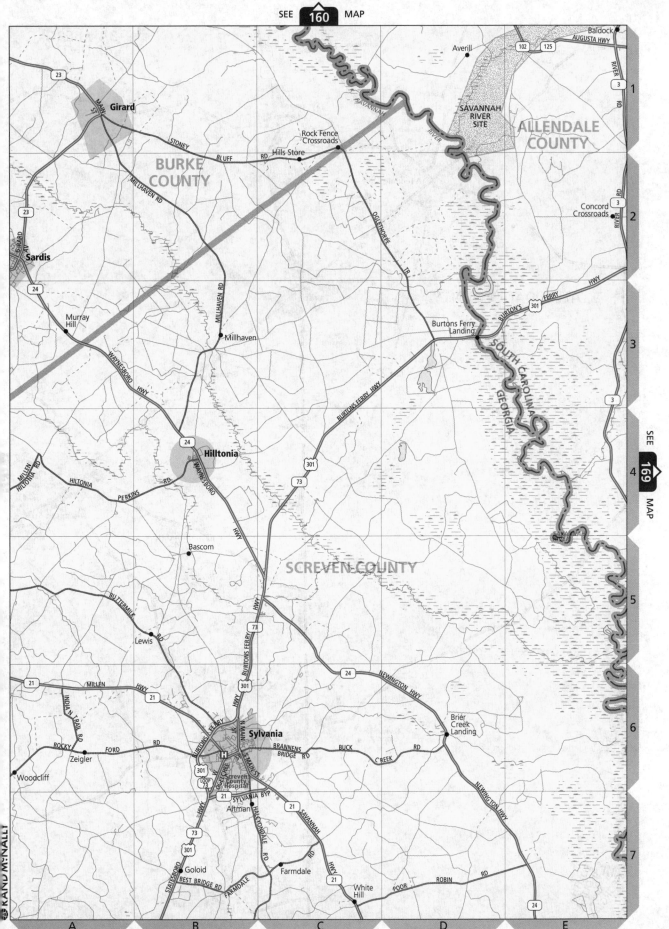

MAP
168

REGIONAL MAP

1:190,080
1 in. = 3 mi.

0   2   4
miles

SEE **160** MAP

Baldock
AUGUSTA HWY
102 125
RIVER RD
3

SAVANNAH RIVER SITE

Averill

ALLENDALE COUNTY

23

Girard

STONEY

BLUFF RD

Rock Fence Crossroads

Hills Store

BURKE COUNTY

MILLHAVEN RD

23

RIVER RD

3

Concord Crossroads

2

Girard

Sardis

24

Murray Hill

MILLHAVEN RD

WAYNESBORO HWY

Millhaven

OGLETHORPE TR

BURTONS FERRY HWY

Burtons Ferry Landing

BURTON'S FERRY

301

SOUTH CAROLINA

GEORGIA

3

3

MILLEN HILLTONIA RD

HILTONIA

PERKINS RD

24

Hilltonia

WAYNESBORO HWY

301

73

SEE **169** MAP

4

Bascom

SCREVEN COUNTY

5

BUTTERMILK RD

Lewis

BURTONS FERRY HWY

73

21

MILLEN HWY

21

INDIAN TRAIL RD

ROCKY FORD RD

Zeigler

Woodcliff

BURTONS FERRY HWY

301

Sylvania

H

Screven County Hospital

301

LOOP 73

21

SYLVANIA BYP

Altman

HACKONDALE RD

21

NEWINGTON HWY

24

Brier Creek Landing

BRANNENS BRIDGE RD

BUCK CREEK RD

6

NEWINGTON HWY

73

301

Goloid

STATESBORO RD

BEST BRIDGE RD

FARMDALE RD

Farmdale

SAVANNAH HWY

21

White Hill

POOR

ROBIN RD

24

7

RAND McNALLY

A   B   C   D   E

MAP
169

REGIONAL MAP

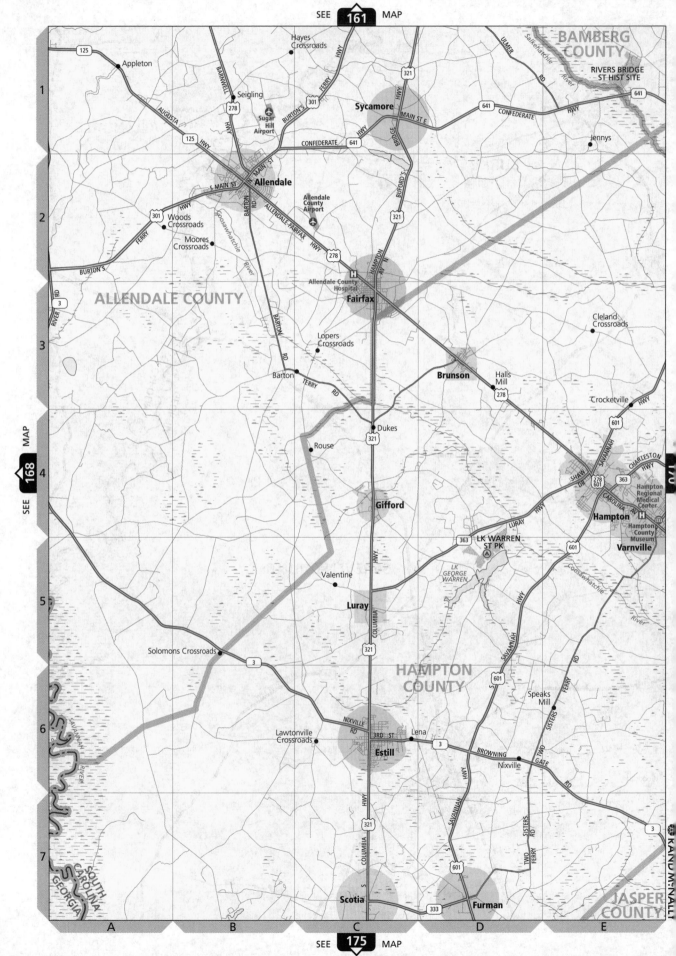

1:190,080
1 in. = 3 mi.

0   2   4
miles

N

BAMBERG COUNTY

RIVERS BRIDGE ST HIST SITE

125
Appleton

Hayes Crossroads

Seigling

278

Sugar Hill Airport

301
BURTON'S FERRY HWY

Sycamore

641

CONFEDERATE

Jennys

641

125 HWY

AUGUSTA HWY

BARNWELL HWY

S MAIN ST

N MAIN ST

Allendale

321

MAIN ST E

BRIDGE

CONFEDERATE

641

301
Woods Crossroads

Moores Crossroads

BARTON RD

Allendale County Airport

321

BUFORD'S

FERRY

Coosawhatchie River

ALLENDALE-FAIRFAX HWY

278

RIVER RD

3

BURTON'S

ALLENDALE COUNTY

BARTON RD

Allendale County Hospital

H

HAMPTON AV N

Fairfax

Cleland Crossroads

Lopers Crossroads

Barton

TERRY RD

Brunson

Halls Mill

278

Crocketville

HWY

601

Dukes

321

Rouse

SHAW DR

SAVANNAH

278
601

CHARLESTON HWY

363

Hampton Regional Medical Center

170

RAND McNALLY

SEE **168** MAP

Gifford

363

LK WARREN ST PK

LK GEORGE WARREN

LURAY HWY

601

Hampton

H

Hampton County Museum

CAROLINA AV

Varnville

Valentine

Luray

COLUMBIA HWY

321

SAVANNAH HWY

Coosawhatchie River

Solomons Crossroads

3

HAMPTON COUNTY

601

Speaks Mill

SISTERS FERRY RD

SAVANNAH

SAVANNAH RD

Lawtonville Crossroads

NIXVILLE RD

3RD ST

Estill

Lena

3

BROWNING

Nixville

TWO GATE RD

321

COLUMBIA HWY

601

SISTERS FERRY RD

TWO GATE RD

3

SOUTH CAROLINA

GEORGIA

Scotia

333

Furman

601

JASPER COUNTY

A   B   C   D   E

MAP
170

REGIONAL MAP

1:190,080
1 in. = 3 mi.

0   2   4
miles

N

SEE 162 MAP

BAMBERG COUNTY

601

BROXTON BRIDGE RD

64
Lodge

LODGE HWY
217
Padgetts

BELLS HWY

21

641

CONFEDERATE HWY 641

601

64
Caldwell

362
LUMBER DR
LUMBER RD
Colleton

212
GEORGE WARREN RD

Williams

Ashton

64

212

BROXTON BRIDGE HWY

Moselle

601

Salkehatchie River

BELLS HWY

WILLIAMS RD

Little Salkehatchie River

Bells Crossroads

21

64

Ruffin

Ashepoo River

SAVANNAH HWY

OLD SALKEHATCHIE HWY

21

Hudsons Mill

COLLETON COUNTY

CHARLESTON HWY

363

63

63
Tobys Bluff

WALTERBORO HWY

SNIDERS HWY

63

SNIDERS HWY

63

Varnville

OLD SALKEHATCHIE HWY

Sniders Crossroads

21

SEE 171 MAP

278

Almeda

Camp Branch

YEMASSEE HWY

HAMPTON COUNTY

Salkehatchie River

LOW COUNTRY HWY

21

95

Cummings

68
Fechtig

GRAYS HWY

Coosawhatchie River

278

GRAYS HWY

OLD SALKEHATCHIE HWY

42

ALT 17

Horsegall

YEMASSEE HWY

95

Jonesville

HENDERSONVILLE HWY

Davidson

EDISTO RIVER

ALT 17

21

Salkehatchie

Blake

JASPER COUNTY

Barkersville

38

SALKEHATCHIE RD

ACE BASIN NAT'L WLD REF

3

McPhersonville

68
Yemassee

21

CASTLE HALL RD

RIVER

Possum Corner

278

Tuliffiny River

95

ALT 17

Grays

BEAUFORT COUNTY

A   B   C   D   E

SEE 176 MAP

MAP
171

REGIONAL MAP

1:190,080
1 in. = 3 mi.

0   2   4
miles

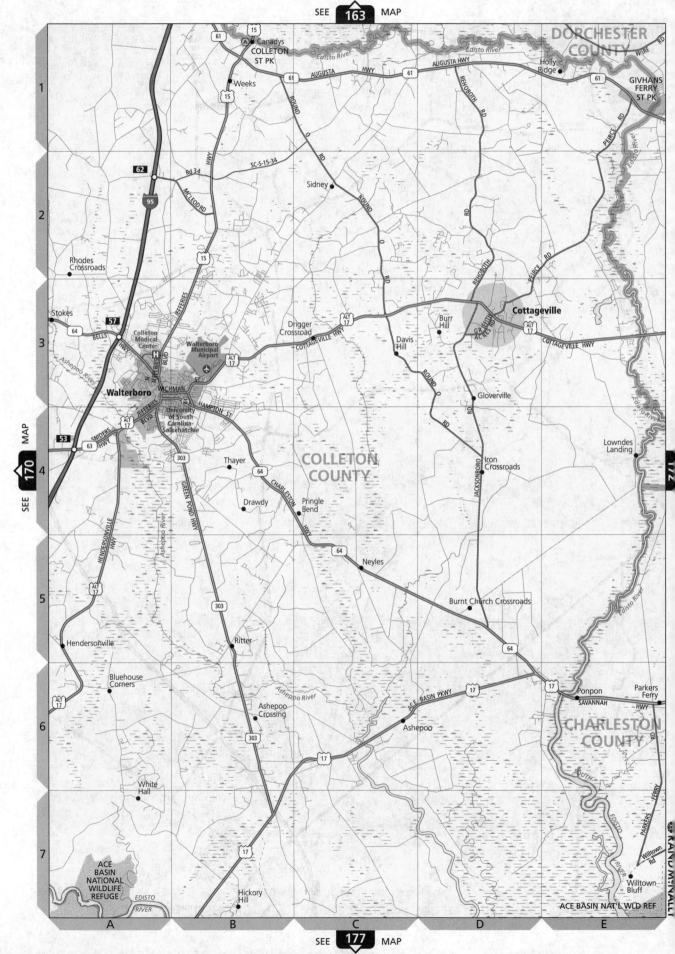

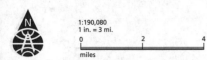

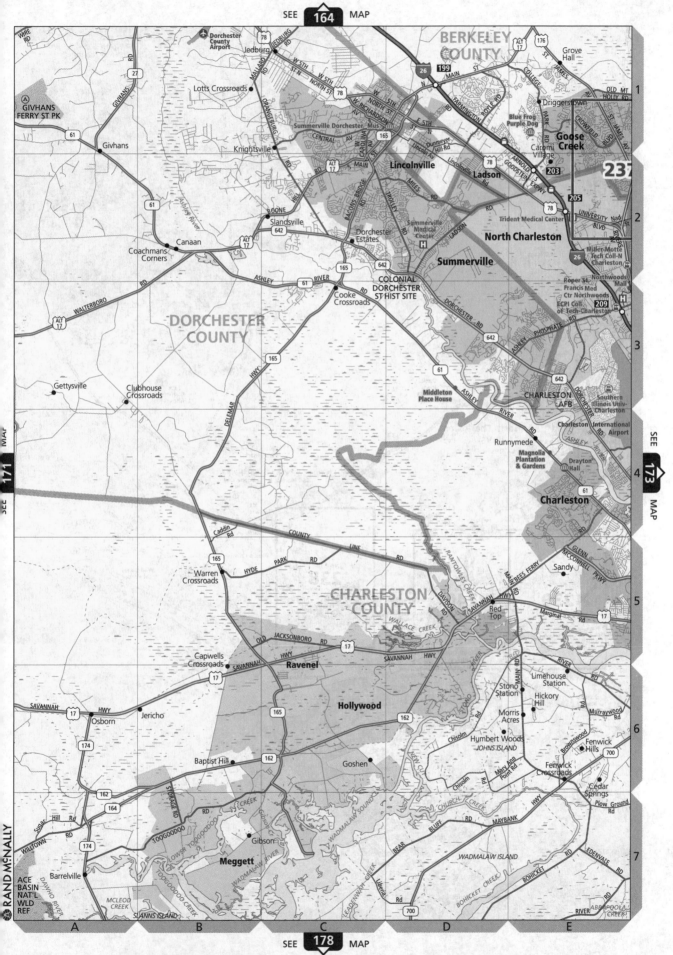

MAP
172

REGIONAL MAP

N

1:190,080
1 in. = 3 mi.

0   2   4
miles

SEE **164** MAP

BERKELEY
COUNTY

WIRE
RD

Dorchester
County
Airport

Jedburg

HEDBURG

78

W 5TH
ST N

MALLARD RD

W 5TH

NORTH ST

W RICHARDSON

I-26

199
MAIN
N

176

ALT
17

Grove
Hall

ST
JAMES
ST

College
ST

Old Mt
Holly Rd

27

Lotts Crossroads

78

NORTH ST
AV

CENTRAL AV

W
N CAROLINA

Summerville Dorchester Mus

78

FARMINGTON

ROYLE RD

PARK

Driggerstown

1

CROWFIELD
BLVD

ST JAMES AV

Blue Frog
Purple Dog

**Goose
Creek**

61

Givhans

GIVHANS RD

Knightsville

ORANGEBURG RD

E 5TH

165

ALT
17

Caromi
Village

GOODSTEIN

ARNOLD

78

203

205

237

61

BOONE
HILL RD

642

Slandsville

BACONS BRIDGE RD

THROLLEY RD

MILES RD

Lincolnville Rd

LADSON RD

78

Trident Medical Center

UNIVERSITY
BLVD

Nad
St

2

Lincolnville

Ladson

26

Miller-Motte
Tech Coll-N
Charleston

Dorchester
Estates

Summerville
Medical
Center
H

North Charleston

Northwoods
Mall

GIVHANS FERRY ST PK

Coachmans
Corners

Canaan

642

ALT
17

165

642

Summerville

Roper St
Francis Med
Ctr Northwoods
ECPI Coll
of Tech-Charleston

209
H

ASHLEY

RIVER

61

ASHLEY RIVER RD

COLONIAL
DORCHESTER
ST HIST SITE

Cooke
Crossroads

DORCHESTER RD

642

ASHLEY PHOSPHATE RD

3

**DORCHESTER
COUNTY**

165

61

Middleton
Place House

642

**CHARLESTON
AFB**

DORCHESTER RD

Southern
Illinois Univ-
Charleston

Gettysville

Clubhouse
Crossroads

DELMAR RD

ASHLEY

RIVER

Runnymede

Magnolia
Plantation
& Gardens

Charleston
International
Airport

ASHLEY RIVER RD

SEE **173** MAP

4

Drayton
Hall

61

Charleston

Caddin
Rd

COUNTY

HYDE PARK RD

LINE

RD

RANTOWLES CREEK

GLENN MCCONNELL PKWY

Sandy

5

165

Warren
Crossroads

DAVRON RD

SAVANNAH HWY

BEES FERRY RD

MAIN RD

Red
Top

Marginal Rd

17

**CHARLESTON
COUNTY**

WALLACE CREEK

OLD JACKSONBORO RD

17

SAVANNAH HWY

STONO RIVER

Limehouse
Station

Stono
Station

RIVER

Capwells
Crossroads

SAVANNAH HWY

Ravenel

162

Hickory
Hill

MAIN RD

Murraywood
Rd

6

SAVANNAH

HWY

17

Osborn

Jericho

165

Hollywood

162

Morris
Acres

Humbert Woods

JOHNS ISLAND

CHISOLM RD

Brownswood
Rd

Fenwick
Hills

700

174

Baptist Hill

162

Goshen

NEW CUT

Mary Ann
Point Rd

Fenwick
Crossroads

162

164

STORAGE RD

TOOGOODOO RD

CREEK

Gibson

CHISOLM RD

CHURCH CREEK

Cedar
Springs

Plow Ground
Rd

Sugar
Hill Rd

174

WILLTOWN RD

LOWER TOOGOODOO CREEK

Meggett

WADMALAW SOUND

BLUFF RD

BEAR RD

MAYBANK HWY

EDENVALE RD

7

WADMALAW ISLAND

ACE
BASIN
NAT'L
WLD
REF

Barrelville

DAWHO RIVER

MCLEOD
CREEK

SLANNS ISLAND

TOOGOODOO CREEK

LEADENWAH CREEK

Liberia
Rd

700

BOHICKET CREEK

ABBAPOOLA
CREEK

BOHICKET RIVER

A   B   C   D   E

SEE **178** MAP

MAP
173

SEE 165 MAP

REGIONAL MAP

N

1

Pine Grove

Hagan

Woodland

Old Joe

FRANCIS MARION NATIONAL FOREST

Green Bay

2

Goose Creek

BERKELEY COUNTY

Moreland

Charity

CHARLESTON COUNTY

US NAVAL RESERVATION

City Colleges of Chicago

Hanahan

Voorhees College-North Charleston

Trident Technical College

Highland Park

Berkeley Hills

Belvedere Estates

The Farms

US AIRFORCE RESERVATION

US ARMY DEPOT

COOPER RIVER

Daniel Island Marina Village

Wando

Cainhoy

Woodville

Awendaw

Mt Pleasant

East Cooper Airport

Chandler

Ten Mile

3

Charleston International Airport

Webster Univ-Charleston

North Charleston

US NAVAL RESERVATION

MONTAGUE AV

CLARK EXPWY

Whitehall Terrace

4

North Charleston Col

Charleston Area Convention Ctr Complex

Southern Wesleyan University Charleston

CHARLESTON NAVAL COMPLEX

Dolphin Cove Marina

CHARLES PICKNEY NAT'L HIST SITE

K&B Marina

Boone Hall Plantation

Splash Island Waterpark

Mt Pleasant Towne Ctr

Wando Crossing

COPAHEE SOUND

CAPERS I

DEWEES ISLAND

5

St Francis

CHARLES TOWNE LNDG ST PK

239

Art Forms & Theatre Concepts

Citadel

Johnson & Wales Univ

South Carolina Aquarium

The Citadel

Johnson Hagood Stad

Joseph P Riley Jr Pk

Charleston Mus

Gaillard Municipal Auditorium

Gibbes Mus of Art

240

East Cooper Reg Med Ctr

238

Shem Creek Marina

Vil Playhouse

PATRIOTS POINT PARK

Wild Dunes Yacht Harbor

Isle of Palms

Citadel Mall

Family Circle Tennis Center

South Carolina Ripley

Ripley Light Marina

Calhoun Mansion

CHARLESTON HARBOR

Fort Sumter National Monument

Sullivans Island

BREACH INLET

6

Stono Marina

JAMES ISLAND

HARBOR VIEW RD

Parrot Point

Oyster Point

MORRIS ISLAND

ATLANTIC OCEAN

7

Charleston Executive Airport

Miller Hill

Riverland

Fort Lamar Historic Site

FT LAMAR HERITAGE PRES

Secessionville

Folly Beach

JOHNS ISLAND

Mariners Cay Marina

RAND McNALLY

SEE 179 MAP

A   B   C   D   E

1:190,080
1 in. = 3 mi.

0   2   4
miles

MAP
174

REGIONAL MAP

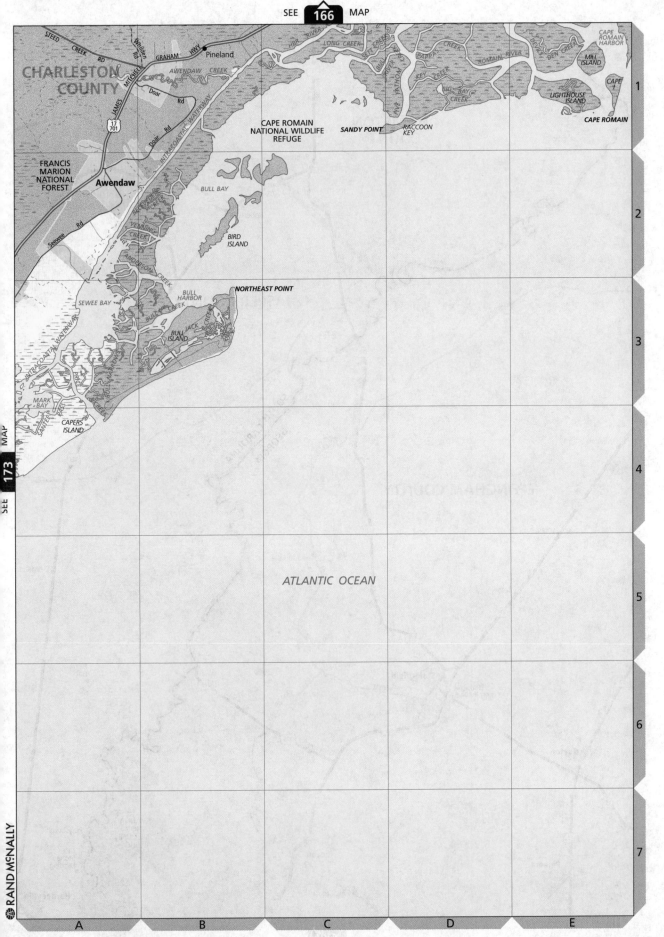

SEE **166** MAP

**CHARLESTON
COUNTY**

STEED CREEK RD

Whilden Rd

GRAHAM HWY

Pineland

JAMES MITCHELL

Doar Rd

17 701

AWENDAW CREEK

Doar Rd

INTRACOASTAL WATERWAY

CAPE ROMAIN
NATIONAL WILDLIFE
REFUGE

HBR RIVER

LONG CREEK

SEE CREEK

FIVE FATHOM CREEK

KEY CREEK

BULL CREEK

ROMAIN RIVER

RAPPEL CREEK

DEN CREEK

CAPE
ROMAIN
HARBOR

MILL
ISLAND

CAPE
1

LIGHTHOUSE
ISLAND

CAPE ROMAIN

SANDY POINT

RACCOON
KEY

BIG
BAY
CREEK

**FRANCIS
MARION
NATIONAL
FOREST**

Awendaw

BETHERA CREEK

Sewee Rd

VENNING CREEK

ANDERSON CREEK

BULL BAY

BIRD
ISLAND

NORTHEAST POINT

BULL
HARBOR

BULL CREEK

JACK CREEK

SEWEE BAY

BULL ISLAND

BULL NARROWS

MARK
BAY

SANTEE PASS

PRICE CREEK

CAPERS
ISLAND

INTRACOASTAL WATERWAY

1

2

3

4

5

6

7

ATLANTIC OCEAN

RAND M?NALLY

A   B   C   D   E

MAP
175

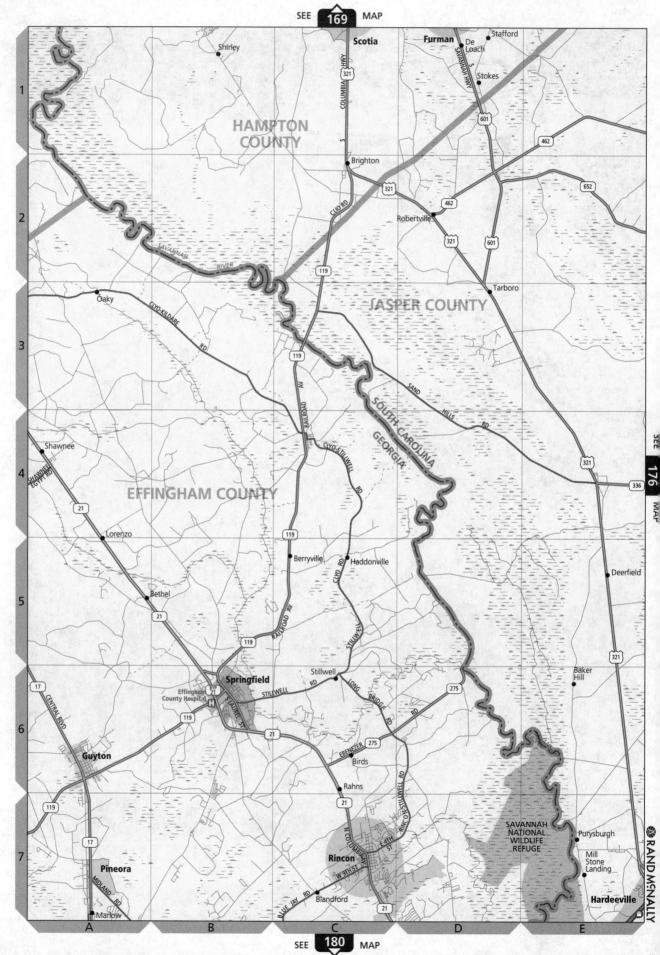

1:190,080
1 in. = 3 mi.
0   2   4
miles

SEE **169** MAP

SEE **176** MAP

RAND McNALLY

SEE **180** MAP

Shirley

Scotia

Furman
De Loach   Stafford

Stokes

HAMPTON
COUNTY

321

COLUMBIA HWY

601

462

652

Brighton

321

CLIO RD

462

601

Robertville

321

119

Tarboro

JASPER COUNTY

Oaky

CLYO-KILDARE
RD

119

SAND
HILLS
RD

321

RAILROAD AV

SOUTH CAROLINA
GEORGIA

336

Shawnee

CLYO-STILLWELL
RD

SHAWNEE EGYPT RD

EFFINGHAM COUNTY

21

Deerfield

Lorenzo

119

Berryville   Haddonville

CLYO RD

Bethel

RAILROAD AV

17

21

STILLWELL

Baker
Hill

321

119

Stillwell   LONG BRIDGE RD   275

Springfield

Effingham
County Hospital
H

BYP
21

STILLWELL RD

EBENEZER RD

275

119

21

275

CENTRAL BLVD

S LAUREL ST

Birds

Guyton

Rahns

21

119

N COLUMBIA HWY

RINCON-STILLWELL RD

E 4TH ST

SAVANNAH
NATIONAL
WILDLIFE
REFUGE

Purysburgh

17

Rincon

W 9TH ST

Mill
Stone
Landing

Pineora

MIDLAND RD

BLUE JAY RD   Blandford

21

Hardeeville

Marlow

A   B   C   D   E

SAVANNAH   RIVER

MAP
176

REGIONAL MAP

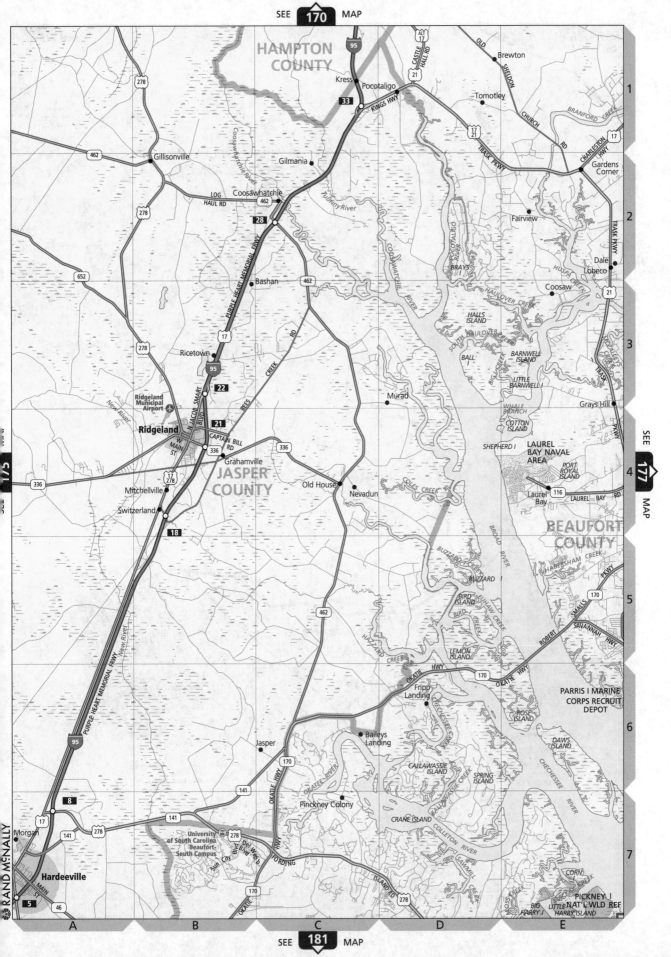

SEE **170** MAP

1:190,080
1 in. = 3 mi.

0   2   4
miles

HAMPTON
COUNTY

ALT 17

OLD

Brewton

95

CASTLE HALL RD

SHELDON

Kress

Pocotaligo

21

Tomotley

BRANFORD CREEK

33

KINGS HWY

CHURCH

1

462

Gillisonville

Gilmania

TRASK PKWY

17 21

Gardens
Corner

17

CHARLESTON HWY

Coosawhatchie River

LOG HAUL RD

Coosawhatchie

462

Fairview

TRASK PKWY

2

278

28

Tulifiny River

PURPLE HEART MEMORIAL PKWY

BRAYS

Dale
Lobeco

21

652

462

Bashan

Coosaw

HUSPA CREEK

COOSAWHATCHIE RIVER

HAULOVER CREEK

HALLS
ISLAND

278

CREEK RD

17

Ricetown

HAULOVER CREEK

BIG CREEK

SOUTH CREEK

BALL I

BARNWELL
ISLAND

LITTLE
BARNWELL I

3

95

New River

22

BEES CREEK

Murad

Grays Hill

TRASK PKWY

Ridgeland
Municipal
Airport

N JACOB SMART BLVD

WHALE BRANCH

COTTON
ISLAND

Ridgeland

21

CAPTAIN BILL RD

SHEPHERD I

LAUREL
BAY NAVAL
AREA

SEE

W MAIN ST

336

Grahamville

336

Old House

PORT
ROYAL
ISLAND

177

JASPER
COUNTY

Nevadun

Laurel
Bay

116

LAUREL BAY RD

MAP

336

17 278

Mitchellville

COLES CREEK

BROAD RIVER

BEAUFORT
COUNTY

4

Switzerland

HABERSHAM CREEK

18

BUZZARD CREEK

PKWY

PURPLE HEART MEMORIAL HWY

New River

462

BIRD
ISLAND

BUZZARD I

BIRD CREEK

RUHAW CREEK

ROBERT SMALLS PKWY

SAVANNAH HWY

170

5

HAZZARD CREEK

LEMON
ISLAND

OKATIE HWY

170

OKATIE HWY

PARRIS I MARINE
CORPS RECRUIT
DEPOT

95

Fripp
Landing

CHECHESSEE CREEK

ROSE
ISLAND

DAWS
ISLAND

6

8

Jasper

Baileys
Landing

170

CALLAWASSIE
ISLAND

SPRING
ISLAND

CHECHESSEE RIVER

141

OKATIE HWY

OKATIE RIVER

CALLAWASSIE CREEK

Morgan

17

Pinckney Colony

CRANE ISLAND

141

141

278

University
of South Carolina
Beaufort-
South Campus

278

Del Webb Blvd

Sun City Blvd

COLLETON RIVER

SAWMILL CREEK

7

RAND MCNALLY

Hardeeville

OKATIE

ISLAND RD

FORDING

170

278

CORN CREEK

PICKNEY I
NAT'L WLD REF

5

46

BIG
HARRY I

LITTLE
HARRY ISLAND

A   B   C   D   E

SEE **181** MAP

MAP
177

REGIONAL MAP

1:190,080
1 in. = 3 mi.

0   2   4
miles

SEE 171 MAP

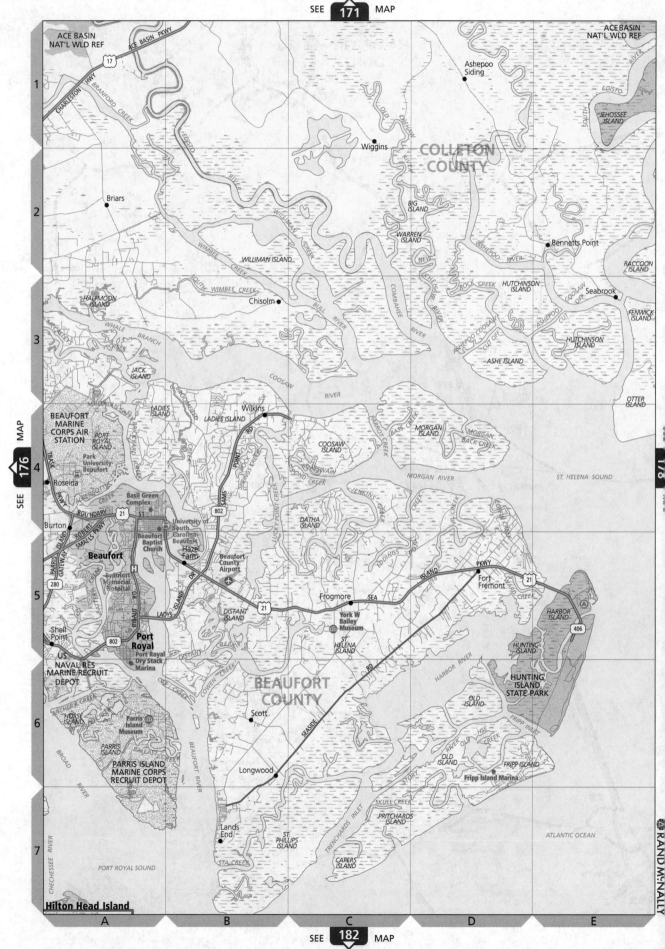

ACE BASIN
NAT'L WLD REF

ACE BASIN
NAT'L WLD REF

**COLLETON
COUNTY**

Ashepoo
Siding

Wiggins

Briars

BIG
ISLAND

WARREN
ISLAND

Bennetts Point

RACCOON
ISLAND

Chisolm

HUTCHINSON
ISLAND

Seabrook

FENWICK
ISLAND

HALFMOON
ISLAND

HUTCHINSON
ISLAND

ASHE ISLAND

OTTER
ISLAND

JACK
ISLAND

COOSAW
RIVER

Wilkins

BEAUFORT
MARINE
CORPS AIR
STATION

LADIES
ISLAND

LADIES ISLAND

COOSAW
ISLAND

MORGAN
ISLAND

MORGAN
ISLAND

Park
University-
Beaufort

ST. HELENA SOUND

Roseida

MORGAN RIVER

Basil Green
Complex

DATHA
ISLAND

Burton

University of
South
Carolina-
Beaufort

Beaufort

Beaufort
Baptist Church

Hazel
Farm

Beaufort
County
Airport

Frogmore

Fort
Fremont

Beaufort
Memorial
Hospital

HARBOR
ISLAND

Shell
Point

DISTANT
ISLAND

York W
Bailey
Museum

**Port
Royal**

ST
HELENA
ISLAND

HUNTING
ISLAND

US
NAVAL RES
MARINE RECRUIT
DEPOT

Port Royal
Dry Stack
Marina

**HUNTING
ISLAND
STATE PARK**

HORSE
ISLAND

Parris
Island
Museum

**BEAUFORT
COUNTY**

OLD
ISLAND

PARRIS
ISLAND

Scott

FRIPP INLET

**PARRIS ISLAND
MARINE CORPS
RECRUIT DEPOT**

OLD
ISLAND

FRIPP ISLAND

Longwood

OLD
ISLAND

Fripp Island Marina

SKULL CREEK

PRITCHARDS
ISLAND

Lands
End

ST.
PHILLIPS
ISLAND

ATLANTIC OCEAN

PORT ROYAL SOUND

STA. CREEK

CAPERS
ISLAND

Hilton Head Island

SEE 176 MAP

SEE 182 MAP

A   B   C   D   E

RAND MCNALLY

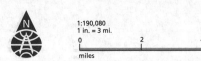

1:190,080
1 in. = 3 mi.

0   2   4
miles

MAP
178

SEE **172** MAP

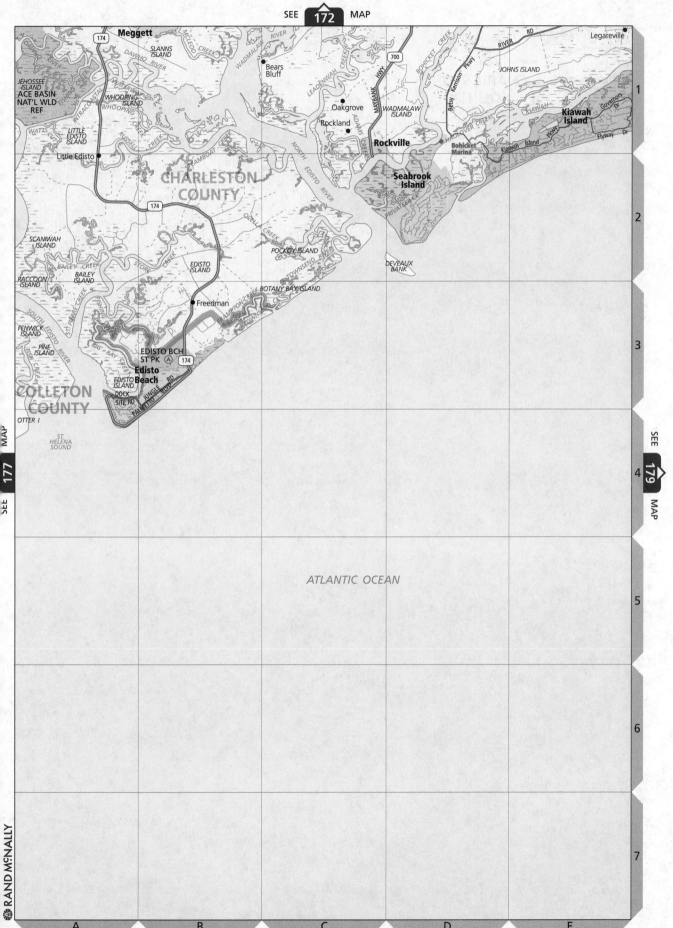

Meggett

Legareville

SLANNS
ISLAND

Bears
Bluff

JEHOSSEE
ISLAND
ACE BASIN
NAT'L WLD
REF

WHOOPING
ISLAND
WHOOPING

JOHNS ISLAND

Oakgrove

WADMALAW
ISLAND

Kiawah
Island

LITTLE
EDISTO
ISLAND

Rockland

Little Edisto

Rockville

Bohicket
Marina

Kiawah Island

Governors
Dr

**CHARLESTON
COUNTY**

Seabrook
Island

Flyway Dr

SCANIWAH
ISLAND

POCKOY ISLAND

DEVEAUX
BANK

RACCOON
ISLAND

BAILEY CREEK

BAILEY
ISLAND

EDISTO
ISLAND

BOTANY BAY ISLAND

Freedman

FENWICK
ISLAND

PINE
ISLAND

EDISTO BCH
ST PK

**Edisto
Beach**

EDISTO
ISLAND

**COLLETON
COUNTY**

DOCK
SITE RD

JUNGLE

OTTER I

ST.
HELENA
SOUND

ATLANTIC OCEAN

SEE 177 MAP

SEE 179 MAP

A   B   C   D   E

MAP
179

1:190,080
1 in. = 3 mi.

0   2   4

miles

SEE 173 MAP

JOHNS
ISLAND

SOL-LEGARE
ISLAND

FOLLY RIVER

FOLLY I

Folly Folly Marina
Beach

KIAWAH RIVER

STONO RIVER

**Kiawah
Island**

BASS CREEK

CHARLESTON
COUNTY

MAP
178
SEE

1

2

3

4

ATLANTIC OCEAN

5

6

7

A   B   C   D   E

MAP
180

REGIONAL MAP

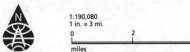

1:190,080
1 in. = 3 mi.

0   2   4
miles

SEE 175 MAP

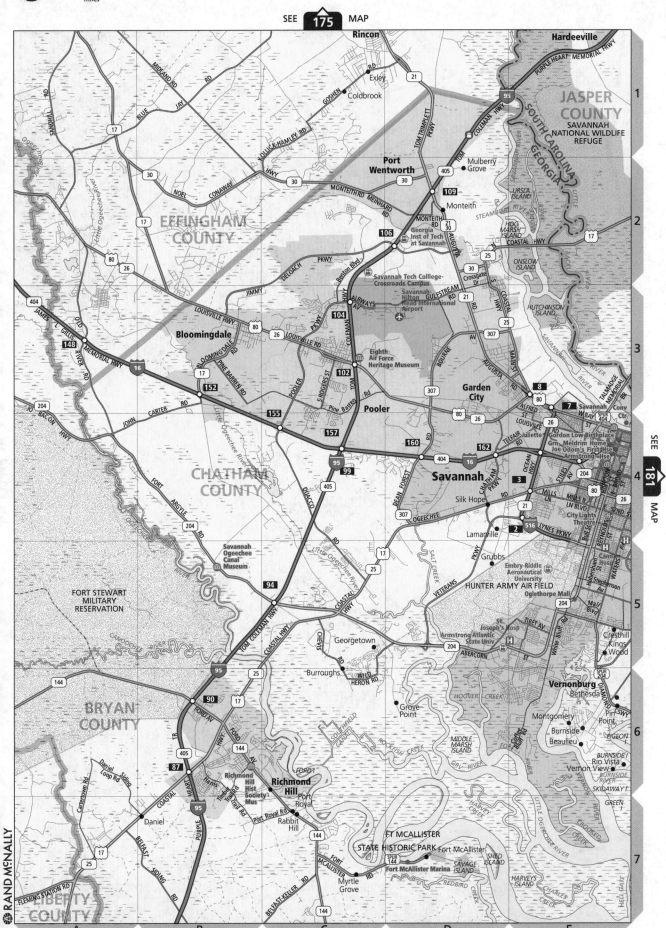

RAND M°NALLY

SEE 181 MAP

Rincon

Hardeeville

JASPER
COUNTY

SAVANNAH
NATIONAL WILDLIFE
REFUGE

Exley
Coldbrook

**Port
Wentworth**

Mulberry
Grove

Monteith

Georgia
Inst of Tech
at Savannah

EFFINGHAM
COUNTY

Savannah Tech Colllege-
Crossroads Campus

Savannah-
Hilton
Head International
Airport

Bloomingdale

Eighth
Air Force
Heritage Museum

**Garden
City**

Savannah Conv
Ctr

Gordon Low Birthplace
Grn Meldrim Home
Joe Odom's First Hse
Armstrong Hse

Pooler

Savannah

Silk Hope

CHATHAM
COUNTY

City Lights
Theatre

Lamarville

Grubbs

Embry-Riddle
Aeronautical
University

Savannah
Ogeechee
Canal
Museum

HUNTER ARMY AIR FIELD

Oglethorpe Mall

FORT STEWART
MILITARY
RESERVATION

St.
Joseph's Hosp

Armstrong Atlantic
State Univ

ABERCORN

Cresthill
Kings
Wood

Georgetown

Vernonburg
Bethesda

Burroughs

Grove
Point

Montgomery

Burnside
Beaulieu

Pin
Point

**BRYAN
COUNTY**

HOOVER CREEK

MIDDLE
MARSH
ISLAND

Rio Vista

Vernon View

Daniel Siding
Loop Rd

Richmond
Hill
Hist
Society
Mus

**Richmond
Hill**

Port
Royal

Daniel

Rabbit
Hill

FT MCALLISTER
STATE HISTORIC PARK

Fort McAllister

Fort McAllister Marina

SHED
ISLAND

SAVAGE
ISLAND

Myrtle
Grove

HARVEYS
ISLAND

MAP
181

REGIONAL MAP

1:190,080
1 in. = 3 mi.

0   2   4
miles

SEE **176** MAP

SEE **180** MAP

SEE **182** MAP

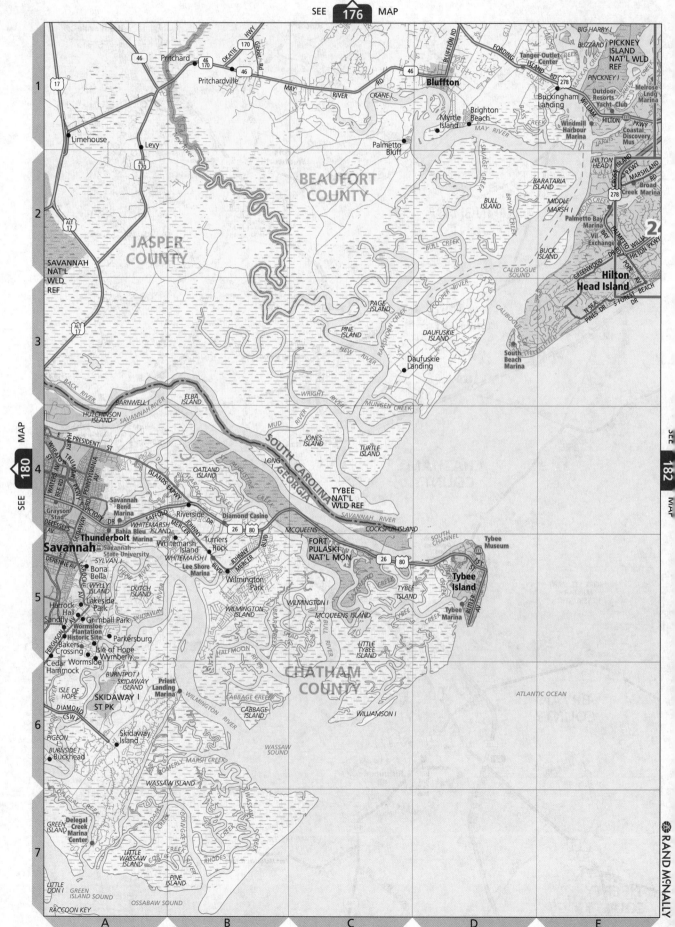

RAND McNALLY

A   B   C   D   E

MAP
182

REGIONAL MAP

1:190,080
1 in. = 3 mi.

0   2   4
miles

SEE ⌃ 177 MAP

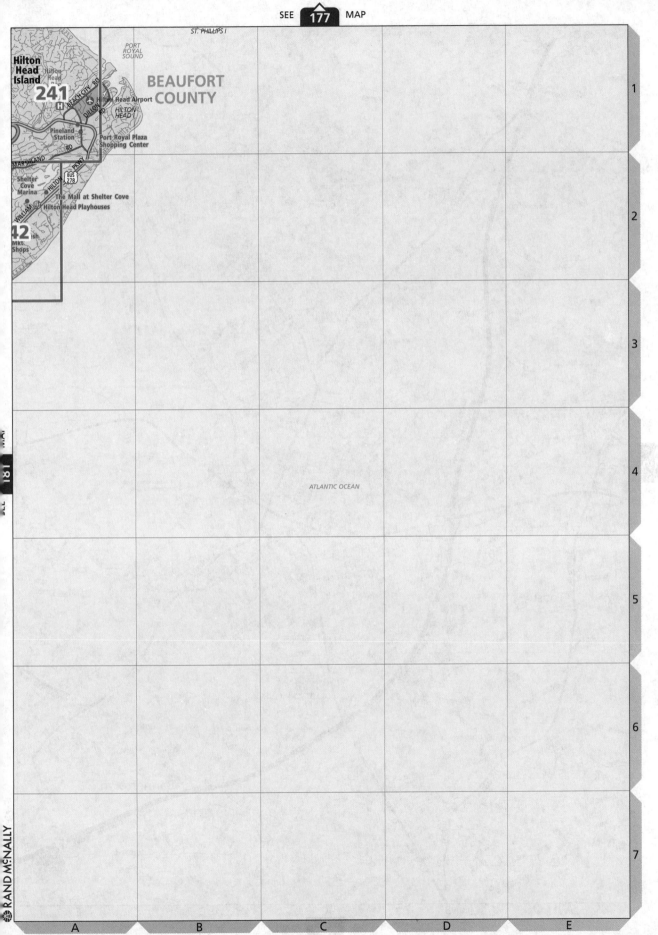

ST. PHILLIPS I

Hilton Head Island

241

PORT ROYAL SOUND

BEAUFORT COUNTY

Hilton Head Airport

HILTON HEAD

Pineland Station

Port Royal Plaza Shopping Center

MARSHLAND

Shelter Cove Marina

BUS 278

The Mall at Shelter Cove

Hilton Head Playhouses

WILLIAM

42

Mkt. Shops

ATLANTIC OCEAN

RAND M°NALLY

A   B   C   D   E

1   2   3   4   5   6   7

MAP
183

1:30,000
1 in. = 2500 ft.
0   0.25   0.5
miles

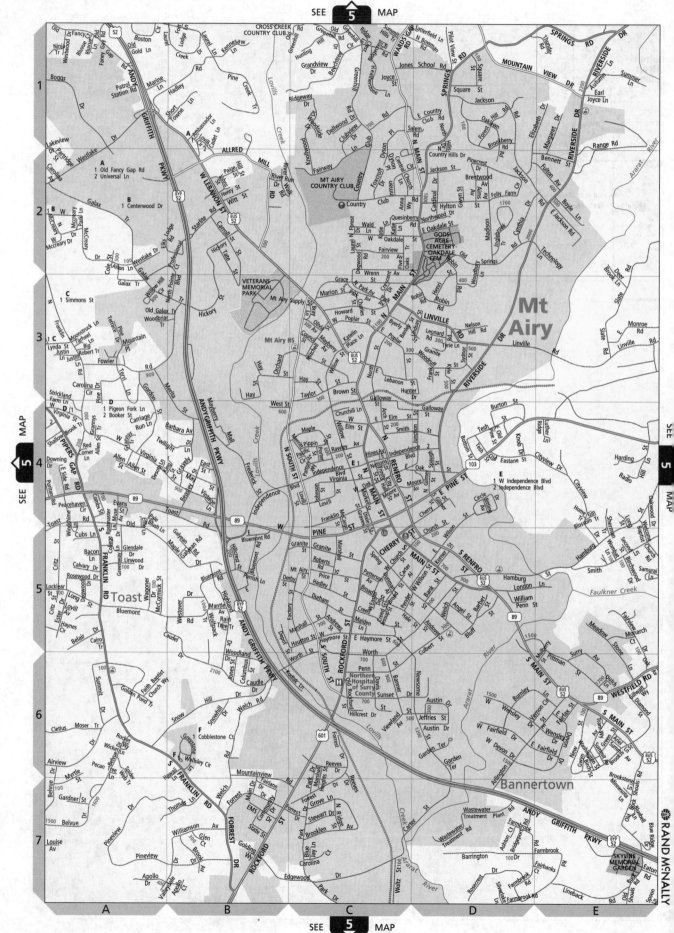

DETAIL MAP

A
1 Old Fancy Gap Rd
2 Universal Ln

B
1 Centerwood Dr

C
1 Simmons St

D
1 Pigeon Fork Ln
2 Booker St

E
1 W Independence Blvd
2 Independence Blvd

F
Cobblestone Ct

Mt Airy Country Club

Veterans Memorial Park

Mt Airy HS

Mt Airy Supply

Mt Airy

Toast

Northern Hospital of Surry County

Bannertown

Skyline Memorial Garden

RAND McNALLY

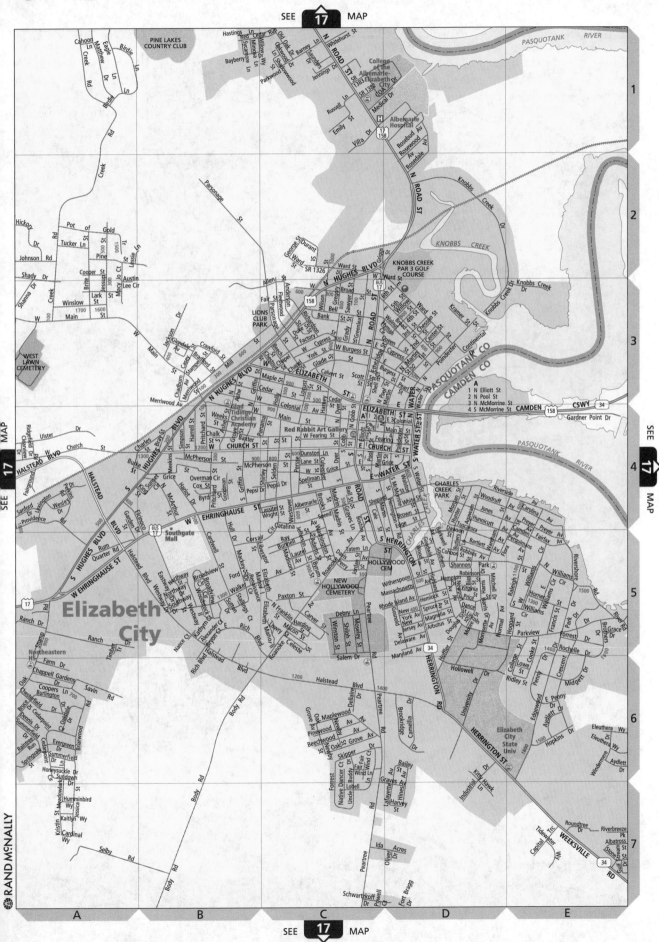

MAP
184

DETAIL MAP

1:30,000
1 in. = 2500 ft.
0   0.25   0.5
miles

SEE 17 MAP

PASQUOTANK RIVER

1

2

3

4

5

6

7

PINE LAKES
COUNTRY CLUB

Pasquotank RIVER

College of the Albemarle-
Elizabeth City

Albemarle
Hospital

KNOBBS CREEK

Knobbs Creek Dr

KNOBBS CREEK
PAR 3 GOLF
COURSE

CAMDEN CO
PASQUOTANK CO

A
1 N Elliott St
2 N Pool St
3 N McMorrine St
4 S McMorrine St

CAMDEN CSWY 34
Gardner Point Dr

WEST
LAWN
CEMETERY

LIONS
CLUB
PARK

Glad
Tidings
Christian
Academy

Red Rabbit Art Gallery
W Fearing St

ELIZABETH ST
CHURCH ST

PASQUOTANK RIVER

CHARLES
CREEK
PARK

SEE 17 MAP

HALSTEAD BLVD

Southgate
Mall

W EHRINGHAUSE ST

HUGHES BLVD

**Elizabeth
City**

Northeastern
HS

Chappell Gardens

HOLLYWOOD CEM

NEW
HOLLYWOOD
CEMETERY

HERRINGTON RD

CHARLES CREEK

Elizabeth
City
State
Univ

HERRINGTON ST

WEEKSVILLE RD

SEE 17 MAP

A   B   C   D   E

MAP
185

DETAIL MAP

1:30,000
1 in. = 2500 ft.
0   0.25   0.5
miles
N

SEE 23 MAP

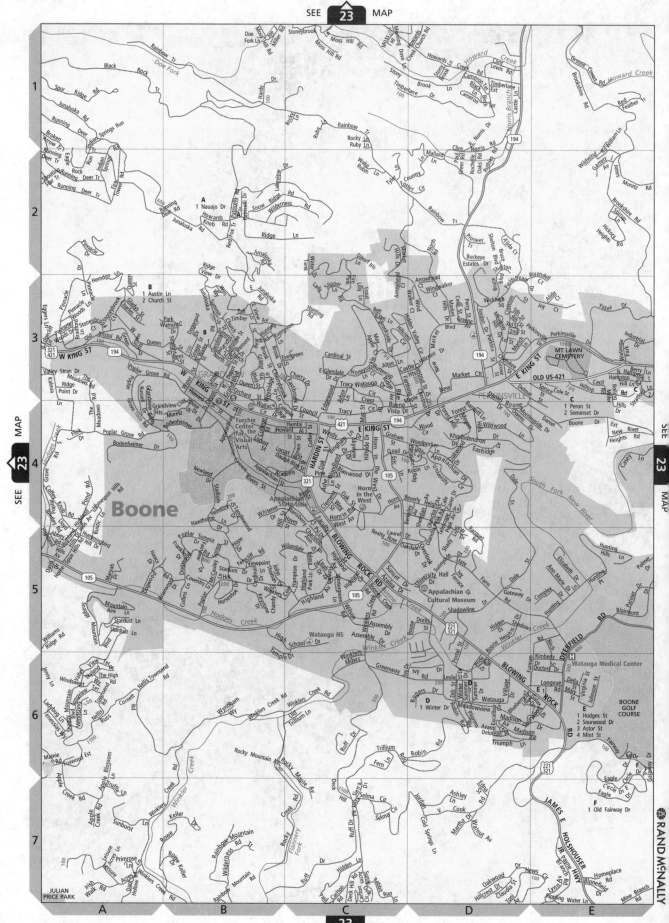

Boone

SEE 23 MAP

SEE 23 MAP

SEE 23 MAP

RAND McNALLY

A   B   C   D   E

MAP
186

DETAIL MAP

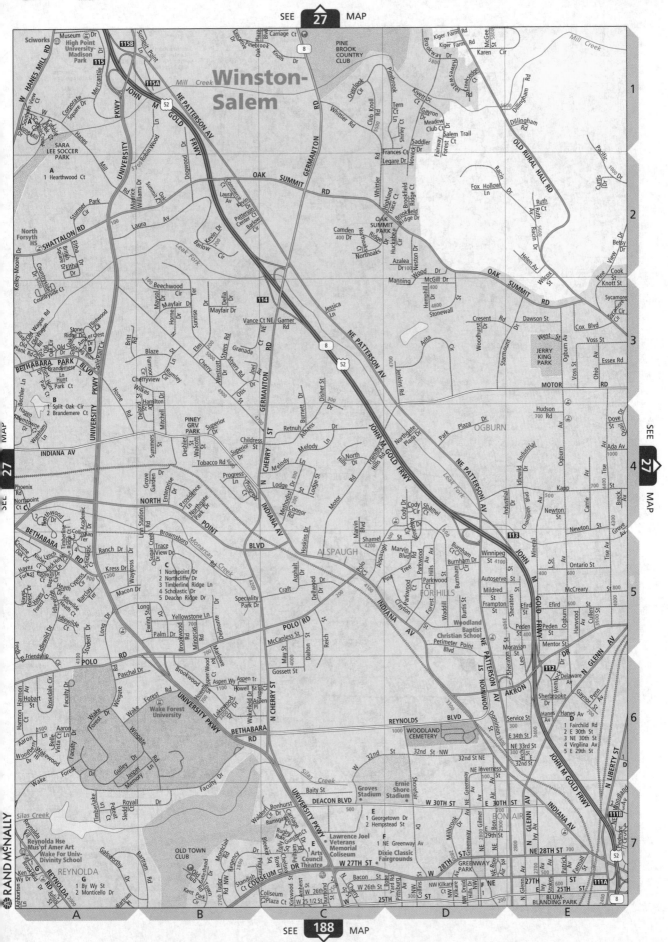

1:30,000
1 in. = 2500 ft.

0   0.25   0.5
miles

Winston-Salem

SEE **27** MAP

SEE **27** MAP

MAP
187

1:30,000
1 in. = 2500 ft.
0   0.25   0.5
miles

SEE 26 MAP

SEE 188 MAP

SEE 27 MAP

RAND McNALLY

MAP
188

DETAIL MAP

1:30,000
1 in. = 2500 ft.

0   0.25   0.5
miles

SEE 186 MAP

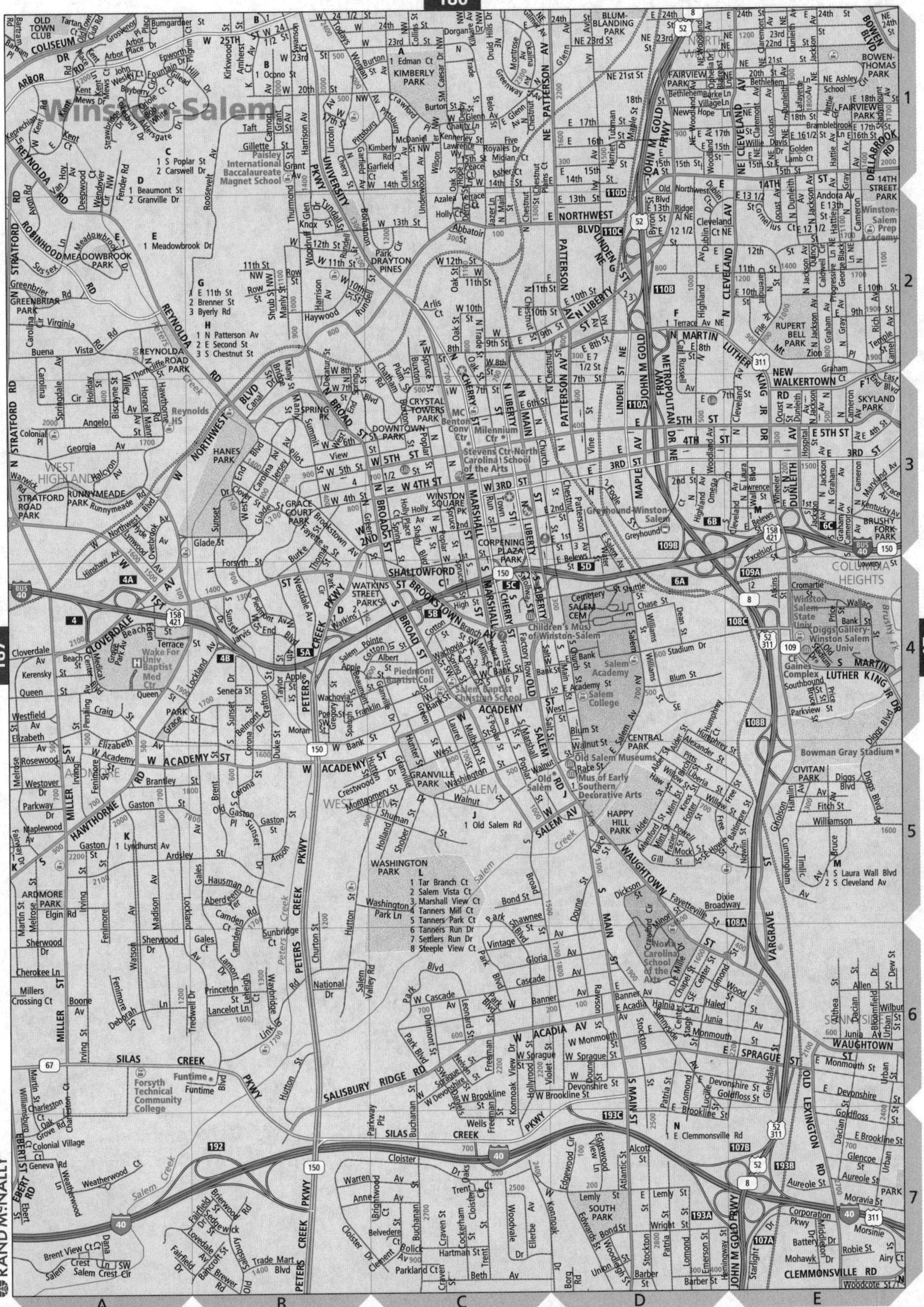

SEE 27 MAP

SEE 187 MAP

SEE 27 MAP

Winston-Salem

RAND McNALLY

MAP
189

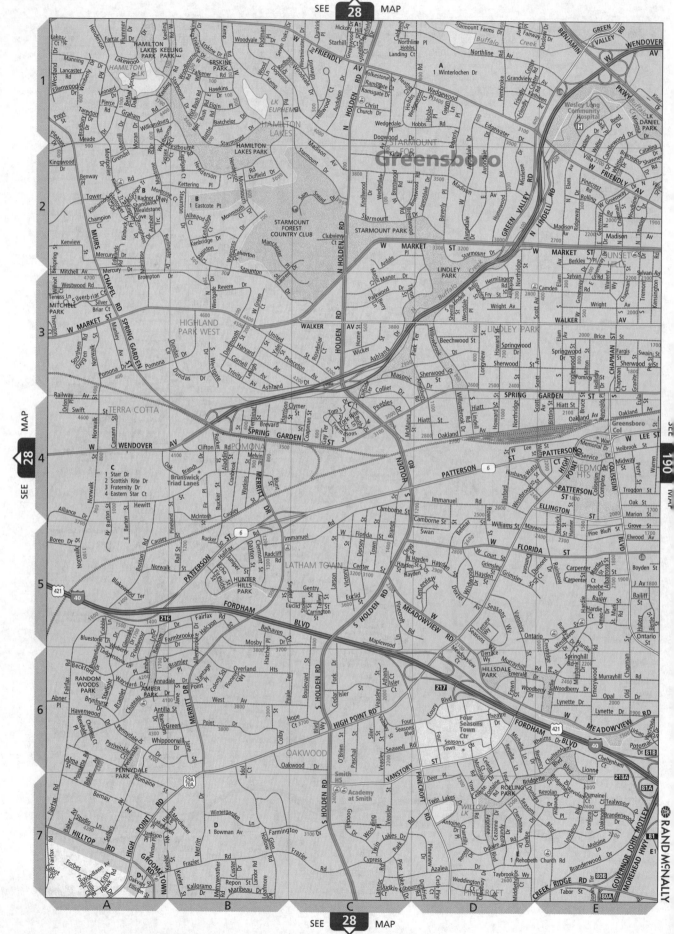

1:30,000
1 in. = 2500 ft.
0   0.25   0.5
miles

SEE 28 MAP

SEE 28 MAP

SEE 190 MAP

SEE 28 MAP

RAND McNALLY

Greensboro

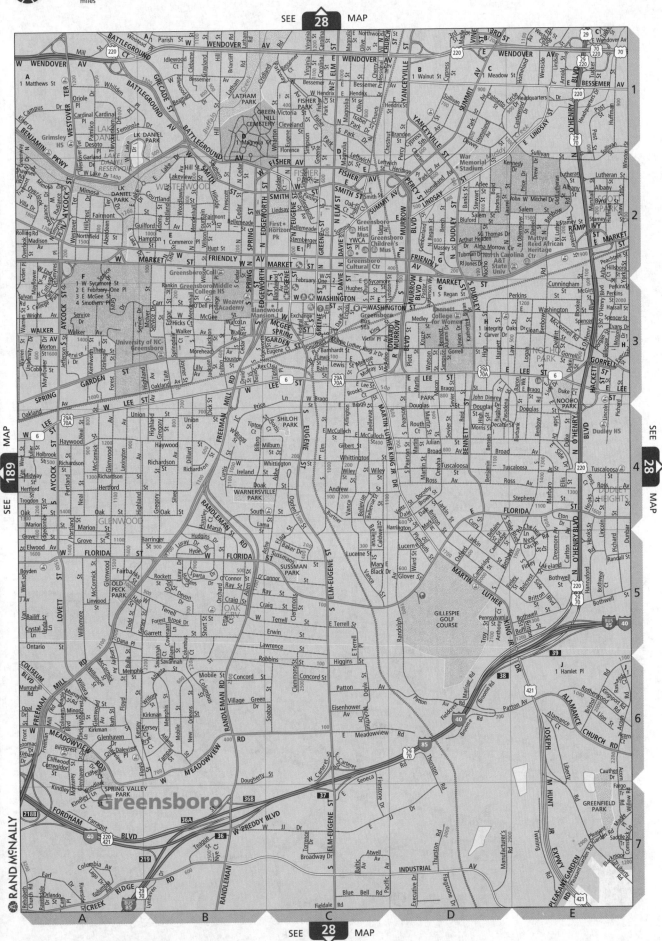

MAP
190

1:30,000
1 in. = 2500 ft.
0   0.25   0.5
miles

SEE MAP 28

DETAIL MAP

SEE 189 MAP

SEE 28 MAP

SEE 28 MAP

Greensboro

RAND McNALLY

1   2   3   4   5   6   7

A   B   C   D   E

MAP
191

DETAIL MAP

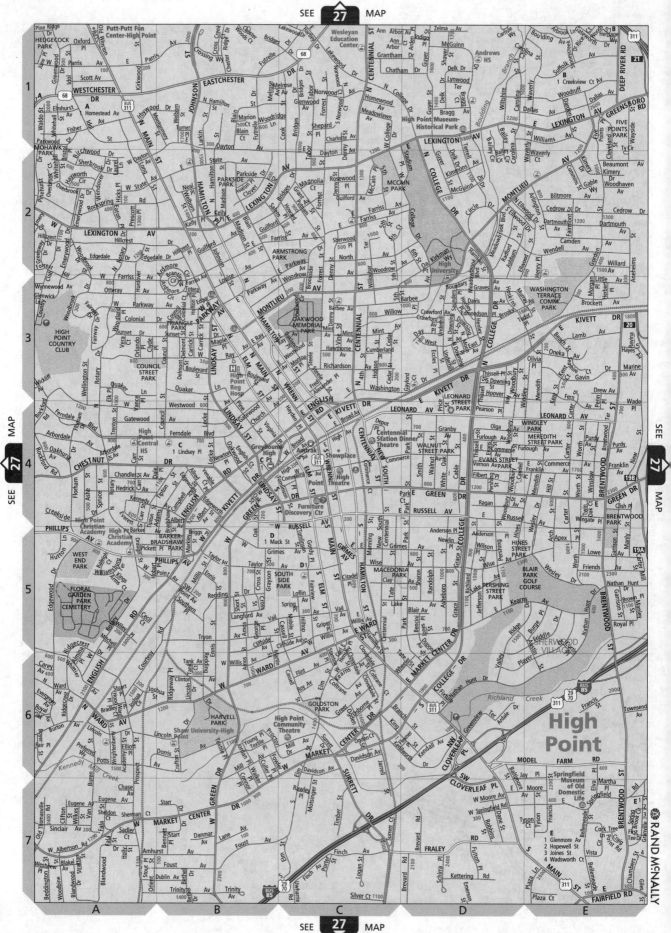

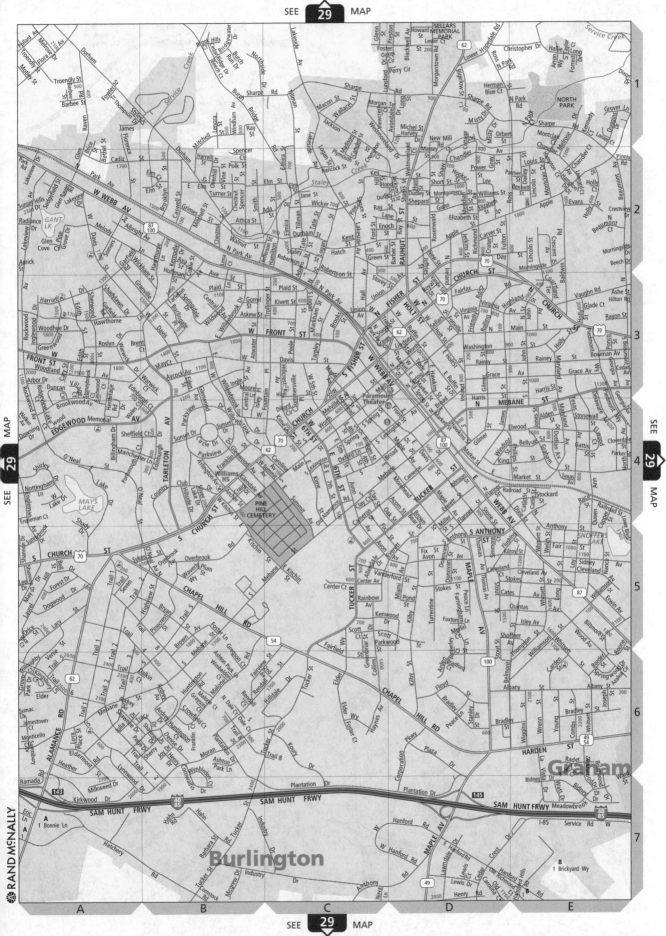

MAP
192

DETAIL MAP

1:30,000
1 in. = 2500 ft.

0   0.25   0.5
miles

SEE 29 MAP

SEE 29 MAP

Burlington

Graham

RAND McNALLY

MAP
193

1:30,000
1 in. = 2500 ft.

0   0.25   0.5
miles

SEE 30 MAP

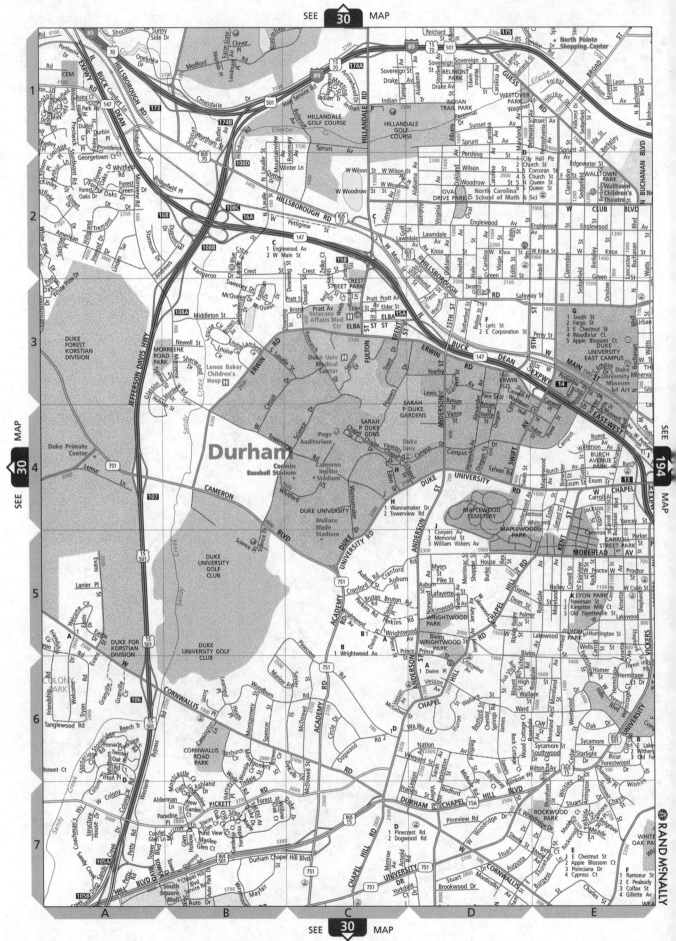

Durham

SEE 30 MAP

SEE 30 MAP

SEE 194 MAP

RAND MC NALLY

MAP
194

DETAIL MAP

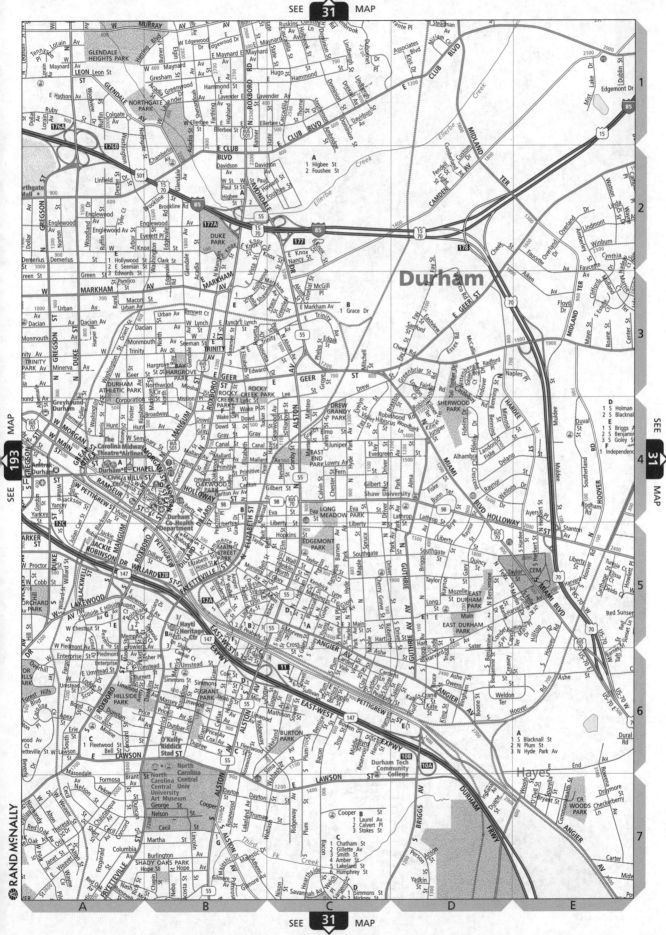

1:30,000
1 in. = 2500 ft.

0   0.25   0.5
miles

SEE 31 MAP

SEE 193 MAP

SEE 31 MAP

SEE 31 MAP

Durham

Hayes

RAND M°NALLY

MAP
195

1:30,000
1 in. = 2500 ft.
0   0.25   0.5
miles

DETAIL MAP

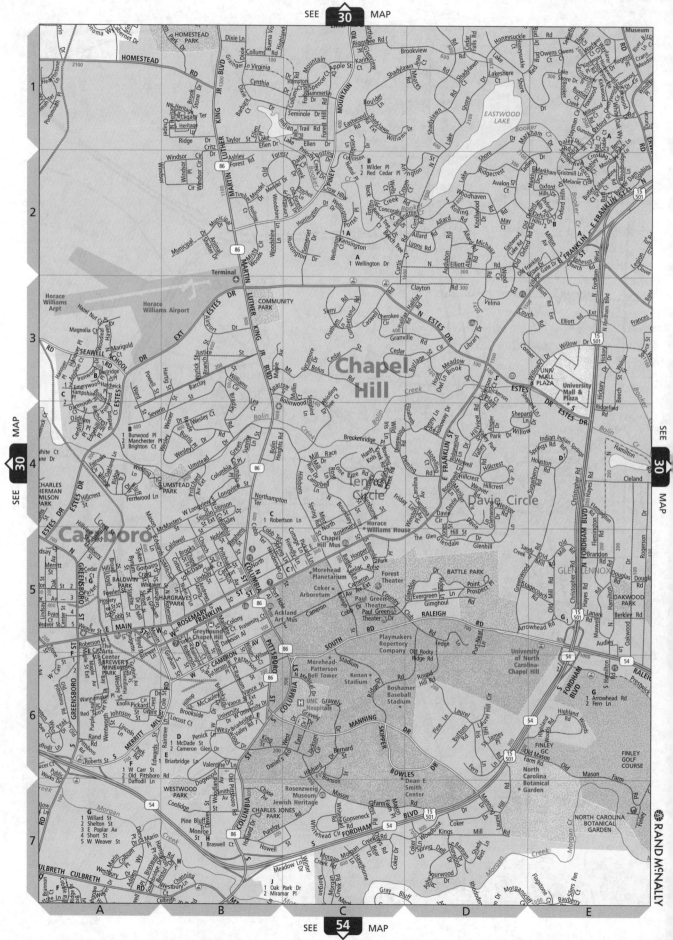

Chapel Hill

Carrboro

SEE 30 MAP

SEE 30 MAP

RAND M^{c}NALLY

MAP
196

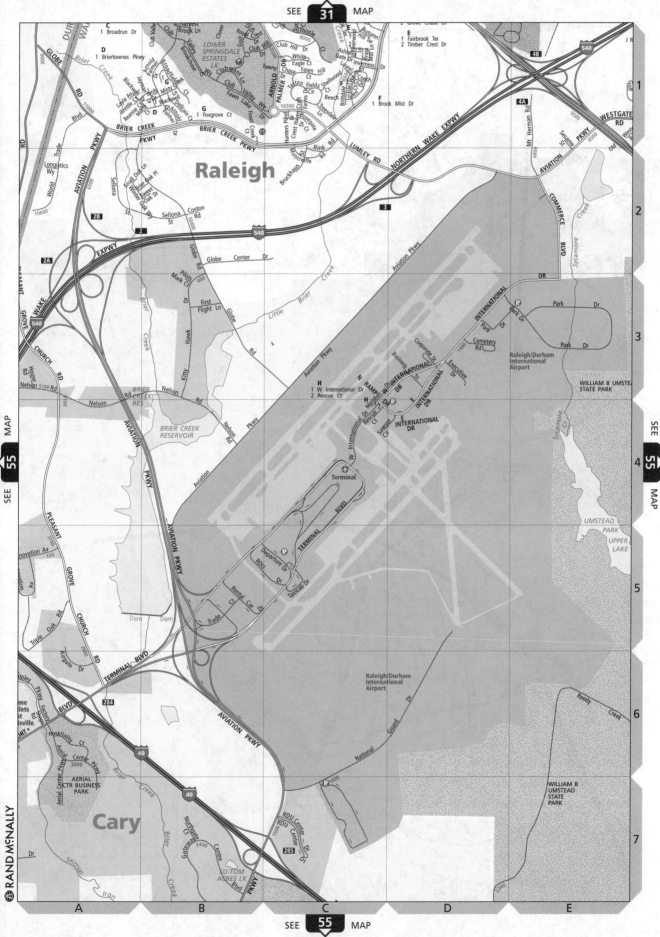

SEE 31 MAP

N

1:30,000
1 in. = 2500 ft.

0   0.25   0.5
miles

DETAIL MAP

Raleigh

DUR
WAKE

GLOBE RD

Brier Creek

BRIER CREEK PKWY

AVIATION PKWY

Trade

Logistics Wy

World

Small Oak Ln

Sellona

Winter Oak Wy

Brier Oak Pl

Sweet Oak Wy

Sellona St

540

EXPWY

2A

WAKE

540

GROVE CHURCH RD

Nelson House Rd

Nelson Rd

PLEASANT GROVE CHURCH RD

AVIATION PKWY

BRIER CREEK RES

BRIER CREEK RESERVOIR

Brier Creek

Little Brier Creek

Globe Center Dr

Globe Rd

Pilots Mark Ct

First Flight Ln

Kitty Hawk

Nelson Rd

Dam

Dam

Trade

Aviation Pkwy

Aviation

Aviation Pkwy

Terminal

TERMINAL BLVD

Departure Dr

RDU Dr

Rental Car Ct

Taxicab Dr

P

P

RDU

LOWER SPRINGDALE ESTATES

C 1 Broadrun Dr

D 1 Briertownes Pkwy

Club Valley

Valley Club

Broadfield

Arnold Palmer

Blackwood

Layla Av

Reane

D

G 1 Foxgrove Ct

Clover

Brook Ln

Golf Club

Club Hill

Club Hill Dr

White Eagle Ct

Clubmont Ln

Fawn Lake

Club Valley Wy

ARNOLD PALMER DR

Tawny

Chase Ct

Fawn Hill

Hunters Pond

Crest Dr

Rosegate Ct

Rink Rd

Moncrieffe

Bruckhaus

LUMLEY RD

540

3

E

E 1 Fairbrook Ter
2 Timber Crest Dr

Gate Dr

Inverness Dr

Beech

Treedale

Shellwood

F 1 Brook Mist Dr

Coach

NORTHERN WAKE EXPWY

48

540

4A

Mt Herman Rd

AVIATION COMMERCE BLVD

Seagate

Old

WESTGATE RD

Gulf

Sycamore Creek

DR

Aviation Pkwy

Park Dr

INTERNATIONAL

P

Park Dr

Park Dr

Park Dr

Cemetery Rd

Corporate Jd

Business

H RAMP-W

INTERNATIONAL DR

INTERNATIONAL DR

Executive Dr

Raleigh/Durham International Airport

Sycamore Ct

WILLIAM B UMSTEAD STATE PARK

H 1 W International Dr
2 Rescue Ct

N

W International Dr

Meridian Dr

Rescue Ct

Sawyer Ct

P

E

E

INTERNATIONAL DR

SEE 55 MAP

SEE 55 MAP

UMSTEAD PARK UPPER LAKE

Sycamore Creek

Raleigh/Durham International Airport

National Guard Dr

Reedy Creek

WILLIAM B UMSTEAD STATE PARK

Cary

Innovation Av

Av

Triple Oak Rd

Allsgate Dr

TERMINAL BLVD

284

40

AERIAL CTR BUSINESS PARK

Aerial Center Pkwy

Aerial Center Pkwy

Hospitality Ct

Aerial Center Pkwy

40

Brier Creek

Northgate Ct

Gateway Centre

RDU Center Dr

RDU Center Dr

285

U-TOM ACRES LK

PKWY

Stirrup Iron

RAND MCNALLY

SEE 55 MAP

A   B   C   D   E

MAP
197

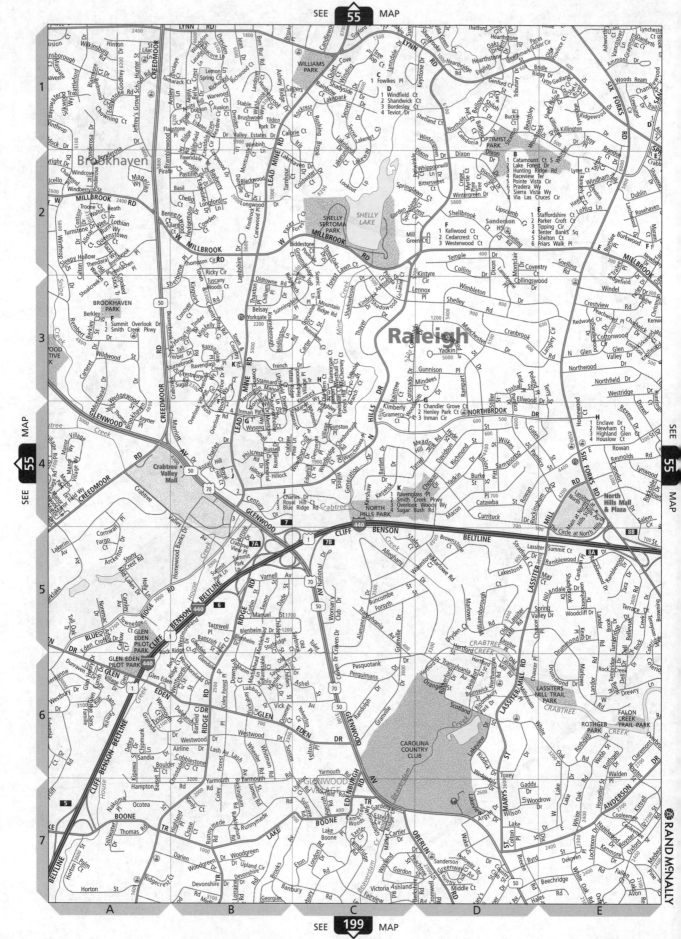

RAND MCNALLY

DETAIL MAP

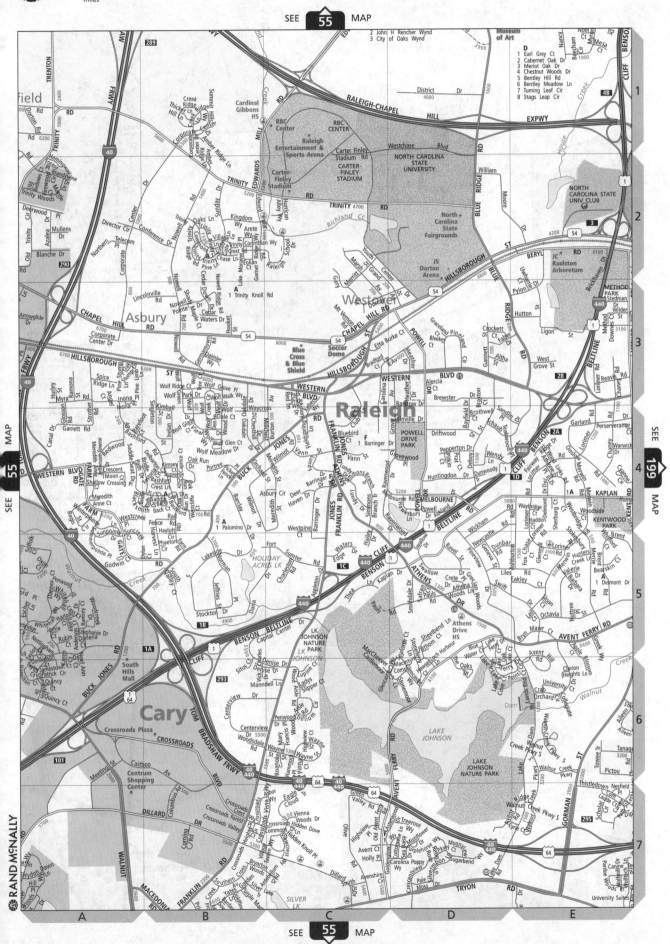

MAP
198

DETAIL MAP

1:30,000
1 in. = 2500 ft.

0   0.25   0.5
miles

N

SEE ⬦ 55 ⬦ MAP

2 John H Rencher Wynd
3 City of Oaks Wynd

Museum of Art

D
1 Earl Grey Ct
2 Cabernet Oak Dr
3 Merlot Oak Dr
4 Chestnut Woods Dr
5 Bentley Hill Rd
6 Bentley Meadow Ln
7 Turning Leaf Cir
8 Stags Leap Cir

RALEIGH-CHAPEL HILL EXPWY

RBC Center

Raleigh Entertainment & Sports Arena

Carter-Finley Stadium

CARTER-FINLEY STADIUM

Westchase Blvd

NORTH CAROLINA STATE UNIVERSITY

NORTH CAROLINA STATE UNIV CLUB

Cardinal Gibbons HS

North Carolina State Fairgrounds

JS Dorton Arena

JC Raulston Arboretum

METHOD PARK

Asbury

CHAPEL HILL RD

Westover

Raleigh

Blue Cross & Blue Shield

Soccer Dome

WESTERN BLVD

POWELL DRIVE PARK

HOLIDAY ACRES LK

LK JOHNSON NATURE PARK

LK JOHNSON

Athens Drive HS

Cary

South Hills Mall

Crossroads Plaza

Caitboo Centrum Shopping Center

Crossroads

DILLARD

LAKE JOHNSON

LAKE JOHNSON NATURE PARK

SILVER LK

University Suites

SEE ⬦ 55 ⬦ MAP

SEE 199 MAP

SEE 55 MAP

A   B   C   D   E

1   2   3   4   5   6   7

MAP
199

1:30,000
1 in. = 2500 ft.

0   0.25   0.5
miles

DETAIL MAP

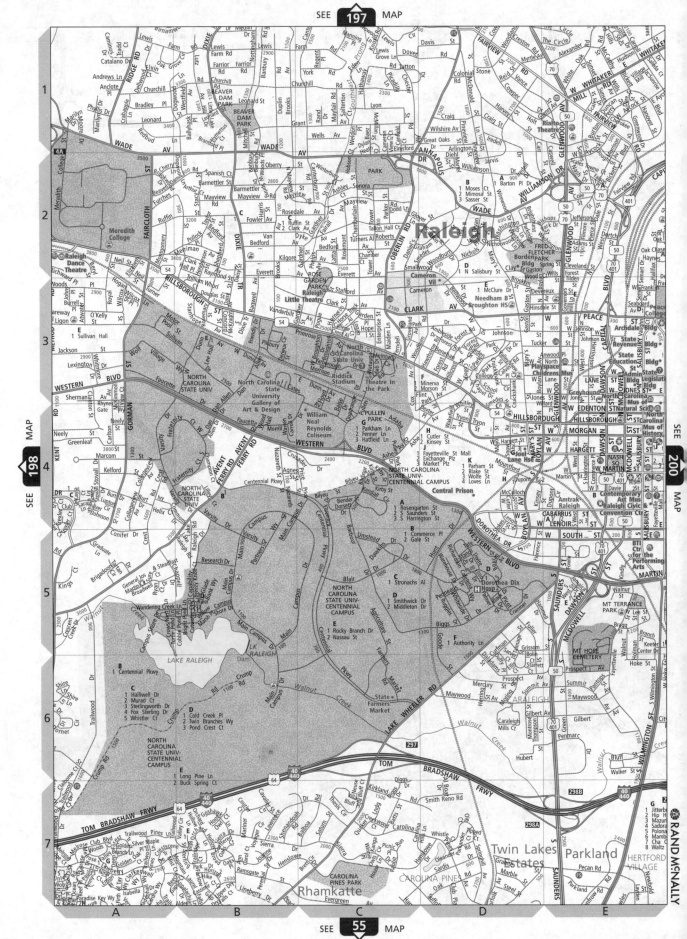

SEE ◄ 198 ► MAP

SEE ◄ 200 ► MAP

Raleigh

RAND McNALLY

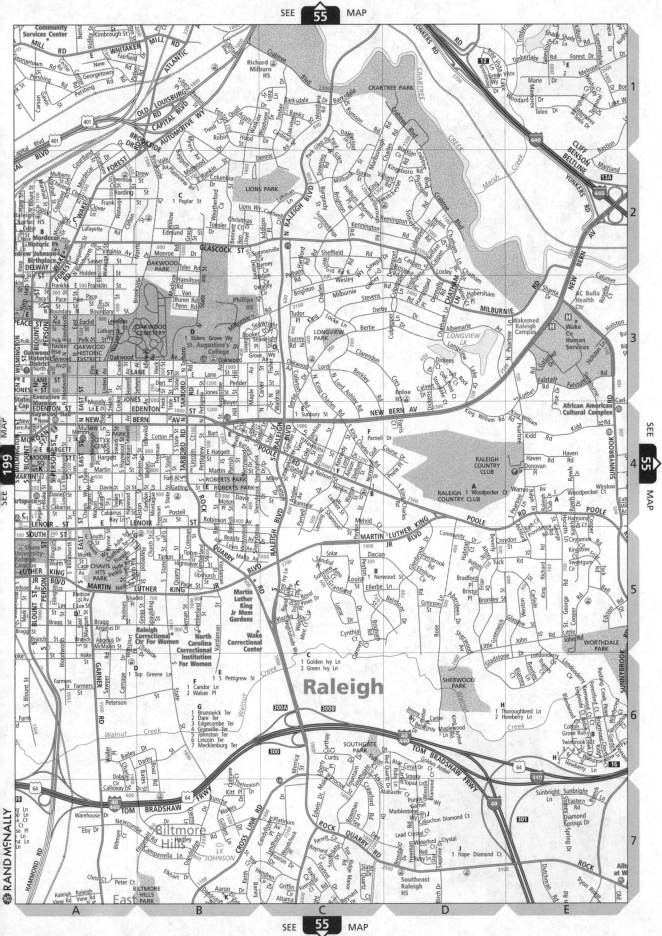

MAP
200

DETAIL MAP

1:30,000
1 in. = 2500 ft.
0   0.25   0.5
miles

SEE ⬆ MAP **55**

SEE **55** MAP

SEE **199** MAP

RAND McNALLY

Raleigh

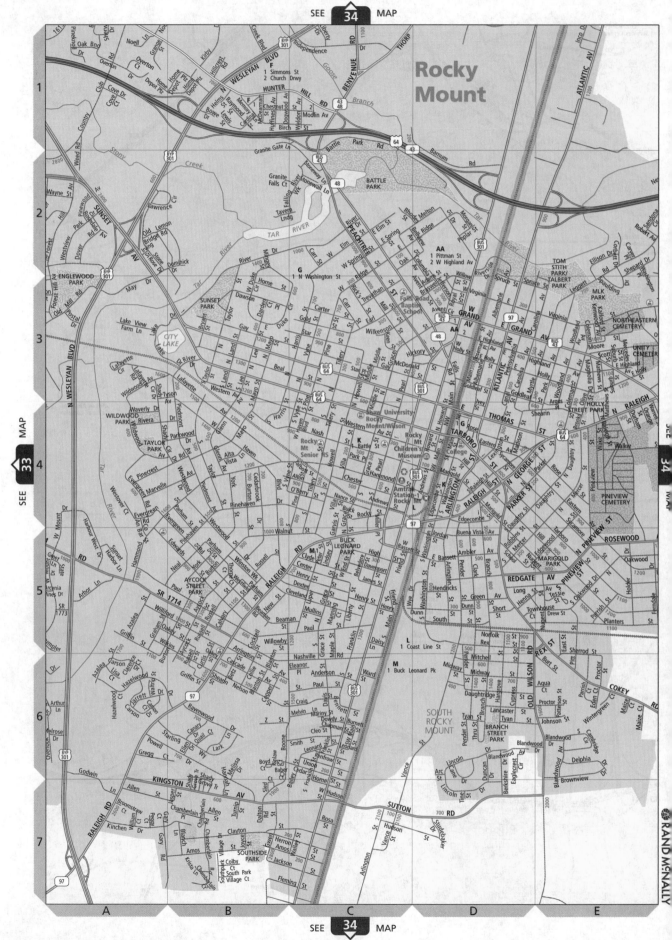

MAP
201

1:30,000
1 in. = 2500 ft.
0   0.25   0.5
miles

SEE 34 MAP

Rocky Mount

DETAIL MAP

SEE 33 MAP

SEE 34 MAP

SEE 34 MAP

RAND McNALLY

MAP
202

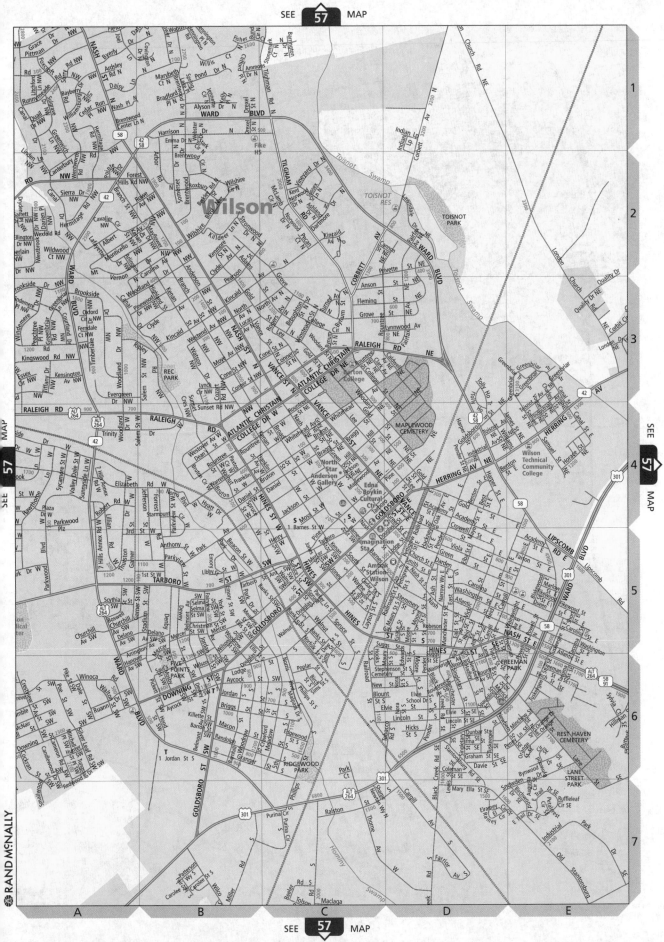

1:30,000
1 in. = 2500 ft.

0   0.25   0.5
miles

DETAIL MAP

SEE 57 MAP

SEE 57 MAP

RAND M?NALLY

MAP
203

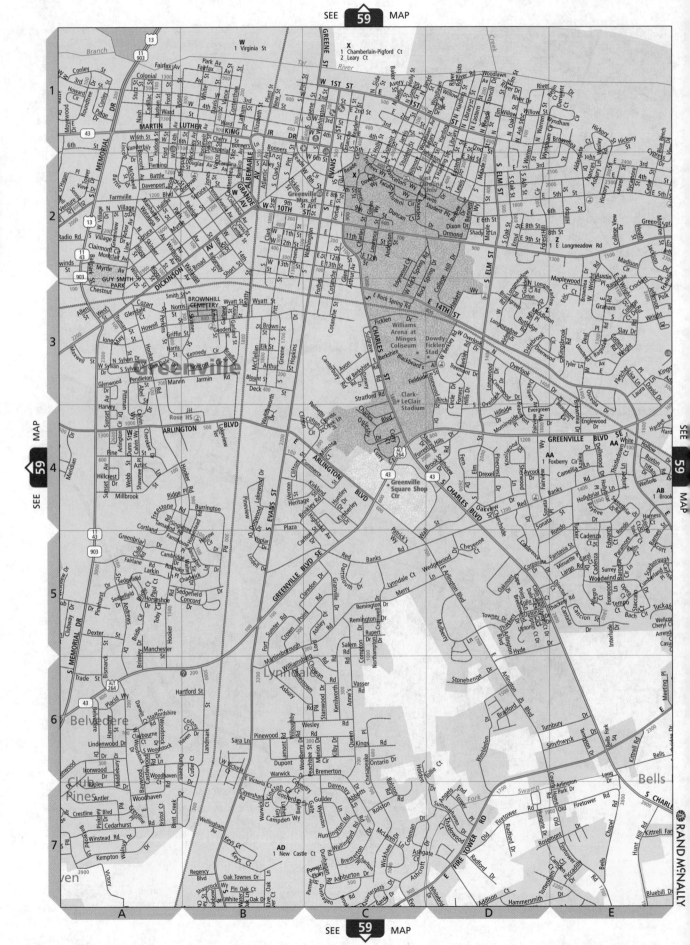

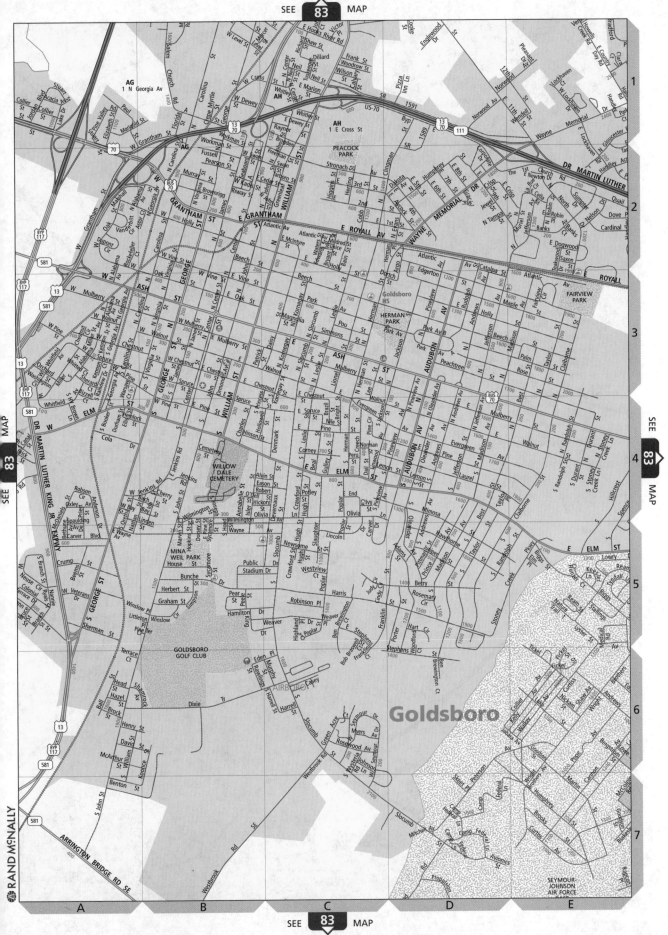

MAP
204

DETAIL MAP

SEE 83 MAP

SEE 83 MAP

Goldsboro

RAND MCNALLY

MAP
205

1:30,000
1 in. = 2500 ft.
0   0.25   0.5
miles
N

DETAIL MAP

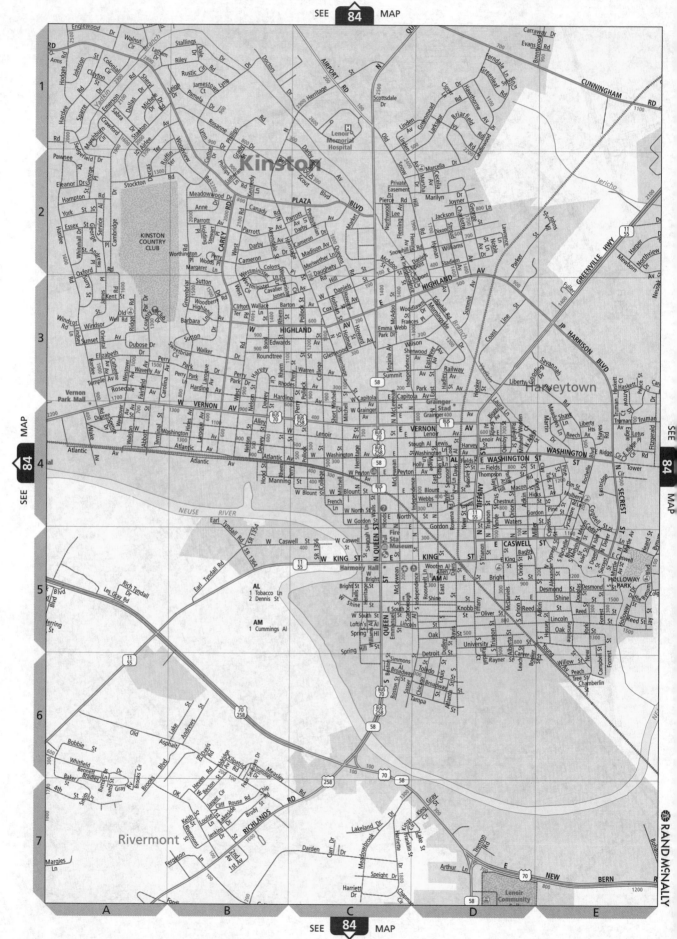

AL
1 Tobacco Ln
2 Dennis St

AM
1 Cummings Al

SEE 84 MAP

SEE 84 MAP

RAND McNALLY

SEE 84 MAP

A   B   C   D   E

MAP
206

1:30,000
1 in. = 2500 ft.

0   0.25   0.5
miles

N

SEE 44 MAP

DETAIL MAP

SEE 44 MAP

SEE 44 MAP

Asheville

Biltmore Forest

RIVERSIDE DR

BROADWAY

MERRIMON AV

CHARLOTTE ST

MARTIN LUTHER KING JR

MCDOWELL ST

BILTMORE AV

HENDERSONVILLE

SWANNANOA RD

TUNNEL RD

GROVE PARK INN RESORT & SPA

University of North Carolina Asheville

Asheville Botanical Gardens at Asheville

Riverside Cemetery

WEAVER PARK

MAGNOLIA PARK

HILLSIDE

ALBEMARLE

Thomas Wolfe Mem State Historical Site

Pack Place Education Arts & Science Center

ASTON PARK

Memorial Mission Hospital

KENILWORTH PARK

SEVEN SPRINGS PARK

LAKEWOOD PARK

Lake Kenilworth

Asheville Mall

Innsbruck Mall

FRENCH BROAD RIVER PARK

WALTON STREET PARK

Asheville-Buncombe Tech Comm Coll

Asheville-Buncombe Tech Comm Coll

Smith McDowell Hse Museum

Biltmore Estate

Biltmore Vil Historic Museum

Thomas Kinkade at Biltmore Vil

MEADOW RD

AMBOY RD

LYMAN ST

WINERY RD

Swannanoa River

French Broad River

A   B   C   D   E

SEE 44 MAP

MAP
207

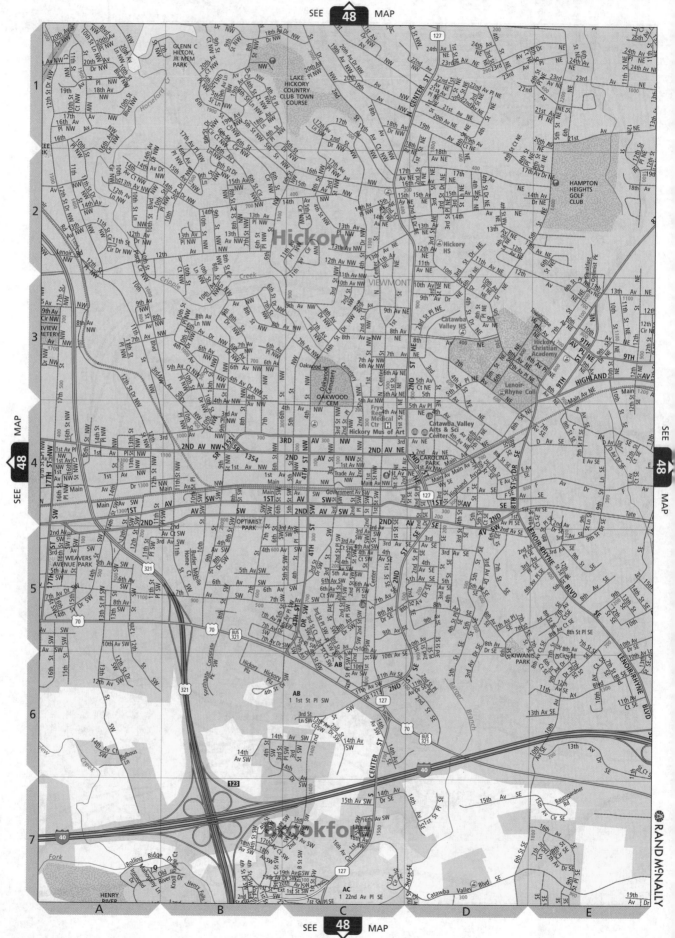

1:30,000
1 in. = 2500 ft.
0   0.25   0.5
miles

N

SEE 48 MAP

SEE 48 MAP

RAND M?NALLY

SEE 48 MAP

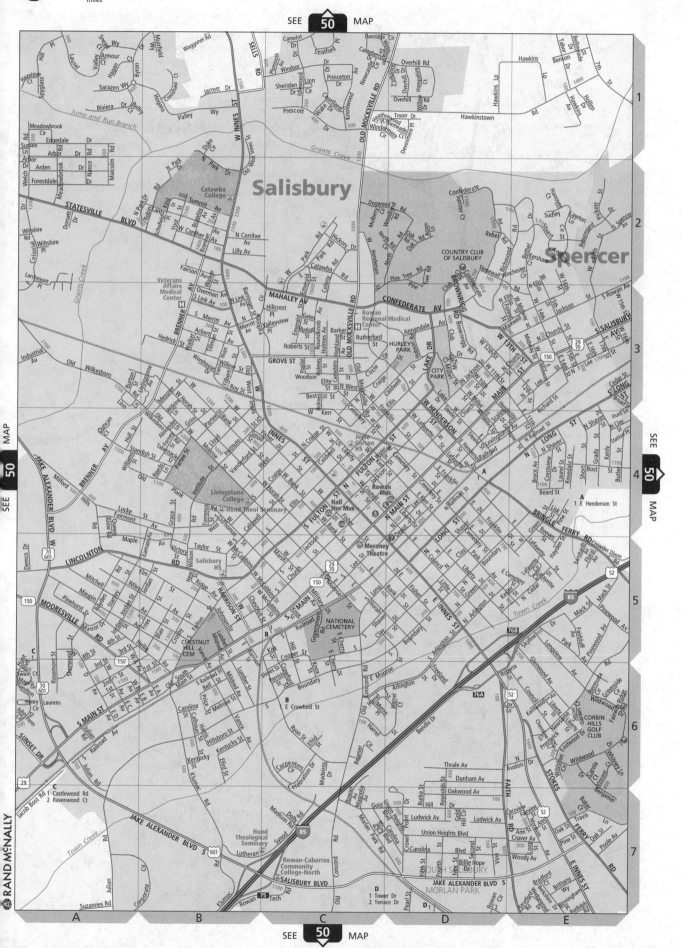

MAP
208

DETAIL MAP

1:30,000
1 in. = 2500 ft.

0   0.25   0.5
miles

SEE 50 MAP

Salisbury

Spencer

SEE 50 MAP

SEE 50 MAP

SEE 50 MAP

RAND MNALLY

MAP
209

1:30,000
1 in. = 2500 ft.

0   0.25   0.5
miles

SEE 52 MAP

DETAIL MAP

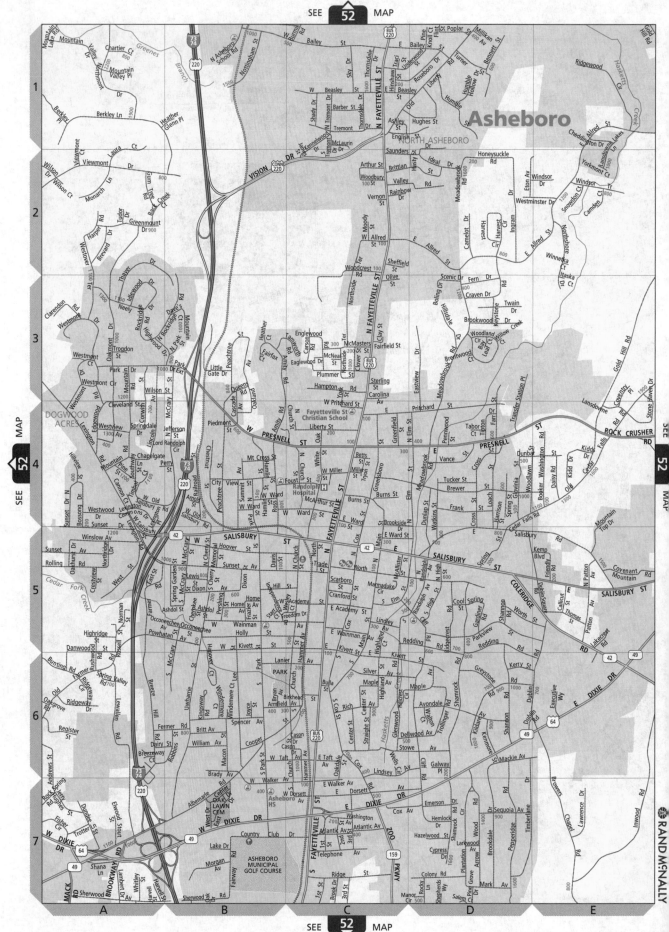

Asheboro

NORTH ASHEBORO

DOGWOOD ACRES

SEE 52 MAP

SEE 52 MAP

ROCK CRUSHER RD

ASHEBORO MUNICIPAL GOLF COURSE

RAND McNALLY

SEE 52 MAP

A   B   C   D   E

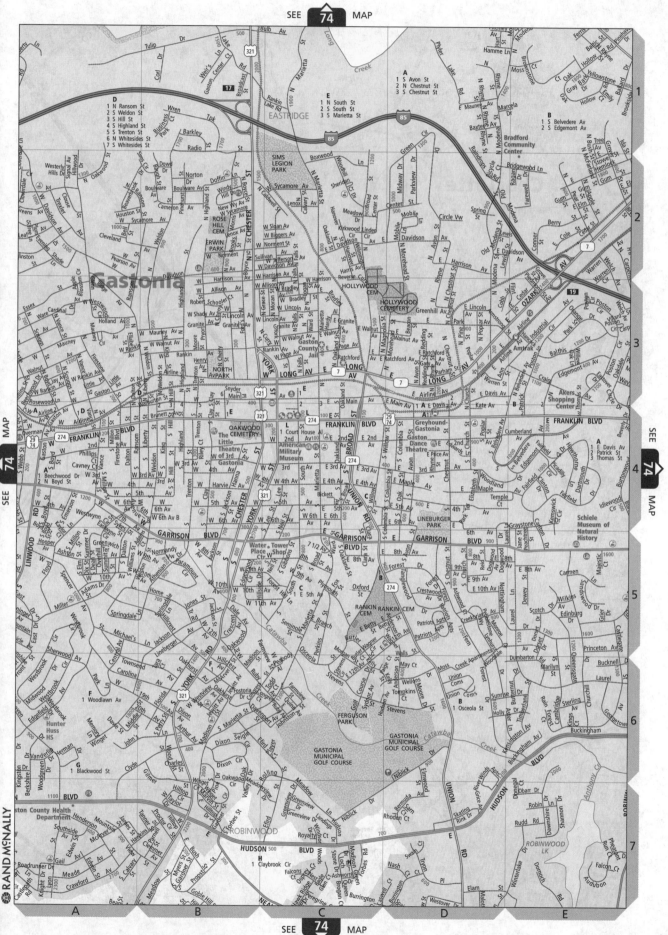

MAP
210

DETAIL MAP

RAND McNALLY

MAP
211

1:30,000
1 in. = 2500 ft.

0   0.25   0.5
miles

SEE 75 MAP

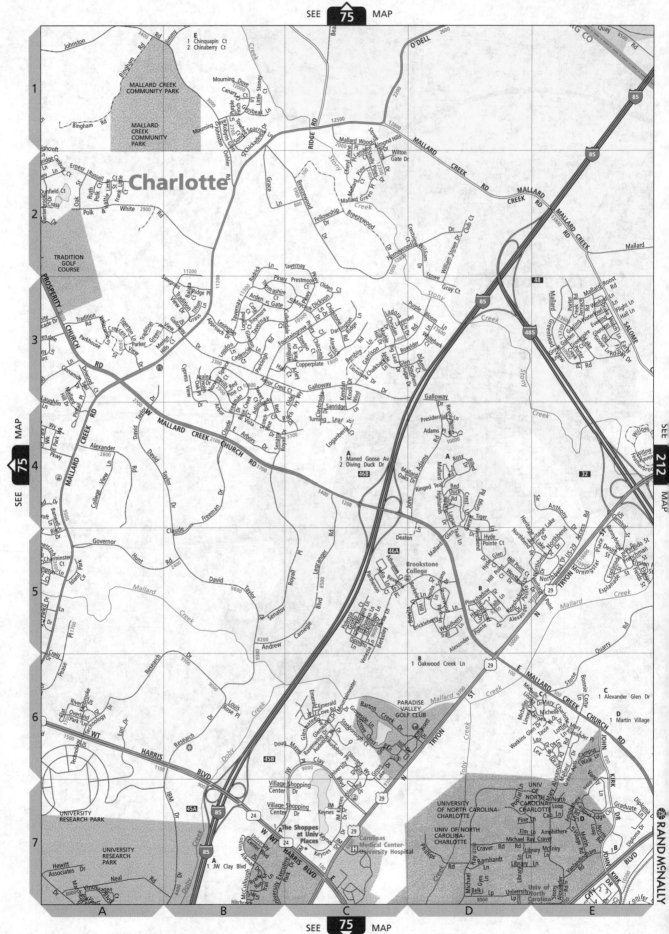

Charlotte

SEE 75 MAP

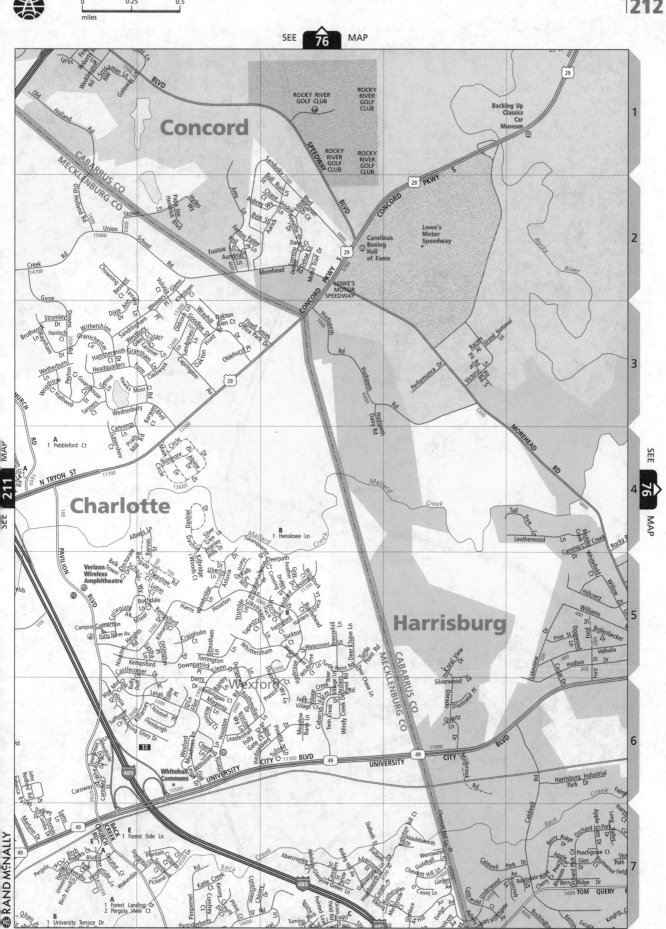

MAP
212

DETAIL MAP

1:30,000
1 in. = 2500 ft.

0   0.25   0.5
miles

SEE 76 MAP

US 29

Backing Up
Classics
Car
Museum

ROCKY RIVER
GOLF CLUB

ROCKY
RIVER
GOLF
CLUB

ROCKY
RIVER
GOLF
CLUB

ROCKY
RIVER
GOLF
CLUB

Concord

CABARRUS CO
MECKLENBURG CO

Old Holland Rd

Lowe's
Motor
Speedway

CONCORD PKWY S

SPEEDWAY BLVD

Carolinas
Boxing
Hall
of Fame

US 29

LOWE'S
MOTOR
SPEEDWAY

Rocky River

Grand National

Performance Dr

Victory

MOREHEAD RD

Charlotte

Pebbleford Ct

N TRYON ST

Mallard Creek

Henslowe Ln

Harrisburg

CABARRUS CO
MECKLENBURG CO

Tall
Tree
Leatherwood

Hillcrest

Williams

Bollenbecker

Valhalla

Verizon
Wireless
Amphitheatre

PAVILION BLVD

Wexford

Silverwood

Coral View Dr

Dorado

Diamond Pl

Quartz Ln

33

Whitehall
Commons

485

UNIVERSITY CITY BLVD

49   UNIVERSITY CITY BLVD   49

Millbrook

Harrisburg Industrial
Park Dr

49

BACK CREEK

CHURCH RD

Forest Side Ln

Caldwell Park

Back Creek

485

1 Forest Landing Ct
2 Pergola View Ct

University Terrace Dr

Abercromby

TOM QUERY

SEE 211 MAP

SEE 76 MAP

SEE 76 MAP

RAND MCNALLY

A   B   C   D   E

MAP
213

SEE 75 MAP

DETAIL MAP

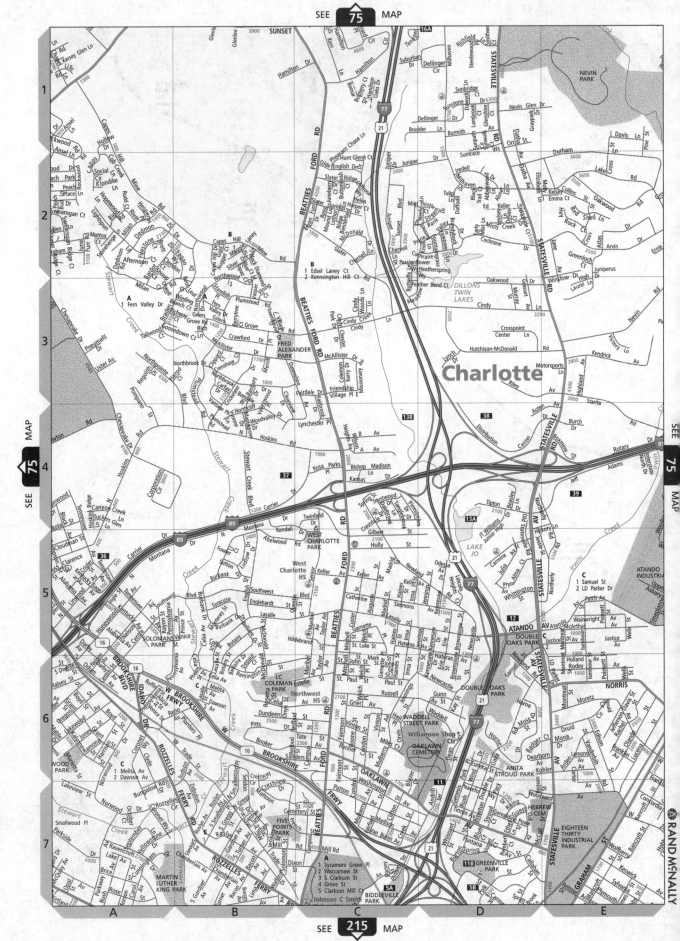

Charlotte

SEE 215 MAP

RAND MÇNALLY

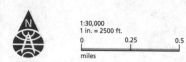

1:30,000
1 in. = 2500 ft.

0   0.25   0.5
miles

MAP
214

DETAIL MAP

SEE **75** MAP

SEE **215** MAP

SEE **75** MAP

Charlotte

RAND McNALLY

LITTLE ROCK INDUSTRIAL PARK

WILKINSON BLVD

BIRMINGHAM

Charlotte/Douglas Int'l Airport

Terminal

Carolinas Aviation Museum

North Carolina Air Nat'l Guard

YORKMONT RD

Charlotte/Douglas International Airport

MULBERRY

WESTERLY HILLS PARK

Central Piedmont Community College West Campus

WINGALE PARK

SOUTHWEST PARK

SOUTHWEST PARK

B
1 Fordwood Dr
2 Denview Ln
3 Parkmont Dr

D
1 Holabird Ln

G
1 Denver Av

AMAY JAMES PARK

BILLY GRAHAM PKWY

PAUL BROWN BLVD

WEST BLVD

Charlotte Correctional Center

LAKE POINT BUSINESS PARK

YORKMONT RD

WHIPPOORWILL LAKE

YORKMONT RD

SUGAR CREEK

Coliseum Centre Dr

CHARLOTTE COLISEUM

Charlotte Coliseum

RENAISSANCE PK

STEELE CREEK

MAP
215

1:30,000
1 in. = 2500 ft.

0   0.25   0.5
miles

SEE **213** MAP

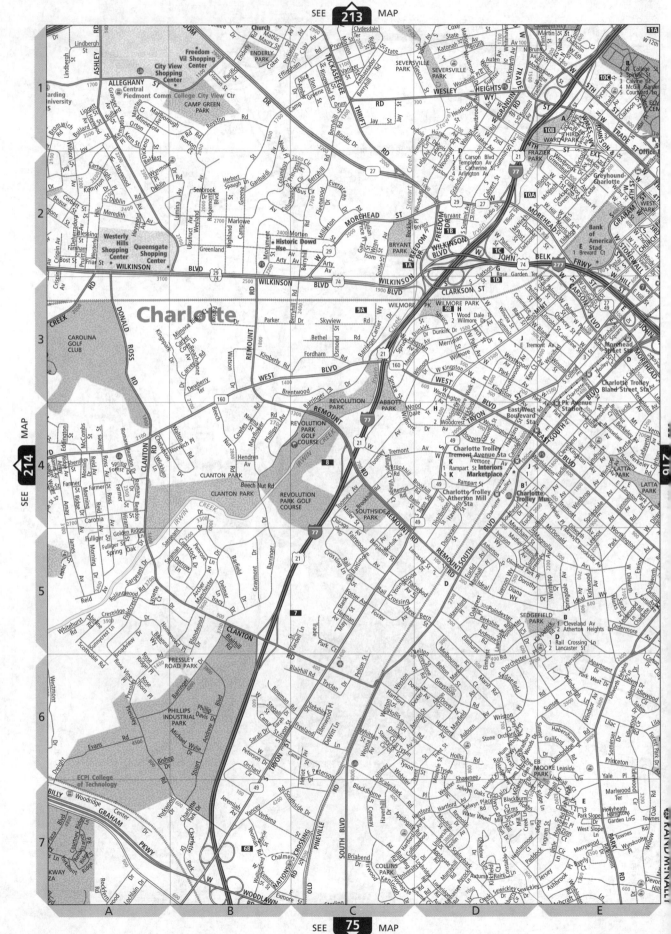

Charlotte

SEE **214** MAP

SEE **216** MAP

SEE **75** MAP

A   B   C   D   E

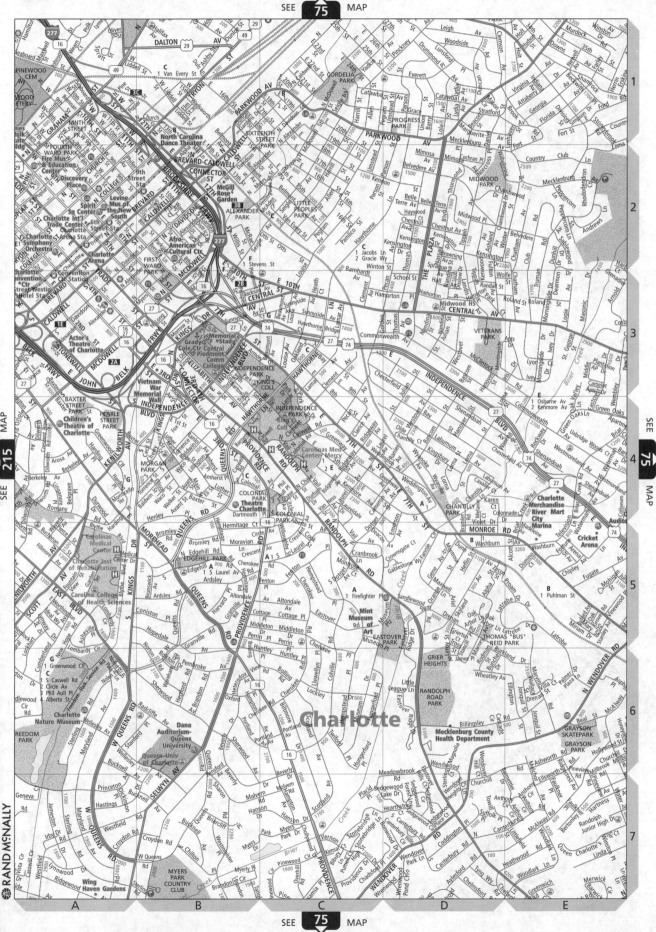

MAP
216

DETAIL MAP

SEE 75 MAP

SEE 215 MAP

SEE 75 MAP

SEE 75 MAP

1:30,000
1 in. = 2500 ft.
0   0.25   0.5
miles

Charlotte

RAND McNALLY

MAP
217

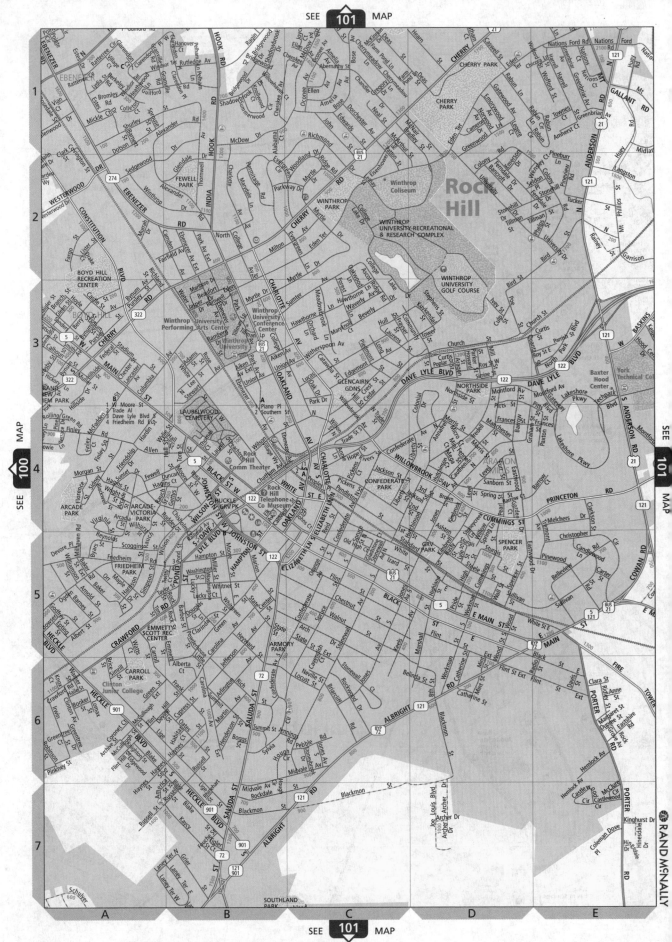

MAP
218

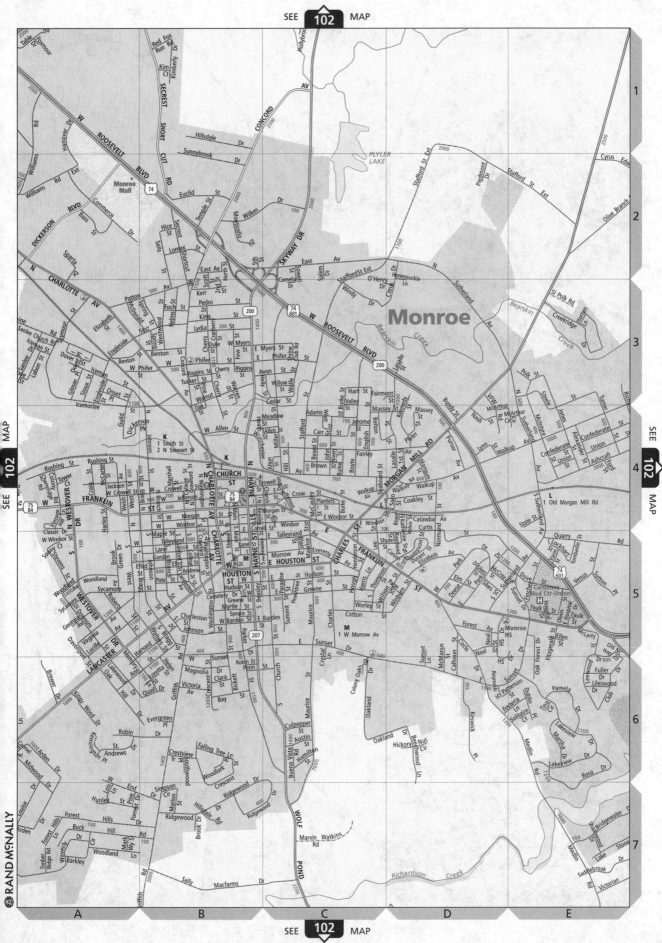

1:30,000
1 in. = 2500 ft.

0   0.25   0.5

miles

Monroe

DETAIL MAP

SEE **102** MAP

SEE **102** MAP

RAND MɔNALLY

A   B   C   D   E

MAP
219

1:30,000
1 in. = 2500 ft.

0   0.25   0.5
miles

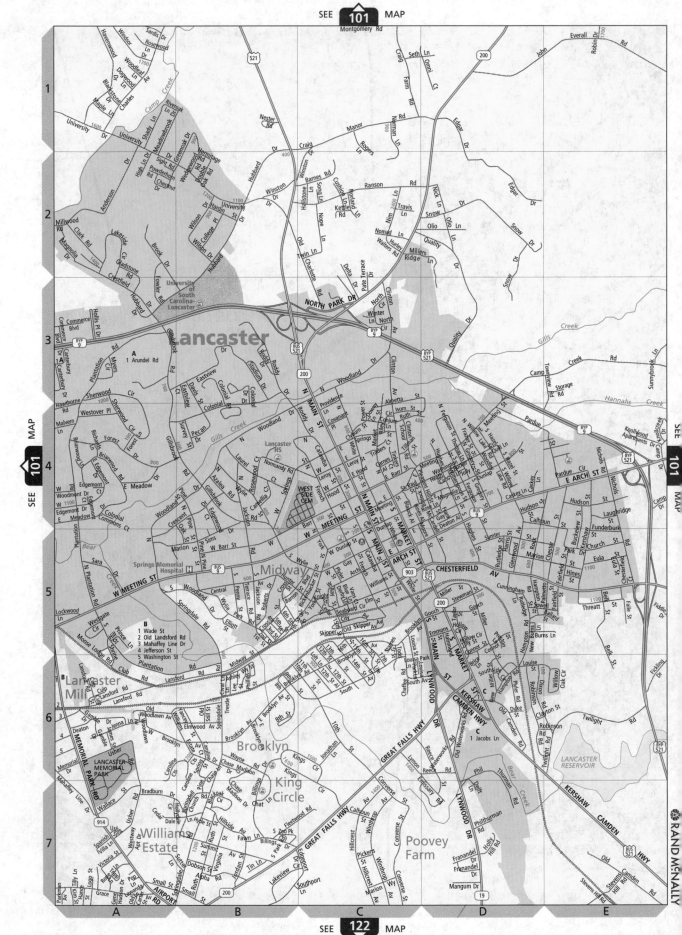

SEE 101 MAP

DETAIL MAP

SEE 101 MAP

SEE 101 MAP

SEE 122 MAP

RAND McNALLY

MAP
220

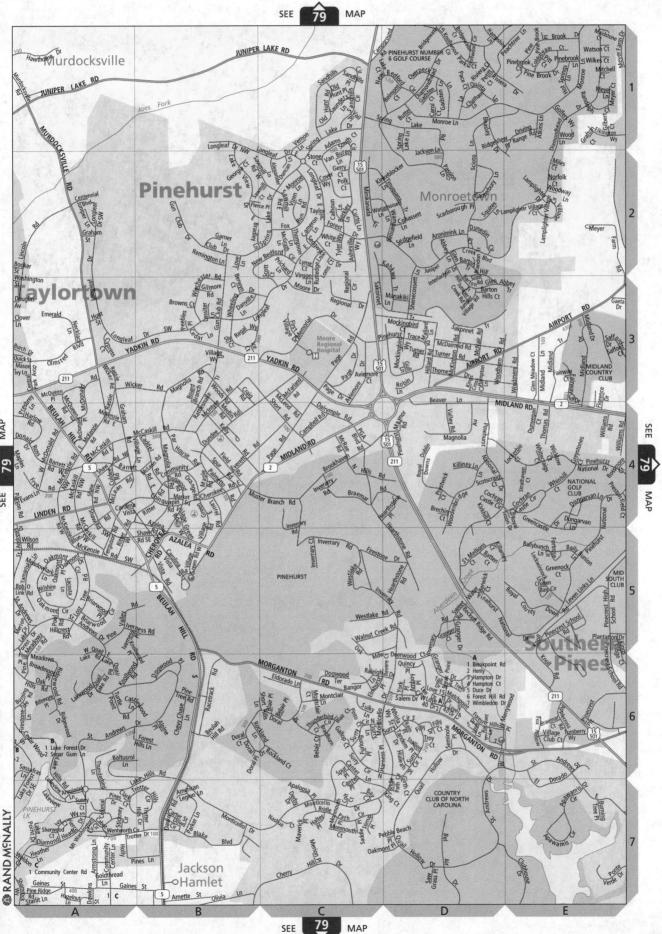

1:30,000
1 in. = 2500 ft.
0   0.25   0.5
miles

SEE 79 MAP

SEE 79 MAP

SEE 79 MAP

RAND McNALLY

MAP
221

1:30,000
1 in. = 2500 ft.

0   0.25   0.5
miles

N

SEE 80 MAP

Spring
Lake

POPE AIR
FORCE BASE

Webster University
Pope Air Force Base
Campbell University
Pope Air Force Base

WILLOW
LAKES
GOLF
COURSE

MCFAYDEN
PND

FORT BRAGG MILITARY
RESERVATION

LONGSTREET RD

FORT
BRAGG
RYDER
GOLF
COURSE

HONEYCUTT

ALL AMERICAN EXPWY

82nd
Airborne
Division
Museum

Fort
Bragg

FORT
BRAGG
STRYKER
GOLF
COURSE

GRUBER RD

SEE 80 MAP

SEE 80 MAP

SEE 80 MAP

RAND M!NALLY

A   B   C   D   E

1   2   3   4   5   6   7

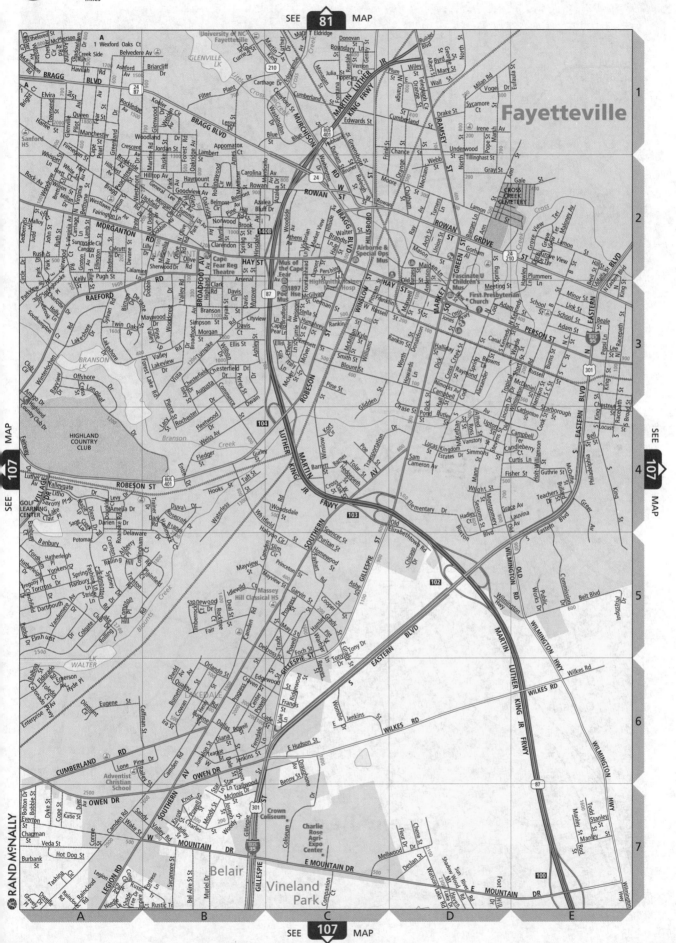

MAP
222

DETAIL MAP

1:30,000
1 in. = 2500 ft.

0   0.25   0.5
miles

SEE ⬆ 81 MAP

Fayetteville

SEE 107 MAP

SEE ➤ 107 MAP

SEE ⬇ 107 MAP

RAND M°NALLY

1   2   3   4   5   6   7

A   B   C   D   E

MAP
223

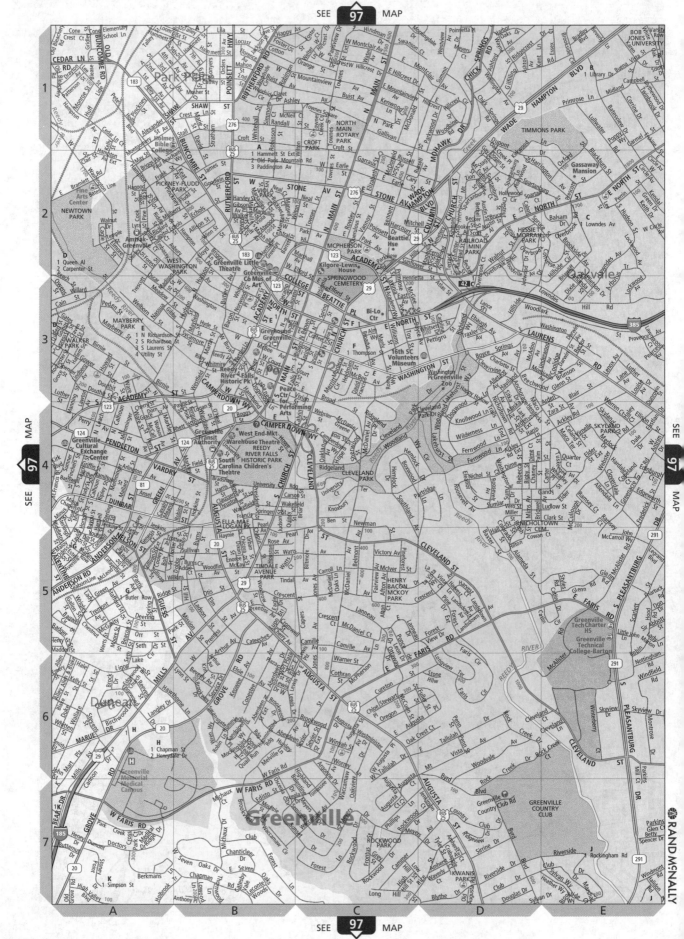

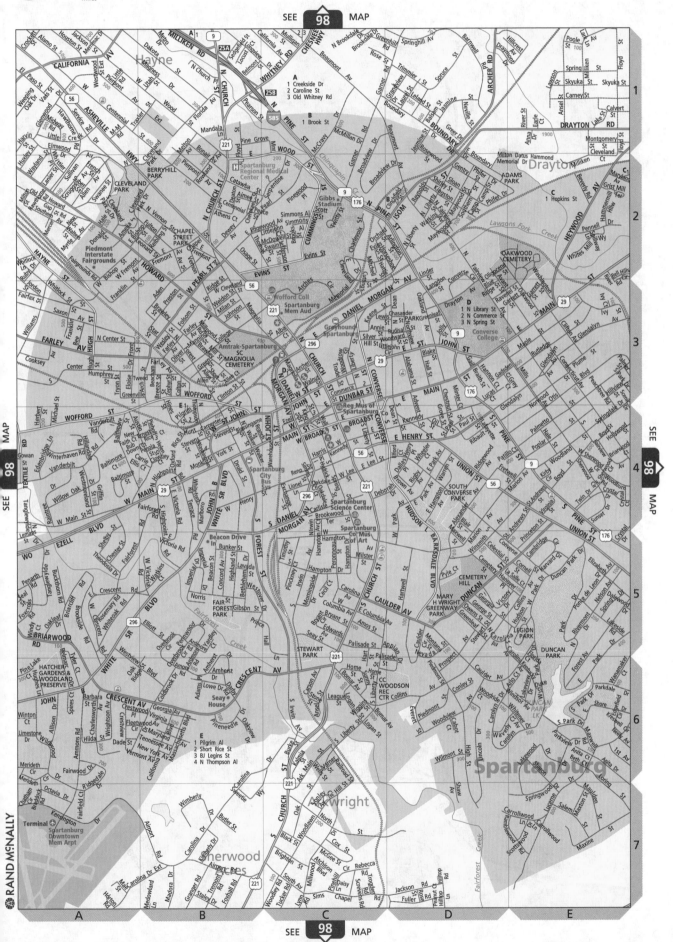

MAP
224

1:30,000
1 in. = 2500 ft.
0   0.25   0.5
miles

SEE 98 MAP

A
1 Creekside Dr
2 Caroline St
3 Old Whitney Rd

B
1 Brook St

C
1 Hopkins St

D
1 N Library St
2 N Commerce St
3 N Spring St

E
1 Pilgrim Al
2 Short Rice St
3 BJ Legins St
4 N Thompson Al

SEE 98 MAP

SEE 98 MAP

SEE 98 MAP

RAND McNALLY

A   B   C   D   E

1   2   3   4   5   6   7

MAP
225

1:30,000
1 in. = 2500 ft.
0   0.25   0.5
miles

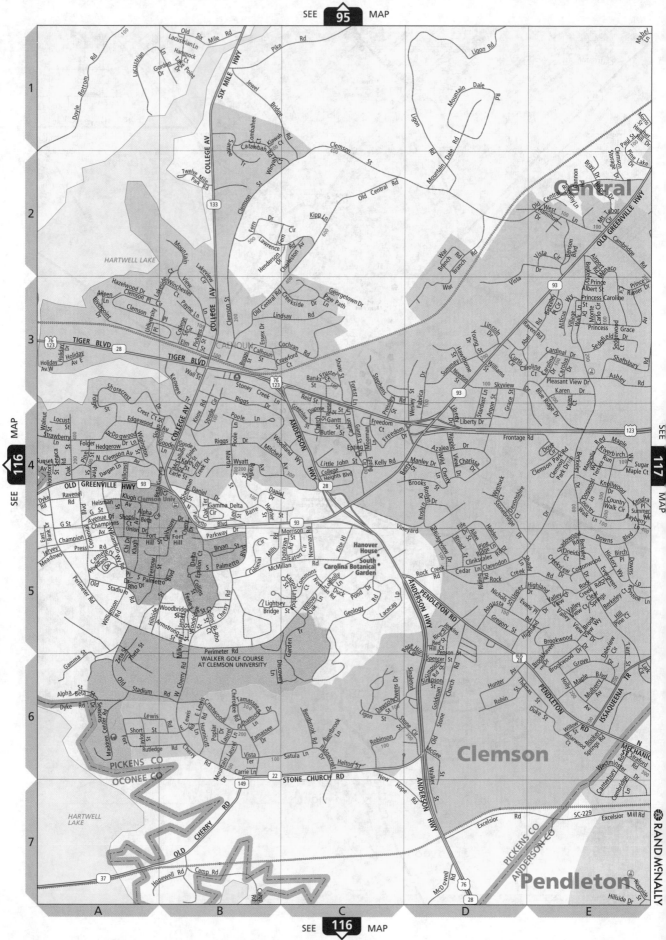

Central

Clemson

Pendleton

HARTWELL LAKE

HARTWELL LAKE

WALKER GOLF COURSE
AT CLEMSON UNIVERSITY

Hanover House

South
Carolina Botanical
Garden

OLD GREENVILLE HWY

TIGER BLVD

PICKENS CO
OCONEE CO

PICKENS CO
ANDERSON CO

SEE 116 MAP

SEE 117 MAP

A   B   C   D   E

MAP
226

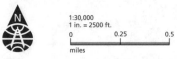

SEE 117 MAP

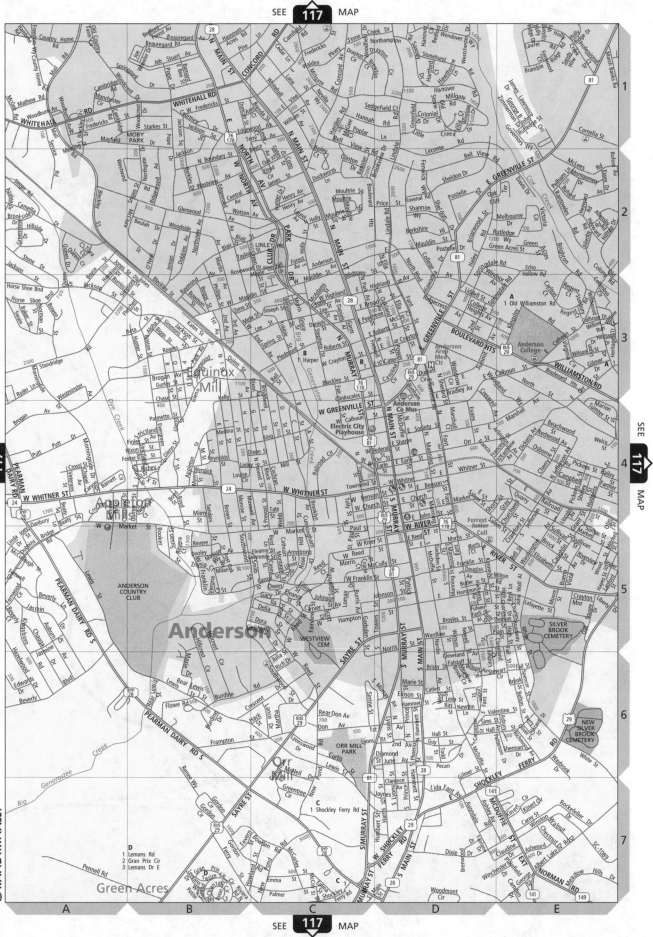

SEE 117 MAP

SEE 117 MAP

DETAIL MAP

1:30,000
1 in. = 2500 ft.
0   0.25   0.5
miles

MAP
227

1:30,000
1 in. = 2500 ft.
0   0.25   0.5
miles

SEE **111** MAP

DETAIL MAP

SEE **111** MAP

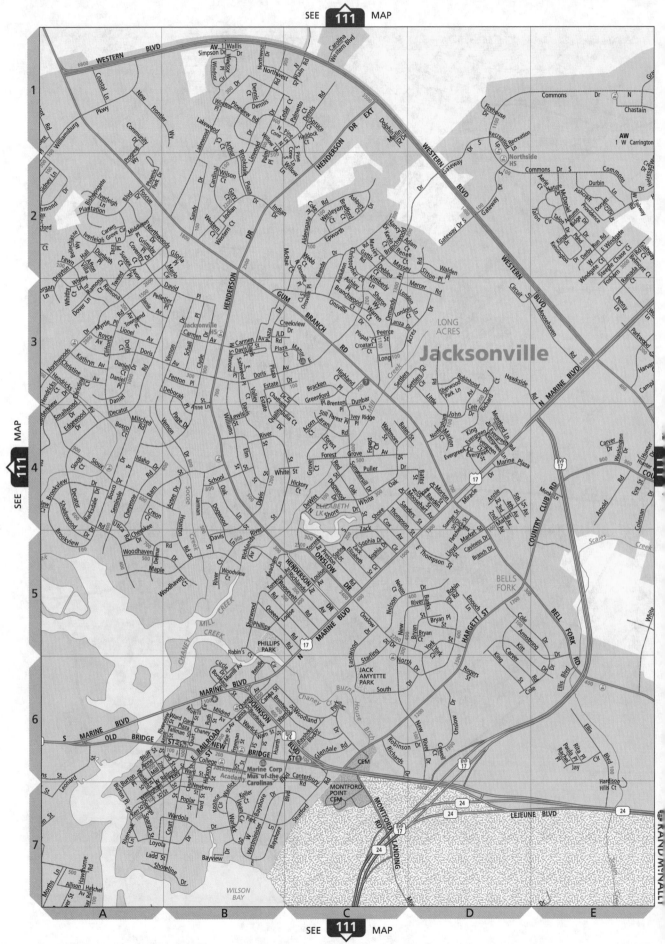

Jacksonville

SEE **111** MAP

A   B   C   D   E

RAND M°NALLY

1:30,000
1 in. = 2500 ft.

0   0.25   0.5
miles

MAP
228

DETAIL MAP

SEE 113 MAP

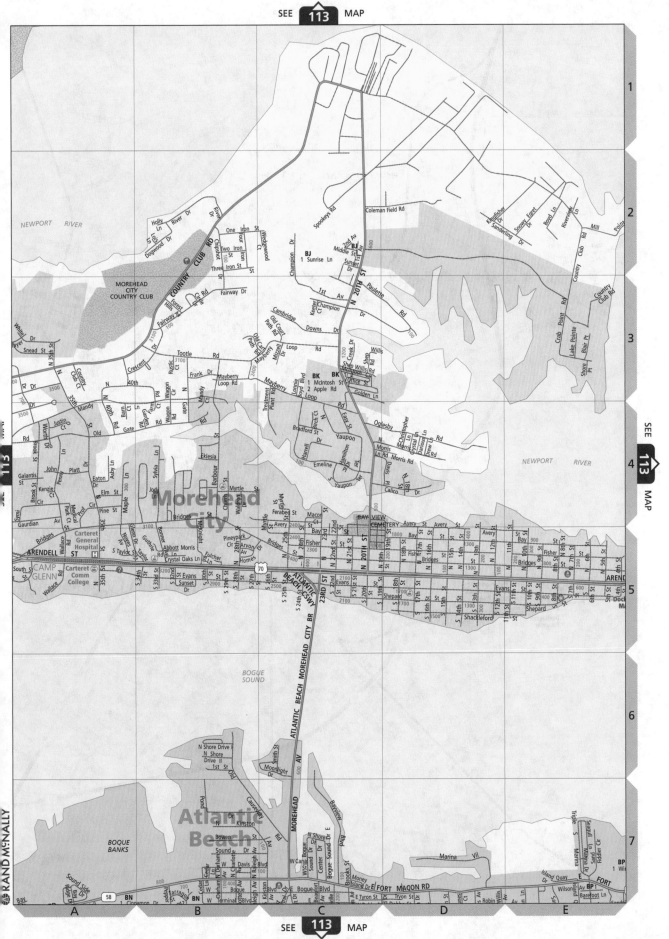

SEE 113 MAP

SEE 113 MAP

RAND MCNALLY

MAP
229

DETAIL MAP

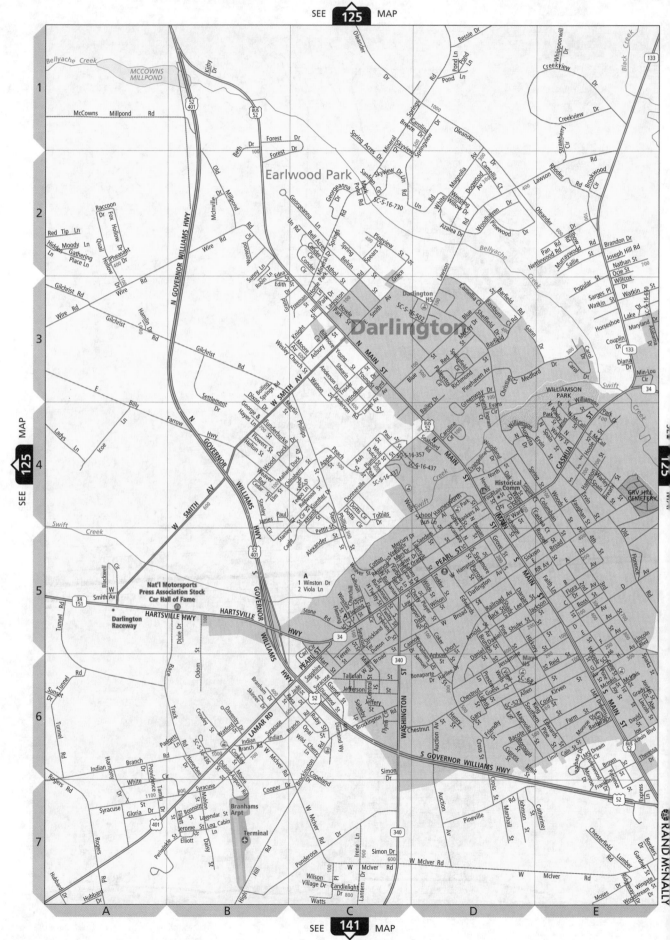

Earlwood Park

Darlington

SEE 125 MAP

SEE 125 MAP

SEE 141 MAP

RAND McNALLY

MAP
230

DETAIL MAP

1:30,000
1 in. = 2500 ft.
0   0.25   0.5
miles

SEE [141] MAP

Brook
Green
Park

Florence

Spaulding
Heights

FLORENCE
COUNTRY CLUB

LUCAS PARK

TIMROD
PARK

MT
HOPE
CEMETERY

Florence
Museum

IOLA
JONES
PARK

KING
MAPLE
PARK

McLeod
Regional
Medical
Center

Healthsouth
Rehabilitation
Hospital

2ND LOOP RD

Jeffries Creek

McCall Branch

RANDALL S HEWITT MEMORIAL HWY

MECHANICSVILLE RD

N CASHUA DR

CASHUA DR

W SUMTER ST

W PALMETTO ST

CHEROKEE RD

S EDISTO DR

N IRBY ST

S IRBY ST

S CHURCH ST

E PALMETTO ST

E ASHBY RD

SEE [141] MAP

SEE [141] MAP

A   B   C   D   E

1   2   3   4   5   6   7

MAP
231

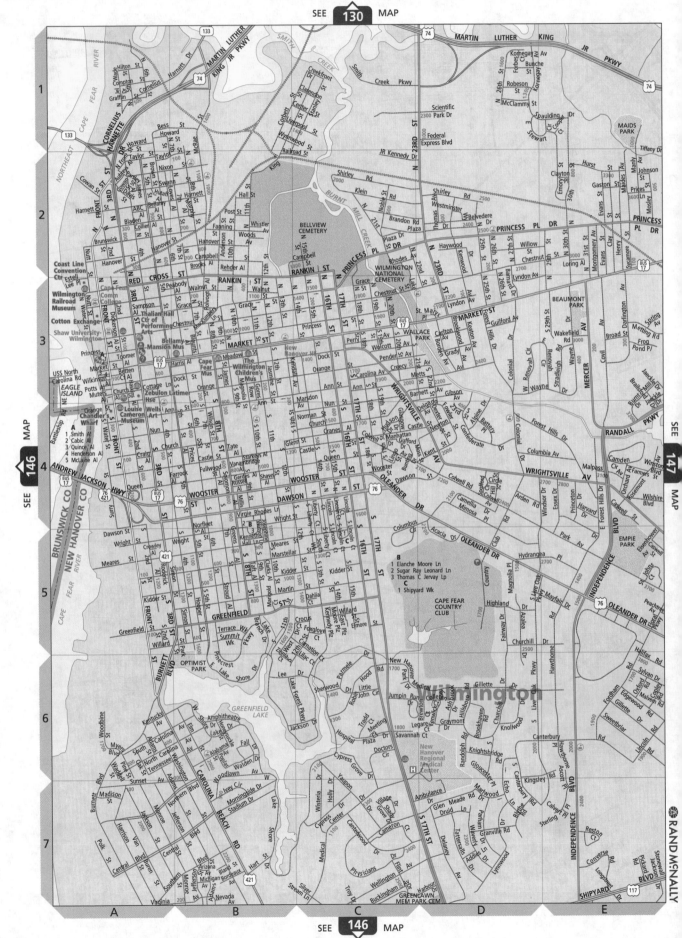

1:30,000
1 in. = 2500 ft.

0   0.25   0.5
miles

DETAIL MAP

SEE ▲ **130** MAP

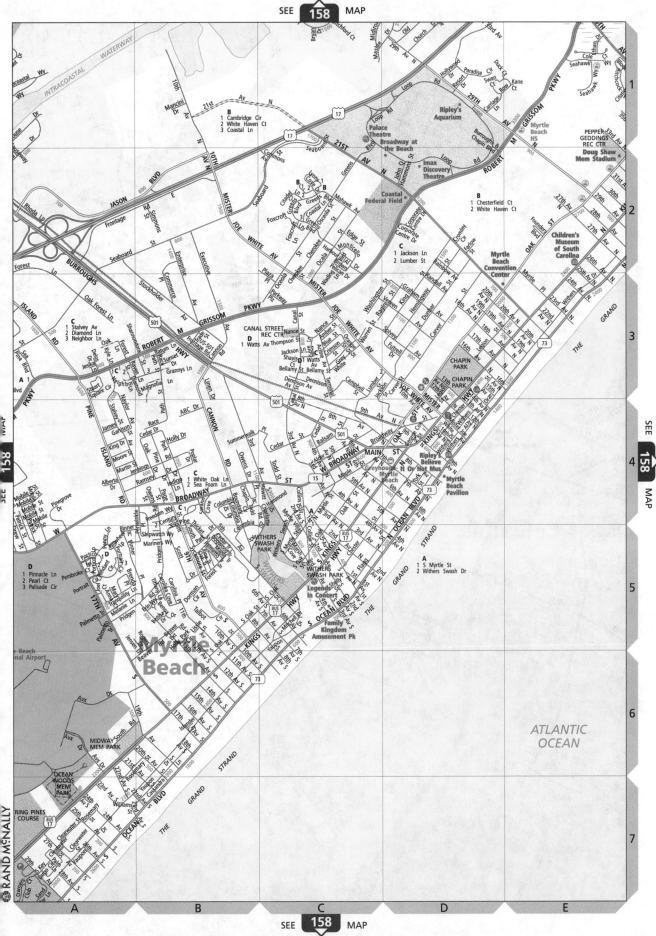

MAP
232

DETAIL MAP

SEE 158 MAP

SEE 158 MAP

SEE 158 MAP

1:30,000
1 in. = 2500 ft.
0   0.25   0.5
miles

B
1 Cambridge Cir
2 White Haven Ct
3 Coastal Ln

B
1 Chesterfield Ct
2 White Haven Ct

C
1 Jackson Ln
2 Lumber St

C
1 Stalvey Av
2 Diamond Ln
3 Neighbor Ln

D
1 Watts Av

C
1 White Oak Ln
2 Sea Foam Ln

D
1 Pinnacle Ln
2 Pearl Ct
3 Palisade Cir

A
1 S Myrtle St
2 Withers Swash Dr

Ripley's Aquarium

Palace Theatre

Broadway at the Beach

Imax Discovery Theatre

Coastal Federal Field

Myrtle Beach HS

PEPPER GEDDINGS REC CTR

Doug Shaw Mem Stadium

Children's Museum of South Carolina

Myrtle Beach Convention Center

CHAPIN PARK

CANAL STREET REC CTR

Greyhound Myrtle Beach

Ripley's Believe It Or Not Mus

Myrtle Beach Pavilion

WITHERS SWASH PARK

WITHERS SWASH PARK

Legends In Concert

Family Kingdom Amusement Pk

Myrtle Beach

MIDWAY MEM PARK

OCEAN WOODS MEM PARK

RING PINES COURSE

ATLANTIC OCEAN

INTRACOASTAL WATERWAY

RAND McNALLY

A   B   C   D   E

1 2 3 4 5 6 7

MAP
233

1:30,000
1 in. = 2500 ft.
0   0.25   0.5
miles

SEE 138 MAP

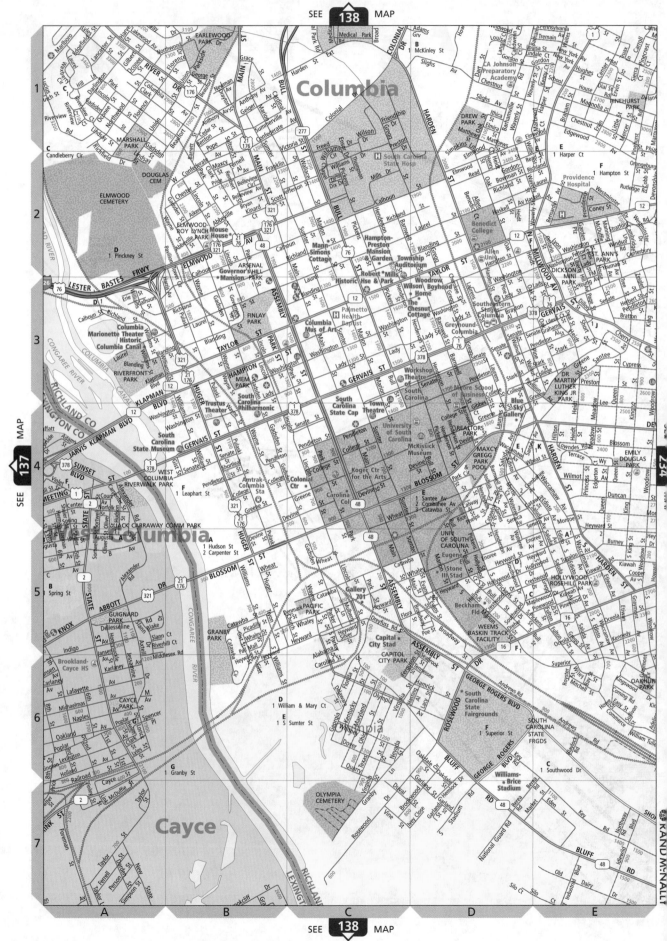

SEE 137 MAP

SEE 234 MAP

SEE 138 MAP

RAND McNALLY

A   B   C   D   E

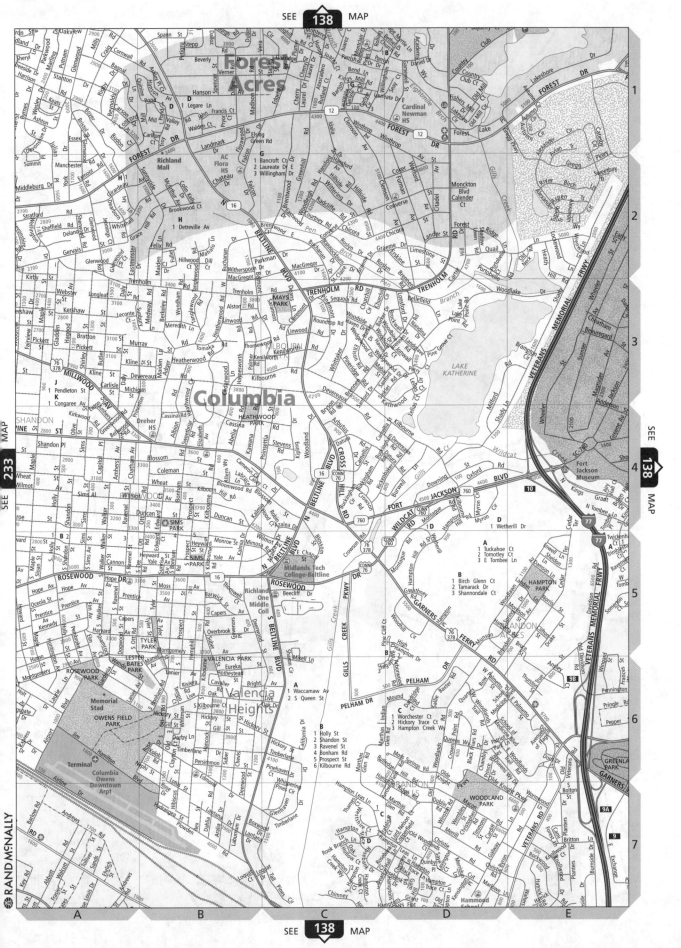

MAP
234

DETAIL MAP

SEE 138 MAP

SEE 233 MAP

SEE 138 MAP

SEE 138 MAP

RAND MCNALLY

MAP
235

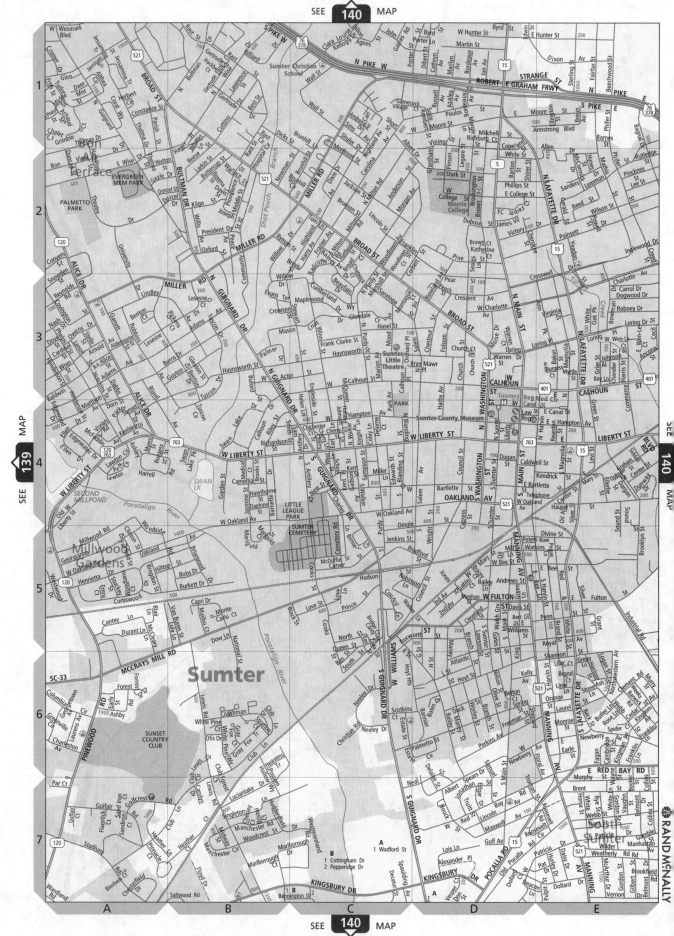

MAP
236

DETAIL MAP

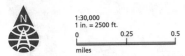

SEE 150 MAP

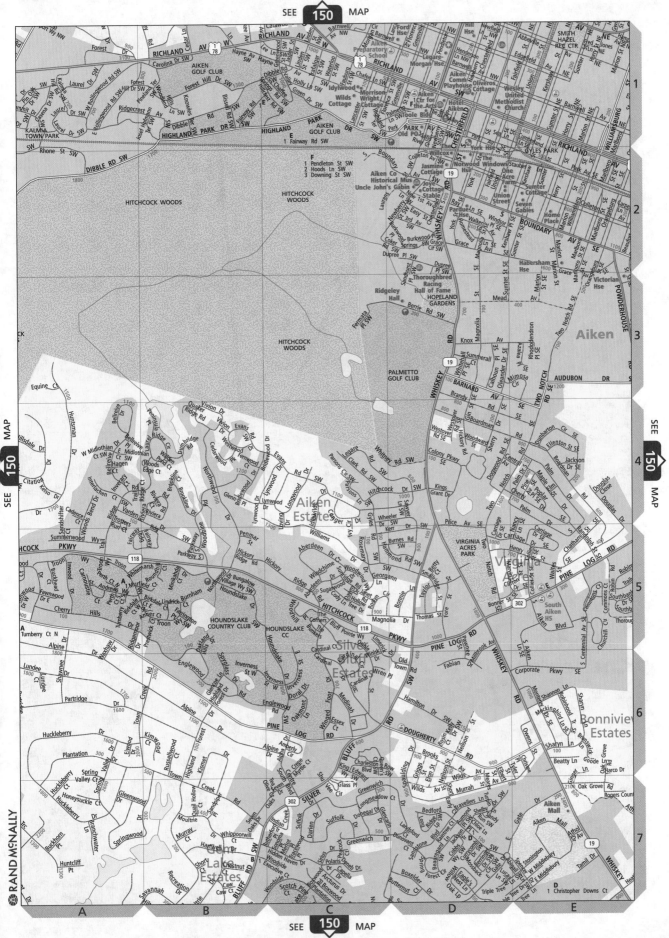

SEE 150 MAP

SEE 150 MAP

SEE 150 MAP

RAND MCNALLY

MAP
237

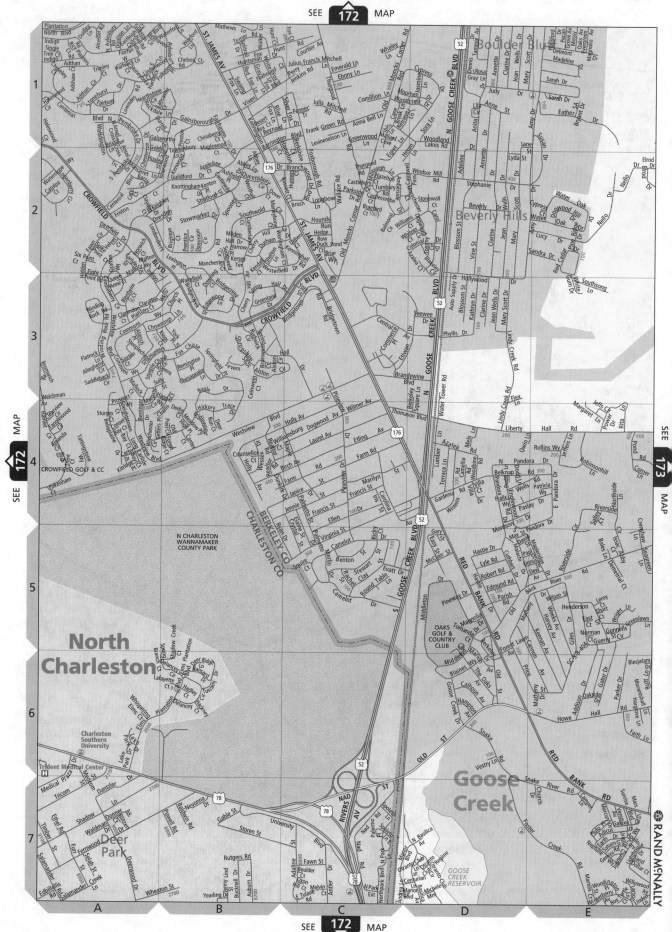

1:30,000
1 in. = 2500 ft.

0   0.25   0.5
miles

DETAIL MAP

SEE 172 MAP

SEE 173 MAP

North Charleston

Beverly Hills

Boulder Bluff

Goose Creek

Deer Park

CROWFIELD GOLF & CC

N CHARLESTON WANNAMAKER COUNTY PARK

Charleston Southern University

Trident Medical Center

OAKS GOLF & COUNTRY CLUB

GOOSE CREEK RESERVOIR

BERKELEY CO
CHARLESTON CO

A   B   C   D   E

RAND MCNALLY

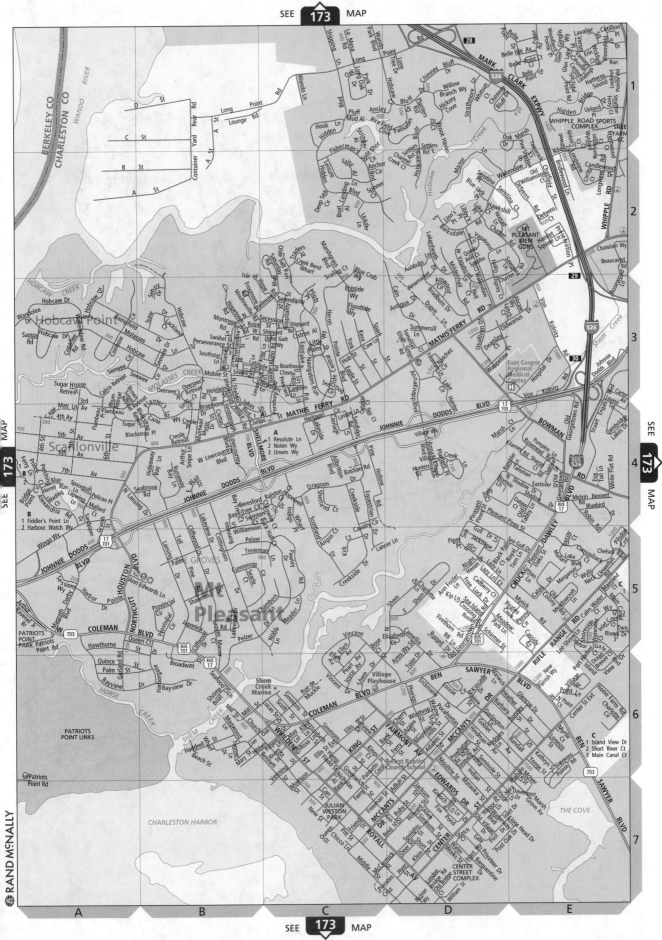

MAP
238

DETAIL MAP

1:30,000
1 in. = 2500 ft.
0   0.25   0.5
miles

SEE ⬆ 173 MAP

SEE 173 MAP

SEE 173 MAP

SEE 173 MAP

RAND M⁹NALLY

A   B   C   D   E

1   2   3   4   5   6   7

MAP
239

1:30,000
1 in. = 2500 ft.
0   0.25   0.5
miles

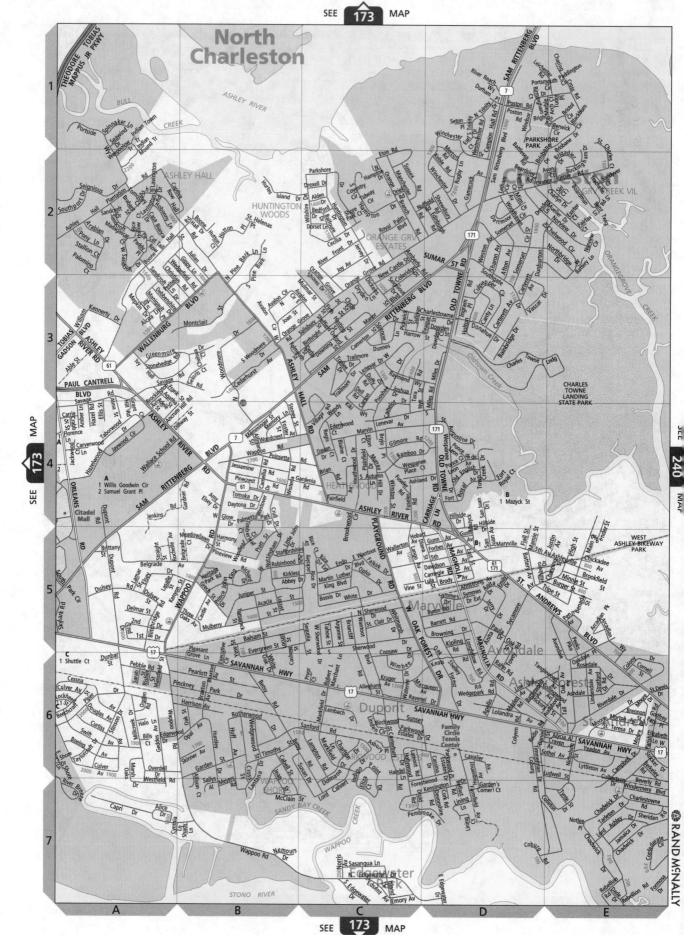

SEE [173] MAP

North
Charleston

DETAIL MAP

SEE [173] MAP

SEE 240 MAP

1
2
3
4
5
6
7

A   B   C   D   E

SEE [173] MAP

RAND MCNALLY

MAP
240

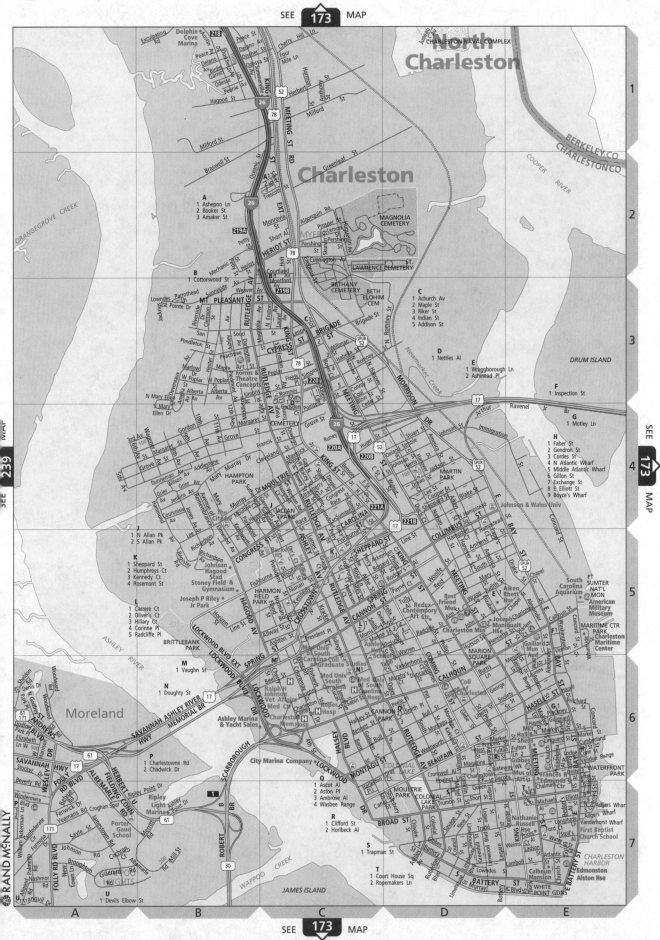

SEE 239 MAP

SEE 173 MAP

DETAIL MAP

1:30,000
1 in. = 2500 ft.
0   0.25   0.5
miles

RAND McNALLY

North Charleston

Charleston

CHARLESTON NAVAL COMPLEX

BERKELEY CO
CHARLESTON CO

COOPER RIVER

DRUM ISLAND

MAGNOLIA CEMETERY

LAWRENCE CEMETERY

A
1 Ashepoo Ln
2 Booker St
3 Amaker St

B
1 Cottonwood St

C
1 Achurch Av
2 Maple St
3 Riker St
4 Indian St
5 Addison St

D
1 Nettles Al

E
1 Wraggborough Ln
2 Ashimead Pl

F
1 Inspection St

G
1 Motley Ln

H
1 Faber St
2 Gendron St
3 Cordes St
4 N Atlantic Wharf
5 Middle Atlantic Wharf
6 Gillon St
7 Exchange St
8 E. Elliott St
9 Boyce's Wharf

J
1 N Allan Pk
2 S Allan Pk

K
1 Sheppard St
2 Humphreys Ct
3 Kennedy Ct
4 Rosemont St

L
1 Carrere Ct
2 Oliver's Ct
3 Hillary Ct
4 Corinne Pl
5 Radcliffe Pl

M
1 Vaughn St

N
1 Doughty St

P
1 Charlestowne Rd
2 Chadwick Dr

Q
1 Ascot Al
2 Aston Pl
3 Ambrose Al
4 Wasbee Range

R
1 Clifford St
2 Horlbeck Al

S
1 Trapman St

T
1 Court House Sq
2 Ropemakers Ln

U
1 Devils Elbow St

Moreland

ASHLEY RIVER

ORANGEGROVE CREEK

JAMES ISLAND

WAPPOO CREEK

CHARLESTON HARBOR

FT SUMTER NAT'L MON
American Military Museum

South Carolina Aquarium

MARITIME CTR PARK
Charleston Maritime Center

Johnson & Wales Univ

WATERFRONT PARK

MARION SQUARE PARK

COLONIAL LAKE PARK

WHITE POINT GDNS

A   B   C   D   E

MAP
241

1:30,000
1 in. = 2500 ft.

0   0.25   0.5
miles

SEE ▲ 177 MAP

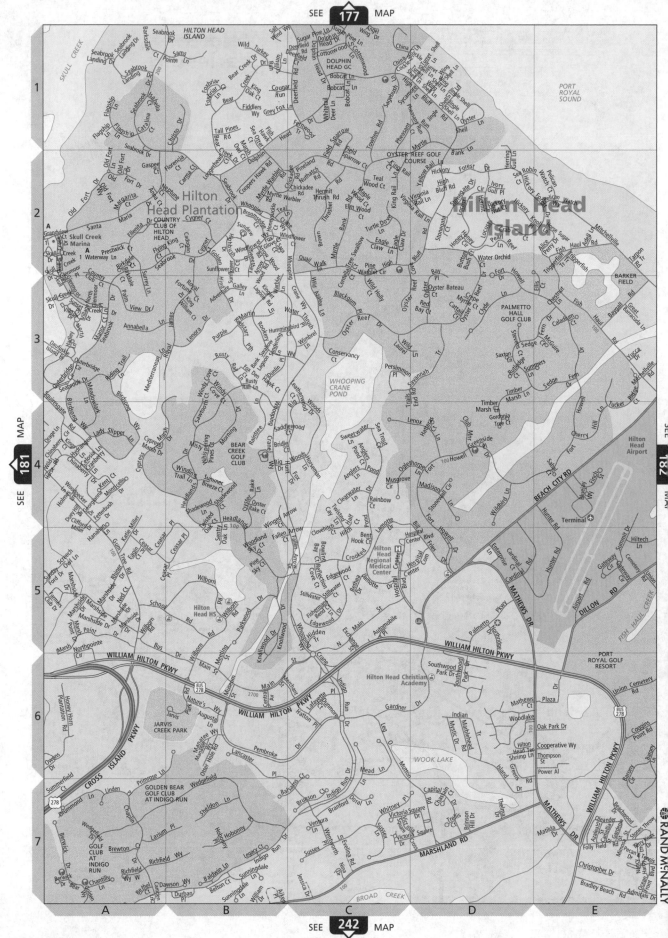

SEE ▲ 242 MAP

SEE ◀ 181 MAP

SEE 182 MAP

RAND M?NALLY

MAP
242

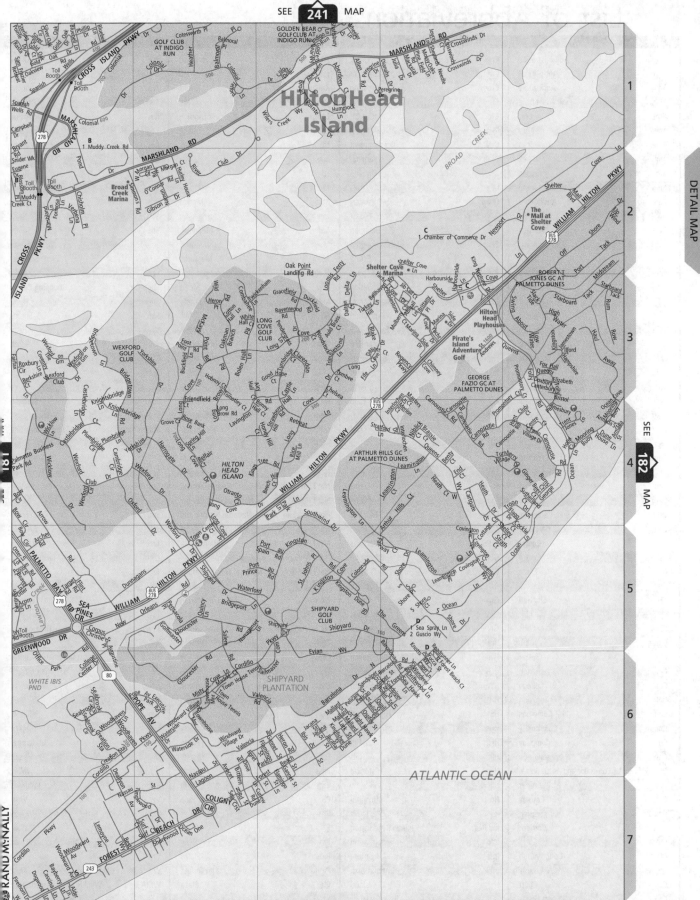

1:30,000
1 in. = 2500 ft.

0   0.25   0.5
miles

SEE 241 MAP

DETAIL MAP

Hilton Head Island

CROSS ISLAND PKWY

MARSHLAND RD

GOLDEN BEAR GOLF CLUB AT INDIGO RUN

GOLF CLUB AT INDIGO RUN

Broad Creek Marina

278

B 1 Muddy Creek Rd

C 1 Chamber of Commerce Dr

The Mall at Shelter Cove

WILLIAM HILTON PKWY

BUS 278

Shelter Cove Marina

ROBERT T JONES GC AT PALMETTO DUNES

Oak Point Landing Rd

LONG COVE GOLF CLUB

WEXFORD GOLF CLUB

Hilton Head Playhouses

Pirate's Island Adventure Golf

GEORGE FAZIO GC AT PALMETTO DUNES

HILTON HEAD ISLAND

ARTHUR HILLS GC AT PALMETTO DUNES

WILLIAM HILTON PKWY

BUS 278

SEE 182 MAP

SEE 181

PALMETTO BAY RD

SEA PINES RD CIR

WILLIAM HILTON PKWY

278

SHIPYARD GOLF CLUB

D 1 Sea Spray Ln
2 Guscio Wy

GREENWOOD DR

80

WHITE IBIS PND

SHIPYARD PLANTATION

POPE AV

ATLANTIC OCEAN

COLIGNY DR CIR

FOREST BEACH

243

RAND McNALLY

A   B   C   D   E

SEE 182 MAP

1 2 3 4 5 6 7

List of Abbreviations

Abbr	Full	Abbr	Full	Abbr	Full	Abbr	Full
Admin	Administration	Cr	Creek	Jct	Junction	PO	Post Office
Agri	Agricultural	Cres	Crescent	Knl	Knoll	Pres	Preserve
Ag	Agriculture	Cross	Crossing	Knls	Knolls	Prov	Provincial
AFB	Air Force Base	Curv	Curve	Lk	Lake	Rwy	Railway
Arpt	Airport	Cto	Cut Off	Lndg	Landing	Rec	Recreation
Al	Alley	Dept	Department	Ln	Lane	Reg	Regional
Amer	American	Dev	Development	Lib	Library	Res	Reservoir
Anx	Annex	Diag	Diagonal	Ldg	Lodge	Rst	Rest
Arc	Arcade	Div	Division	Lp	Loop	Rdg	Ridge
Arch	Archaeological	Dr	Drive	Mnr	Manor	Rd	Road
Aud	Auditorium	Drwy	Driveway	Mkt	Market	Rds	Roads
Avd	Avenida	E	East	Mdw	Meadow	St.	Saint
Av	Avenue	El	Elevation	Mdws	Meadows	Ste.	Sainte
Bfld	Battlefield	Env	Environmental	Med	Medical	Sci	Science
Bch	Beach	Est	Estate	Mem	Memorial	Sci	Sciences
Bnd	Bend	Ests	Estates	Metro	Metropolitan	Sci	Scientific
Bio	Biological	Exh	Exhibition	Mw	Mews	Shop Ctr	Shopping Center
Blf	Bluff	Expm	Experimental	Mil	Military	Shr	Shore
Blvd	Boulevard	Expo	Exposition	Ml	Mill	Shrs	Shores
Brch	Branch	Expwy	Expressway	Mls	Mills	Skwy	Skyway
Br	Bridge	Ext	Extension	Mon	Monument	S	South
Brk	Brook	Frgds	Fairgrounds	Mtwy	Motorway	Spr	Spring
Bldg	Building	ft	Feet	Mnd	Mound	Sprs	Springs
Bur	Bureau	Fy	Ferry	Mnds	Mounds	Sq	Square
Byp	Bypass	Fld	Field	Mt	Mount	Stad	Stadium
Bywy	Byway	Flds	Fields	Mtn	Mountain	St For	State Forest
Cl	Calle	Flt	Flat	Mtns	Mountains	St Hist Site	State Historic Site
Cljn	Callejon	Flts	Flats	Mun	Municipal	St Nat Area	State Natural Area
Cmto	Caminito	For	Forest	Mus	Museum	St Pk	State Park
Cm	Camino	Fk	Fork	Nat'l	National	St Rec Area	State Recreation Area
Cap	Capitol	Ft	Fort	Nat'l For	National Forest	Sta	Station
Cath	Cathedral	Found	Foundation	Nat'l Hist Pk	National Historic Park	St	Street
Cswy	Causeway	Frwy	Freeway	Nat'l Hist Site	National Historic Site	Smt	Summit
Cem	Cemetery	Gdn	Garden	Nat'l Mon	National Monument	Sys	Systems
Ctr	Center	Gdns	Gardens	Nat'l Park	National Park	Tech	Technical
Ctr	Centre	Gen Hosp	General Hospital	Nat'l Rec Area	National Recreation Area	Tech	Technological
Cir	Circle	Gln	Glen	Nat'l Wld Ref	National Wildlife Refuge	Tech	Technology
Crlo	Circulo	GC	Golf Course	Nat	Natural	Ter	Terrace
CH	City Hall	Grn	Green	NAS	Naval Air Station	Terr	Territory
Clf	Cliff	Grds	Grounds	Nk	Nook	Theol	Theological
Clfs	Cliffs	Grv	Grove	N	North	Thwy	Throughway
Clb	Club	Hbr	Harbor/Harbour	Orch	Orchard	Toll Fy	Toll Ferry
Cltr	Cluster	Hvn	Haven	Ohwy	Outer Highway	TIC	Tourist Information Center
Col	Coliseum	HQs	Headquarters	Ovl	Oval	Trc	Trace
Coll	College	Ht	Height	Ovlk	Overlook	Trfwy	Trafficway
Com	Common	Hts	Heights	Ovps	Overpass	Tr	Trail
Coms	Commons	HS	High School	Pk	Park	Tun	Tunnel
Comm	Community	Hwy	Highway	Pkwy	Parkway	Tpk	Turnpike
Co.	Company	Hl	Hill	Pas	Paseo	Unps	Underpass
Cons	Conservation	Hls	Hills	Psg	Passage	Univ	University
Conv & Vis Bur	Convention and Visitors Bureau	Hist	Historical	Pass	Passenger	Vly	Valley
Cor	Corner	Hllw	Hollow	Pth	Path	Vet	Veterans
Cors	Corners	Hosp	Hospital	Pn	Pine	Vw	View
Corp	Corporation	Hse	House	Pns	Pines	Vil	Village
Corr	Corridor	Ind Res	Indian Reservation	Pl	Place	Wk	Walk
Cte	Corte	Info	Information	Pln	Plain	Wall	Wall
CC	Country Club	Inst	Institute	Plns	Plains	Wy	Way
Co	County	Int'l	International	Plgnd	Playground	W	West
Ct	Court	I	Island	Plz	Plaza	WMA	Wildlife Management Area
Ct Hse	Court House	Is	Islands	Pt	Point		
Cts	Courts	Isl	Isle	Pnd	Pond		

Street Index

INDEX 3

SR-12 Klapman Blvd

Street Index

SR

STREET City State Map# Grid

SR-12 Klapman Blvd
Richland Co SC 233 A4
SR-12 Ocean Tr
Currituck Co NC 18 C6
SR-12 Percival Rd
Columbia SC 138 B5
Kershaw Co SC 138 E3
SR-12 Taylor St
Richland Co SC 233 B3
SR-12 N Virginia Dare Tr
Kitty Hawk NC 39 E2
SR-12 S Virginia Dare Tr
Nags Head NC 40 A4
SR-13
Habersham Co GA 115 B3
Mt Airy GA 115 A3
SR-13 Dicks Hill Pkwy
Habersham Co GA 115 B3
Mt Airy GA 115 A3
SR-14
Fountain Inn SC 118 D1
Greenville Co SC 97 D7
Greer SC 97 D3
Laurens Co SC 118 E2
Laurens Co SC 119 A3
Rockingham Co NC 7 D6
SR-14 N Main St
Greer SC 97 D3
SR-14 S Main St
Fountain Inn SC 118 D1
SR-14 SE Main St
Greenville Co SC 97 D7
SR-15
Habersham Co GA 94 B7
Habersham Co GA 115 A2
Myrtle Beach SC 232 C4
SR-15 W Broadway St
Myrtle Beach SC 232 C4
SR-16
Ashe Co NC 3 A7
Charlotte NC 75 C5
Charlotte NC 101 D1
Gaston Co NC 75 A2
Grayson Co VA 2 E2
Marvin NC 101 D3
Newton NC 48 E7
Richland Co SC 233 D5
Taylorsville NC 48 C1
Troutdale VA 2 E1
Union Co NC 101 E3
Wilkes Co NC 24 C6
Wilkesboro NC 24 C4
SR-16 N Beltline Blvd
Richland Co SC 234 C4
SR-16 Brookshire Blvd
Charlotte NC 75 C5
SR-16 Jefferson Hwy
Grayson Co VA 2 E3
SR-16 S McDowell St
Charlotte NC 216 A3
SR-16 Providence Rd
Charlotte NC 75 D7
Charlotte NC 101 D1
SR-16 Providence Rd S
Marvin NC 101 D3
Weddington NC 101 D2
SR-16 Rosewood Dr
Richland Co SC 233 D5
SR-16 Troutdale Hwy
Grayson Co VA 2 E2
Grayson Co VA 3 A3
Troutdale VA 2 E1
SR-17
Bloomingdale GA 180 B3
Canon GA 116 A6
Clarkesville GA 115 A2
Effingham Co GA 180 B2
Franklin Co GA 116 A7
Hiawassee GA 93 B4
SR-17 ALT
Habersham Co GA 115 B2
SR-17 Bloomingdale Rd
Bloomingdale GA 180 B3
SR-17 Central Blvd
Effingham Co GA 175 A6
SR-17 N Main St
Towns Co GA 93 B4
SR-17 ALT Talmadge Dr
Habersham Co GA 115 B2
SR-17 Toccoa Hwy
Habersham Co GA 115 A2
SR-17 Tommy Irvin Pkwy
Habersham Co GA 115 B2
SR-17 Unicoi Tpk
Towns Co GA 93 C4
SR-17 Veterans Memorial Wy
Stephens Co GA 115 C3
SR-17 Washington Hwy
Elbert Co GA 133 A6
SR-18
Alleghany Co NC 3 D5
Alleghany Co NC 4 A4
Belwood NC 73 D1
Cedar Rock NC 23 D7
Cherokee Co SC 99 B3
Cleveland Co NC 73 D3
Fallston NC 73 D3
Morganton NC 47 B4
Shelby NC 73 C5
Wilkes Co NC 24 C2
SR-18 BUS
Lenoir NC 47 C1
SR-18 Fallston Rd
Belwood NC 73 D1
Cleveland Co NC 73 D4
Fallston NC 73 D3
SR-18 Gaffney Hwy
Union Co SC 99 B5
SR-18 BUS Harper Av
Lenoir NC 47 C1
SR-18 Jonesville Hwy
Union Co SC 99 B7
SR-18 S Jonesville Hwy
Union Co SC 99 B6
SR-18 S Lafayette St
Cleveland Co NC 73 C6
Shelby NC 73 C5
SR-18 Morganton Blvd SW
Caldwell Co NC 47 B2
SR-18 Shelby Hwy
Cherokee Co SC 73 C6
SR-18 Sparta Rd
Wilkes Co NC 24 C2
SR-18 S Sterling St
Morganton NC 47 B4
SR-18 Union Hwy
Cherokee Co SC 99 B3
SR-18 Wilkesboro Blvd
Caldwell Co NC 23 D7
Caldwell Co NC 24 B6
SR-19
Aiken SC 150 A7
Aiken Co SC 149 E4
Aiken Co SC 150 A5
Aiken Co SC 160 B1
Aiken Co SC 236 D2
Lancaster Co SC 219 D7
SR-19 Chesterfield St S
Aiken Co SC 236 D2
SR-19 Edgefield Hwy
Aiken Co SC 149 E4
Aiken Co SC 150 A5
SR-19 Lynwood Dr
Lancaster Co SC 219 D7
SR-19 Whiskey Rd
Aiken Co SC 150 A7
Aiken Co SC 160 B1
Aiken Co SC 236 E7
SR-20
Abbeville Co SC 118 A7
Abbeville Co SC 134 B1
Anderson Co SC 117 E3
Due West SC 118 B7
Greenville SC 223 B5
Hoke Co NC 106 B3
Lumber Bridge NC 106 D4
Pelzer SC 117 E2
Robeson Co NC 107 A5
SR-20 Augusta St
Greenville SC 223 B5
SR-20 Due West Rd
Anderson Co SC 117 E6
SR-20 Grove Rd
Greenville Co SC 97 A6
Greenville Co SC 223 A7
SR-20 N Piedmont Hwy
Greenville Co SC 97 A7
SR-20 S Piedmont Hwy
Greenville Co SC 118 A1
SR-20 River St
Greenville SC 223 B4
SR-20 St. Pauls Rd
Hoke Co NC 106 B3
SR-21
Cherokee Co SC 73 E7
Cherokee Co SC 74 A7
Effingham Co GA 180 D1
Georgetown Co SC 156 B7
Georgetown Co SC 166 B1
Port Wentworth GA 180 D3
Rincon GA 175 C7
Savannah GA 180 E4
Springfield GA 175 B6
SR-21 BYP
Springfield GA 175 B6
SR-21 Antioch Rd
Cherokee Co SC 73 E7
Cherokee Co SC 74 A7
SR-21 Augusta Rd
Port Wentworth GA 180 D3
SR-21 County Line Rd
Georgetown Co SC 156 B7
Georgetown Co SC 166 B1
SR-21 Lynes Pkwy
Chatham Co GA 180 E4
SR-21 Millen Hwy
Screven Co GA 168 B6
SR-21 Savannah Hwy
Screven Co GA 168 C7
SR-21 Sylvania Byp
Screven Co GA 168 B7
SR-22
Chatham Co NC 53 B7
Guilford Co NC 28 D7
Horry Co SC 143 E6
Horry Co SC 158 C1
Moore Co NC 79 C3
Pickens Co SC 225 B6
Randolph Co NC 52 D2
Southern Pines NC 79 D5
SR-22 McNeill St
Moore Co NC 79 C3
SR-22 Stone Church Rd
Clemson SC 225 B6
SR-22 Veterans Hwy
Horry Co SC 143 E6
Horry Co SC 144 B7
Horry Co SC 158 C1
SR-23
Batesburg-Leesville SC 136 D7
Burke Co GA 159 E7
Burke Co GA 168 A1
Edgefield Co SC 149 C2
McCormick Co SC 148 E3
Monetta SC 150 C1
Saluda Co SC 150 B1
Unicoi Co TN 20 D5
SR-23 E Church St
Batesburg-Leesville SC 136 D7
SR-23 Columbia Rd
Edgefield Co SC 149 D2
SR-23 Flag Pond Rd
Unicoi Co TN 20 D5
SR-24
Albemarle NC 77 C3
Anderson Co SC 116 E3
Anderson Co SC 117 A4
Autryville NC 107 D2
Bogue NC 112 D5
Burke Co GA 159 B7
Burke Co GA 168 A3
Carteret Co NC 113 A5
Cedar Point NC 112 A6
Charlotte NC 75 D4
Charlotte NC 211 C7
Duplin Co NC 109 D3
Duplin Co NC 110 A2
Fayetteville NC 80 E7
Fayetteville NC 107 B1
Harnett Co NC 80 C4
Hilltonia GA 168 B4
Jacksonville NC 111 B5
Montgomery Co NC 77 E4
Onslow Co NC 111 E6
Sampson Co NC 108 C2
Stanly Co NC 76 E5
SR-24 BUS
Duplin Co NC 109 C2
Jacksonville NC 227 C6
Warsaw NC 109 B1
SR-24 W 6th St
Burke Co GA 159 B7
SR-24 Albemarle Rd
Charlotte NC 75 E6
Charlotte NC 76 A6
Troy NC 78 A3
SR-24 Autry Hwy
Sampson Co NC 108 A2
SR-24 Beulaville Hwy
Onslow Co NC 110 D2
SR-24 Bragg Blvd
Cumberland Co NC 221 E4
Fayetteville NC 80 E7
Fayetteville NC 222 C2
SR-24 N Bragg Blvd
Spring Lake NC 221 D1
SR-24 Cedar Point Blvd
Cedar Point NC 112 A6
SR-24 Clinton Rd
Autryville NC 107 D2
SR-24 Freedom Wy
Jacksonville NC 111 C6
Onslow Co NC 111 E6
SR-24 S Kenansville Byp
Duplin Co NC 109 D3
SR-24 KIA MIA POW Frwy
Jacksonville NC 111 B5
SR-24 E Main St
Albemarle NC 77 C3
SR-24 BUS Marine Blvd
Jacksonville NC 227 C6
SR-24 Newington Hwy
Screven Co GA 168 E7
SR-24 Oak Hwy
Oconee Co SC 116 C2
SR-24 W Oak Hwy
Oconee Co SC 116 B2
SR-24 Portman Rd
Anderson Co SC 117 B4
SR-24 Richlands Hwy
Onslow Co NC 110 E3
Onslow Co NC 111 A4
SR-24 Roseboro Hwy
Sampson Co NC 108 C2
SR-24 Rowan St
Fayetteville NC 222 D2
SR-24 Turkey Hwy
Sampson Co NC 108 E2
Sampson Co NC 109 A2
SR-24 Waynesboro Hwy
Screven Co GA 168 B4
SR-24 W Whitner St
Anderson Co SC 226 A4
SR-24 E Wt Harris Blvd
Charlotte NC 75 E5
SR-24 W Wt Harris Blvd
Charlotte NC 75 D4
SR-24 W WT Harris Blvd
Charlotte NC 211 B7
SR-25
Chatham Co GA 180 D2
Garden City GA 180 D3
SR-25 Coastal Hwy
Liberty Co GA 180 B6
SR-25 N Coastal Hwy
Port Wentworth GA 180 D2
SR-25 Main St
Chatham Co GA 180 D3
SR-25 Ogeechee Rd
Chatham Co GA 180 C5
SR-26
Bloomingdale GA 180 C3
Chatham Co GA 181 B4
Effingham Co GA 180 A2
Garden City GA 180 D4
Savannah GA 180 E4
Tybee Island GA 181 C5
SR-26 Louisville Hwy
Bloomingdale GA 180 C3
SR-26 Ocean Hwy
Savannah GA 180 E4
SR-26 Saffold Dr
Chatham Co GA 181 B4
SR-26 E Victory Dr
Savannah GA 180 E4
SR-27
Berkeley Co SC 164 A4
Biscoe NC 78 E3
SR-27
Charlotte NC 75 B5
Charlotte NC 76 A6
Charlotte NC 216 A3
Dorchester Co SC 172 A1
Harnett Co NC 81 E2
Lillington NC 81 B2
Lincoln Co NC 47 D7
Lincoln Co NC 73 E1
Lincolnton NC 74 B1
Locust NC 76 E5
Midland NC 76 D5
Montgomery Co NC 77 E4
Montgomery Co NC 78 C3
Moore Co NC 79 D3
SR-27 Albemarle Rd
Charlotte NC 75 E6
Charlotte NC 76 A6
Troy NC 78 A3
SR-27 Freedom Dr
Charlotte NC 75 B5
Charlotte NC 215 D2
SR-27 Givhans Rd
Dorchester Co SC 164 A7
Dorchester Co SC 172 A1
SR-27 E Main St
Albemarle NC 77 C3
SR-27 N McDowell St
Charlotte NC 216 B3
SR-27 S McDowell St
Charlotte NC 216 A3
SR-27 W Morehead St
Charlotte NC 215 E3
SR-27 Mt Holly Rd
Gaston Co NC 75 A4
SR-27 Old Gilliard Rd
Berkeley Co SC 164 A4
SR-27 Paul Green Memorial Hwy
Lillington NC 81 B2
SR-27 Ridgeville Rd
Dorchester Co SC 164 B6
SR-28
Abbeville Co SC 133 E1
Abbeville Co SC 134 A3
Aiken Co SC 159 D1
Anderson SC 117 B3
Anderson SC 226 D6
Anderson Co SC 117 A2
Augusta GA 149 B7
Augusta GA 159 B1
Clemson SC 225 C4
Graham Co NC 67 C2
Macon Co NC 68 B6
Martinez GA 149 A7
McCormick Co SC 148 D3
Oconee Co SC 116 C1
Parksville SC 148 D2
Pickens Co SC 225 D7
Rabun Co GA 94 E3
Walhalla SC 95 A6
SR-28 BUS
Pickens Co SC 225 D6
SR-28 BYP
Abbeville Co SC 134 A3
Anderson Co SC 117 B4
Anderson Co SC 226 C7
SR-28 Abbeville Hwy
Anderson Co SC 117 C5
SR-28 Anderson Hwy
Clemson SC 225 C4
Pickens Co SC 225 D7
SR-28 Blue Ridge Blvd
Oconee Co SC 95 B7
SR-28 Bryson City Rd
Macon Co NC 68 B6
SR-28 Calhoun Expwy
Augusta GA 159 B1
SR-28 Clemson Blvd
Anderson Co SC 117 B3
SR-28 Fontana Rd
Graham Co NC 67 C2
SR-28 Franklin Rd
Highlands NC 94 E1
SR-28 Furrys Ferry Rd
McCormick Co SC 148 E5
SR-28 Furys Ferry Rd
Martinez GA 149 A7
SR-28 Highlands Hwy
Oconee Co SC 95 A6
SR-28 Highlands Rd
Macon Co NC 68 D7
SR-28 N Main St
Anderson SC 226 C3
SR-28 S Main St
Anderson Co SC 226 D7
SR-28 N Murray St
Anderson SC 226 C4
SR-28 S Murray St
Anderson SC 226 D5
SR-28 BYP Pearman Dairy Rd
Anderson Co SC 117 B4
Anderson Co SC 226 A4
SR-28 BYP Pearman Dairy Rd S
Anderson Co SC 226 C7
SR-28 BUS Pendleton Rd
Pickens Co SC 225 D6
SR-28 Sand Bar Ferry Rd
Aiken Co SC 159 D1
SR-28 Sayre St
Anderson SC 226 D6
SR-28 Tiger Blvd
Clemson SC 225 A3
SR-28 Washington Rd
Augusta GA 149 B7
SR-30
Charleston SC 173 B6
Charleston SC 240 B7
Effingham Co GA 180 C2
SR-30
McMinn Co TN 65 A3
Pitt Co NC 59 D3
Port Wentworth GA 180 D2
SR-30 Augusta Rd
Port Wentworth GA 180 D2
SR-30 Bonnybridge Rd
Port Wentworth GA 180 D2
SR-30 David W Lillard Mem Hwy
McMinn Co TN 65 A3
SR-30 James Island Expwy
Charleston SC 173 B6
SR-30 Kimsey Hwy
Polk Co TN 65 A6
SR-30 Noel Conaway Hwy
Effingham Co GA 180 C2
SR-30 Robert B Scarborough Br
Charleston SC 240 B7
SR-30 Tennessee Av
McMinn Co TN 65 A3
SR-31
Horry Co SC 144 D7
Horry Co SC 157 E3
Horry Co SC 158 D1
SR-31 Carolina Bays Pkwy
Horry Co SC 144 D7
Horry Co SC 157 E3
Horry Co SC 158 D1
SR-32
Beaufort Co NC 60 E4
Beaufort Co NC 61 A2
Chowan Co NC 16 B7
Chowan Co NC 37 D4
Cocke Co TN 42 E3
Cocke Co TN 43 A3
Darlington Co SC 140 E2
Plymouth NC 37 A7
Suffolk VA 16 B1
SR-32 Broad Creek Rd
Beaufort Co NC 60 E4
SR-32 Carolina Rd
Suffolk VA 16 B1
SR-32 Cosby Hwy
Cocke Co TN 42 E2
SR-32 Haughton Rd
Chowan Co NC 37 D4
SR-32 Lee State Park Rd
Darlington Co SC 140 E2
SR-32 River Rd
Beaufort Co NC 60 B6
SR-32 TG Sonny Boy Joyner Hwy
Washington Co NC 37 A7
Washington Co NC 61 A1
SR-32 Virginia Rd
Chowan Co NC 16 B7
Chowan Co NC 37 B2
SR-33
Aurora NC 87 B3
Beaufort Co NC 86 D1
Calhoun Co SC 153 A6
Chocowinity NC 60 B7
Edgecombe Co NC 58 E1
Etowah TN 65 A3
Greenville NC 59 C4
Leggett NC 34 D6
McMinn Co TN 65 B1
Pamlico Co NC 87 D3
Tarboro NC 34 E7
SR-33 Belvoir Hwy
Greenville NC 59 B4
SR-33 Blounts Creek Rd
Beaufort Co NC 86 D1
SR-33 Cameron Rd
Calhoun Co SC 153 A6
Orangeburg Co SC 152 E7
SR-33 Hobucken Rd
Pamlico Co NC 87 D3
SR-33 N Main St
Tarboro NC 34 E7
SR-33 Pactolus Hwy
Greenville NC 59 C4
SR-33 Tennessee Av
McMinn Co TN 65 A3
SR-33 N Tennessee Av
Etowah TN 65 B3
SR-34
Camden Co NC 184 E4
Chappells SC 135 E2
Darlington Co SC 125 C7
Darlington Co SC 229 A5
Dillon Co SC 126 C5
Elizabeth City NC 17 C6
Elizabeth City NC 184 D5
Fairfield Co SC 122 B7
Greene Co TN 19 C3
Greeneville TN 20 A3
Greenwood SC 134 E3
Johnson Co TN 1 E7
Jonesborough TN 20 E1
Mosheim TN 19 D3
Mountain City TN 1 E5
Newberry SC 136 C1
Newberry Co SC 136 B2
Pasquotank Co NC 17 D7
Pasquotank Co NC 38 D1
Washington Co TN 21 A1
SR-34 Andrew Johnson Hwy
Washington Co TN 20 D2
SR-34 E Andrew Johnson Hwy
Greeneville TN 20 A3
Hamblen Co TN 19 A2
Tusculum TN 20 B2
SR-34 W Andrew Johnson Hwy
Greene Co TN 19 C3
SR-34 Bishopville Hwy
Kershaw Co SC 139 C1
SR-34 Camden Cswy
Camden Co NC 184 E4
SR-34 Camden Hwy
Lee Co SC 140 A2
SR-34 Cashua St
Darlington SC 229 C5
SR-34 Cashua Ferry Rd
Darlington Co SC 125 C7
SR-34 Dixie Dr
Newberry Co SC 136 C1
SR-34 Hartsville Hwy
Darlington Co SC 125 A7
Darlington Co SC 229 A5
Lee Co SC 140 C1
SR-34 W Jackson Blvd
Jonesborough TN 20 E1
SR-34 E Lydia Hwy
Darlington Co SC 124 E7
SR-34 W Lydia Hwy
Darlington Co SC 124 D7
SR-34 W Market St
Washington Co TN 21 A1
SR-34 Newberry Rd
Fairfield Co SC 121 C6
SR-34 Ninety Six Hwy
Greenwood SC 134 E3
Greenwood Co SC 135 A3
SR-34 Ridgeway Rd
Kershaw Co SC 138 E2
SR-34 S Road St
Elizabeth City NC 184 D5
SR-34 Robert F Smith Pkwy
Mosheim TN 19 D3
SR-34 Salem Church Rd
Pasquotank Co NC 17 D7
SR-34 N Shady St
Mountain City TN 1 D5
SR-34 S Shady St
Mountain City TN 1 E5
SR-34 Shawboro Rd
Currituck Co NC 17 D3
SR-34 Soundneck Rd
Pasquotank Co NC 38 D1
SR-34 Weeksville Rd
Elizabeth City NC 17 C6
SR-35
Boykins VA 14 D2
Greene Co TN 19 C5
Sevier Co TN 41 B2
Sevier Co TN 42 B1
Sevierville TN 42 A1
Woodland NC 14 D6
SR-35 Chapman Hwy SE
Sevier Co TN 41 D2
SR-35 N Church St
Conway NC 14 C5
SR-35 Dolly Parton Pkwy
Sevierville TN 42 A1
SR-35 Maryville Hwy
Sevier Co TN 41 B2
SR-35 Meherrin Rd
Boykins VA 14 D2
Southampton Co VA 14 D1
SR-35 Newport Hwy
Greene Co TN 19 C5
Sevier Co TN 42 B1
SR-36
Carter Co TN 21 A4
Unicoi Co TN 20 E4
SR-36 Erwin Hwy
Carter Co TN 21 A4
SR-36 James H Quillen Pkwy
Unicoi Co TN 20 E4
Unicoi Co TN 21 A4
SR-36 Spivey Mountain Rd
Unicoi Co TN 20 E6
Unicoi Co TN 21 A6
SR-37
Barnwell Co SC 161 A3
Carter Co TN 21 D2
Chowan Co NC 37 D4
Elko SC 161 B2
Gates Co NC 15 E5
Gates Co NC 16 B5
Oconee Co SC 225 A7
SR-37 Haughton Rd
Chowan Co NC 37 D4
SR-37 Ocean Hwy S
Perquimans Co NC 37 C2
SR-37 Veterans Memorial Pkwy
Carter Co TN 21 D2
Carter Co TN 22 A3
SR-38
Bennettsville SC 125 E2
Marlboro Co SC 125 E1
Marlboro Co SC 126 A4
Richmond Co NC 104 E5
SR-38 Blenheim Hwy
Marlboro Co SC 125 E2
SR-38 EB Cottingham Blvd N
Bennettsville SC 125 E2
SR-38 Louis Breeden Blvd
Richmond Co NC 104 E5
SR-39
Aiken Co SC 150 E4
Aiken Co SC 151 A5
Barnwell Co SC 160 E2
Barnwell Co SC 161 A1
Chappells SC 135 D4
Franklin Co NC 32 D3
SR-39
Franklin Co NC 56
Henderson NC 11
Laurens Co SC 119
Laurens Co SC 135
Saluda Co SC 136
SR-39 Blue Ridge Spring Hwy
Saluda Co SC 136
Saluda Co SC 150
SR-39 Festival Trail Rd
Aiken Co SC 151
SR-39 Liberty Hill Rd
McMinn Co TN 65
SR-39 Mecca Pike
Monroe Co TN 65
Tellico Plains TN 65
SR-39 Old 96 Indian Tr
Aiken Co SC 150
Aiken Co SC 151
SR-39 Old Englewood Rd
McMinn Co TN 65
SR-39 Springfield Rd
Barnwell Co SC 161
SR-39 William S Corbitt Hwy
Franklin Co NC 32
Henderson NC 11
SR-40
Ducktown TN 91
Florence Co SC 142
Polk Co TN 65
Polk Co TN 91
SR-40 Old Copper Rd
Ducktown TN 91
Polk Co TN 65
Polk Co TN 91
SR-40 River Rd
Florence Co SC 142
SR-41
Berkeley Co SC 165
Berkeley Co SC 173
Beulaville NC 110
Bladen Co NC 108
Bladen Co NC 129
Duplin Co NC 109
Duplin Co NC 110
Fairmont NC 127
Georgetown Co SC 166
Harrells NC 109
Jamestown SC 165
Jones Co NC 85
Marion Co SC 143
Robeson Co NC 127
Trenton NC 85
SR-41 ALT
Dillon Co SC 127
Marion Co SC 142
SR-41 County Line Rd
Georgetown Co SC 156
Georgetown Co SC 166
SR-41 Franklin Tpk
Pittsylvania Co VA 8
SR-41 Kingsburg Hwy
Florence Co SC 156
SR-41 N Morgan Av
Andrews SC 166
SR-41 S Morgan Av
Georgetown Co SC 166
SR-41 Old Tram Rd
Marion Co SC 142
SR-41 Tomahawk Hwy
Sampson Co NC 108
Sampson Co NC 109
SR-42
Asheboro NC 52
Bertie Co NC 14
Bertie Co NC 35
Bertie Co NC 36
Chatham Co NC 53
Chatham Co NC 54
Edgecombe Co NC 58
Fuquay-Varina NC 55
Harnett Co NC 55
Hertford Co NC 15
Johnston Co NC 56
Johnston Co NC 57
Lee Co NC 80
Lewiston Woodville NC 35
Oak City NC 35
Sanford NC 80
Wilson NC 57
SR-42 Avents Ferry Rd
Chatham Co NC 54
Sanford NC 80
SR-42 Carbonton Rd
Lee Co NC 53
Lee Co NC 54
Lee Co NC 80
SR-42 Coleridge Rd
Asheboro NC 52
SR-42 S Horner Blvd
Sanford NC 80
SR-42 N Main St
Fuquay-Varina NC 55
SR-42 E Salisbury St
Asheboro NC 52
Asheboro NC 209
SR-42 W Salisbury St
Asheboro NC 209
SR-42 Ward Blvd
Wilson NC 57
Wilson NC 202
SR-43
Craven Co NC 86
Dortches NC 33
Edgecombe Co NC 34
Edgecombe Co NC 58
Greenville NC 59
Greenville NC 203
Halifax Co NC 33

INDEX 4
-43 Street Index SR-75 Bowmantown Rd

TREET
State Map# Grid
R-43
incoln Co GA 148 A1
itt Co NC 59 C6
itt Co NC 85 E1
ocky Mount NC 34 A6
ocky Mount NC 201 C2
Varren Co NC 12 C7
R-43 BUS
dgecombe Co NC 34 A6
ocky Mount NC 201 D3
R-43 W 5th St
reenville NC 59 A4
R-43 BUS Benvenue Rd
ocky Mount NC 201 C2
R-43 S Charles Blvd
reenville NC 203 A6
R-43 Coach Jimmy
mith Hwy
incoln Co GA 148 A1
R-43 Cokey Rd
dgecombe Co NC 34 B7
R-43 Dortches Blvd
ortches NC 33 E5
R-43 Greenville Blvd
W
Greenville NC 59 B5
R-43 S Memorial Dr
Greenville NC 59 B4
Greenville NC 203 A2
R-43 Red Oak Blvd
Nash Co NC 33 D3
R-43 Washington Post
d
Craven Co NC 86 A4
R-44
Greenwood Co SC 135 A4
Lincoln Co GA 133 C7
Martin Co NC 35 B6
Sullivan Co TN 1 A3
R-44 Epworth Camp Rd
Greenwood Co SC 135 A4
R-44 Graball Rd
Lincoln Co GA 133 C7
R-45
Berkeley Co SC 164 E1
Berkeley Co SC 165 C2
Berkeley Co SC 166 C6
Bertie Co NC 36 E2
Bertie Co NC 37 A5
Eutawville SC 164 A2
Harrellsville NC 15 E7
Hyde Co NC 61 D4
Hyde Co NC 62 B7
Plymouth NC 37 A7
Winton NC 15 C5
SR-45 Branchdale Hwy
Orangeburg Co SC 163 E2
Orangeburg Co SC 164 A2
SR-45 DeWitt Williams
Blvd
Berkeley Co SC 165 A1
SR-45 French Santee Rd
Berkeley Co SC 166 C6
SR-45 NC-45 N
Bertie Co NC 36 E2
SR-45 Santee River Rd
Berkeley Co SC 165 C2
SR-45 TG Sonny Boy
Joyner Hwy
Hyde Co NC 62 A6
Washington Co NC 37 A7
Washington Co NC 61 A1
SR-45 Trojan Rd
Berkeley Co SC 164 D2
SR-46
Beaufort Co SC 181 C1
Jasper Co SC 176 A7
Northampton Co NC 12 E3
Northampton Co NC 13 B3
SR-46 Christanna Hwy
Brunswick Co VA 12 D1
SR-46 Lawrenceville Rd
Northampton Co NC 12 E3
Northampton Co NC 13 B3
SR-46 May River Rd
Beaufort Co SC 181 C1
SR-46 Okatie Hwy
Beaufort Co SC 181 B1
SR-47
Davidson Co NC 50 E3
Denton NC 51 D6
Elloree SC 153 B7
Lincoln Co GA 148 B4
Orangeburg Co SC 153 C7
Orangeburg Co SC 163 B1
SR-47 Belmont Rd
Davidson Co NC 50 E3
SR-47 Cleveland St
Orangeburg Co SC 153 B7
Orangeburg Co SC 163 B1
SR-47 Scotts Ferry Rd
Columbia Co GA 148 C6
SR-47 Washington Rd
Columbia Co GA 148 C5
SR-48
Nash Co NC 33 E4
Nash Co NC 34 A5
Northampton Co NC 13 C3
Richland Co SC 138 B7
Richland Co SC 152 C1
Richland Co SC 153 A1
Richland Co SC 233 E7
Rocky Mount NC 201 C2
SR-48 Assembly St
Richland Co SC 233 B2
SR-48 S Assembly St
Richland Co SC 233 D7
SR-48 Bluff Rd
Richland Co SC 138 B7
Richland Co SC 152 C1
Richland Co SC 153 A1

STREET
City State Map# Grid
SR-48 Bluff Rd
Richland Co SC 233 E7
SR-48 Pleasant Hill Rd
Northampton Co NC 13 C3
SR-49
Alamance Co NC 29 D3
Burlington NC 192 D7
Caswell Co NC 30 B1
Charlotte NC 75 E4
Charlotte NC 212 A7
Chester Co SC 99 E6
Davidson Co NC 51 C7
Graham NC 29 D4
Laurens Co SC 119 C3
Lockhart SC 99 D6
Person Co NC 10 A4
Ramseur NC 52 E3
Randolph Co NC 53 A2
Union Co SC 120 A1
York Co SC 74 E7
York Co SC 100 D2
SR-49 Burlington Rd
Caswell Co NC 30 B1
Person Co NC 9 C7
SR-49 Buster Boyd Br
York Co SC 101 A1
SR-49 Charlotte Hwy
York Co SC 74 E7
York Co SC 100 D2
SR-49 Cross Keys Hwy
Spartanburg Co SC 119 E2
Union Co SC 120 A1
SR-49 E Dixie Dr
Asheboro NC 209 D6
SR-49 W Dixie Dr
Asheboro NC 209 B7
SR-49 Earl Davis
Gregory Hwy
Mecklenburg Co VA 10 C3
SR-49 E Elm St
Graham NC 29 D4
SR-49 N Graham St
Charlotte NC 216 A1
SR-49 Harden St
Burlington NC 192 E6
SR-49 Lockhart Hwy
Chester Co SC 99 E6
Lockhart SC 99 D6
SR-49 Lockhart Rd
York Co SC 99 E5
York Co SC 100 A4
SR-49 Maple Av
Alamance Co NC 29 C5
Burlington NC 192 D7
SR-49 W Morehead St
Charlotte NC 215 E3
SR-49 Sharon Rd
York Co SC 100 B3
SR-49 N Tryon St
Charlotte NC 75 D5
Charlotte NC 216 B1
SR-49 S Tryon St
Charlotte NC 75 B7
SR-49 University City
Blvd
Charlotte NC 75 E4
Mecklenburg Co NC 212 A7
SR-49 Virgilina Rd
Person Co NC 9 E5
Person Co NC 10 A4
SR-50
Duplin Co NC 83 B7
Duplin Co NC 109 C2
Duplin Co NC 110 A4
Granville Co NC 31 C4
Johnston Co NC 55 E6
Johnston Co NC 82 B3
Onslow Co NC 131 E2
Raleigh NC 55 D3
Raleigh NC 197 D7
Raleigh NC 199 E1
Surf City NC 131 E4
Warsaw NC 109 B1
SR-50 Benson Rd
Wake Co NC 55 E4
SR-50 Creedmoor Rd
Raleigh NC 55 D1
Raleigh NC 197 B4
Wake Co NC 31 C7
SR-50 Glenwood Av
Raleigh NC 197 D7
Raleigh NC 199 E1
SR-50 Julius Sutton
Hwy
Sampson Co NC 82 E5
SR-50 Mt Olive Hwy
Sampson Co NC 82 E4
SR-50 W Ocean Rd
Onslow Co NC 131 E2
SR-50 S Saunders St
Raleigh NC 55 D3
SR-50 S Shore Dr
Surf City NC 131 E4
SR-50 Suttontown Rd
Sampson Co NC 83 A5
SR-50 Wade Av
Raleigh NC 199 E2
SR-51
Bowersville GA 116 B6
Canon GA 116 A6
Charlotte NC 101 C1
Danville VA 8 B2
Florence SC 141 C2
Florence Co SC 141 E3
Florence Co SC 142 A5
Georgetown Co SC 156 D6
Georgetown Co SC 167 A1
Hartwell GA 116 C6
Homer GA 115 A7
Matthews NC 75 E7
York Co SC 101 B1

STREET
City State Map# Grid
SR-51 2nd Loop Rd
Florence Co SC 141 C2
Florence Co SC 230 A7
SR-51 Blair Rd
Mint Hill NC 76 A6
SR-51 Bowersville Hwy
Bowersville GA 116 B6
Hart Co GA 116 C6
SR-51 Browns Ferry Rd
Georgetown Co SC 156 E7
Georgetown Co SC 157 A7
SR-51 County Line Rd
Georgetown Co SC 156 D5
SR-51 Hatton Ford Rd
Hart Co GA 116 D4
SR-51 Historic Homer
Hwy
Homer GA 115 A7
SR-51 Kingsburg Hwy
Florence Co SC 156 D1
SR-51 Matthews-Mint
Hill Rd
Mint Hill NC 76 A7
SR-51 Matthews
Township Pkwy
Matthews NC 75 E7
SR-51 Old Federal Rd
Franklin Co GA 115 B6
SR-51 Pamplico Hwy
Florence Co SC 141 E3
SR-51 N Pamplico Hwy
Florence Co SC 142 A5
SR-51 S Pamplico Hwy
Florence Co SC 142 B6
SR-51
Pineville-Matthews Rd
Charlotte NC 101 D1
SR-51 Reed Creek Hwy
Hart Co GA 116 D5
SR-51 Sandy Cross Rd
Franklin Co GA 115 D7
SR-51 Stars Bridge Rd
Canon GA 116 A7
Franklin Co GA 115 E7
SR-51 Westover Dr
Danville VA 8 B2
SR-52
Gilmer Co GA 91 A7
SR-52 Chatsworth Hwy
Gilmer Co GA 91 A7
SR-53
Atkinson NC 130 B2
Bladen Co NC 107 D6
Bladen Co NC 128 E1
Bladen Co NC 129 E4
Bladen Co NC 130 A4
Burgaw NC 130 E2
Onslow Co NC 110 E6
Pender Co NC 131 A1
Sumter Co SC 140 D7
Sumter Co SC 141 A5
SR-53 Burgaw Hwy
Onslow Co NC 110 E6
Onslow Co NC 111 A5
SR-53 Cedar Creek Rd
Cumberland Co NC 107 B2
SR-53 Narrow Paved Rd
Sumter Co SC 140 D7
Sumter Co SC 141 A5
SR-54
Alamance Co NC 29 E6
Burlington NC 29 C5
Carrboro NC 30 B7
Chapel Hill NC 30 C7
Durham NC 30 E7
Graham NC 29 D5
Orange Co NC 30 A7
Wake Co NC 55 B2
Wake Co NC 198 B3
SR-54 Chapel Hill Rd
Burlington NC 29 C5
Raleigh NC 198 B3
Wake Co NC 55 B2
SR-54 S Fordham Blvd
Chapel Hill NC 30 C7
SR-54 Harden St
Burlington NC 192 E6
SR-54 E Harden St
Graham NC 29 D5
SR-54 Hillsborough St
Raleigh NC 198 E2
SR-55
Alliance NC 87 A5
Angier NC 55 C7
Cherokee Co SC 99 E1
Craven Co NC 86 C5
Dunn NC 81 E3
Durham NC 30 E6
Durham NC 31 A6
Durham Co NC 55 A1
Erwin NC 81 D3
Fuquay-Varina NC 55 B6
Grantsboro NC 86 E5
Harnett Co NC 81 D2
Holly Springs NC 55 A4
Johnston Co NC 82 C4
Kinston NC 84 D4
Wayne Co NC 83 B5
SR-55 Greenville Hwy
Kinston NC 84 D4
SR-55 Harnett-Dunn Hwy
Johnston Co NC 82 C4
SR-55 E Jackson Blvd
Erwin NC 81 D3
SR-55 Main St
Alliance NC 87 A5
SR-55 N Main St
Fuquay-Varina NC 55 B6
SR-55 Mt Olive Hwy
Sampson Co NC 82 E4
SR-56
Burke Co GA 159 B7

STREET
City State Map# Grid
SR-56
Franklin Co NC 32 A3
Franklin Co NC 33 B3
Granville Co NC 31 C3
Laurens Co SC 119 D5
Louisburg NC 32 C4
Newberry Co SC 135 D1
Spartanburg SC 98 D4
Spartanburg Co SC 98 D6
Spartanburg Co SC 224 A1
SR-56 SPUR
Augusta GA 159 B2
Burke Co GA 159 C5
SR-56 TRK
Clinton SC 119 D4
SR-56 W 6th St
Burke Co GA 159 B7
SR-56 Asheville Hwy
Spartanburg Co SC 98 C3
Spartanburg Co SC 224 A1
SR-56 Cedar Springs Rd
Spartanburg SC 98 D4
SR-56 N Church St
Spartanburg SC 224 B3
SR-56 S Church St
Spartanburg SC 224 C4
SR-56 Cross Anchor Hwy
Spartanburg Co SC 119 D3
SR-56 SPUR Doug
Barnard Pkwy
Augusta GA 159 B2
SR-56 E Green St
Franklin Co NC 32 B4
SR-56 W Green St
Franklin Co NC 32 A3
SR-56 E Henry St
Spartanburg SC 224 D4
SR-56 Mike Padgett Hwy
Augusta GA 159 C4
SR-56 SPUR River Rd
Burke Co GA 159 C5
SR-56 TRK Springdale
Dr
Clinton SC 119 D4
SR-57
Caswell Co NC 9 A4
Dillon Co SC 126 E6
Dillon Co SC 127 A7
Martinsville VA 7 B1
Orange Co NC 30 D2
Roxboro NC 9 D7
SR-57 Appalachian Dr
Henry Co VA 7 A1
SR-57 Bradford Blvd
Dillon Co SC 126 D4
SR-57 Chatham Rd
Henry Co VA 7 B1
SR-57 E Church Rd
Martinsville VA 7 B1
SR-57 Durham Rd
Person Co NC 9 D7
Person Co NC 30 E1
SR-57 Fairystone Park
Hwy
Patrick Co VA 6 A1
SR-57 Semora Rd
Person Co NC 9 C5
SR-58
Atlantic Beach NC 113 A6
Castalia NC 33 C4
Franklin Co NC 33 A1
Indian Beach NC 112 C6
Jones Co NC 85 C7
Jones Co NC 111 E2
Jones Co NC 112 A4
Kinston NC 84 C1
Lenoir Co NC 84 E5
Nashville NC 33 D6
Warren Co NC 12 A7
Warrenton NC 12 A5
Wilson NC 57 D3
Wilson NC 202 E6
Wilson NC 57 D2
SR-58 S 1st St
Nashville NC 33 D6
SR-58 Fort Macon Dr W
Atlantic Beach NC 113 A6
SR-58 W Fort Macon Rd
Atlantic Beach NC 228 A7
SR-58 Lipscomb Rd E
Wilson Co NC 202 E5
SR-58 E Macon St
Warrenton NC 12 A5
SR-58 Nash St N
Wilson Co NC 57 D2
SR-58 Nash St SE
Wilson NC 202 E6
SR-58 Pleasant Grove
Rd
Lee Co SC 140 E5
SR-58 Pudding Swamp Rd
Sumter Co SC 140 E7
SR-58 N Queen St
Kinston NC 84 E3
Kinston NC 205 C4
SR-58 Salter Path Rd
Indian Beach NC 112 C6
SR-58 Trenton Hwy
Kinston NC 205 C7
SR-58 Ward Blvd
Wilson NC 57 D3
Wilson NC 202 D4
SR-59
Banks Co GA 115 B7
Cumberland Co NC 106 E2
Cumberland Co NC 107 A3
Franklin Co GA 116 B5
SR-59 Chickenfoot Rd
Cumberland Co NC 107 A3
SR-59 Hope Mills Rd
Cumberland Co NC 106 E2

STREET
City State Map# Grid
SR-59 Knox Bridge
Crossing Rd
Hart Co GA 116 B4
SR-59 Tokeena Rd
Oconee Co SC 116 C2
SR-60
Fannin Co GA 91 E5
Fannin Co GA 92 B7
Lexington Co SC 137 D4
SR-60 SPUR
Fannin Co GA 91 E3
SR-60 Lake Murray Blvd
Lexington Co SC 137 D4
SR-60 Mineral Bluff
Hwy
Fannin Co GA 91 D3
SR-60 Morganton Hwy
Fannin Co GA 91 E5
Fannin Co GA 92 A7
SR-60 SPUR Murphy Hwy
Fannin Co GA 91 E3
SR-61
Bamberg Co SC 162 D5
Charleston SC 172 E4
Charleston SC 240 A6
Charleston Co SC 239 B4
Colleton Co SC 163 A7
Colleton Co SC 171 B1
Guilford Co NC 28 E2
Whitsett NC 29 A4
SR-61 Ashley River Rd
Charleston Co SC 172 E4
Charleston Co SC 239 B4
SR-61 Augusta Hwy
Colleton Co SC 162 E6
Colleton Co SC 163 A7
Colleton Co SC 171 B1
SR-61 Edisto River Rd
Bamberg Co SC 162 D5
SR-61 Herbert U
Fielding Conn
Charleston SC 240 B7
SR-61 St. Andrews Blvd
Charleston SC 240 A6
Charleston Co SC 239 D5
SR-62
Alamance Co NC 29 B6
Burlington NC 29 B4
Burlington NC 192 D3
Caswell Co NC 9 A4
Guilford Co NC 28 E7
Pittsylvania Co VA 8 E3
Trinity NC 51 E1
Yanceyville NC 8 D7
SR-62 Alamance Rd
Burlington NC 192 A6
SR-62 N Church St
Burlington NC 192 D3
SR-62 S Church St
Burlington NC 29 B4
Burlington NC 192 C4
SR-62 Milton Hwy
Pittsylvania Co VA 8 E3
SR-62 Rauhut St
Burlington NC 192 D1
SR-63
Banks Co GA 115 B6
Buncombe Co NC 44 B5
Colleton Co SC 170 C4
Colleton Co SC 171 A4
Florence Co SC 230 B1
Madison Co NC 43 E4
SR-63 Martin Bridge Rd
Banks Co GA 115 B6
SR-63 Mechanicsville
Rd
Florence Co SC 230 B1
SR-63 Mize Rd
Stephens Co GA 115 C4
SR-63 New Leicester
Hwy
Buncombe Co NC 44 B5
SR-63 Sniders Hwy
Colleton Co SC 170 C4
Colleton Co SC 171 A4
SR-63 Sunshine Rd
Franklin Co GA 115 B5
SR-63 Walterboro Hwy
Colleton Co SC 170 B3
SR-64
Bamberg Co SC 161 D7
Bamberg Co SC 162 A7
Barnwell SC 161 A5
Colleton Co SC 170 D2
Colleton Co SC 171 B4
Lodge SC 170 B1
Snelling SC 160 E5
SR-64 Bells Hwy
Colleton Co SC 170 D2
Colleton Co SC 171 A3
Lodge SC 170 B1
SR-64 Charleston Hwy
Colleton Co SC 171 B4
SR-64 Dunbarton Blvd
Barnwell SC 161 A5
Snelling SC 160 E5
SR-64 Low Country Hwy
Bamberg Co SC 161 D6
Bamberg Co SC 162 A7
SR-65
Forsyth Co NC 26 E3
Forsyth Co NC 27 B1
Rockingham Co NC 7 C6
Rockingham Co NC 28 A1
Stokesdale NC 27 E2
Walnut Cove NC 27 C1
SR-65 Belews Creek Rd
Stokesdale NC 27 E2
SR-65 Bethania-Rural
Hall Rd
Forsyth Co NC 26 E3
Forsyth Co NC 27 A2

STREET
City State Map# Grid
SR-66
Forsyth Co NC 27 A3
Hawkins Co TN 19 C1
Kernersville NC 27 D4
Laurens Co SC 119 E6
Laurens Co SC 120 B5
Stokes Co NC 5 E7
Stokes Co NC 26 E1
Towns Co GA 92 E3
Walkertown NC 27 C3
SR-66 Milton Rd
Laurens Co SC 119 E6
SR-66 W Mountain St
Kernersville NC 27 D4
SR-66 Old Hollow Rd
Forsyth Co NC 27 A3
Walkertown NC 27 C3
SR-66 Winfield Dunn
Pkwy
Sevierville TN 41 E1
SR-67
Carter Co TN 21 E1
Carter Co TN 22 A1
Forsyth Co NC 26 C2
Greenwood Co SC 134 E5
Johnson City TN 21 B1
Johnson Co TN 1 E7
Johnson Co TN 2 A7
Jonesville NC 25 D2
Winston-Salem NC 26 E3
Winston-Salem NC 27 A5
Winston-Salem NC 187 C1
Winston-Salem NC 188 A6
Yadkin Co NC 25 E2
SR-67 Callison Hwy
Greenwood Co SC 134 E5
SR-67 Cherokee Rd
Johnson City TN 21 B1
Washington Co TN 21 A2
SR-67 Doe Valley Rd
Johnson Co TN 1 C6
SR-67 Reynolda Rd
Forsyth Co NC 26 C2
Winston-Salem NC 26 E3
Winston-Salem NC 27 A4
SR-67 S Shady St
Mountain City TN 1 E5
SR-67 Silas Creek Pkwy
Winston-Salem NC 27 A5
Winston-Salem NC 187 C1
Winston-Salem NC 188 A6
SR-67 University Pkwy
Johnson City TN 21 B1
SR-68
Guilford Co NC 27 E4
Guilford Co NC 28 A5
Hampton Co SC 170 B6
High Point NC 27 D7
High Point NC 191 A1
Monroe Co TN 65 D5
Polk Co TN 91 C2
Stokesdale NC 27 E3
SR-68 Eastchester Dr
High Point NC 27 E6
High Point NC 191 C1
SR-68 Thomas A.
Burton Hwy
Rockingham Co NC 28 A1
SR-68 Westchester Dr
High Point NC 27 D7
High Point NC 191 A1
SR-68 Yemassee Hwy
Hampton Co SC 170 B6
SR-69
Clay Co NC 93 A2
SR-70
Barnwell SC 161 A5
Barnwell Co SC 161 C4
Greene Co TN 19 E3
Greene Co TN 20 A6
Orangeburg Co SC 162 B1
SR-70 BYP
Greeneville TN 19 E3
SR-70 Asheville Hwy
Greene Co TN 19 E6
Greene Co TN 20 A6
SR-70 Barnwell Rd
Barnwell Co SC 161 C4
SR-70 Binnicker
Bridge Rd
Orangeburg Co SC 162 B1
SR-70 Country Club Rd
Bamberg Co SC 161 E3
SR-70 Lonesome Pine Tr
Greene Co TN 19 E3
SR-70 Main St
Barnwell SC 161 A5
SR-71
Abbeville Co SC 133 C2
Lumber Bridge NC 106 C4
Maxton NC 105 E6
Pigeon Forge TN 41 E3
Robeson Co NC 106 A5
Sevier Co TN 41 D2
Sevier Co TN 42 A3
Sevierville TN 41 E2
SR-71 Chapman Hwy SE
Knox Co TN 41 B1
SR-71 Forks of the
River Pkwy
Sevierville TN 41 E2
SR-71 Parkway
Pigeon Forge TN 41 E3
Sevier Co TN 42 A3
SR-72
Abbeville Co SC 134 A3
Chester Co SC 100 E5
Chester Co SC 121 B2
Clinton SC 119 E4
Elbert Co GA 133 C5
Greenwood Co SC 135 B1
Laurens Co SC 119 C6

STREET
City State Map# Grid
SR-72
Laurens Co SC 120 B4
Middleton GA 133 A4
Robeson Co NC 106 B5
Rock Hill SC 217 B7
SR-72 BYP
Greenwood Co SC 134 D2
Rock Hill SC 217 C6
SR-72 BYP Albright Rd
Rock Hill SC 217 C6
SR-72 Calhoun Falls
Hwy
Elbert Co GA 133 C5
Middleton GA 133 A4
SR-72 Carlisle
Whitmire Hwy
Union Co SC 120 D3
SR-72 Caton Rd
Robeson Co NC 127 C1
SR-72 Charles L
Powell Hwy
Greenwood Co SC 134 C2
SR-72 Laurens Hwy
Greenwood Co SC 135 B1
SR-72 Reynolds St
Greenwood Co SC 134 E2
SR-72 Saluda Rd
Chester Co SC 100 E5
SR-72 Saluda St
Rock Hill SC 217 B7
SR-72 West End Rd
Chester Co SC 121 B2
SR-72 Whitmire Hwy
Newberry Co SC 120 C4
SR-72 Willard Rd
Laurens Co SC 119 E4
SR-72 Wilmington Hwy
Robeson Co NC 127 E4
SR-73
Albemarle NC 77 C3
Blount Co TN 41 D4
Cabarrus Co NC 75 E2
Cabarrus Co NC 76 D3
Cocke Co TN 19 A7
Cocke Co TN 42 E3
Cocke Co TN 43 A1
Concord NC 76 B2
Gatlinburg TN 42 B4
Huntersville NC 75 D2
Lincoln Co NC 74 E1
Myrtle Beach SC 158 B3
Myrtle Beach SC 232 B6
Richmond Co NC 78 E6
Screven Co GA 168 C4
Stanly Co NC 77 A3
Sylvania GA 168 B5
Townsend TN 41 C5
Screven Co GA 168 B6
SR-73 Burtons Ferry
Hwy
Screven Co GA 168 C4
SR-73 Church St N
Concord NC 76 B2
SR-73 Concord Rd
Stanly Co NC 77 A3
SR-73 Cosby Hwy
Cocke Co TN 42 E2
SR-73 Davidson Hwy
Cabarrus Co NC 75 E2
Concord NC 76 A2
SR-73 E Pkwy
Gatlinburg TN 42 B4
SR-73 Edwina Rd
Cocke Co TN 19 A7
Cocke Co TN 43 A1
SR-73 Hooper Hwy
Cocke Co TN 42 E3
SR-73 N Main St
Sylvania GA 168 B5
SR-73 N Ocean Blvd
Myrtle Beach SC 158 B3
Myrtle Beach SC 232 D4
SR-73 S Ocean Blvd
Myrtle Beach SC 232 B6
SR-73 Parkway
Pigeon Forge TN 41 E3
Sevier Co TN 42 A3
SR-73 Pittman Pkwy
Pittman Center TN 42 C3
SR-73 Sam Furr Rd
Huntersville NC 75 B2
Mecklenburg Co NC 75 D2
SR-73 Smoky Mountains
Hwy
Townsend TN 41 C5
SR-73 Spaulding St
Albemarle NC 77 C3
SR-73 Statesboro Hwy
Screven Co GA 168 B7
SR-73 Walland Hwy
Blount Co TN 41 A3
SR-73 Wears Valley Rd
Blount Co TN 41 D4
SR-73 Wilton Springs
Rd
Cocke Co TN 42 E1
SR-75
Hiawassee GA 93 B4
Lancaster Co SC 101 D5
Monroe NC 218 A4
Towns Co GA 93 B3
Union Co NC 102 A3
Washington Co TN 20 D2
Washington Co VA 1 B2
Waxhaw NC 101 E4
SR-75 ALT
White Co GA 93 B7
SR-75 Barkley Rd
Washington Co TN 20 C2
SR-75 Bowmantown Rd
Washington Co TN 20 D1

INDEX 5

SR-75 Charlotte Hwy — Street Index — SR-13

Street Index

STREET / City State / Map# Grid

SR-75 Charlotte Hwy
Lancaster Co SC 101 D4
SR-75 W Franklin St
Monroe NC 218 A4
SR-75 Green Spring Rd
Washington Co VA 1 B2
SR-75 W Jefferson St
Monroe NC 218 B4
SR-75 N Main St
Hiawassee GA 93 B4
SR-75 W Rebound Rd
Lancaster Co SC 101 D5
SR-75 Unicoi Tpk
Towns Co GA 93 C4
SR-75 Waxhaw Hwy
Mineral Springs NC 102 A3
Union Co NC 101 E4
SR-77
Hart Co GA 116 C6
Hartwell GA 116 D7
SR-77 CONN
Hart Co GA 116 B5
SR-77 SPUR
Hart Co GA 116 E7
SR-77 Bowersville Hwy
Hartwell GA 116 C6
SR-77 S Carter St
Hartwell GA 116 D7
SR-77 SPUR Cokesbury Hwy
Hart Co GA 116 E7
SR-77 Elberton Hwy
Hart Co GA 116 D7
SR-77 Lavonia Hwy
Hart Co GA 116 C6
SR-77 CONN Lavonia Hwy
Hart Co GA 116 B5
SR-77 Providence Church Rd
Hart Co GA 116 B5
SR-78
Lee Co NC 80 B1
SR-78 Tramway Rd
Sanford NC 80 B1
SR-79
Elbert Co GA 133 C6
Marlboro Co SC 104 D7
Scotland Co NC 105 A6
SR-79 Elberton Hwy
Lincoln Co GA 133 C7
SR-79 Gibson Rd
Scotland Co NC 105 A6
SR-79 Lincolnton Hwy
Elbert Co GA 133 C6
SR-80
Burke Co GA 159 A7
Hilton Head Island SC 242 A6
McDowell Co NC 45 D3
McDowell Co NC 46 A4
Mitchell Co NC 21 E6
Waynesboro GA 159 B7
SR-80 Buck Creek Rd
McDowell Co NC 45 D3
McDowell Co NC 46 A4
SR-80 Pope Av
Hilton Head Island SC 242 A6
SR-81
Abbeville Co SC 133 D5
Anderson SC 117 C3
Anderson Co SC 96 E7
Anderson Co SC 117 B5
Anderson Co SC 226 C7
Asheville NC 44 D7
Buncombe Co NC 206 D6
Greenville Co SC 223 A4
McCormick Co SC 134 A6
Starr SC 117 B7
Washington Co TN 20 E2
SR-81 Anderson Rd
Greenville Co SC 96 E6
Greenville Co SC 223 A4
SR-81 Flag Pond Rd
Unicoi Co TN 20 D5
SR-81 E Greenville St
Anderson SC 117 C3
Anderson SC 226 D3
SR-81 James H Quillen Pkwy
Unicoi Co TN 20 E4
Unicoi Co TN 21 A4
SR-81 Murray St
Anderson SC 226 C7
SR-81 N Murray St
Anderson SC 226 C4
SR-81 S Murray St
Anderson SC 226 D5
SR-81 Swannanoa River Rd
Asheville NC 44 D7
Buncombe Co NC 206 D6
SR-81 Williamsburg Rd
Anderson Co SC 117 D1
SR-82
Harnett Co NC 81 D4
SR-82 Herb Farm Rd
Cumberland Co NC 81 E6
SR-83
Robeson Co NC 105 D7
Robeson Co NC 126 D1
SR-84
Monroe NC 218 A4
Union Co NC 102 A2
Wesley Chapel NC 101 E2
SR-84 W Franklin St
Monroe NC 218 A4
SR-84 W Jefferson St
Monroe NC 218 B4
SR-84 Weddington Rd
Union Co NC 102 A2
Wesley Chapel NC 101 E2
SR-86
Anderson Co SC 96 D7
SR-86
Caswell Co NC 8 E6
Caswell Co NC 9 A7
Chapel Hill NC 30 C7
Danville VA 8 C4
Greenville Co SC 118 A1
Hillsborough NC 30 C5
Yanceyville NC 8 D6
SR-86 Anderson Hwy
Anderson Co SC 96 D7
SR-86 Bessie Rd
Greenville Co SC 118 A1
SR-86 N Churton St
Hillsborough NC 30 C4
SR-86 Martin L King Jr Blvd
Chapel Hill NC 30 C7
Chapel Hill NC 195 B2
SR-87
Alamance Co NC 29 B3
Bladen Co NC 107 B5
Bladen Co NC 128 D1
Boiling Spring Lakes NC 146 D4
Brunswick Co NC 146 C1
Chatham Co NC 54 A6
Columbus Co NC 130 B6
Cumberland Co NC 221 E4
Elizabethtown NC 129 C3
Fayetteville NC 80 E7
Fayetteville NC 107 A1
Graham NC 29 C4
Harnett Co NC 80 D5
Pittsboro NC 54 A4
Reidsville NC 7 D7
Rockingham Co NC 7 C5
Rockingham Co NC 28 E1
Sandyfield NC 129 E5
Sanford NC 54 B7
Sanford NC 80 C2
SR-87 BYP
Bladen Co NC 128 E1
Elizabethtown NC 129 A1
SR-87 Andrew Jackson Hwy
Columbus Co NC 130 B6
SR-87 Bragg Blvd
Fayetteville NC 80 E7
Fayetteville NC 222 A1
Spring Lake NC 221 E4
SR-87 N Bragg Blvd
Spring Lake NC 221 D1
SR-87 Freeway Dr
Reidsville NC 7 D7
Rockingham Co NC 7 E7
SR-87 George II Hwy SE
Brunswick Co NC 146 D4
SR-87 Graham Rd
Chatham Co NC 54 A3
SR-87 Harrington Hwy
Rockingham Co NC 7 C5
SR-87 S Horner Blvd
Sanford NC 80 B1
SR-87 Leaksville Rd
Henry Co VA 7 B3
SR-87 Maco Rd NE
Brunswick Co NC 130 B7
Brunswick Co NC 146 C1
SR-87 S Main St
Graham NC 29 C4
SR-87 Martin L King Jr Frwy
Fayetteville NC 107 A1
Fayetteville NC 222 C3
SR-87 Ocean Hwy E
Brunswick Co NC 146 C2
SR-87 Old Stage Rd
Columbus Co NC 130 A6
Sandyfield NC 129 E5
SR-87 River Rd SE
Brunswick Co NC 146 D5
SR-87 E Webb Av
Burlington NC 192 E5
SR-87 W Webb Av
Burlington NC 192 B2
SR-88
Anderson Co SC 96 C7
Anderson Co SC 117 A1
Ashe Co NC 2 E6
Ashe Co NC 3 A6
Hephzibah GA 159 A3
Jefferson NC 2 D6
SR-88 E Main St
Jefferson NC 2 D6
SR-88 Old Greenville Hwy
Anderson Co SC 96 C7
Anderson Co SC 117 C1
SR-89
Mt Airy NC 5 B5
Mt Airy NC 183 E6
Stokes Co NC 5 E5
Stokes Co NC 6 B6
Stokes Co NC 27 C1
Surry Co NC 4 E4
Surry Co NC 183 B4
SR-89 S Main St
Mt Airy NC 5 A5
Mt Airy NC 183 D5
SR-89 W Pine St
Surry Co NC 4 E4
Surry Co NC 5 A4
SR-89 Skyline Hwy
Grayson Co VA 4 B2
SR-89 Westfield Rd
Mt Airy NC 183 E6
Surry Co NC 5 C4
SR-90
Alexander Co NC 24 B7
Alexander Co NC 48 C1
Caldwell Co NC 22 E6
Caldwell Co NC 23 C7
Horry Co SC 157 E1
SR-90
Horry Co SC 158 B1
Iredell Co NC 49 A2
SR-90 Collettsville Rd
Caldwell Co NC 23 C7
SR-90 Edgemont Rd
Caldwell Co NC 22 E6
SR-90 E Garner Bagnal Blvd
Iredell Co NC 49 B3
SR-90 N Main St
Lenoir NC 47 C1
SR-90 National Forest Rd
Caldwell Co NC 22 E6
SR-90 Taylorsville Hwy
Iredell Co NC 49 B2
SR-90 Taylorsville Rd
Caldwell Co NC 47 E1
SR-91
Carter Co TN 1 C4
Damascus VA 1 E3
Johnson City TN 21 B1
Mountain City TN 1 D5
Saratoga NC 58 B4
Walstonburg NC 58 C5
Wilson NC 202 E6
Wilson Co NC 58 A3
SR-91 Jeb Stuart Hwy
Damascus VA 1 E3
SR-91 E Main St
Johnson City TN 21 B1
SR-91 Monroe Rd
Washington Co VA 1 E1
SR-91 Nash St SE
Wilson NC 202 E6
SR-91 N Shady St
Mountain City TN 1 D5
SR-91 Stony Creek Rd
Carter Co TN 1 A6
SR-91 N Wilson St
Greene Co NC 58 B5
SR-92
Bath NC 60 E7
Beaufort Co NC 60 D6
Beaufort Co NC 61 A7
Mecklenburg Co VA 11 B1
Spartanburg Co SC 119 C1
SR-92 W R Bill Roberson Jr Hwy
Beaufort Co NC 60 D6
SR-93
Alleghany Co NC 3 B3
Greene Co TN 20 A3
Oconee Co SC 116 E1
Pickens Co SC 96 A7
Pickens Co SC 225 C4
SR-93 Greenville Hwy
Pickens Co SC 96 C6
SR-93 Kingsport Hwy
Greene Co TN 20 A3
SR-93 Liberty Dr
Pickens Co SC 96 A7
SR-93 Old Greenville Hwy
Oconee Co SC 116 E1
Pickens Co SC 225 C4
SR-94
Chowan Co NC 37 D5
Grayson Co VA 4 A1
Hyde Co NC 62 C6
SR-94 Haughton Rd
Chowan Co NC 37 D4
SR-94 Riverside Dr
Grayson Co VA 4 A2
SR-94 Scenic Rd
Grayson Co VA 4 A1
SR-94 Soundside Dr
Chowan Co NC 37 C4
SR-96
Franklin Co NC 31 E3
Franklin Co NC 32 A4
Granville Co NC 10 B4
Johnston Co NC 56 D4
Johnston Co NC 82 C1
Oxford NC 10 E7
Youngsville NC 32 A5
SR-96 Linden Av
Oxford NC 10 E7
SR-96 Little Batterwhite Rd
Granville Co NC 10 B4
SR-96 Virgilian Rd
Halifax Co VA 9 E3
Halifax Co VA 10 A3
SR-96 Zebulon Rd
Wake Co NC 32 C7
Wake Co NC 56 C1
SR-97
Carroll Co VA 4 C2
Chester Co SC 100 B6
Chester Co SC 121 D2
Chester Co SC 122 B2
Edgecombe Co NC 34 C6
Edgecombe Co NC 35 A4
Franklin Co NC 56 E1
Nash Co NC 33 A7
Nash Co NC 57 D1
Rocky Mount NC 34 A5
York Co SC 99 E2
SR-97 Atlantic Av
Edgecombe Co NC 34 A5
SR-97 Cedar Creek Rd
Lancaster Co SC 122 D4
SR-97 Center Rd
Chester Co SC 100 B6
SR-97 Great Falls Rd
Chester Co SC 121 D2
Chester Co SC 122 B2
SR-97 John G Richards Rd
Kershaw Co SC 122 E5
SR-97 John G Richards Rd
Kershaw Co SC 123 A7
SR-97 Pipers Gap Rd
Carroll Co VA 4 C2
SR-98
Durham Co NC 31 A6
Franklin Co NC 32 B6
Nash Co NC 33 A7
SR-98 Commerce St
Homer GA 115 A7
SR-98 Durham Rd
Wake Co NC 31 E6
SR-98 Wait Av
Wake Co NC 32 A6
SR-98 Wake Forest Hwy
Durham Co NC 31 A6
SR-99
Chester Co SC 122 B2
Washington Co NC 61 B1
SR-99 Pungo Rd
Beaufort Co NC 61 B4
SR-99 Richburg Rd
Chester Co SC 122 B2
SR-100
Burlington NC 29 C4
Burlington NC 192 D6
Guilford Co NC 29 A4
SR-100 Maple Av
Burlington NC 29 C4
Burlington NC 192 D6
SR-100 W Webb Av
Burlington NC 192 B2
SR-101
Carteret Co NC 113 B3
Craven Co NC 112 E3
Greenville Co SC 97 C2
Greer SC 97 E4
Laurens Co SC 118 E2
Laurens Co SC 119 A1
Spartanburg Co SC 98 A6
SR-101 W Georgia Rd
Spartanburg Co SC 98 A7
SR-101 New Bern Rd
Carteret Co NC 113 B3
Craven Co NC 112 E3
SR-101 Ware Shoals Rd
Laurens Co SC 118 E2
SR-102
Ayden NC 59 C7
Beaufort Co NC 59 E7
Beaufort Co NC 60 A7
Chesterfield SC 103 D7
Chesterfield Co SC 124 D1
SR-102 Patrick Hwy
Darlington Co SC 124 E4
SR-103
Mt Airy NC 183 D4
Patrick Co VA 6 A3
Surry Co NC 5 B4
SR-103 Claudville Hwy
Patrick Co VA 5 C3
SR-103 Dry Pond Hwy
Patrick Co VA 5 E3
Patrick Co VA 6 A3
SR-103 E Pine St
Mt Airy NC 183 D4
Surry Co NC 5 B4
SR-104
Augusta GA 149 B7
Augusta GA 159 B1
Columbia Co GA 148 E6
Evans GA 148 E7
Martinez GA 149 A7
Surry Co NC 5 B4
SR-104 Riverside Dr
Surry Co NC 5 B4
SR-104 Riverwatch Pkwy
Augusta GA 149 B7
Augusta GA 159 B1
SR-104 Washington Rd
Columbia Co GA 148 E6
Evans GA 148 E7
Martinez GA 149 A7
SR-105
Avery Co NC 22 D4
Banks Co GA 115 A5
Boone NC 185 C5
Cherokee Co SC 99 C3
Watauga Co NC 23 A3
SR-105 Mt Tabor Church Rd
Union Co SC 99 D6
SR-105 National Hwy
Cherokee Co SC 99 A1
SR-105 Wilkinsville Hwy
Cherokee Co SC 99 C3
SR-106
Franklin Co GA 115 D6
Macon Co NC 94 D2
SR-106 Athens Rd
Franklin Co GA 115 D7
SR-106 Dillard Rd
Macon Co NC 94 D2
SR-106 Mize Rd
Stephens Co GA 115 C4
SR-107
Cocke Co TN 43 C1
Greene Co TN 19 E6
Greene Co TN 20 B4
Greeneville TN 20 A3
Jackson Co NC 68 E4
Jackson Co NC 69 A7
Oconee Co SC 95 B2
Sylva NC 68 E3
Tusculum TN 20 B3
Unicoi Co TN 21 D4
SR-107 Asheville Hwy
Greene Co TN 19 E6
SR-107 Dixie Hwy
Cocke Co TN 19 C7
SR-107 Erwin Hwy
Greene Co TN 20 B4
Unicoi Co TN 21 B3
SR-107 Houston Valley Rd
Greene Co TN 19 D7
SR-107 John Sevier Hwy
Washington Co TN 20 D4
SR-107 Limestone Cove Rd
Unicoi Co TN 21 D4
SR-107 W Main St
Sylva NC 68 D3
SR-107 Tusculum Blvd
Greeneville TN 20 A3
SR-107 Upper Wolf Creek Rd
Cocke Co TN 43 C1
SR-108
Polk Co NC 71 E4
Rutherford Co NC 72 B4
SR-108 Tryon Rd
Rutherford Co NC 72 B4
SR-109
Anson Co NC 103 C4
Chesterfield Co SC 124 C1
Davidson Co NC 51 D6
Montgomery Co NC 78 A2
Richmond Co NC 77 E6
Thomasville NC 27 C7
Thomasville NC 51 D3
Troy NC 78 A4
Winston-Salem NC 188 E4
SR-109 Albemarle Rd
Troy NC 78 A4
SR-109 Camden Rd
Anson Co NC 103 B6
SR-109 Market St
Ruby SC 103 C7
SR-109 Randolph St
Thomasville NC 51 D3
SR-109 Stadium Dr
Winston-Salem NC 188 E4
SR-109 Thomasville Rd
Forsyth Co NC 27 B5
SR-110
Cherokee Co SC 72 E7
Haywood Co NC 69 E1
SR-110 Battleground Rd
Cherokee Co SC 72 D7
Spartanburg Co SC 98 E2
SR-110 Cowpens Hwy
Cherokee Co SC 98 D1
SR-110 Pisgah Dr
Haywood Co NC 69 E1
SR-111
Duplin Co NC 84 A7
Duplin Co NC 110 A1
Edgecombe Co NC 35 B6
Edgecombe Co NC 58 B2
Goldsboro NC 83 D1
Onslow Co NC 111 A4
Stantonsburg NC 58 A5
Tarboro NC 34 D7
Wayne Co NC 57 E7
SR-111 Catherine Lake Rd
Duplin Co NC 110 D4
Onslow Co NC 111 A4
SR-111 Dr ML King Jr Expwy
Goldsboro NC 83 D1
SR-111 Pinetops Rd
Edgecombe Co NC 34 D7
Edgecombe Co NC 58 C1
SR-111 Saratoga Rd
Edgecombe Co NC 58 C1
SR-111 W Wilson St
Tarboro NC 34 D7
SR-113
Aiken Co SC 151 A4
Alleghany Co NC 3 B5
Hawkins Co TN 19 B1
SR-113 S Dixie Rd
Aiken Co SC 151 A6
SR-113 Sand Dam Rd
Aiken Co SC 151 A4
SR-113 Silver City Rd
Hamblen Co TN 19 A2
SR-113 Simpson Rd
Hamblen Co TN 19 A1
SR-114
Burke Co NC 47 B4
Union Co SC 99 B6
SR-114 Bobby Faucett Rd
Union Co SC 99 B5
SR-114 Bob Little Rd
Union Co SC 99 B6
SR-114 Drexel Rd
Burke Co NC 47 B4
SR-115
Blount Co TN 66 E1
Cornelius NC 75 C1
Habersham Co GA 115 A2
Huntersville NC 75 C2
Iredell Co NC 25 A5
Iredell Co NC 49 C7
Mecklenburg Co NC 75 D4
North Wilkesboro NC 24 D3
Statesville NC 49 C3
Wilkes Co NC 24 E4
SR-115 Charlotte Hwy
Iredell Co NC 49 D6
SR-115 N Main St
Cornelius NC 75 C1
SR-115 Mt Ulla Hwy
Iredell Co NC 49 C7
SR-115 Old Statesville Rd
Mecklenburg Co NC 75 C4
SR-115 N Old Statesville Rd
Huntersville NC 75 C2
SR-115 Shelton Av
Statesville NC 49 C3
SR-115 Statesville Rd
North Wilkesboro NC 24 D3
Wilkes Co NC 24 E4
SR-115 Toccoa Hwy
Habersham Co GA 115 A2
SR-115 Tommy Irvin Rd SE
Habersham Co GA 115 B3
SR-115 Wilkesboro Hwy
Iredell Co NC 25 B7
Iredell Co NC 49 B1
SR-116
Beaufort Co SC 176 E4
SR-116 Laurel Bay Rd
Beaufort Co SC 176 E4
SR-117
Greenville Co SC 97 B1
SR-117 N Tigerville Rd
Greenville Co SC 97 B1
SR-118
Aiken Co SC 149 E6
Aiken Co SC 150 A6
Aiken Co SC 236 C5
Pitt Co NC 85 B2
SR-118 Hitchcock Pkwy
Aiken SC 149 E6
Aiken SC 150 A7
Aiken Co SC 236 C5
SR-118 University Pkwy
Aiken Co SC 150 A6
SR-119
Caswell Co NC 8 E7
Caswell Co NC 9 A4
Caswell Co NC 29 E1
Effingham Co GA 175 A7
Guyton GA 175 B6
Mebane NC 29 E3
Swepsonville NC 29 D5
SR-119 S 5th St
Mebane NC 29 E3
SR-119 Railroad Av
Effingham Co GA 175 B5
SR-120
Rutherford Co NC 72 E5
Rutherford Co NC 73 A4
Sumter SC 235 A5
Sumter Co SC 139 E7
Sumter Co SC 153 E1
SR-120 Alice Dr
Sumter SC 139 E7
Sumter SC 235 A2
SR-120 W Liberty St
Sumter SC 235 A5
Sumter Co SC 235 A4
SR-120 Pinewood Rd
Sumter Co SC 139 E7
Sumter Co SC 153 E1
SR-121
Burke Co GA 159 A5
Chester Co SC 121 B2
Farmville NC 58 D4
Johnston SC 149 E2
Newberry Co SC 120 C7
Newberry Co SC 136 B1
Rock Hill SC 101 A3
Saluda Co SC 135 E7
Saluda Co SC 149 E1
Trenton SC 149 D3
Waynesboro GA 159 B7
York Co SC 217 E5
SR-121 Albright Rd
Rock Hill SC 101 A4
Rock Hill SC 217 B7
SR-121 N Anderson Rd
Rock Hill SC 101 A3
SR-121 S Anderson Rd
Rock Hill SC 217 E3
SR-121 Carlisle Whitmire Hwy
Union Co SC 120 D3
SR-121 Edgefield Rd
Aiken Co SC 149 C7
SR-121 Gordon Hwy
Augusta GA 159 B1
SR-121 Johnston Hwy
Saluda Co SC 135 E7
Saluda Co SC 149 E1
SR-121 Lee St
Edgefield Co SC 149 E2
SR-121 N Liberty St
Burke Co GA 159 B7
SR-121 E Main St
York Co SC 217 E5
SR-121 Newberry Hwy
Saluda Co SC 135 E5
SR-121 Peach Orchard Rd
Augusta GA 159 B2
SR-121 Saluda Rd
Chester Co SC 100 E5
SR-121 West End Rd
Chester Co SC 121 B2
SR-121 Whitmire Hwy
Newberry Co SC 120 C4
SR-122
Edgecombe Co NC 35 A6
Edgecombe Co NC 58 C2
Rock Hill SC 101 A4
Rock Hill SC 217 B4
Tarboro NC 34 D7
SR-122 N 2nd St
Edgecombe Co NC 58 C2
SR-122 Dave Lyle Blvd
Rock Hill SC 101 A4
Rock Hill SC 217 B4
SR-122 Johnston St
Rock Hill SC 217 B5
SR-122 McNair Rd
Edgecombe Co NC 34 D7
SR-122 Pinetops Rd
Edgecombe Co NC 34 D7
Edgecombe Co NC 58 C1
SR-122 Pinetops-Tarboro Rd
Edgecombe Co NC 58 C1
SR-123
Greene Co NC 84 D1
Polk Co TN 65 D7
SR-123 Saw Mill Rd
Polk Co TN 65 D7
SR-124
Edgecombe Co NC 58 D2
Greenville SC 223 B4
Greenville Co SC 97 A5
SR-124 Old Easley Hwy
Greenville Co SC 97 A5
SR-124 Pendleton St
Greenville SC 223 B4
SR-125
Aiken Co SC 149 C7
Aiken Co SC 159 E3
Allendale Co SC 168 E1
Allendale Co SC 169 A1
Halifax Co NC 13 C6
Halifax Co NC 34 D1
Halifax Co NC 35 A2
Martin Co NC 36 A7
Scotland Neck NC 35 A4
SR-125 Atomic Rd
Aiken Co SC 149 C7
Aiken Co SC 160 A4
Jackson SC 159 E3
SR-125 Augusta Hwy
Allendale Co SC 168 E1
Allendale Co SC 169 A1
SR-125 Grapevine Rd
Halifax Co NC 13 C6
SR-126
Aiken Co SC 149 C7
Burke Co NC 46 C3
Burke Co NC 47 A4
SR-126 Belvedere Clearwater Rd
Aiken Co SC 149 C7
SR-126 Yellow Mountain Rd
Burke Co NC 46 C3
SR-127
Brookford NC 207 C7
Catawba Co NC 48 A5
Hickory NC 207 C6
Laurens Co SC 119 B4
SR-127 2nd St NE
Hickory NC 207 D4
SR-127 2nd St SE
Hickory NC 207 C6
SR-127 S Center St
Brookford NC 207 C7
SR-127 Duncan Hill Ln
Alexander Co NC 48 B1
SR-127 William L Patterson Hwy
Laurens Co SC 119 B4
SR-128
Buncombe Co NC 45 C4
SR-129
Spartanburg Co SC 98 A3
SR-129 Fort Prince Blvd
Spartanburg Co SC 98 A3
SR-130
Brunswick Co NC 145 A3
Columbus Co NC 128 B5
Maxton NC 105 E7
Robeson Co NC 126 D1
Robeson Co NC 127 C4
Shallotte NC 145 D5
Whiteville NC 128 D7
SR-130 BUS
Fairmont NC 127 C4
SR-130 Holden Beach Rd SW
Brunswick Co NC 145 E6
SR-130 Joe Brown Hwy
Columbus Co NC 128 B6
SR-130 Main St
Shallotte NC 145 D5
SR-130 New Britton Rd
Columbus Co NC 144 D1
Columbus Co NC 145 A2
SR-130 Rochester Hwy
Oconee Co SC 95 D7
SR-130 Stamp Creek Rd
Oconee Co SC 95 D5
SR-130 Whiteville Rd NW
Brunswick Co NC 145 A3
SR-130 Whitewater Falls Rd
Oconee Co SC 95 C4
SR-131
Bladen Co NC 107 C7
Bladen Co NC 128 C2
SR-131 Bladenboro Rd
Columbus Co NC 128 C4
SR-132
New Hanover Co NC 131 A7
New Hanover Co NC 147 A2
Wilmington NC 147 A1
SR-132 N College Rd
New Hanover Co NC 131 A7
SR-132 S College Rd
New Hanover Co NC 147 A2
Wilmington NC 147 A1
SR-133
Belville NC 146 D1
Brunswick Co NC 146 D5
Johnson Co TN 1 E3
New Hanover Co NC 130 E7

INDEX 6
-133 Street Index SR-215 S Duncan Byp

TREET
State Map# Grid
R-133
lew Hanover Co NC 131 A5
lew Hanover Co NC 231 A1
ak Island NC 146 C6
ickens Co SC 95 E4
ickens Co SC 225 B2
ix Mile SC 95 E6
Vilmington NC 231 B1
R-133 Castle Hayne Rd
lew Hanover Co NC 130 E7
lew Hanover Co NC 131 A5
R-133 College Av
ickens Co SC 225 B2
R-133 Cornelius
arnett Dr
Vilmington NC 231 B1
R-133 Country Club Dr
aswell Beach NC 146 C6
R-133 Crow Creek Rd
ickens Co SC 95 E4
R-133 Dosher Cto SE
runswick Co NC 146 D5
R-133 Mt Olivet Rd
ix Mile SC 95 E6
R-133 River Rd SE
elville NC 146 D1
runswick Co NC 146 D5
R-133 Shady Grove Rd
ickens Co SC 95 E4
R-133 Six Mile Hwy
ickens Co SC 95 E7
R-133
outhport-Supply Rd SE
runswick Co NC 146 D5
R-134
Montgomery Co NC 78 B2
andolph Co NC 52 B7
R-135
ickens Co SC 96 C6
ockingham Co NC 6 E6
ockingham Co NC 7 B5
R-135 Anderson Hwy
ickens Co SC 96 C6
R-135 Dacusville Hwy
ickens Co SC 96 C5
R-135 JJ Webster Hwy
ockingham Co NC 7 B5
R-136
edell Co NC 49 D7
Aooresville NC 49 D6
R-136 Coddle Creek Rd
edell Co NC 49 D7
R-136 W Iredell Av
Aooresville NC 49 D6
R-137
iates Co NC 15 D4
ickens Co SC 96 A5
R-137 Clemson
x-Mile Hwy
ickens Co SC 96 A5
R-137 Norris Hwy
ickens Co SC 96 A6
R-138
hester Co SC 122 B3
tanly Co NC 77 B5
R-138 Aquadale Rd
tanly Co NC 77 B5
R-138 Golf Course Rd
hester Co SC 122 B3
R-141
nderson Co SC 117 C5
nderson Co SC 226 D7
herokee Co NC 66 E7
herokee Co NC 92 D1
ardeeville SC 176 A7
asper Co SC 176 B7
R-141 McDuffie St Ext
nderson Co SC 226 D7
R-141 Warren St
asper Co SC 176 A7
R-142
dgecombe Co NC 35 B6
assell NC 35 C6
R-143
arter Co TN 22 A4
raham Co NC 66 E4
R-143 Burbank Rd
arter Co TN 22 A3
R-143 Cherohala Skwy
raham Co NC 66 C4
R-143 Massey Branch
d
raham Co NC 67 A4
R-143 Roan Rd
arter Co TN 21 E4
arter Co TN 22 A4
R-143 Santeetlah Rd
raham Co NC 66 E4
R-143 Snowbird Rd
raham Co NC 67 A4
R-143 Sweetwater Rd
raham Co NC 67 B3
R-144
ryan Co GA 180 A6
chmond Hill GA 180 B6
cotland Co NC 105 D4
R-144 SPUR
ryan Co GA 180 D7
R-144 Ford Av
chmond Hill GA 180 B6
R-144 SPUR Fort
cAllister Rd
ryan Co GA 180 D7
R-144 Old Wire Rd
cotland Co NC 105 D4
R-145
nson Co NC 104 A4
hesterfield Co SC 103 D7
hesterfield Co SC 124 B3
ranklin Co GA 115 D6
occoa GA 115 C3

STREET
City State Map# Grid
SR-145 Liberty Hill Rd
Toccoa GA 115 C3
SR-145 Toms Creek Rd
Stephens Co GA 115 D4
SR-146
Buncombe Co NC 70 D1
Greenville SC 97 B5
Greenville Co SC 97 E6
Spartanburg Co SC 98 B7
Spartanburg Co SC 119 C1
SR-146 Cross Anchor
Hwy
Spartanburg Co SC 98 B7
Spartanburg Co SC 119 C1
SR-146 Long Shoals Rd
Buncombe Co NC 70 D1
SR-146 Woodruff Rd
Greenville SC 97 B5
Greenville Co SC 97 E6
SR-147
Durham NC 30 E5
Durham NC 193 D3
Durham Co NC 31 A6
SR-147 Durham Frwy
Durham Co NC 31 A7
SR-147 IL Buck Dean
Expwy
Durham NC 193 D3
SR-147 I L Buck Dean
Frwy
Durham NC 30 E5
Durham Co NC 31 A6
SR-149
Pickens Co SC 225 B7
Washington Co NC 36 E7
SR-149 Ken Trowbridge
Rd
Washington Co NC 36 E7
SR-149 Norman Rd
Anderson Co SC 226 E7
SR-149 Old Cherry Rd
Clemson SC 225 B7
SR-150
Catawba Co NC 49 A6
Cherokee Co SC 99 A3
Cleveland Co NC 73 E4
Davidson Co NC 26 E7
Davidson Co NC 27 A7
Davidson Co NC 51 A1
Guilford Co NC 28 E1
Lincoln Co NC 74 B2
Mooresville NC 49 D6
Oak Ridge NC 27 E3
Rockingham Co NC 8 B7
Salisbury NC 50 D4
Shelby NC 73 C5
Summerfield NC 28 D2
Winston-Salem NC 27 C4
SR-150 Boiling
Springs Hwy
Cherokee Co SC 73 B7
SR-150 Cherryville Rd
Cleveland Co NC 73 E4
SR-150 Cobbham Rd
Columbia Co GA 148 A6
SR-150 College Av
Cleveland Co NC 73 B5
SR-150 S DeKalb St
Cleveland Co NC 73 C5
SR-150 Gaffney Rd
Cleveland Co NC 73 B6
SR-150 Glenn Springs
Rd
Spartanburg Co SC 98 D6
SR-150 Jake Pollard
Hwy
Columbia Co GA 148 D5
SR-150 N Main St
Forsyth Co NC 27 D3
Salisbury NC 50 D4
Spencer NC 208 E3
SR-150 S Main St
Salisbury NC 208 C5
SR-150 E Marion St
Shelby NC 73 D4
SR-150 Mooresville Rd
Rowan Co NC 49 E6
Rowan Co NC 50 A5
Salisbury NC 208 A6
SR-150 Oak Ridge Rd
Guilford Co NC 27 E3
Summerfield NC 28 A2
SR-150 Pacolet Hwy
Cherokee Co SC 99 A3
SR-150 Peters Creek
Pkwy
Winston-Salem NC 27 A5
Winston-Salem NC 188 B7
SR-150 E Plaza Dr
Mooresville NC 49 D6
SR-150 River Hwy
Iredell Co NC 49 C6
SR-151
Buncombe Co NC 44 B7
Buncombe Co NC 70 B1
Chesterfield Co SC 102 E7
Chesterfield Co SC 123 E3
Chesterfield Co SC 124 C5
Darlington Co SC 125 A7
Darlington Co SC 229 A5
SR-151 BYP
Jefferson SC 123 E1
Pageland SC 102 E6
SR-151 E Bobo Newsome
Hwy
Darlington Co SC 124 E7
SR-151 Hartsville Hwy
Darlington Co SC 125 A7
Darlington Co SC 229 A5
SR-151 Pisgah Hwy
Buncombe Co NC 44 B7
Buncombe Co NC 70 B1

STREET
City State Map# Grid
SR-151 BYP Van Lngl
Mungo Blvd
Pageland SC 102 E6
SR-152
Rowan Co NC 49 E6
Rowan Co NC 50 B6
SR-153
Anderson Co SC 96 E6
Rowan Co NC 50 A7
SR-153 EE Morris Jr
Mem Hy
Pickens Co SC 96 E6
SR-153 Earl E Morris
Jr Hwy
Anderson Co SC 96 E6
SR-154
Lee Co SC 140 B3
SR-154 St. Charles Rd
Lee Co SC 140 B3
SR-157
Durham Co NC 30 E4
Kershaw Co SC 123 C3
Person Co NC 9 C7
SR-157 Guess Rd
Durham Co NC 30 E4
Person Co NC 9 C7
SR-157 Jones Rd
Kershaw Co SC 123 C3
SR-159
Asheboro NC 209 C7
Carter Co TN 22 B1
Randolph Co NC 52 C5
SR-159 Zoo Pkwy
Asheboro NC 209 C7
Randolph Co NC 52 C5
SR-160
Charlotte NC 75 B7
Charlotte NC 101 A1
Cocke Co TN 19 A4
Fort Mill SC 101 B2
Lancaster Co SC 101 C2
Mecklenburg Co NC 75 B6
SR-160 Dixie Rd
Mecklenburg Co NC 75 B6
SR-160 Steele Creek Rd
Charlotte NC 75 B7
Charlotte NC 101 A1
SR-160 Tom Hall St
York Co SC 101 C2
SR-161
Bessemer City NC 74 B5
Cleveland Co NC 74 A5
York Co SC 100 B1
SR-161 Cleveland Av
Cleveland Co NC 74 A5
SR-161 W Old York Rd
York Co SC 100 D2
SR-162
Charleston Co SC 172 A7
Hollywood SC 172 D6
Meggett SC 172 C6
SR-163
Ashe Co NC 2 E7
Ashe Co NC 23 E1
Ashe Co NC 24 A1
McMinn Co TN 65 A4
SR-163 Gen Lee
Aderholt Mem Hy
McMinn Co TN 65 A4
SR-164
Banks Co GA 115 A7
SR-164 Historic Homer
Hwy
Banks Co GA 115 A7
SR-165
Dorchester Co SC 172 C3
Hollywood SC 172 C6
Monroe Co TN 65 E3
Monroe Co TN 66 A3
Ravenel SC 172 B5
Summerville SC 172 C1
SR-165 BYP
Tellico Plains TN 65 E3
SR-165 Bacons Bridge
Rd
Dorchester Co SC 172 C2
SR-165 Delemar Hwy
Dorchester Co SC 172 C3
SR-165 Indian
Boundary Rd
Monroe Co TN 66 A3
SR-165 S Main St
Summerville SC 172 C1
SR-165 River Rd
Monroe Co TN 65 E3
SR-167
Johnson Co TN 1 C7
Johnson Co TN 2 A5
Mountain City TN 1 E6
SR-167 Forge Creek Rd
Johnson Co TN 2 A5
Mountain City TN 1 E6
SR-167 Roan Creek Rd
Johnson Co TN 1 C7
SR-168
Chesapeake VA 17 C1
Currituck Co NC 17 E3
Currituck Co NC 18 A4
Knox Co TN 41 A1
SR-168 Caratoke Hwy
Currituck Co NC 17 E3
Currituck Co NC 18 A4
SR-168 Chesapeake
Expwy
Chesapeake VA 17 C1
SR-168 E Gov John
Sevier Hwy
Knox Co TN 41 A1
SR-170
Beaufort Co SC 176 C6
Beaufort Co SC 181 B1

STREET
City State Map# Grid
SR-170 ALT
Jasper Co SC 181 A2
SR-170 Okatie Hwy
Beaufort Co SC 176 C6
Beaufort Co SC 181 B1
SR-170 Robert Smalls
Pkwy
Beaufort Co SC 176 E5
SR-171
Beaufort Co NC 60 B2
Charleston SC 173 A5
Charleston SC 239 D2
Charleston SC 240 A7
Charleston Co SC 173 B7
Charleston Co SC 239 D5
SR-171 Folly Rd
Charleston SC 173 B6
Charleston Co SC 173 B7
SR-171 Old Towne Rd
Charleston SC 173 A5
Charleston SC 239 D4
SR-171 St. Andrews
Blvd
Charleston SC 240 A6
Charleston Co SC 239 D5
SR-171 Wesley Dr
Charleston SC 240 A7
SR-172
Calhoun Co SC 152 B5
Greene Co TN 19 E3
Greene Co TN 20 A1
Hart Co GA 116 D7
Onslow Co NC 111 E6
Onslow Co NC 132 B2
SR-172 Baileyton Rd
Greene Co TN 19 E3
Greene Co TN 20 A1
SR-172 Bowman Hwy
Hart Co GA 116 D7
SR-172 Old Swamp Rd
Calhoun Co SC 152 B5
SR-173
Carter Co TN 21 D3
SR-173 Erwin Hwy
Unicoi Co TN 21 B3
SR-173 Limestone Cove
Rd
Unicoi Co TN 21 C3
SR-173 Simerly Creek
Rd
Carter Co TN 21 D3
SR-174
Charleston Co SC 172 A6
Charleston Co SC 178 A1
SR-175
Towns Co GA 93 B3
SR-177
Hamlet NC 104 D4
Richmond Co NC 104 E3
Richmond Co NC 105 A3
SR-177 Frank C Wilson
Hwy
Hamlet NC 104 D4
Richmond Co NC 104 E3
Richmond Co NC 105 A3
SR-179
Brunswick Co NC 145 C6
Calabash NC 145 A7
SR-179 BUS
Sunset Beach NC 145 B7
SR-179 Beach Dr SW
Brunswick Co NC 145 C6
Carolina Shores NC 145 A7
SR-179 Seaside Rd SW
Brunswick Co NC 145 B6
SR-179 BUS Sunset
Blvd N
Sunset Beach NC 145 B7
SR-180
Cleveland Co NC 73 D4
Union Co GA 92 D7
Union Co GA 93 A5
SR-180 N Post Rd
Cleveland Co NC 73 D4
SR-180 S Post Rd
Cleveland Co NC 73 D5
SR-180 Wolf Pen Gap Rd
Union Co GA 92 D7
SR-181
Avery Co NC 22 D5
Burke Co NC 46 E2
Burke Co NC 47 A3
Hart Co GA 116 E7
Hart Co GA 117 A7
Newland NC 22 C5
SR-181 N Green St
Burke Co NC 47 A3
SR-181 Jonas Ridge Hwy
Avery Co NC 22 C6
SR-181 Linville Falls
Hwy
Avery Co NC 22 D5
SR-181 Smith McGee Hwy
Hart Co GA 116 E7
SR-181 Smith McGee Rd
Anderson Co SC 117 B6
SR-182
Lincoln Co NC 73 E2
Lincoln Co NC 74 A2
Oconee Co SC 116 B3
Polkville NC 73 C2
SR-182 Oakway Rd
Oconee Co SC 116 B2
SR-182 W Stage Coach
Tr
Polkville NC 73 C2
SR-183
Burke Co NC 22 C7
Greenville SC 223 B2
Greenville Co SC 223 A1
Oconee Co SC 95 B7
Pickens SC 96 B4

STREET
City State Map# Grid
SR-183
Pickens Co SC 96 E4
SR-183 Cedar Ln Rd
Greenville Co SC 223 A1
SR-183 Farrs Bridge Rd
Pickens SC 96 B4
Pickens Co SC 96 E4
SR-183 W North St
Greenville SC 223 B2
SR-183 Pickens Hwy
Oconee Co SC 95 C6
SR-183 Rochester Hwy
Oconee Co SC 95 D6
SR-183 Walhalla Hwy
Pickens Co SC 95 E5
Pickens Co SC 96 A5
SR-183 Westminster Hwy
Oconee Co SC 95 B7
SR-184
Abbeville Co SC 118 C6
Anderson Co SC 117 D7
Anderson Co SC 133 B1
Banks Co GA 115 A6
Banner Elk NC 22 D3
Due West SC 118 B7
Sugar Mountain NC 22 D4
SR-184 Antreville Hwy
Anderson Co SC 117 D7
SR-184 Beachmountain
Pkwy
Banner Elk NC 22 D3
SR-184 Damascus Rd
Banks Co GA 115 A6
SR-184 Dicks Hill Pkwy
Stephens Co GA 115 C3
SR-184 Elberton Hwy
Anderson Co SC 133 B1
SR-184 Homer Rd
Stephens Co GA 115 B4
SR-184 N Main St
Due West SC 118 B7
SR-184 Prather Bridge
Rd
Stephens Co GA 115 D2
SR-184 Tynecastle Hwy
Sugar Mountain NC 22 D4
SR-185
Abbeville Co SC 117 E6
Abbeville Co SC 118 A7
Abbeville Co SC 134 B1
Due West SC 118 B7
SR-185 Due West Hwy
Anderson Co SC 117 D5
SR-186
Northampton Co NC 13 D4
Northampton Co NC 14 A3
Pickens Co SC 96 D3
Seaboard NC 13 E3
SR-186 Earls Bridge Rd
Greenville Co SC 96 D3
SR-186 Pittman Rd
Southampton Co VA 14 C2
SR-187
Anderson Co SC 117 A4
Anderson Co SC 133 A1
SR-188
Oconee Co SC 95 C7
SR-188 Keowee School
Rd
Oconee Co SC 95 C7
SR-189
Southampton Co VA 15 C1
SR-189 S Quay Rd
Southampton Co VA 15 C1
SR-191
Aiken Co SC 149 E4
Aiken Co SC 150 A4
Asheville NC 44 C7
Buncombe Co NC 44 D7
Buncombe Co NC 70 D1
Johnston SC 149 E3
SR-191 Boylston Hwy
Henderson Co NC 70 D3
SR-191 Brevard Rd
Buncombe Co NC 44 C7
Buncombe Co NC 70 D1
SR-191 Charles F
Simons Jr Hwy
Aiken Co SC 149 E4
Aiken Co SC 150 A4
SR-191 Haywood Rd
Henderson Co NC 70 D3
SR-191 Old
Graniteville Hwy
Aiken Co SC 149 E5
SR-191 Senn St
Aiken Co SC 149 E6
SR-193
Florence Co SC 230 A3
Saluda Co SC 135 E7
Saluda Co SC 150 A1
SR-193 W Sumter St
Florence Co SC 230 A3
SR-194
Ashe Co NC 2 C7
Ashe Co NC 23 B2
Avery Co NC 22 C4
Newland NC 22 C5
Saluda Co SC 136 A5
Watauga Co NC 185 D1
SR-194 Banner Elk Hwy
Avery Co NC 22 C3
SR-194 Elk Park Hwy
Avery Co NC 22 C4
SR-194 E King St
Boone NC 185 C4
SR-194 W King St
Boone NC 185 A3
SR-194 Linville Falls
Hwy
Avery Co NC 22 C6

STREET
City State Map# Grid
SR-194 Pineola St
Newland NC 22 C5
SR-194 Robert G Barr
Expwy
Ashe Co NC 2 D6
SR-194 Three Mile Hwy
Avery Co NC 22 B7
SR-197
Buncombe Co NC 44 E3
Buncombe Co NC 45 A3
Habersham Co GA 93 D7
Habersham Co GA 115 A2
Mitchell Co NC 21 B5
SR-197 Barnardsville
Hwy
Buncombe Co NC 44 E3
SR-197 N Fork Rd
Buncombe Co NC 45 A3
SR-198
Banks Co GA 115 B6
Blacksburg SC 73 D7
Cleveland Co NC 73 D6
SR-198 Blacksburg Rd
Cleveland Co NC 73 D6
SR-198 N Mountain St
Blacksburg SC 73 D7
SR-200
Cabarrus Co NC 76 D4
Fairfield Co SC 121 E6
Great Falls SC 122 C3
Lancaster SC 101 D7
Lancaster SC 219 D5
Lancaster Co SC 219 B7
Locust NC 76 D6
Monroe NC 102 B3
Union Co NC 101 E5
Union Co NC 102 A4
Unionville NC 102 C2
SR-200 N Central Av
Locust NC 76 D6
SR-200 Chester Av
Chester Co SC 122 C3
SR-200 Great Falls Hwy
Lancaster Co SC 122 D1
Lancaster Co SC 219 B7
SR-200 Lancaster Av
Monroe NC 102 B3
SR-200 Lancaster Hwy
Union Co NC 101 E5
Union Co NC 102 A4
SR-200 N Market St
Lancaster SC 219 D5
SR-200 S Market St
Lancaster SC 101 D7
SR-200 Monroe Hwy
Lancaster Co SC 101 E6
SR-200 Morgan Mill Rd
Union Co NC 76 D7
Unionville NC 102 C2
SR-200 W Roosevelt
Blvd
Monroe NC 102 C2
Monroe NC 218 C3
SR-200 Skyway Dr
Monroe NC 218 B3
SR-201
Abbeville Co SC 134 A1
Anderson Co SC 117 E7
SR-202
Newberry Co SC 136 E2
SR-203
Abbeville Co SC 134 B2
SR-203 Old Douglas
Mill Rd
Abbeville Co SC 134 B2
SR-204
Bryan Co GA 180 A3
Savannah GA 180 E5
SR-204 SPUR
Chatham Co GA 180 E6
SR-204 37th St Conn
Savannah GA 180 E4
SR-204 Abercorn St
Chatham Co GA 180 D5
Savannah GA 180 E5
SR-204 Fort Argyle Rd
Chatham Co GA 180 B4
SR-204 Jo Bacon Hwy
Bryan Co GA 180 A3
SR-204 SPUR Whitfield
Av
Chatham Co GA 180 E6
SR-205
Stanly Co NC 76 E6
Union Co NC 102 E1
SR-207
Chesterfield Co SC 102 C6
Monroe NC 218 B5
SR-207 N Hayne St
Monroe NC 218 B5
SR-207 Wolf Pond Rd
Union Co NC 102 C3
SR-208
Madison Co NC 20 A7
Madison Co NC 44 A1
SR-209
Haywood Co NC 43 D5
SR-209 Crabtree Rd
Haywood Co NC 43 D7
SR-209 Rush Fork Rd
Haywood Co NC 43 D5
SR-210
Bladen Co NC 108 D7
Bladen Co NC 129 E3
Cumberland Co NC 80 E7
Fayetteville NC 81 A7
Fayetteville NC 222 D2
Harnett Co NC 83 B1
Johnston Co NC 56 C7
North Topsail Beach NC 132 B3
Onslow Co NC 132 B2
Orangeburg Co SC 162 E4

STREET
City State Map# Grid
SR-210
Orangeburg Co SC 163 A3
Pender Co NC 131 A4
SR-210 Bowman Branch
Hwy
Orangeburg Co SC 162 E4
Orangeburg Co SC 163 A3
SR-210 S Bragg Blvd
Spring Lake NC 221 E3
SR-210 Cedar Creek Rd
Cumberland Co NC 107 B2
SR-210 Island Dr
North Topsail Beach NC 132 B3
Onslow Co NC 132 B2
SR-210 Lillington Hwy
Spring Lake NC 221 E1
SR-210 Murchison Rd
Cumberland Co NC 80 E7
Cumberland Co NC 221 E3
Fayetteville NC 81 A7
Fayetteville NC 222 C1
SR-210 Rifle Range Rd
Onslow Co NC 132 B1
SR-210 Rowan St
Fayetteville NC 222 D2
SR-210 Vance Rd
Orangeburg Co SC 163 A3
SR-211
Bladen Co NC 129 B5
Brunswick Co NC 146 D5
Candor NC 78 E4
Cherokee Co SC 99 C4
Hoke Co NC 79 D7
Hoke Co NC 105 E1
Hoke Co NC 106 B3
Lumberton NC 127 D1
Montgomery Co NC 78 D4
Red Springs NC 106 C6
Robeson Co NC 127 E2
Robeson Co NC 128 A2
Southern Pines NC 220 E6
York Co SC 100 A3
SR-211 BYP
Bladen Co NC 128 B2
SR-211 E 4th Av
Red Springs NC 106 C6
SR-211 Aberdeen Rd
Hoke Co NC 79 D7
Hoke Co NC 105 E1
Hoke Co NC 106 A2
SR-211 Asbury Rd
Cherokee Co SC 99 B4
SR-211 Gowdeysville Rd
Cherokee Co SC 99 C4
SR-211 Green Swamp Rd
NW
Brunswick Co NC 145 E4
SR-211 Hickory Grove
Rd
York Co SC 100 A3
SR-211 Irene Bridge
Hwy
York Co SC 99 D3
SR-211 Red Springs Rd
Hoke Co NC 106 B3
SR-211 N Roberts Av
Lumberton NC 127 D1
SR-211
Southport-Supply Rd SE
Brunswick Co NC 146 D5
SR-211 Union Hwy
Cherokee Co SC 99 B4
SR-211 Wilkinsville
Hwy
Cherokee Co SC 99 D4
SR-212
Colleton Co SC 170 D1
Madison Co NC 20 B7
SR-212 George Warren
Rd
Colleton Co SC 170 D1
SR-213
Fairfield Co SC 121 B7
Fairfield Co SC 137 B1
Madison Co NC 44 D2
SR-213 Parr Rd
Newberry Co SC 137 B1
SR-214
Bolton NC 129 C6
Columbus Co NC 128 E6
Columbus Co NC 130 A6
SR-214 Andrew Jackson
Hwy
Columbus Co NC 129 E6
Columbus Co NC 130 A6
SR-214 Sam Potts Hwy
Bolton NC 129 C6
Columbus Co NC 128 E6
Columbus Co NC 129 A6
SR-215
Canton NC 43 E7
Fairfield Co SC 121 B6
Fairfield Co SC 137 C1
Haywood Co NC 69 D4
Spartanburg Co SC 98 D5
Union SC 99 B7
Union Co SC 99 A7
Union Co SC 120 E2
SR-215 E Blackstock Rd
Spartanburg Co SC 98 B4
SR-215 Blackwell Dr
Canton NC 43 E7
SR-215 Buffalo-W
Springs Hwy
Union Co SC 98 E7
SR-215 Carlisle
Chester Hwy
Union Co SC 120 E2
SR-215 N Duncan Byp
Union Co SC 99 B7
SR-215 S Duncan Byp
Union SC 120 C1

Street Index

STREET / City State / Map# Grid

US-64 ALT
Edgecombe Co NC 34 C6
Edgecombe Co NC 58 E1
Edgecombe Co NC 59 A1
Nash Co NC 33 A6
US-64 BUS
Chatham Co NC 54 B3
Rocky Mount NC 201 C3
Tarboro NC 34 D6
Wake Co NC 56 B2
US-64 BYP
Dare Co NC 39 E5
Morganton NC 47 A4
US-64 Chimney Rock Rd
Hendersonville NC 71 B3
US-64 Cong L H Fountain Hwy
Edgecombe Co NC 34 B6
US-64 E Dixie Dr
Asheboro NC 209 E6
US-64 W Dixie Dr
Randolph Co NC 209 A7
US-64 BYP W Fleming Dr
Morganton NC 47 A4
US-64 Harper Av
Lenoir NC 47 D1
US-64 Highlands Rd
Macon Co NC 68 C7
Macon Co NC 94 E1
US-64 Lindsey C Warren Br
Dare Co NC 39 B6
US-64 BUS Mack Todd Rd
Wake Co NC 56 C2
US-64 BUS N Main St
Tarboro NC 34 D6
US-64 Major RH Wilkins Mem Hy
Tyrrell Co NC 38 A6
US-64 Martin Luther King Blvd
Hendersonville NC 71 A4
US-64 Mocksville Rd
Davidson Co NC 51 A2
US-64 Morganton Blvd SW
Burke Co NC 47 C1
US-64 Murphy Rd
Macon Co NC 67 E7
Macon Co NC 68 A7
Macon Co NC 93 E1
US-64 New Hendersonville Hwy
Transylvania Co NC 70 C5
US-64 Old Copper Rd
Polk Co TN 65 A7
Polk Co TN 91 C2
US-64 Rosman Hwy
Transylvania Co NC 69 E7
Transylvania Co NC 70 A6
US-64 Scuppernong Dr
Columbia NC 38 E5
US-64 Sylva Rd
Macon Co NC 68 B7
US-64 Taylorsville Rd
Lenoir NC 47 E1
US-64 Tom Bradshaw Frwy
Cary NC 55 E3
US-64 BYP Virginia Dare Mem Br
Dare Co NC 39 E5
US-64 BUS Wendell Blvd
Wake Co NC 56 B2
US-70
Black Mountain NC 45 B6
Buncombe Co NC 45 D6
Buncombe Co NC 206 B3
Burlington NC 29 C4
Burlington NC 192 D3
Carteret Co NC 114 A3
Claremont NC 48 E4
Connelly Springs NC 47 D4
Davidson Co NC 51 E2
Durham NC 193 C1
Durham Co NC 31 B7
Garner NC 55 E3
Goldsboro NC 83 D2
Greensboro NC 28 C5
Guilford Co NC 28 A6
Hickory NC 48 B4
High Point NC 27 E7
High Point NC 191 E6
Johnston Co NC 57 A7
Johnston Co NC 83 B1
Madison Co NC 44 A1
Morehead City NC 113 B5
New Bern NC 86 A5
Old Fort NC 45 E5
Orange Co NC 30 A4
Raleigh NC 197 C6
Raleigh NC 199 E1
Thomasville NC 51 D1
Woodfin NC 44 D5
US-70 BUS
Durham NC 30 E6
Durham NC 193 D2
Goldsboro NC 204 B2
Johnston Co NC 56 C6
New Bern NC 86 B6
US-70 Arendell St
Morehead City NC 228 C5
US-70 BUS E Ash St
Goldsboro NC 83 D2
Goldsboro NC 204 B2
US-70 Burlington Rd
Guilford Co NC 28 D4
Guilford Co NC 29 B4
US-70 Capital Blvd
Raleigh NC 199 E2
US-70 Charlotte St
Buncombe Co NC 206 C3
US-70 N Church St
Burlington NC 192 D3
US-70 S Church St
Burlington NC 29 C4
US-70 Conover Blvd W
Newton NC 48 C4
US-70 Dixie Hwy
Cocke Co TN 19 B7
Cocke Co TN 43 C1
US-70 Dr ML King Jr Expwy
Goldsboro NC 83 D2
Goldsboro NC 204 D1
US-70 N Fisher St
Burlington NC 192 D2
US-70 W Fleming Dr
Morganton NC 47 A4
US-70 Glenwood Av
Raleigh NC 55 C1
Raleigh NC 197 C6
Raleigh NC 199 E1
US-70 Hickory Hwy
Iredell Co NC 49 B3
US-70 BUS Hillsborough Rd
Durham NC 193 C2
US-70 BUS Holloway St
Durham NC 30 E6
US-70 Jake Alexander Blvd S
Salisbury NC 208 A6
US-70 Jake Alexander Blvd W
Salisbury NC 208 A5
US-70 S Main St
Salisbury NC 50 D4
Salisbury NC 208 C5
US-70 Morris L McGough Frwy
Woodfin NC 44 D5
US-70 BUS Neuse Blvd
New Bern NC 86 B6
US-70 E New Bern Rd
Kinston NC 205 D7
US-70 New Raleigh Hwy
Durham Co NC 31 B7
US-70 N O'Henry Blvd
Greensboro NC 190 E5
US-70 BUS N Queen St
Kinston NC 205 C4
US-70 S Salisbury Av
Salisbury NC 208 E3
US-70 W State St
Black Mountain NC 45 B6
US-70 Statesville Blvd
Rowan Co NC 49 E3
Rowan Co NC 50 A4
US-70 Tunnel Rd
Asheville NC 44 E6
US-70 BUS W Vernon Av
Kinston NC 205 B4
US-70 Wade Av
Raleigh NC 199 E2
US-70 E Wendover Av
Greensboro NC 190 E1
US-70A
Greensboro NC 190 D3
Guilford Co NC 189 B7
US-70A High Point Rd
Guilford Co NC 189 B7
US-70A E Lee St
Greensboro NC 190 D3
US-70A W Lee St
Greensboro NC 190 C3
US-74
Anson Co NC 103 D3
Anson Co NC 104 B3
Asheville NC 44 C7
Buncombe Co NC 70 D1
Charlotte NC 75 C6
Charlotte NC 215 C3
Columbus Co NC 130 A6
Gastonia NC 74 C5
Haywood Co NC 43 D7
Haywood Co NC 69 C1
Henderson Co NC 71 A4
Indian Trail NC 102 A1
Kings Mountain NC 74 A5
Lilesville NC 104 A3
Marshville NC 102 E2
Monroe NC 218 E5
Polk Co TN 65 A7
Polkton NC 103 C2
Robeson Co NC 127 E3
Rutherford Co NC 72 E4
Scotland Co NC 105 E6
Shelby NC 73 B4
Swain Co NC 68 A2
US-74 ALT
Asheville NC 44 E7
Buncombe Co NC 206 A4
Rutherford Co NC 71 E2
Spindale NC 72 C4
US-74 BUS
Columbus Co NC 128 B6
Forest City NC 72 E4
Laurinburg NC 105 D6
Rockingham NC 104 D4
Rutherford Co NC 73 A5
Shelby NC 73 D5
US-74 BYP
Shelby NC 73 C5
US-74 Andrew Jackson Hwy
Columbus Co NC 128 E6
Columbus Co NC 129 A6
Robeson Co NC 127 E3
Scotland Co NC 105 A5
US-74 BUS Andrew Jackson Hwy
Scotland Co NC 105 D6
US-74 ALT Charlotte Hwy
Buncombe Co NC 44 E7
Buncombe Co NC 71 B1
US-74 ALT Charlotte St
Buncombe Co NC 206 D3
US-74 ALT Chimney Rock Rd
Rutherford Co NC 72 B3
US-74 E Dixon Blvd
Cleveland Co NC 73 E5
US-74 W Dixon Blvd
Cleveland Co NC 73 A4
Shelby NC 73 B4
US-74 BYP W Dixon Blvd
Shelby NC 73 C5
US-74 E Franklin Blvd
Gastonia NC 210 D4
US-74 W Franklin Blvd
Gastonia NC 74 C5
Gastonia NC 210 A4
US-74 Great Smoky Mtns Expwy
Haywood Co NC 43 D7
Haywood Co NC 69 C1
Swain Co NC 68 A2
US-74 Gr Kendley Frwy
Richmond Co NC 104 D4
US-74 E Independence Blvd
Charlotte NC 75 E7
US-74 BUS Joe Brown Hwy
Columbus Co NC 128 B6
US-74 W John Belk Frwy
Charlotte NC 215 D2
US-74 BUS E Marion St
Cleveland Co NC 73 D5
US-74 Martin L King Jr Pkwy
Wilmington NC 131 A7
Wilmington NC 231 B1
US-74 Old Copper Rd
Polk Co NC 65 A7
Polk Co TN 91 C2
US-74 W Roosevelt Blvd
Monroe NC 218 E5
US-74 Salisbury St
Anson Co NC 103 D3
US-74 Solon David Smart Mem Hy
Rutherford Co NC 72 E4
US-74 ALT Swannanoa River Rd
Asheville NC 44 E7
US-74 Wilkinson Blvd
Charlotte NC 75 C6
Charlotte NC 214 D2
Charlotte NC 215 C3
Mecklenburg Co NC 75 A5
US-74 W Wilkinson Blvd
Gaston Co NC 74 E5
US-76
Anderson SC 226 C3
Anderson Co SC 117 B3
Anderson Co SC 118 B4
Columbia SC 137 E5
Columbus Co NC 127 D7
Columbus Co NC 128 E6
Columbus Co NC 129 A6
East Ellijay GA 91 C6
Fannin Co GA 91 E4
Florence SC 230 B5
Florence Co SC 141 C2
Florence Co SC 142 A2
Irmo SC 137 D4
Laurens Co SC 119 C5
Lee Co SC 140 D5
Newberry SC 136 C1
Newberry Co SC 120 B7
Newberry Co SC 136 E2
Oconee Co SC 115 E1
Oconee Co SC 116 B1
Rabun Co GA 94 A5
Richland Co SC 138 E7
Richland Co SC 233 D3
Sumter Co SC 139 D6
Wilmington NC 147 A1
Wilmington NC 231 A4
US-76 BYP
Laurens SC 119 B4
US-76 CONN
Columbia SC 138 B6
Richland Co SC 234 C5
US-76 Anderson Hwy
Clemson SC 116 E1
Pickens Co SC 225 D7
US-76 Andrew Jackson Hwy
Columbus Co NC 128 E6
Columbus Co NC 129 A6
US-76 Andrew Jackson Hwy SW
Columbus Co NC 127 E6
Columbus Co NC 128 A6
US-76 Andrew Jackson Rd SW
Columbus Co NC 128 B6
US-76 Appalachian Hwy
Blue Ridge GA 91 D4
Fannin Co GA 91 E4
Fannin Co GA 92 A4
US-76 CONN N Beltline Blvd
Richland Co SC 234 C4
US-76 Belton Honea Path Hwy
Anderson Co SC 118 A5
US-76 Broad St
Sumter Co SC 139 D6
US-76 Chapin Rd
Lexington Co SC 137 B3
US-76 Charles Aiken Hwy
Greenville Co SC 118 C4
US-76 Clemson Blvd
Anderson Co SC 117 B3
Seneca SC 116 E1
US-76 Clemson Hwy
Anderson Co SC 117 B3
US-76 CONN Cross Hill Rd
Columbia SC 138 B6
US-76 Dawson St
Wilmington NC 231 C4
US-76 Devine St
Richland Co SC 234 C5
US-76 CONN Devine St
Richland Co SC 234 C5
US-76 Dutch Fork Rd
Richland Co SC 137 C3
US-76 Elmwood Av
Richland Co SC 233 B2
US-76 Florence Hwy
Lee Co SC 140 D5
US-76 Garners Ferry Rd
Richland Co SC 138 E7
Richland Co SC 234 D5
US-76 Gervais St
Richland Co SC 233 D3
US-76 BYP Hillcrest Dr
Laurens SC 119 B4
US-76 James F Byrnes Expwy
Irmo SC 137 D4
US-76 Lester Bastes Frwy
Columbia SC 137 E5
Richland Co SC 233 A3
US-76 Long Creek Hwy
Oconee Co SC 94 C5
Oconee Co SC 115 E1
US-76 Lookout Mtn Scenic Hwy
Rabun Co GA 93 E5
Rabun Co GA 94 A5
US-76 McMillan Hwy
Marion Co SC 143 B1
US-76 E North Av
Anderson SC 226 C3
US-76 Oleander Dr
Wilmington NC 147 A1
US-76 E Palmetto St
Florence Co SC 141 E2
Florence Co SC 142 A2
US-76 W Palmetto St
Florence SC 230 B5
US-76 Robert E Graham Frwy
Sumter SC 235 E1
US-76 CONN Rosewood Dr
Richland Co SC 234 C5
US-76 Sandifer Blvd
Oconee Co SC 116 B1
US-76 E Smith St
Florence Co SC 141 C2
US-76 W Smith St
Florence Co SC 141 A4
US-76 Southern Highroads Tr
Blairsville GA 92 E4
US-76 Southern Hghrds Scnc Hwy
East Ellijay GA 91 B7
US-76 Tails Creek Rd
Gilmer Co GA 91 A7
US-76 Tiger Blvd
Clemson SC 225 B3
US-76 Wilson Rd
Newberry SC 136 C1
US-76 Wooster St
Wilmington NC 231 E5
US-78
Aiken Co SC 150 C7
Aiken Co SC 160 D1
Aiken Co SC 236 C1
Augusta GA 159 B1
Bamberg Co SC 161 C3
Bamberg Co SC 162 D5
Burnettown SC 149 D7
Charleston SC 240 C2
Charleston Co SC 172 D2
Denmark SC 161 E3
Dorchester Co SC 163 A5
Dorchester Co SC 164 A6
North Charleston SC 172 E2
North Charleston SC 173 A4
Reevesville SC 163 B5
Williston SC 161 B3
US-78 Charleston Hwy
Aiken Co SC 150 C7
Aiken Co SC 160 D1
US-78 Dorange Rd
Dorchester Co SC 163 A5
Orangeburg Co SC 162 E5
US-78 Gordon Hwy
Augusta GA 159 A1
US-78 Heritage Hwy
Bamberg Co SC 161 E3
Bamberg Co SC 162 D5
US-78 Jefferson Davis Hwy
Aiken Co SC 149 D7
US-78 Johnston Av
Dorchester Co SC 163 B5
US-78 King St Ext
Charleston SC 240 C2
US-78 Richland Av SE
Aiken Co SC 236 F2
US-78 Richland Av SW
Aiken Co SC 236 C1
US-78 Richland Av W
Aiken Co SC 236 B1
US-78 Rivers Av
North Charleston SC 173 A4
North Charleston SC 237 C7
US-80
Chatham Co GA 181 B4
Effingham Co GA 180 A2
Pooler GA 180 D4
Savannah GA 180 E4
Tybee Island GA 181 C5
US-80 W Bay St
Garden City GA 180 E3
US-80 Butler Av
Tybee Island GA 181 C5
US-80 E Louisville Rd
Pooler GA 180 B3
US-80 W Victory Dr
Savannah GA 180 E4
US-117
Burgaw NC 130 E2
Duplin Co NC 109 D5
Goldsboro NC 83 C1
Goldsboro NC 204 A6
New Hanover Co NC 131 A7
Pender Co NC 130 E1
Warsaw NC 109 C2
Wayne Co NC 57 D7
Wayne Co NC 83 D1
Wayne Co NC 204 A3
Wilmington NC 231 E7
US-117 ALT
Duplin Co NC 83 B5
US-117 BYP
Wayne Co NC 83 C2
US-117 Castle Hayne Rd
New Hanover Co NC 131 A5
US-117 N College Rd
New Hanover Co NC 131 A6
US-117 Dr ML King Jr Expwy
Goldsboro NC 204 A3
US-117 RB Nelson Hwy
Wayne Co NC 204 A6
US-117 BYP Rb Nelson Hwy
Wayne Co NC 83 C2
US-117 Shipyard Blvd
Wilmington NC 231 E7
US-123
Clemson SC 116 E1
Clemson SC 117 A1
Clemson SC 225 B3
Greenville SC 223 A4
Habersham Co GA 115 A3
Oconee Co SC 116 A2
Pickens Co SC 96 B7
US-123 Academy St N
Greenville SC 223 B3
US-123 S Academy St
Greenville SC 223 A4
US-123 Clemson Blvd
Seneca SC 116 E1
US-123 Dicks Hill Pkwy
Habersham Co GA 115 A3
US-123 Sandifer Blvd
Oconee Co SC 116 B1
US-123 Tiger Blvd
Clemson SC 225 B3
US-123 Toccoa Hwy
Oconee Co SC 115 E2
Oconee Co SC 116 A2
US-129
Cherokee Co NC 67 A6
Lumpkin Co GA 92 E7
Murphy NC 66 D7
Murphy NC 92 C1
US-129 Gainesville Hwy
Union Co GA 92 E6
US-129 Murphy Hwy
Union Co GA 92 C3
US-129 Tallulah Rd
Graham Co NC 67 B4
US-129 Tapoco Rd
Graham Co NC 66 E2
Graham Co NC 67 A2
US-158
Caswell Co NC 9 A6
Currituck Co NC 18 C7
Davie Co NC 50 B1
Elizabeth City NC 17 C5
Garysburg NC 13 E5
Gates Co NC 16 C4
Guilford Co NC 28 D1
Halifax Co NC 12 E4
Halifax Co NC 13 A4
Kitty Hawk NC 39 D2
Middleburg NC 11 D5
Northampton Co NC 14 A5
Person Co NC 10 B7
Reidsville NC 7 D7
Rockingham Co NC 7 E7
Roxboro NC 9 D6
Stokesdale NC 27 E2
Stokesdale NC 28 A2
Vance Co NC 11 C6
Walkertown NC 27 C3
Weldon NC 13 D4
Winston-Salem NC 27 B4
US-158 BUS
Granville Co NC 11 A7
Warren Co NC 12 A5
US-158 BYP
Vance Co NC 11 A7
US-158
Granville Co NC 10 E7
US-158 Caratoke Hwy
Currituck Co NC 18 C7
Currituck Co NC 39 C2
US-158 S Croatan Hwy
Nags Head NC 40 A4
US-158 Freeway Dr
Reidsville NC 7 D7
US-158 N Hughes Blvd
Elizabeth City NC 184 C3
US-158 E Jefferson St
Jackson NC 14 B4
US-158 Julian Allsbrook Hwy
Halifax Co NC 13 A4
Roanoke Rapids NC 13 B4
US-158 Leasburg Rd
Person Co NC 9 B6
US-158 S Madison Blvd
Roxboro NC 9 D6
US-158 N Main St
Davie Co NC 50 B1
US-158 Oxford Rd
Person Co NC 9 E6
Person Co NC 10 B7
US-158 Reidsville Rd
Forsyth Co NC 27 D2
Walkertown NC 27 C3
US-158 N Road St
Elizabeth City NC 184 C1
US-158 Shortcut Rd
Currituck Co NC 17 E4
Currituck Co NC 18 A4
US-158 E South Main St
Littleton NC 12 C5
US-158 S Stratford Rd
Winston-Salem NC 187 E4
US-158 Walter Reid Mem Hwy
Hertford Co NC 14 E4
US-158 Wright Memorial Br
Kitty Hawk NC 39 D2
US-176
Berkeley Co SC 164 D7
Berkeley Co SC 172 E1
Calhoun Co SC 152 A2
Calhoun Co SC 153 A6
Cayce SC 137 E6
Columbia SC 137 E4
Goose Creek SC 237 C4
Henderson Co NC 71 A5
Lexington Co SC 233 B5
Newberry Co SC 137 A1
Orangeburg Co SC 163 E3
Richland Co SC 233 B2
Spartanburg SC 98 D4
Tryon NC 71 D6
Union Co SC 120 C2
US-176 BUS
Union SC 99 B7
US-176 BYP
Spartanburg Co SC 98 E4
US-176 TRK
Orangeburg Co SC 163 E4
Orangeburg Co SC 164 A4
US-176 Asheville Hwy
Spartanburg Co SC 71 E7
Spartanburg Co SC 97 E1
US-176 TRK Boyer Rd
Orangeburg Co SC 163 E4
Orangeburg Co SC 164 A4
US-176 Broad River Rd
Columbia SC 137 E4
Richland Co SC 137 C3
US-176 Charleston Hwy
Lexington Co SC 137 E7
US-176 Elmwood Av
Richland Co SC 233 B2
US-176 Furman L Fendley Hwy
Union Co SC 99 A6
US-176 Huger St
Richland Co SC 233 B4
US-176 Knox Abbott Dr
Lexington Co SC 233 B5
US-176 Main St
Richland Co SC 233 B1
US-176 Old State Rd
Calhoun Co SC 152 C3
Calhoun Co SC 153 A6
Orangeburg Co SC 163 E3
US-176 N Pine St
Spartanburg SC 98 C3
Spartanburg SC 224 C2
US-176 S Pine St
Spartanburg SC 224 D3
US-176 Spartanburg Hwy
Henderson Co NC 71 A5
US-176 St. James Av
Berkeley Co SC 172 E1
Goose Creek SC 237 C4
US-176 State Rd
Berkeley Co SC 164 D7
US-176 BUS Thompson Blvd
Union SC 99 B7
US-176 Whitmire Hwy
Newberry Co SC 120 C4
US-178
Abbeville Co SC 118 B6
Anderson SC 117 C4
Anderson SC 226 C3
Anderson Co SC 117 B2
Dorchester Co SC 163 E6
Dorchester Co SC 164 A6
Greenwood Co SC 134 E4
Greenwood Co SC 135 A4
Lexington Co SC 151 A3
Liberty SC 96 B5
Orangeburg Co SC 152 A5
Orangeburg Co SC 162 D1
Pickens Co SC 95 E1
Pickens Co SC 96 C7
Transylvania Co NC 69 E7
US-178 BUS
Orangeburg SC 152 C7
US-178 Batesburg Hwy
Saluda SC 135 E6
Saluda Co SC 136 B6
US-178 Belton Honea Path Hwy
Anderson Co SC 118 A5
US-178 BUS Broughton St
Orangeburg SC 152 C7
US-178 Charleston Hwy
Orangeburg Co SC 162 E2
Orangeburg Co SC 163 A2
US-178 Clemson Blvd
Anderson Co SC 117 B3
US-178 Fairview Rd
Lexington Co SC 150 D1
Lexington Co SC 151 A3
US-178 Greenwood Hwy
Saluda Co SC 135 D5
US-178 Joe S Jeffords Hwy
Orangeburg Co SC 162 D1
US-178 Liberty Hwy
Anderson Co SC 96 B7
Anderson Co SC 117 B2
US-178 E Main St
Dorchester Co SC 163 E6
Dorchester Co SC 164 A6
US-178 W Main St
Dorchester Co SC 163 D5
US-178 Moorefield Memorial Hwy
Pickens Co SC 95 E1
Pickens Co SC 96 B5
US-178 E North Av
Anderson SC 226 C3
US-178 North Rd
Orangeburg Co SC 151 E5
Orangeburg Co SC 152 A5
US-178 Pickens Hwy
Transylvania Co NC 69 E7
Transylvania Co NC 96 A1
US-178 E River St
Anderson SC 117 C4
US-220
Greensboro NC 28 B4
Greensboro NC 190 A1
Guilford Co NC 28 A2
Henry Co VA 6 E1
Henry Co VA 7 B2
Montgomery Co NC 78 D4
Randolph Co NC 209 A7
Richmond Co NC 104 D2
Summerfield NC 28 A3
US-220 ALT
Montgomery Co NC 78 D4
Randolph Co NC 52 C7
US-220 BUS
Asheboro NC 52 C3
Asheboro NC 209 C6
Martinsville VA 7 A1
Randolph Co NC 52 C1
Rockingham Co NC 6 E6
Rockingham Co NC 7 A5
US-220 BYP
Henry Co VA 7 B2
US-220 CONN
Randolph Co NC 209 B2
US-220 Battleground Av
Greensboro NC 28 B4
Greensboro NC 190 A1
US-220 BUS W Decatur St
Madison NC 6 E6
US-220 BUS N Fayetteville St
Asheboro NC 209 C3
US-220 BUS S Fayetteville St
Asheboro NC 209 C6
Randolph Co NC 52 C5
US-220 Fordham Blvd
Greensboro NC 190 A7
US-220 Gov John M Morehead Hy
Guilford Co NC 28 B7
US-220 Greensboro Rd
Henry Co VA 7 B3
US-220 BUS Greensboro Rd
Henry Co VA 7 B2
US-220 BUS Memorial Blvd S
Martinsville VA 7 A1
US-220 N O'Henry Blvd
Greensboro NC 28 C5
Greensboro NC 190 E5
US-220 Thomas A. Burton Hwy
Rockingham Co NC 7 A7
Rockingham Co NC 28 A1
US-220 BYP Thomas A. Burton Hy
Rockingham Co NC 7 A4
US-220 CONN Vision Dr
Asheboro NC 209 B2
US-220 E Wendover Av
Greensboro NC 190 E1
US-220 W Wendover Av
Greensboro NC 190 D1
US-220 William F Stone Hwy
Henry Co VA 6 E1
Henry Co VA 7 B2
US-220 BYP William F Stone Hwy
Henry Co VA 7 B2
US-221
Ashe Co NC 2 E6
Grayson Co VA 4 A2
Greenwood Co SC 134 E2
Independence VA 3 D3
Laurens Co SC 119 B3
Laurens Co SC 135 A1
Marion NC 46 B5

Street Index

US-221   US-521 Kershaw Hwy

INDEX 12
US-521 Kershaw Camden — Street Index — Asheville Rd US-23 BUS

STREET / City State Map# Grid

US-521 Kershaw Camden Hwy
Lancaster Co SC 122 E1
Lancaster Co SC 123 A2
US-521 Manning Av
Sumter SC 140 A7
Sumter Co SC 235 E7
US-521 BUS N Market St
Lancaster SC 219 D5
US-521 BUS S Market St
Lancaster SC 219 E7
US-521 Oakland Av
Sumter SC 235 A1
US-521 Sumter Hwy
Kershaw Co SC 139 C3
US-521 Thomas Sumter Hwy
Sumter Co SC 139 E6
US-601
Bamberg Co SC 162 A3
Boonville NC 25 E3
Cabarrus Co NC 76 B1
Calhoun Co SC 152 D5
Chesterfield Co SC 123 D1
Colleton Co SC 170 A1
Columbia SC 139 A5
Concord NC 76 B3
Davie Co NC 26 A6
Fairview NC 76 C7
Hampton SC 169 E4
Jasper Co SC 175 D2
Monroe NC 218 E5
Mt Airy NC 183 C6
Pageland SC 102 E6
Salisbury NC 208 B7
Surry Co NC 4 E7
Surry Co NC 25 E2
Union Co NC 102 D4
Unionville NC 102 C2
US-601 TRK
Orangeburg Co SC 152 D7
US-601 Bamberg Rd
Orangeburg Co SC 162 B2
US-601 Broxton Bridge Hwy
Colleton Co SC 170 A1
US-601 Broxton Bridge Rd
Bamberg Co SC 162 A4
US-601 TRK Chestnut St
Orangeburg Co SC 152 D7
US-601 Colonel Thompson Hwy
Calhoun Co SC 153 A3
US-601 Concord Hwy
Fairview NC 76 C7
Unionville NC 102 C2
US-601 Gold Mine Hwy
Chesterfield Co SC 123 D1
US-601 Jake Alexander Blvd S
Salisbury NC 208 B7
US-601 Jake Alexander Blvd W
Rowan Co NC 208 A5
US-601 Jefferson Davis Hwy
Camden SC 139 A1
US-601 Kershaw Hwy
Kershaw Co SC 123 B5
US-601 Magnolia St NE
Orangeburg Co SC 152 D7
US-601 McCords Ferry Rd
Richland Co SC 139 A5
Richland Co SC 153 B3
US-601 Pageland Hwy
Union Co NC 102 D4
US-601 N Pearl St
Chesterfield Co SC 102 E6
US-601 Rockford St
Surry Co NC 4 E6
Surry Co NC 5 A5
US-601 W Roosevelt Blvd
Monroe NC 218 C3
US-601 Savannah Hwy
Hampton Co SC 169 E4
Hampton Co SC 170 A3
US-601 S Savannah Hwy
Hampton Co SC 169 E5
US-601 St. Matthews Rd
Calhoun Co SC 152 D5
US-701
Bladen Co NC 108 B7
Bladen Co NC 128 E2
Bladen Co NC 129 A1
Charleston Co SC 166 D6
Conway SC 157 D1
Elizabethtown NC 128 E1
Georgetown Co SC 157 C4
Horry Co SC 143 E5
Horry Co SC 144 B3
Mt Pleasant SC 173 C5
Mt Pleasant SC 238 A5
US-701 BYP
Horry Co SC 144 B2
Sampson Co NC 108 D1
Whiteville NC 128 D6
US-701 4th Av
Conway SC 157 D1
US-701 Faircloth Frwy
Sampson Co NC 108 D2
US-701 Frank Melvin Rd
Bladen Co NC 129 A1
US-701 N Fraser St
Georgetown Co SC 157 C4
Georgetown Co SC 167 A1
US-701 Garland Hwy
Sampson Co NC 108 D4
US-701 Hobbton Hwy
Sampson Co NC 82 D6
US-701 James B White Hwy N
Columbus Co NC 128 D5
US-701 James B White Hwy S
Columbus Co NC 144 C2
US-701 James M Graham Hy
Awendaw SC 174 A1
Charleston Co SC 166 C7
US-701 Johnnie Dodds Blvd
Mt Pleasant SC 173 C5
Mt Pleasant SC 238 D5
US-701 N Main St
Conway SC 157 D1
US-701 S Poplar St
Bladen Co NC 128 E1

A

N A St
Easley SC 96 C5
N A St SR-135
Easley SC 96 C5
W A St
Cabarrus Co NC 76 A1
Kannapolis NC 50 A7
Aarons Creek Rd
Halifax Co VA 10 B2
Aarron Burr Rd
Chester Co SC 100 D6
Aarron Burr Rd SR-909
Chester Co SC 100 D6
Abbeville Hwy
Anderson Co SC 117 D7
Greenwood Co SC 134 D2
Abbeville Hwy SR-28
Anderson Co SC 117 D7
Abbeville Hwy SR-72
Greenwood Co SC 134 D2
Abercorn St
Savannah GA 180 D5
Abercorn St SR-204
Savannah GA 180 D5
Aberdeen Rd
Hoke Co NC 79 D7
Hoke Co NC 105 D1
Hoke Co NC 106 A2
Aberdeen Rd SR-211
Hoke Co NC 79 D7
Hoke Co NC 105 D1
Hoke Co NC 106 A2
Aberdeen Rd US-15
Scotland Co NC 105 C5
Aberdeen Rd US-501
Scotland Co NC 105 C5
Abner Rd
Montgomery Co NC 52 B7
Montgomery Co NC 78 B1
Abner Creek Rd
Spartanburg Co SC 97 D5
Abram Penn Hwy
Patrick Co VA 6 C2
Academy St N
Greenville SC 223 C2
Academy St N US-123
Greenville SC 223 C2
E Academy St
Fuquay-Varina NC 55 B6
S Academy St
Greenville SC 223 A3
S Academy St US-123
Greenville SC 223 A3
W Academy St
Cherryville NC 74 A3
Fuquay-Varina NC 55 B6
Randleman NC 52 C2
Winston-Salem NC 188 C4
W Academy St SR-42
Wake Co NC 55 B6
W Acadia Av
Winston-Salem NC 188 C6
Ace Basin Pkwy
Colleton Co SC 171 C6
Colleton Co SC 177 A1
Ace Basin Pkwy US-17
Colleton Co SC 171 C6
Colleton Co SC 177 A1
Acorn Hill Rd
Gates Co NC 16 C5
Adako Rd
Caldwell Co NC 47 A1
Adams Mill Rd
Greenville Co SC 97 C6
Addor Rd
Hoke Co NC 105 C1
Moore Co NC 79 B7
Adelaide St
Newberry Co SC 136 C1
Adelaide St US-76 BUS
Newberry Co SC 136 C1
Aderholdt Rd
Gaston Co NC 74 B3
Adkins Rd
York Co SC 100 D2
Affinity Rd
Robeson Co NC 127 C6
Aiken Rd
Buncombe Co NC 44 D5
Ridge Spring SC 150 B1
Aiken Rd SR-392
Ridge Spring SC 150 B1
Air Base Rd
Richland Co SC 138 C7
Airbase Rd
Scotland Co NC 105 D5
Air Harbor Rd
Guilford Co NC 28 B3
Airline-Goldmine Rd
Hart Co GA 116 B7
Air Line School Rd
Hart Co GA 116 B6
Airport Blvd
Morrisville NC 55 A1
Springdale SC 137 E7
Airport Blvd SR-302
Cayce SC 137 E7
Airport Blvd NW
Wilson Co NC 57 D2
Airport Rd
Buncombe Co NC 70 D2
Cherokee Co NC 66 E6
Cherokee Co NC 67 A6
Greenwood Co SC 134 E2
Lancaster Co SC 219 A7
Lenoir Co NC 84 D3
Monroe NC 102 A2
Moore Co NC 79 C5
Richmond Co NC 104 D4
Rowan Co NC 50 B5
Scotland Co NC 105 D5
Trenton SC 149 E3
Airport Rd SR-280
Buncombe Co NC 70 D2
Airport Rd SR-914
Lancaster Co SC 219 A7
Airways Av
Pooler GA 180 C3
Akron Dr
Winston-Salem NC 186 E6
Alabama Av
Spartanburg Co SC 72 D7
Alabama Av US-221
Spartanburg Co SC 72 D7
S Alabama Av
Spartanburg Co SC 72 D7
S Alabama Av US-221
Chesnee SC 72 D7
Alamance Rd
Alamance Co NC 29 B5
Burlington NC 192 A6
Alamance Rd SR-62
Alamance Co NC 29 B5
Burlington NC 192 A6
Alamance Church Rd
Greensboro NC 190 E6
Guilford Co NC 28 C5
Guilford Co NC 29 A6
Albemarle Av
Greenville NC 203 B2
Albemarle Rd
Charleston SC 240 A6
Charlotte NC 75 E6
Troy NC 78 A3
Albemarle Rd SR-24
Charlotte NC 76 A6
Troy NC 78 A3
Albemarle Rd SR-27
Charlotte NC 75 E6
Charlotte NC 76 A6
Troy NC 78 A3
Albemarle Rd SR-109
Troy NC 78 A3
Albert St
Dublin NC 128 D1
Albert St SR-87
Dublin NC 128 D1
Albright Rd
Rock Hill SC 101 A4
Rock Hill SC 217 B7
Albright Rd SR-72 BYP
Rock Hill SC 101 A4
Rock Hill SC 217 B7
Albright Rd SR-121
Rock Hill SC 101 A4
Rock Hill SC 217 B7
Alexander Rd
Buncombe Co NC 44 C5
Matthews NC 75 D7
Rowan Co NC 75 E1
E Alexander Love Hwy
York Co SC 100 C2
E Alexander Love Hwy SR-5 BYP
York SC 100 C2
E Alexander Love Hwy SR-161
York Co SC 100 C2
W Alexander Love Hwy
York Co SC 100 C2
W Alexander Love Hwy SR-5
York Co SC 100 C2
Alex Harvin Hwy
Clarendon Co SC 154 A5
Alex Harvin Hwy US-301
Clarendon Co SC 154 A5
Alexis High Shoals Rd
Gaston Co NC 74 D3
Alexis Lucia Rd
Gaston Co NC 74 D3
Gaston Co NC 75 A3
Alfred St
Garden City GA 180 E3
Alice Dr
Sumter SC 235 A3
Sumter Co SC 139 E6
Alice Dr SR-120
Sumter SC 139 E6
Sumter SC 235 A3
All American Expwy
Cumberland Co NC 80 D6
Cumberland Co NC 221 B5
All American Frwy
Fayetteville NC 80 E7
Fayetteville NC 106 E1
Alleghany St
Charlotte NC 75 B5
Charlotte NC 215 A1
Allendale-Fairfax Hwy
Fairfax SC 169 B2
Allendale-Fairfax Hwy US-278
Fairfax SC 169 B2
Allen E Vaughn Frwy
Greenville Co SC 97 C6
Allen E Vaughn Frwy I-385
Greenville Co SC 97 C6
Alliance Church Rd
Guilford Co NC 28 C6
Alligator Rd
Florence Co SC 141 C3
Allman Hill Rd
Buncombe Co NC 44 D3
Allred Mill Rd
Mt Airy NC 183 B2
AL Philpott Hwy
Henry Co VA 6 E2
Henry Co VA 7 A2
AL Philpott Hwy US-58
Henry Co VA 6 E2
Al Philpott Hwy US-58
Henry Co VA 7 C1
AL Philpott Hwy US-58 BUS
Henry Co VA 7 A2
Al Philpott Memorial Hwy
Grayson Co VA 3 B3
Al Philpott Memorial Hwy US-58
Grayson Co VA 3 B3
Alpine Rd
Richland Co SC 138 B4
N Alston Av
Durham NC 31 A6
N Alston Av SR-55
Durham NC 31 A6
S Alston Av
Durham NC 31 A7
Durham Co NC 55 A1
Altamont Rd
Greenville Co SC 97 A3
Alton Post Office Rd
Halifax Co VA 9 C3
Alvin Hough Rd
Cabarrus Co NC 76 B5
Amboy Rd
Asheville NC 44 D7
Buncombe Co NC 206 A6
S Amhurst Pl
Englewood TN 65 B2
S Amhurst Pl SR-33
Englewood TN 65 B2
S Amhurst Pl US-411
Englewood TN 65 B2
Amity Hill Rd
Rowan Co NC 49 E4
N Anderson Blvd
Topsail Beach NC 131 E5
N Anderson Blvd SR-50
Topsail Beach NC 131 E5
S Anderson Blvd
Topsail Beach NC 131 D5
S Anderson Blvd SR-50
Topsail Beach NC 131 D5
Anderson Dr
Anderson Co SC 117 E2
Laurens SC 119 A4
Liberty SC 96 B6
Raleigh NC 55 D2
Raleigh NC 197 E7
Anderson Dr SR-20 CONN
Williamston SC 117 E2
Anderson Dr US-29 CONN
Anderson Co SC 117 E2
Anderson Dr US-76 BYP
Laurens SC 119 A4
Anderson Dr US-178
Liberty SC 96 B6
Anderson Hwy
Anderson Co SC 96 E7
Anderson Co SC 117 D2
Clemson SC 116 E1
Clemson SC 225 C4
Elbert Co GA 133 A1
Hart Co GA 116 D7
Anderson Hwy SR-8
Hart Co GA 116 D7
Anderson Hwy SR-20 CONN
Anderson Co SC 117 D2
Anderson Hwy SR-28
Clemson SC 116 E1
Clemson SC 225 C4
Pickens Co SC 225 D6
Anderson Hwy SR-86
Anderson Co SC 96 D7
Anderson Hwy SR-135
Pickens Co SC 96 C7
Anderson Hwy SR-368
Elbert Co GA 133 A2
Anderson Hwy US-29
Hart Co GA 116 D7
Anderson Hwy US-29 CONN
Anderson Co SC 117 D2
Anderson Hwy US-76
Clemson SC 116 E1
Clemson SC 225 C4
Pickens Co SC 225 D6
Anderson Rd
Anderson Co SC 96 E6
Greenville Co SC 97 A6
Greenville Co SC 223 A5
Anderson Rd SR-81
Anderson Co SC 96 E6
Greenville Co SC 97 A6
Greenville Co SC 223 A5
N Anderson Rd
York Co SC 101 A3
York Co SC 217 E2
N Anderson Rd SR-121
Rock Hill SC 101 A3
York Co SC 217 E2
N Anderson Rd US-21
Rock Hill SC 217 E2
York Co SC 101 A3
S Anderson Rd
Rock Hill SC 217 E4
York Co SC 101 B4
S Anderson Rd SR-72 BYP
Rock Hill SC 217 E4
S Anderson Rd SR-121
Rock Hill SC 217 E4
S Anderson Rd US-21
York Co SC 101 B4
S Anderson Rd US-21 BYP
Rock Hill SC 217 E4
Anderson St
Anderson Co SC 117 E4
Greenville SC 223 A5
Anderson St SR-81
Greenville SC 223 A5
Anderson St SR-86
Anderson Co SC 117 E1
Anderson St US-76
Anderson Co SC 117 E4
Anderson St US-178
Anderson Co SC 117 E4
Anderson Mill Rd
Spartanburg Co SC 98 B4
Anderson Ridge Rd
Greenville Co SC 97 D5
Anderson Valley Rd
Guilford Co NC 28 D3
Andrew Jackson Hwy
Brunswick Co NC 130 B7
Brunswick Co NC 231 A4
Columbus Co NC 128 B6
Columbus Co NC 129 D6
Leland NC 130 D7
Robeson Co NC 127 D2
Scotland Co NC 105 B5
Andrew Jackson Hwy US-17
Belville NC 130 D7
Andrew Jackson Hwy US-17 BUS
Brunswick Co NC 231 A4
Andrew Jackson Hwy US-74
Belville NC 130 D7
Brunswick Co NC 130 B7
Columbus Co NC 128 B6
Columbus Co NC 129 D6
Robeson Co NC 127 D2
Scotland Co NC 105 B5
Andrew Jackson Hwy US-74 BUS
Scotland Co NC 105 D6
Andrew Jackson Hwy US-76
Belville NC 130 D7
Brunswick Co NC 130 B7
Brunswick Co NC 231 A4
Columbus Co NC 128 B6
Columbus Co NC 129 D6
Andrew Jackson Hwy US-421
Brunswick Co NC 231 A4
Andrew Jackson Hwy SW
Columbus Co NC 127 E6
Fair Bluff NC 127 D7
Andrew Jackson Hwy SW US-76
Columbus Co NC 127 E6
Fair Bluff NC 127 D7
Andrew Jackson Rd SW
Columbus Co NC 128 B6
Andrew Jackson Rd SW US-76
Columbus Co NC 128 B6
Andrew Johnson Hwy
Bulls Gap TN 19 A2
Greene Co TN 20 C2
Andrew Johnson Hwy SR-34
Bulls Gap TN 19 A2
Washington Co TN 20 D2
Andrew Johnson Hwy US-11E
Bulls Gap TN 19 A2
Greene Co TN 20 C2
Andrew Johnson Hwy US-321
Greene Co TN 20 C2
E Andrew Johnson Hwy
Greeneville TN 20 B3
Hamblen Co TN 19 A2
E Andrew Johnson Hwy SR-34
Greeneville TN 20 B3
Hamblen Co TN 19 A2
E Andrew Johnson Hwy SR-113
Hamblen Co TN 19 A2
E Andrew Johnson Hwy US-11E
Greeneville TN 20 B3
Hamblen Co TN 19 A2
E Andrew Johnson Hwy US-321
Greeneville TN 20 B3
W Andrew Johnson Hwy
Greene Co TN 19 B2
W Andrew Johnson Hwy SR-34
Greene Co TN 19 B2
W Andrew Johnson Hwy US-11E
Greene Co TN 19 B2
E Andrews Av
Henderson NC 11 B7
E Andrews Av SR-39
Henderson NC 11 B7
W Andrews Av
Henderson NC 11 B6
W Andrews Av SR-39
Henderson NC 11 B6
Andrews Rd
Cumberland Co NC 81 A6
Andy Griffith Pkwy
Mt Airy NC 5 A4
Mt Airy NC 183 B5
Surry Co NC 183 D7
Andy Griffith Pkwy US-52 BYP
Mt Airy NC 5 A4
Surry Co NC 183 D7
Angelus Rd
Chesterfield Co SC 124 B2
Angier Av
Durham NC 31 A6
Ankum Rd
Brunswick Co VA 12 D2
Ann St
Pickens SC 96 B4
Ann St US-178
Pickens SC 96 B4
Annapolis Dr
Raleigh NC 199 D2
Ansonville Rd
Union Co NC 102 D2
Anthony Dr
Patrick Co VA 6 C1
S Anthony St
Burlington NC 192 D5
S Anthony St SR-100
Burlington NC 192 D5
Antioch Rd
Pickens Co SC 96 E5
Antioch Amez Church Rd
Richland Co SC 138 E7
Antioch Church Rd
Habersham Co GA 115 A2
Union Co NC 101 E2
Antreville Hwy
Anderson Co SC 117 C7
Antreville Hwy SR-184
Anderson Co SC 117 C7
Appalachian Dr
Henry Co VA 7 A1
Appalachian Dr SR-57
Henry Co VA 7 A1
Appalachian Hwy
Fannin Co GA 91 D5
Fannin Co GA 92 A4
Appalachian Hwy SR-2
Fannin Co GA 91 D5
Fannin Co GA 92 A4
Appalachian Hwy SR-5
Fannin Co GA 91 D5
Appalachian Hwy SR-515
Fannin Co GA 91 D5
Fannin Co GA 92 A4
Appalachian Hwy US-76
Fannin Co GA 91 D5
Fannin Co GA 92 A4
Apple Valley Rd
Spartanburg Co SC 97 E5
Appling Harlem Rd
Columbia Co GA 148 B7
Appling Harlem Rd SR-47
Columbia Co GA 148 B7
Appling Harlem Rd US-221
Columbia Co GA 148 B7
Aquadale Rd
Stanly Co NC 77 B6
Aquadale Rd SR-138
Stanly Co NC 77 B6
Ararat Hwy
Patrick Co VA 5 B3
Ararat Rd
Surry Co NC 5 A6
Arbor Dr
Lancaster Co SC 123 B3
Arbor Dr SR-157
Kershaw Co SC 123 B3
Arbor Rd
Winston-Salem NC 187 E1
Winston-Salem NC 188 A1
E Arcadia Rd
Bladen Co NC 129 D5
E Arch St
Lancaster Co SC 101 E7
Lancaster Co SC 219 C5
E Arch St SR-9
Lancaster Co SC 101 E7
Lancaster Co SC 219 C5
Archer Rd
Spartanburg Co SC 98 C3
Spartanburg Co SC 224 D1
Archibald Rd
Cabarrus Co NC 76 B3
N Arendell Av
Zebulon NC 56 C1
N Arendell Av SR-96
Zebulon NC 56 C1
N Arendell Av US-64 BUS
Zebulon NC 56 C1
S Arendell Av
Wake Co NC 56 D1
S Arendell Av SR-96
Wake Co NC 56 D1
Arendell St
Morehead City NC 113 B5
Morehead City NC 228 A5
Arendell St US-70
Morehead City NC 113 B5
Morehead City NC 228 A5
E Arlington Blvd
Greenville NC 203 C4
W Arlington Blvd
Greenville NC 59 A5
Greenville NC 203 A4
Arlington Rd
Greer SC 97 D3
Arlington Rd SR-357
Greer SC 97 D3
Arlington St
Rocky Mount NC 201 D4
Arlington St SR-97
Rocky Mount NC 201 D4
Arlington Church Rd
Mecklenburg Co NC 76 B6
Armory Rd
Chester Co SC 100 C7
Armstrong Rd
Gaston Co NC 75 A7
Armstrong Rd SR-273
Gaston Co NC 75 A7
Armstrong Ford Rd
Cramerton NC 74 E6
Armstrong Park Rd
Gastonia NC 74 D5
Arnett Blvd
Danville VA 8 C2
Arnette Rd
Dillon Co SC 127 A5
Arnold Rd
Davidson Co NC 51 A1
Washington Co TN 21 A3
Arnold Palmer Dr
Raleigh NC 196 C1
Arnold S Goodstein Expwy
Berkeley Co SC 172 E2
Arnold S Goodstein Expwy I-26
Berkeley Co SC 172 E1
Arrington Bridge Rd SE
Wayne Co NC 83 C2
Wayne Co NC 204 A7
Arrington Bridge Rd SE SR-581
Wayne Co NC 83 C2
Wayne Co NC 204 A7
Arrowhead Dr NE
Catawba Co NC 48 B3
Arrowood Rd
Mecklenburg Co NC 75 B7
W Arrowood Rd
Charlotte NC 75 B7
Arthur Ravenel Jr Br
Charleston SC 173 B5
Arthur Ravenel Jr Br US-17
Charleston SC 173 B5
Asbury Rd
Cherokee Co SC 99 A3
Asbury Rd SR-211
Cherokee Co SC 99 A3
Asbury Chapel Rd
Mecklenburg Co NC 75 D3
Ascauga Lake Rd
Aiken Co SC 149 D6
E Ash St
Goldsboro NC 83 D2
Goldsboro NC 204 C3
E Ash St US-70 BUS
Goldsboro NC 83 D2
Goldsboro NC 204 C3
W Ash St
Goldsboro NC 83 C2
Goldsboro NC 204 B3
W Ash St SR-581
Goldsboro NC 83 C2
Ashbrook Park Rd
Gaston Co NC 74 C4
E Ashby Rd
Florence Co SC 141 D1
Florence Co SC 230 E1
E Ashby Rd SR-358
Florence Co SC 230 E1
Ashe Rd
Mountain City TN 1 E6
Ashe Rd SR-167
Mountain City TN 1 E6
Asheville Hwy
Haywood Co NC 44 A7
Madison Co NC 20 A6
Spartanburg Co SC 71 E7
Spartanburg Co SC 97 E1
Spartanburg Co SC 98 B2
Spartanburg Co SC 224 A1
Sylva NC 68 E3
Transylvania Co NC 70 B4
Asheville Hwy SR-56
Spartanburg Co SC 98 B3
Spartanburg Co SC 224 A1
Asheville Hwy SR-70
Greene Co TN 20 A6
Asheville Hwy SR-280
Transylvania Co NC 70 B4
Asheville Hwy US-19
Haywood Co NC 43 E7
Haywood Co NC 44 A7
Asheville Hwy US-23
Haywood Co NC 43 E7
Haywood Co NC 44 A7
Asheville Hwy US-23 BUS
Sylva NC 68 E3
Asheville Hwy US-176
Spartanburg Co SC 71 E7
Spartanburg Co SC 97 E1
Spartanburg Co SC 98 B2
Asheville Rd
Haywood Co NC 69 C1
Asheville Rd US-23 BUS
Haywood Co NC 69 C1

Ashford Rd — Street Index — Billy Graham Frw

INDEX 14
y Graham Frwy — Street Index — Brownswood Rd

STREET
City State Map# Grid

y Graham Frwy
40
heville NC 44 D7
y Graham Pkwy
arlotte NC 75 B6
tmore Av
incombe Co NC 206 C4
gham Dr
mberland Co NC 106 E1
nicker Bridge Rd
angeburg Co SC 162 A2
nicker Bridge Rd
-70
angeburg Co SC 162 A2
d Creek Rd
vier Co TN 42 B3
d Creek Rd SR-454
vier Co TN 42 B3
scoe Rd
ontgomery Co NC 78 B3
scoe Rd SR-24
ry NC 78 B3
scoe Rd SR-27
ontgomery Co NC 78 B3
shop Rd
nion Co SC 120 A1
shopville Hwy
ershaw Co SC 139 D1
shopville Hwy SR-34
ershaw Co SC 139 D1
vins Rd
range Co NC 30 D4
ack Hwy
ork Co SC 100 A1
ack Hwy SR-5
ork Co SC 100 A1
ack Rd
aston Co NC 74 A2
ack St E
ock Hill SC 101 A4
ock Hill SC 217 C5
ack St W
ock Hill SC 217 B4
ack St W SR-5
ock Hill SC 217 B4
ack Ankle Rd
annin Co GA 91 E7
ack Hollow Rd
ashington Co VA 1 A1
ack Mountain Hwy
uncombe Co NC 45 A6
ack Mountain Hwy
-70
uncombe Co NC 45 A6
ackridge Rd
ecklenburg Co VA 12 B2
ack River Rd
larendon Co SC 154 E1
larendon Co SC 155 A3
ack River Rd SR-527
larendon Co SC 154 E1
larendon Co SC 155 A3
ack Rock School Rd
herryville NC 73 E3
acks Dr
reenville Co SC 97 C5
acksburg Hwy
herokee Co SC 73 C7
acksburg Hwy SR-5
herokee Co SC 73 C7
acksburg Rd
leveland Co NC 73 D6
acksburg Rd SR-198
leveland Co NC 73 D6
ack Snake Rd
tanley NC 74 E3
acksnake Rd
aston Co NC 74 E3
ackstock Rd
airfield Co SC 121 D3
partanburg Co SC 98 A2
Blackstock Rd
partanburg SC 98 B4
Blackstock Rd SR-215
partanburg SC 98 B4
Blackstock Rd
partanburg Co SC 98 B3
ack Tom Rd
erkeley Co SC 164 E6
ack Tom Rd Ext
erkeley Co SC 164 E6
ackwell Rd SE
runswick Co NC 146 D1
adenboro Rd
olumbus Co NC 128 C4
adenboro Rd SR-131
olumbus Co NC 128 C4
air Rd
Mint Hill NC 76 A6
air Rd SR-51
Mint Hill NC 76 A6
air St
andolph Co NC 51 D1
anch Rd
aswell Co NC 8 D4
ane Rd
alifax Co VA 9 D3
aney Franks Rd
Vake Co NC 55 C4
enheim Hwy
lenheim SC 125 E2
Marlboro Co SC 125 E3
enheim Hwy SR-38
Marlboro Co SC 125 E2
oomingdale Rd
loomingdale GA 180 B3
oomingdale Rd SR-17
loomingdale GA 180 B3
ossom St
ichland Co SC 233 D4
ossom St US-21 CONN
ichland Co SC 233 D4

Blossom St US-76 CONN
Richland Co SC 233 D4
N Blount St
Raleigh NC 200 A3
S Blount St
Raleigh NC 55 D3
Blounts Creek Rd
Beaufort Co NC 86 C1
Blounts Creek Rd SR-33
Beaufort Co NC 86 C1
Blowing Rock Blvd
Caldwell Co NC 23 C7
Blowing Rock Blvd US-321
Caldwell Co NC 23 C7
Blowing Rock Hwy
Avery Co NC 22 D5
Blowing Rock Hwy US-221
Avery Co NC 22 D5
Blowing Rock Rd
Boone NC 23 B3
Boone NC 185 C5
Blowing Rock Rd US-221
Boone NC 23 B3
Boone NC 185 C5
Blowing Rock Rd US-321
Boone NC 23 B3
Boone NC 185 C5
Blue Creek Rd
Onslow Co NC 110 E5
Onslow Co NC 111 A5
Blue Jay Rd
Effingham Co GA 175 C7
Effingham Co GA 180 B1
Blue Johnson Rd
Richland Co SC 138 D6
Blue Mill Rd
Cocke Co TN 43 C1
Blue Ridge Blvd
Oconee Co SC 95 B7
Oconee Co SC 116 C1
Blue Ridge Blvd SR-28
Oconee Co SC 95 B7
Oconee Co SC 116 C1
Blue Ridge Dr
Fannin Co GA 91 D4
Blue Ridge Dr SR-5
Fannin Co GA 91 D4
Blue Ridge Pkwy
Ashe Co NC 24 A1
Haywood Co NC 69 C3
Henderson Co NC 70 C2
Jackson Co NC 42 D7
Jackson Co NC 68 E1
Patrick Co VA 5 A2
Watauga Co NC 23 A4
Blue Ridge Rd
Black Mountain NC 45 B6
Wake Co NC 55 C2
Wake Co NC 197 A5
Wake Co NC 198 D2
Blue Ridge Ter
Richland Co SC 138 A4
Blue Ridge Spring Hwy
Saluda Co SC 136 A6
Saluda Co SC 150 A1
Blue Ridge Spring Hwy SR-39
Saluda Co SC 136 A6
Saluda Co SC 150 A1
Blues Farm Rd
Laurinburg NC 105 B6
Blue Star Memorial Hwy
Black Mountain NC 45 C6
Blue Star Memorial Hwy I-40
Black Mountain NC 45 C6
Bluff Rd
Richland Co SC 138 B7
Richland Co SC 152 E1
Richland Co SC 153 A1
Richland Co SC 233 D6
Bluff Rd SR-48
Richland Co SC 138 B7
Richland Co SC 152 E1
Richland Co SC 153 A1
Richland Co SC 233 D6
Bluffton Rd
Bluffton SC 181 D1
Bluffton Rd SR-46
Bluffton SC 181 D1
Blythe St
Hendersonville NC 70 E4
Blythewood Rd
Blythewood SC 138 A2
W B McLean Blvd
Cape Carteret NC 112 B6
W B McLean Blvd SR-24
Cape Carteret NC 112 B6
Bobbitt Rd
Franklin Co NC 32 B1
Bobby Brown State Park Rd
Elbert Co GA 133 C5
Bobby Faucett Rd
Union Co SC 99 B5
Bobby Faucett Rd SR-114
Union Co SC 99 B5
Bobby Jones Expwy
Augusta GA 159 B2
Evans GA 149 A7
Bobby Jones Expwy I-520
Augusta GA 159 B2
Bobby Jones Expwy SR-232
Martinez GA 149 A7
Bob Little Rd
Union Co SC 99 B6

Bob Little Rd SR-114
Union Co SC 99 B6
Bobo Rd
Spartanburg Co SC 97 E3
E Bobo Newsome Hwy
Darlington Co SC 124 E7
Darlington Co SC 125 A7
E Bobo Newsome Hwy SR-151
Darlington Co SC 124 E7
Darlington Co SC 125 A7
W Bobo Newsome Hwy
Darlington Co SC 124 C6
W Bobo Newsome Hwy SR-151
Darlington Co SC 124 C6
Bob's Creek Rd
Henderson Co NC 71 A6
Bob's Creek Rd SR-225
Henderson Co NC 71 A6
Bohicket Rd
Charleston Co SC 172 E7
E Boiling Spring Rd
Boiling Spring Lakes NC 146 C4
Boiling Springs Hwy
Cherokee Co SC 73 B7
Cherokee Co SC 99 B1
Boiling Springs Hwy SR-150
Cherokee Co SC 73 B7
Cherokee Co SC 99 B1
Boiling Springs Rd
Spartanburg Co SC 98 C2
Boiling Springs Rd SR-9
Spartanburg Co SC 98 C2
Bold Springs Rd
Franklin Co GA 115 C7
Bold Springs Rd SR-164
Franklin Co GA 115 C7
Boleman Hill Rd
Hart Co GA 116 C5
Bolling Rd
Halifax Co NC 13 B4
Bolton St
Winston-Salem NC 187 D6
Bonanza Dr
Fayetteville NC 80 E7
Bonlee Carbonton Rd
Chatham Co NC 53 D7
Bonlee Carbonton Rd SR-42
Chatham Co NC 53 D7
Bonner Rd
Cherokee Co SC 72 E7
Bonner Rd CO-36
Cherokee Co SC 72 E7
Bonnerton Rd
Beaufort Co NC 86 D2
Bookman Rd
Richland Co SC 138 C3
Boone Tr
Wilkes Co NC 24 C3
Boone Hill Rd
Dorchester Co SC 172 C2
Boone Hill Rd US-17 ALT
Dorchester Co SC 172 C2
Boones Creek Rd
Washington Co TN 20 E1
Boones Creek Rd SR-354
Washington Co TN 20 E1
Boone Trail Rd
Lee Co NC 54 A7
Boone Trail Rd US-421
Lee Co NC 54 A7
Boots Branch Rd
Sumter Co SC 140 B7
Bostian Rd
Rowan Co NC 50 B7
Bostic Sunshine Rd
Bostic NC 72 D3
Rutherford Co NC 72 E2
Boston Rd
Person Co NC 9 E4
Boston Rd US-501
Person Co NC 9 E4
Boulevard Hts
Anderson SC 226 D3
Boulevard Hts US-29 BUS
Anderson SC 226 D3
S Boundary Av SE
Aiken Co SC 236 E2
Boundary Dr
Spartanburg Co SC 224 D1
Boundary St
Beaufort SC 177 A4
Newberry Co SC 136 B1
Boundary St SR-34 BUS
Newberry Co SC 136 B1
Boundary St US-21 BUS
Beaufort SC 177 A4
Bourne Av
Garden City GA 180 D3
Bourne Av SR-307
Port Wentworth GA 180 D3
Bowen Blvd
Winston-Salem NC 27 B4
Winston-Salem NC 188 E1
Bowersville Hwy
Hart Co GA 116 B6
Bowersville Hwy SR-51
Hart Co GA 116 B6
Bowlan Rd
Anderson Co SC 117 D3
Bowman Hwy
Hart Co GA 116 C7
Bowman Hwy SR-172
Hart Co GA 116 C7
Bowman Rd
Mt Pleasant SC 173 C5

Bowman Rd
Mt Pleasant SC 238 E4
Bowman Branch Hwy
Branchville SC 162 D4
Orangeburg Co SC 162 E4
Orangeburg Co SC 163 A3
Bowman Branch Hwy SR-210
Branchville SC 162 D4
Orangeburg Co SC 162 E4
Orangeburg Co SC 163 A3
Bowmantown Rd
Washington Co TN 20 D1
Bowmantown Rd SR-75
Washington Co TN 20 D1
E Boyce St
Manning SC 154 C4
E Boyce St SR-261
Manning SC 154 C4
E Boyce St US-521
Manning SC 154 C4
W Boyce St
Manning SC 154 C4
W Boyce St SR-261
Manning SC 154 C4
Boyd Rd
Chester Co SC 121 D2
Boyds Creek Hwy
Sevier Co TN 41 C1
Boyds Creek Hwy SR-338
Sevier Co TN 41 C1
Boyer Rd
Orangeburg Co SC 163 E3
Boyer Rd SR-453 TRK
Orangeburg Co SC 163 E3
Boyer Rd US-176 TRK
Orangeburg Co SC 163 E3
Boyer St
Charlotte NC 214 D2
Boyette Rd
Johnston Co NC 82 C1
Boykin Rd
Camden SC 139 B1
Kershaw Co SC 139 B4
Boykin Rd SR-261
Kershaw Co SC 139 B4
Boykin Bridge Rd
Sampson Co NC 108 C3
Boykins Rd
Severn NC 14 D3
Boykins Rd SR-35
Severn NC 14 D3
Boylston Hwy
Transylvania Co NC 70 C4
Boylston Hwy SR-280
Henderson Co NC 70 C3
Brad Dixon Rd
Elbert Co GA 133 C6
Bradford Blvd
Dillon Co SC 126 D4
Bradford Blvd SR-9
Dillon Co SC 126 D4
Bradford Blvd SR-57
Dillon Co SC 126 D4
Bradshaw Cir
Buncombe Co NC 44 B7
Bragg Blvd
Cumberland Co NC 221 E4
Fayetteville NC 80 E6
Fayetteville NC 107 A1
Fayetteville NC 222 B1
Bragg Blvd SR-24
Cumberland Co NC 221 E4
Fayetteville NC 80 E6
Fayetteville NC 107 A1
Fayetteville NC 222 B1
Bragg Blvd SR-87
Cumberland Co NC 221 E4
Fayetteville NC 80 E6
Fayetteville NC 107 A1
Fayetteville NC 222 B1
N Bragg Blvd
Cumberland Co NC 80 E5
Spring Lake NC 221 D1
N Bragg Blvd SR-24
Cumberland Co NC 80 E5
Spring Lake NC 221 D1
N Bragg Blvd SR-87
Spring Lake NC 80 E5
Spring Lake NC 221 D1
S Bragg Blvd
Spring Lake NC 221 E3
S Bragg Blvd SR-24
Spring Lake NC 221 E3
S Bragg Blvd SR-87
Spring Lake NC 221 E3
S Bragg Blvd SR-210
Spring Lake NC 221 E3
Bragg St
Sanford NC 80 B1
Branchdale Hwy
Orangeburg Co SC 163 D2
Orangeburg Co SC 164 A2
Branchdale Hwy SR-45
Orangeburg Co SC 163 D2
Orangeburg Co SC 164 A2
Branchdale Hwy SR-453 TRK
Orangeburg Co SC 164 A2
Branchview Dr NE
Concord NC 76 B2
Branchview Dr NE SR-3
Concord NC 76 B2
Branchview Dr SE
Concord NC 76 B2
Brandon Rd
York Co SC 74 D7
Branham Rd
Richland Co SC 138 B2
Brannens Bridge Rd
Screven Co GA 168 C6

Brantley Rd
Cabarrus Co NC 76 B1
Brattonsville Rd
York Co SC 100 D5
Braxton Rd
Cumberland Co NC 107 A3
S Breazeale Av
Mt Olive NC 83 B5
S Breazeale Av US-117 ALT
Mt Olive NC 83 B5
Breazeale Rd
Anderson Co SC 117 D2
Brenner Av
Salisbury NC 50 C5
Salisbury NC 208 A4
Brentwood St
High Point NC 27 E7
Brevard Rd
Asheville NC 44 D7
Buncombe Co NC 70 D1
Brevard Rd SR-191
Asheville NC 44 D7
Buncombe Co NC 70 D1
Brevard Rd US-64
Henderson Co NC 70 D4
N Brevard St
Charlotte NC 216 B2
S Brevard St
Charlotte NC 216 A3
N Brevard-Caldwell Conn St
Charlotte NC 216 B2
E Brewington Rd
Sumter Co SC 140 A6
W Brewington Rd
Sumter Co SC 139 E6
Sumter Co SC 140 A6
Briarwood Rd
Spartanburg SC 224 A5
Brice Rd
Spartanburg Co SC 98 B4
Brices Store Rd
Duplin Co NC 109 D4
N Brick Church Rd
Lee Co SC 140 C6
N Brick Church Rd SR-527
Lee Co SC 140 C6
S Brick Church Rd
Sumter Co SC 140 D7
S Brick Church Rd SR-527
Sumter Co SC 140 D7
Bricklanding Rd SW
Brunswick Co NC 145 D6
Bricklanding Rd SW SR-179
Brunswick Co NC 145 D6
N Brickyard Rd
Richland Co SC 138 B3
Bridford Pkwy
Greensboro NC 28 A5
Bridge St
Eden NC 7 C4
Hot Springs NC 43 E1
Bridge St US-25
Hot Springs NC 43 E1
Bridge St US-70
Hot Springs NC 43 E1
E Bridge St
St. Matthews SC 152 E4
E Bridge St SR-6
St. Matthews SC 152 E4
N Bridge St
Elkin NC 25 C1
N Bridge St US-21 BUS
Elkin NC 25 C2
W Bridge St
St. Matthews SC 152 D4
W Bridge St SR-6
St. Matthews SC 152 D4
Bridge Creek Rd
Rabun Co GA 93 E6
Rabun Co GA 94 A5
Bridges Rd
Greenville Co SC 97 C6
Bridges St
Morehead City NC 113 A5
Brief Rd
Mint Hill NC 76 B6
Brief Rd W
Fairview NC 76 B6
Brier Creek Pkwy
Raleigh NC 31 B7
Raleigh NC 196 B1
Brigade St
Charleston SC 240 C3
S Briggs Av
Durham NC 31 A6
N Brightleaf Blvd
Smithfield NC 56 D7
N Brightleaf Blvd SR-96
Smithfield NC 56 D7
N Brightleaf Blvd US-301
Smithfield NC 56 D7
S Brightleaf Blvd
Smithfield NC 56 C7
S Brightleaf Blvd SR-96
Smithfield NC 56 C7
S Brightleaf Blvd US-301
Smithfield NC 56 C7
Bringle Ferry Rd
Davidson Co NC 51 A6
Rowan Co NC 50 D5
Salisbury NC 208 E4
Brink Rd
Greensville Co VA 13 A2

E Broad Av
Rockingham NC 104 D3
E Broad Av US-74 BUS
Rockingham NC 104 D3
Broad St
Augusta GA 159 C1
Bennettsville SC 125 E2
Camden SC 139 B1
Charleston SC 240 C7
Loris SC 144 B4
Middleburg NC 11 C5
Milton NC 9 A3
New Bern NC 86 B6
Oriental NC 87 B7
Rural Hall NC 27 A2
Sumter SC 139 E6
Sumter SC 140 A7
Sumter SC 235 C2
Sumter Co SC 139 D6
Wake Co NC 55 B5
Broad St SR-9 BUS
Bennettsville SC 125 E2
Broad St SR-28
Augusta GA 159 C1
Broad St SR-38 BUS
Marlboro Co SC 125 E2
Broad St SR-55
New Bern NC 86 B6
Pamlico Co NC 87 B7
Wake Co NC 55 B5
Broad St SR-57
Milton NC 9 A3
Broad St SR-66
Rural Hall NC 27 A2
Broad St US-1
Middleburg NC 11 C5
Broad St US-17
New Bern NC 86 B6
Broad St US-70 BUS
New Bern NC 86 B6
Broad St US-76
Sumter Co SC 139 D6
Broad St US-76 BUS
Sumter SC 139 E6
Sumter SC 140 A7
Sumter SC 235 C2
Broad St US-158
Middleburg NC 11 C5
Broad St US-378
Sumter Co SC 139 D6
Broad St US-378 BUS
Sumter SC 139 E6
Sumter SC 140 A7
Sumter SC 235 C2
Broad St US-521
Camden SC 139 B1
Sumter SC 139 E6
Sumter SC 140 A7
Sumter SC 235 C2
Broad St US-601
Camden SC 139 B1
Broad St US-701
Loris SC 144 B4
E Broad St
Elizabethtown NC 129 A1
Hemingway SC 156 D2
Savannah GA 180 E4
Spartanburg SC 224 C4
St. Pauls NC 106 E5
Statesville NC 49 C3
E Broad St SR-20
St. Pauls NC 106 E5
E Broad St SR-87
Elizabethtown NC 129 A1
E Broad St SR-261
Hemingway SC 156 D2
N Broad St
Brevard NC 70 B5
Camden SC 139 B1
Chowan Co NC 37 C3
Clinton SC 119 D4
Winston-Salem NC 27 A4
N Broad St SR-56
Clinton SC 119 D4
N Broad St SR-72
Clinton SC 119 D4
N Broad St US-17 BUS
Chowan Co NC 37 C3
N Broad St US-64
Brevard NC 70 B5
N Broad St US-276
Brevard NC 70 B5
N Broad St US-521
Camden SC 139 B1
N Broad St US-601
Camden SC 139 B1
S Broad St
Clinton SC 119 D5
Gastonia NC 210 C4
Mooresville NC 49 D6
Toccoa GA 115 C3
Winston-Salem NC 27 A5
S Broad St SR-63
Toccoa GA 115 C3
S Broad St SR-72
Laurens Co SC 119 D5
S Broad St SR-106
Toccoa GA 115 C3
S Broad St SR-115
Mooresville NC 49 D6
S Broad St SR-274
Gastonia NC 210 C4
W Broad St
Elizabethtown NC 128 E1
Spartanburg SC 224 C4
Williamsburg Co SC 156 D2
W Broad St SR-41
Elizabethtown NC 128 E1
W Broad St SR-87
Elizabethtown NC 128 E1
W Broad St SR-261
Hemingway SC 156 D2

Broad Creek Rd
Beaufort Co NC 60 C6
Broad Creek Rd SR-32
Beaufort Co NC 60 C6
Broadfoot Av
Fayetteville NC 222 B3
Broad River Rd
Richland Co SC 137 B2
Broad River Rd US-176
Richland Co SC 137 B2
Broadway Rd
Lee Co NC 80 C1
Broadway St
Asheville NC 44 D6
Buncombe Co NC 206 B1
S Broadway St
Alexander Mills NC 72 D4
S Broadway St US-221 ALT
Alexander Mills NC 72 D4
W Broadway St
Johnsonville SC 156 D1
Myrtle Beach SC 232 B4
W Broadway St SR-341
Johnsonville SC 156 D1
Broadway School Rd
Anderson Co SC 117 D4
N Brockington St
Timmonsville SC 141 A3
N Brockington St SR-403
Timmonsville SC 141 A3
Brockman McClimon Rd
Spartanburg Co SC 97 D4
Brodie Rd
Batesburg-Leesville SC 136 D7
Brodnax Rd
Brunswick Co VA 12 C1
Brogden Rd
Johnston Co NC 82 E1
Johnston Co NC 83 A1
Smithfield NC 56 D7
Brookbend Rd
Pickens Co SC 95 E7
Brookhaven Rd
Stephens Co GA 115 E4
Brooklyn Rd
Halifax Co VA 9 A1
N Brooks St
Manning SC 154 C4
N Brooks St US-301
Manning SC 154 C4
Brookshire Blvd
Mecklenburg Co NC 75 B4
Brookshire Blvd SR-16
Mecklenburg Co NC 75 B4
E Brookshire Frwy
Charlotte NC 216 B2
E Brookshire Frwy I-277
Charlotte NC 216 B2
E Brookshire Frwy SR-16
Charlotte NC 216 B2
W Brookshire Frwy
Charlotte NC 75 C5
W Brookshire Frwy SR-16
Charlotte NC 75 C5
Brookside Dr
Raleigh NC 200 A1
Brookstown Av
Winston-Salem NC 188 C4
Brookway Rd
Randolph Co NC 209 A7
Brothers Rd
Lenoir Co NC 84 B2
Broughton St
Orangeburg SC 152 C7
Broughton St US-178 BUS
Orangeburg SC 152 C7
Brown Av
Anderson Co SC 117 E4
Waynesville NC 69 C1
Brown Av SR-20
Anderson Co SC 117 E4
Brown Rd
Anderson Co SC 117 C3
Augusta GA 159 B3
Greenville Co SC 97 A7
N Brown St
Chadbourn NC 128 B6
N Brown St SR-410
Chadbourn NC 128 B6
Browne Rd
Charlotte NC 75 D3
Browning Gate Rd
Hampton Co SC 169 D6
Browning Gate Rd SR-3
Hampton Co SC 169 D6
Brown Mountain Beach Rd
Burke Co NC 46 E2
Brownrigg Rd
Salisbury NC 208 D2
Browns Creek Rd
Pamlico Co NC 87 C5
Browns Ferry Rd
Georgetown Co SC 156 E6
Georgetown Co SC 157 A7
Georgetown Co SC 167 A1
Browns Ferry Rd SR-51
Georgetown Co SC 156 E6
Georgetown Co SC 157 A7
Georgetown Co SC 167 A1
Browns Mill Rd
Moore Co NC 78 E2
Brown Summit Rd
Guilford Co NC 28 D2
Brownswood Rd
Charleston Co SC 172 E6

INDEX 15
N Browntown Rd — Street Index — S Cente

Street Index

STREET / City State / Map# Grid

N Browntown Rd
Nash Co NC 33 D3
S Browntown Rd
Dortches NC 33 E5
Broxton Bridge Hwy
Bamberg Co SC 170 A2
Broxton Bridge Hwy US-601
Bamberg Co SC 170 A2
Broxton Bridge Rd
Bamberg Co SC 162 A7
Bamberg Co SC 170 A1
Broxton Bridge Rd US-601
Bamberg Co SC 162 A7
Bamberg Co SC 170 A1
Brunson Spring Rd
Horry Co SC 143 B7
Brushy Creek Rd
Easley SC 96 D6
Greenville Co SC 97 C4
Brushy Mountain Rd
Wilkes Co NC 24 D5
Bryant Blvd
York Co SC 100 E3
Bryant Rd
Spartanburg Co SC 98 C2
Bryantown Rd
Northampton Co NC 14 A6
Bryson Rd
Buncombe Co NC 44 B7
N Buchanan Blvd
Durham NC 193 E2
Buck Creek Rd
McDowell Co NC 45 E3
Screven Co GA 168 C6
Buck Creek Rd SR-80
McDowell Co NC 45 E3
Buckingham Rd
Greene Co TN 20 A4
Buck Jones Rd
Raleigh NC 55 C2
Bud Black Rd
Gaston Co NC 74 A2
Bud Henderson Rd
Huntersville NC 75 B2
Buff Blvd
Clarendon Co SC 154 A5
Buffalo Rd
Johnston Co NC 56 D6
Buffaloe Rd
Garner NC 55 D4
Wake Co NC 55 D4
Wake Co NC 56 A1
Buffalo-West Springs Hwy
Union Co SC 98 E6
Union Co SC 99 A7
Buffalo-W Springs Hwy SR-215
Union Co SC 98 E6
Union Co SC 99 A7
Bufords Branch Rd
Blackville SC 161 C3
Bufords Branch Rd SR-304
Blackville SC 161 C3
Buford's Bridge Hwy
Allendale Co SC 161 D7
Sycamore SC 169 C2
Ulmer SC 161 C7
Buford's Bridge Hwy US-301
Ulmer SC 161 D7
Buford's Bridge Hwy US-321
Allendale Co SC 161 C7
Sycamore SC 169 C2
Buggs Island Rd
Mecklenburg Co VA 11 C2
Buggs Island Rd SR-4
Mecklenburg Co VA 11 C2
Bull St
Bladen Co NC 108 B6
Richland Co SC 233 B1
Savannah GA 180 E4
Bull St SR-277
Richland Co SC 233 B1
Bull St US-76
Richland Co SC 233 C2
Bulldog Miller Rd
Washington Co TN 20 E2
Bull Hill Rd
Bertie Co NC 36 C3
Bull Mountain Rd
Cocke Co TN 43 B2
Bull Swamp Rd
Orangeburg Co SC 152 A5
Bull Swamp Rd SR-172
Orangeburg Co SC 152 A5
Bultman Dr
Sumter SC 235 B2
Bultman Dr US-15 CONN
Sumter SC 235 B2
Bultman Dr US-521 CONN
Sumter SC 235 B2
Bunce Rd
Cumberland Co NC 106 D1
Bunch Ford Rd
Orangeburg Co SC 163 D3
Bunch Ford Rd SR-314
Orangeburg Co SC 163 D3
S Buncombe Rd
Greenville Co SC 97 C4
Buncombe St
Edgefield SC 149 C2
Greenville SC 223 B1
Buncombe St SR-183
Greenville SC 223 B1
Buncombe St US-25
Edgefield SC 149 C2
Buncombe St US-25 BUS
Greenville SC 223 B1
N Buncombe School Rd
Buncombe Co NC 44 D4
Burbank Rd
Carter Co TN 22 A3
Burbank Rd SR-143
Carter Co TN 22 A3
Burcale Rd
Horry Co SC 158 A3
Burgaw Hwy
Onslow Co NC 110 D6
Onslow Co NC 111 A6
Burgaw Hwy SR-53
Onslow Co NC 110 D6
Onslow Co NC 111 A6
Burke Rd
Calhoun Co SC 152 D5
Burke St
Rhodhiss NC 47 E3
Burke Mill Rd
Winston-Salem NC 27 A5
Winston-Salem NC 187 D7
Burlington Rd
Greensboro NC 28 D4
Guilford Co NC 28 E4
Person Co NC 9 C7
Person Co NC 30 B1
Whitsett NC 29 A5
Burlington Rd SR-49
Person Co NC 30 B1
Roxboro NC 9 C7
Burlington Rd US-70
Guilford Co NC 28 E4
Whitsett NC 29 A5
Burlington Mills Rd
Wake Co NC 32 A7
Burnett Blvd
Wilmington NC 231 A6
Burnett Blvd US-421
Wilmington NC 231 A6
Burnett Rd
Cumberland Co NC 81 D4
Burnett Rd SR-82
Cumberland Co NC 81 D4
Burnt Branch Rd
Clarendon Co SC 155 B1
S Burris Rd
Chester Co SC 100 B5
Burton Rd
Durham Co NC 31 B5
Burton Dam Rd
Rabun Co GA 93 E6
Burton's Ferry Hwy
Allendale Co SC 169 A2
Burtons Ferry Hwy
Screven Co GA 168 C4
Burton's Ferry Hwy
Screven Co GA 168 D3
Ulmer SC 161 C7
Burtons Ferry Hwy SR-21
Screven Co GA 168 B6
Burtons Ferry Hwy SR-73
Screven Co GA 168 C4
Burton's Ferry Hwy US-301
Allendale Co SC 169 A2
Burtons Ferry Hwy US-301
Screven Co GA 168 C4
Burton's Ferry Hwy US-301
Screven Co GA 168 D3
Ulmer SC 161 C7
Bush St
Raleigh NC 55 D1
Bush River Rd
Richland Co SC 137 D5
Butler Av
Tybee Island GA 181 D5
Butler Av SR-26
Tybee Island GA 181 D5
Butler Av US-80
Tybee Island GA 181 D5
Butler Rd
Columbus Co NC 144 C2
E Butler Rd
Mauldin SC 97 C6
W Butler Rd
Greenville Co SC 97 B6
Butner Rd
Granville Co NC 31 D1
Oxford NC 10 D7
Buttermilk Rd
Screven Co GA 168 A5
Bynum Rd
Chatham Co NC 54 B3
Bypass 225 S
Greenwood SC 134 D3
Bypass 225 S SR-225
Greenwood SC 134 D3
By-Pass SE
Greenwood Co SC 134 E3
By-Pass SE US-25 BYP
Greenwood Co SC 134 E3
By-Pass SE US-178 BYP
Greenwood SC 134 E3
By-Pass SE US-221 BYP
Greenwood Co SC 134 E3
Byrd Rd
Stanly Co NC 77 D3
Byrnes Dr
St. Stephen SC 165 B1
Byrnes Dr US-52
St. Stephen SC 165 B1

C

E C St
Granville Co NC 31 B3
E C St SR-56
Granville Co NC 31 B3
W C St
Cabarrus Co NC 76 A1
Rowan Co NC 50 A7
Cabarrus Av W
Concord NC 76 B2
Cabarrus Rd
Mecklenburg Co NC 76 B6
Cabarrus Station Rd
Midland NC 76 B5
Cabin Creek Rd
Richland Co SC 138 D7
Caddin Rd
Charleston Co SC 172 B4
Cade Rd
Williamsburg Co SC 155 D2
Williamsburg Co SC 156 A3
Cade Rd SR-512
Williamsburg Co SC 155 D2
Williamsburg Co SC 156 A2
Cades Cove Loop Rd
Blount Co TN 41 A6
Cadwell Mountain Rd
Madison Co NC 43 D3
Caesers Head Hwy
Pickens Co SC 96 C1
Caesers Head Hwy SR-8
Pickens Co SC 96 C1
Cain Rd
Fayetteville NC 81 A7
Cajah Mountain Rd
Caldwell Co NC 47 D2
N Caldwell St
Charlotte NC 216 B2
S Caldwell St
Charlotte NC 216 A3
S Caledonia Rd
Laurinburg NC 105 C6
Cale Yarborough Hwy
Florence Co SC 141 A4
Cale Yarborough Hwy SR-403
Florence Co SC 141 A4
Cal Floyd Rd
Northampton Co NC 13 B3
Calhoun Rd
Greenwood Co SC 134 D2
Calhoun St
Abbeville Co SC 133 D3
Charleston SC 240 D6
Johnston SC 149 E2
Calhoun St SR-23
Edgefield Co SC 149 E2
Calhoun St SR-81
Abbeville Co SC 133 D3
E Calhoun St
Sumter SC 235 E3
E Calhoun St US-401
Sumter SC 235 E3
S Calhoun St
Calhoun Falls SC 133 C4
S Calhoun St SR-81
Calhoun Falls SC 133 C4
W Calhoun St
Sumter SC 235 D3
W Calhoun St US-401
Sumter SC 235 D3
Calhoun Falls Hwy
Elbert Co GA 133 A4
Calhoun Falls Hwy SR-72
Elbert Co GA 133 A4
Calhoun Memorial Hwy
Easley SC 96 D5
Calhoun Memorial Hwy US-123
Easley SC 96 D5
California Av
Spartanburg Co SC 224 A1
Calks Ferry Rd
Lexington Co SC 151 B1
Callison Hwy
Greenwood Co SC 134 E5
Callison Hwy SR-67
Greenwood Co SC 134 E5
Calvary Rd
Halifax Co VA 9 B3
Calvary Rd SR-119
Halifax Co VA 9 B3
E Cambridge Av
Greenwood SC 134 E2
W Cambridge Av
Greenwood Co SC 134 D2
W Cambridge Av SR-72
Greenwood Co SC 134 D2
Camden Av
Durham NC 31 A5
Durham NC 194 D2
Camden Cswy
Camden Co NC 17 C6
Camden Co NC 184 E4
Camden Cswy SR-34
Camden Co NC 184 E4
Elizabeth City NC 17 C6
Camden Cswy US-158
Camden Co NC 17 C6
Camden Co NC 184 E4
Camden Hwy
Lee Co SC 140 A1
Sumter SC 139 E6
Camden Hwy SR-34
Lee Co SC 139 E2
Lee Co SC 140 A1
Camden Hwy US-521
Sumter Co SC 139 E6
Camden Rd
Anson Co NC 103 D3
Mt Croghan SC 103 B6
Orangeburg Co SC 163 E3
Camden Rd SR-109
Chesterfield Co SC 103 B6
Camden Rd SR-310
Orangeburg Co SC 163 E3
Camden Rd SR-453 TRK
Orangeburg Co SC 163 E3
Camden St
Mt Croghan SC 103 B6
Camden St SR-9
Mt Croghan SC 103 B6
Cameron Rd
Calhoun Co SC 153 B5
Cameron SC 152 E7
Cameron SC 153 A6
Henry Co VA 7 A2
Cameron Rd SR-33
Calhoun Co SC 153 B5
Cameron SC 152 E7
Cameron SC 153 A6
Cameron Rd E-752
Henry Co VA 7 A2
Camp Rd
Charleston SC 173 B6
Campbell Rd
Wake Co NC 55 C3
E Camperdown Wy
Greenville SC 223 B4
E Camperdown Wy SR-124
Greenville SC 223 B4
W Camperdown Wy
Greenville SC 223 B3
W Camperdown Wy US-25 BUS
Greenville SC 223 B3
Camp Ground Rd
Richland Co SC 137 E3
Richland Co SC 138 A3
Campground Rd
Spartanburg Co SC 98 A3
Camp Julia Rd
Cabarrus Co NC 76 B1
Camp MacBoykin Rd
Sumter Co SC 153 C4
Camp Rawls Rd
Aiken Co SC 150 D5
Aiken Co SC 151 A5
Camp Rotary Rd
Gaston Co NC 74 B5
Camp Stewart Rd
Mecklenburg Co NC 76 A5
Camp Welfare Rd
Fairfield Co SC 122 A5
Canaan Rd
Spartanburg Co SC 98 C4
Canal St
Aiken Co SC 149 E6
Canal St SR-191
Aiken Co SC 149 E6
Candy Mountain Rd
Cherokee Co NC 65 E7
Cherokee Co NC 91 E1
Cane Creek Rd
Buncombe Co NC 70 E2
Buncombe Co NC 71 A1
N Cannon Blvd
Kannapolis NC 76 B1
Kannapolis NC 50 B7
N Cannon Blvd US-29
Cabarrus Co NC 76 B1
Rowan Co NC 50 B7
S Cannon Blvd
Cabarrus Co NC 76 B1
S Cannon Blvd US-29
Cabarrus Co NC 76 B1
Cannon Rd
Banks Co GA 115 B5
Horry Co SC 232 B4
Myrtle Beach SC 158 B3
Cannon Rd SR-105
Banks Co GA 115 B5
Cannon St
Charleston SC 240 C5
Cannon Bridge Rd
Orangeburg Co SC 162 C2
Cannon Farm Rd
Rowan Co NC 50 A7
Cannons Campground Rd
Spartanburg Co SC 98 D3
N Cansler St
Kings Mountain NC 74 A5
Cape Hatteras National Park Rd
Nags Head NC 40 B5
Cape Hatteras NP Rd SR-12
Nags Head NC 40 B5
Cape Hickory Rd
Rhodhiss NC 47 E3
Capital Blvd
Franklin Co NC 32 A5
Raleigh NC 55 E1
Raleigh NC 199 E3
Wake Co NC 31 E7
Capital Blvd SR-50
Raleigh NC 199 E3
Capital Blvd US-1
Franklin Co NC 32 A5
Raleigh NC 55 E1
Wake Co NC 31 E7
Capital Blvd US-70
Raleigh NC 199 E3
Capital Blvd US-401
Raleigh NC 55 E1
Raleigh NC 199 E3
Capital Wy
Orangeburg Co SC 151 C7
Orangeburg Co SC 161 C1
Capital Wy SR-3
Orangeburg Co SC 151 C7
Orangeburg Co SC 161 C1
Captain Bill Rd
Ridgeland SC 176 B4
Captain Bill Rd SR-77
Ridgeland SC 176 B4
Caratoke Hwy
Currituck Co NC 17 C2
Currituck Co NC 18 B5
Currituck Co NC 39 C1
Caratoke Hwy SR-168
Currituck Co NC 17 C2
Caratoke Hwy US-158
Currituck Co NC 18 B5
Currituck Co NC 39 C1
Carbon City Rd
Burke Co NC 46 E4
Morganton NC 47 A4
Carbon City Rd US-70
Burke Co NC 46 E4
Morganton NC 47 A4
Carbonton Rd
Lee Co NC 53 E7
Sanford NC 80 A1
Carbonton Rd SR-42
Lee Co NC 53 E7
Sanford NC 80 A1
Carey Rd
Kinston NC 84 D3
Carl Eller Rd
Madison Co NC 44 D2
Carl Eller Rd SR-213
Madison Co NC 44 D2
Carlisle Chester Hwy
Union Co SC 120 E2
Carlisle Chester Hwy SR-72
Union Co SC 120 E2
Carlisle Chester Hwy SR-121
Union Co SC 120 E2
Carlisle Chester Hwy SR-215
Union Co SC 120 E2
Carlisle Whitmire Hwy
Union Co SC 120 C3
Carlisle Whitmire Hwy SR-72
Union Co SC 120 C3
Carlisle Whitmire Hwy SR-121
Union Co SC 120 C3
Carl Sanders Hwy
Augusta GA 149 A7
Carl Sanders Hwy I-20
Augusta GA 149 A7
Carl Sanders Hwy SR-402
McDuffie Co GA 148 A7
Carmel Rd
Charlotte NC 75 D7
Charlotte NC 101 C1
Carner Av
North Charleston SC 173 B4
Carner Av US-52
North Charleston SC 173 B4
Carolina Av
Beaufort NC 113 C5
Hampton SC 169 E4
Washington NC 60 A5
Carolina Av US-17
Washington NC 60 A5
Carolina Av US-70
Beaufort NC 113 C5
Carolina Av US-278
Hampton SC 169 E4
E Carolina Av
Clinton SC 119 D5
Darlington Co SC 124 E6
Darlington Co SC 125 A6
E Carolina Av US-76
Clinton SC 119 D5
W Carolina Av
Hartsville SC 124 D6
Summerville SC 172 C2
W Carolina Av SR-151 BUS
Hartsville SC 124 D6
Carolina Dr
Dunn NC 81 E3
Carolina Hwy
Olar SC 161 E3
Carolina Hwy US-321
Olar SC 161 E3
Carolina Rd
Gates Co NC 16 B1
Carolina Rd SR-32
Gates Co NC 16 B1
Carolina St
Charleston SC 240 C4
Carolina Bays Pkwy
Horry Co SC 144 D7
Horry Co SC 157 E3
Horry Co SC 158 B2
Carolina Bays Pkwy SR-31
Horry Co SC 144 D7
Horry Co SC 157 E3
Horry Co SC 158 B2
Carolina Beach Rd
New Hanover Co NC 147 A2
Wilmington NC 146 E1
Wilmington NC 231 B6
Carolina Beach Rd US-421
New Hanover Co NC 147 A2
Wilmington NC 146 E1
Wilmington NC 231 B6
Carolina Country Club Rd
Spartanburg Co SC 98 C5
Carowinds Blvd
York Co SC 101 B1
Carpenter Rd
Durham Co NC 31 A5
Carpenter Fletcher Rd
Durham NC 30 E7
Carpenter Pond Rd
Durham Co NC 31 B7
Carpenter Upchurch Rd
Wake Co NC 55 A2
Carriage Ln
Charleston SC 239 D4
Carrollton Pike
Carroll Co VA 4 C1
Carrollton Pike US-58
Carroll Co VA 4 C1
Carrollton Pike US-221
Carroll Co VA 4 C1
Carr Store Rd
Orange Co NC 30 A3
W Carson Blvd
Charlotte NC 215 E3
Carson Rd
Gastonia NC 74 C5
York Co SC 100 C3
Carsonville Rd
Grayson Co VA 3 D1
Carsonville Rd E-660
Grayson Co VA 3 D1
Carteret St
Bath NC 60 E6
Carteret St SR-92
Bath NC 60 E6
Cartertown Rd
Bryan Co GA 180 A7
Carthage Rd
Lumberton NC 127 D1
Carthage St
Cameron NC 80 A3
Sanford NC 80 B1
Carthage St SR-24
Cameron NC 80 A3
Carthage St SR-27
Cameron NC 80 A3
Carthage St US-1 BUS
Sanford NC 80 B1
Cartledge Creek Rd
Richmond Co NC 78 B6
Carver St
Durham NC 30 E5
Carver School Rd
Winston-Salem NC 27 B4
NW Cary Pkwy
Cary NC 55 B2
SE Cary Pkwy
Cary NC 55 C3
SW Cary Pkwy
Cary NC 55 B3
Casar Rd
Casar NC 73 B1
Cleveland Co NC 47 C7
Casar Rd SR-10
Casar NC 73 B2
Cleveland Co NC 47 C7
Cascade Rd
Pittsylvania Co VA 7 D3
Cascade Lake Rd
Transylvania Co NC 70 C5
Cascade Mill Rd
Pittsylvania Co VA 7 D3
N Cashua Dr
Florence SC 230 A4
Florence Co SC 141 D2
Florence SC 230 A2
S Cashua Dr
Florence SC 230 A5
Florence Co SC 141 C2
Cashua St
Darlington SC 125 B7
Darlington SC 229 E4
Cashua St SR-34
Darlington SC 125 B7
Darlington SC 229 E4
Cashua Ferry Rd
Darlington Co SC 125 C7
Dillon Co SC 126 B4
Cashua Ferry Rd SR-34
Darlington SC 125 C7
Cason Oldfield Rd
Anson Co NC 103 D5
Castle Hall Rd
Beaufort Co SC 176 D1
Yemassee SC 170 D7
Castle Hall Rd SR-3
Yemassee SC 170 D7
Castle Hall Rd US-17 ALT
Beaufort Co SC 176 D1
Castle Hall Rd US-21
Beaufort Co SC 176 D1
Castle Hayne Rd
New Hanover Co NC 130 E6
Castle Hayne Rd SR-133
New Hanover Co NC 130 E6
E Caswell St
Kinston NC 205 D5
Wadesboro NC 103 D3
E Caswell St US-52
Wadesboro NC 103 D3
E Caswell St US-74
Wadesboro NC 103 D3
S Caswell St
La Grange NC 84 A3
S Caswell St SR-903
La Grange NC 84 A3
Caswell Beach Rd
Caswell Beach NC 146 D6
Oak Island NC 146 C6
W Catawba Av
Gaston Co NC 75 A4
Huntersville NC 75 C2
Catawba St
Belmont NC 75 A5
Catawba St SR-7
Belmont NC 75 A5
Catawba River Rd
Chester Co SC 122 C2
Fort Lawn SC 101 B7
Catawba River Rd US-21
Chester Co SC 122
Fort Lawn SC 101
N Catherine St
Walhalla SC 95
N Catherine St SR-183
Walhalla SC 95
Catherine Lake Rd
Onslow Co NC 110
Catherine Lake Rd SR-111
Onslow Co NC 110
Cato St
Pageland SC 102
Caton Rd
Lumberton NC 127
Robeson Co NC 106
Caton Rd SR-72
Robeson Co NC 106
Robeson Co NC 127
Caulder Av
Spartanburg SC 224
Causby Rd
Morganton NC 46
Causeway Dr
Wrightsville Beach NC 147
Causeway Dr US-76
Wrightsville Beach NC 147
Causeway Dr SW
Ocean Isle Beach NC 145
Causeway Dr SW SR-904
Ocean Isle Beach NC 145
Causey Lake Rd
Guilford Co NC 28
Cavel Chub Lake Rd
Person Co NC 9
Cawcaw Hwy
Calhoun Co SC 152
Cawcaw Hwy SR-6
Calhoun Co SC 152
CCC Rd
Aiken Co SC 159
CC Camp Rd
Surry Co NC 25
Cedar St
Beaufort NC 113
Cedar St US-70
Beaufort NC 113
Cedar Creek Rd
Cumberland Co NC 107
Greene Co TN 19
Hart Co GA 116
Lancaster Co SC 122
Richland Co SC 137
Washington Co VA 1
Cedar Creek Rd SR-53
Cumberland Co NC 107
Cedar Creek Rd SR-97
Lancaster Co SC 122
Cedar Creek Rd SR-210
Cumberland Co NC 107
Cedar Crest Rd
Spartanburg Co SC 98
Cedar Island Rd
Carteret Co NC 88
Carteret Co NC 114
Cedar Island Rd SR-12
Carteret Co NC 88
Carteret Co NC 114
Cedar Ln Rd
Greenville Co SC 97
Greenville Co SC 223
Cedar Ln Rd SR-183
Greenville Co SC 97
Greenville Co SC 223
Cedar Point Blvd
Cedar Point NC 112
Cedar Point Blvd SR-24
Cedar Point NC 112
Cedar Springs Rd
Spartanburg Co SC 98
Cedar Springs Rd SR-56
Spartanburg Co SC 98
Celanese Rd
Rock Hill SC 100
York Co SC 101
Celanese Rd SR-161
Rock Hill SC 100
York Co SC 101
Cel-River Rd
York Co SC 101
N Centennial St
High Point NC 27
High Point NC 191
Center Rd
Chester Co SC 100
Yadkin Co NC 25
Center Rd SR-97
Chester Co SC 100
Center St
Apex NC 55
Chester SC 100
Mt Pleasant SC 173
Mt Pleasant SC 238
Center St SR-9 BUS
Chester SC 100
Center St SR-97 BUS
Chester SC 100
Center St US-321 BUS
Chester SC 100
Center St E
Perry SC 151
N Center St
Catawba Co NC 48
Statesville NC 49
N Center St SR-115
Statesville NC 49
N Center St SR-127
Catawba Co NC 48
S Center St
Hickory NC 48
Hickory NC 207

INDEX 16
Center St SR-127 — Street Index — Coach Jimmy Smith Hwy

STREET
City State Map# Grid

S Center St SR-127
Hickory NC 48 A4
Hickory NC 207 C6
W Center St
Monroe NC 218 C5
W Center St
Alamance Co NC 29 E4
Lexington NC 51 A2
W Center St US-70
Alamance Co NC 29 E4
Center Church Rd
Davidson Co NC 51 A1
Centergrove Rd
Cabarrus Co NC 76 B1
Center Hill Hwy
Hertford NC 37 C1
Center Hill Rd
Calhoun Co SC 152 B3
Chowan Co NC 16 B7
Chowan Co NC 37 B1
Center Hill Rd SR-6
Calhoun Co SC 152 B3
Central Av
Augusta GA 159 B1
Charlotte NC 75 D6
Dorchester Co SC 172 C1
Granville Co NC 31 B3
N Central Av
Stanly Co NC 76 D4
N Central Av SR-200
Stanly Co NC 76 D4
S Central Av
Locust NC 76 D5
S Central Av SR-200
Locust NC 76 D5
Central Blvd
Danville VA 8 C3
Guyton GA 175 A6
Central Blvd SR-17
Guyton GA 175 A6
Central Blvd SR-86
Danville VA 8 C3
Central Dr
Southern Pines NC 79 D5
Central Dr SR-22
Southern Pines NC 79 D5
Central Rd
Williamsburg Co SC 155 E5
Central Park Rd
Charleston Co SC 173 A6
Century Cir
Cumberland Co NC 106 D2
Cerdar Falls Rd
Greenville Co SC 118 C2
CF Harvey Pkwy
Lenoir Co NC 84 D2
Chadbourn Hwy
Columbus Co NC 128 C6
Chadbourn Hwy SR-130
Columbus Co NC 128 C6
Chadbourn Hwy US-74 BUS
Columbus Co NC 128 C6
Chadbourn Hwy US-76 BUS
Columbus Co NC 128 C6
Chalk Rd
Richmond Co NC 104 D4
Chamblin Rd
Columbia Co GA 148 D7
Champion Dr
Canton NC 43 E7
Champion Dr SR-215
Haywood Co NC 43 E7
Chance Creek Rd
Carroll Co VA 4 D2
Chandler Rd
Durham NC 31 A6
Chapel Grove Rd
Gaston Co NC 74 C6
Chapel Hill Rd
Burlington NC 29 C4
Burlington NC 192 C6
Durham NC 30 E6
Morrisville NC 55 A1
Raleigh NC 198 C3
Tyrrell Co NC 38 A6
Wake Co NC 55 B2
Chapel Hill Rd SR-54
Burlington NC 29 C4
Burlington NC 192 C6
Morrisville NC 55 A1
Raleigh NC 198 C3
Chapel Hill Rd US-15
Chatham Co NC 54 B2
Chapel Hill Rd US-501
Chatham Co NC 54 B2
Chapel Hill Nelson Hwy
Durham NC 30 E7
Chapel Hill Nelson Hwy SR-54
Durham NC 30 E7
Chapin Rd
Lexington Co SC 137 A3
Chapin Rd US-76
Chapin SC 137 A3
Chapman Hwy SE
Knox Co TN 41 C2
Chapman Hwy SE SR-35
Sevier Co TN 41 D2
Chapman Hwy SE SR-71
Knox Co TN 41 C2
Chapman Hwy SE US-411
Sevier Co TN 41 D2
Chapman Hwy SE US-441
Knox Co TN 41 C2
Chapman St
Greensboro NC 189 E3
Charles Blvd
Greenville NC 59 B5
Greenville NC 203 E7
Charles Blvd SR-43
Greenville NC 59 B5
Greenville NC 203 E7

Charles Rd
Shelby NC 73 C5
Charles St
Monroe NC 218 C5
S Charles St
Greenville NC 59 B5
Greenville NC 203 C3
Charles Aiken Hwy
Greenville Co SC 118 B3
Charles Aiken Hwy US-25
Greenville Co SC 118 B3
Charles L Griffin III Hwy
Sumter Co SC 139 C7
CL Griffin III Hy SR-261
Sumter Co SC 139 C6
Charles L Powell Hwy
Abbeville Co SC 134 C3
Charles L Powell Hwy SR-72
Abbeville Co SC 134 B3
Charles M Shelton Hwy
Surry Co NC 4 D4
Surry Co NC 25 D1
Charles M Shelton Hwy I-74
Surry Co NC 4 D4
Charles M Shelton Hwy I-77
Surry Co NC 4 D4
Surry Co NC 25 D1
Charles Raper Jonas Hwy
Gaston Co NC 74 E3
Charles Raper Jonas Hwy SR-27
Gaston Co NC 74 E3
Charleston Hwy
Aiken Co SC 150 C7
Aiken Co SC 160 D1
Beaufort Co SC 176 E2
Beaufort Co SC 177 A1
Colleton Co SC 171 B4
Dorchester Co SC 163 A3
Hampton SC 169 E4
Hampton Co SC 170 A4
Lexington Co SC 137 E7
Charleston Hwy SR-64
Colleton Co SC 171 B4
Charleston Hwy SR-363
Hampton SC 169 E4
Hampton Co SC 170 A4
Charleston Hwy US-17
Beaufort Co SC 176 E2
Beaufort Co SC 177 A1
Charleston Hwy US-21
Lexington Co SC 137 E6
Lexington Co SC 152 A1
Charleston Hwy US-78
Aiken Co SC 150 C7
Aiken Co SC 160 D1
Charleston Hwy US-176
Lexington Co SC 137 E6
Lexington Co SC 152 A1
Charleston Hwy US-178
Dorchester Co SC 163 A3
Orangeburg Co SC 162 D1
S Charleston Rd
Darlington Co SC 125 D7
Darlington Co SC 141 D1
Charlie Walker Rd
Cabarrus Co NC 76 A1
Charlotte Av
Rock Hill SC 217 B3
Charlotte Av S
Rock Hill SC 217 C4
N Charlotte Av
Monroe NC 102 B2
Monroe NC 218 A3
N Charlotte Av SR-200
Monroe NC 218 B4
S Charlotte Av
Monroe NC 218 B5
S Charlotte Av SR-200
Monroe NC 218 B4
Charlotte Hwy
Buncombe Co NC 44 E7
Buncombe Co NC 45 A7
Buncombe Co NC 71 B1
Cowpens SC 98 E2
Iredell Co NC 49 C6
Lancaster Co SC 101 C3
York Co SC 100 D1
Charlotte Hwy SR-49
York Co SC 74 E7
York Co SC 100 D1
Charlotte Hwy SR-115
Iredell Co NC 49 C6
Charlotte Hwy SR-274
York Co SC 100 D1
Charlotte Hwy US-21
Iredell Co NC 49 C6
Charlotte Hwy US-29
Cowpens SC 98 E2
Charlotte Hwy US-74 ALT
Buncombe Co NC 44 E7
Buncombe Co NC 45 A7
Buncombe Co NC 71 B1
Charlotte Hwy US-521
Lancaster Co SC 101 D6
W Charlotte Hwy
York Co SC 100 D2
W Charlotte Hwy SR-49
York Co SC 100 D2
Charlotte Rd
Rutherfordton NC 72 C3
Charlotte Rd US-74 BUS
Rutherfordton NC 72 C3

Charlotte Rd US-221 ALT
Rutherfordton NC 72 C3
Charlotte St
Buncombe Co NC 206 C2
S Charlotte St
Buncombe Co NC 206 C4
Charlottes Rd
Laurens Co SC 119 C5
Charter Oak Rd
Lexington Co SC 137 B6
Chase High Rd
Rutherford Co NC 72 D5
Chatham Ln
Raleigh NC 200 D3
Chatham Pkwy
Chatham Co GA 180 D4
Chatham Rd
Henry Co VA 7 B1
Chatham Rd SR-57
Henry Co VA 7 B1
Chatham Rd SR-457
Henry Co VA 7 B1
Chatham St
Newport NC 112 E4
E Chatham St
Cary NC 55 B2
W Chatham St
Cary NC 55 B2
S Chatham Av Ext
Chatham Co NC 53 C4
Chatooga Ridge Rd
Oconee Co SC 94 D6
Chatsworth Hwy
Gilmer Co GA 91 A6
Chatsworth Hwy SR-2
Gilmer Co GA 91 A6
Chatsworth Hwy SR-52
Gilmer Co GA 91 A6
Checker Rd
Guilford Co NC 28 A7
Cheddar Rd
Anderson Co SC 117 D3
Cheek Rd
Durham Co NC 31 B5
Chelsea Rd
Craven Co NC 86 A6
Cheraw Hwy
Marlboro Co SC 125 E1
Cheraw Hwy SR-9 BUS
Marlboro Co SC 125 E1
Cherokee Av
Cherokee Co SC 99 B1
Cherokee Av US-29
Cherokee Co SC 99 B1
Cherokee Dr
Greenville Co SC 97 B4
Cherokee Rd
Florence SC 141 D2
Florence SC 230 C6
Johnson City TN 21 A2
Pinehurst NC 220 B5
Cherokee Rd SR-2
Pinehurst NC 220 B5
Cherokee Rd SR-67
Johnson City TN 21 A2
Cherokee St
Cherokee Co SC 72 D7
Cherokee St SR-11
Cherokee Co SC 72 D7
Cherokee St US-221 ALT
Cherokee Co SC 72 D7
E Cherokee St
Cherokee Co SC 73 D7
E Cherokee St US-29
Cherokee Co SC 73 D7
W Cherokee St
Cherokee Co SC 99 C1
W Cherokee St US-29
Cherokee Co SC 99 C1
Cherokee Tr
Pickens Co SC 96 D4
Cherokee Foothills Scenic Hwy
Greenville Co SC 71 D7
Greenville Co SC 97 A1
Pickens Co SC 95 E4
Pickens Co SC 96 A3
Spartanburg Co SC 72 B7
Cherokee Fthls Scnc Hy SR-11
Greenville Co SC 71 D7
Greenville Co SC 97 A1
Pickens Co SC 95 E4
Pickens Co SC 96 A3
Spartanburg Co SC 72 B7
Cherry Rd
Rock Hill SC 101 A3
Rock Hill SC 217 C2
Washington Co NC 37 E6
Cherry Rd SR-322
Rock Hill SC 101 A3
Cherry Rd US-21
York Co SC 101 A3
Cherry Rd US-21 BUS
Rock Hill SC 217 C2
S Cherry Rd
Rock Hill SC 217 A3
S Cherry Rd SR-322
Rock Hill SC 217 A3
Cherry St
Mt Airy NC 183 C5
Pendleton SC 117 A1
N Cherry St
Winston-Salem NC 27 A3
Winston-Salem NC 186 C4
Winston-Salem NC 188 C3
S Cherry St
Winston-Salem NC 188 C4
Cherry Grove Rd
Caswell Co NC 8 C7
Caswell Co NC 29 A1

Cherry Run Rd
Beaufort Co NC 59 E2
Cherryville Rd
Cleveland Co NC 73 D4
Cherryville Rd SR-150
Cleveland Co NC 73 D4
Chesapeake Expwy
Chesapeake VA 17 C1
Chesapeake Expwy SR-168
Chesapeake VA 17 C1
Chesnee Hwy
Cherokee Co SC 72 E7
Cherokee Co SC 73 A7
Cherokee Co SC 99 A1
Spartanburg Co SC 98 C3
Spartanburg Co SC 224 C1
Chesnee Hwy SR-11
Cherokee Co SC 72 E7
Cherokee Co SC 73 A7
Cherokee Co SC 99 A1
Chesnee Hwy US-221
Spartanburg Co SC 98 C3
Spartanburg Co SC 224 C1
Chester Av
Great Falls SC 122 C3
Chester Av SR-99
Great Falls SC 122 C3
Chester Hwy
York Co SC 100 C5
Chester Hwy US-321
York Co SC 100 C5
N Chester St
Gastonia NC 74 C5
N Chester St US-321
Gastonia NC 74 C5
S Chester St
Gastonia NC 74 C5
Gastonia NC 210 B4
S Chester St US-321
Gastonia NC 74 C5
Gastonia NC 210 B4
Chesterfield Av
Lancaster SC 219 D5
Chesterfield Av SR-903
Lancaster SC 219 D5
Chesterfield Hwy
Cheraw SC 104 A7
Chesterfield Co SC 103 E7
Chesterfield Hwy SR-9
Cheraw SC 104 A7
Chesterfield Co SC 103 E7
Chesterfield St S
Aiken Co SC 236 D1
Chesterfield St S SR-19
Aiken Co SC 236 D2
Chestnut Dr
Davidson Co NC 27 D7
High Point NC 27 E7
High Point NC 191 A4
Chestnut Ln
Union Co NC 101 E1
Chestnut St
Orangeburg SC 152 C7
St. Matthews SC 152 D5
Chestnut St US-21
Orangeburg SC 152 C7
Chestnut St US-178
Orangeburg SC 152 C7
Chestnut St NE
Orangeburg SC 152 C7
Chestnut St NE US-178
Orangeburg SC 152 C7
E Chestnut St
Stanley NC 74 E3
Chestnut Hill Rd
Buncombe Co NC 45 C7
Chestnut Ridge Rd
Cleveland Co NC 74 A5
Chevis Rd
Chatham Co GA 180 C5
Chewing Rd
Clarendon Co SC 153 D4
Cheyenne Rd
York Co SC 99 E2
Chickasha Dr
Forsyth Co NC 26 D4
Chicken Rd
Robeson Co NC 127 C3
Chicken Farm Rd
Harnett Co NC 81 E4
Chicken Foot Rd
Cumberland Co NC 107 A3
Chick Springs Rd
Greenville SC 223 D1
Chime Bell Church Rd
Aiken Co SC 160 A2
Chimney Rock Rd
Greensboro NC 28 A5
Henderson Co NC 71 A3
Rutherford Co NC 72 B3
Chimney Rock Rd US-64
Henderson Co NC 71 A3
Rutherford Co NC 72 B3
Chimney Rock Rd US-74 ALT
Rutherford Co NC 72 B3
China Grove Rd
Kannapolis NC 76 B1
Mecklenburg Co VA 11 C2
Rowan Co NC 50 B7
Chisolm Rd
Charleston Co SC 172 D6
Choppee Rd
Georgetown Co SC 156 E3
Georgetown Co SC 157 A4
Choppee Rd SR-261
Georgetown Co SC 156 E3
Georgetown Co SC 157 A4
Chrismon Rd
Guilford Co NC 28 E2

Christanna Hwy
Brunswick Co VA 12 D2
Christanna Hwy SR-46
Brunswick Co VA 12 D2
Chub Lake Rd
Person Co NC 9 D5
Chuck Dawley Blvd
Mt Pleasant SC 238 E5
Chuck Dawley Blvd I-526 BUS
Mt Pleasant SC 238 E5
Chuck Dawley Blvd US-17 BUS
Mt Pleasant SC 238 E5
Chuck Dawley Blvd US-701 BUS
Mt Pleasant SC 238 E5
Chuckey Rd
Greene Co TN 20 B3
Chuckey Rd SR-351
Greene Co TN 20 B3
Church Ln
Spartanburg Co SC 98 B4
Church Lp N
Black Creek NC 57 D4
Church Lp S
Black Creek NC 57 D5
Church Rd
Alamance Co NC 29 D7
St. Stephen SC 165 B2
Church Rd SR-45
St. Stephen SC 165 B2
E Church Rd
Martinsville VA 7 B1
E Church Rd SR-57
Martinsville VA 7 B1
E Church Rd US-58 BUS
Martinsville VA 7 B1
Church St
Clarendon Co SC 154 A5
Conway SC 157 D1
Georgetown SC 167 A2
Henry Co VA 7 B3
Laurens SC 119 A4
Lynchburg SC 140 E4
McConnells SC 100 C5
Rockingham Co NC 28 C1
Sharpsburg NC 33 E7
Society Hill SC 125 C4
Wake Co NC 55 A1
Williston SC 160 E2
Church St SR-14
Laurens SC 119 A4
Church St SR-322
McConnells SC 100 C5
Church St SR-341
Lynchburg SC 140 E4
Church St US-15
Clarendon Co SC 154 A5
Church St US-17
Georgetown SC 167 A2
Church St US-78
Williston SC 160 E2
Church St US-220 BUS
Henry Co VA 7 B3
Church St US-301
Sharpsburg NC 33 E7
Church St US-501
Conway SC 157 D1
Church St N
Concord NC 76 B2
Church St N SR-73
Concord NC 76 B2
E Church St
Batesburg-Leesville SC 136 D7
Bishopville SC 140 B2
Elizabeth City NC 184 C4
Greene Co TN 20 A3
Laurinburg NC 105 C6
Stanly Co NC 77 B1
E Church St SR-23
Batesburg-Leesville SC 136 D7
E Church St SR-150
Cherryville NC 74 A3
E Church St SR-341
Bishopville SC 140 B2
E Church St US-52
Stanly Co NC 77 B1
E Church St US-74 BUS
Laurinburg NC 105 C6
N Church St
Burlington NC 192 D3
Charlotte NC 216 A2
Greensboro NC 190 D1
Greenville SC 223 C3
Guilford Co NC 28 C2
Haw River NC 29 C4
Monroe NC 218 B4
Mountain City TN 1 E5
Rocky Mount NC 34 A5
Spartanburg Co SC 224 B2
Wayne Co NC 83 C5
N Church St SR-37
Hertford NC 37 D1
N Church St SR-56
Spartanburg SC 224 C3
N Church St SR-91
Mountain City TN 1 E5
N Church St SR-200
Monroe NC 218 B4
N Church St US-17 BUS
Hertford NC 37 D1
N Church St US-29
Greenville SC 223 C3
N Church St US-70
Burlington NC 192 D3
Haw River NC 29 C4
N Church St US-221
Spartanburg SC 224 C3
Spartanburg Co SC 224 B2

N Church St US-301 BUS
Rocky Mount NC 34 A5
N Church St US-521
Manning SC 154 C4
S Church St
Burlington NC 29 C4
Burlington NC 192 B5
Greenville SC 223 B4
Rocky Mount NC 34 A7
Rutherford Co NC 72 D4
Spartanburg SC 224 C5
Spartanburg Co SC 224 C7
S Church St SR-62
Burlington NC 29 C4
Burlington NC 192 B5
S Church St US-29
Greenville SC 223 B4
S Church St US-70
Burlington NC 29 C4
Burlington NC 192 B5
S Church St US-221
Spartanburg SC 98 C4
Spartanburg SC 224 C5
Spartanburg Co SC 224 C7
S Church St US-301 BUS
Rocky Mount NC 34 A7
W Church St
Batesburg-Leesville SC 136 D7
Elizabeth City NC 184 B4
Laurinburg NC 105 C6
Lee Co SC 140 B2
Richfield NC 77 A1
Saluda SC 135 E6
W Church St SR-23
Batesburg-Leesville SC 136 D7
W Church St SR-34
Lee Co SC 140 B2
W Church St US-52
Richfield NC 77 A1
W Church St US-74 BUS
Laurinburg NC 105 C6
W Church St US-378
Saluda SC 135 E6
Church Hill Rd
Warren Co NC 12 B4
Church Park Dr
York Co SC 100 C1
Church Park Dr SR-55
York Co SC 100 C1
S Church St Ext
Spartanburg Co SC 98 C5
S Church St Ext US-221
Spartanburg Co SC 98 C5
S Churton St
Orange Co NC 30 B5
Clanton Rd
Charlotte NC 75 C6
Clarence E Coker Hwy
Clarendon Co SC 140 E7
Clarence E Coker Hwy US-378
Clarendon Co SC 140 E7
Clarence Robert Koon Mem Hwy
Newberry Co SC 136 C1
Clarence R Koon Mem Hy US-76
Newberry Co SC 136 C1
Clark Av
Raleigh NC 199 C3
Clark Rd
Augusta GA 159 B4
Clark St
Sumter Co SC 153 D3
Clark St SR-261
Pinewood SC 153 D3
E Clark St
Pinewood SC 153 D3
E Clark St SR-261
Pinewood SC 153 D3
Clark's Rd
Craven Co NC 85 E6
Clarksbury Rd
Southampton Co VA 14 D1
Clarksbury Rd E-668
Southampton Co VA 14 C1
Clarkson Rd
Richland Co SC 138 C7
Richland Co SC 152 D1
S Clarkson St
Charlotte NC 215 D3
Clarksville Rd
Halifax Co VA 10 B3
Clarksville Rd SR-49
Halifax Co VA 10 B3
Claude E Pope Memorial Hwy
Chatham Co NC 54 E5
Wake Co NC 55 A4
Claude E Pope Mem Hwy US-1
Chatham Co NC 54 E5
Wake Co NC 55 A4
Claude Lee Rd
Cumberland Co NC 107 A2
Claudville Hwy
Patrick Co VA 5 C3
Claudville Hwy SR-103
Patrick Co VA 5 C3
Claussen Rd
Florence Co SC 141 E3
Florence Co SC 142 A3
Clayton Rd
Durham Co NC 31 A5
Clear Branch Rd
Unicoi Co TN 20 E5
Clear Run School Rd
Sampson Co NC 108 E6
Clemmons Rd
Clemmons NC 26 D6
Clemmons Rd US-158
Clemmons NC 26 D6

Clemmonsville Rd
Winston-Salem NC 188 E7
W Clemmonsville Rd
Winston-Salem NC 27 A5
Clemson Blvd
Seneca SC 116 D1
Clemson Blvd SR-28
Seneca SC 116 D1
Clemson Blvd US-76
Seneca SC 116 D1
Clemson Blvd US-123
Seneca SC 116 D1
Clemson Hwy
Anderson Co SC 117 A2
Clemson Hwy SR-28
Anderson Co SC 117 A2
Clemson Hwy US-76
Anderson Co SC 117 A2
Clemson Rd
Richland Co SC 138 B3
Clemson Six-Mile Hwy
Pickens Co SC 96 A6
Clemson Six-Mile Hwy SR-137
Pickens Co SC 96 A6
Cleveland Av
Grover NC 73 D6
Kings Mountain NC 74 A5
Cleveland Av SR-161
Kings Mountain NC 74 A5
Cleveland Av SR-226
Grover NC 73 D6
N Cleveland Av
Winston-Salem NC 188 E2
NE Cleveland Av
Winston-Salem NC 188 E1
Cleveland St
Greenville SC 223 E6
Orangeburg Co SC 153 B7
Orangeburg Co SC 163 B1
Cleveland St SR-47
Elloree SC 153 B7
Orangeburg Co SC 163 B1
Cleveland Pike Rd
Oconee Co SC 115 D1
Cliff Benson Beltline
Raleigh NC 55 C2
Raleigh NC 197 A7
Raleigh NC 200 E1
Cliff Benson Beltline I-440
Raleigh NC 55 C2
Raleigh NC 197 A7
Raleigh NC 200 E1
Cliff Benson Beltline US-1
Raleigh NC 197 A7
Cliffdale Rd
Cumberland Co NC 106 D1
Cliffside Hwy
Cherokee Co SC 72 E7
Cliffside Hwy US-221 ALT
Cherokee Co SC 72 E7
Cliffside Rd
Cleveland Co NC 73 A5
Cliffview Rd
Galax VA 4 B1
Clinard Farms Rd
Guilford Co NC 27 E5
Clingman Av
Buncombe Co NC 206 B4
N Clinton Av
Peachland NC 103 B2
S Clinton Av
Dunn NC 81 E4
S Clinton Av US-301
Dunn NC 81 E4
Clinton Hwy
Newberry Co SC 120 B4
Clinton Hwy SR-72
Newberry Co SC 120 B4
Clinton Rd
Fayetteville NC 107 B1
Stedman NC 107 C1
Clinton Rd SR-24
Stedman NC 107 C1
Clio Rd
Hampton Co SC 175 C2
Clio Rd SR-119
Hampton Co SC 175 C2
Cloniger Dr
Trinity NC 51 D1
Cloniger Dr SR-62
Trinity NC 51 D1
Cloverdale Av
Winston-Salem NC 188 A4
NW Cloverleaf Pl
High Point NC 191 D6
NW Cloverleaf Pl US-311
High Point NC 191 D6
SW Cloverleaf Pl
High Point NC 191 D7
E Club Blvd
Durham NC 31 A5
Durham NC 194 C1
Club Dr
Anderson SC 226 C2
Club Dr US-76
Anderson SC 226 C2
Club Dr US-178
Anderson SC 226 C2
Cluster Springs Rd
Halifax Co VA 9 D2
Clyo-Kildare Rd
Effingham Co GA 175 A3
Clyo-Stillwell Rd
Effingham Co GA 175 C4
Coach Jimmy Smith Hwy
Lincoln Co GA 148 A2

INDEX 17
Coach Jimmy Smith Hwy — Street Index — E Daniel Morgan A

STREET City State Map# Grid

Coach Jimmy Smith Hwy SR-43
Lincoln Co GA 148 A2
Coach Jimmy Smith Hwy US-378
Lincoln Co GA 148 A2
Coal Creek Rd
Carroll Co VA 4 C3
Coastal Hwy
Chatham Co GA 180 C5
Coastal Hwy SR-25
Chatham Co GA 180 C5
Coastal Hwy US-17
Chatham Co GA 180 C5
N Coastal Hwy
Jasper Co SC 180 E2
Port Wentworth GA 180 D2
N Coastal Hwy SR-25
Port Wentworth GA 180 D2
S Coastal Hwy
Port Wentworth GA 180 D3
S Coastal Hwy SR-25
Port Wentworth GA 180 D3
Cobbham Rd
Columbia Co GA 148 B5
Cobbham Rd SR-150
Columbia Co GA 148 B5
Coddle Creek Rd
Iredell Co NC 49 D7
Coddle Creek Rd SR-136
Iredell Co NC 49 D7
Coffee Bluff Rd
Savannah GA 180 E6
Coghill Rd
McMinn Co TN 65 A4
N Coit St
Florence SC 141 D2
Florence SC 230 D4
N Coit St US-52 CONN
Florence SC 141 D2
Florence SC 230 D4
Cokesbury Hwy
Hart Co GA 116 E7
Cokesbury Hwy SR-77 SPUR
Hart Co GA 116 E7
Cokesbury Rd
Greenwood Co SC 134 D1
Cokesbury Rd SR-254
Greenwood Co SC 134 D1
Cokey Rd
Edgecombe Co NC 34 B7
Rocky Mount NC 201 E6
Cokey Rd SR-43
Edgecombe Co NC 34 B7
Cold Springs Rd
Cabarrus Co NC 76 C2
Cold Springs Rd E
Cabarrus Co NC 76 C3
Cold Springs Rd S
Cabarrus Co NC 76 C3
Coleman Blvd
Mt Pleasant SC 173 C5
Mt Pleasant SC 238 C6
Coleman Blvd SR-703
Mt Pleasant SC 173 C5
Mt Pleasant SC 238 C6
Coleman Blvd US-17 BUS
Mt Pleasant SC 173 C5
Mt Pleasant SC 238 C6
Coleman Blvd US-701 BUS
Mt Pleasant SC 173 C5
Mt Pleasant SC 238 C6
W Coleman Blvd
Mt Pleasant SC 173 C5
Mt Pleasant SC 238 A5
W Coleman Blvd SR-703
Mt Pleasant SC 173 C5
Mt Pleasant SC 238 A5
W Coleman Blvd US-17 BUS
Mt Pleasant SC 173 C5
Mt Pleasant SC 238 A5
W Coleman Blvd US-701 BUS
Mt Pleasant SC 173 C5
Mt Pleasant SC 238 A5
Cole Mill Rd
Durham NC 30 D4
Coleridge Rd
Ramseur NC 52 E3
Randolph Co NC 209 D5
Coleridge Rd SR-22
Ramseur NC 52 E3
Coleridge Rd SR-42
Randolph Co NC 209 D5
Coley Rd
Richland Co SC 138 B7
Coligny Cir
Hilton Head Island SC 242 B7
Coliseum Blvd
Greensboro NC 28 B5
Greensboro NC 189 E4
Greensboro NC 190 A6
Coliseum Dr
Winston-Salem NC 186 B7
Winston-Salem NC 187 E1
Winston-Salem NC 188 A1
College Av
Clemson SC 116 E1
Clemson SC 225 B2
Cleveland Co NC 73 C5
College Av SR-133
Clemson SC 116 E1
Clemson SC 225 B2
College Av SR-150
Cleveland Co NC 73 C5
E College Av
Boiling Springs NC 73 B5
E College Av SR-150
Boiling Springs NC 73 B5
W College Av
Boiling Springs NC 73 B5
College Dr
High Point NC 191 D5
N College Dr
High Point NC 191 D2
S College Dr
High Point NC 191 D6
College Rd
Greensboro NC 28 A5
N College Rd
New Hanover Co NC 131 A6
N College Rd SR-132
New Hanover Co NC 131 A6
N College Rd US-117
New Hanover Co NC 131 A6
S College Rd
Wilmington NC 131 A7
Wilmington NC 147 A2
S College Rd SR-132
Wilmington NC 131 A7
Wilmington NC 147 A2
S College Rd US-117
Wilmington NC 131 A7
College St
Buncombe Co NC 206 C3
Greenville SC 223 B3
Oxford NC 10 D7
College St SR-183
Greenville SC 223 B3
College St US-15
Oxford NC 10 D7
N College St
Charlotte NC 216 A2
S College St
Charlotte NC 216 A2
W College St
Warsaw NC 109 B1
Washington Co TN 20 E1
W College St SR-24 BUS
Warsaw NC 109 B1
W College St SR-81
Jonesborough TN 20 E1
College Park Rd
Berkeley Co SC 172 E1
Collettsville Rd
Caldwell Co NC 23 B7
Collettsville Rd SR-90
Caldwell Co NC 23 B7
Collins Rd
Toccoa GA 115 C3
Colon Rd
Lee Co NC 54 B7
Colonel Maham Dr
Berkeley Co SC 165 A1
Colonel Thompson Hwy
Calhoun Co SC 152 E4
Calhoun Co SC 153 A4
Colonel Thompson Hwy US-601
Calhoun Co SC 152 E4
Calhoun Co SC 153 A4
Colonial Dr
Richland Co SC 233 C1
Colonial Dr SR-555
Richland Co SC 233 C1
Colony Rd
Charlotte NC 75 D7
Columbia Av
Chapin SC 137 A3
E Columbia Av
Batesburg-Leesville SC 136 D7
E Columbia Av US-1
Batesburg-Leesville SC 136 D7
N Columbia Av
Rincon GA 175 C7
N Columbia Av SR-21
Rincon GA 175 C7
W Columbia Av
Batesburg-Leesville SC 136 C7
W Columbia Av US-1
Batesburg-Leesville SC 136 C7
Columbia Hwy
Gifford SC 169 C5
Pomaria SC 136 E1
Saluda Co SC 136 D5
Columbia Hwy US-176
Pomaria SC 136 E1
Columbia Hwy US-321
Gifford SC 169 C5
Columbia Hwy US-378
Saluda Co SC 136 D5
Columbia Hwy N
Aiken Co SC 150 B4
Columbia Hwy N US-1
Aiken Co SC 150 B4
S Columbia Hwy
Hampton Co SC 175 C1
Scotia SC 169 C7
S Columbia Hwy US-321
Hampton Co SC 175 C1
Scotia SC 169 C7
Columbia Rd
Calhoun Co SC 152 B2
Edgefield Co SC 149 D2
Fairfield Co SC 121 E7
Orangeburg Co SC 152 C7
Columbia Rd SR-23
Edgefield Co SC 149 D2
Columbia Rd SR-232
Evans GA 148 E7
Columbia Rd US-21
Calhoun Co SC 152 B2
Columbia Rd US-321 BUS
Fairfield Co SC 121 E7
Columbia Rd NE
Orangeburg Co SC 152 C6
Columbia Rd NE US-21
Orangeburg Co SC 152 C6
Columbia St
Chester Co SC 121 C1
Columbia St US-321
Chester Co SC 121 C1
S Columbia St
Chapel Hill NC 30 C7
S Columbia St SR-86
Chapel Hill NC 30 C7
Columbus St
Charleston SC 240 D5
Column St
Greenville SC 223 D2
Column St US-29
Greenville SC 223 D2
Comers Rock Rd
Grayson Co VA 3 B1
Comfort Rd
Onslow Co NC 110 E3
Onslow Co NC 111 A2
Coming St
Charleston SC 240 D6
Commerce Blvd
Wake Co NC 196 E2
Community Center Rd
Cumberland Co NC 221 C6
Concord Av
Monroe NC 102 C2
Union Co NC 218 B1
Concord Hwy
Fairview NC 76 C7
Union Co NC 102 C1
Concord Hwy US-601
Fairview NC 76 C7
Union Co NC 102 C1
Concord Pkwy N
Concord NC 76 B2
Concord Pkwy N US-29
Concord NC 76 B2
Concord Pkwy N US-601
Concord NC 76 B2
Concord Pkwy S
Concord NC 76 A3
Concord NC 212 C3
Concord Pkwy S US-29
Concord NC 76 A3
Concord NC 212 C3
Concord Rd
Albemarle NC 77 A3
Anderson SC 117 C3
Anderson SC 226 B1
Buncombe Co NC 70 E1
Buncombe Co NC 71 A1
Davidson NC 75 C1
Concord Rd SR-73
Albemarle NC 77 A3
Concord Ceffo Rd
Person Co NC 9 C5
Concord Church Rd
Lewisville NC 26 D5
E Cone Blvd
Greensboro NC 28 C4
W Cone Blvd
Greensboro NC 28 B4
Confederate Av
Salisbury NC 208 C3
Confederate Hwy
Allendale Co SC 169 D1
Colleton Co SC 170 A1
Confederate Hwy SR-641
Allendale Co SC 169 C1
Colleton Co SC 170 A1
Congaree Rd
Richland Co SC 138 D7
Richland Co SC 152 D1
Congaree Rd SR-769
Richland Co SC 138 D7
Richland Co SC 152 D1
Congress Pkwy
McMinn Co TN 65 A1
Congress Pkwy SR-2
McMinn Co TN 65 A1
Congress Pkwy US-11
McMinn Co TN 65 A1
Congress St
Charleston SC 240 B5
N Congress St
York SC 100 C2
N Congress St SR-49
York SC 100 C2
Congressman L H Fountain Hwy
Edgecombe Co NC 34 B6
Cong L H Fountain Hwy US-64
Edgecombe Co NC 34 B6
Conklin Rd
Washington Co TN 20 E3
Connaritsa Rd
Bertie Co NC 35 E2
Connelly Springs Rd
Cajah's Mountain NC 47 C2
Conover Blvd E
Conover NC 48 C4
Conover Blvd E US-70
Conover NC 48 C4
Conrad Rd
Lewisville NC 26 D4
Constitution Blvd
Rock Hill SC 217 A2
N Converse St
Spartanburg SC 224 C3
S Converse St
Spartanburg SC 224 C4
Conway Rd
Fair Bluff NC 127 D7
Conway Rd SR-904
Fair Bluff NC 127 D7
Cook Rd
Alamance Co NC 29 B4
Durham NC 30 E6
Cooks Bridge Rd
Aiken Co SC 150 B5
Cooley Bridge Rd
Anderson Co SC 117 E3
Anderson Co SC 118 A3
Cooley Bridge Rd SR-247
Anderson Co SC 117 E4
Anderson Co SC 118 A3
Cool Springs Rd
Lee Co NC 54 A7
Rowan Co NC 49 E2
Rowan Co NC 50 B3
E Cooper St
Winterville NC 59 B6
Cooper Hill Rd
Bertie Co NC 36 D5
Cooper Hill Rd SR-308
Bertie Co NC 36 D5
Cooper Lake Rd
Greenville Co SC 97 D7
Cooper Mill Rd
Lee Co SC 140 B3
Cooper Store Rd
Berkeley Co SC 164 E5
Copas Rd SW
Shallotte NC 145 D5
Cope Rd
Orangeburg Co SC 161 E1
Orangeburg Co SC 162 A2
Cope Rd SR-332
Norway SC 161 E1
Orangeburg Co SC 162 A2
Copperfield Blvd NE
Concord NC 76 B2
Copperhead Rd
Berkeley Co SC 165 C6
Corban Av SE
Concord NC 76 B2
Corban Av SE SR-73
Concord NC 76 B2
Corbett Av
Wilson NC 202 C3
W Corbett Av
Swansboro NC 112 A6
W Corbett Av SR-24
Swansboro NC 112 A6
Corbett Hill Rd SW
Wayne Co NC 83 A4
Corby Bridge Rd
Washington Co TN 20 C3
Cordova Rd
Orangeburg Co SC 162 C1
Cordova Rd SW
Orangeburg Co SC 162 C1
Core Point Rd
Craven Co NC 86 C3
Corinth Rd
Chatham Co NC 54 D6
Cornatzer Rd
Davie Co NC 26 C7
Cornelius St
Orange Co NC 30 B4
Cornelius St US-70
Orange Co NC 30 B4
Cornelius Harnette Dr
Wilmington NC 231 A1
Cornwallis Rd
Johnston Co NC 56 A4
E Cornwallis Rd
Durham NC 31 A7
W Cornwallis Rd
Durham NC 30 D5
Cosby Hwy
Cocke Co TN 42 D2
Cosby Hwy SR-32
Cocke Co TN 42 E1
Cosby Hwy SR-73
Cocke Co TN 42 D2
Cosby Hwy US-321
Cocke Co TN 42 E1
Costner School Rd
Gaston Co NC 74 C4
Cotswold Av
Greensboro NC 28 B3
Cottageville Hwy
Colleton Co SC 171 C3
Cottageville Hwy US-17 ALT
Colleton Co SC 171 C3
Cotton Grove Rd
Davidson Co NC 51 A4
Lexington NC 51 A3
Cotton Grove Rd SR-8
Davidson Co NC 51 A4
Lexington NC 51 A3
Country Club Dr
Fayetteville NC 81 A7
Waynesville NC 69 C1
Country Club Dr US-401 BYP
Fayetteville NC 81 A7
Country Club Rd
Bamberg Co SC 161 E3
Carolina Shores NC 145 A6
Carteret Co NC 228 B3
Jacksonville NC 111 C5
Lincolnton NC 74 C1
New Bern NC 86 B6
Warren Co NC 12 A5
Winston-Salem NC 26 E4
Winston-Salem NC 27 A4
Country Club Rd SR-58
Warren Co NC 12 A5
Country Club Rd SR-70
Bamberg Co SC 161 E3
Country Junction Rd
Oconee Co SC 95 B6
Countryside Dr
Pittsylvania Co VA 8 E2
County Home Rd
Catawba Co NC 48 B3
Davie Co NC 50 B1
County Line Rd
Andrews SC 166 B1
Charleston Co SC 172 C4
Gaston Co NC 74 A4
Georgetown Co SC 156 C6
Georgetown Co SC 166 A3
Greenwood Co SC 134 E5
County Line Rd SR-21
Andrews SC 166 B1
County Line Rd SR-41
Georgetown Co SC 156 C6
Williamsburg Co SC 166 A3
County Line Rd SR-216
Gaston Co NC 74 A4
County Line Rd SR-513
Georgetown Co SC 156 D5
County Line Rd US-17 ALT
Georgetown Co SC 166 A3
Court St
Gatesville NC 15 E4
Court St SR-137
Gatesville NC 15 E4
E Court St
McDowell Co NC 46 B5
E Court St US-70
Marion NC 46 B5
Courtney-Huntsville Rd
Yadkin Co NC 26 B5
Cove Rd
McDowell Co NC 46 A7
Rutherford Co NC 72 A1
Cove Creek Rd
Haywood Co NC 43 C6
Covered Bridge Rd
Johnston Co NC 56 B4
Cowan Rd
York Co SC 217 E5
Cowan Rd SR-121
York Co SC 217 E5
Cowpens Hwy
Cherokee Co SC 98 E1
Cowpens Hwy SR-110
Cherokee Co SC 98 E1
Cox Rd
Evans GA 148 E7
Gastonia NC 74 D5
Cpcc Ln
Matthews NC 102 A1
CR-618
Monroe Co TN 65 E5
CR-648
Habersham Co GA 94 B7
Habersham Co GA 115 A1
Crab Creek Rd
Henderson Co NC 70 D5
Crabtree Rd
Haywood Co NC 43 C7
Crabtree Rd SR-209
Haywood Co NC 43 C7
Craggy Gdns
Buncombe Co NC 45 A4
Craig Rd
Durham Co NC 30 D4
Crane Church Rd
Richland Co SC 138 A4
Craven St
Buncombe Co NC 206 A4
Crawford Rd
Gaston Co NC 74 C6
Rock Hill SC 217 A5
Creech Rd
Greene Co NC 84 A1
Wake Co NC 55 E3
Creedmoor Rd
Raleigh NC 31 D7
Raleigh NC 197 A4
Wake Co NC 55 D1
Creedmoor Rd SR-50
Raleigh NC 31 D7
Raleigh NC 197 A4
Wake Co NC 55 D1
Creek Rd
Robeson Co NC 127 D5
N Creek Rd
Robeson Co NC 127 E4
Creek Ridge Rd
Greensboro NC 28 B5
Greensboro NC 189 E7
Greensboro NC 190 A7
Creekview Rd
Guilford Co NC 28 D4
Creekway Dr NW
Lenoir NC 47 C1
Crescent Av
Spartanburg SC 98 C4
Spartanburg SC 224 B6
Crest Rd
Edgefield SC 149 C2
Crest Rd SR-430
Edgefield SC 149 C2
Crestline Rd
Scotland Co NC 105 C7
Scotland Co NC 126 C1
Crestview Rd
Easley SC 96 D6
C Richard Vaughn Hwy
Surry Co NC 4 E5
Surry Co NC 5 A5
C Richard Vaughn Hwy I-74
Surry Co NC 4 E5
Surry Co NC 5 A5
Cripple Creek Rd
Cocke Co TN 43 A2
Croasdaile Farm Pkwy
Durham NC 30 E5
N Croatan Hwy
Kill Devil Hills NC 39 E3
Kitty Hawk NC 39 E2
N Croatan Hwy US-158
Kill Devil Hills NC 39 E3
Kitty Hawk NC 39 E2
S Croatan Hwy
Nags Head NC 40 A3
S Croatan Hwy US-158
Nags Head NC 40 A3
W Croatan Hwy
Kill Devil Hills NC 39 E2
W Croatan Hwy US-158
Kill Devil Hills NC 39 E2
Cronly Rd
Columbus Co NC 130 A6
Crooked Creek Rd
Towns Co GA 93 A3
Crooked Creek Rd SR-339
Towns Co GA 93 A3
Cross Rd
York Co SC 74 D7
Cross Anchor Hwy
Spartanburg Co SC 98 B7
Spartanburg Co SC 119 C1
Cross Anchor Hwy SR-146
Spartanburg Co SC 98 B7
Spartanburg Co SC 119 C1
Cross Anchor Rd
Woodruff SC 98 B7
Cross Anchor Rd SR-146
Woodruff SC 98 B7
Crossgate Dr
Port Wentworth GA 180 D2
Cross Hill Rd
Richland Co SC 234 C4
Crosshill Rd
Richland Co SC 138 C7
Cross Hill Rd SR-16 CONN
Richland Co SC 234 C4
Cross Hill Rd US-76 CONN
Richland Co SC 234 C4
Crossing Creek Rd
Richland Co SC 138 D7
Cross Island Pkwy
Hilton Head Island SC 181 E2
Hilton Head Island SC 241 A7
Hilton Head Island SC 242 A2
Cross Island Pkwy US-278
Hilton Head Island SC 181 E2
Hilton Head Island SC 241 A7
Hilton Head Island SC 242 A2
Cross Keys Hwy
Union Co SC 119 E2
Union Co SC 120 A1
Cross Keys Hwy SR-49
Union Co SC 119 E2
Union Co SC 120 A1
Cross Link Rd
Raleigh NC 55 D3
Cross Roads Dr
Grayson Co VA 4 A3
Crosstown
Charleston SC 240 C5
Crosstown US-17
Charleston SC 240 C5
Crow Creek Rd
Pickens Co SC 95 E5
Crow Creek Rd SR-133
Pickens Co SC 95 E5
Crowder Rd
Wake Co NC 55 D4
Crowders Creek Rd
Gaston Co NC 74 B7
Crowders Mountain Rd
Bessemer City NC 74 B5
Crowe Creek Rd
Pickens Co SC 95 E4
Crowe Creek Rd SR-133
Pickens Co SC 95 E4
Crowfield Blvd
Goose Creek SC 172 E1
Goose Creek SC 237 B3
Cruso Rd
Haywood Co NC 69 E1
Haywood Co NC 70 A2
Cruso Rd US-276
Haywood Co NC 69 E1
Haywood Co NC 70 A2
Crymes Cove Rd
Waynesville NC 69 C1
Culbreth Rd
Chapel Hill NC 30 C7
Cumberland Rd
Cumberland Co NC 106 E2
Cumberland Co NC 107 A1
Cumberland Co NC 222 A6
E Cumberland St
Dunn NC 81 E4
E Cumberland St US-421
Harnett Co NC 81 E4
W Cumberland St
Dunn NC 81 E3
W Cumberland St SR-55
Erwin NC 81 E3
W Cumberland St US-421
Dunn NC 81 E3
Cummings Rd
Henderson Co NC 70 D4
Cummings St
Rock Hill SC 217 D4
Spartanburg SC 224 C2
Cunningham Rd
Kinston NC 84 E3
Kinston NC 205 E1
Person Co NC 9 B4
Cureton Ferry Rd
York Co SC 101 B5
E Currahee St
Toccoa GA 115 D3
E Currahee St SR-13
Toccoa GA 115 C3
E Currahee St SR-365
Toccoa GA 115 C3
E Currahee St US-123
Toccoa GA 115 C3
W Currahee St
Toccoa GA 115 C3
W Currahee St SR-13
Toccoa GA 115 C3
W Currahee St SR-184
Toccoa GA 115 C3
W Currahee St SR-365
Toccoa GA 115 C3
W Currahee St US-123
Toccoa GA 115 C3
E Curtis St
Simpsonville SC 97 C7
E Curtis St SR-417
Simpsonville SC 97 C7
Curtis Grove Rd
Granville Co NC 31 D1
Cypress St
Charleston SC 240 C3
Cypress Campground Rd
Berkeley Co SC 164 B7
Cypress Creek Rd
Onslow Co NC 110 C4
Cypress Gardens Rd
Berkeley Co SC 164 E7
Berkeley Co SC 165 A7

D

D St
Bridgeton NC 86 B6
North Wilkesboro NC 24 D3
D St US-17
Bridgeton NC 86 B6
D St US-421 BUS
North Wilkesboro NC 24 D3
E D St
Newton NC 48 C5
E D St SR-10
Newton NC 48 C5
E D St SR-16
Newton NC 48 C5
Dabney Dr
Henderson NC 11 B7
Dacusville Hwy
Pickens Co SC 96 C3
Dacusville Hwy SR-135
Pickens Co SC 96 C3
Dacusville Rd
Greenville Co SC 96 D3
Dacusville Rd SR-186
Greenville Co SC 96 D3
Daisy Rd
Horry Co SC 144 A5
Dale Earnhardt Blvd
Cabarrus Co NC 76 A1
Dale Earnhardt Blvd SR-3
Cabarrus Co NC 76 A1
Dallas-Bessemer City Hwy
Gastonia NC 74 C4
Dallas-Bessemr City Hwy SR-275
Gastonia NC 74 C4
Dallas-Cherryville Hwy
Gaston Co NC 74 B3
Dallas-Cherryville Hwy SR-279
Gaston Co NC 74 B3
Dallas-High Shoals Hwy
Dallas NC 74 C3
Dallas-Hgh Shls Hwy US-321 BUS
Dallas NC 74 C3
Dallas-Spencer Mountain Rd
Gaston Co NC 74 D
Dallas-Stanley Hwy
Dallas NC 74 D
Dallas-Stanley Hwy SR-275
Dallas NC 74 D
Dalton Av
Charlotte NC 216 B
Dalton Av SR-49
Charlotte NC 216 B
Dalton Av US-29
Charlotte NC 216 B
Damascus Rd
Banks Co GA 115 B
Damascus Rd SR-184
Banks Co GA 115 B
Damascus Church Rd
Orange Co NC 54 B
Dameron Rd
Gaston Co NC 74 B
Danetower Rd
Anderson Co SC 117 B
Danford Rd SE
Brunswick Co NC 146 B
Daniel Av
Saluda Co SC 135 E
Ward SC 150 A
Daniel Av SR-193
Saluda Co SC 135 E
Saluda Co SC 150 A
Daniel Boone Tr
Johnson Co TN 1 C
Daniel Boone Tr SR-34
Johnson Co TN 1 C
Daniel Boone Tr US-421
Johnson Co TN 1 C
E Daniel Morgan Av
Spartanburg SC 224 C
E Daniel Morgan Av SR-296
Spartanburg SC 224 C

INDEX 18

aniel Morgan Av — Street Index — Eckerson Rd

REET State Map# Grid
Daniel Morgan Av
partanburg SC 224 C3
Daniel Morgan Av
R-296
partanburg SC 224 C3
Daniel Morgan Av
partanburg SC 224 C4
Daniel Morgan Av
R-296
partanburg SC 224 C4
aniels Rd
ates Co NC 16 B2
aniels Creek Rd
enry Co VA 7 A1
aniel Siding Loop Rd
ryan Co GA 180 A6
an K Moore Frwy
urham Co NC 31 A7
ake Co NC 55 B1
an K Moore Frwy I-40
ary NC 55 B1
urham Co NC 31 A7
anville Expwy
anville VA 8 A3
anville Expwy US-29
anville VA 8 A3
anville Expwy US-58
anville VA 8 A3
anville Pike
arroll Co VA 5 B1
anville Pike US-58
arroll Co VA 5 B1
Danzler Rd
partanburg Co SC 97 E4
arby Rd
hester Co SC 100 D6
Darby Rd
reenville Co SC 97 B3
Darby Rd
reenville Co SC 97 B3
arlington Hwy E
ee Co SC 140 C4
arlington Hwy E
S-401
ee Co SC 140 C4
arlington Hwy W
ee Co SC 140 B4
arlington Hwy W
S-401
ee Co SC 140 B5
ave Lyle Blvd
ock Hill SC 101 A3
ock Hill SC 217 E3
ave Lyle Blvd SR-122
ock Hill SC 101 A3
ock Hill SC 217 D3
Dave Lyle Blvd
ock Hill SC 101 A3
Dave Lyle Blvd
R-122
ock Hill SC 101 A3
Dave Lyle Blvd
ock Hill SC 217 B5
aves Rd
ork Co SC 100 C4
avidson Hwy
abarrus Co NC 75 E2
oncord NC 76 A2
avidson Hwy SR-73
abarrus Co NC 75 E2
oncord NC 76 A2
avidson Rd
abarrus Co NC 75 D1
Davidson St
harlotte NC 216 B2
avidson-Concord Rd
abarrus Co NC 75 D2
annapolis NC 75 D1
avidson-Concord Rd
R-73
abarrus Co NC 75 D1
avid W Lillard
emorial Hwy
owah TN 65 A2
avid W Lillard Mem
wy SR-30
owah TN 65 A2
avie Av
atesville NC 49 C3
avie Av US-21
atesville NC 49 C3
avie Av US-64
atesville NC 49 C3
Davie St
reensboro NC 190 C2
Davie St
reensboro NC 190 C3
avis Dr
ary NC 55 A2
urham Co NC 31 A7
avis St
amar SC 140 D3
avis St US-401
amar SC 140 D3
avison Rd
ollywood SC 172 D5
avis Park Rd
aston Co NC 74 C5
avy Crockett Rd
ashington Co TN 20 C2
Dawson Dr
hester SC 100 C7
Dawson Dr SR-97 BYP
hester Co SC 100 C7
Dawson Dr US-321 BYP
hester Co SC 100 C7
Dawson Dr
hester Co SC 100 C7
Dawson Dr US-321
ONN
hester SC 100 C7

STREET City State Map# Grid
Dawson St
Wilmington NC 146 E1
Wilmington NC 231 B4
Dawson St US-17
Wilmington NC 146 E1
Dawson St US-74
Wilmington NC 146 E1
Dawson St US-76
Wilmington NC 146 E1
Wilmington NC 231 B4
Dawson Cabin Rd
Onslow Co NC 110 E6
Onslow Co NC 111 A6
Deacon Blvd
Winston-Salem NC 186 C7
Deal Rd
Rowan Co NC 49 E7
Dean Forest Rd
Chatham Co SC 180 D4
Dean Forest Rd SR-307
Savannah GA 180 D4
Deans St
Bailey NC 57 A2
Deans St US-264 ALT
Nash Co NC 57 A2
Deans Bridge Rd
Augusta GA 159 A2
Deans Bridge Rd SR-4
Augusta GA 159 A2
Dearborn Dr
Durham NC 31 A5
Decker Blvd
Arcadia Lakes SC 138 B5
Deep Creek Rd
Anson Co NC 103 C5
Deep River Rd
High Point NC 27 E6
High Point NC 191 E1
Deepstep Rd
Edgefield Co SC 149 A5
Deerfield Rd
Boone NC 185 E6
Watauga Co NC 23 B3
S DeKalb St
Shelby NC 73 C5
S DeKalb St SR-150
Shelby NC 73 C5
Delaware Rd
Southampton Co VA 15 B1
Delaware Rd E-687
Southampton Co VA 15 B1
Delemar Hwy
Dorchester Co SC 172 B4
Delemar Hwy SR-165
Dorchester Co SC 172 B4
Delesseps Av
Savannah GA 181 A4
Delhart Rd
Grayson Co VA 4 A3
Delhi Rd
Lincoln Co GA 133 B7
Dellabrook Rd
Winston-Salem NC 188 E1
Dellwood Rd
Haywood Co NC 43 C7
Dellwood Rd US-19
Haywood Co NC 43 C7
Dellwood Rd US-276
Haywood Co NC 43 C7
Delview Rd
Cherryville NC 73 E3
Delway Hwy
Sampson Co NC 109 A5
Delway Hwy US-421
Sampson Co NC 109 A5
Delway St
Raleigh NC 200 A2
Denmark Rd
Barnwell Co SC 161 C4
Denmark Rd SR-70
Barnwell Co SC 161 C4
Denniston Rd
Halifax Co VA 9 E3
Denny Hwy
Saluda Co SC 136 C4
Denny Hwy SR-194
Saluda Co SC 136 C4
Denton Rd
Cocke Co TN 42 E1
Cocke Co TN 43 A1
Davidson Co NC 51 C6
Denton Rd SR-73
Cocke Co TN 42 E1
Cocke Co TN 43 A1
Depot St
Buncombe Co NC 206 B5
E Depot St
Angier NC 55 C7
E Depot St SR-210
Angier NC 55 C7
E Derenne Av
Savannah GA 181 A5
Derita Rd
Cabarrus Co NC 75 E3
Desert Rd
Suffolk VA 16 C1
Desert Rd E-604
Suffolk VA 16 C1
Devil Fork Rd
Unicoi Co TN 20 D6
Devil Fork Rd SR-352
Unicoi Co TN 20 D6
Devils Racetrack Rd
Johnston Co NC 82 C1
Devine St
Richland Co SC 233 E4
Devine St US-21 CONN
Richland Co SC 233 E4
Devine St US-76 CONN
Richland Co SC 233 E4
Dewey Cox Rd
Williamsburg Co SC 155 E2

STREET City State Map# Grid
DeWitt Williams Blvd
Berkeley Co SC 165 A1
DeWitt Williams Blvd
SR-45
Berkeley Co SC 165 A1
Dexter St
Blackville SC 161 B3
Dexter St US-78
Blackville SC 161 B3
Dial Rd
Fannin Co GA 92 A6
Diamond Cswy
Chatham Co GA 180 E6
Chatham Co GA 181 A6
Diamond Cswy SR-204
SPUR
Chatham Co GA 180 E6
Chatham Co GA 181 A6
Dibble Rd SW
Aiken Co SC 236 A2
Dicey Creek Rd
Kershaw Co SC 139 B1
Dicey Ford Rd
Camden SC 139 B1
Dickerson Blvd
Monroe NC 218 A2
Dickinson Av
Greenville NC 59 A5
Greenville NC 203 A3
Dickinson Av US-13
Greenville NC 59 A5
Dick Pond Rd
Horry Co SC 157 E4
Horry Co SC 158 A4
Dick Pond Rd SR-544
Horry Co SC 157 E4
Horry Co SC 158 A4
Dicks Creek Rd
Macon Co NC 67 C6
SE Diggs Rd
Edgefield Co SC 149 D3
SE Diggs Rd SR-19 CONN
Trenton SC 149 D3
SE Diggs Rd SR-121
CONN
Trenton SC 149 D3
Dillard Dr
Cary NC 55 C3
Dillard Rd
Highlands NC 94 D2
Dillard Rd SR-106
Highlands NC 94 D2
Dillingham Rd
Buncombe Co NC 45 A3
Dillon Hwy
Dillon Co SC 127 B6
Dillon Hwy SR-9
Dillon Co SC 127 B5
Dillon Rd
Hilton Head Island SC 182 A1
Hilton Head Island SC 241 E5
Dillons Fork Rd
Henry Co VA 6 E1
Dix Creek Road 1
Buncombe Co NC 44 B6
Dix Creek Road 2
Buncombe Co NC 44 B6
Dixie Dr
Newberry Co SC 136 B1
Dixie Dr SR-34 BYP
Newberry Co SC 136 B1
E Dixie Dr
Asheboro NC 52 C4
Asheboro NC 209 E6
E Dixie Dr SR-49
Asheboro NC 52 C4
Asheboro NC 209 E6
E Dixie Dr US-64
Asheboro NC 52 C4
Asheboro NC 209 E6
W Dixie Dr
Asheboro NC 52 C4
Randolph Co NC 209 B7
W Dixie Dr SR-49
Randolph Co NC 209 B7
W Dixie Dr US-64
Asheboro NC 52 C4
Randolph Co NC 209 B7
Dixie Hwy
Cocke Co TN 19 B7
Cocke Co TN 43 C1
Woodfin NC 44 D5
Dixie Hwy SR-9
Cocke Co TN 19 B7
Cocke Co TN 43 C1
Dixie Hwy SR-107
Cocke Co TN 19 B7
Dixie Hwy SR-251
Woodfin NC 44 D5
Dixie Hwy US-25
Cocke Co TN 19 B7
Cocke Co TN 43 C1
Dixie Hwy US-70
Cocke Co TN 19 B7
Cocke Co TN 43 C1
Dixie Rd
Charlotte NC 75 B6
S Dixie Rd
Aiken Co SC 151 A5
S Dixie Rd SR-113
Aiken Co SC 151 A5
Dixie Tr
Raleigh NC 55 D2
Raleigh NC 199 B2
Dixie Clay Rd
Aiken Co SC 149 D7
Aiken Co SC 159 D1
Dixie River Rd
Mecklenburg Co NC 75 A6
E Dixon Blvd
Cleveland Co NC 73 D5

STREET City State Map# Grid
E Dixon Blvd US-74 BYP
Cleveland Co NC 73 D5
W Dixon Blvd
Shelby NC 73 B4
W Dixon Blvd US-74
Shelby NC 73 B4
Dixon Airline Rd
Augusta GA 159 B2
Dixon School Rd
Cleveland Co NC 74 A6
Doar Rd
Awendaw SC 174 B1
Dobberville Rd SW
Wayne Co NC 82 E4
Dobbin Holmes Rd
Cumberland Co NC 81 B7
Dobson St
Forsyth Co NC 27 D4
Doby's Bridge Rd
Lancaster Co SC 101 B3
Dock Rd
Columbus Co NC 144 D3
Dock Site Rd
Edisto Beach SC 178 A3
Doc Nichols Rd
Durham Co NC 31 B6
Doc Pugh Rd
Burke Co NC 47 E4
Doctor Purdy Rd
Brunswick Co VA 12 C2
Doc Wehunt Rd
Gaston Co NC 73 E3
Doe Creek Rd
Johnson Co TN 1 B7
Doe Creek Rd SR-167
Johnson Co TN 1 B7
Doe Valley Rd
Johnson Co TN 1 D5
Doe Valley Rd SR-67
Johnson Co TN 1 D5
Doggett Rd
Guilford Co NC 28 C2
Dogwood Blvd
Kannapolis NC 76 A1
Dogwood Dr
Buncombe Co NC 44 D5
Orange Co NC 54 C1
Dogwood Rd
Buncombe Co NC 44 B7
Dolly Parton Pkwy
Sevierville TN 41 E1
Dolly Parton Pkwy
SR-35
Sevierville TN 41 E1
Dolly Parton Pkwy
US-411
Sevierville TN 41 E1
Dominion St
Winston-Salem NC 186 D6
Donald Ross Rd
Charlotte NC 215 A3
Donaldson Rd
Greenville Co SC 97 B7
Don Felmet Rd
Buncombe Co NC 44 B5
Doral Dr
Forsyth Co NC 26 E2
Dorange Rd
Branchville SC 162 E5
Dorchester Co SC 163 A5
Dorange Rd US-78
Branchville SC 162 E5
Dorchester Co SC 163 A5
Dorchester Rd
Dorchester Co SC 172 D3
North Charleston SC 172 E3
Dorchester Rd SR-642
Dorchester Co SC 172 D3
North Charleston SC 172 E3
Dorman Rd
Harnett Co NC 81 D4
Dortches Blvd
Dortches NC 33 E5
Dortches Blvd SR-43
Dortches NC 33 D5
Double Branches Rd
Lincoln Co GA 148 B3
Double Branches Rd
SR-220 SPUR
Lincoln Co GA 148 B3
E Double Shoals Rd
Cleveland Co NC 73 D3
W Double Shoals Rd
Cleveland Co NC 73 C3
Doug Barnard Pkwy
Augusta GA 159 B2
Doug Barnard Pkwy
SR-56 SPUR
Augusta GA 159 B2
Dougherty Rd
Aiken Co SC 236 D6
Douglas Dam Rd
Sevierville TN 41 E1
Douglas Dam Rd SR-338
Sevierville TN 41 E1
Douglas Hill Rd
Abbeville SC 134 B3
Douglas Hill Rd SR-203
Abbeville SC 134 B3
Douglass Rd
Fairfield Co SC 121 C4
Dow Rd S
New Hanover Co NC 147 A4
N Dow Rd
Carolina Beach NC 147 A4
Downing St
Wilson NC 202 B6
Dozier Rd
Columbia Co GA 148 A6
Dragstrip Rd
Aiken Co SC 159 E3

STREET City State Map# Grid
Drake Rd
Marlboro Co SC 125 E4
Marlboro Co SC 126 A4
Drayton Rd
Spartanburg Co SC 98 C3
Spartanburg Co SC 224 E1
Drayton St
Savannah GA 180 E4
Dreher Island Rd
Lexington Co SC 136 E4
Dreher Shoals Rd
Richland Co SC 137 C4
Dreher Shoals Rd SR-6
Richland Co SC 137 C4
Drewry Rd
Vance Co NC 11 C4
Drexel Rd
Burke Co NC 47 B4
Drexel Rd SR-114
Burke Co NC 47 C4
Dr Humphries Rd
Kershaw Co SC 139 C1
Dr Martin Luther King
Jr Blvd
Craven Co NC 86 A6
Warren Co NC 11 D6
Dr Martin L King Jr
Blvd US-17
Craven Co NC 86 A6
Dr Martin Luther King
Jr Expwy
Goldsboro NC 83 D1
Goldsboro NC 204 A4
Dr ML King Jr Expwy
SR-111
Goldsboro NC 204 E2
Dr ML King Jr Expwy
SR-581
Goldsboro NC 204 A4
Dr ML King Jr Expwy
US-13
Goldsboro NC 83 D1
Goldsboro NC 204 A4
Dr ML King Jr Expwy
US-70
Goldsboro NC 83 D1
Goldsboro NC 204 E2
Dr ML King Jr Expwy
US-117
Goldsboro NC 204 A4
Dr Martin Luther King
Jr Hwy
Marlboro Co SC 125 E2
McColl SC 126 A1
Dr Martin L King Jr
Hwy SR-9
Bennettsville SC 125 E2
Dr Martin L King Jr
Hwy SR-38
Marlboro Co SC 125 E2
Dr Martin L King Jr
Hwy US-15
Bennettsville SC 125 E2
McColl SC 126 A1
Dr Martin L King Jr
Hwy US-401
Marlboro Co SC 125 E2
McColl SC 126 A1
Dr Milams Rd
Pittsylvania Co VA 9 A1
Dr Moses A Ray Hwy
Tarboro NC 34 D7
Dr Moses A Ray Hwy
US-64
Tarboro NC 34 D7
Dr William L Wood Sr
Hwy
Yadkin Co NC 25 C4
Dr William L Wood Sr
Hy US-421
Yadkin Co NC 25 C4
Dry Branch Rd
Aiken Co SC 160 A1
Dry Bread Rd
Brunswick Co VA 12 D1
Dry Creek Rd
Carter Co TN 21 C2
Dry Creek Rd SR-361
Carter Co TN 21 C2
Dryman Mountain Rd
Asheville NC 44 C6
Drymonia Rd
Craven Co NC 85 E5
Dry Pond Hwy
Patrick Co VA 5 E3
Patrick Co VA 6 A3
Dry Pond Hwy SR-103
Patrick Co VA 5 E3
Patrick Co VA 6 A3
Dubard Boyle Rd
Richland Co SC 138 A4
Dubose Siding Rd
Sumter Co SC 139 E4
Sumter Co SC 140 A4
Duck Rd
Dare Co NC 18 D7
Dare Co NC 39 D1
Duck Rd SR-12
Dare Co NC 18 D7
Dare Co NC 39 D1
N Dudley St
Greensboro NC 190 D2
S Dudley St
Greensboro NC 190 D3
Due West Hwy
Anderson Co SC 117 D6
Due West Hwy SR-185
Anderson Co SC 117 D6
Due West Rd
Anderson Co SC 117 E5
Due West Rd SR-20
Anderson Co SC 117 E5

STREET City State Map# Grid
Duke St
Granite Falls NC 47 E3
N Duke St
Durham NC 30 E5
N Duke St US-501
Durham NC 30 E5
Dull Rd
Forsyth Co NC 26 D5
Dunbar St
Greenville SC 223 A4
E Dunbar St
Spartanburg SC 224 C3
Dunbarton Blvd
Barnwell SC 161 A5
Snelling SC 160 E5
Dunbarton Blvd SR-64
Barnwell SC 161 A5
Snelling SC 160 E5
N Duncan Byp
Union SC 99 B7
N Duncan Byp US-176
Union SC 99 B7
S Duncan Byp
Union SC 120 B1
S Duncan Byp SR-215
Union SC 120 B1
S Duncan Byp US-176
Union SC 120 B1
Duncan St
Spartanburg SC 98 C4
Spartanburg SC 224 D5
Duncan Chapel Rd
Greenville Co SC 97 A4
Duncan Hill Ln
Alexander Co NC 48 B2
Duncan Hill Ln SR-127
Alexander Co NC 48 B2
Duncan-Reidville Rd
Spartanburg Co SC 97 E4
Duncans Creek Rd
Rutherford Co NC 72 E1
Rutherford Co NC 73 A1
Dunklin Bridge Rd
Greenville Co SC 118 C3
Dunlap Roddey Rd
York Co SC 101 A5
N Dunleith Av
Winston-Salem NC 188 E3
Dunmeyer Hill Rd
Lincolnville SC 172 D1
Dunn Rd
Cumberland Co NC 81 D5
Fayetteville NC 107 B1
Dunn Rd US-301
Cumberland Co NC 81 D5
Dunns Mountain Rd
Granite Quarry NC 50 D6
Duraleigh Rd
Raleigh NC 55 C1
Durant Rd
Raleigh NC 31 D7
Durham Frwy
Durham Co NC 31 A7
Durham Frwy SR-147
Durham Co NC 31 A7
Durham Rd
Person Co NC 9 D7
Person Co NC 30 D1
Roxboro NC 9 D6
Wake Co NC 31 E6
Wake Forest NC 32 A6
Durham Rd SR-57
Person Co NC 9 D6
Person Co NC 30 D1
Durham Rd SR-98
Wake Co NC 31 E6
Wake Forest NC 32 A6
Durham Rd US-501
Person Co NC 9 D6
Person Co NC 30 D1
Durham Chapel Hill
Blvd
Durham NC 30 D6
Durham Chpl Hl Blvd
US-15 BUS
Durham NC 30 D6
Durham Chapel Hill
Blvd US-15A
Durham NC 30 D6
Durham Chpl Hl Blvd
US-501 BUS
Durham NC 30 D6
Durham Creek Rd
Beaufort Co NC 86 D2
Durst Av E
Greenwood SC 134 E2
Dutch Fork Rd
Richland Co SC 137 C3
Dutch Fork Rd US-76
Richland Co SC 137 C3
Dye Plant Rd
Henry Co VA 7 A1
Dye Plant Rd E-706
Henry Co VA 7 A1

E

E Pkwy
Gatlinburg TN 42 A4
Sevier Co TN 42 C3
E Pkwy SR-73
Gatlinburg TN 42 A4
Pittman Center TN 42 C3
E Pkwy US-321
Gatlinburg TN 42 A4
Sevier Co TN 42 C3
Eagle Rd
Belmont NC 74 E5
Eagle Rock Rd
Johnston Co NC 56 C2
Earl Rd
Shelby NC 73 D5

STREET City State Map# Grid
Earl Rd SR-226
Shelby NC 73 D5
Earl Davis Gregory Hwy
Halifax Co VA 10 C3
Earl Davis Gregory
Hwy SR-49
Halifax Co VA 10 C3
Earl E Morris Jr Hwy
Anderson Co SC 96 E5
Earl E Morris Jr Hwy
SR-153
Anderson Co SC 96 E5
Earls Bridge Rd
Pickens Co SC 96 C4
Earls Bridge Rd SR-186
Pickens Co SC 96 C4
Easley Hwy
Anderson Co SC 117 E1
Easley Hwy SR-8
Anderson Co SC 117 E1
Easley Bridge Rd
Greenville Co SC 97 A5
Easley Bridge Rd
US-123
Greenville Co SC 97 A5
S East Av
Lexington Co SC 136 D7
East Blvd
Charlotte NC 75 C6
Chesterfield SC 103 D7
Williamston NC 36 A7
East Blvd SR-9
Chesterfield SC 103 D7
East Blvd US-13
Williamston NC 36 A7
East Blvd US-17
Williamston NC 36 A7
N East Blvd
Clinton NC 108 D1
N East Blvd US-701 BUS
Clinton NC 108 D1
S East Blvd
Clinton NC 108 D1
S East Blvd US-701 BUS
Clinton NC 108 D1
East St
Pittsboro NC 54 B3
East St US-64 BUS
Pittsboro NC 54 B3
N East St
Roseboro NC 108 A2
N East St SR-242
Roseboro NC 108 A2
Eastchester Dr
High Point NC 27 E6
High Point NC 191 B1
Eastchester Dr SR-68
High Point NC 27 E6
High Point NC 191 B1
Eastern Av
Nash Co NC 33 D6
N Eastern Blvd
Fayetteville NC 107 A1
Fayetteville NC 222 E3
N Eastern Blvd I-95
BUS
Fayetteville NC 107 A1
Fayetteville NC 222 E3
N Eastern Blvd US-301
Fayetteville NC 107 A1
Fayetteville NC 222 E3
S Eastern Blvd
Fayetteville NC 222 C6
S Eastern Blvd I-95
BUS
Fayetteville NC 222 C6
S Eastern Blvd US-301
Fayetteville NC 222 E4
Eastern School Rd
Sumter Co SC 140 C7
Eastfield Rd
Mecklenburg Co NC 75 D3
Eastview Rd
York Co SC 100 E3
Eastway Dr
Charlotte NC 75 D6
Eastwood Rd
New Hanover Co NC 131 A7
Eastwood Rd US-74
New Hanover Co NC 131 A7
Eaton Ferry Rd
Warren Co NC 12 C4
Ebenezer Rd
Darlington Co SC 141 C1
Effingham Co GA 175 C6
Rock Hill SC 100 E3
Rock Hill SC 101 A3
Rock Hill SC 217 A2
Ebenezer Rd SR-274
Rock Hill SC 100 E3
Rock Hill SC 101 A3
Rock Hill SC 217 A2
Ebenezer Rd SR-275
Effingham Co GA 175 C6
N Ebenezer Rd
Florence Co SC 141 C2
Ebenezer Church Rd
Raleigh NC 31 C7
Raleigh NC 55 C1
Ebert Rd
Winston-Salem NC 27 A5
Winston-Salem NC 187 E7
Winston-Salem NC 188 A7
Ebert St
Winston-Salem NC 188 A7
Ebony Rd
Brunswick Co VA 12 C3
Ebony Rd SR-903
Warren Co NC 12 C3
Eckerson Rd
Guilford Co NC 28 D3

Street Index

STREET / City State / Map# Grid

Eden Dr
Boiling Spring Lakes NC 146 D4
Eden Ter
Rock Hill SC 101 A3
Edenburgh Rd
Raleigh NC 197 C7
S Edenton Rd St
Hertford NC 37 D1
S Edenton Rd St SR-37
Hertford NC 37 D1
S Edenton Rd St US-17 BUS
Hertford NC 37 D1
Edenvale Rd
Charleston Co SC 172 E7
Ederlee Dr
Cary NC 55 B3
Edgefield Hwy
Aiken Co SC 149 E4
Aiken Co SC 150 A4
Edgefield Hwy SR-19
Aiken Co SC 149 E4
Aiken Co SC 150 A4
Edgefield Hwy SR-191
Aiken Co SC 149 E4
Edgefield Rd
Aiken Co SC 149 C6
North Augusta SC 149 C7
York Co SC 100 B3
Edgefield Rd SR-121
Edgefield Co SC 149 C5
North Augusta SC 149 C7
Edgefield Rd US-25
Edgefield Co SC 149 C5
North Augusta SC 149 C7
Edgeland Rd
Chester Co SC 101 A7
Edgeland Rd SR-901
Chester Co SC 101 A7
Edgemont Rd
Wake Co NC 56 B1
Edgewood Av
Burlington NC 29 B4
Burlington NC 192 A4
Edgewood Rd
Bessemer City NC 74 B5
N Edgeworth St
Greensboro NC 190 C2
S Edgeworth St
Greensboro NC 190 C3
S Edisto Dr
Florence SC 141 D2
Florence SC 230 B7
Edisto River Rd
Bamberg Co SC 162 C5
Edisto River Rd SR-61
Bamberg Co SC 162 C5
Edmonds Rd
Grayson Co VA 4 B3
Edmund Hwy
Lexington Co SC 137 D7
Lexington Co SC 151 C2
Springdale SC 137 E7
Edmund Hwy SR-302
Cayce SC 137 E7
Lexington Co SC 151 C2
South Congaree SC 137 D7
Edward St
Orangeburg Co SC 162 D5
Edward St US-78
Orangeburg Co SC 162 D5
Edward E Burroughs Hwy
Horry Co SC 143 A4
Horry Co SC 157 D1
Myrtle Beach SC 158 A2
Edward E Burroughs Hwy US-501
Conway SC 157 D1
Horry Co SC 143 A4
Myrtle Beach SC 158 A2
Edward R Murrow Blvd
Greensboro NC 190 D3
Edwards Dr
Mt Pleasant SC 238 D7
Edwards Rd
Greenville Co SC 97 B4
Marlboro Co SC 125 D3
Edwards St
Summerton SC 154 A5
Edwards Mill Rd
Raleigh NC 198 B2
Wake Co NC 55 C1
Edwina Rd
Cocke Co TN 43 A1
Edwina Rd SR-73
Cocke Co TN 43 A1
E Effingham Hwy
Florence Co SC 141 E4
E Effingham Hwy SR-327
Florence Co SC 141 E4
W Ehringhaus St
Elizabeth City NC 17 B6
W Ehringhaus St US-17 BUS
Elizabeth City NC 17 B6
W Ehringhause St
Elizabeth City NC 184 A5
W Ehringhause St US-17 BUS
Elizabeth City NC 184 A5
Ela Rd
Swain Co NC 68 C2
Ela Rd US-19
Swain Co NC 68 C2
Elam Rd
Brunswick Co VA 12 C2
Elams Rd
Warren Co NC 12 C3
Elams Rd SR-903
Warren Co NC 12 C3
Elba St
Durham NC 193 C3
Elberton Hwy
Hart Co GA 116 D7
Lincoln Co GA 133 C7
Elberton Hwy SR-17
Wilkes Co GA 133 A7
Elberton Hwy SR-77
Hart Co GA 116 D7
Elberton Hwy SR-79
Lincoln Co GA 133 C7
Elberton Hwy SR-184
Anderson Co SC 133 B1
Elden Rd
Charleston Co SC 166 B7
Eldorado Rd
Troy NC 78 A3
Eldorado Rd SR-109
Troy NC 78 A3
Eliada Home Rd
Asheville NC 44 C6
Elizabeth Ln N
Rock Hill SC 217 C5
Elizabeth Ln S
Rock Hill SC 217 B5
E Elizabeth St
Elizabeth City NC 184 C4
E Elizabeth St US-158
Elizabeth City NC 184 C4
W Elizabeth St
Clinton NC 108 D2
Elizabeth City NC 184 C3
Jefferson SC 123 E1
W Elizabeth St SR-265
Jefferson SC 123 E1
W Elizabeth St US-158
Elizabeth City NC 184 C3
Elizabethton Hwy
Carter Co TN 21 C1
Elizabethton Hwy SR-91
Carter Co TN 21 C1
Elizabethtown Hwy
Sampson Co NC 108 A3
Elizabethtown Hwy SR-242
Sampson Co NC 108 A3
Elk Creek Pkwy
Grayson Co VA 3 C2
Elk Creek Pkwy US-21
Grayson Co VA 3 C2
Elk Creek Rd
Watauga Co NC 23 C3
Elkin Hwy
Wilkes Co NC 24 E3
Wilkes Co NC 25 A2
Elkin Hwy SR-268
Wilkes Co NC 24 E3
Wilkes Co NC 25 A2
Elkin Rd
North Wilkesboro NC 24 D3
Elkin Rd SR-268
North Wilkesboro NC 24 D3
Elkins Branch Rd
Buncombe Co NC 44 E3
Elk Mountain Rd
Woodfin NC 44 D5
Elk Park Hwy
Avery Co NC 22 C4
Elk Park Hwy SR-194
Avery Co NC 22 C4
Ellejoy Rd
Blount Co TN 41 A3
Ellenboro Rd
Cleveland Co NC 73 A4
Ellenboro Rd US-74 BUS
Cleveland Co NC 73 A4
Ellenton St
Barnwell Co SC 161 A4
Ellenton St US-278
Barnwell SC 161 A4
Ellington St
Greensboro NC 189 E4
Elliot Hwy
Lee Co SC 140 C5
Elliot Hwy SR-527
Lee Co SC 140 C5
N Ellis Av
Dunn NC 81 E3
Ellis Rd
Durham NC 31 A6
Ellisboro Rd
Rockingham Co NC 6 E7
Rockingham Co NC 27 E1
Ellison Rd
Stokesdale NC 28 A2
Elm Ln
Charlotte NC 101 D1
Elm Rd
Lowrys SC 100 C6
Elm St
Horry Co SC 143 C5
Elm St SR-319
Horry Co SC 143 C5
E Elm St
Goldsboro NC 83 D2
Goldsboro NC 204 E5
Graham NC 29 D4
E Elm St SR-49
Graham NC 29 C4
N Elm St
Greensboro NC 28 C4
Greensboro NC 190 C2
High Point NC 191 B3
Marshville NC 102 E2
Pageland SC 102 E6
N Elm St SR-205
Marshville NC 102 E2
N Elm St SR-207
Pageland SC 102 E6
S Elm St
Greenville NC 59 B4
Greenville NC 203 D2
High Point NC 191 C5
W Elm St
Goldsboro NC 83 C2
Goldsboro NC 204 A4
Elm City Rd N
Elm City NC 57 E1
Wilson Co NC 57 E2
S Elm-Eugene St
Greensboro NC 28 C5
Greensboro NC 190 C7
Elmwood Av
Richland Co SC 233 B2
Elmwood Av US-21
Richland Co SC 233 B2
Elmwood Av US-76
Richland Co SC 233 B2
Elmwood Av US-176
Richland Co SC 233 B2
Elmwood Av US-321
Richland Co SC 233 B2
Elon Byp
Elon College NC 29 B4
Elon Byp SR-100
Alamance Co NC 29 B4
N Elwell Ferry Rd
Bladen Co NC 129 C4
S Elwell Ferry Rd
Bladen Co NC 129 C4
Emanuel Church Rd
Lexington Co SC 137 D6
Emerald Dr
Emerald Isle NC 112 C6
Emerald Dr SR-58
Emerald Isle NC 112 C6
Emma Rd
Buncombe Co NC 44 D6
Emmanuel Church Rd
Conover NC 48 D5
W End Av
Statesville NC 49 C3
W End Av SR-90
Statesville NC 49 B3
Engineer Rd
Aiken Co SC 150 B2
Engineer Rd SR-392
Aiken Co SC 150 B2
English Rd
High Point NC 27 E7
High Point NC 191 A6
E English Rd
High Point NC 191 C4
Enka Lake Rd
Buncombe Co NC 44 C7
Ennis Rd
Union Co NC 101 D2
N Enochville Av
Rowan Co NC 50 A7
Enochville School Rd
Rowan Co NC 50 A7
Enola Rd
Morganton NC 47 B4
Enon Church Rd
Rowan Co NC 50 B4
Enterprise Rd
Warren Co NC 12 C3
Enterprise Rd SR-903
Warren Co NC 12 C3
Ephesus Church Rd
Durham Co NC 30 D7
Epworth Camp Rd E
Greenwood Co SC 135 A4
Epworth Camp Rd E SR-44
Greenwood Co SC 135 A4
Ernest Johnson Rd
Aiken Co SC 151 A5
Ernest Vandiver Hwy
Banks Co GA 115 B7
Franklin Co GA 116 A5
Ernest Vandiver Hwy I-85
Banks Co GA 115 B7
Franklin Co GA 116 A5
Ernest Vandiver Hwy SR-403
Banks Co GA 115 B7
Lavonia GA 116 A5
Erskine Rd
Anderson Co SC 117 D5
Erwin Hwy
Greene Co TN 20 B4
Unicoi Co TN 21 B3
Erwin Hwy SR-107
Greene Co TN 20 B4
Unicoi Co TN 21 B3
Erwin Hwy SR-351
Greene Co TN 20 B4
Erwin Rd
Chapel Hill NC 30 D6
Durham NC 193 D3
Estes Dr
Carrboro NC 195 A5
Chapel Hill NC 195 B3
N Estes Dr
Chapel Hill NC 30 C7
Chapel Hill NC 195 D3
S Estes Dr
Chapel Hill NC 195 E4
Estes Dr Ext
Chapel Hill NC 30 C7
Chapel Hill NC 195 A4
Ethel Rd
Spartanburg Co SC 98 B3
Etowah Pike
McMinn Co TN 65 B3
Etowah Pike SR-33
McMinn Co TN 65 B3
Etowah Pike US-411
McMinn Co TN 65 B3
Eubanks Rd
Orange Co NC 30 C6
N Eugene St
Greensboro NC 190 C2
S Eugene St
Greensboro NC 190 C4
Eutaw Hwy
Orangeburg Co SC 164 A2
Eutaw Hwy SR-453
Orangeburg Co SC 164 A2
Eutaw Rd
Holly Hill SC 163 E3
Orangeburg Co SC 164 A2
Eutaw Rd SR-453
Holly Hill SC 163 E3
Orangeburg Co SC 164 A2
Evans Rd
Cary NC 55 B1
Macon Co NC 67 D6
Wake Co NC 55 B2
S Evans St
Greenville NC 59 B5
Greenville NC 203 C2
Evans to Locks Rd
Columbia Co GA 149 A6
Everett Rd
Transylvania Co NC 70 C5
Evins St
Spartanburg SC 224 B2
Exchange Dr
Laurens SC 119 B4
Exchange Dr US-76 BYP
Laurens SC 119 B4
Exchange Dr US-221 TRK
Laurens SC 119 B4

F

Fain St
North Charleston SC 173 A3
Fair Bluff Rd
Robeson Co NC 127 D6
Faircloth Frwy
Sampson Co NC 108 D2
Faircloth Frwy US-421
Sampson Co NC 108 D2
Faircloth St
Raleigh NC 199 A2
Fairfield Rd
Chester Co SC 121 A2
Richland Co SC 138 A5
Fairfield Rd SR-215
Chester Co SC 121 A2
Fairfield Rd US-321
Richland Co SC 138 A5
E Fairfield Rd
Guilford Co NC 28 A7
Guilford Co NC 191 E7
E Fairfield Rd SR-610
Archdale NC 28 A7
W Fairfield Rd
High Point NC 27 E7
Fairforest Wy
Greenville Co SC 97 B6
Fairley Rd
Robeson Co NC 126 D2
Fairmont Av
Mt Pleasant SC 238 D6
Fairmont Rd
Iredell Co NC 49 C1
E Fairplay Blvd
Oconee Co SC 116 C4
E Fairplay Blvd SR-243
Oconee Co SC 116 C4
Fairplay Rd
Anderson Co SC 116 E4
Fairplay Rd SR-243
Anderson Co SC 116 E4
Fairview Dr
Lexington NC 51 A3
Fairview Rd
Charlotte NC 75 C7
Greenville Co SC 97 C4
Laurens Co SC 118 C2
Lexington Co SC 150 D1
Lexington Co SC 151 B3
Mint Hill NC 76 A6
Raleigh NC 55 D2
Raleigh NC 199 E1
Fairview Rd SR-218
Mint Hill NC 76 A6
Fairview Rd US-178
Lexington Co SC 150 D1
Lexington Co SC 151 B3
N Fairview Rd
Rocky Mount NC 34 A6
N Fairview Rd SR-43 BUS
Rocky Mount NC 34 A6
Fairview St
Fountain Inn SC 118 D1
Fairwood Rd
Grayson Co VA 2 C1
Faison Dr
Richland Co SC 138 A4
Faison Hwy
Sampson Co NC 82 E7
Sampson Co NC 83 A6
Sampson Co NC 108 E1
Faison Hwy SR-403
Sampson Co NC 82 E7
Sampson Co NC 83 A6
Sampson Co NC 108 E1
Faith Rd
Salisbury NC 208 D6
Falling Creek Rd
Hickory NC 48 B3
Falls Rd
Rocky Mount NC 34 A6
Toccoa GA 115 C2
Falls Rd SR-17 ALT
Toccoa GA 115 C2
Falls Rd SR-43 BUS
Rocky Mount NC 34 A6
Falls Rd SR-48
Rocky Mount NC 34 A6
Falls of Neuse Rd
Raleigh NC 31 D7
Fallston Rd
Cleveland Co NC 73 D3
Fallston Rd SR-18
Cleveland Co NC 73 D3
Fancy Gap Hwy
Carroll Co VA 4 E1
Carroll Co VA 5 A3
Fancy Gap Hwy US-52
Carroll Co VA 4 E1
Carroll Co VA 5 A3
Fancy Hill Rd
Gaston Co NC 74 D3
Fanny Brown Rd
Wake Co NC 55 D5
E Faris Rd
Greenville SC 97 A5
Greenville SC 223 D6
W Faris Rd
Greenville SC 223 A7
Farley Av
Spartanburg Co SC 98 B3
Spartanburg Co SC 224 A3
Farmdale Rd
Screven Co GA 168 B7
Farm Gate Rd
Raleigh NC 55 C2
Farming Creek Rd
Richland Co SC 137 C4
Farmington Rd
Berkeley Co SC 172 D1
Davie Co NC 26 C6
Farrington Rd
Chatham Co NC 54 D2
Farrington Mill Rd
Durham Co NC 54 D1
Farrington Point Rd
Chatham Co NC 54 D1
Farrow Rd
Arcadia Lakes SC 138 B4
Richland Co SC 138 B2
Farrow Rd SR-555
Richland Co SC 138 B4
Farrs Bridge Rd
Pickens Co SC 96 C5
Farrs Bridge Rd SR-183
Pickens Co SC 96 C5
Faust St
Bamberg Co SC 162 A4
Fayette St
Martinsville VA 7 A1
Fayette St SR-457
Martinsville VA 7 A1
Fayetteville Hwy
Newton Grove NC 82 D4
Sampson Co NC 81 E6
Sampson Co NC 82 A6
Fayetteville Hwy US-13
Newton Grove NC 82 D4
Sampson Co NC 81 E6
Sampson Co NC 82 A6
Fayetteville Rd
Durham Co NC 30 E7
Robeson Co NC 106 D7
Rockingham NC 104 D3
Wake Co NC 55 C5
Fayetteville Rd US-1
Rockingham NC 104 D3
Fayetteville Rd US-301
Robeson Co NC 106 D7
Fayetteville Rd US-401
Hoke Co NC 106 B2
Wake Co NC 55 C5
Fayetteville St
Durham NC 30 E6
N Fayetteville St
Asheboro NC 52 C4
Asheboro NC 209 C5
N Fayetteville St US-220 BUS
Asheboro NC 52 C4
Asheboro NC 209 C5
S Fayetteville St
Asheboro NC 52 C5
Asheboro NC 209 C7
S Fayetteville St US-220 BUS
Asheboro NC 52 C5
Asheboro NC 209 C7
Feaster Rd
Greenville Co SC 97 C6
Federal Rd
Benson NC 82 A2
Federal Rd SR-242
Benson NC 82 A2
Ferguson Av
Chatham Co GA 181 A5
Ferguson Rd
Mecklenburg Co NC 76 B6
Ferguson Ridge Rd
Gaston Co NC 74 C6
Fernwood Dr
Spartanburg SC 98 D3
Ferrell Rd
Durham Co NC 31 A5
Ferry Rd
Craven Co NC 112 E2
Craven Co NC 113 A2
Ferry Rd SR-306
Craven Co NC 112 E2
Craven Co NC 113 A2
Fertilizer Rd
Brunswick Co NC 130 A6
Festival Trail Rd
Salley SC 151 B7
Festival Trail Rd SR-39
Aiken Co SC 151 B6
Salley SC 151 B7
Fews Bridge Rd
Greenville Co SC 97 B2
Fews Chapel Rd
Greenville Co SC 97 C2
F Guerry Rd
Williamsburg Co SC 155 E5
F Hugh Atkins Hwy
Spartanburg Co SC 98 A3
F Hugh Atkins Hwy I-85
Spartanburg Co SC 98 A3
S Fieldcrest Rd
Eden NC 7 D4
S Fieldcrest Rd SR-700
Eden NC 7 D4
W Fieldcrest Rd
Eden NC 7 D4
Fields Dr
Sanford NC 80 B1
S Fields St
Pitt Co NC 58 D5
Fieldside Rd
Orangeburg Co SC 162 A2
Fieldside Rd SR-332
Cope SC 162 A2
Fifty Lakes Dr
Boiling Spring Lakes NC 146 D4
W Finch Av
Middlesex NC 56 E2
W Finch Av US-264 ALT
Middlesex NC 56 E2
Fines Creek Rd
Haywood Co NC 43 C5
Finley Cove Rd
Henderson Co NC 70 E4
Firestone Pkwy NE
Wilson Co NC 57 E2
Fire Tower Rd
Dillon Co SC 126 B5
Lee Co NC 80 B1
Rock Hill SC 217 E6
York Co SC 101 A4
Firetower Rd
Irmo SC 137 D4
Fire Tower Rd SR-34
Dillon Co SC 126 B5
E Fire Tower Rd
Greenville NC 59 B5
Pitt Co NC 203 D7
E Fisher Av
Greensboro NC 190 C2
W Fisher Av
Greensboro NC 190 C2
Fisher Rd
Cumberland Co NC 106 D2
Gaston Co NC 73 E2
N Fisher St
Burlington NC 29 C4
Burlington NC 192 D3
N Fisher St SR-62
Burlington NC 29 C4
Burlington NC 192 D3
N Fisher St US-70
Burlington NC 29 C4
Burlington NC 192 D3
S Fisher St
Burlington NC 192 C3
S Fisher St SR-62
Burlington NC 192 C3
S Fisher St US-70
Burlington NC 192 C3
Fishers Farm Rd
Henry Co VA 7 A2
Fishers Gap Rd
Grayson Co VA 4 B3
Fish Hatchery Rd
Burke Co NC 46 D2
Hamblen Co TN 19 A3
Fish Hatchery Rd SR-340
Hamblen Co TN 19 A3
Fishing Creek Church Rd
Chester Co SC 100 E6
Chester Co SC 101 A6
N Fish Trap Rd
Pickens Co SC 96 E5
Five Chop Rd
Orangeburg Co SC 162 D1
Orangeburg Co SC 163 A1
Five Chop Rd US-301
Orangeburg Co SC 162 D1
Orangeburg Co SC 163 A1
Five Forks Rd
Greenville Co SC 97 C6
Warren Co NC 12 A4
Five Forks Rd SR-296
Greenville Co SC 97 C6
Five Notch Rd
Edgefield Co SC 134 E7
Edgefield Co SC 135 A7
Edgefield Co SC 149 A1
Five Notch Rd SR-67
Edgefield Co SC 134 E6
W Five Notch Rd
North Augusta SC 149 C7
Flat Creek Rd
Buncombe Co NC 45 C7
Lancaster Co SC 101 E7
Lancaster Co SC 102 A7
Lancaster Co SC 123 A1
Flat Creek Rd SR-903
Lancaster Co SC 101 E7
Lancaster Co SC 102 A7
Lancaster Co SC 123 A1
Flat Creek Church Rd
Buncombe Co NC 44 D4
Flat Ridge Rd
Grayson Co VA 2 E2
Grayson Co VA 3 A2
Flat Rock Rd
Lancaster Co SC 123 B6
S Flat Swamp Rd
Beaufort Co NC 86 C2
E Fleming Dr
Morganton NC 47
E Fleming Dr US-70
Morganton NC 47
Fleming Rd
Greensboro NC 28
Fleming St
Laurens SC 119
Fleming St US-76 BYP
Laurens SC 119
Fleming St US-221 TRK
Laurens SC 119
Fleming Station Rd
Liberty Co GA 180
Fleming Station Rd SR-196
Liberty Co GA 180
Flemming Mill Rd
Warren Co NC 12
Fletcher Martin Rd
Buncombe Co NC 44
Fletcher's Chapel Rd
Durham Co NC 31
Flint Dr
Burnettown SC 149
Flint Hill Rd
Alleghany Co NC 3
Buncombe Co NC 44
Cleveland Co NC 73
East Bend NC 26
Flint Hill Rd SR-113
Alleghany Co NC 3
Flora Dr
Richland Co SC 138
Florence Hwy
Lynchburg SC 140
Florence Hwy US-76
Lynchburg SC 140
Florence Rd
Pamlico Co NC 87
Florida Av
Greenwood Co SC 134
E Florida St
Greensboro NC 190
W Florida St
Greensboro NC 28
Greensboro NC 189
Greensboro NC 190
Flowes Store Rd
Cabarrus Co NC 76
Floyd Rd
Spartanburg Co SC 98
W Floyd Baker Blvd
Gaffney SC 99
W Floyd Baker Blvd SR-11
Gaffney SC 99
Floyds Rd
Darlington Co SC 125
Flyway Dr
Kiawah Island SC 178
Folk Rd
Richland Co SC 138
Folly Rd
Charleston Co SC 173
Sumter Co SC 139
Folly Rd SR-171
Charleston Co SC 173
Folly Rd SR-441
Sumter Co SC 139
Folly Rd Blvd
Charleston SC 173
Charleston SC 240
Folly Rd Blvd SR-171
Charleston SC 173
Charleston SC 240
Fontana Blvd
Havelock NC 112
Fontana Blvd SR-101
Havelock NC 112
Foothills Pkwy
Blount Co TN 41
Cocke Co TN 42
Foothills Pkwy SR-339
Cocke Co TN 42
Forbes Rd
Gaston Co NC 74
Forbush Rd
Yadkin Co NC 26
Ford Av
Richmond Hill GA 180
Ford Av SR-144
Richmond Hill GA 180
Fordham Blvd
Greensboro NC 28
Greensboro NC 189
Greensboro NC 190
Fordham Blvd I-40
Greensboro NC 28
Greensboro NC 189
Greensboro NC 190
Fordham Blvd US-220
Greensboro NC 190
Fordham Blvd US-421
Greensboro NC 28
Greensboro NC 189
Greensboro NC 190
N Fordham Blvd
Chapel Hill NC 30
N Fordham Blvd US-15
Chapel Hill NC 30
N Fordham Blvd US-501
Chapel Hill NC 30
Fording Island Rd
Beaufort Co SC 176
Beaufort Co SC 181
Fording Island Rd US-278
Beaufort Co SC 176
Beaufort Co SC 181
Forest Dr
Columbia SC 138

INDEX 20
rest Dr
Street Index
Governor John Sevier

STREET
City State Map# Grid

rest Dr
chland Co SC 234 E1
rest Dr SR-12
olumbia SC 138 B5
chland Co SC 234 A2
rest St
nesville SC 99 A5
Forest St
artanburg SC 98 C4
artanburg SC 224 B5
Forest Beach Dr
ilton Head Island SC 181 E3
ilton Head Island SC 242 A7
Forest Beach Dr
-243
ilton Head Island SC 242 A7
restbrook Rd
orry Co SC 157 E3
orry Co SC 158 A3
rest Lawn Dr
dian Trail NC 101 E1
restville Rd
ake Co NC 56 A1
ake Forest NC 32 A6
rge Creek Rd
lount Co TN 41 A7
hnson Co TN 1 E5
hnson Co TN 2 A5
rge Creek Rd SR-167
hnson Co TN 1 E5
hnson Co TN 2 A5
Fork Rd
uilford Co NC 28 A6
Fork Rd
uncombe Co NC 45 B3
Fork Rd SR-197
uncombe Co NC 45 B3
rk Shoals Rd
reenville Co SC 97 B7
reenville Co SC 118 B1
rrest Dr
urry Co NC 183 B7
rrester Dr
auldin SC 97 C6
rt Argyle Rd
hatham Co GA 180 B4
rt Argyle Rd SR-204
hatham Co GA 180 B4
rt Fisher Blvd N
ew Hanover Co NC 147 A4
rt Fisher Blvd N
S-421
ure Beach NC 147 A4
rt Fisher Blvd S
ure Beach NC 147 A5
ew Hanover Co NC 146 E5
rt Fisher Blvd S
S-421
ure Beach NC 147 A5
ew Hanover Co NC 146 E5
rt Jackson Blvd
ichland Co SC 234 D4
rt Jackson Blvd
R-760
ichland Co SC 234 D4
rt Jackson Rd
ershaw Co SC 138 E3
ershaw Co SC 139 A3
rt Jackson Rd SR-12
ershaw Co SC 138 E3
ershaw Co SC 139 A3
rt Johnson Rd
harleston Co SC 173 B6
rt Macon Dr W
tlantic Beach NC 113 B6
rt Macon Dr W SR-58
tlantic Beach NC 113 B6
Fort Macon Rd
tlantic Beach NC 113 B6
tlantic Beach NC 228 C7
arteret Co NC 113 C6
Fort Macon Rd SR-58
tlantic Beach NC 113 B6
tlantic Beach NC 228 C7
rt McAllister Rd
ryan Co GA 180 C7
rt McAllister Rd
R-144 SPUR
ryan Co GA 180 C7
rt Mott Rd
alhoun Co SC 153 B4
rt Mott Rd SR-419
alhoun Co SC 153 B4
rt Prince Blvd
yman SC 97 E3
partanburg Co SC 98 A3
rt Prince Blvd
R-129
yman SC 97 E3
partanburg Co SC 98 A3
rt Prince Blvd
R-292
yman SC 97 E3
oster Rd
partanburg Co SC 72 A7
ountain Inn Rd
partanburg Co SC 98 A7
ountain Inn Rd SR-418
partanburg Co SC 98 A7
ourmile Lp
uilford Co NC 28 D4
ourmile Lp US-70
uilford Co NC 28 D4
Foxworth Mill Rd
umter Co SC 140 A5
raley Rd
igh Point NC 191 D7
rancis Av
reat Falls SC 122 B2
rancis Av SR-97
hester Co SC 122 B2

Francis Marion Rd
Florence Co SC 141 E5
Florence Co SC 142 A5
Francis Marion Rd
SR-327
Florence Co SC 142 A3
Francis Peter Fensel
Hwy
New Hanover Co NC 130 D6
Francis Peter Fensel
Hy US-421
New Hanover Co NC 130 D6
Frank C Wilson Hwy
Richmond Co NC 104 E4
Richmond Co NC 105 A3
Frank C Wilson Hwy
SR-177
Richmond Co NC 104 E4
Richmond Co NC 105 A3
Franklin Blvd
Greensboro NC 28 D5
E Franklin Blvd
Gastonia NC 210 C4
E Franklin Blvd US-29
Gastonia NC 210 C4
E Franklin Blvd US-74
Gastonia NC 210 C4
W Franklin Blvd
Gastonia NC 74 C5
Gastonia NC 210 A4
W Franklin Blvd SR-274
Gastonia NC 210 A4
W Franklin Blvd US-29
Gastonia NC 74 C5
Gastonia NC 210 A4
W Franklin Blvd US-74
Gastonia NC 74 C5
Gastonia NC 210 A4
S Franklin Rd
Surry Co NC 5 A5
Surry Co NC 183 B6
E Franklin St
Chapel Hill NC 195 E2
Hartwell GA 116 D7
Monroe NC 102 C3
Monroe NC 218 C5
E Franklin St SR-8
Hartwell GA 116 D7
E Franklin St US-29
Hartwell GA 116 D7
W Franklin St
Monroe NC 102 B3
Monroe NC 218 A4
W Franklin St SR-75
Monroe NC 102 B3
Monroe NC 218 A4
W Franklin St SR-84
Monroe NC 102 B3
Monroe NC 218 A4
Franklin Tpk
Danville VA 8 C1
Franklin Tpk SR-41
Danville VA 8 C1
Franklin Church Rd
Franklin Co GA 116 A6
Franklin Church Rd
SR-327
Franklin Co GA 116 A6
Frank Stanton Rd
Washington Co TN 20 C3
N Fraser St
Georgetown Co SC 157 B7
Georgetown Co SC 167 A1
N Fraser St US-701
Georgetown Co SC 157 B7
Georgetown Co SC 167 A1
S Fraser St
Georgetown SC 167 A3
Georgetown Co SC 166 E4
S Fraser St US-17
Georgetown SC 167 A3
Georgetown Co SC 166 E4
S Fraser St US-701
Georgetown SC 167 A3
Georgetown Co SC 166 E4
E Frederick St
Gaffney SC 99 B2
E Frederick St SR-18
Gaffney SC 99 B2
Fred W Scott Hwy
Burnettown SC 149 D7
Fred W Scott Hwy
SR-421
Burnettown SC 149 D7
Freedom Dr
Charlotte NC 75 B5
Charlotte NC 215 D2
Freedom Dr SR-27
Charlotte NC 75 B5
Freedom Rd
Branchville SC 162 D5
Orangeburg Co SC 162 D4
Freedom Rd US-21
Branchville SC 162 D5
Orangeburg Co SC 162 D4
Freedom Rd US-78
Branchville SC 162 D5
Freedom Wy
Onslow Co NC 111 D6
Onslow Co NC 112 A6
Freedom Wy SR-24
Onslow Co NC 111 D6
Onslow Co NC 112 A6
Freedom Mill Rd
Gaston Co NC 74 B6
Freeman Rd
Durham Co NC 31 A5
Freeman Mill Rd
Greensboro NC 28 C5
Greensboro NC 190 A6
Freeway Dr
Rockingham Co NC 7 D7

Freeway Dr SR-87
Rockingham Co NC 7 D7
French Santee Rd
Berkeley Co SC 166 A4
French Santee Rd SR-45
Berkeley Co SC 166 A4
Freshly Mill Rd
Richland Co SC 137 C3
Frieden Church Rd
Guilford Co NC 28 E4
Guilford Co NC 29 A3
Friendfield Rd
Coward SC 141 D6
E Friendfield Rd
Florence Co SC 141 E6
S Friendfield Rd
Florence Co SC 142 A6
E Friendly Av
Greensboro NC 190 D2
W Friendly Av
Greensboro NC 28 B4
Greensboro NC 189 E2
Greensboro NC 190 B2
Friendly Woods Rd
Richland Co SC 137 E3
Richland Co SC 138 A3
Friendship Rd
Oconee Co SC 116 D2
Friendship Church Rd
Guilford Co NC 28 E3
Friendship Patterson
Mill Rd
Alamance Co NC 29 B6
Fries Rd
Carroll Co VA 4 A1
Frink St
Cayce SC 137 E6
Lexington Co SC 233 A7
Frink St SR-2
Cayce SC 137 E6
Front St
Pink Hill NC 84 B7
Front St SR-241
Lenoir Co NC 84 B7
E Front St
Iva SC 117 B7
E Front St SR-15
Iva SC 117 B7
N Front St
Wilmington NC 231 A3
S Front St
Wilmington NC 231 A5
W Front St
Burlington NC 29 B4
Burlington NC 192 A3
Lillington NC 81 B2
Statesville NC 49 B3
Ward SC 150 A1
W Front St SR-23
Ward SC 150 A1
W Front St SR-90
Statesville NC 49 B3
W Front St US-64
Statesville NC 49 B3
W Front St US-421
Harnett Co NC 81 B2
Fruitland Rd
Henderson Co NC 71 A3
Fulcher Rd
Hephzibah GA 159 A5
Fullwood Ln
Matthews NC 75 E7
Fulmer Rd
Richland Co SC 138 A2
Fulton St
Durham NC 193 C3
N Fulton St
Salisbury NC 208 C4
S Fulton St
Salisbury NC 208 C4
W Fulton St
Sumter SC 235 D5
Furman L Fendley Hwy
Union Co SC 99 A5
Furman L Fendley Hwy
US-176
Union Co SC 99 A5
Furrys Ferry Rd
Columbia Co GA 148 E5
Furrys Ferry Rd SR-28
Columbia Co GA 148 E5
Furse Mill Rd
Allendale Co SC 160 D7
Furys Ferry Rd
Columbia Co GA 148 E6
Columbia Co GA 149 A6
Furys Ferry Rd SR-28
Columbia Co GA 148 E6
Columbia Co GA 149 A6

G

G St
Elizabethton TN 21 C1
G St SR-67
Elizabethton TN 21 C1
G St US-321
Elizabethton TN 21 C1
W G St
Elizabethton TN 21 C1
W G St SR-67
Elizabethton TN 21 C1
Gaddys Mill Rd
Robeson Co NC 126 D1
Gaffney Hwy
Union Co SC 99 B5
Gaffney Hwy SR-18
Union Co SC 99 B5
Gaffney Rd
Cleveland Co NC 73 B6
Gaffney Rd SR-150
Cleveland Co NC 73 B6

Gaillard Rd
Berkeley Co SC 164 E6
Gaines Store Rd
Greenwood Co SC 135 A5
Gainesville Hwy
Union Co GA 92 E7
Gainesville Hwy SR-11
Union Co GA 92 E7
Gainesville Hwy SR-180
Union Co GA 92 E6
Gainesville Hwy US-19
Union Co GA 92 E7
Gainesville Hwy US-129
Union Co GA 92 E7
Galatia Rd
Northampton Co NC 14 B4
Gallbush Rd
Chesapeake VA 17 C1
Galloway Crossroads
Pitt Co NC 59 D7
E Gannon Av
Zebulon NC 56 D1
E Gannon Av SR-97
Zebulon NC 56 D1
E Gannon Av US-64 BUS
Zebulon NC 56 D1
W Gannon Av
Zebulon NC 56 C1
W Gannon Av SR-97
Zebulon NC 56 C1
Gap Creek Rd
Buncombe Co NC 71 A1
Carter Co TN 21 D2
Duncan SC 97 D3
Greene Co TN 19 C2
Gap Creek Rd SR-362
Carter Co TN 21 D2
E Gap Creek Rd
Greenville Co SC 97 D3
Garden City Conn
Horry Co SC 157 E5
Gardner Blvd
Holly Hill SC 163 E4
Gardner Blvd SR-453
Holly Hill SC 163 E4
Garland Hwy
Garland NC 108 C6
Sampson Co NC 108 D3
Garland Hwy US-701
Garland NC 108 C6
Sampson Co NC 108 D3
Garland Airport Rd
Sampson Co NC 108 C5
Garlington Rd
Greenville Co SC 97 C5
Garner Rd
Raleigh NC 55 D2
E Garner Rd
Garner NC 55 E3
Johnston Co NC 56 A4
W Garner Rd
Garner NC 55 D3
Garners Ferry Rd
Richland Co SC 138 C7
Richland Co SC 139 A7
Richland Co SC 234 E6
Garners Ferry Rd US-76
Richland Co SC 138 C7
Richland Co SC 139 A7
Richland Co SC 234 E6
Garners Ferry Rd
US-378
Richland Co SC 138 C7
Richland Co SC 139 A7
Richland Co SC 234 E6
N Garnett St
Henderson NC 11 B6
N Garnett St US-1 BUS
Henderson NC 11 B6
N Garnett St US-158
Henderson NC 11 B6
Garren Creek Rd
Buncombe Co NC 45 B7
Buncombe Co NC 71 B1
Garrett Rd
Durham NC 30 D6
E Garrison Blvd
Gastonia NC 74 D5
Garrison Rd
Greenville Co SC 118 B1
Gasburg Rd
Brunswick Co VA 12 D2
S Gaston St
Dallas NC 74 D4
Gaston Day School Rd
Gastonia NC 74 D6
Gastonia Hwy
Lincoln Co NC 74 C2
Gastonia Hwy US-321
BUS
Lincoln Co NC 74 C2
Gaston-Webbs Chapel Rd
Lincoln Co NC 74 B2
Gates Rd
Suffolk VA 15 D1
Gates Rd E-615
Suffolk VA 15 D1
Gate Two Rd
Granville Co NC 31 C3
Geer Hwy
Greenville Co SC 96 E2
Greenville Co SC 97 A3
Transylvania Co NC 70 C7
Geer Hwy US-276
Greenville Co SC 96 E2
Greenville Co SC 97 A3
Transylvania Co NC 70 C7
E Geer St
Durham Co NC 31 B5
General Howe Rd
Columbus Co NC 129 E6

General Howe Rd SR-11
Columbus Co NC 129 E6
N Generals Blvd
Lincolnton NC 74 C1
N Generals Blvd
US-321 BUS
Lincolnton NC 74 C1
S Generals Blvd
Lincolnton NC 74 C1
S Generals Blvd SR-150
Lincolnton NC 74 C1
S Generals Blvd
US-321 BUS
Lincolnton NC 74 C1
General Thomas Hwy
Newsoms VA 14 D1
General Thomas Hwy
E-671
Newsoms VA 14 D1
Genoble Rd
Spartanburg Co SC 97 D4
N George St
Goldsboro NC 204 B3
Rocky Mount NC 201 D4
N George St US-64 BUS
Rocky Mount NC 201 D4
N George St US-70 BUS
Goldsboro NC 204 B3
S George St
Goldsboro NC 83 C2
Goldsboro NC 204 A5
S George St US-117 BUS
Goldsboro NC 83 C2
George Hildebran
School Rd
Burke Co NC 47 D5
George II Hwy SE
Boiling Spring Lakes NC 146 C4
George II Hwy SE SR-87
Boiling Spring Lakes NC 146 C4
George Rogers Blvd
Richland Co SC 233 D7
George S Coble
Memorial Hwy
Davidson Co NC 27 B7
Davidson Co NC 51 A2
George S Coble Mem
Hwy SR-8
Davidson Co NC 51 A2
George S Coble Mem
Hwy US-52
Davidson Co NC 27 B7
Davidson Co NC 51 A2
S Georgetown Hwy
Florence Co SC 156 D2
S Georgetown Hwy SR-41
Florence Co SC 156 D2
S Georgetown Hwy SR-51
Florence Co SC 156 D2
George Warren Rd
Colleton Co SC 170 D1
George Warren Rd
SR-212
Colleton Co SC 170 D1
Georgia Av
North Augusta SC 149 C7
Georgia Av US-25 BUS
North Augusta SC 149 C7
Georgia Rd
Macon Co NC 68 B7
Macon Co NC 94 B2
Georgia Rd US-23
Macon Co NC 68 B7
Macon Co NC 94 B2
Georgia Rd US-441
Macon Co NC 68 B7
Macon Co NC 94 B2
E Georgia Rd
Greenville Co SC 97 D7
Woodruff SC 98 B7
E Georgia Rd SR-417
Greenville Co SC 97 D7
W Georgia Rd
Greenville Co SC 97 C7
Greenville Co SC 118 B1
Woodruff SC 98 A7
W Georgia Rd SR-101
Woodruff SC 98 A7
German Hill Rd
Anson Co NC 103 A2
Germanton Rd
Winston-Salem NC 27 A3
Winston-Salem NC 186 C4
Germanton Rd SR-8
Winston-Salem NC 27 A3
Winston-Salem NC 186 C2
S Germanton Rd
Forsyth Co NC 27 A2
S Germanton Rd SR-8
Forsyth Co NC 27 A2
Gerton Hwy
Henderson Co NC 71 B1
Gerton Hwy US-74 ALT
Henderson Co NC 71 B1
Gervais St
Richland Co SC 233 B4
Gervais St US-1
Richland Co SC 233 B4
Gervais St US-76
Richland Co SC 233 B4
Gervais St US-378
Richland Co SC 233 B4
Gibbet Rd
Beaufort Co SC 181 B1
Gibbon Rd
Charlotte NC 75 D4
Gibbs Rd
Spartanburg Co SC 98 A3
Gibson Hwy
Marlboro Co SC 125 E1
Gibson Hwy SR-385
Marlboro Co SC 125 E1

Gibson Rd
Scotland Co NC 105 B6
Gibson Rd SR-79
Scotland Co NC 105 B6
Gilbert Rd
Buncombe Co NC 44 B5
Gilead Rd
Huntersville NC 75 C2
Gillespie St
Cumberland Co NC 107 A2
Cumberland Co NC 222 C5
Fayetteville NC 107 A1
Fayetteville NC 222 B7
Gillespie St I-95 BUS
Cumberland Co NC 107 A2
Cumberland Co NC 222 B7
Gillespie St US-301
Cumberland Co NC 107 A2
Cumberland Co NC 222 B7
Gills Creek Pkwy
Richland Co SC 234 C6
Girard Av
Sardis GA 168 A2
Girard Av SR-23
Sardis GA 168 A2
Givhans Rd
Dorchester Co SC 164 B7
Dorchester Co SC 172 A1
Ridgeville SC 164 A7
Givhans Rd SR-27
Dorchester Co SC 172 A1
Ridgeville SC 164 A7
Glascock St
Raleigh NC 55 E2
Raleigh NC 200 B2
S Glenburnie Rd
New Bern NC 86 A6
S Glenburnie Rd SR-43
New Bern NC 86 A6
Glendale Av
Durham NC 194 A1
Glendon-Carthage Rd
Moore Co NC 79 D2
Gleneagles Rd
Charlotte NC 75 C7
Glen Eden Dr
Raleigh NC 197 B6
Wake Co NC 55 C1
Wake Co NC 197 A6
N Glenn Av
Winston-Salem NC 27 B4
Winston-Salem NC 186 E6
Glenn Rd
Durham Co NC 31 A5
Glenn St
Denton NC 51 D5
Glenn St SR-109
Denton NC 51 D5
Glenn Hi Rd
Forsyth Co NC 27 C5
Glenn McConnell Pkwy
Charleston SC 172 E5
Glenn McConnll Pkwy
SR-61 SPUR
Charleston SC 172 E5
Glenns Bay Rd
Horry Co SC 157 E5
Glenn Springs Rd
Spartanburg Co SC 98 E6
Glenn Springs Rd
SR-150
Spartanburg Co SC 98 E6
Glenwood Av
Raleigh NC 31 B7
Raleigh NC 55 C1
Raleigh NC 197 C6
Raleigh NC 199 E2
Glenwood Av SR-50
Raleigh NC 197 C6
Raleigh NC 199 E2
Glenwood Av US-70
Raleigh NC 31 B7
Raleigh NC 55 C1
Raleigh NC 197 C6
Raleigh NC 199 E2
Gliden Rd
Chowan Co NC 16 B6
Gliden Rd SR-37
Chowan Co NC 16 B6
Globe Rd
Caldwell Co NC 23 A5
Durham Co NC 196 A1
Raleigh NC 31 A7
Glover St
Orangeburg SC 162 C1
Godwin Av
Lumberton NC 127 E1
Godwin-Falcon Rd
Cumberland Co NC 81 D5
Godwin-Falcon Rd SR-82
Cumberland Co NC 81 D5
Gold St
Shelby NC 73 C5
E Gold St
McCormick SC 134 C7
E Gold St US-221
McCormick SC 134 C7
E Gold St US-378
McCormick SC 134 C7
W Gold St
McCormick SC 134 C7
W Gold St US-221
McCormick SC 134 C7
W Gold St US-378
McCormick SC 134 C7
Golden View Dr
Washington Co VA 1 A2
Gold Hill Rd
Cabarrus Co NC 76 C2
York Co SC 101 A1
Gold Mine Hwy
Lancaster Co SC 123 C2

Gold Mine Hwy US-601
Lancaster Co SC 123 C2
Goldmine Rd
Wesley Chapel NC 102 A2
Gold Rock Rd
Nash Co NC 34 A5
Gold Rock Rd SR-48
Nash Co NC 34 A5
Gold Sand Rd
Franklin Co NC 32 E2
Goldsboro Hwy
Sampson Co NC 82 D4
Goldsboro Hwy US-13
Sampson Co NC 82 D4
Goldsboro Rd
Cumberland Co NC 81 D6
Goldsboro Rd US-13
Cumberland Co NC 81 D6
Goldsboro St E
Wilson NC 202 C4
Goldsboro St SW
Wilson NC 57 D3
Wilson NC 202 B5
Goldview Rd
Buncombe Co NC 44 C5
Golf Club Rd
Pittsylvania Co VA 8 B2
Golf Course Rd
Chester Co SC 122 A3
Robeson Co NC 127 C4
Golf Course Rd SR-130
Robeson Co NC 127 C4
Golf Course Rd SR-138
Chester Co SC 122 A3
Goodes Rd
Halifax Co VA 9 A1
Goodes Ferry Rd
Mecklenburg Co VA 11 E1
Good Hope Church Rd
Anderson Co SC 117 B7
Goodjoin Rd
Spartanburg Co SC 97 D2
Goodjoin Rd SR-357
Spartanburg Co SC 97 D2
Good News Church Rd
Wilson Co NC 58 B3
Good News Church Rd
SR-111
Wilson Co NC 58 B3
Good Springs Rd
Aiken Co SC 149 E5
Aiken Co SC 150 A5
Goodwin Rd
Durham Co NC 30 E4
Durham Co NC 31 A4
Richland Co SC 152 D1
Goodyear Blvd
Danville VA 8 C3
N Goose Creek Blvd
Goose Creek SC 173 A1
Goose Creek SC 237 D3
N Goose Creek Blvd
US-52
Goose Creek SC 173 A2
Goose Creek SC 237 D3
S Goose Creek Blvd
Goose Creek SC 237 C5
S Goose Creek Blvd
US-52
Goose Creek SC 237 C5
Gordon Hwy
Augusta GA 159 B1
Gordon Hwy SR-10
Augusta GA 159 B1
Gordon Hwy US-78
Augusta GA 159 B1
Gordon Hwy US-278
Augusta GA 159 B1
Gordon Rd
New Hanover Co NC 131 A7
York Co SC 100 D4
Gorman St
Raleigh NC 55 C3
Gorrell St
Greensboro NC 190 E3
Goshen Rd
Effingham Co GA 180 C1
Hyde Co NC 63 A6
Goshen Back Rd
Hyde Co NC 63 A5
Gossett Rd
Spartanburg Co SC 98 D2
Gov Rd
Haywood Co NC 43 C4
Govenors Rd
Bertie Co NC 35 D2
Govenors Rd SR-308
Bertie Co NC 35 D2
Governor James B Hunt
Jr Hwy
Greene Co NC 58 C4
Gov James B Hunt Jr
Hwy US-264
Greene Co NC 58 C4
Gov John Motley
Morehead Hwy
Greensboro NC 189 E7
Guilford Co NC 28 B7
Gov John M Morehead
Hy US-220
Greensboro NC 189 E7
Guilford Co NC 28 B7
Governor John Sevier
Hwy
Cocke Co TN 19 A6
Parrottsville TN 19 B6
Governor John Sevier
Hwy SR-35
Cocke Co TN 19 A6
Parrottsville TN 19 B6

Ivy River Rd US-70 BUS **Street Index** E King

Street Index

INDEX 26

Main St SR-341 — Street Index — E Market St

STREET
City State Map# Grid

Main St SR-341
Lake City SC 155 E1
E Main St SR-385
Bennettsville SC 125 E2
E Main St SR-705
Randolph Co NC 52 C7
E Main St SR-903
Magnolia NC 109 C3
E Main St US-1
Lexington SC 137 C6
E Main St US-11
Abingdon VA 1 C1
E Main St US-15 BUS
Bennettsville SC 125 E2
E Main St US-21 BUS
Rock Hill SC 101 A4
York Co SC 217 E5
E Main St US-29
Spartanburg SC 98 D3
Spartanburg SC 224 E3
E Main St US-58
Independence VA 3 D2
E Main St US-64 BUS
Jamesville NC 60 C1
E Main St US-70
Havelock NC 112 D3
Old Fort NC 45 E6
E Main St US-74 BUS
Forest City NC 72 D4
E Main St US-76
Westminster SC 116 B1
E Main St US-76 BUS
Laurens SC 119 B4
E Main St US-78
Williston SC 160 E2
Williston SC 161 A2
E Main St US-123
Westminster SC 116 B1
E Main St US-158
Conway NC 14 C4
E Main St US-178
Dorchester Co SC 164 A6
Harleyville SC 163 E5
E Main St US-221
Independence VA 3 D2
E Main St US-221 ALT
Forest City NC 72 D4
E Main St US-221 BUS
Jefferson NC 2 E6
E Main St US-258
Murfreesboro NC 14 E4
E Main St US-321 BUS
Maiden NC 48 C7
E Main St US-411
Sevierville TN 41 E1
E Main St US-441 BUS
Franklin NC 68 C6
E Main St US-501
Rowland NC 127 A3
N Main St
Abbeville SC 134 A3
Anderson SC 117 C4
Archdale NC 27 E7
Belton SC 117 E3
Bishopville SC 140 B1
Bladenboro NC 128 C2
Boiling Springs NC 73 B5
Bulls Gap TN 19 B2
Clover SC 74 C7
Due West SC 118 B7
Fountain Inn SC 118 D1
Franklin Co NC 32 D3
Hemingway SC 156 D2
High Point NC 27 D6
Hoke Co NC 106 A2
Holly Springs NC 55 A4
Hope Mills NC 106 E2
Jefferson SC 123 E1
Kannapolis NC 50 A7
Kernersville NC 27 D4
Kershaw Co SC 123 E4
Lancaster SC 101 D7
Laurinburg NC 105 C6
Montgomery Co NC 78 C3
Mullins SC 143 A1
Newberry Co SC 120 B4
Newton NC 48 C5
Ninety Six SC 135 B3
Oakboro NC 77 A5
Salisbury NC 50 D5
Saluda SC 135 E5
Sylvania GA 168 B6
Wake Forest NC 32 A6
Walnut Cove NC 27 C1
N Main St SR-2
Towns Co GA 93 B3
N Main St SR-5
Sumter SC 235 D3
N Main St SR-5 ALT
Ellijay GA 91 B7
N Main St SR-9
Jonesville SC 99 A5
N Main St SR-9 BUS
Lancaster SC 219 C4
N Main St SR-10
Catawba NC 48 E4
N Main St SR-11
Kenansville NC 109 D2
N Main St SR-11 BUS
Bethel NC 59 B1
N Main St SR-14
Greenville Co SC 118 D1
Greer SC 97 D3
N Main St SR-16
Newton NC 48 C5
N Main St SR-17
Towns Co GA 93 B3
N Main St SR-20
Belton SC 117 E3
N Main St SR-27
Lillington NC 81 B1
N Main St SR-28
Abbeville SC 134 A2
Anderson SC 117 C4
Anderson SC 226 B1
N Main St SR-33
Tarboro NC 34 D6
N Main St SR-34
Bishopville SC 140 B1
Ninety Six SC 135 B3
N Main St SR-35
Greeneville TN 19 E3
N Main St SR-39
Cross Hill SC 119 B7
N Main St SR-41
Hemingway SC 156 D2
Mullins SC 143 A1
N Main St SR-51
Hemingway SC 156 D2
N Main St SR-55 BUS
Holly Springs NC 55 A4
N Main St SR-59
Hope Mills NC 106 E2
N Main St SR-66
Bulls Gap TN 19 B2
N Main St SR-71
Abbeville SC 134 A2
N Main St SR-72
Newberry Co SC 120 B4
N Main St SR-73
Mt Gilead NC 77 E5
Sylvania GA 168 B6
N Main St SR-90
Lenoir NC 23 C7
N Main St SR-101
Woodruff SC 98 A7
N Main St SR-115
Cornelius NC 75 C1
Iredell Co NC 49 B4
N Main St SR-121
Farmville NC 58 D5
Saluda SC 135 E6
N Main St SR-131
Bladenboro NC 128 C3
N Main St SR-134
Troy NC 78 B3
N Main St SR-146
Woodruff SC 98 A7
N Main St SR-150
Kernersville NC 27 D4
Salisbury NC 50 D5
Salisbury NC 208 D3
N Main St SR-151
Jefferson SC 123 E1
N Main St SR-152
Mooresville NC 49 D6
N Main St SR-184
Abbeville Co SC 118 B7
N Main St SR-200
Lancaster SC 219 C4
N Main St SR-205
Oakboro NC 77 A5
N Main St SR-210
Lillington NC 81 B1
N Main St SR-242
Bladenboro NC 128 C3
Salemburg NC 108 B1
N Main St SR-273
Mt Holly NC 75 A4
N Main St SR-293
Danville VA 8 C2
N Main St SR-302
South Congaree SC 137 D7
N Main St SR-341
Bishopville SC 140 B1
Kershaw Co SC 123 E4
N Main St SR-381
McColl SC 126 B1
N Main St SR-410
Bladenboro NC 128 C3
N Main St SR-903
Kenansville NC 109 D2
N Main St SR-917
Mullins SC 143 A1
N Main St US-1 ALT
Wake Forest NC 32 A6
N Main St US-13 BUS
Bethel NC 59 B1
N Main St US-15
Bishopville SC 140 B1
Society Hill SC 125 C3
Sumter Co SC 140 A6
N Main St US-15 BUS
Laurinburg NC 105 C6
N Main St US-17 ALT
Summerville SC 172 D1
N Main St US-21
Richland Co SC 138 A5
Sparta NC 3 D4
Troutman NC 49 B4
N Main St US-23 BUS
Waynesville NC 69 C1
N Main St US-29
Rowan Co NC 50 B6
Salisbury NC 50 D5
Salisbury NC 208 D3
N Main St US-29 BUS
Lexington NC 51 B2
N Main St US-52 BUS
Darlington SC 125 B7
Darlington SC 229 C3
N Main St US-64 BUS
Tarboro NC 34 D6
N Main St US-70
Salisbury NC 50 D5
Salisbury NC 208 D3
N Main St US-70 BUS
Lexington NC 51 B2
N Main St US-76
Honea Path SC 118 A5
Laurens Co SC 119 E5
Towns Co GA 93 B3
N Main St US-158
Mocksville NC 50 B1
N Main St US-178
Honea Path SC 118 A5
N Main St US-220 ALT
Montgomery Co NC 78 C3
N Main St US-220 BUS
Asheboro NC 52 C2
N Main St US-221
Rutherfordton NC 72 C3
Woodruff SC 98 A7
N Main St US-221 BUS
Marion NC 46 B4
N Main St US-258
Rich Square NC 14 C7
N Main St US-276
Mauldin SC 97 C6
N Main St US-278
Allendale SC 169 B2
N Main St US-301
Allendale SC 169 B2
N Main St US-301 BUS
Sylvania GA 168 B6
N Main St US-311
Archdale NC 27 E7
Walnut Cove NC 27 C1
N Main St US-311 BUS
High Point NC 27 E6
High Point NC 191 A1
N Main St US-321
Greeneville TN 19 E3
Lexington Co SC 151 E2
York Co SC 74 C7
N Main St US-321 ALT
Caldwell Co NC 47 E2
Lenoir NC 23 C7
N Main St US-401
Fuquay-Varina NC 55 B6
Lillington NC 81 B1
Rolesville NC 32 B7
Society Hill SC 125 C3
N Main St US-401 BUS
Laurinburg NC 105 C6
N Main St US-421
Lillington NC 81 B1
N Main St US-501
Roxboro NC 9 D5
N Main St US-501 BUS
Laurinburg NC 105 C6
Marion SC 142 D2
N Main St US-521 BUS
Lancaster SC 101 D7
Lancaster SC 219 C3
N Main St US-701
Conway SC 143 D7
NE Main St
Simpsonville SC 97 C7
NE Main St SR-14
Simpsonville SC 97 C7
NE Main St SR-417
Simpsonville SC 97 C7
S Main St
Alamance Co NC 29 C5
Anderson Co SC 226 D7
Belmont NC 74 E5
Belton SC 117 E4
Bethune SC 124 A5
Blenheim SC 125 E3
Cabarrus Co NC 76 A1
Caswell Co NC 8 C3
Chester Co SC 101 A7
Clio SC 126 B2
Clover SC 100 C1
Darlington Co SC 125 C7
Davidson Co NC 27 B6
Drexel NC 47 B3
Edgecombe Co NC 34 E7
Farmville NC 58 D5
Fountain Inn SC 118 D1
Franklinton NC 32 A4
Granville Co NC 31 C4
Greenville Co SC 97 A3
Hemingway SC 156 D3
Hope Mills NC 106 E2
Kernersville NC 27 D4
King NC 26 E1
Landis NC 50 C7
Laurinburg NC 105 C6
Lexington NC 51 A2
McColl SC 126 B1
Mt Airy NC 5 B5
Newberry Co SC 136 D2
Saluda SC 135 E6
Summerville SC 172 C2
Wake Forest NC 32 A6
Winston-Salem NC 188 D6
S Main St SR-2
Hiawassee GA 93 B3
S Main St SR-5 ALT
Ellijay GA 91 B7
S Main St SR-8
Lincolnton NC 51 A2
S Main St SR-9
Clio SC 126 B2
Lake View SC 127 B6
Union Co SC 99 A5
S Main St SR-9 BUS
Lancaster SC 219 C5
S Main St SR-11 BUS
Bethel NC 59 B1
S Main St SR-14
Fountain Inn SC 118 D1
Greer SC 97 D4
S Main St SR-17
Hiawassee GA 93 B3
S Main St SR-18
Jonesville SC 99 A5
S Main St SR-21 BUS
Sylvania GA 168 B6
S Main St SR-28
Anderson Co SC 117 C5
Anderson Co SC 226 D7
S Main St SR-33
Princeville NC 34 E7
S Main St SR-34
Greenwood SC 134 E3
S Main St SR-38
Blenheim SC 125 E4
S Main St SR-41
Fairmont NC 127 C4
Hemingway SC 156 D3
Mullins SC 143 A2
S Main St SR-41 ALT
Marion SC 142 D2
S Main St SR-50
Granville Co NC 31 C4
S Main St SR-51
Hemingway SC 156 D3
S Main St SR-55 BUS
Wake Co NC 55 B5
S Main St SR-59
Hope Mills NC 106 E2
S Main St SR-72
Red Springs NC 106 B5
S Main St SR-73
Mt Gilead NC 77 E6
S Main St SR-75
Hiawassee GA 93 B3
S Main St SR-86
Caswell Co NC 8 C3
S Main St SR-87
Alamance Co NC 29 C5
S Main St SR-89
Galax VA 4 B2
Mt Airy NC 5 B5
Mt Airy NC 183 E6
S Main St SR-111
Stantonsburg NC 58 A5
S Main St SR-114
Drexel NC 47 B3
S Main St SR-115
Troutman NC 49 C4
S Main St SR-121
Saluda SC 135 E6
S Main St SR-150
Boiling Springs NC 73 B5
S Main St SR-151
Jefferson SC 123 E1
S Main St SR-157
Person Co NC 9 D6
S Main St SR-184
Due West SC 118 A7
S Main St SR-210
Lillington NC 81 B2
S Main St SR-211
Raeford NC 106 A2
S Main St SR-222
Stantonsburg NC 58 A5
S Main St SR-242
Bladenboro NC 128 C3
Salemburg NC 108 B2
S Main St SR-273
Mt Holly NC 75 A5
S Main St SR-275
Stanley NC 74 E3
S Main St SR-308
Roxobel NC 35 C1
S Main St SR-341
Bethune SC 124 A5
S Main St SR-381
McColl SC 126 B1
S Main St SR-410
Bladen Co NC 128 C3
S Main St SR-561
Northampton Co NC 14 C7
S Main St SR-710
Red Springs NC 106 B5
S Main St SR-731
Candor NC 78 D4
S Main St SR-901
Chester Co SC 101 A7
S Main St SR-903
Robersonville NC 59 D1
S Main St SR-917
Mullins SC 143 A2
S Main St US-1 ALT
Franklin Co NC 32 A4
Wake Forest NC 32 A6
S Main St US-13 BUS
Bethel NC 59 B1
S Main St US-15
Darlington Co SC 125 C4
Lee Co SC 140 B2
S Main St US-15 BUS
Laurinburg NC 105 C6
S Main St US-17 ALT
Summerville SC 172 C2
S Main St US-21
Sparta NC 3 D5
Troutman NC 49 C4
S Main St US-21 BUS
Arlington NC 25 C2
S Main St US-23 BUS
Waynesville NC 69 C1
S Main St US-25
Greenville Co SC 97 A3
S Main St US-29
Cowpens SC 98 E2
Salisbury NC 208 C5
S Main St US-29 BUS
Lexington NC 51 A2
S Main St US-52
Darlington Co SC 125 C4
S Main St US-52 BUS
Darlington SC 125 C7
Darlington SC 229 E6
Mt Airy NC 5 B5
S Main St US-64 BUS
Edgecombe Co NC 34 E7
S Main St US-70
Salisbury NC 208 C5
S Main St US-70 BUS
Lexington NC 51 A2
S Main St US-76
Belton SC 117 E4
Hiawassee GA 93 B3
S Main St US-158
Mocksville NC 50 B1
S Main St US-178
Belton SC 117 E4
S Main St US-220 ALT
Biscoe NC 78 C3
Candor NC 78 D4
S Main St US-220 BUS
Asheboro NC 52 C2
S Main St US-221
Rutherfordton NC 72 C3
S Main St US-221 BUS
Jefferson NC 2 D6
S Main St US-258
Farmville NC 58 D5
Northampton Co NC 14 C7
S Main St US-276
Greenville Co SC 97 A3
Mauldin SC 97 C6
S Main St US-301
Allendale SC 169 B2
S Main St US-311
Archdale NC 52 A1
High Point NC 191 E7
S Main St US-311 BUS
High Point NC 191 C5
S Main St US-321
Clover SC 100 C1
Gaston SC 151 E2
S Main St US-321 ALT
Caldwell Co NC 47 E3
S Main St US-401
Darlington Co SC 125 C4
Fuquay-Varina NC 55 B6
Lillington NC 81 B2
Wagram NC 105 D4
Wake Co NC 32 A7
Warrenton NC 11 E6
S Main St US-401 BUS
Laurinburg NC 105 C6
S Main St US-501 BUS
Marion SC 142 D2
SE Main St
Simpsonville SC 97 D7
SE Main St SR-14
Simpsonville SC 97 D7
W Main St
Abingdon VA 1 B1
Albemarle NC 77 B3
Belhaven NC 61 C5
Benson NC 82 A2
Berkeley Co SC 164 E5
Berkeley Co SC 165 A5
Beulaville NC 110 B2
Boonville NC 25 E2
Brunswick Co NC 145 B7
Burnsville NC 45 C1
Carrboro NC 30 C7
Chesterfield SC 103 D7
Chesterfield Co SC 103 C6
Conway NC 14 C4
Everetts NC 35 E7
Franklinville NC 52 D3
Glen Alpine NC 46 E4
Harleyville SC 163 D5
Independence VA 3 D2
Jamestown NC 28 A6
Laurens SC 119 A4
Lawndale NC 73 C2
Liberty SC 96 B6
Mt Olive NC 83 B5
Northampton Co NC 14 D6
Ridgeland SC 176 B4
Rock Hill SC 100 E3
Rock Hill SC 217 A3
Sevierville TN 41 E1
Spartanburg SC 98 C3
Thomasville NC 51 D1
Wilkesboro NC 24 D4
Williamston NC 36 A7
W Main St SR-5
Rock Hill SC 100 E3
Rock Hill SC 101 A4
Rock Hill SC 217 A3
W Main St SR-6
Berkeley Co SC 164 E5
Berkeley Co SC 165 A5
W Main St SR-9
Ruby SC 103 C6
W Main St SR-9 BUS
Chesterfield SC 103 D7
W Main St SR-18
Wilkesboro NC 24 D4
W Main St SR-20
Lumber Bridge NC 106 C3
W Main St SR-22
Franklinville NC 52 D3
W Main St SR-23
Ridge Spring SC 150 B1
W Main St SR-24
Beulaville NC 110 B2
Locust NC 76 D5
W Main St SR-27
Locust NC 76 D5
W Main St SR-28
Walhalla SC 95 B6
W Main St SR-35
Greeneville TN 19 E4
Sevierville TN 41 E1
W Main St SR-39
Ridge Spring SC 150 B1
W Main St SR-41
Wallace NC 109 D6
W Main St SR-49
Union SC 99 B7
W Main St SR-50
Benson NC 82 A2
Faison NC 83 A6
W Main St SR-67
Boonville NC 25 E2
Mountain City TN 1 D5
W Main St SR-71
Sevierville TN 41 E1
W Main St SR-78
Sanford NC 80 B1
W Main St SR-81
Jonesborough TN 20 E1
W Main St SR-88
Jefferson NC 2 D6
W Main St SR-91
Johnson City TN 21 B1
W Main St SR-93
Central SC 96 A7
Easley SC 96 C5
Liberty SC 96 B6
W Main St SR-107
Sylva NC 68 E3
W Main St SR-109
Chesterfield Co SC 103 C6
W Main St SR-130
Oconee Co SC 95 C4
W Main St SR-182
Lawndale NC 73 C2
W Main St SR-183
Pickens SC 96 B5
W Main St SR-268
Wilkesboro NC 24 D4
W Main St SR-290
Duncan SC 97 E4
W Main St SR-293
Danville VA 8 B3
W Main St SR-336
Ridgeland SC 176 B4
W Main St SR-341
Florence Co SC 141 D7
W Main St SR-385
Marlboro Co SC 125 E2
W Main St SR-403
Faison NC 83 A6
W Main St SR-917
Latta SC 126 D6
W Main St US-1
Lexington SC 137 C6
W Main St US-11
Abingdon VA 1 B1
W Main St US-11 BUS
Aulander NC 35 E1
W Main St US-13 ALT
Everetts NC 35 E7
Williamston NC 36 A7
W Main St US-15 BUS
Marlboro Co SC 125 E2
W Main St US-29
Spartanburg SC 98 C3
Spartanburg SC 224 A4
W Main St US-52
Boonville NC 25 E2
Rockwell NC 50 D7
W Main St US-58
Independence VA 3 D2
W Main St US-64
Williamston NC 36 A7
W Main St US-64 ALT
Everetts NC 35 E7
W Main St US-70
Glen Alpine NC 46 E4
Havelock NC 112 D2
W Main St US-70 BUS
Durham NC 193 E3
W Main St US-74 BUS
Forest City NC 72 C3
W Main St US-76 BUS
Laurens SC 119 A4
W Main St US-158
Conway NC 14 C4
W Main St US-178
Harleyville SC 163 D5
W Main St US-221 ALT
Forest City NC 72 C3
W Main St US-258
Murfreesboro NC 14 E4
Northampton Co NC 14 C6
W Main St US-264 BUS
Belhaven NC 61 C5
W Main St US-321
Greeneville TN 19 E4
W Main St US-378
Lexington SC 137 C6
W Main St US-378 BUS
Florence Co SC 141 D7
W Main St US-401
Lamar SC 140 E2
W Main St US-411
Sevierville TN 41 E1
W Main St US-441
Sevierville TN 41 E1
Majolica Rd
Rowan Co NC 50 C5
N Major Rd
Anderson Co SC 117 D4
Major Raymond H Wilkins Mem Hy
Tyrrell Co NC 38 A6
Major RH Wilkins Mem Hy US-64
Tyrrell Co NC 38 A6
Malcolm Blvd
Rutherford College NC 47 D3
Mall Blvd
Savannah GA 180 E5
Mallard Rd
Dorchester Co SC 172 B1
Mallard Creek Rd
Charlotte NC 75 D3
Charlotte NC 211 A4
Mecklenburg Co NC 211 E2
E Mallard Creek Church Rd
Mecklenburg Co NC 211 D6
W Mallard Creek Church Rd
Charlotte NC 211 A4
Mallet Hill Rd
Richland Co SC 138 C4
Malmaison Rd
Pittsylvania Co VA 8 D1
Mandella Rd
Berkeley Co SC 165 A3
Maney Branch Rd
Buncombe Co NC 44 E4
Manning Av
Sumter SC 235 E6
Sumter Co SC 140 A7
Sumter Co SC 235 E7
Manning Av US-521
Sumter SC 235 E6
Sumter Co SC 140 A7
Sumter Co SC 235 E7
Manning Dr
Brunswick Co VA 12 E2
Brunswick Co VA 13 A2
Manning Dr E-600
Brunswick Co VA 13 A2
Manning Hwy
Clarendon Co SC 155 A4
Manning Hwy SR-261
Clarendon Co SC 155 A4
Mannville-St. Charles Rd
Lee Co SC 140 B3
Mannville-Wisacky Rd
Lee Co SC 140 B3
Maple Av
Alamance Co NC 29 C5
Burlington NC 192 D5
Winston-Salem NC 188 D3
Maple Av SR-49
Burlington NC 29 C5
Burlington NC 192 D5
W Maple Dr
Henry Co VA 7 D3
Maple Cypress Rd
Craven Co NC 85 C3
Marengo Rd
Mecklenburg Co VA 12 A1
Marginal Rd
Charleston Co SC 172 E5
Margrace Rd
Cleveland Co NC 73 E6
Cleveland Co NC 74 A6
Marian Av
Pasquotank Co NC 17 A7
Marietta Rd
Marietta NC 127 C6
Marine Blvd
Jacksonville NC 227 B6
Marine Blvd US-17
Jacksonville NC 227 B6
N Marine Blvd
Jacksonville NC 111 B5
Jacksonville NC 227 C5
N Marine Blvd US-17
Jacksonville NC 111 B5
Jacksonville NC 227 C5
S Marine Blvd
Jacksonville NC 111 B5
Jacksonville NC 227 A6
S Marine Blvd SR-24 BUS
Jacksonville NC 111 B5
Jacksonville NC 227 A6
S Marine Blvd US-17
Jacksonville NC 111 B5
Jacksonville NC 227 A6
E Marion St
Shelby NC 73 D4
E Marion St US-74 BUS
Cleveland Co NC 73 D4
W Marion St
Shelby NC 73 C4
W Marion St US-74W BUS
Shelby NC 73 C4
Marion P Carnell Hwy
Greenwood Co SC 134 D1
Marion P Carnell Hwy US-25
Greenwood Co SC 134 D1
Marion P Carnell Hwy US-178
Greenwood Co SC 134 D1
Marion Stage Rd
Robeson Co NC 127 C3
Mariposa Rd
Gaston Co NC 74 E3
Mark Clark Expwy
Berkeley Co SC 173 B4
Mt Pleasant SC 238 D1
Mark Clark Expwy I-526
Berkeley Co SC 173 B4
Mt Pleasant SC 238 D1
Market Sq
Fayetteville NC 222 D3
Market St
Cheraw SC 104 B7
New Hanover Co NC 131 B6
Wilmington NC 130 E7
Wilmington NC 131 A7
Wilmington NC 231 B3
York Co SC 101 B2
Market St SR-9
Cheraw SC 104 B7
Market St US-17
New Hanover Co NC 131 B6
Market St US-17 BUS
Wilmington NC 130 E7
Wilmington NC 131 A7
Wilmington NC 231 B3
E Market St
Greensboro NC 28 C5
Greensboro NC 190 E2
Johnston Co NC 56 D7

INDEX 28

ohawk Dr — Street Index — Ninety Nine Ford

STREET
City State Map# Grid

Mohawk Dr
Greenville SC 223 D2
N Mohawk Dr
Erwin TN 21 A4
Mohican Tr
New Hanover Co NC 147 A2
Mollie Iron Hill Rd
Columbus Co NC 144 C2
Momeyer Wy
Momeyer NC 33 B6
Momeyer Wy US-64 ALT
Momeyer NC 33 B6
Monarch Hwy
Union Co SC 99 C7
Union Co SC 120 C1
Monarch Hwy SR-49 CONN
Union Co SC 99 C7
Union Co SC 120 C1
Monarch Hwy SR-215 CONN
Union Co SC 99 C7
Union Co SC 120 C1
Moncure-Pittsboro Rd
Pittsboro NC 54 B4
S Monk St
Magnolia NC 109 C3
S Monk St US-117
Magnolia NC 109 C3
Monroe Hwy
Lancaster Co SC 101 E6
Monroe Hwy SR-200
Lancaster Co SC 101 E6
Monroe Rd
Charlotte NC 75 E6
Southampton Co VA 15 A2
Washington Co VA 1 E1
Monroe Rd SR-91
Washington Co VA 1 E1
Monroe Rd E-684
Southampton Co VA 15 A2
Monroe St
Carthage NC 79 C3
Wingate NC 102 D3
Monroe St SR-24
Carthage NC 79 C3
Monroe St SR-27
Carthage NC 79 C3
Monroe St US-74
Wingate NC 102 D3
Monroe White Store Rd
Anson Co NC 103 A4
Montagu St
Charleston SC 240 C6
E Montague Av
North Charleston SC 173 A4
Montague St
Greenwood SC 134 D2
Montague St US-25
Greenwood SC 134 D2
Montague St US-178
Greenwood SC 134 D2
Monteith Rd
Port Wentworth GA 180 C2
Monteith Rd SR-30
Port Wentworth GA 180 C2
Monte Vista Rd
Buncombe Co NC 44 B7
Montford Cove Rd
McDowell Co NC 46 A7
Montford Landing Rd
Jacksonville NC 227 C7
Montgomery Ln
Richland Co SC 138 B7
Monticello Rd
Buncombe Co NC 44 C4
Richland Co SC 137 E3
Richland Co SC 138 A5
Monticello Rd SR-215
Columbia SC 138 A5
Richland Co SC 137 E3
Montlieu Av
High Point NC 27 E6
High Point NC 191 B3
Monument Dr
Edgefield Co SC 149 E1
Moore Rd
Barnwell Co SC 160 E5
Kelford NC 35 D1
E Moore St
Brunswick Co NC 146 D6
E Moore St SR-211
Brunswick Co NC 146 D6
Moore-Duncan Hwy
Spartanburg Co SC 98 A5
Moore-Duncan Hwy SR-290
Spartanburg Co SC 98 A5
Moorefield Bridge Rd
Pittsylvania Co VA 8 B2
Moorefield Memorial Hwy
Pickens Co SC 96 A3
Moorefield Memorial Hwy US-178
Pickens Co SC 96 B5
Moores Chapel Rd
Charlotte NC 75 B5
Mecklenburg Co NC 75 A5
Moores Ferry Rd
Greensville Co VA 13 C2
Moores Spring Rd
Stokes Co NC 5 E6
Stokes Co NC 6 A6
Moores Spring Rd SR-268
Stokes Co NC 5 E6
Stokes Co NC 6 A6
Mooresville Rd
Cabarrus Co NC 75 E1
Cabarrus Co NC 76 A1
Rowan Co NC 49 E6
Rowan Co NC 50 B5
Salisbury NC 208 A5
Mooresville Rd SR-3
Cabarrus Co NC 75 E1
Cabarrus Co NC 76 A1
Mooresville Rd SR-150
Rowan Co NC 49 E6
Rowan Co NC 50 B5
Salisbury NC 208 A5
Morehead Av
Carteret Co NC 228 C7
Morehead Rd
Cabarrus Co NC 76 A4
Cabarrus Co NC 212 E4
W Morehead St
Charlotte NC 215 D2
W Morehead St SR-27
Charlotte NC 215 D2
W Morehead St US-29
Charlotte NC 215 D2
S Morgan Av
Andrews SC 166 B1
S Morgan Av SR-41
Andrews SC 166 B1
Morgan Rd
Eden NC 7 C4
Morgan Branch Rd
Buncombe Co NC 44 B6
Morgan Ford Rd
Henry Co VA 7 C3
Morgan J Rd
Rennert NC 106 C5
Morgan Mill Rd
Monroe NC 218 D4
Union Co NC 76 D7
Union Co NC 102 C1
Morgan Mill Rd SR-200
Union Co NC 76 D7
Union Co NC 102 C1
Morganton Blvd SW
Lenoir NC 47 C2
Morganton Blvd SW SR-18 BYP
Lenoir NC 47 C2
Morganton Blvd SW US-64
Lenoir NC 47 C2
Morganton Hwy
Fannin Co GA 91 E4
Morganton Hwy SR-60
Fannin Co GA 91 E4
Morganton Rd
Fayetteville NC 80 D7
Fayetteville NC 106 E1
Fayetteville NC 222 A2
Pinehurst NC 79 C6
Pinehurst NC 220 D6
W Morganton Rd
Southern Pines NC 79 C6
Morning Side Dr
Henry Co VA 6 D1
S Morris St
Florence Co SC 155 D1
Morris Callaway Rd
Columbia Co GA 148 B7
Morris L McGough Frwy
Buncombe Co NC 44 D4
Woodfin NC 44 D5
Morris L McGough Frwy I-26
Buncombe Co NC 44 D5
Morris L McGough Frwy US-19
Buncombe Co NC 44 D5
Morris L McGough Frwy US-23
Buncombe Co NC 44 D5
Morris L McGough Frwy US-25
Buncombe Co NC 44 D5
Morris L McGough Frwy US-70
Buncombe Co NC 44 D5
Morrison Dr
Charleston SC 240 D3
Morrison Dr US-52 SPUR
Charleston SC 240 D3
Morrisville Pkwy
Morrisville NC 55 A2
Morrisville Carpenter Rd
Morrisville NC 55 A2
Morven Rd
Wadesboro NC 103 D3
Moses Dingle Rd
Clarendon Co SC 154 A5
Motley Rd
Richland Co SC 138 C7
Motor Rd
Winston-Salem NC 27 A3
Winston-Salem NC 186 E3
Moultrie St
Charleston SC 240 C4
E Mountain Dr
Cumberland Co NC 222 D7
Fayetteville NC 107 A2
Fayetteville NC 222 C7
W Mountain Dr
Cumberland Co NC 222 B7
Mountain Rd
Cocke Co TN 43 C1
Henderson Co NC 70 E3
W Mountain Rd
Nash Co NC 33 D7
E Mountain St
Forsyth Co NC 27 D4
N Mountain St
Blacksburg SC 73 D7
Cherryville NC 74 A3
N Mountain St SR-198
Cherokee Co SC 73 D7
N Mountain St SR-274
Cherryville NC 74 A3
W Mountain St
Forsyth Co NC 27 C4
W Mountain St SR-66
Kernersville NC 27 D4
Mountain City Rd
Washington Co VA 1 E3
Mountain City Rd SR-91
Washington Co VA 1 E2
E Mountain Creek Rd
Greenville Co SC 97 B4
E Mountain Creek Rd SR-253
Greenville Co SC 97 B4
Mountain Gap Rd
Chester Co SC 122 A3
Mountain Gap Rd SR-901
Chester Co SC 122 A3
Mountain Island Hwy
Gaston Co NC 75 A3
Mt Holly NC 75 A4
Mountain Island Hwy SR-273
Mt Holly NC 75 A4
Mountain Park Rd
Surry Co NC 4 C7
Mountain Valley Rd
Henry Co VA 7 D1
Mountain View Dr
Surry Co NC 183 D1
Mountain View Rd
Wilkes Co NC 24 D3
Mountainview Rd
Greenville Co SC 97 B2
Mountainview Rd SR-253
Greenville Co SC 97 B2
Mt Beulah Rd
Aiken Co SC 160 D1
Windsor SC 160 D2
Mt Carmel Rd
Abbeville Co SC 134 A4
Buncombe Co NC 44 C6
Chatham Co NC 54 D1
Mt Carmel Rd SR-823
Abbeville Co SC 134 A4
Mt Carmel Church Rd
Chapel Hill NC 54 C1
Mt Cross Rd
Danville VA 8 B2
Mt Gallant Rd
Rock Hill SC 101 A3
Rock Hill SC 217 E1
York Co SC 100 E2
York Co SC 101 A2
W Mt Gallant Rd
York Co SC 100 D3
Mt Holly Rd
Charlotte NC 75 B4
York Co SC 101 A4
Mt Holly Rd SR-27
Charlotte NC 75 B4
Mt Holly Rd SR-901
York Co SC 101 A4
Mt Holly-Huntersville Rd
Charlotte NC 75 A4
Mecklenburg Co NC 75 B4
Mt Hope Church Rd
Guilford Co NC 28 D4
Mt Lebanon Rd
Spartanburg Co SC 97 D2
Mt Lebanon Church Rd
Greenville Co SC 97 D2
Mt Misery Rd NE
Northwest NC 130 B6
Mt Moriah Church Rd
Landis NC 50 A7
Mt Olive Dr
Newton Grove NC 82 D4
Mt Olive Dr SR-50
Newton Grove NC 82 D4
Mt Olive Dr SR-55
Newton Grove NC 82 D4
Mt Olive Hwy
Sampson Co NC 82 D4
Mt Olive Hwy SR-50
Sampson Co NC 82 D4
Mt Olive Hwy SR-55
Sampson Co NC 82 D4
Mt Olivet Rd
Cabarrus Co NC 76 A2
Hart Co GA 116 C5
Pickens Co SC 95 E7
Six Mile SC 95 E5
Mt Olivet Rd SR-133
Pickens Co SC 95 E7
Six Mile SC 95 E5
Mt Pleasant Rd N
Cabarrus Co NC 76 D1
Mt Pleasant Rd S
Cabarrus Co NC 76 D3
Midland NC 76 C4
Mt Pleasant Rd W
Cabarrus Co NC 76 D3
Mt Pleasant St
Charleston SC 240 B3
Mt Sinai Rd
Durham Co NC 30 C6
Mt Sterling Rd
Haywood Co NC 43 B3
Mt Tabor Church Rd
Union Co SC 99 D5
Mt Tabor Church Rd SR-105
Union Co SC 99 D5
Mt Valley Rd
Richland Co SC 138 A3
Mt Vernon Rd
Williamsburg Co SC 155 A3
Mt Vernon Church Rd
Wake Co NC 31 D7
Mt View Rd
Pittsylvania Co VA 8 C1
Mt Wesley Rd
Washington Co TN 20 E3
Mt Zion Rd
Horry Co SC 144 D7
Spartanburg Co SC 98 A3
Sumter Co SC 141 A5
Mt Zion Rd SR-341
Sumter Co SC 141 A5
Mt Zion Church Rd
Robeson Co NC 106 B6
Moye-Turnage Rd
Farmville NC 58 E5
Moyton Av
Stantonsburg NC 58 A5
Moyton Av SR-58
Stantonsburg NC 58 A5
Muirs Chapel Rd
Greensboro NC 28 B4
Greensboro NC 189 A2
Mulberry Church Rd
Charlotte NC 214 D1
Muller Rd
Richland Co SC 138 A2
Murchison Rd
Fayetteville NC 81 A7
Fayetteville NC 222 C1
Spring Lake NC 80 E6
Spring Lake NC 221 E3
Murchison Rd SR-210
Fayetteville NC 81 A7
Fayetteville NC 222 C1
Spring Lake NC 80 E6
Spring Lake NC 221 E3
Murdock Rd
Iredell Co NC 49 C4
Murdocksville Rd
Moore Co NC 220 A1
Pinehurst NC 79 C5
Murphy Hwy
Fannin Co GA 91 E3
Fannin Co GA 92 A3
Murphy Hwy SR-11
Union Co GA 92 C3
Murphy Hwy SR-60 SPUR
Fannin Co GA 91 E3
Fannin Co GA 92 A3
Murphy Hwy US-19
Union Co GA 92 C3
Murphy Hwy US-129
Union Co GA 92 C3
Murphy Rd
Macon Co NC 67 E7
Macon Co NC 68 A7
Macon Co NC 93 E1
Murphy Rd US-64
Macon Co NC 67 E7
Macon Co NC 68 A7
Macon Co NC 93 E1
Murphy St
Towns Co GA 93 A3
Murphy St SR-66
Towns Co GA 93 A3
Murrah Rd
Edgefield Co SC 149 B6
E Murray Av
Durham NC 194 B1
S Murray Av
Anderson Co SC 117 C5
S Murray Av SR-81
Anderson Co SC 117 C5
W Murray Av
Durham NC 194 A1
Murray Rd
Winston-Salem NC 27 A3
Murray St
Anderson Co SC 226 C7
N Murray St
Anderson SC 117 C4
Anderson SC 226 C3
N Murray St US-76
Anderson SC 117 C4
Anderson SC 226 C3
N Murray St US-178
Anderson SC 117 C4
Anderson SC 226 C3
S Murray St
Anderson SC 226 D4
Anderson Co SC 117 C4
Anderson Co SC 226 C7
S Murray St SR-28
Anderson SC 226 D4
S Murray St SR-81
Anderson SC 226 D4
Anderson Co SC 117 C4
Anderson Co SC 226 C7
S Murray St US-29 BUS
Anderson SC 226 D4
S Murray St US-76
Anderson SC 226 D4
S Murray St US-178
Anderson SC 226 D4
Murrays Mill Rd
Catawba Co NC 48 E5
Murraywood Rd
Charleston Co SC 172 E6
N Murrow Blvd
Greensboro NC 190 D2
S Murrow Blvd
Greensboro NC 190 D3
Museum Rd
Rock Hill SC 100 E3
Mutual Blvd
Princeville NC 34 E7
Mutual Blvd SR-111
Princeville NC 34 E7
Mutual Blvd SR-122
Princeville NC 34 E7
Mutual Blvd US-258
Princeville NC 34 E7
Myers Rd
Monroe NC 102 B1
Myers Mayo Rd
Dorchester Co SC 164 B7
Myrtle Beach Hwy
Sumter Co SC 140 C7
Myrtle Beach Hwy US-378
Sumter Co SC 140 C7
E Myrtle Beach Hwy
Florence Co SC 141 E7
Florence Co SC 142 D7
E Myrtle Beach Hwy SR-41
Florence Co SC 142 D7
E Myrtle Beach Hwy US-378
Florence Co SC 141 E7
Florence Co SC 142 D7
E Myrtle Beach Hwy US-378 BUS
Lake City SC 141 D7
W Myrtle Beach Hwy
Florence Co SC 142 C7
W Myrtle Beach Hwy SR-51
Florence Co SC 142 C7
W Myrtle Beach Hwy US-378
Florence Co SC 142 C7
Myrtle Grove Rd
New Hanover Co NC 147 A3
S Myrtle School Rd
Gastonia NC 74 C5

N

N Blvd
Coward SC 141 D6
N Blvd US-52
Coward SC 141 D6
Nad St
North Charleston SC 172 E2
North Charleston SC 237 C7
Nakina Rd
Columbus Co NC 144 E2
Nakina Rd SR-905
Columbus Co NC 144 E2
Nance St
Newberry SC 136 B1
Nance St SR-395
Newberry SC 136 B1
Narrow Gauge Rd
Gaston Co NC 74 D3
Narrow Paved Rd
Sumter Co SC 140 D7
Sumter Co SC 141 A6
Narrow Paved Rd SR-53
Sumter Co SC 140 D7
Sumter Co SC 141 A6
Narrow Paved Rd SR-58
Sumter Co SC 140 D7
Nash St E
Wilson NC 202 E5
Nash St N
Wilson NC 202 B3
Wilson Co NC 57 D2
Nash St N SR-58
Wilson Co NC 57 D2
Nash St SE
Wilson NC 57 E3
Nash St SE SR-58
Wilson NC 57 E3
Nash St SE US-264
Wilson NC 57 E3
E Nash St
Spring Hope NC 33 B6
E Nash St US-64 ALT
Spring Hope NC 33 B6
N Nash St
Middlesex NC 56 E2
N Nash St SR-231
Middlesex NC 56 E2
W Nash St
Nash Co NC 33 A6
W Nash St US-64 ALT
Nash Co NC 33 A6
Natal St
Cumberland Co NC 107 A2
National Hwy
Cherokee Co SC 99 A1
Thomasville NC 27 D7
Thomasville NC 51 D1
National Hwy SR-68
Thomasville NC 27 D7
National Hwy SR-105
Cherokee Co SC 99 A1
National Forest Rd
Caldwell Co NC 22 E6
Macon Co NC 67 D7
Macon Co NC 93 E1
National Forest Rd SR-90
Caldwell Co NC 22 E6
National Park Rd
Haywood Co NC 43 A4
Nations Ford Rd
Charlotte NC 75 C7
Pineville NC 101 B1
Natures Wy
Columbia Co GA 148 C7
N Navassa Rd
Navassa NC 130 D7
Nazareth Rd
Lexington Co SC 137 C7
Lexington Co SC 151 B1
Spartanburg Co SC 98 A4
Nazareth Church Rd
Spartanburg Co SC 98 A4
NC-11-Byp S
Lewiston Woodville NC 35 D3
NC-11-Byp S SR-42
Lewiston Woodville NC 35 D3
NCHS East Rd
Northampton Co NC 14 B4
Neal Rd
Durham NC 30 D5
Neal Hawkins Rd
Gaston Co NC 74 C6
Gastonia NC 74 C5
Nebo Rd
Yadkin Co NC 26 A2
Nebraska Rd
Hyde Co NC 63 A6
Neel Rd
Rowan Co NC 50 B5
Neely Rd
Transylvania Co NC 70 B5
Neely Ferry Rd
Laurens Co SC 118 D4
Waterloo SC 119 A6
Neelys Creek Rd
York Co SC 101 A5
Neely Store Rd
York Co SC 101 B4
Neeses Hwy
Neeses SC 151 D7
Orangeburg Co SC 152 A7
Neeses Hwy SR-4
Neeses SC 151 D7
Orangeburg Co SC 152 A7
Nelson Blvd
Kingstree SC 155 C4
Nelson Blvd SR-527
Kingstree SC 155 C4
Nelson St
Greenville SC 223 A5
Nesmith Rd
Williamsburg Co SC 156 B4
Neuse Blvd
New Bern NC 86 A5
Neuse Blvd SR-43
New Bern NC 86 A5
Neuse Blvd SR-55
New Bern NC 86 A5
Neuse Rd
Arapahoe NC 86 D6
Neuse River Br
New Bern NC 86 B6
Neuse River Br SR-55
Craven Co NC 86 B6
Neuse River Br US-17
Craven Co NC 86 B6
New Bern Av
Raleigh NC 55 E2
New Bern Av US-64
Raleigh NC 55 E2
New Bern Av US-264
Raleigh NC 55 E2
New Bern Hwy
Onslow Co NC 111 C4
New Bern Hwy US-17
Jacksonville NC 111 C4
New Bern Rd
Carteret Co NC 113 B4
Craven Co NC 112 E3
New Bern Rd SR-101
Carteret Co NC 113 B4
Craven Co NC 112 E3
E New Bern Rd
Kinston NC 84 E4
Kinston NC 205 E7
E New Bern Rd US-70
Kinston NC 84 E4
Kinston NC 205 E7
W New Bern Rd
Lenoir Co NC 84 D4
W New Bern Rd US-70
Lenoir Co NC 84 D4
W New Bern Rd US-258
Lenoir Co NC 84 D4
Newberry Hwy
Saluda Co SC 135 E5
Saluda Co SC 136 A4
Newberry Hwy SR-121
Saluda Co SC 135 E5
Saluda Co SC 136 A4
Newberry Rd
Fairfield Co SC 121 D5
Newberry Rd SR-34
Fairfield Co SC 121 D5
Newberry Rd SR-200
Fairfield Co SC 121 D6
New Bethel Rd
Johnston Co NC 56 A5
New Bethel Church Rd
Wake Co NC 55 E4
New Bridge Rd
Aiken Co SC 150 B6
New Bridge St
Jacksonville NC 227 B6
New Britton Rd
Columbus Co NC 128 D7
Columbus Co NC 144 E1
Columbus Co NC 145 A2
New Britton Rd SR-130
Columbus Co NC 128 D7
Columbus Co NC 144 E1
Columbus Co NC 145 A2
New Clyde Hwy
Clyde NC 43 D7
New Clyde Hwy US-19
Haywood Co NC 43 D7
New Clyde Hwy US-23
Haywood Co NC 43 D7
New Cut Rd
Spartanburg Co SC 98 A3
New Easley Hwy
Greenville Co SC 96 E5
New Easley Hwy US-123
Greenville Co SC 96 E5
Newfound Rd
Buncombe Co NC 44 A7
Haywood Co NC 43 E7
New Garden Rd
Greensboro NC 28 B4
New Hendersonville Hwy
Transylvania Co NC 70 B5
New Hendersonville Hwy US-64
Transylvania Co NC 70 B5
New Hill Rd
Chatham Co NC 54 E3
New Hill Rd SR-751
Chatham Co NC 54 E3
New Hill-Olive Chapel Rd
Wake Co NC 54 E3
New Holland Rd
Aiken Co SC 150 C5
New Hope Rd
Lancaster Co SC 122 D2
Lancaster Co SC 123 A2
Perquimans Co NC 38 B1
Spartanburg Co SC 98 A4
Wake Co NC 55 E1
N New Hope Rd
Gastonia NC 74 D4
N New Hope Rd SR-279
Gastonia NC 74 D4
S New Hope Rd
Gastonia NC 74 E6
Raleigh NC 55 E3
S New Hope Rd SR-279
Gastonia NC 74 E6
New Hope Church Rd
Orange Co NC 30 C6
Raleigh NC 55 E1
New House Rd
Cleveland Co NC 73 A3
Newington Hwy
Screven Co GA 168 D6
Newington Hwy SR-24
Screven Co GA 168 D6
Newland Hwy
Avery Co NC 22 C5
Newland Hwy SR-181
Avery Co NC 22 C5
Newland Rd
Washington Co NC 37 C7
New Leicester Hwy
Asheville NC 44 B5
New Leicester Hwy SR-63
Asheville NC 44 B5
New Light Rd
Wake Co NC 31 D6
New Market St
Greenwood SC 134 E3
New Pee Dee Rd
Horry Co SC 157 C3
Newport Hwy
Cocke Co TN 19 D5
Sevier Co TN 42 B1
Newport Hwy SR-35
Cocke Co TN 19 D5
Sevier Co TN 42 B1
Newport Hwy US-321
Cocke Co TN 19 D5
Newport Hwy US-411
Sevier Co TN 42 B1
New Raleigh Hwy
Durham Co NC 31 A6
New Raleigh Hwy US-70
Durham Co NC 31 A6
New Rand Rd
Garner NC 55 E4
N New River Dr
Surf City NC 132 A4
N New River Dr SR-210
Surf City NC 132 A4
New River Pkwy
Grayson Co VA 3 D3
New River Pkwy US-21
Grayson Co VA 3 D3
New River Pkwy US-221
Grayson Co VA 3 D3
New Salem Rd
Randolph Co NC 52 C2
New South Centennial St
High Point NC 191 C4
New Stock Rd
Buncombe Co NC 44 D4
Newt Good Rd
Washington Co TN 20 D2
Newton Grove Hwy
Sampson Co NC 82 B5
Newton Grove Hwy US-13
Sampson Co NC 82 B5
New Town Rd
Union Co NC 101 D3
Weddington NC 101 D2
New Walkertown Rd
Walkertown NC 27 B4
Winston-Salem NC 188 E3
New Walkertown Rd US-311
Walkertown NC 27 B4
Winston-Salem NC 188 E3
New Zion Rd
Williamsburg Co SC 155 C1
NF-40
Cherokee Co NC 65 E5
Nichols Hwy
Dillon Co SC 127 C6
Nichols Hwy SR-9
Dillon Co SC 127 C6
N Nichols Hwy
Horry Co SC 143 C3
S Nichols Hwy
Horry Co SC 143 C4
Ninety Nine Ford
Wilkes Co NC 23 D4

STREET / City State / Map# / Grid

Ninety Six Hwy
Greenwood Co SC 134 E3
Greenwood Co SC 135 A3
Ninety Six Hwy SR-34
Greenwood Co SC 134 E3
Greenwood Co SC 135 A3
Nixon Rd
Augusta GA 159 B2
Nixville Rd
Estill SC 169 C6
Nixville Rd SR-3
Estill SC 169 C6
Noah Hayes Rd
Surry Co NC 4 C7
Surry Co NC 25 C1
Noah Helms Rd
Union Co NC 76 B7
Noel Conaway Hwy
Effingham Co GA 180 B2
Noel Conaway Hwy SR-30
Effingham Co GA 180 B2
Noles Dr
Mt Holly NC 75 A4
Norman Rd
Anderson Co SC 226 E7
Norman Rd SR-149
Anderson Co SC 226 E7
Norris Av
Charlotte NC 75 D5
N Norris Dr
Norris SC 96 A6
N Norris Dr SR-93
Norris SC 96 A6
S Norris Dr
Norris SC 96 A7
S Norris Dr SR-93
Norris SC 96 A7
Norris Hwy
Pickens Co SC 96 A6
Norris Hwy SR-137
Pickens Co SC 96 A6
North Av W
Westminster SC 116 A1
North Av W US-76
Westminster SC 116 A1
E North Av
Anderson SC 117 B3
Anderson SC 226 B2
E North Av US-76
Anderson SC 117 B3
Anderson SC 226 B1
E North Av US-178
Anderson SC 117 B3
Anderson SC 226 B1
W North Av
Anderson SC 226 B2
W North Av US-76
Anderson SC 226 B2
W North Av US-178
Anderson SC 226 B2
North Blvd
Clinton NC 108 D1
North Rd
North SC 151 D5
Orangeburg Co SC 152 A5
North Rd US-178
North SC 151 D5
Orangeburg Co SC 152 A5
E North St
Greenville SC 223 E2
Greenville Co SC 97 B5
E North St I-385 BUS
Greenville SC 223 C3
W North St
Greenville SC 223 B3
W North St SR-183
Greenville SC 223 B3
E North 1st St
Seneca SC 116 D1
E North 1st St US-76 BUS
Seneca SC 116 D1
E North 1st St US-123 BUS
Seneca SC 116 D1
W North 1st St
Seneca SC 116 C1
W North 1st St US-76 BUS
Seneca SC 116 C1
W North 1st St US-123 BUS
Seneca SC 116 C1
Northbrook Dr
Raleigh NC 197 D4
Northeast Creek Pkwy
Durham NC 31 A7
Northern Wake Expwy
Wake Co NC 31 B7
Wake Co NC 55 E1
Wake Co NC 56 A1
Northern Wake Expwy I-540
Wake Co NC 31 B7
Wake Co NC 55 E1
Wake Co NC 56 A1
North Lake Rd
Hyde Co NC 62 D5
Hyde Co NC 63 A5
North Park Dr
Lancaster SC 219 C3
North Point Blvd
Winston-Salem NC 186 B4
Northside Dr W
Greenwood Co SC 134 D2
E Northside Dr
Greenwood Co SC 134 E2
E Northwest Blvd
Winston-Salem NC 188 D2
W Northwest Blvd
Winston-Salem NC 188 B3

Northwest Rd NE
Northwest NC 130 B6
Norway Rd
Norway SC 161 D1
Orangeburg Co SC 152 B7
Orangeburg Co SC 161 E1
Orangeburg Co SC 162 A1
Norway Rd SR-332
Norway SC 161 D1
Norway Rd SR-400
Orangeburg Co SC 152 B7
Orangeburg Co SC 161 E1
Orangeburg Co SC 162 A1
Norwell Blvd
Cary NC 55 B1
Norwood Rd
Wake Co NC 31 C7
Norwood St SW
Lenoir NC 47 D1
Norwood St SW US-321 ALT
Lenoir NC 47 D1
N Norwood St
Wallace NC 109 D6
N Norwood St US-117
Wallace NC 109 D5
S Norwood St
Duplin Co NC 109 D6
S Norwood St US-117
Duplin Co NC 109 D6
Nottely Dam Rd
Union Co GA 92 B5
Nottely Dam Rd SR-325
Union Co GA 92 B5
Number Nine Rd
Lee Co SC 140 A4

O

Oak Av
Bailey NC 57 A2
Oak Av SR-581
Bailey NC 57 A2
Oak Dr
Lexington Co SC 137 D6
Oak Hwy
Oconee Co SC 116 C3
Oak Hwy SR-24
Oconee Co SC 116 C2
W Oak Hwy
Oconee Co SC 116 B2
W Oak Hwy SR-24
Oconee Co SC 116 B2
Oak St
Forest City NC 72 D4
Myrtle Beach SC 158 B3
S Oak St
Seneca SC 116 C1
S Oak St SR-59
Seneca SC 116 C1
Oakcrest Rd
Arcadia Lakes SC 138 B4
Oakdale Rd
Charlotte NC 75 C4
W Oak Forest Dr
Charleston SC 239 C5
Oak Grove Rd
Spartanburg Co SC 98 B4
Winston-Salem NC 27 C4
Oak Hill Rd
Buncombe Co NC 44 C7
E Oak Island Dr
Oak Island NC 146 C6
W Oak Island Dr
Oak Island NC 146 B6
Oakland Av
Rock Hill SC 101 A3
Rock Hill SC 217 B3
Sumter SC 235 D4
Oakland Av SR-274
Rock Hill SC 101 A3
Rock Hill SC 217 B3
Oakland Av US-521
Sumter SC 235 D4
Oakland Av S
Rock Hill SC 217 C4
Oakland Av S US-21 BUS
Rock Hill SC 217 B4
Oakland Rd
Spindale NC 72 C4
Oakley Pirkle Rd
Evans GA 148 E7
Oak Ridge Rd
Oak Ridge NC 27 E3
Summerfield NC 28 A2
Oakridge Rd
York Co SC 74 E7
Oak Ridge Rd SR-150
Oak Ridge NC 27 E3
Summerfield NC 28 A2
Oak Ridge Farm
Mooresville NC 49 D6
Oak Ridge Farm SR-150
Mooresville NC 49 D6
Oaks Rd
New Bern NC 86 B5
Oak Summit Rd
Forsyth Co NC 186 D2
Winston-Salem NC 27 A3
W Oakview Rd
Buncombe Co NC 44 C7
Oakway Rd
Oconee Co SC 116 B3
Oakway Rd SR-182
Oconee Co SC 116 B3
Oakwood Av
Cabarrus Co NC 76 A1
Oakwoods Rd
Wilkes Co NC 24 D4
Oates Hwy
Darlington Co SC 124 D7
Darlington Co SC 140 E1

Oates Hwy
Darlington Co SC 141 A2
Oates Hwy SR-403
Darlington Co SC 140 E1
Darlington Co SC 141 A2
Oates Hwy US-15
Darlington Co SC 124 D7
Oberlin Rd
Raleigh NC 197 C7
Ocean Blvd
Southern Shores NC 39 E1
Ocean Blvd SR-12
Southern Shores NC 39 E1
Ocean Blvd E
Holden Beach NC 146 A6
Ocean Blvd N
North Myrtle Beach SC 158 E1
Surfside Beach SC 158 A5
Ocean Blvd N SR-65
North Myrtle Beach SC 158 E1
Ocean Blvd S
North Myrtle Beach SC 158 D1
Surfside Beach SC 158 A5
Ocean Blvd S SR-65
North Myrtle Beach SC 158 D1
Ocean Blvd W
Holden Beach NC 145 D6
N Ocean Blvd
Myrtle Beach SC 158 B3
Myrtle Beach SC 232 D5
N Ocean Blvd SR-73
Myrtle Beach SC 158 B3
Myrtle Beach SC 232 D5
S Ocean Blvd
Myrtle Beach SC 158 B4
Myrtle Beach SC 232 A7
S Ocean Blvd SR-73
Myrtle Beach SC 158 B4
Myrtle Beach SC 232 A7
Ocean Hwy
Chowan Co NC 37 B3
Georgetown Co SC 157 D6
Georgetown Co SC 167 B2
Savannah GA 180 E4
Ocean Hwy I-516
Savannah GA 180 E4
Ocean Hwy SR-21
Savannah GA 180 E4
Ocean Hwy SR-25
Savannah GA 180 E4
Ocean Hwy US-17
Edenton NC 37 B3
Georgetown Co SC 157 D7
Georgetown Co SC 167 B2
Ocean Hwy E
Brunswick Co NC 146 C3
Ocean Hwy E US-17
Brunswick Co NC 146 A4
Ocean Hwy N
Perquimans Co NC 17 A7
Winfall NC 16 E7
Winfall NC 37 D1
Ocean Hwy N US-17
Perquimans Co NC 17 A7
Winfall NC 16 E7
Winfall NC 37 D1
Ocean Hwy S
Chowan Co NC 37 D2
Ocean Hwy S US-17
Chowan Co NC 37 D2
Ocean Hwy W
Brunswick Co NC 145 B6
Ocean Hwy W US-17
Brunswick Co NC 145 B6
E Ocean Rd
Onslow Co NC 131 E3
E Ocean Rd SR-50
Onslow Co NC 131 E3
W Ocean Rd
Onslow Co NC 110 D7
Onslow Co NC 131 E1
W Ocean Rd SR-50
Holly Ridge NC 131 E1
Onslow Co NC 110 D7
Ocean Tr
Currituck Co NC 18 D6
Ocean Tr SR-12
Currituck Co NC 18 D6
Ocean Isle Beach Rd SW
Brunswick Co NC 145 C6
O'Dell School Rd
Cabarrus Co NC 75 E2
Odonnald Rd
Buncombe Co NC 44 C6
Ogden Rd
Rock Hill SC 100 E4
Ogeechee Rd
Chatham Co GA 180 D4
Ogeechee Rd SR-25
Chatham Co GA 180 D4
Ogeechee Rd US-17
Chatham Co GA 180 D4
W Ogeechee St
Screven Co GA 168 B6
W Ogeechee St SR-73
Screven Co GA 168 B6
W Ogeechee St US-301 BUS
Screven Co GA 168 B6
Oglethorpe Tr
Burke Co GA 168 C2
N O'Henry Blvd
Greensboro NC 28 C4
Greensboro NC 190 E1
Guilford Co NC 28 D4
N O'Henry Blvd US-29
Greensboro NC 190 E1
Guilford Co NC 28 C4
N O'Henry Blvd US-70
Greensboro NC 190 E1
N O'Henry Blvd US-220
Greensboro NC 190 E1

Ohio Av
Erwin TN 21 A4
Oine Rd
Warren Co NC 11 D3
Okatie Hwy
Beaufort Co SC 176 B7
Beaufort Co SC 181 B1
Okatie Hwy SR-46
Beaufort Co SC 181 B1
Okatie Hwy SR-170
Beaufort Co SC 176 B7
Beaufort Co SC 181 B1
Oklahoma Rd
Washington Co TN 20 D3
Okolona Rd
Carter Co TN 21 C1
Okolona Rd SR-359
Carter Co TN 21 C1
Olanta Hwy
Florence Co SC 141 C7
Olanta Hwy SR-341
Florence Co SC 141 C7
Olanta Hwy US-301
Florence Co SC 141 C5
W Old Rd
Harnett Co NC 81 B2
W Old Rd SR-27
Harnett Co NC 81 B2
Old St
Goose Creek SC 237 D6
Old 6 Hwy
Calhoun Co SC 153 A5
St. Matthews SC 152 E4
Old 6 Hwy SR-6
Calhoun Co SC 152 E4
Calhoun Co SC 153 A5
Old 96 Indian Tr
Aiken Co SC 151 A4
Old 96 Indian Tr SR-39
Aiken Co SC 151 A4
Old 421 Rd
Liberty NC 53 A1
Randolph Co NC 28 E7
Randolph Co NC 53 A2
Old Airport Rd
Cabarrus Co NC 76 C3
Old Allenton Rd
Robeson Co NC 128 A2
Old Apex Rd
Cary NC 55 B3
Old Athens Madisonville Rd
Athens TN 65 A1
Old Athens Madisnvle Rd SR-307
Athens TN 65 A1
S Old Barnwell Av
Denmark SC 161 D3
S Old Barnwell Av SR-70
Denmark SC 161 D3
Old Barnwell Rd
Aiken Co SC 150 B7
Aiken Co SC 160 D1
Lexington Co SC 137 C7
Old Beatty Ford Rd
Rowan Co NC 50 B7
Old Bible Creek Dr
Grayson Co VA 3 B2
Old Boardman Rd
Boardman NC 128 A4
Old Boones Creek Rd
Washington Co TN 21 A1
Old Branchville Rd
Southampton Co VA 14 C1
Old Branchville Rd E-666
Southampton Co VA 14 C1
Old Bridge St
Jacksonville NC 227 A6
Old Buncombe Rd
Greenville Co SC 97 A4
Greenville Co SC 223 A1
Union Co SC 119 E2
Union Co SC 120 A2
Old Camden Rd
Mecklenburg Co NC 76 B5
Unionville NC 102 C1
E Old Camden Rd
Darlington Co SC 124 E5
Darlington Co SC 125 A4
W Old Camden Rd
Darlington Co SC 124 C6
Old Canaan Rd
Spartanburg Co SC 98 C4
Old Caroleen Rd
Forest City NC 72 D4
Old Cedar Island Rd
Carteret Co NC 114 B2
Old Chapel Hill Rd
Chapel Hill NC 30 D7
Old Chpl Hill-Hillsborough Rd
Orange Co NC 30 B5
Old Chapin Rd
Lexington Co SC 137 C6
Old Charlotte Hwy
Monroe NC 102 A2
Old Charlotte Rd SW
Concord NC 76 B3
Old Cherokee Rd
Lexington Co SC 137 B6
Old Cherry Rd
Oconee Co SC 116 E1
Oconee Co SC 225 B7
Old Cherry Rd SR-149
Oconee Co SC 225 B7
Old Chester Rd
Cherokee Co SC 99 D1
Old Church Rd
Southampton Co VA 14 B1

Old Concord Rd
Charlotte NC 75 E5
Rowan Co NC 50 C7
Old Copper Rd
Ducktown TN 91 C2
Polk Co TN 65 A7
Polk Co TN 91 B1
Old Copper Rd SR-40
Ducktown TN 91 C2
Polk Co TN 65 A7
Polk Co TN 91 B1
Old Copper Rd US-64
Ducktown TN 91 C2
Polk Co TN 65 A7
Polk Co TN 91 B1
Old Copper Rd US-74
Ducktown TN 91 C2
Polk Co TN 65 A7
Polk Co TN 91 B1
Old County Home Rd
Buncombe Co NC 44 C6
Old Crews Rd
Wake Co NC 56 A1
Old Darlington Hwy
Darlington Co SC 141 D1
Old Dibble Rd
Aiken Co SC 150 B7
Old Douglas Mill Rd
Abbeville Co SC 134 B2
Old Douglas Mill Rd SR-203
Abbeville Co SC 134 B2
Old Douglass Rd
Fairfield Co SC 121 C5
Old Dowd Rd
Charlotte NC 214 B2
Mecklenburg Co NC 75 A5
Old Dutch Rd
Fairview NC 76 B6
Old Easley Hwy
Greenville Co SC 96 E5
Old Easley Hwy SR-124
Greenville Co SC 96 E5
Old Eastover Rd
Richland Co SC 138 E7
Richland Co SC 153 A1
Old Eastover Rd SR-764
Richland Co SC 138 E7
Richland Co SC 153 A1
Old Englewood Rd
McMinn Co TN 65 A2
Old Englewood Rd SR-39
McMinn Co TN 65 A2
Olde South Rd
Wake Co NC 55 C3
Old Evans Rd
Columbia Co GA 148 E7
Evans GA 149 A7
Old Faison Rd
Wake Co NC 56 A2
Old Falston Rd
Gaston Co NC 73 E2
Old Farrington Rd
Chatham Co NC 54 D1
Old Fayetteville Rd
Bladen Co NC 107 E4
Bladen Co NC 108 A5
Orange Co NC 30 C7
Old Fayetteville Rd NE
Leland NC 130 D7
Old Federal Rd
Franklin Co GA 115 B6
Old Federal Rd SR-51
Franklin Co GA 115 B6
Old Fort Rd
Buncombe Co NC 45 D7
Old Fort Sugar Hill Rd
McDowell Co NC 45 E6
McDowell Co NC 46 A6
Old GA-76
Fannin Co GA 91 E4
Old GA-76 SR-60
Fannin Co GA 91 E4
Old GA-197 S
Habersham Co GA 115 A3
Old GA-441
Rabun Co GA 94 B6
Old Georgetown Rd SW
Brunswick Co NC 145 B6
Old Georgetown Rd SW SR-179
Brunswick Co NC 145 B6
Old Georgia Hwy
Cherokee Co SC 98 E2
Cherokee Co SC 99 A2
Old Georgia Hwy US-29
Cherokee Co SC 98 E2
Cherokee Co SC 99 A2
Old Georgia Rd
Spartanburg Co SC 98 B5
Old Gilliard Rd
Berkeley Co SC 164 A5
Old Gilliard Rd SR-27
Berkeley Co SC 164 A5
Old Graniteville Hwy
Aiken Co SC 149 E5
Old Graniteville Hwy SR-191
Aiken Co SC 149 E5
Old Greensboro Rd
Orange Co NC 30 A7
N Old Greensboro Rd
Davidson Co NC 27 D7
Old Greenville Hwy
Anderson Co SC 96 C7
Anderson Co SC 117 B1
Clemson SC 116 E1
Pickens Co SC 225 A4
Old Greenville Hwy SR-88
Anderson Co SC 96 C7
Anderson Co SC 117 B1

Old Greenville Hwy SR-93
Clemson SC 116 E1
Pickens Co SC 225 A4
Old Haywood Rd
Henderson Co NC 70 D2
Old Haywood Rd SR-191
Henderson Co NC 70 D2
Old Hendersonville Hwy
Brevard NC 70 B5
Old Hickory Grove Rd
Gaston Co NC 74 E4
Old Highway 19
Buncombe Co NC 44 D4
Old Highway 20
Buncombe Co NC 44 B4
Old Highway 27
Gaston Co NC 74 E3
Old Hollow Rd
Walkertown NC 27 A3
Old Hollow Rd SR-66
Walkertown NC 27 A3
Old Holly Springs Apex Rd
Wake Co NC 55 A4
Old Hopkins Rd
Richland Co SC 138 C7
Old Jackson Hwy
Aiken Co SC 159 D2
Old Jacksonboro Rd
Ravenel SC 172 B5
Old Jefferson Hwy
Chesterfield Co SC 123 C2
Old Jefferson Hwy SR-265
Chesterfield Co SC 123 C2
Old Jenks Rd
Wake Co NC 55 A3
Old Jonesboro Rd
Greene Co TN 19 E5
Greene Co TN 20 A5
Washington Co VA 1 A3
Old Jonesboro Rd SR-351
Greene Co TN 19 E5
Greene Co TN 20 A5
Old Jonesborough Rd
Washington Co TN 21 A1
Old Knight Rd
Wake Co NC 56 A2
N Old Lake Rd
Bladen Co NC 129 D5
Old Lake City Rd
Williamsburg Co SC 155 D4
Old Lakey Gap Rd
Black Mountain NC 45 B6
Old Laurens Rd
Greenwood Co SC 134 E2
Old Leaksville Rd
Ridgeway VA 7 B3
Old Leicester Hwy
Buncombe Co NC 44 C6
Old Leicester Rd
Buncombe Co NC 44 C5
Old Lexington Rd
Davidson Co NC 27 B6
Winston-Salem NC 188 E6
Old Liberty Rd
Randolph Co NC 53 A1
Old Louisburg Rd
Raleigh NC 200 B1
Old Lumberton Rd
Columbus Co NC 128 B5
E Old Marion Hwy
Florence Co SC 141 E1
Old Marshall Hwy
Buncombe Co NC 44 C4
Old Marshall Hwy SR-251
Buncombe Co NC 44 C4
Old Mars Hill Hwy
Buncombe Co NC 44 D4
Old Milburnie Rd
Wake Co NC 56 A1
Old Mill Rd
Mauldin SC 97 C6
Old Mill Rd NE
Navassa NC 130 D7
Old Mocksville Rd
Salisbury NC 50 D4
Salisbury NC 208 C1
Old Monroe Rd
Stallings NC 102 A1
Old Mountain Rd
Iredell Co NC 49 A3
Old Mt Holly Rd
Berkeley Co SC 172 E1
Old Mullins Rd
Dillon Co SC 127 B7
Old Murphy Rd
Franklin NC 68 B6
Old Nation Rd
York Co SC 101 B2
Old Nation Rd US-21 BUS
York Co SC 101 B2
Old NC-10
Burke Co NC 47 E4
Orange Co NC 30 C5
Old NC-18
Wilkes Co NC 24 C4
Old NC-20
Buncombe Co NC 44 C4
Old NC-49
Randolph Co NC 51 E5
Randolph Co NC 52 A5
Old NC-54
Durham NC 30 D7
Old NC-86
Caswell Co NC 8 C4
Orange Co NC 30 B6

Old NC-87
Columbus Co NC 130
Old NC-98
Wake Forest NC 31
Old NC-150
Lincoln Co NC 74
Old NC-903
Duplin Co NC 109
Old Newport Hwy
Sevier Co TN 42
Old Newport Hwy SR-339
Sevier Co TN 42
Old Nichols Hwy
Marion Co SC 143
W Old Number Four Hwy
Florence Co SC 141
W Old Number Four Hwy SR-541
Florence Co SC 141
Old Oak Ridge Rd
Guilford Co NC 28
Old Ocean Hwy E
Brunswick Co NC 146
Old Ocean Hwy E US-17 BUS
Brunswick Co NC 146
S Old Oregon Inlet Rd
Nags Head NC 40
Old Oxford Hwy
Durham Co NC 31
Old Oxford Rd
Durham NC 31
Old Pacolet Rd
Spartanburg Co SC 98
Old Peachland Rd
Union Co NC 103
Old Percival Rd
Richland Co SC 138
Old Petersburg Rd
Lincoln Co GA 148
Martinez GA 149
Old Pinckney Rd
York Co SC 100
Old Pink Hill Rd
Lenoir Co NC 84
Old Pink Hill Rd SR-11
Lenoir Co NC 84
Old Pink Hill Rd SR-55
Lenoir Co NC 84
Old Pipers Gap Rd
Carroll Co VA 4
Old Plank Rd
Charlotte NC 75
Edgefield Co SC 149
Saluda Co SC 150
Old Post Rd
Cherokee Co SC 99
Erwin NC 81
W Old Post Rd
Cherryville NC 74
Old Quarry Rd
Pittsylvania Co VA 8
Old Raleigh Rd
Apex NC 55
Old Reidsville Rd
Guilford Co NC 28
Old Richburg Rd
Chester Co SC 100
Chester Co SC 101
Old Richmond Rd
Pittsylvania Co VA 8
Old Richmond Rd SR-360
Pittsylvania Co VA 8
Old River Rd
Fairfield Co SC 122
Florence Co SC 142
Haywood Co NC 69
Old River Rd SR-215
Haywood Co NC 69
N Old River Rd
Florence Co SC 142
S Old River Rd
Florence Co SC 142
Old Rosman Hwy
Transylvania Co NC 70
Old Rural Hall Rd
Forsyth Co NC 27
Forsyth Co NC 186
Old Salem Rd
Forsyth Co NC 27
Hilda SC 161
Old Salisbury Rd
Davidson Co NC 27
Old Salisbury-Concord Rd
Cabarrus Co NC 76
Old Salkehatchie Hwy
Hampton Co SC 170
Old Sandy Run Rd
Calhoun Co SC 152
Old Savannah Rd
Augusta GA 159
Old SC-11
Oconee Co SC 95
Old Seneca Rd
Oconee Co SC 116
Old Sheldon Church Rd
Beaufort Co SC 176
Old Sitton Mill Rd
Oconee Co SC 116
Old Smithfield Rd SW
Goldsboro NC 83
Johnston Co NC 83
Old Smithfield Rd SW SR-581
Goldsboro NC 83
Old Spartanburg Rd
Greenville Co SC 97
Old Stage Rd
Bladen Co NC 129
Columbus Co NC 130
Garner NC 55

INDEX 30

ld Stage Rd — Street Index — Pinckney Rd SR-9

STREET / City State / Map# Grid

ld Stage Rd
arnett Co NC 81 C2
cotland Co NC 105 B7
ld Stage Rd SR-27
arnett Co NC 81 C2
ld Stage Rd SR-87
laden Co NC 129 E5
olumbus Co NC 130 A6
ld Stagecoach Rd
Vashington Co TN 20 D1
ld State Rd
alhoun Co SC 152 E5
alhoun Co SC 163 B1
ameron SC 153 A6
rangeburg Co SC 164 A4
ld State Rd US-176
alhoun Co SC 152 E5
alhoun Co SC 163 B1
ameron SC 153 A6
rangeburg Co SC 164 A4
ld Statesville Rd
harlotte NC 75 D4
untersville NC 75 C2
ld Statesville Rd
R-115
untersville NC 75 C2
ld Statesville Rd
S-21
harlotte NC 75 D4
Old Statesville Rd
untersville NC 75 C2
Old Statesville Rd
R-115
untersville NC 75 C2
ld St Tammany Rd
ecklenburg Co VA 12 A2
ld Swamp Rd
alhoun Co SC 152 B4
amden Co NC 17 A3
ld Swamp Rd SR-172
alhoun Co SC 152 B4
ld Thomasville Rd
igh Point NC 27 D7
ld TN-34
Vashington Co TN 20 C2
ld TN-34 SR-353
Vashington Co TN 20 D2
ld TN-68
onroe Co TN 65 C1
ld TN-73
evier Co TN 41 D5
ld Tory Tr
iken Co SC 150 C7
ld Towne Rd
harleston SC 239 D4
ld Towne Rd SR-171
harleston SC 239 D4
ld Tram Rd
Marion Co SC 142 D6
ld Tram Rd SR-41
Marion Co SC 142 D6
ld Tuckaleechee Rd
lount Co TN 41 B5
ld Two Notch Rd
ichland Co SC 138 C3
ld Union Church Rd
East Spencer NC 50 D5
ld US-1
Chatham Co NC 54 D5
Wake Co NC 55 A4
ld US-11E
Greene Co TN 19 E3
ld US-13
Hertford Co NC 15 B5
ld US-13 SR-461
Hertford Co NC 15 B5
ld US-17
Perquimans Co NC 17 A7
ld US 19 23 Hwy
Buncombe Co NC 44 A7
ld US-19E
Yancey Co NC 45 B1
ld US-25
Henderson Co NC 71 A6
ld US-25 SR-225
Henderson Co NC 71 A6
ld US-52
Berkeley Co SC 165 A7
Davidson Co NC 27 B7
Davidson Co NC 51 A1
Forsyth Co NC 26 E1
Pilot Mountain NC 5 C6
Stanly Co NC 77 B1
Stokes Co NC 5 D7
ld US-52 SR-8
Davidson Co NC 51 A1
ld US-64
Chatham Co NC 53 B3
Martin Co NC 36 E7
Martin Co NC 60 D1
Tyrrell Co NC 38 D5
ld US-64 W
Clay Co NC 92 E2
Old US-64
Lexington NC 51 B2
ld US-70
Carteret Co NC 112 E4
Craven Co NC 85 B4
Rowan Co NC 50 A4
ld US-70 W
Craven Co NC 85 D5
Craven Co NC 86 A5
Johnston Co NC 56 A4
ld US-264
Wake Co NC 56 D1
ld US-421
Boone NC 185 E3
Forsyth Co NC 26 B4
Watauga Co NC 22 E1
Watauga Co NC 23 C2
Wilkes Co NC 24 D4
Wilkesboro NC 24 C3

Old US-421
Yadkin Co NC 25 E4
Old US-421 US-221
Watauga Co NC 23 C2
Old US-421 N
Chatham Co NC 53 B3
Old US-421 S
Chatham Co NC 53 C4
Old US-601
Surry Co NC 4 E6
Surry Co NC 5 A5
Old US-601 US-601 BUS
Surry Co NC 4 E6
Old Valley School Rd
Forsyth Co NC 27 C3
Old Vaucluse Rd
Aiken Co SC 149 E5
Old Vineyard Rd
Winston-Salem NC 187 A5
Old Walkertown Rd
Forsyth Co NC 27 B3
Old Washington Rd
Columbia Co GA 148 D6
Old Waynesboro Rd
Augusta GA 159 B3
Old Weaver Tr
Wake Co NC 31 C4
Old Westfield Rd
Pilot Mountain NC 5 C6
Old Whiskey Rd N
New Ellenton SC 160 A2
Old Whiskey Rd S
New Ellenton SC 160 A2
Old White Horse Rd
Greenville Co SC 96 E4
Old Whitesville Rd
Berkeley Co SC 164 E6
Old Whiteville Rd
Columbus Co NC 128 A2
Old Willis School Rd
Gaston Co NC 74 D3
Old Wilmington Rd
Cumberland Co NC 222 E5
Old Wilson Rd
Rocky Mount NC 34 A6
Rocky Mount NC 201 D6
Old Wire Rd
Kershaw Co SC 123 D7
Kershaw Co SC 124 A6
Kershaw Co SC 139 C1
Scotland Co NC 105 C5
Old Wire Rd SR-144
Scotland Co NC 105 C5
Old York Rd
Chester Co SC 100 C7
Old York Rd SR-161
York Co SC 100 E3
Old York Rd SR-274
York Co SC 100 E3
Old York Rd SR-909
Chester Co SC 100 C6
E Old York Rd
York Co SC 100 D2
E Old York Rd SR-161
York Co SC 100 D2
W Old York Rd
York Co SC 100 C2
W Old York Rd SR-161
York Co SC 100 C3
Oleander Dr
Wilmington NC 147 A1
Wilmington NC 231 D5
Oleander Dr US-76
Wilmington NC 147 A1
Wilmington NC 231 D5
Olive Rd
Augusta GA 159 B1
Olive St
Pickens Co SC 96 D5
Olive Branch Rd
Durham Co NC 31 B6
Oliver Church Rd
Marietta NC 127 C5
Olivette Rd
Buncombe Co NC 44 C5
N O'Neil St
Clayton NC 56 B4
Onslow Dr
Jacksonville NC 227 C5
Opie Arnold Rd
Washington Co TN 20 C2
Opie Arnold Rd SR-75
Washington Co TN 20 C2
Optimist Farm Rd
Wake Co NC 55 B4
Ora Rd
Laurens Co SC 119 A2
Ora Rd SR-92
Laurens Co SC 119 A2
Orangeburg Rd
Dorchester Co SC 172 C1
Organ Church Rd
Rowan Co NC 50 D7
Oriental Rd
Pamlico Co NC 87 B7
Orleans Rd
Charleston Co SC 239 A4
Orphanage Rd
Cabarrus Co NC 76 A2
Pittsylvania Co VA 8 C2
Osteen Hill Rd
Anderson Co SC 117 E1
Ostwalt Amity Rd
Iredell Co NC 49 C4
Oswego Hwy
Sumter Co SC 140 A6
Oswego Hwy US-401
Sumter Co SC 140 A6
Oswego Rd
Sumter SC 140 A7
Oswego Rd US-401
Sumter Co SC 140 A7

Otis Baughman Sr Memorial Hwy
Aiken Co SC 151 B4
Otis Baughman Sr Mem Hy SR-302
Aiken Co SC 151 B4
Outing Club Rd
Aiken Co SC 149 E6
Oven Creek Rd
Cocke Co TN 19 B5
Oven Creek Rd SR-340
Cocke Co TN 19 B5
Overlook Rd
Asheville NC 70 D1
Owen Dr
Cumberland Co NC 222 B6
Fayetteville NC 106 E1
Fayetteville NC 107 A1
Owl Creek Rd
Towns Co GA 93 B5
Oxford Rd
Henderson NC 11 B7
Person Co NC 9 E6
Person Co NC 10 A7
Oxford Rd US-158
Person Co NC 9 E6
Person Co NC 10 A7
Oxford Rd US-158 BUS
Henderson NC 11 B7
Oxford Outer Lp
Oxford NC 10 D7
Oxford Outer Lp US-158
Granville Co NC 10 D7
Oxford School Rd
Catawba Co NC 48 D3
E Ozark Av
Gastonia NC 74 D5
E Ozark Av SR-7
Gastonia NC 74 D5
Ozone Dr
Polk Co NC 71 B5

P

Pacolet Hwy
Cherokee Co SC 99 A3
Pacolet Hwy SR-150
Cherokee Co SC 99 A3
Pacolet Rd
Gaffney SC 99 B2
Pacolet Rd SR-150
Gaffney SC 99 B2
Pactolus Hwy
Greenville NC 59 B4
Pactolus Hwy SR-33
Greenville NC 59 B4
Page Rd
Durham NC 55 A1
Durham Co NC 31 B7
Pageland Hwy
Lancaster Co SC 101 E7
Union Co NC 102 C3
Pageland Hwy SR-9
Lancaster Co SC 101 E7
Lancaster Co SC 102 B7
Pageland Hwy US-601
Union Co NC 102 C3
Paint Fork Rd
Buncombe Co NC 44 E4
Buncombe Co NC 45 A3
Palm Blvd
Isle of Palms SC 173 D5
Palm Blvd SR-703
Isle of Palms SC 173 D5
W Palmer St
Franklin NC 68 B6
Palmer Springs Rd
Mecklenburg Co VA 11 D3
Palmetto Blvd
Edisto Beach SC 178 A4
Palmetto Blvd SR-174
Edisto Beach SC 178 A4
Palmetto Pkwy
North Augusta SC 159 C1
Palmetto Pkwy I-520
North Augusta SC 159 C1
E Palmetto St
Florence SC 141 D2
Florence SC 230 D5
Florence Co SC 141 E2
Florence Co SC 142 A2
E Palmetto St SR-327
Florence Co SC 142 A2
E Palmetto St US-76
Florence SC 141 D2
Florence SC 230 D5
Florence Co SC 141 E2
Florence Co SC 142 A2
E Palmetto St US-301
Florence SC 141 D2
Florence SC 230 D5
Florence Co SC 141 E2
Florence Co SC 142 A2
W Palmetto St
Florence SC 141 D2
Florence SC 230 A5
Florence Co SC 141 C2
W Palmetto St US-76
Florence SC 141 D2
Florence SC 230 A5
Florence Co SC 141 C3
Palmetto Bay Rd
Hilton Head Island SC 181 E2
Hilton Head Island SC 242 A5
Palmetto Bay Rd US-278
Hilton Head Island SC 181 E2
Hilton Head Island SC 242 A5
Pamalee Dr
Fayetteville NC 80 E7
Pamalee Dr US-401 BYP
Fayetteville NC 80 E7

Pamlico St
Beaufort Co NC 61 C5
Pamlico St US-264 BUS
Beaufort Co NC 61 C5
Pamplico Hwy
Florence SC 141 D3
Florence Co SC 141 E3
Pamplico Hwy SR-51
Florence SC 141 D2
Florence Co SC 141 E3
N Pamplico Hwy
Florence Co SC 142 A5
N Pamplico Hwy SR-51
Florence Co SC 142 A5
S Pamplico Hwy
Florence Co SC 142 B6
S Pamplico Hwy SR-51
Florence Co SC 142 B6
S Paraham Rd
York Co SC 100 D2
Park Av
Danville VA 8 C3
Franklin Co NC 32 A4
Transylvania Co NC 70 B5
Park Av US-1 ALT
Franklin Co NC 32 A4
Park Av SW
Aiken Co SC 236 D1
W Park Av
Mooresville NC 49 D6
W Park Av SR-801
Mooresville NC 49 D6
Park Dr
Anderson SC 117 C4
Anderson SC 226 C2
Washington NC 60 B5
Park Dr SR-32
Washington NC 60 B5
Park Dr US-76
Anderson SC 117 C4
Anderson SC 226 C2
Park Dr US-178
Anderson SC 117 C4
Anderson SC 226 C2
Park Rd
Charlotte NC 75 C7
Charlotte NC 101 C1
Spartanburg Co SC 98 A2
York Co SC 74 A7
Park St
Richland Co SC 233 B3
Park St SR-12
Richland Co SC 233 B3
W Park St
Canton NC 43 E7
W Park St US-19
Canton NC 43 E7
W Park St US-23
Canton NC 43 E7
Parker Rd
Johnston Co NC 82 B1
Spartanburg Co SC 119 C1
Parker Rd SR-92
Spartanburg Co SC 119 C1
E Parker Rd
Morganton NC 47 B4
W Parker Rd
Greenville Co SC 97 A5
Parker St
Rocky Mount NC 201 D4
E Parker St
Graham NC 29 C4
Parkers Ferry Rd
Charleston Co SC 171 E7
E Parkins Mill Rd
Greenville SC 97 B6
Parklane Rd
Arcadia Lakes SC 138 B4
Park Place Rd
York Co SC 100 D3
Parks Lafferty Rd
Cabarrus Co NC 76 C4
Parkway
Gatlinburg TN 42 A3
Pigeon Forge TN 41 E2
Parkway SR-71
Gatlinburg TN 42 A3
Pigeon Forge TN 41 E2
Parkway SR-73
Gatlinburg TN 42 A3
Parkway US-321
Gatlinburg TN 42 A3
Parkway US-441
Gatlinburg TN 42 A3
Pigeon Forge TN 41 E2
W Parkway Av
High Point NC 191 B3
Parkwood Av
Charlotte NC 216 B1
N Parler Av
St. George SC 163 C5
N Parler Av US-15
St. George SC 163 C5
S Parler Av
St. George SC 163 C6
S Parler Av US-15
St. George SC 163 C6
Parr Rd
Newberry Co SC 137 A1
Parr Rd SR-213
Newberry Co SC 137 A1
Parris Bridge Rd
Spartanburg Co SC 72 C7
Spartanburg Co SC 98 C2
Parris Island Gateway
Beaufort Co SC 177 A5
Parris Island Gateway SR-280
Beaufort Co SC 177 A5
Parson Branch Rd
Blount Co TN 41 A7
Blount Co TN 66 E1

Pasture Branch Rd
Greenevers NC 109 E4
Patch Rd
Haywood Co NC 43 D4
Pat Colwell Rd
Union Co GA 92 C4
NE Patetown Rd
Goldsboro NC 83 D1
NE Patetown Rd SR-111
Goldsboro NC 83 D1
Patrick Hwy
Darlington Co SC 124 E5
Patrick Hwy SR-102
Darlington Co SC 124 E6
Patrick Rd
Gaston Co NC 74 D6
Patrick Society Hill Rd
Chesterfield Co SC 124 E3
Chesterfield Co SC 125 A3
Patterson Av
Winston-Salem NC 188 D3
NE Patterson Av
Winston-Salem NC 27 A3
Winston-Salem NC 186 D4
Winston-Salem NC 188 D1
Patterson Ct
Greensboro NC 189 E4
Patterson Ct SR-6
Greensboro NC 189 E4
Patterson Rd
Kings Mountain NC 74 A5
Rabun Co GA 94 A4
Patterson St
Barnwell SC 161 A5
Greensboro NC 28 B5
Patterson St SR-6
Greensboro NC 28 B5
Patterson St SR-64
Barnwell SC 161 A5
Patterson Gap Rd
Rabun Co GA 94 A3
Patterson Mill Dr
Allendale Co SC 160 D7
Patterson Mill Rd
Barnwell Co SC 160 D6
Patton Av
Asheville NC 44 C7
Buncombe Co NC 206 B3
Patton Av US-19
Asheville NC 44 C7
Patton Av US-23
Asheville NC 44 C7
Patton Av US-74 ALT
Asheville NC 44 C7
Paul Brown Blvd
Charlotte NC 75 B6
Paul Brown Blvd SR-160
Charlotte NC 75 B6
Paul Cantrell Blvd
Charleston Co SC 239 A3
Pauley Swamp Rd
Horry Co SC 157 C2
Pauley Swamp Rd SR-109
Horry Co SC 157 C2
Paul Green Memorial Hwy
Harnett Co NC 80 D1
Harnett Co NC 81 A2
Paul Green Memorial Hwy SR-27
Harnett Co NC 81 B2
Paul Green Memorial Hwy US-421
Harnett Co NC 80 D1
Harnett Co NC 81 A2
Paul's Path Rd
Greene Co NC 84 B2
Pavilion Blvd
Charlotte NC 212 A5
Paxville Hwy
Paxville SC 154 A3
Paxville Hwy SR-261
Paxville SC 154 A3
W Peace St
Raleigh NC 199 E3
Peace Haven Rd
Forsyth Co NC 26 D5
Winston-Salem NC 187 B1
N Peace Haven Rd
Winston-Salem NC 26 E4
Winston-Salem NC 187 B2
S Peace Haven Rd
Forsyth Co NC 26 E5
Peach Dr
Anderson Co SC 117 B1
Peach Festival Rd
Lexington Co SC 137 A6
Peachoid Rd
Cherokee Co SC 99 A1
Peach Orchard Rd
Augusta GA 159 A3
Cabarrus Co NC 76 A5
Sumter Co SC 139 D6
Peach Orchard Rd SR-121
Augusta GA 159 A3
Peach Orchard Rd SR-441
Sumter SC 139 D6
Peach Orchard Rd US-25
Augusta GA 159 A3
Peachtree Rd
Charlotte NC 75 C4
Lattimore NC 73 B4
Peachtree St
Rocky Mount NC 201 C2
Peacock Rd
Columbus Co NC 128 C5
Columbus Co NC 144 C2
Peake Rd
Richland Co SC 138 C1

Pea Landing Rd NW
Brunswick Co NC 145 A6
Peanut Rd
Elizabethtown NC 128 E1
Pearces Rd
Franklin Co NC 32 D7
Wake Co NC 56 D1
Pea Ridge Rd
Polk Co NC 71 E4
Polk Co NC 72 A4
Pearl St
Darlington SC 125 B7
Darlington SC 229 D5
Darlington Co SC 229 C6
Pageland SC 102 E6
Pearl St SR-34
Darlington SC 125 B7
Darlington SC 229 D5
Pearl St SR-151 BUS
Pageland SC 102 E6
Pearl St US-401
Darlington Co SC 229 C6
N Pearl St
Pageland SC 102 E6
N Pearl St SR-151 BUS
Chesterfield Co SC 102 E6
N Pearl St US-601
Chesterfield Co SC 102 E6
W Pearl St
Spartanburg SC 224 B3
Pearman Dairy Rd
Anderson Co SC 117 B4
Anderson Co SC 226 A4
Pearman Dairy Rd SR-28 BYP
Anderson Co SC 117 B4
Anderson Co SC 226 A4
Pearman Dairy Rd S
Anderson Co SC 117 B4
Anderson Co SC 226 B6
Pearman Dairy Rd S SR-28 BYP
Anderson Co SC 117 B4
Anderson Co SC 226 B6
Pee Dee Hwy
Horry Co SC 143 B7
Horry Co SC 157 B1
Pee Dee Rd
Moore Co NC 79 D6
Peeler Rd
Rowan Co NC 50 C6
Peirce Rd
Colleton Co SC 171 E1
Cottageville SC 171 D2
Pekin Rd
Montgomery Co NC 78 B5
Pelham Dr
Columbia SC 138 B6
Richland Co SC 234 C6
Pelham Rd
Greenville Co SC 97 C5
Pelzer Hwy
Easley SC 96 C6
Greenville Co SC 118 A2
Pelzer Hwy SR-8
Easley SC 96 C6
Greenville Co SC 118 A2
Pemberton Rd
Sullivan Co TN 1 A4
Pence Rd
Charlotte NC 75 E5
Pendergrass Blvd
Great Falls SC 122 C3
Pendergrass Blvd SR-200
Great Falls SC 122 C3
Pendergrass Blvd US-21
Great Falls SC 122 C3
Pendleton Rd
Clemson SC 225 E6
Pendleton Rd SR-28 BUS
Clemson SC 225 E6
Pendleton St
Greenville SC 97 A5
Greenville SC 223 A4
Pendleton St SR-124
Greenville SC 97 A5
Greenville SC 223 A4
Penninger Rd
Cabarrus Co NC 76 B1
Pennsylvania Av
Chatham Co GA 181 A4
Vandemere NC 87 B4
Pennsylvania Av SR-307
Vandemere NC 87 B4
Penny Rd
Cary NC 55 B3
Guilford Co NC 28 A6
Wake Co NC 55 C3
Penry Rd
Guilford Co NC 28 D4
Perch Rd
Stokes Co NC 26 C1
Percival Rd
Richland Co SC 138 C4
Percival Rd SR-12
Richland Co SC 138 C4
Percy St
Greensboro NC 190 D2
Perimeter Rd
Burke Co GA 159 B7
Greenville Co SC 97 A7
Perimeter Rd SR-873
Burke Co GA 159 B7
Perry Creek Rd
Raleigh NC 31 E7
Perry's Bridge Rd
Perquimans Co NC 16 C5
Perrys Chapel Rd
Franklin Co NC 32 B4
Persimmon Rd
Carolina Shores NC 145 A6

Persimmon Rd
Rabun Co GA 94 A4
Person Rd
Franklin Co NC 32 E1
Person St
Fayetteville NC 222 E3
N Person St
Raleigh NC 200 A3
Pete Brittain Rd
Burke Co NC 47 A4
Peters Creek Pkwy
Winston-Salem NC 27 A6
Winston-Salem NC 188 B7
Peters Creek Pkwy SR-150
Winston-Salem NC 27 A6
Winston-Salem NC 188 B7
Pharr Mill Rd
Harrisburg NC 76 B4
Philadelphia Church Rd
Gaston Co NC 74 D3
Phillips Av
Greensboro NC 28 C4
High Point NC 191 B5
Phillips Rd
Clay Co NC 93 A2
Phillis Rd
Mecklenburg Co VA 11 B1
Philpott Rd
Halifax Co VA 9 C2
Philpott Rd US-58
Halifax Co VA 9 C2
Philpott Rd US-360
Halifax Co VA 9 C2
Phinizy Rd
Augusta GA 159 B2
Pickens Dr
Liberty SC 96 B6
Pickens Dr US-178
Liberty SC 96 B6
Pickens Hwy
Oconee Co SC 95 C6
Pickens Co SC 96 B5
Rosman NC 69 E7
Pickens Hwy SR-8
Pickens Co SC 96 B5
Pickens Hwy SR-183
Oconee Co SC 95 C6
Pickens Hwy US-178
Rosman NC 69 E7
Pickett Rd
Durham NC 30 D6
Pickney Rd
Chester Co SC 99 E6
Chester Co SC 100 A7
Pickney Rd SR-9
Chester Co SC 99 E6
Chester Co SC 100 A7
N Piedmont Av
Cleveland Co NC 74 A5
N Piedmont Av SR-216
Cleveland Co NC 74 A5
Piedmont Dr
Danville VA 8 C3
Piedmont Hwy
Greenville Co SC 97 A7
Piedmont Hwy SR-20
Greenville Co SC 97 A7
N Piedmont Hwy
Greenville Co SC 97 A7
N Piedmont Hwy SR-20
Greenville Co SC 97 A7
S Piedmont Hwy
Greenville Co SC 118 A1
S Piedmont Hwy SR-20
Greenville Co SC 118 A1
Piedmont Pkwy
High Point NC 28 A5
Piedmont Rd
York Co SC 74 A7
York Co SC 100 A1
Piedmont Park Rd
Greenville Co SC 97 B4
Pigeon Rd
Haywood Co NC 69 D1
Pigeon Rd US-276
Haywood Co NC 69 D1
Pigeon St
Waynesville NC 69 C1
Pigeon St US-276
Waynesville NC 69 C1
Pigott Rd
Carteret Co NC 113 E5
N Pike E
Sumter SC 235 E1
N Pike W
Sumter SC 235 C1
Sumter Co SC 139 E6
S Pike E
Sumter SC 235 E1
S Pike W
Sumter SC 235 B1
Pikeville Princeton Rd NW
Wayne Co NC 57 B7
Pilgram Church Rd
Alexander Co NC 24 E6
Alexander Co NC 25 A6
Pilgrim Church Rd
Lexington Co NC 137 C5
Pilot Mountain Pkwy
Surry Co NC 5 C6
Pilot Mountain Pkwy US-52
Surry Co NC 5 C6
Pilot-Riley Rd
Franklin Co NC 32 C6
Pinckney Rd
Chester Co SC 100 B7
Pinckney Rd SR-9
Chester Co SC 100 B7

STREET
City State Map# Grid

Roy Eaker Rd
Cherryville NC 74 A3
Royle Rd
Berkeley Co SC 172 D1
Royston Hwy
Hart Co GA 116 C7
Royston Hwy SR-8
Hart Co GA 116 C7
Royston Hwy US-29
Hart Co GA 116 C7
Rozzelles Ferry Rd
Mecklenburg Co NC 75 B4
R Stoudemayer Rd
Richland Co SC 137 B2
Ruby Rd
Darlington Co SC 124 D5
Ruby Hartsville Rd
Chesterfield Co SC 124 D3
Ruckersville Rd
Elbert Co GA 133 A2
Rudisill Rd
Gaston Co NC 74 B3
Rugby Rd
Grayson Co VA 2 D3
Rugby Rd E-743
Grayson Co VA 2 E3
Ruhammah Rd
Pickens Co SC 96 B6
Running Creek Church Rd
Stanly Co NC 76 E4
Stanly Co NC 77 A3
Rush St
Raleigh NC 55 D3
Rush Fork Rd
Haywood Co NC 43 D6
Rush Fork Rd SR-209
Haywood Co NC 43 D6
Russ Av
Haywood Co NC 43 C7
Waynesville NC 69 C1
Russ Av US-276
Haywood Co NC 43 C7
Waynesville NC 69 C1
E Russell Av
High Point NC 191 D4
W Russell Av
High Point NC 191 C4
Russell Rd
Durham Co NC 30 E4
Russell Rd NW
Abingdon VA 1 B1
Russell Rd NW US-58 ALT
Abingdon VA 1 B1
Russell St
Orangeburg SC 152 D7
Russell St SR-33
Orangeburg SC 152 D7
Rutherford Rd
Burke Co NC 47 A5
Greenville Co SC 97 B4
Greenville Co SC 223 B1
Marion NC 46 B5
Rutherford Rd US-64
Burke Co NC 47 A5
Rutherford Rd US-221 BUS
McDowell Co NC 46 B5
N Rutherford Rd
Greenville Co SC 97 C3
Rutherford St
Greenville SC 223 B2
Rutherford St US-25 BUS
Greenville SC 223 B2
Rutherford St US-276 BUS
Greenville SC 223 B2
E Rutherford St
Landrum SC 71 D6
E Rutherford St SR-14
Landrum SC 71 D6
Rutherfordton Hwy
Cherokee Co SC 72 D7
Rutherfordton Hwy US-221
Cherokee Co SC 72 D7
Rutledge Av
Charleston SC 240 D6
Ryland Rd
Chowan Co NC 16 B6

S

Saddle Club Rd
Burlington NC 29 B4
Saffold Dr
Thunderbolt GA 181 A4
Saffold Dr SR-26
Thunderbolt GA 181 A4
Saffold Dr US-80
Thunderbolt GA 181 A4
Sage Rd
Chapel Hill NC 30 D6
St. Andrews Blvd
Charleston SC 173 A5
Charleston SC 239 D5
Charleston SC 240 A6
St. Andrews Blvd SR-61
Charleston SC 173 A5
Charleston SC 239 D5
Charleston SC 240 A6
St. Andrews Blvd SR-171
Charleston SC 173 A5
Charleston SC 239 D5
Charleston SC 240 A6
St. Andrews Rd
Lexington Co SC 137 D5
St. Charles Rd
Lee Co SC 140 B2
St. Charles Rd SR-154
Lee Co SC 140 B2
St. Clair Rd
Hamblen Co TN 19 A1
St. Clair Rd SR-344
Hamblen Co TN 19 A1
St. Clairs Creek Rd
Smyth Co VA 2 B1
St. David Rd
Washington Co NC 38 A6
St. James Av
Berkeley Co SC 172 E1
Goose Creek SC 237 B1
St. James Av US-176
Goose Creek SC 172 E1
Goose Creek SC 237 B1
St. James Rd
Greene Co TN 19 C6
St. John St
Spartanburg SC 224 C4
St. John St US-29
Spartanburg SC 224 C4
E St. John St
Spartanburg SC 224 D3
E St. John St US-29
Spartanburg SC 224 D3
W St. John St
Spartanburg SC 224 B4
W St. John St US-29
Spartanburg SC 224 C3
St. Johns Church Rd
Cabarrus Co NC 76 C2
St. Mark Rd
Greenville Co SC 97 C3
St. Marks Church Rd
Lincoln Co NC 74 B3
St. Marys Rd
Orange Co NC 30 C4
St. Marys St
Raleigh NC 197 D7
St. Matthews Rd
Calhoun Co SC 152 D6
Lexington Co SC 151 E3
St. Matthews Rd SR-6
Lexington Co SC 151 E3
Lexington Co SC 152 A3
St. Matthews Rd US-601
Calhoun Co SC 152 D6
St. Paul Rd
Clarendon Co SC 153 E6
St. Paul Rd US-15
Clarendon Co SC 153 E6
St. Paul Rd US-301
Clarendon Co SC 153 E6
St. Pauls Rd
Raeford NC 106 B3
St. Pauls Rd SR-20
Raeford NC 106 B3
St. Pauls Church Rd
Sumter Co SC 139 D7
S St. Pauls Church Rd
Sumter Co SC 153 D1
St. Peters Church Rd
Lexington Co SC 137 A3
Saints Delight Rd
Georgetown Co SC 166 C2
Saints Delight Rd US-17 ALT
Georgetown Co SC 166 C2
St. Stephens Church Rd
Cabarrus Co NC 76 E1
Rowan Co NC 50 E7
W Salem Av
Winston-Salem NC 188 C5
Salem Hwy
Stokes Co NC 6 A3
Salem Hwy SR-8
Stokes Co NC 6 A3
Salem Rd
Clarendon Co SC 154 E1
Clarendon Co SC 155 B1
Florence Co SC 141 C6
Marlboro Co SC 125 E4
Morganton NC 47 A5
Salem Rd SR-541
Florence Co SC 141 C6
Salem St
Thomasville NC 51 D1
Salem St SR-109
Thomasville NC 51 D1
N Salem St
Wake Co NC 55 A3
S Salem St
Wake Co NC 55 A3
N Salemburg Hwy
Sampson Co NC 82 B7
Sampson Co NC 108 B1
N Salemburg Hwy SR-242
Sampson Co NC 82 B7
Sampson Co NC 108 B1
S Salemburg Hwy
Sampson Co NC 108 A2
S Salemburg Hwy SR-242
Sampson Co NC 108 A2
Salem Chapel Rd
Forsyth Co NC 27 C2
Salem Church Rd
Lincolnton NC 74 C2
Pasquotank Co NC 17 C7
Pasquotank Co NC 38 D1
Rutherford Co NC 72 E3
Wake Co NC 55 A3
Salem Church Rd SR-34
Pasquotank Co NC 17 C7
Pasquotank Co NC 38 D1
N Salisbury Av
Granite Quarry NC 50 D5
Spencer NC 50 D4
N Salisbury Av SR-150
Spencer NC 50 D4
N Salisbury Av US-29
Spencer NC 50 D4
N Salisbury Av US-52
Rowan Co NC 50 D5
N Salisbury Av US-70
Spencer NC 50 D4
S Salisbury Av
Granite Quarry NC 50 D6
Salisbury NC 50 D4
Salisbury NC 208 E3
S Salisbury Av SR-150
Salisbury NC 208 E3
Spencer NC 50 D4
S Salisbury Av US-29
Salisbury NC 208 E3
Spencer NC 50 D4
S Salisbury Av US-52
Granite Quarry NC 50 D6
S Salisbury Av US-70
Spencer NC 50 D4
Spencer NC 208 E3
Salisbury Blvd
Salisbury NC 208 C7
Salisbury Hwy
Iredell Co NC 49 C3
Salisbury Hwy US-70
Iredell Co NC 49 C3
Salisbury Rd
Davie Co NC 50 B1
Statesville NC 49 C3
Salisbury Rd US-601
Davie Co NC 50 B1
Salisbury St
Kernersville NC 27 D4
E Salisbury St
Asheboro NC 209 E5
E Salisbury St SR-42
Asheboro NC 209 D5
N Salisbury St
Raleigh NC 199 E3
W Salisbury St
Asheboro NC 209 B5
Wrightsville Beach NC 147 B1
W Salisbury St SR-42
Asheboro NC 209 B5
W Salisbury St US-74
Wrightsville Beach NC 147 B1
Salisbury Ridge Rd
Winston-Salem NC 188 B6
Salkehatchie Rd
Hampton Co SC 170 D7
Salley Rd
Aiken Co SC 150 E6
Orangeburg Co SC 151 D5
Salley Rd SR-394
Aiken Co SC 150 E6
Orangeburg Co SC 151 D5
Sally Hill Rd
Darlington Co SC 141 B2
N Sally Hill Rd
Florence Co SC 141 B2
Salome Church Rd
Mecklenburg Co NC 211 E3
Salter Path Rd
Indian Beach NC 112 E6
Pine Knoll Shores NC 113 A6
Salter Path Rd SR-58
Indian Beach NC 112 E6
Pine Knoll Shores NC 113 A6
Saluda Av
Batesburg-Leesville SC 136 C7
Saluda Av US-178
Batesburg-Leesville SC 136 C7
Saluda Hwy
Saluda Co SC 150 B1
Saluda Hwy SR-39
Saluda Co SC 150 B1
Saluda Rd
Chester SC 100 E6
Saluda Rd SR-121
Chester SC 100 E6
Saluda Rd SR-276
Chester SC 100 E6
Saluda St
Ninety Six SC 135 B3
Rock Hill SC 101 A4
Rock Hill SC 217 B7
Saluda St SR-72
Rock Hill SC 101 A4
Rock Hill SC 217 B7
Saluda St SR-121
Rock Hill SC 101 A4
Saluda St SR-246
Ninety Six SC 135 B3
Saluda Dam Rd
Pickens Co SC 96 D5
Sam Black Rd
Cabarrus Co NC 76 B5
Sam Furr Rd
Huntersville NC 75 C2
Sam Furr Rd SR-73
Huntersville NC 75 C2
Sam Hunt Frwy
Alamance Co NC 29 D5
Alamance Co NC 192 A7
Sam Hunt Frwy I-40
Alamance Co NC 192 A7
Graham NC 29 D5
Sam Hunt Frwy I-85
Alamance Co NC 29 D5
Alamance Co NC 192 A7
Sam Newell Rd
Matthews NC 75 E7
Sam Potts Hwy
Bolton NC 129 C6
Columbus Co NC 128 E6
Columbus Co NC 129 A6
Sam Potts Hwy SR-214
Bolton NC 129 C6
Columbus Co NC 128 E6
Columbus Co NC 129 A6
Sampson St
Clinton NC 108 D1
Sam Rittenberg Blvd
Charleston SC 173 A5
Charleston SC 239 D1
Charleston Co SC 239 A4
Sam Rittenberg Blvd SR-7
Charleston SC 173 A5
Charleston SC 239 D1
Charleston Co SC 239 A4
Sams Point Rd
Beaufort Co SC 177 B4
Sams Point Rd SR-802
Beaufort Co SC 177 B4
Sam Wilson Rd
Mecklenburg Co NC 75 A5
Sand Bar Ferry Rd
Augusta GA 159 C1
Sand Bar Ferry Rd SR-28
Augusta GA 159 C1
Sand Dam Rd
Aiken Co SC 151 A4
Sand Dam Rd SR-113
Aiken Co SC 151 A4
Sanders Rd
New Hanover Co NC 147 A2
Sanderson Rd
Chesapeake VA 17 C1
Sandfield Rd
Richland Co SC 138 B2
Sand Hill Rd
Asheville NC 44 C7
Sandhill Rd
Effingham Co GA 180 A1
N Sandhills Blvd
Aberdeen NC 79 C7
N Sandhills Blvd SR-211
Aberdeen NC 79 C7
N Sandhills Blvd US-1
Aberdeen NC 79 C7
N Sandhills Blvd US-15
Aberdeen NC 79 C7
N Sandhills Blvd US-501
Aberdeen NC 79 C7
Sand Hills Rd
Jasper Co SC 175 D3
Sand Hole Rd
Robeson Co NC 127 B2
Sandifer Blvd
Oconee Co SC 116 B1
Sandifer Blvd US-76
Oconee Co SC 116 B1
Sandifer Blvd US-123
Oconee Co SC 116 B1
Sandifer Rd
York Co SC 100 C4
Sand Pit Rd
Moore Co NC 79 C7
Sand Ridge Rd
Onslow Co NC 111 E6
Sandy Bluff Rd
Mullins SC 143 A2
Sandy Bluff Rd SR-917
Mullins SC 143 A2
Sandy Cross Rd
Franklin Co GA 115 C7
Gates Co NC 16 B5
Sandy Cross Rd SR-51
Franklin Co GA 115 C7
Sandy Flat Rd
Greenville Co SC 97 B3
Sandy Flat Rd SR-253
Greenville Co SC 97 B3
Sandy Ford Rd
Gaston Co NC 75 A3
Sandy Forks Rd
Raleigh NC 55 D1
Sandy Ridge Rd
Chowan Co NC 37 B1
Forsyth Co NC 27 E5
Southampton Co VA 15 A1
Sandy Ridge Rd E-685
Southampton Co VA 15 A1
Sandy Springs Rd
Greenville Co SC 118 B1
Sanford Av
Mocksville NC 50 B1
Sanford Dr
Morganton NC 47 A3
Sanford Dr US-64
Morganton NC 47 A3
Sanford Rd
Pittsboro NC 54 B4
Sanford Rd US-15
Pittsboro NC 54 B4
Sanford Rd US-501
Pittsboro NC 54 B4
Sans Souci Rd
Bertie Co NC 36 E6
Santa Fe Dr
Fayetteville NC 80 E7
Santee Rd
Williamsburg Co SC 165 D2
Williamsburg Co SC 166 A2
Santee River Rd
Berkeley Co SC 165 B2
Santee River Rd SR-45
Berkeley Co SC 165 B2
Santeetlah Rd
Graham Co NC 66 E3
Graham Co NC 67 A4
Santeetlah Rd SR-143
Graham Co NC 67 A4
Santuc Carlisle Hwy
Union Co SC 120 C1
Santuc Carlisle Hwy SR-215
Union Co SC 120 C1
Saratoga Rd
Edgecombe Co NC 58 B2
Saratoga Rd SR-111
Edgecombe Co NC 58 B2
Sardis Rd
Buncombe Co NC 44 C7
Matthews NC 75 D7
Union Co SC 120 B2
Sardis Rd SR-112
Buncombe Co NC 44 C7
Sardis Rd N
Charlotte NC 75 E7
Sardis Church Rd
Indian Trail NC 102 A1
Sassafras Ln
Camden Co NC 17 E5
Satterfield Rd
Person Co NC 30 C1
Saulston Rd NE
Wayne Co NC 83 E1
S Saunders St
Raleigh NC 55 D3
S Saunders St SR-50
Raleigh NC 55 D3
S Saunders St US-70
Raleigh NC 55 D3
S Saunders St US-401
Raleigh NC 55 D3
Savage Rd
Charleston SC 173 A5
Savannah Hwy
Beaufort Co SC 176 E5
Charleston Co SC 171 E6
Charleston Co SC 172 A6
Charleston Co SC 173 A5
Charleston Co SC 239 C6
Hampton SC 169 E4
Hampton Co SC 170 A3
Norway SC 161 E1
Orangeburg Co SC 161 E2
Ravenel SC 172 D5
Screven Co GA 168 C7
Savannah Hwy SR-21
Screven Co GA 168 C7
Savannah Hwy SR-802
Beaufort Co SC 176 E5
Savannah Hwy US-17
Charleston SC 239 C6
Charleston SC 240 A6
Charleston Co SC 171 E6
Charleston Co SC 173 A5
Ravenel SC 172 C5
Savannah Hwy US-321
Norway SC 161 E1
Orangeburg Co SC 151 E6
Orangeburg Co SC 161 E2
Savannah Hwy US-601
Hampton SC 169 E4
Hampton Co SC 170 A3
S Savannah Hwy
Furman SC 175 D1
Hampton SC 169 D5
Hampton Co SC 169 D7
S Savannah Hwy US-601
Furman SC 175 D1
Hampton SC 169 D5
Hampton Co SC 169 D7
N Savannah Rd
Beaufort Co NC 61 B6
E Savannah St
Calhoun Falls SC 133 D4
E Savannah St SR-72
Calhoun Falls SC 133 C4
Saw Rd
Rowan Co NC 50 A7
Saw Mill Rd
Polk Co TN 65 D7
Saw Mill Rd SR-123
Polk Co TN 65 D7
Saxapahaw Bethlehem Church Rd
Alamance Co NC 29 E7
Sayre St
Anderson SC 117 C4
Anderson SC 226 C6
Sayre St US-29 BUS
Anderson SC 117 C4
Anderson SC 226 C6
SC-31 E
Horry Co SC 144 B7
SC-33
Sumter Co SC 235 A6
SC-57 N
Horry Co SC 144 E7
N Scales St
Reidsville NC 7 D6
S Scales St
Reidsville NC 7 E7
Scalesville Rd
Summerfield NC 28 A2
Scenic Rd
Grayson Co VA 4 A1
Scenic Rd SR-94
Grayson Co VA 4 A1
Scheafer St
Bowersville GA 116 B6
Scheafer St SR-51
Bowersville GA 116 B6
Schloss Rd
Franklin Co NC 32 E1
School Rd E
Buncombe Co NC 44 E7
School St
Dorchester Co SC 164 B7
S Scientific St
High Point NC 28 A6
Scott Av
Paxville SC 154 A3
Scott Av US-15
Paxville SC 154 A3
Scott Rd
Guilford Co NC 28 C3
Scott St
Dillon Co SC 127 B7
Scott St
Tellico Plains TN 65 E3
Scott King Rd
Durham Co NC 54 E1
Scotts Ferry Rd
Columbia Co GA 148 C6
Scotts Ferry Rd SR-47
Columbia Co GA 148 C6
Scotts Ferry Rd US-221
Columbia Co GA 148 C6
Screaming Eagle Rd
Columbia SC 138 D4
SC-S-15-34
Colleton Co SC 171 B2
Scuffletown Rd
Greenville Co SC 97 D6
Seaboard Rd
Williamsburg Co SC 155 D7
E Seaboard St
Bladenboro NC 128 C3
E Seaboard St SR-211 BUS
Bladen Co NC 128 C3
W Seaboard St
Bladenboro NC 128 B3
W Seaboard St SR-211 BUS
Bladenboro NC 128 B3
Sea Island Pkwy
Beaufort Co SC 177 C5
Sea Island Pkwy US-21
Beaufort Co SC 177 C5
Sea Mountain Hwy
Horry Co SC 144 E7
Sea Pines Cir
Hilton Head Island SC 242 A5
N Sea Pines Dr
Hilton Head Island SC 181 E3
Seashore Dr
Carteret Co NC 114 B2
Seashore Dr US-70
Carteret Co NC 114 B2
Seaside Rd
Beaufort Co SC 177 C6
Seaside Rd SW
Sunset Beach NC 145 B6
Seaside Rd SW SR-179
Sunset Beach NC 145 B6
Seaside Rd SW SR-904
Sunset Beach NC 145 B6
Seawell School Rd
Chapel Hill NC 30 C7
Orange Co NC 195 A3
N Secrest St
Kinston NC 205 E4
Secret Short Cut Rd
Monroe NC 102 B1
Seddon Rusty Goode Jr Frwy
Mecklenburg Co NC 75 B6
Seddon R Goode Jr Frwy I-485
Mecklenburg Co NC 75 B6
Sedge Garden Rd
Forsyth Co NC 27 C4
Seed Lake Rd
Rabun Co GA 93 E6
Rabun Co GA 94 A6
Seewee Rd
Charleston Co SC 173 E3
Charleston Co SC 174 A2
Sellars Rd
Gaston Co NC 74 A4
Sells Rd
Salisbury NC 50 C4
Salisbury NC 208 B1
S Selma Rd
Wendell NC 56 C2
S Selma Rd SR-231
Wendell NC 56 C2
Semora Rd
Person Co NC 9 C5
Semora Rd SR-57
Person Co NC 9 C5
Senator David W. Hoyle Hwy
Gaston Co NC 74 C3
Sen David W. Hoyle Hwy US-321
Gaston Co NC 74 C3
Sen Marshall Arthur Rauch Hwy
Gaston Co NC 74 B5
Sen Marshall A Rauch Hy I-85
Gaston Co NC 74 B5
Senn St
Aiken Co SC 149 E6
Senn St SR-191
Aiken Co SC 149 E6
Settawig Rd
Clay Co NC 92 D1
Settlement Rd
Greenville Co SC 96 E3
Seven Creeks Rd
Columbus Co NC 144 E3
Seven Creeks Rd SR-905
Columbus Co NC 144 E1
Seven Pines Rd
Barnwell Co SC 160 E4
E Seven Pines St
Darlington Co SC 140 E1
Darlington Co SC 141 A1
Sevierville Rd
Blount Co TN 41 A2
Sevierville Rd SR-35
Blount Co TN 41 A2
Sevierville Rd US-411
Blount Co TN 41 A2
Seward Rd
Forsyth Co NC 26 D3
Shacktown Rd
Yadkin Co NC 26
S Shady Av
Damascus VA 1
N Shady St
Johnson Co TN 1
N Shady St SR-34
Johnson Co TN 1
N Shady St SR-91
Johnson Co TN 1
N Shady St US-421
Johnson Co TN 1
S Shady St
Mountain City TN 1
S Shady St SR-34
Mountain City TN 1
S Shady St SR-67
Mountain City TN 1
S Shady St US-421
Mountain City TN 1
Shady Grove Rd
Pickens Co SC 95
Pickens Co SC 96
Richland Co SC 137
W Shady Grove Rd
Richland Co SC 137
Shakespeare Rd
Arcadia Lakes SC 138
Shallowford Rd
Forsyth Co NC 26
Lewisville NC 26
Shallowford St
Winston-Salem NC 188
Shallowford Church Rd
Alamance Co NC 29
Shamrock Rd
Cabarrus Co NC 76
Orangeburg Co SC 151
Shannon Rd
Robeson Co NC 106
Sharon SC 100
York Co SC 100
Sharon Ln
Charlotte NC 75
Sharon Rd
Buncombe Co NC 71
Charlotte NC 75
York SC 100
Sharon Rd SR-49
York SC 100
Sharon Rd W
Charlotte NC 75
N Sharon Amity Rd
Charlotte NC 75
Sharon School Rd
Iredell Co NC 48
Sharp Rd
Richland Co SC 138
Shattalon Dr
Winston-Salem NC 26
Shattalon Rd
Winston-Salem NC 26
Winston-Salem NC 27
Winston-Salem NC 186
Shaw Dr
Hampton SC 169
Shaw Dr SR-363
Hampton SC 169
Shaw Rd
Cumberland Co NC 80
Sampson Co NC 108
Shaw St
Greenville Co SC 223
Shawboro Rd
Currituck Co NC 17
Shawboro Rd SR-34
Currituck Co NC 17
Shaw Mill Rd
Cumberland Co NC 81
Shawnee Egypt Rd
Effingham Co GA 175
Shawspring Rd
Warren Co NC 12
Shawspring Rd SR-903
Warren Co NC 12
Shearer Rd
Mecklenburg Co NC 75
Shelby Hwy
Cherokee Co SC 99
Gaston Co NC 73
Shelby Hwy SR-18
Cherokee Co SC 99
Cherokee Co SC 99
Shelby Hwy SR-150
Gaston Co NC 73
Shelby Rd
Cleveland Co NC 73
Kings Mountain NC 74
Shelby Rd US-74 BUS
Cleveland Co NC 73
Kings Mountain NC 74
Shell Rd
Carteret Co NC 114
S Shellmore Blvd
Mt Pleasant SC 238
Shelton Av
Iredell Co NC 49
Shelton Av SR-115
Iredell Co NC 49
Shelton Av US-21
Iredell Co NC 49
Sheppard St
Charleston SC 240
Sheppard Branch Rd
Buncombe Co NC 44
Sherer Rd
York Co SC 100
Sherrill-Lever Rd
Richland Co SC 137
Sherrills Ford Rd
Catawba Co NC 48
Catawba Co NC 49

INDEX 34

errills Ford Rd

Street Index

W Stuart Dr US-221

STREET
City State Map# Grid

errills Ford Rd
owan Co NC 50 B4
erron Rd
urham Co NC 31 A6
iloh Rd
conee Co SC 116 D1
urbeville SC 140 E7
usculum TN 20 A4
iloh Rd SR-58
urbeville SC 140 E7
Shiloh Rd
ork Co SC 100 D2
Shiloh Rd
ork Co SC 100 D3
iloh Church Rd
erson Co NC 9 C4
iloh Farm Rd
dgecombe Co NC 34 E7
ipyard Blvd
ilmington NC 146 E1
ilmington NC 231 E7
ipyard Blvd US-117
ilmington NC 146 E1
ilmington NC 231 E7
oal Rd
ncoln Co NC 74 A2
Shockley Ferry Rd
nderson SC 226 D7
nderson Co SC 117 C4
Shockley Ferry Rd
S-29
nderson SC 226 D7
nderson Co SC 117 C4
Shockley Ferry Rd
nderson Co SC 117 B5
nderson SC 226 D7
Shockley Ferry Rd
S-29
nderson Co SC 117 B5
nderson SC 226 D7
op Rd
olumbia SC 138 B6
ichland Co SC 233 E7
op Rd SR-768
olumbia SC 138 B6
opton Rd
harlotte NC 75 B6
opton Rd W
ecklenburg Co NC 75 A7
Shore Dr
oiling Spring Lakes NC 146 D4
Shore Dr
urf City NC 131 E4
Shore Dr SR-50
urf City NC 131 E4
ore Rd
orsyth Co NC 26 E2
orsyth Co NC 27 A2
oreline Dr W
unset Beach NC 145 B7
oreline Dr W SR-179
US
unset Beach NC 145 B7
ort Cut Rd
orchester Co SC 163 D6
ortcut Rd
urrituck Co NC 17 D4
ortcut Rd US-158
urrituck Co NC 17 D4
ucraft Rd
olumbia Co GA 148 B7
uffond St
art Co GA 116 A6
uffond St SR-17
art Co GA 116 A6
ding Rd
ertie Co NC 35 D1
las Creek Pkwy
Vinston-Salem NC 27 A4
Vinston-Salem NC 187 C2
Vinston-Salem NC 188 C7
las Creek Pkwy SR-67
Vinston-Salem NC 27 A4
Vinston-Salem NC 187 C2
Vinston-Salem NC 188 A6
ler City Snow Camp
d
hatham Co NC 53 C3
lk Hope Rd
hatham Co NC 53 C3
berty NC 53 A1
lk Hope Gum Springs
d
hatham Co NC 53 D3
lk Hope Liberty Rd
hatham Co NC 53 B2
loam Rd
urry Co NC 5 A6
adkin Co NC 26 B2
lver Bluff Rd
iken Co SC 150 A7
iken Co SC 159 E2
lver Bluff Rd SR-302
iken Co SC 150 A7
iken Co SC 159 E2
lver City Rd
amblen Co TN 19 A2
lver City Rd SR-113
amblen Co TN 19 A2
lver Dollar Rd
arteret Co NC 113 C1
lver Lake Rd
partanburg Co SC 97 E5
lverstein Rd
ransylvania Co NC 69 D6
Silverton St
iken Co SC 159 E3
iken Co SC 160 A3
merly Creek Rd
arter Co TN 21 C3

Simerly Creek Rd
SR-173
Carter Co TN 21 C3
Simmons St
New Bern NC 86 B6
Simms Reach Rd
Williamsburg Co SC 155 E6
Simpkins Rd
Wake Co NC 55 D4
Simpson Rd
Anderson Co SC 117 A2
Hamblen Co TN 19 A1
Simpson Rd SR-113
Hamblen Co TN 19 A1
Sims Bridge Rd
Franklin Co NC 32 B3
Six Forks Rd
Raleigh NC 55 D1
Raleigh NC 197 E1
Wake Co NC 31 D7
E Six Forks Rd
Raleigh NC 55 D1
Six Mile Hwy
Pickens Co SC 95 E7
Pickens Co SC 225 B1
Six Mile Hwy SR-133
Pickens Co SC 95 E7
Pickens Co SC 225 B1
Six Mile Rd
Charleston Co SC 173 D4
Skeet Club Rd
High Point NC 27 D5
Skibo Rd
Fayetteville NC 80 E7
Fayetteville NC 106 E1
Skibo Rd US-401 BYP
Fayetteville NC 80 E7
Fayetteville NC 106 E1
Skidaway Rd
Savannah GA 181 A5
Skippers Rd
Greensville Co VA 13 D1
Skippers Rd US-301
Greensville Co VA 13 D1
Skipwith Rd
Mecklenburg Co VA 11 A1
Skyline Hwy
Grayson Co VA 4 B3
Skyline Hwy SR-89
Grayson Co VA 4 B3
Skylyn Dr
Spartanburg Co SC 98 D3
Skyway Dr
Monroe NC 102 C2
Skyway Dr SR-200
Monroe NC 102 C3
Skyway Dr US-601
Union Co NC 218 C2
Slab Landing Rd
Orangeburg Co SC 162 A2
Slab Landing Rd SR-332
Orangeburg Co SC 162 A2
Sloan Rd
Monroe Co TN 66 A1
Richland Co SC 138 B4
Sloan Rd SR-360
Monroe Co TN 66 A1
Sluder Branch Rd
Buncombe Co NC 44 B5
W Smith Av
Darlington Co SC 125 B7
Darlington Co SC 229 B3
Smith Rd
Lenoir Co NC 84 B2
Rowan Co NC 49 E7
Rowan Co NC 50 A7
Smith St
Ware Shoals SC 118 C6
Smith St SR-420
Ware Shoals SC 118 C6
E Smith St
Greensboro NC 190 C2
Timmonsville SC 141 B3
E Smith St US-76
Timmonsville SC 141 B3
W Smith St
Florence Co SC 140 E4
Florence Co SC 141 A3
Greensboro NC 190 C2
W Smith St SR-403
Florence Co SC 141 A3
W Smith St US-76
Florence Co SC 140 E4
Florence Co SC 141 A3
Smith Church Rd
Halifax Co NC 13 B4
N Smithfield Rd
Knightdale NC 56 A2
S Smithfield Rd
Knightdale NC 56 B2
Smithfield St
Newton Grove NC 82 C4
Smithfield St US-701
Newton Grove NC 82 C4
Smith Level Rd
Chatham Co NC 54 C1
Smith McGee Hwy
Hart Co GA 116 E7
Smith McGee Hwy SR-181
Hart Co GA 116 E7
Smith McGee Rd
Anderson Co SC 117 B7
Smith McGee Rd SR-181
Anderson Co SC 117 B7
Smiths Ferry Rd
Southampton Co VA 15 B2
Smiths Ferry Rd US-258
Southampton Co VA 15 B2
Smithtown Rd
Yadkin Co NC 26 B2
Smokey Park Hwy
Asheville NC 44 B7

Smokey Park Hwy US-19
Asheville NC 44 B7
Smokey Park Hwy US-23
Asheville NC 44 B7
Smokey Park Hwy US-74
ALT
Asheville NC 44 B7
Smoky Mountains Hwy
Blount Co TN 41 B5
Smoky Mountains Hwy
SR-73
Blount Co TN 41 B5
Smoky Mountains Hwy
SR-337
Blount Co TN 41 B5
Smyrna Church Rd
Richland Co SC 138 C2
Snake Rd
Goose Creek SC 173 A2
Snapp Bridge Rd
Washington Co TN 20 C3
Snider Rd
Yadkin Co NC 26 A3
Sniders Hwy
Colleton Co SC 170 D4
Walterboro SC 171 A4
Sniders Hwy SR-63
Colleton Co SC 170 D4
Walterboro SC 171 A4
Snipes Pond Rd
Aiken Co SC 150 C4
Snow Rd
Greenville Co SC 118 B1
Snowbird Rd
Robbinsville NC 67 A4
Snowbird Rd SR-143 BUS
Graham Co NC 67 A4
Snow Camp Rd
Alamance Co NC 29 C7
Alamance Co NC 53 C2
Snow Hill Rd
Durham Co NC 30 E4
Durham Co NC 31 A4
Soapstone Rd
Henry Co VA 7 A2
Socastee Blvd
Horry Co SC 157 E3
Horry Co SC 158 A3
Socastee Blvd SR-707
Horry Co SC 157 E3
Horry Co SC 158 A3
Society St
Clio SC 126 B2
Greeleyville SC 155 A6
Society St SR-381
Clio SC 126 B2
Society St US-521
Greeleyville SC 155 A6
Society Hill Rd
Chesterfield Co SC 125 A2
Soco Rd
Haywood Co NC 69 A1
Jackson Co NC 68 D1
Maggie Valley NC 43 B7
Maggie Valley NC 69 B1
Soco Rd US-19
Haywood Co NC 69 A1
Maggie Valley NC 43 B7
Maggie Valley NC 69 B1
Soco Rd US-441 BUS
Jackson Co NC 68 C1
So Hi Dr
Durham Co NC 31 A7
Solomon Blatt Av
Blackville SC 161 B3
Solomon Blatt Av SR-3
Blackville SC 161 B3
Solon David Smart
Memorial Hwy
Rutherford Co NC 72 D4
Solon David Smart Mem
Hy US-74
Rutherford Co NC 72 D4
Somers Rd
Wilkes Co NC 25 B4
Soundneck Rd
Pasquotank Co NC 38 D1
Soundneck Rd SR-34
Pasquotank Co NC 38 D1
Soundside Dr
Chowan Co NC 37 C3
Soundside Dr SR-94
Chowan Co NC 37 C3
South Blvd
Charlotte NC 75 C7
Coward SC 141 D6
South Blvd US-52
Coward SC 141 D6
N South St
Mt Airy NC 183 B4
S South St
Mt Airy NC 183 C6
South Boston Hwy
Pittsylvania Co VA 8 E3
South Boston Hwy US-58
Pittsylvania Co VA 8 E3
South Boston Hwy
US-360
Pittsylvania Co VA 8 E3
South Boston Rd
Danville VA 8 D3
South Boston Rd US-58
Danville VA 8 D3
South Boston Rd US-360
Danville VA 8 D3
Southbound Rd
Lexington Co SC 151 E3
Southbound Rd US-321
Lexington Co SC 151 E3
Southeast Blvd
Sampson Co NC 108 D2

Southeast Blvd US-701
BUS
Sampson Co NC 108 D2
Southern Av
Fayetteville NC 107 A1
Fayetteville NC 222 B7
Southern Connector
Greenville Co SC 97 A7
Southern Connector
I-185
Greenville Co SC 97 A7
Southern Highroads Tr
Blairsville GA 92 D4
Southern Highroads Tr
SR-2
Blairsville GA 92 D4
Southern Highroads Tr
SR-11
Blairsville GA 92 D4
Southern Highroads Tr
SR-515
Blairsville GA 92 D4
Southern Highroads Tr
US-19
Blairsville GA 92 D4
Southern Highroads Tr
US-76
Blairsville GA 92 D4
Southern Highroads Tr
US-129
Blairsville GA 92 D4
Southern Highroads
Scenic Hwy
East Ellijay GA 91 B7
Southern Highrds Scnc
Hwy SR-2
East Ellijay GA 91 B7
Southern Highrds Scnc
Hwy SR-5
East Ellijay GA 91 B7
Southrn Hghrds Scnc
Hwy SR-515
East Ellijay GA 91 B7
Southern Hghrds Scnc
Hwy US-76
East Ellijay GA 91 B7
South Fork Lp
Patrick Co VA 6 B3
Southpoint Rd
Belmont NC 75 A6
Southpoint Rd SR-273
Belmont NC 75 A6
Southport Rd
Spartanburg SC 98 C4
Spartanburg Co SC 98 D4
Southport Rd SR-295
Spartanburg SC 98 C4
Southport-Supply Rd SE
Brunswick Co NC 146 A5
Southport-Supply Rd
SE SR-211
Brunswick Co NC 146 A5
Southside Av
Buncombe Co NC 206 C4
Southside Av US-25
Buncombe Co NC 206 C4
Southside Rd
Carter Co TN 21 D1
Elizabethton TN 21 C1
Southwest Blvd
Lenoir NC 47 C1
Spainhour Mill Rd
Forsyth Co NC 26 D2
Sparkleberry Ln
Richland Co SC 138 C4
Sparrow Springs Rd
Gaston Co NC 74 B5
Sparta Rd
Wilkes Co NC 3 C7
Wilkes Co NC 24 C1
Sparta Rd SR-18
Wilkes Co NC 3 C7
Wilkes Co NC 24 C1
Spartanburg Hwy
Henderson Co NC 71 A4
Union Co SC 99 A5
Spartanburg Hwy SR-9
Union Co SC 99 A5
Spartanburg Hwy US-25
BUS
Henderson Co NC 71 A4
Spartanburg Hwy US-176
Henderson Co NC 71 B5
Spartanburg Rd
Lyman SC 97 E3
Spartanburg Rd SR-292
Lyman SC 97 E4
Spaulding St
Albemarle NC 77 C3
Spaulding St SR-24
Albemarle NC 77 B3
Spaulding St SR-27
Albemarle NC 77 B3
Spaulding St SR-73
Albemarle NC 77 B3
Spaulding St US-52
Albemarle NC 77 B3
Spears Creek Church Rd
Richland Co SC 138 D4
Speedway Blvd
Concord NC 75 E3
Concord NC 212 C1
S Spencer St
Duncan SC 97 E4
Spencer Branch Rd
Grayson Co VA 2 D3
Spencer Branch Rd
E-797
Grayson Co VA 2 D3
Spencer-Dixon Rd
Guilford Co NC 28 C2

Spicewood Dr
Forsyth Co NC 26 E4
Spies Rd
Montgomery Co NC 78 C2
Spivey Mountain Rd
Unicoi Co TN 20 E5
Spivey Mountain Rd
SR-36
Unicoi Co TN 20 E5
Spivey Mountain Rd
US-19W
Unicoi Co TN 20 E5
Spivey's Corner Hwy
Sampson Co NC 82 B5
Spivey's Corner Hwy
SR-242
Sampson Co NC 82 B5
Spivey's Corner Hwy
US-421
Sampson Co NC 82 B5
E Sprague St
Winston-Salem NC 188 E6
Spratt St
York Co SC 101 B3
Spratt St US-21 BUS
Fort Mill SC 101 B3
Spring Dr
Garner NC 55 D3
Spring Ln
Sanford NC 54 A7
Spring Rd
Patrick Co VA 6 B1
Spring Rd E-680
Patrick Co VA 6 B1
Spring St
Charleston SC 240 B6
Jonesborough TN 20 E1
E Spring St
Lancaster Co SC 123 A2
E Spring St US-521
Heath Springs SC 123 A2
N Spring St
Greensboro NC 190 B2
S Spring St
Greensboro NC 190 B3
Spring Branch Rd
Windsor SC 160 D1
Springdale Dr
Camden SC 139 A1
Clinton SC 119 D4
Springdale Dr SR-56
TRK
Clinton SC 119 D4
E Springdale Rd
York Co SC 101 B4
Springfield Pkwy
York Co SC 101 B2
Springfield Rd
Rocky Mount NC 34 A5
Springfield SC 151 B7
Williston SC 161 A2
Springfield Rd SR-4
Springfield SC 151 B7
Springfield Rd SR-39
Williston SC 161 A2
Spring Forest Rd
Raleigh NC 55 E1
Raleigh NC 197 E2
Spring Garden St
Greensboro NC 28 B5
Greensboro NC 189 D3
Greensboro NC 190 C3
Spring Haven Dr
Edgefield Co SC 149 B6
Springs Rd
Catawba Co NC 48 C3
Hickory NC 48 B4
Mt Airy NC 5 A4
Surry Co NC 183 E1
Springs Rd NE
Catawba Co NC 48 B3
N Springs Rd
Richland Co SC 138 C3
Spring Valley Rd
Grayson Co VA 3 E1
Spruce St
Martinsville VA 7 B1
Spruill Av
North Charleston SC 173 A4
Squire Davis Rd
Guilford Co NC 27 D5
Squirrel Spur Rd
Patrick Co VA 5 C1
SR 1225
Greene Co NC 58 C6
SR 1316
Como NC 15 A2
SR 1354
Hickory NC 207 B4
SR 1355
Hickory NC 207 B4
SR 1714
Rocky Mount NC 201 A5
Stafford Mill Rd
Forsyth Co NC 27 B2
Stagecoach Rd NE
McDuffie Co GA 148 A7
E Stage Coach Tr
Fallston NC 73 D2
E Stage Coach Tr
SR-182
Fallston NC 73 D2
W Stage Coach Tr
Polkville NC 73 B2
W Stage Coach Tr
SR-182
Polkville NC 73 B2
Stagville Rd
Durham Co NC 31 A3
Stallings Rd
Durham NC 31 B5
Durham Co NC 31 B6

Stallings Rd
Greenville Co SC 97 B4
Harrisburg NC 76 A4
Union Co NC 76 A7
Stamp Creek Rd
Oconee Co SC 95 C5
Stamp Creek Rd SR-130
Oconee Co SC 95 C5
Stanley Rd
Greensboro NC 28 B5
Warren Co NC 12 D2
Stanley Rd E-666
Warren Co NC 12 D2
Stanley Lucia Rd
Gaston Co NC 74 E3
Gaston Co NC 75 A3
Stanley-Spencer
Mountain Rd
Spencer Mountain NC 74 E4
S Stanly School Rd
Stanly Co NC 77 B5
Stantonsburg Rd
Greenville NC 58 D4
Greenville NC 59 A5
Stars Bridge Rd
Franklin Co GA 115 E7
Franklin Co GA 116 A7
Stars Bridge Rd SR-51
Franklin Co GA 115 E7
Franklin Co GA 116 A7
Startown Rd
Lincoln Co NC 48 B7
State Rd
Berkeley Co SC 164 A4
State Rd US-176
Berkeley Co SC 164 A4
State St
Lexington Co SC 233 A5
State St SR-2
Lexington Co SC 233 A5
E State St
Buncombe Co NC 45 C6
E State St US-70
Buncombe Co NC 45 C6
N State St
Yadkinville NC 26 A4
N State St US-601
Yadkinville NC 26 A4
S State St
Yadkinville NC 26 A4
S State St US-601
Yadkinville NC 26 A4
W State St
Black Mountain NC 45 B6
W State St US-70
Black Mountain NC 45 B6
Stateline Rd
York Co SC 74 E7
N State of Franklin Rd
Johnson City TN 21 A1
N State of Franklin
Rd SR-381
Johnson City TN 21 A1
State Park Rd
Aiken Co SC 150 D7
Dillon Co SC 127 A6
Greenville Co SC 97 A4
Newberry Co SC 136 E4
Travelers Rest SC 97 A3
State Park Rd SR-253
Greenville Co SC 97 A4
Statesboro Hwy
Screven Co GA 168 B7
Statesboro Hwy SR-73
Screven Co GA 168 B7
Statesboro Hwy US-301
Screven Co GA 168 B7
Statesview Hwy
Iredell Co NC 49 D6
Statesview Hwy SR-115
Mooresville NC 49 D6
Statesville Blvd
Cleveland NC 49 E3
Rowan Co NC 50 A4
Salisbury NC 50 C4
Salisbury NC 208 A2
Statesville Blvd US-70
Cleveland NC 49 E3
Rowan Co NC 50 A4
Statesville Rd
Charlotte NC 75 C4
Cornelius NC 75 C1
Hertford Co NC 15 A2
Southampton Co VA 14 E2
Wilkes Co NC 24 E4
Wilkes Co NC 25 A5
Statesville Rd SR-115
Wilkes Co NC 24 E4
Wilkes Co NC 25 A5
Statesville Rd E-673
Hertford Co NC 15 A2
Southampton Co VA 14 E2
Statesville Rd US-21
Charlotte NC 75 C4
Cornelius NC 75 C1
Stecoa Av
Mountain City GA 94 B4
Stecoa Av SR-15
Mountain City GA 94 B4
Stecoa Av US-23
Mountain City GA 94 B4
Stecoa Av US-441
Rabun Co GA 94 B4
Steed Creek Rd
Berkeley Co SC 165 D7
Charleston Co SC 174 A1
Steele Creek Rd
Mecklenburg Co NC 75 A7
Mecklenburg Co NC 101 A1
Steele Creek Rd SR-160
Mecklenburg Co NC 75 A7
Mecklenburg Co NC 101 A1

Stella Rd
Carteret Co NC 112 A5
Stephenson Av
Savannah GA 180 E5
S Sterling St
Morganton NC 47 B4
S Sterling St SR-18
Morganton NC 47 B4
Stevens Creek Rd
Augusta GA 149 A7
McCormick Co SC 148 E5
Stevens Mill Rd
Goldsboro NC 83 C2
Stallings NC 76 A7
Stevens Mill Rd SW
Wayne Co NC 83 A2
Stiles Av
Savannah GA 180 E4
Stillwell Rd
Effingham Co GA 175 B6
Stillwell Clyo Rd
Effingham Co GA 175 C5
Stockton Rd
Buncombe Co NC 44 E3
Stockwell Rd
Orangeburg Co SC 151 D6
Stokes Rd
Greenville Co SC 97 C7
Stokes Ferry Rd
Rowan Co NC 50 D5
Salisbury NC 208 E6
E Stone Av
Greenville SC 223 C2
E Stone Av US-276
Greenville SC 223 C2
W Stone Av
Greenville SC 223 B2
W Stone Av US-276
Greenville SC 223 B2
Stoneboro Rd
Kershaw Co SC 122 E3
Lancaster Co SC 123 A2
Stoneboro Rd SR-522
Kershaw Co SC 122 E3
Lancaster Co SC 123 A3
Stone Chimney Rd SW
Brunswick Co NC 145 E5
Brunswick Co NC 146 A5
Stone Church Rd
Pickens Co SC 225 C7
Stone Church Rd SR-22
Pickens Co SC 225 C7
Stones Dairy Rd
Henry Co VA 6 D1
Stone Station Rd
Spartanburg Co SC 98 C5
Stone Station Rd
SR-215
Spartanburg Co SC 98 C5
W Stonewall St
Charlotte NC 215 E2
Stoney Bluff Rd
Burke Co GA 168 B1
Stoney Mountain Rd
Alamance Co NC 29 C2
Stoney Point Rd
Cumberland Co NC 106 C1
Stony Creek Rd
Carter Co TN 1 A6
Stony Creek Rd SR-91
Carter Co TN 1 A6
Stony Mill Rd
Pittsylvania Co VA 8 A2
Storage Rd
Charleston Co SC 172 B6
Storm Branch Rd
Aiken Co SC 159 D1
Straight Rd
Pamlico Co NC 87 B6
Strait Rd
York Co SC 100 E5
Straits Rd
Carteret Co NC 113 D5
Strange St
Sumter Co SC 235 D1
N Stratford Rd
Winston-Salem NC 187 E3
Winston-Salem NC 188 A3
S Stratford Rd
Winston-Salem NC 26 E6
Winston-Salem NC 27 A5
Winston-Salem NC 187 B7
S Stratford Rd US-158
Winston-Salem NC 26 E6
Winston-Salem NC 27 A5
Winston-Salem NC 187 B7
Strawberry Blvd N
Columbus Co NC 128 A5
Strawberry Rd
Berkeley Co SC 165 D6
Summerfield NC 28 B3
Strickland Rd
Wake Co NC 31 C7
Strickland Bridge Rd
Cumberland Co NC 106 D2
Strom Thurmond Frwy
Florence Co SC 141 C2
Strom Thurmond Frwy
I-20
Florence Co SC 141 B2
E Stuart Dr
Galax VA 4 B1
E Stuart Dr US-58
Galax VA 4 B1
E Stuart Dr US-221
Galax VA 4 B1
W Stuart Dr
Galax VA 4 B2
W Stuart Dr US-58
Galax VA 4 B2
W Stuart Dr US-221
Galax VA 4 B2

Points of Interest Index

Points of Interest Index

Points of Interest Index

Points of Interest Index

Entertainment & Sports

Golf Courses   **Points of Interest Index**   Golf Courses

Points of Interest Index

Points of Interest Index

Hospitals

FEATURE NAME Address City State	MAP#	GRID
John Umstead Hosp 1003 12th St, Granville Co, NC	31	B3
Kershaw County Med Ctr Camden, SC	139	B1
Kings Mountain Hosp Kings Mountain, NC	74	A5
Lake Norman Regional Med Ctr Mooresville, NC	49	C7
Laughlin Memorial Hosp Greeneville, TN	20	A3
Laurens County Health Care System Laurens Co, SC	119	C4
Lenoir Memorial Hosp Airport Rd, Kinston, NC	205	C1
Lenox Baker Children's Hosp 3000 Erwin Rd, Durham, NC	30	E5
Lexington Med Ctr Lexington Co, SC	137	E6
Lexington Memorial Hosp Davidson Co, NC	51	A2
LifeCare Hosps of North Carolina 1031 Noell Dr, Rocky Mount, NC	34	A5
Lincoln County Hosp 200 Doctors Pk, Lincolnton, NC	74	C1
Loris Healthcare System 3655 Mitchell St, Loris, SC	144	A4
Margaret R Pardee Memorial Hosp Hendersonville, NC	70	E4
Maria Parham Hosp 566 Ruin Creek Rd, Vance Co, NC	11	A7
Marion County Med Ctr Marion Co, SC	142	E2
Marlboro Park Hosp 1138 Cheraw Hwy, Marlboro Co, SC	125	E1
Martin General Hosp 310 S McCaskey Rd, Williamston, NC	36	A7
Mary Black Hosp Spartanburg Co, SC	98	C3
McDowell Hosp 430 Rankin Dr, McDowell Co, NC	46	B5
McLeod Med Ctr-Dillon 301 E Jackson St, Dillon, SC	126	E5
McLeod Regional Med Ctr 555 E Cheves St, Florence, SC	230	E4
Medical University of South Carolina Hosp 169 Ashley Av, Charleston, SC	240	C6
Memorial Health University Med Ctr Savannah, GA	180	E4
Memorial Hosp-Martinsville 320 Hospital Dr, Martinsville, VA	7	B1
Memorial Mission Hosp 509 McDowell St, Asheville, NC	206	C5
Mission Hosp Memorial Asheville, NC	44	D7
Montgomery Memorial Hosp Troy, NC	78	B3
Moore Regional Hosp 155 Memorial Dr, Pinehurst, NC	220	C3
Morehead Memorial Hosp 117 E Kings Hwy, Eden, NC	7	C4
Moses H Cone Memorial Hosp Greensboro, NC	28	C4
Murdoch Center 1600 Murdoch Center St Hospital, Granville Co, NC	31	C3
Murphy Med Ctr Cherokee Co, NC	92	D1
Nash General Hosp Rocky Mount, NC	33	E5
Newberry County Memorial Hosp 2669 Kinard St, Newberry, SC	136	C1
New Hanover Regional Med Ctr 2131 S 17th St, Wilmington, NC	231	D6
North Carolina Memorial Hosp Chapel Hill, NC	30	C7
Northeast Med Ctr 900 Hospital St NE, Concord, NC	76	B2
Northern Hosp of Surry County 830 Rockford St, Mt Airy, NC	183	C6
North Greenville Hosp Travelers Rest, SC	97	A3
Oconee Memorial Hosp 298 Memorial Dr, Oconee Co, SC	116	C1
Onslow Memorial Hosp Jacksonville, NC	111	C5
Our Community Hosp 921 Junior High School Rd, Scotland Neck, NC	35	A3
Outer Banks Hosp Nags Head, NC	40	A4
Palmetto Health-Baptist 1300 Taylor St, Columbia, SC	233	C3
Palmetto Health Baptist Easley 200 Fleetwood Dr, Easley, SC	96	C5
Palmetto Health Richland 5 Medical Park Rd, Columbia, SC	138	A5
Palmetto Health-Richland Columbia, SC	233	C1
Park Ridge Hosp 50 Hospital Dr, Henderson Co, NC	70	E3
Pender Memorial Hosp 507 E Freemont St, Burgaw, NC	130	E2
Person Memorial Hosp 615 Ridge Rd, Roxboro, NC	9	D6
Piedmont Med Ctr Rock Hill, SC	100	E3
Pitt County Memorial Hosp Greenville, NC	59	B4
Presbyterian Hosp Charlotte, NC	75	D6
Presbyterian Hosp Huntersville Huntersville, NC	75	C2
Presbyterian Hosp of Matthews Matthews, NC	75	E7
Providence Hosp Forest Dr, Columbia, SC	233	E2
Providence Hosp Northeast 120 Gateway Corporate Blvd, Richland Co, SC	138	B4
Pungo District Hosp 210 E Water St, Belhaven, NC	61	C5
Rabun County Memorial Hosp 196 Ridgecrest Cir, Clayton, GA	94	B4
Ralph H Johnson Veterans Affairs Med Ctr 109 Bee St, Charleston, SC	240	C6
Randolph Hosp 364 White Oak St, Asheboro, NC	209	C4
Regional Med Ctr Orangeburg Co, SC	152	D6
Rex Healthcare Raleigh, NC	55	C2
RJ Reynolds Patrick County Hosp 18688 Jeb Stuart Hwy, Patrick Co, VA	6	A2
Roanoke Chowan Hosp Ahoskie, NC	15	B7
Roper Hosp 316 Calhoun St, Charleston, SC	240	C6
Roper St. Francis Med Ctr Northwoods 2233 Northwood Blvd, North Charleston, SC	172	E3
Rowan Regional Med Ctr 612 Old Mocksville Rd, Salisbury, NC	208	C3
Rutherford County Hosp 2270 Twitty Ford Rd, Rutherfordton, NC	72	B3
St. Francis Hosp Greenville Co, SC	97	A5
St. Joseph Hosp Augusta, GA	159	B1
St. Joseph's Hosp Biltmore Av, Asheville, NC	206	C5
St. Joseph's Hosp Savannah, GA	180	E5
St. Luke's Hosp 101 Hospital Dr, Columbus, NC	71	D5
Sampson Regional Med Ctr 607 Beaman St, Clinton, NC	108	D1
Sandhills Regional Med Ctr 1000 W Hamlet Av, Hamlet, NC	104	D4
Scotland Memorial Hosp 500 E Lauchwood Dr, Laurinburg, NC	105	C6
Screven County Hosp 215 Mims Rd, Sylvania, GA	168	B6
Self Memorial Hosp Greenwood, SC	134	E3
Sevier Med Ctr-Fort Sanders 709 Middle Creek Rd, Sevierville, TN	41	E2
South Carolina State Hosp 2100 Williams Dr, Columbia, SC	233	C2
Southeastern Regional Med Ctr 300 W 27th St, Lumberton, NC	127	E1
Southern Wake Hosp 400 W Ransom St, Fuquay-Varina, NC	55	B6
Spartanburg Regional Med Ctr 101 E Wood St, Spartanburg, SC	224	B2
Springs Memorial Hosp 800 W Meeting St, Lancaster, SC	219	A5
Spruce Pine Community Hosp 125 Hospital Dr, Spruce Pine, NC	46	A1
Stanly Memorial Hosp Albemarle, NC	77	B3
Stephens County Hosp 2003 Falls Rd, Toccoa, GA	115	C2
Stokes-Reynolds Memorial Hosp Stokes Co, NC	6	B6
Summerville Med Ctr Summerville, SC	172	D2
Swain County Hosp 45 Plateau St, Bryson City, NC	68	B2
Takoma Adventist Hosp 401 Takoma Av, Greeneville, TN	19	E4
Thomasville Med Ctr Thomasville, NC	51	C1
Transylvania Community Hosp 90 Hospital Rd, Brevard, NC	70	B5
Trident Med Ctr 9330 Medical Plaza Dr, North Charleston, SC	237	A6
Tuomey Regional Med Ctr N Sumter St, Sumter, SC	235	D3
Twin County Regional Hosp Galax, VA	4	B2
Unicoi County Memorial Hosp 100 Greenway Cir, Erwin, TN	21	A4
Union General Hosp 214 Hospital Cir, Union Co, GA	92	D4
Union Regional Med Ctr 600 Hospital Dr, Monroe, NC	102	C3
University Hosp Augusta, GA	159	B1
Upstate Carolina Med Ctr 1530 N Limestone St, Cherokee Co, SC	99	B1
Valdese Hosp 720 Malcolm Blvd, Burke Co, NC	47	D4
Veterans Affairs Med Ctr 1100 Tunnel Rd, Asheville, NC	44	E6
Veterans Affairs Med Ctr 1 Freedom Wy, Augusta, GA	159	B1
Veterans Affairs Med Ctr 508 Fulton St, Durham, NC	193	C3
Veterans Affairs Med Ctr 2300 Ramsey St, Fayetteville, NC	81	A7
Veterans Affairs Med Ctr 1601 Brenner Av, Salisbury, NC	208	B2
Wake Forest University Baptist Med Ctr Queen St, Winston-Salem, NC	188	A4
WakeMed Cary Hosp Cary, NC	55	B3
Wakemed Raleigh Campus 3000 New Bern Av, Raleigh, NC	200	E3
Wallace Thompson Hosp 322 W South St, Union, SC	159	B7
Washington County Hosp Plymouth, NC	37	A7
Watauga Med Ctr 336 Deerfield Rd, Boone, NC	185	E6
Wayne Memorial Hosp 2700 N Wayne Memorial Dr, Goldsboro, NC	83	D1
Wesley Long Community Hosp N Elam Av, Greensboro, NC	189	E1
Wilkes Regional Med Ctr 1370 Locust St, North Wilkesboro, NC	24	D3
Williamsburg Regional Hosp 500 Nelson Blvd, Kingstree, SC	155	C4
Wilson Med Ctr Wilson, NC	57	D3
Woods Memorial Hosp 886 Tennessee Av, Etowah, TN	65	A4

Military Installations

FEATURE NAME Address City State	MAP#	GRID
Beaufort Marine Corps Air Station, Beaufort-Co, SC	177	A4
Camp Butner NC St Nat'l Guard Training Site, -Granville Co, NC	31	B3
Camp Lejeune Marine Corps Base, Onslow Co,-NC	227	B7
Camp Mackall Military Reservation, Scotland-Co, NC	105	C2
Charleston Air Force Base, North-Charleston, SC	172	E3
Charleston Naval Complex, North Charleston,-SC	240	D1
Cherry Point Marine Corps Air Station, -Craven Co, NC	112	D2
Dare County Bombing Range, Dare Co, NC	63	C1
Fort Bragg Military Reservation, Hoke Co,-NC	80	B6
Fort Bragg Military Reservation, Spring-Lake, NC	221	D4
Fort Gordon Military Reservation, Richmond-Co, GA	159	A2
Fort Jackson Military Reservation, -Columbia, SC	234	E2
Fort Stewart Military Reservation, Bryan-Co, GA	180	A5
Harvey Point Defense Testing Activity, -Perquimans Co, NC	38	A2
Hunter Army Air Field, Savannah, GA	180	D5
Laurel Bay Naval Area, Beaufort Co, SC	176	E4
McEntire Air National Guard Station, -Richland Co, SC	138	D7
New River Marine Corps Air Station, -Jacksonville, NC	111	B6
North Army Air Base, Orangeburg Co, SC	151	E5
Parris Island Marine Corps Recruit Depot, -Beaufort Co, SC	177	A6
Pope Air Force Base, Cumberland Co, NC	221	B1
Savannah River Site, Barnwell Co, SC	160	B5
Seymour-Johnson Air Force Base, Goldsboro,-NC	204	C7
Shaw Air Force Base, Sumter, SC	139	D6
Shaw Air Force Base Middle Marker Annex, -Sumter Co, SC	139	C7
Sunny Point Army Terminal, Kure Beach, NC	147	A4
Sunny Point Military Ocean Terminal, -Brunswick Co, NC	146	E4
US Airforce Reservation, Hanahan, SC	173	A3
US Army Depot, Berkeley Co, SC	173	B3
US Coast Guard Air Station, Pasquotank Co,-NC	17	C6
US Military Res, Bogue, NC	112	C6
US Naval Reservation, Berkeley Co, SC	173	B4
US Naval Res Marine Recruit Depot, Beaufort-Co, SC	177	A5
US Navy Northwest Radio Station, -Chesapeake, VA	17	A1

Museums

FEATURE NAME Address City State	MAP#	GRID
16th SC Volunteers Mus 15 Boyce Av, Greenville, SC	223	C3
82nd Airborne Division Mus Ardennes St, Cumberland Co, NC	221	A7
1897 Poe House Mus 206 Bradford Av, Fayetteville, NC	222	C3
Ackland Art Mus S Columbia St, Chapel Hill, NC	30	C7
African American Cultural Complex 119 Sunnybrook Rd, Raleigh, NC	55	E2
Afro-American Cultural Center 401 N Myers St, Charlotte, NC	216	B2
Aiken Center for the Arts 122 Laurens St SW, Aiken, SC	236	D1
Aiken County Historical Mus 433 Newberry St SW, Aiken, SC	236	C2
Airborne & Special Ops Mus 100 Bragg Blvd, Fayetteville, NC	222	C2
Alamance County Historical Mus Alamance Co, NC	29	B5
Alamants Battle Grounds Alamance Co, NC	29	B6
American Historical Wax Mus Parkway, Gatlinburg, TN	42	A4
American Military Mus 360 Concord St, Charleston, SC	240	E5
American Military Mus 115 W 2nd Av, Gastonia, NC	210	C4
Anderson County Mus 202 E Greenville St, Anderson, SC	226	D4
Appalachian Cultural Mus University Hall Dr, Boone, NC	185	D5
Appalachian Heritage Mus 175 Mystery Hill Ln, Watauga Co, NC	23	B3
Asheville Art Mus 2 S Pack Sq, Asheville, NC	206	C3
Augusta Mus of History 560 Reynolds St, Augusta, GA	159	C1
Aurora Fossil Mus 400 Main St, Aurora, NC	87	A2
Backing Up Classics Car Mus 4545 Concord Pkwy S, Concord, NC	212	D1
Bellamy Mansion Mus Market St, Wilmington, NC	231	A3
Best Friend Mus 31 Ann St, Charleston, SC	240	D5
Biltmore Village Historic Mus 7 Angle St, Asheville, NC	206	C7
Black Mountain College Mus 56 Broadway St, Asheville, NC	206	C3
Blue Frog Purple Dog 201 Goucher Ct, Berkeley Co, SC	172	E1
Blue Heaven Basketball Mus 2460 Sedgefield Dr, Chapel Hill, NC	195	E1
BMW Zentrum Mus Greer, SC	97	E4
Brevard Station Mus 112 S Main St, Stanley, NC	74	E3
Broach Nascar Tours 2727 Selwyn Av, Charlotte, NC	75	C6
Burke County Mus 536 S Liberty St, Waynesboro, GA	159	B7
Burwell School Historic Site 319 N Churton St, Hillsborough, NC	30	C4
Calhoun County Mus 313 Butler St, St. Matthews, SC	152	E4
Camden Archives & Mus 1314 Broad St, Camden, SC	139	B1
Canton Historical Mus 36 W Park St, Canton, NC	43	E7
Cape Fear Mus 814 Market St, Wilmington, NC	231	B3
Carbo's Police Mus 3311 Parkway, Pigeon Forge, TN	41	E3
Carolinas Aviation Mus 4108 Airport Dr, Charlotte, NC	214	B2
Carolinas Boxing Hall of Fame 5555 Concord Pkwy S, Concord, NC	212	C2
Catawba County Firefighters Mus 3957 Herman Sipe Rd, Conover, NC	48	C4
Catawba County Mus of History 15 N College Av, Newton, NC	48	C5
Catawba Cultural Center 1536 Tom Steven Rd, York Co, SC	101	C4
Catawba Valley Arts & Sciences Center 243 3rd Av NE, Hickory, NC	207	D4

Points of Interest Index

Points of Interest Index

Points of Interest Index

Parks & Recreation

Shopping Centers

Ski Areas

Visitor Information

RAND M?NALLY

Thank you for purchasing this Rand McNally Road Atlas!
We value your comments and suggestions.

Please help us serve you better by completing this postage-paid reply card.
This information is for internal use ONLY and will not be distributed or sold to any external third party.

Missing pages? Maybe not... Please refer to the "Using Your Road Atlas" page for further explanation.

Road Atlas Title: The Carolinas Road Atlas   ISBN-13# 978-0-5288-6661-6   MKT: SRA

Todayís Date: _____   Gender: ☐M ☐F   Age Group: ☐18-24 ☐25-31 ☐32-40 ☐41-50 ☐51-64 ☐65+

1. What type of industry do you work in?

☐Real Estate	☐Trucking	☐Delivery	☐Construction	☐Utilities ☐Government
☐Retail	☐Sales	☐Transportation	☐Landscape	☐Service & Repair
☐Courier	☐Automotive	☐Insurance	☐Medical	☐Police/Fire/First Response

☐Other, please specify: _____

2. What type of job do you have in this industry?_____
3. Where did you purchase this Road Atlas? (store name & city) _____
4. Why did you purchase this Road Atlas? _____
5. How often do you purchase an updated Road Atlas?   ☐Annually   ☐2 yrs.   ☐3-5 yrs.   ☐Other: _____
6. Where do you use it?   ☐Primarily in the car   ☐Primarily in the office   ☐Primarily at home   ☐Other: _____
7. How do you use it?   ☐Exclusively for business   ☐Primarily for business but also for personal or leisure use
    ☐Both work and personal evenly   ☐Primarily for personal use   ☐Exclusively for personal use
8. What do you use your Road Atlas for?
    ☐Find Addresses   ☐In-route navigation   ☐Planning routes   ☐Other: _____
    Find points of interest: ☐Schools   ☐Parks   ☐Buildings   ☐Shopping Centers   ☐Other:_____
9. How often do you use it?   ☐Daily   ☐Weekly   ☐Monthly   ☐Other:_____
10. Do you use the internet for maps and/or directions?   ☐Yes   ☐No
11. How often do you use the internet for directions?   ☐Daily   ☐Weekly   ☐Monthly   ☐Other:_____
12. Do you use any of the following mapping products in addition to your Road Atlas?
    ☐Folded paper maps   ☐Folded laminated maps   ☐Wall maps   ☐GPS   ☐PDA   ☐In-car navigation   ☐Phone maps
13. What features, if any, would you like to see added to your Road Atlas? _____
    _____
14. What features or information do you find most useful in your Rand McNally Road Atlas? (please specify)
    _____
    _____
15. Please provide any additional comments or suggestions you have. _____
    _____
    _____

We strive to provide you with the most current updated information available if you know of a map correction, please notify us here.

Where is the correction?   Map Page #:_____   Grid #:_____   Index Page #:_____

Nature of the correction: ☐Street name missing   ☐Street name misspelled   ☐Street information incorrect
    ☐Incorrect location for point of interest   ☐Index error   ☐Other: _____

Detail: _____

I would like to receive information about updated editions and special offers from Rand McNally
    ☐via e-mail   E-mail address: _____
    ☐via postal mail
    Your Name: _____   Company (if used for work): _____
    Address:_____   City/State/ZIP: _____

Thank you for your time and help. We are working to serve you better.
This information is for internal use ONLY and will not be distributed or sold to any external third party.

TAPE SHUT
TAPE SHUT

CUT ALONG DOTTED LINE

2ND FOLD LINE

1ST FOLD LINE

CUT ALONG DOTTED LINE

RAND McNALLY
The most trusted name on the map.

You'll never need to ask for directions again with these Rand McNally products!

- EasyFinder® Laminated Maps
- Folded Maps
- Street Guides
- Wall Maps
- CustomView Wall Maps
- Road Atlases
- Motor Carriers' Road Atlases

SGTG_07